# Advertising and Public Relations Law

D0062444

Addressing a critical need, *Advertising and Public Relations Law* explores the issues and ideas that affect the regulation of advertising and public relations speech. Coverage includes the categorization of different kinds of speech afforded varying levels of First Amendment protection; court-created tests for laws and regulations of speech; and non-content-based restrictions on speech and expression.

Features of this edition include:

- A discussion in each chapter of new-media implications
- Extended excerpts from major court decisions
- Appendices providing

  — a chart of the judicial system
  — a summary of the judicial process
  — an overview of alternative dispute resolution mechanisms
  — the professional codes for media industry and business associations, including the American Association of Advertising Agencies, the Public Relations Society of America and the Society of Professional Journalists

- Online resources for instructors.

The volume is developed for upper-level undergraduate and graduate students in media, advertising and public relations law or regulation courses. It also serves as an essential reference for advertising and public relations practitioners.

**Roy L. Moore** is professor of journalism and dean of the College of Mass Communication at Middle Tennessee State University. He holds a Ph.D. in mass communication from the University of Wisconsin and a juris doctorate from the Georgia State University College of Law.

**Carmen Maye** is a South Carolina-based lawyer and an instructor in the School of Journalism and Mass Communications at the University of South Carolina, where she teaches courses in media law and advertising. Her undergraduate degree is from the University of North Carolina at Chapel Hill. Her master's and juris doctorate degrees are from the University of South Carolina.

**Erik L. Collins** is the associate director for graduate studies and research in the School of Journalism and Mass Communications at the University of South Carolina. He teaches courses in media law, mass communication research methods and integrated communications management. Dr. Collins holds a Ph.D. from the Newhouse School of Public Communications, Syracuse University, and a juris doctorate from the Ohio State University School of Law.

Instructor materials are available on this book's web page at www. routledge.com

# Communication Series
General Editors Jennings Bryant and
Dolf Zillmann

# Advertising and Public Relations Law

Second Edition

Roy L. Moore, Carmen Maye and Erik L. Collins

Routledge
Taylor & Francis Group

NEW YORK AND LONDON

First edition published 1998
by Lawrence Erlbaum Associates, Inc.

This edition published 2011
by Routledge
270 Madison Avenue, New York, NY 10016

Simultaneously published in the UK
by Routledge
2 Park Square, Milton Park, Abingdon, Oxon OX14 4RN

Routledge is an imprint of the Taylor & Francis Group, an informa
business

Typeset in Sabon and GillSans by Swales & Willis Ltd,
Exeter, Devon
Printed by CPI Antony Rowe, Chippenham, Wiltshire

Library of Congress Cataloging-in-Publication Data
Moore, Roy L.
    Advertising and public relations law / Roy L. Moore,
    Carmen Maye, Erik L. Collins. — 2nd ed.
    p. cm.
    Includes bibliographical references.
    Advertising laws—United States. 2. Public relations and law—
    United States. I. Maye, Carmen. II. Collins, Erik. III. Title.
    KF1614.M66 2010
    343.73'082—dc22
    2010010838

ISBN13: 978–0–8058–5346–9 (hbk)
ISBN13: 978–0–415–96548–4 (pbk)
ISBN13: 978–0–203–84587–5 (ebk)

This book is dedicated in memory of Essie and Lila and to Pam, Derek and Michelle; to Sidney, Archie and Earnie; and to Lilly and Lolly.

# Contents

*Appendices*

# Preface

In the early days of the twentieth century, the original curriculum of the world's first school of journalism included a required course in communication law. The class dealt with libel and, to a substantial degree, with postal regulations. That made sense at the time: 85 percent of all journalism graduates went to work for community newspapers, and an understanding of law affecting the mail was important.

Today, we operate in a mass-media environment. Advertising and public relations professionals, and those hoping to enter the professional world, not only need to possess many of the same skills as traditional journalists, but also need to learn a great deal about public opinion and human behavior, management techniques and strategic problem solving. And, as was the case with those pioneering journalists nearly a century ago, today's advertising and public relations professionals must be aware of the laws and jurisprudence affecting their chosen fields.

Some of the legal issues facing journalists equally affect advertising and public relations professionals. However, many other law-related issues and concerns of those in the advertising and public relations professions are different from those of editors and reporters. Designed to serve both the practitioner and the student, this second edition of *Advertising and Public Relations Law* addresses this wide range of legal topics.

Although there are some excellent general media law texts available, none has been developed to the extent this one has to reflect the distinctive needs of advertising and public relations professionals and aspiring professionals. Some of the specific differences you will notice are (a) two entire chapters devoted to the commercial speech doctrine, including its history and development; (b) separate chapters on public-interest speech, patents and trademarks, and trade secrets and business schemes; (c) extensive discussions of how federal agencies beyond the Federal Trade Commission regulate advertising and product promotion; (d) two chapters focusing on privacy rights and concerns; and (e) an appendix with model release forms, professional codes of ethics, a diagram of the United States court system and a copy of the United States Constitution. Our concluding chapter deals with traditional journalistic concerns such as privilege, free-press-versus-fair-trial issues and access. Readers also will note a chapter-by-chapter discussion of the effects of new media and breakthroughs in digital information technologies in terms of how they impact the laws and regulations governing advertising and public relations.

Lawyers sometimes characterize seemingly unimportant, minute differentiations of facts or law as "distinctions without a difference." We believe you will find this volume, in comparison with others on the topic, a distinction *with* a difference. We hope that practitioners and students alike will find our efforts interesting, enjoyable and, most of all, highly informative.

# Acknowledgments

Many individuals contributed to the completion of this text. We especially want to note the contributions of our colleagues Jay Bender and Lisa Sisk and graduate students Lauren Von Herbulis, Anna Saunders, Jamie Stancil, Renée Williamson, Matthew Telleen and Rachel Amanda Farris who endured countless hours of discussion, argumentation and copy editing. Christopher S. McDonald, of the McNair Law Firm in Columbia, S.C., is largely responsible for the discussion of contract law in Chapter 9 and contributed his expertise in a number of other areas.

We would also like to take this opportunity to acknowledge and thank the contributions to media law made by our contemporaries in schools and departments of journalism and mass communications around the country, including, but not limited to, Jay Wright, Steve Helle, Bob Trager, Bill Chamberlain, Bob Drechsel, Kent Middleton, Ruth Walden, Dwight Teeter, Barton Carter, Kyu Ho Youm, Michael D. Murray, J. Michael Farrell and others too numerous to mention, but nonetheless, deeply deserving of our great respect, who have paved the way for today's younger generation of scholars who make this field vibrant and dynamic.

Equally, if not more deserving of acknowledgment, are the true pioneers of commercial speech law: Jim Goodale, Cam DeVore, Conrad Schumadine, Bruce Johnson, Steve Brody, Diane Zimmerman, Bob Sack and others whose labors have created robust constitutional protection for a category of speech that originally was accorded none at all.

# Chapter 1

# The First Amendment

Advertising and public relations practitioners picking up a 450-plus page book filled with examples and discussions of laws regulating commercial speech could be pardoned for being somewhat puzzled. After all, the language of the First Amendment to the Federal Constitution clearly mandates that "Congress [and by logical extension any lesser unit of government] shall make no law . . . abridging freedom of speech or of the press . . ."[1] How can there be laws regulating any speech (let alone advertising or public relations speech) in the face of the Constitution's emphatic statement that there can be "no law?"

This puzzle requires us to begin with a brief overview of the First Amendment and how it is interpreted before we turn our attention to the principal subject matter of this book.

## Development of First Amendment Jurisprudence

Courts faced with cases challenging the constitutionality of laws and regulations affecting speech and press have developed a body of mass media law by weighing and balancing the interests of those supporting freedom of expression against those favoring competing interests.

The dilemma faced by the courts in such situations today is that despite the emphatic "no law" language of the Amendment, it is almost impossible to believe that those who helped add the First Amendment to the Federal Constitution more than 200 years ago meant to protect all speech without exception, even speech, for example, that is treasonous or criminally threatening or harmful to reputation. Yet judges and justices cannot simply ignore the First Amendment because they personally disapprove of the speech in question. Therefore, they have been obliged to develop a logical, rational and defensible method of interpretation. To understand how they have accomplished this, we need to take a brief look both at how judges interpret law and how historians interpret history.

Role play the part of judge for a moment—not a Supreme Court justice but a judge in a low-level court in which the cases usually involve petty crimes and minor disagreements. The next case on the docket is *City v. Jones*. Testifying for the city is the arresting officer, who reports that the defendant was apprehended at 10 a.m. Saturday and charged with operating a motorized, self-propelled vehicle within a city park. A municipal ordinance makes such operation illegal for all "persons regardless of status or circumstances." The ordinance specifies that all persons so doing shall be sentenced to (a) no more than 30 and no fewer than 10 days in the city jail, and (b) a fine of no more than $100 and no less than $30. Because the defendant, Jones, is pleading guilty, this seems like an open-and-shut case.

However, before passing judgment, it seems only fair to hear what the defendant has to say. Unfortunately, Mr. Jones apparently is no place to be seen. When you ask the arresting officer "Where's Jones?" the policeman gestures for you to lean forward and look over the front of your large, desk-like bench. Upon so doing, you discover that "Mr. Jones" is a curly headed, 9-year-old, clutching a giant toy truck on which a child can sit and ride by winding up a big key on the truck's cab.

You're the judge. Now what do you do? You can't very well issue a fine and throw the kid in the slammer, but you also aren't free to ignore the law that clearly says it applies to all "persons regardless of status or circumstances."

This rather exaggerated case is an example that illustrates a very real dilemma that daily confronts those who must interpret the law and apply it to a set of facts. We know what the law says—we can read it over and over. The question is—what does the law mean? This is exactly what judges face when asked to interpret the First Amendment.

Let's go back to the courtroom where everyone is awaiting your decision. If you thought about looking at the precedents set by other judges who have looked at this municipal ordinance in the past, you are on the right track. Judges do look to prior decisions and the rationales employed by the judges in those earlier cases. But they generally don't stop there. They may study as well the literal language of the law or regulation and may take the added step of researching the records of the debate and discussion surrounding its adoption by those who passed it in the first place. Judges often find this legislative history a helpful guide in interpreting and applying the language of the law to the unique set of facts in the cases before them. In addition, they may examine any other historical records that could cast light on the meaning and purpose of a law or regulation.

As it happens in this case, the minutes taken at the city council meeting when the ordinance was passed reveal that the purpose of the municipal ordinance was to block off the streets going though city parks to prevent cars, trucks and buses from running over joggers and bike riders and in-line skaters (and children riding toy trucks) using the paved surfaces in city parks on weekends. Support for this interpretation is reflected in

When the war ended in Europe, federal laws regulating speech involving political issues fell into disuse, but a new and potentially more dangerous threat to the free discussion of public issues was growing. The years between 1920 and 1940 marked the growth of labor unions—to a minor degree influenced by socialist and communist ideologies—as workers organized to improve working conditions, hours and benefits. These efforts were bitterly opposed by the captains of industry and their friends in state legislatures and statehouses, particularly when labor resorted to the ultimate weapon of a strike.

This era of industrial warfare frightened many in power with the specter of organized workers dominated by evil forces bent on destroying the democratic capitalist system by less than peaceful means, if necessary. State lawmakers responded to these fears with the passage of criminal syndicalism or criminal anarchy statutes. Eventually, 21 states adopted such laws aimed at punishing those who spoke out in favor of the duty, propriety or necessity of overturning lawful governments by force or violence.[13]

Historically, such state laws would have raised no federal First Amendment issues, but this all changed in 1925 when the Supreme Court of the United States decided the case of *Gitlow v. New York*.[14] Benjamin Gitlow had been convicted of criminal anarchy for printing material urging labor unrest and the highest appeals court in New York had upheld the conviction, deciding that it did not violate the state constitution's protection of speech. Despite the odds and a century-old history of precedent against the success of such an appeal, Gitlow petitioned the Supreme Court of the United States to hear his case, and the Court surprised many observers by agreeing to do so.

Unfortunately for Gitlow, the Court agreed with the New York court and upheld his conviction. Fortunately for free-speech advocates, the Court also found that the Due Process Clause of the Fourteenth Amendment to the Federal Constitution gave jurisdiction to federal courts to review state court decisions that arguably infringe upon free speech rights.

During the decade following *Gitlow*, the Court reviewed a dozen or so speech regulation cases emanating from state courts. These decisions usually upheld the convictions of speakers, but also created a series of precedents and contained dissenting opinions (usually by Justices Holmes and Brandeis) filled with ideas, historical analyses and philosophical points for future arguments in favor of a limited ability for government at any level to regulate speech.

In one of the most important cases of the era, *Near v. Minnesota*,[15] the Court tackled the case of an alternative newspaper editor who had so outraged authorities in Minneapolis/St. Paul that he was denied the right to continue to publish any newspaper in the state on the basis that for him to do so would constitute a public nuisance. Rightfully seeing this as a prior restraint of speech about important public issues, the Court struck down the state regulation. In so doing, the Court affirmed that the most dangerous threats to free speech, and, therefore, those most disfavored by the First Amendment, are prior restraints. Such censorship measures not only include the public nuisance law in *Near*, but also court orders, censorship boards, discriminatory taxation policies, licensing schemes, limiting access to the means of production and other government actions aimed at preventing speech from entering the marketplace of ideas. State efforts to regulate protected speech declined in the mid-1930s as the country concentrated on pulling itself out of the Great Depression. With little sympathy for either Germany or Japan in World War II, and with the Soviet Union as an ally, virtually no public speech favored fascism or advocated organized popular resistance to fighting the war. Therefore, no cases occurred triggering the prosecution of speech-related activities like those of Schenck or Abrams. This hiatus came to an abrupt end, however, at the end of World War II with the heating up of the so-called Cold War in the mid-to-late 1940s. With the scare of a Moscow-inspired, sinister communist penetration into all aspects of American life by the early 1950s, federal prosecutors and legislative investigating committees pursued a spate of espionage-related speech cases.

Two of the more famous were *Dennis v. U.S.*[16] and *Yates v. U.S.*[17] The Court in *Dennis*, the low point of First Amendment protection for political speech, upheld a conviction apparently based solely on membership in the Communist Party. The Court noted that the defendant's participation in a "highly organized conspiracy"[18] ready for violence when "the time had come for action"[19] was enough of a threat to warrant criminal sanctions. The Court appeared to feel that simply by being a communist, Dennis was advocating treasonous activity. By 1957 and the *Yates* decision, however, cooler judgment prevailed and the Court returned to the rationale that a showing of actual advocacy of illegal activity was necessary before the government could punish mere speech.

This trend toward greater protection of civil rights and fundamental personal liberties (including freedom of speech), begun in the late 1950s, accelerated in the decade of the 1960s. By 1969, the Court had evolved its thinking about the extent of protection for public-interest speech to the degree that in *Brandenburg v. Ohio*[20] it struck down the conviction of a Ku Klux Klan member who spoke out in favor of prejudicially motivated violence. The Court held unconstitutional an Ohio statute with wording almost identical to that found in similar statutes in other states upheld in earlier Court decisions in the 1920s and 1930s. The new test, said the *Brandenburg* Court, requires the state to prove the speech was intended to produce "imminent, lawless activity" likely to occur.[21]

The Court reaffirmed its position that prior restraint is the most serious violation of the First Amendment in the so-called "Pentagon Papers

Case."[22] In this 1971 case, the federal government asked the courts for injunctions to stop publication by *The New York Times* and *The Washington Post* of classified defense documents. The Court, in a 6–3 decision, noted that "any system of prior restraints of expression comes to the court bearing heavy presumption against its constitutionality"[23] and that the government had not met that heavy burden. Therefore, the Court struck down a lower court order prohibiting *The New York Times* from continuing to publish the papers.

More recent developments, particularly the continuing terrorist threats to national security post 9/11 and the use of Web sites by radical groups to foment violent protests, pose new challenges for those defending freedom of speech. Nonetheless, it is still true today that the government at both the federal and state levels faces a difficult task in defending a law or regulation that either prohibits or punishes speech about important political or social issues.

## The Tests, Constitutional and Otherwise, for "Fully Protected" Speech

If Congress or a federal agency wishes to regulate most everyday activities and the government action is subsequently challenged in court as unconstitutional, the government usually will prevail if it can demonstrate a well-drafted law or regulation designed to accomplish a reasonable government purpose. Sometimes referred to as a "rationality" test, this historic, court-made rule places the burden on those challenging the government action as unconstitutional to demonstrate a lack of rational basis for the law or regulation, often a difficult burden for the challenger to meet.[24]

Challenging the regulation of protected speech, however, automatically differentiates such a case from the norm. The first major exception to treating speech cases differently was Justice Holmes' "clear and present danger" test in *Schenck*.[25] Although the test's exact meaning has been altered over the years, a modern-day court normally will require the government to meet the equivalent of that test when the government seeks an immediate cessation or punishment of protected speech.

Even if the government interest in regulating speech is compelling, the government will not automatically win a case involving regulation of protected speech. A court still must weigh and balance the government's interests against the other side's speech interests. How to do this represents another example of conflicting judicial philosophies and theories.

Envision the statue of Lady Justice holding a set of scales. One school of judicial thought suggests that in speech cases a court first should pile extra weight on the speech side of the scale and then look to the government to pile enough weight on its side to overcome the handicap created in favor of the speech interests. This approach, sometimes referred to as giving speech a "preferred position,"[26] suggests that a court require the government to meet an extra "heavy burden"[27] when it wants to regulate fully protected speech (e.g., speech about important political or social issues). This "definitional balancing"[28] permits the formulation of rules that can be applied uniformly from case to case. For example, such a test often is interpreted to mean that when the government seeks to regulate an individual's fundamental constitutional right to speak and the government's action is challenged in court on constitutional grounds, the court will treat the law or regulation as presumptively *un*constitutional.

Borrowing from Fourteenth Amendment Equal Protection cases,[29] those who feel this approach best protects speech, yet accommodates important competing interests, suggest that only if the government can demonstrate a "compelling need" for its actions will the opposing speech interests be subject to the possibility of regulation. Such an approach, sometimes referred to as requiring "strict scrutiny" of any attempt to regulate speech about important political or social issues, is often used by the Court when protecting so-called "fundamental liberties."[30] The Court has spent more than eight decades developing an appropriate test to preserve constitutional values when a legislature or agency wishes to regulate "those functions essential to effective democracy."[31] Although the Court has never set out a definitive list of these "functions," clearly the right to freedom of speech and press is among them.

This "compelling government interest test" has proven to be a major bulwark in the defense of individual liberties. The test places a heavy burden on the government body wishing to regulate, requiring that it must demonstrate (a) an overriding necessity for its actions; (b) that the law or regulation actually advances the government interest; (c) that it is "narrowly tailored" to accomplish just the limited purpose the government may be permitted; and (d) that it is the least restrictive (of speech) means available to the government for accomplishing its ends.[32]

This imbalanced approach to deciding speech cases is by no means the only approach a court might follow, however. Many jurists and legal scholars argue that the correct approach for a court to take is to first determine if both the government and speech interests are substantial and, if so, to adjudicate the actual case before the court by simply balancing the interests of both parties and arriving at a decision, based upon which has the greater weight on its side. For example, as Justice Harlan noted in his opinion in *Barenblatt v. United States*,[33] "[w]here First Amendment rights are asserted to bar government interrogation, resolution of the issue always involves a balancing by the courts of the competing private and public interests at stake in the particular circumstances."[34]

Courts have not been uniform in electing to follow either this "ad hoc balancing"[35] approach or the preferred-position approach discussed above. This has created some confusion for those trying to predict the outcomes of cases, as well as those who believe First Amendment law should develop in a neat and orderly manner.

## Content-Based Regulation of "Less Protected" Speech

As discussed previously, the development of First Amendment law during the last eight decades of the twentieth century focused on the attempts to regulate "political speech." Today it is generally agreed that, in most circumstances, a legislature or agency wishing to regulate this constitutionally protected speech faces a heavy burden of convincing a court that there is a compelling need for the government's actions. Unfortunately for free speech advocates, courts have proven less vigilant in striking down attempts to regulate speech that does not easily fit under the political speech rubric.

As noted earlier, because of confusion about what the framers of the First Amendment actually meant when they wrote "no law," courts historically have differentiated among different kinds of speech by the degree of constitutional protection afforded each. This differentiation is critical to understanding the reasons underlying the degree of constitutionally permissible regulation of advertising, public relations and other forms of commercial speech (discussed in more detail in Chapter 2). Suffice it to say that courts have consistently held that "purely" commercial speech does not receive the same level of protection as speech about important public issues.

Similarly, courts have held that lessened First Amendment protection applies to over-the-air broadcast speech. The logic employed by the courts for so holding is slightly different, however. Initially unregulated, radio broadcasters went to Congress in the 1920s seeking help because broadcasters were impinging on each others' radio frequencies. What they got was the Radio Act of 1927.[36] This soon was supplanted by the more comprehensive Communications Act of 1934,[37] that also created the Federal Communications Commission (FCC) to not only regulate use of frequencies and technical specifications, but also to police the content of broadcasts to ensure broadcasters operated "in the public interest convenience and necessity."[38]

Eventually, broadcasters challenged the FCC (and the law itself) as unconstitutionally infringing on their protected speech rights. In the combined *NBC v. U.S.* and *CBS v. U.S.*[39] cases in 1943, the Supreme Court of the United States upheld the constitutionality of the Act. It decided that Congress could set content restrictions on broadcasters to police the use of the airwaves, which the government labeled a scarce public resource. The underlying legal premise was that the authors of the First Amendment could not have anticipated over-the-air broadcast speech and that the government was therefore entitled to more leeway in regulating such speech. The continuing need for such laws and regulations, given today's multitude of media and communication channels, will be one of the major areas of potential free-speech litigation facing lawmakers and communicators in this century.

Unlike commercial and broadcast speech, which are protected to some degree from government regulation, courts have held that pornographic speech and speech that is criminal in nature (e.g., threatening, extorting or fraudulent) are totally without First Amendment protection. Although an extensive discussion of this court-sanctioned form of content restriction is beyond the scope of this book, readers should understand that almost always the issue in cases challenging government restrictions of these kinds of speech is a definitional one (e.g., is the speech pornographic or does it contain a real threat?).

The Court has spent decades wrestling with the definitional problems involved in pornography cases. The wording of the current test is from *Miller v. California*,[40] a case decided by the Court in 1973, involving a conviction under state law of a man accused of mailing sexually explicit advertisements for books and films. Upholding the conviction, the Court said that for a work to be defined as legally pornographic, the average person, applying contemporary community standards, must find that the work, taken as a whole, appeals to prurient interest in sex. In addition, the material must describe specifically defined content in a patently offensive manner and the work, taken as a whole, must lack serious literary, artistic, political or scientific value.[41]

## Non-Content-Based Speech Regulations

The First Amendment clearly places barriers in the government's attempts to restrain or punish speech based upon its content. However, other speech-related laws and regulations, although infringing on a speaker's ability to get his or her message across, may not raise the same degree of First Amendment concern for the courts.

One example is regulation based on "time, place and manner." The criteria for such regulations are that they (a) advance a legitimate government interest; (b) be content neutral; (c) be reasonable; and (d) not be used to ban or make speech practically impossible. Challenges to time, place and manner regulations often occur when authorities try to regulate such speech activities as door-to-door solicitations, parades, demonstrations on public property and so forth. Recently, courts have been faced with a series of cases involving billboards and news racks resulting from municipalities' attempts to limit the number and placement of signs and vending machines on city streets for safety or aesthetic reasons. A number of these cases involve advertising or commercial speech are discussed later.

New media technology provides yet another problem area for time, place and manner regulations. Government attempts to limit spam e-mail messages and prevent unsolicited telephone marketing efforts raise interesting, and as yet unresolved, First Amendment issues that have been winding their way through state and federal systems.

Other types of cases raising non-content speech issues involve efforts to gain access to government information, avoid disclosing the sources of information to government agencies or being required by law to publish information. Whether seeking to gain or avoid giving information, those so doing typically claim a right of free speech as the basis for their actions. Government representatives counter that the First Amendment gives lawmakers greater leeway to regulate such speech-related activities because the laws are not content based. Courts dealing with such claims have reacted inconsistently, sometimes recognizing First Amendment claims and sometimes giving them short shrift. These issues are discussed in subsequent chapters.

Finally, a non-content-based rationale employed by those who wish to regulate speech is frequently raised in cases involving expressive conduct rather than pure speech. Some of these controversial decisions have concerned flag burning, nude dancing, spray-painting "hate speech" messages and picketing of abortion clinics. Those wishing to engage in such actions argue that their activities are protected by the First Amendment because of the message inherent in their actions. An alternative interpretation, often advanced by the government, argues that conduct is different from speech and can therefore legally be more controlled.

This so-called speech/action dichotomy has created conflicting rulings from courts grappling with the issues that such cases raise. Often the outcome has turned on an ad hoc evaluation of the "importance" of the expression versus the strength of the competing government interest. Thus the Supreme Court has held that flag burning[42] is expressive conduct that is protected because of its political nature. Nude dancing, on the other hand, is expressive conduct that often is not protected because the message conveyed is of such a minor artistic nature that the government can ban or control it simply on public policy grounds.[43]

## Importance of Free Speech

As this introductory chapter concludes, it may occur to the reader that a great number of people have gone to an awful lot of trouble to theorize, legislate, argue and fight for the right of the individual to speak free of unwarranted government restraint or censure. The logical question that follows is: Why is free speech so important that many believe almost all other interests are subservient to it?

One of the reasons we might ask that question is that we have always lived in a society where free speech is protected. We take it for granted that we have the right to speak or write about almost anything we please without first getting it cleared by the official government censor or fearing the heavy tread of the storm trooper's boot outside our door. However, the founders of this nation knew what it was like to fear both the censor and the authorities. Therefore, they were adamant in their belief that only in a society where people were free to criticize government and official conduct, as well as to speak out on other important public issues, could a democratic form of government flourish.

This has led scholars like Melvin Nimmer to the conclusion that the chief function of unfettered speech is the "enlightenment function."[44] Nimmer quotes Justice Brandeis, one of the Court's generally acknowledged great champions of freedom of speech and press, to the effect that "freedom to think as you will and to speak as you think are means indispensable to the discovery and spread of political truth. . . ."[45] But Nimmer argues that focusing solely on political truth is too limiting:

> The search for all forms of "truth," which is to say the search for all aspects of knowledge and the formulation of enlightened opinion on all subjects, is dependent upon open channels of communication. Unless one is exposed to all the data on a given subject, it is not possible to make an informed judgment as to which "facts" and which views deserve to be accepted.[46]

Free speech, however, is important to our society beyond its critical role in governance. In a country not controlled by an ideology or dogma, free speech is seen as both a means for continually examining the status quo and as the mechanism for introducing new ideas and concepts into society as a leavening agent of change. The seventeenth-century philosopher John Milton was one of the first to publicly argue that the best path to truth is through uncensored exchange of ideas.[47] Two centuries later, John Stuart Mill urged the correlative idea that even speech proven to be false is important and needs protection because it forces us to reexamine old ideas rather than just assume them to be true.[48]

Critical to the enlightenment function of free speech is that the system for arriving at the outcome should be equally unrestricted. As Nimmer points out, "[a]bsolute certainty on any issue of fact or opinion is beyond human capability. All determinations of 'truth' are necessarily tentative, subject to modifying or contradictory 'truths' which may later emerge."[49] However, if information that could lead to "contradictory truths" is limited or prohibited, the system becomes stagnant.

Justice Oliver Wendell Holmes, Jr. likened this process to the free marketplace of goods and services in his famous dissenting view in *Abrams*. Writing with a touch of irony, Justice Holmes first noted that "[p]ersecution for the expression of opinions seems to me perfectly logical. If you have no doubt of your premises or your power and want a certain result with all your heart, you naturally express your wishes in law and sweep away all opposition."[50] However, Justice Holmes was quick to point out that

> when men have realized that time has upset many fighting faiths, they may come to believe even more than they believe the very foundations of their own conduct that the ultimate good desired is better reached by free trade in ideas—that the best test of truth is the power of the thought to get itself accepted in the competition of the market and that truth is the only ground upon which their wishes can be carried out. That at any rate is the theory of our Constitution. It is an experiment, as all life is an experiment.[51]

The authors of this text would not be surprised to learn that those reading the passage from Justice Holmes' dissent quoted above would strongly affirm his views as their own. Yet when given specific examples of the kinds of ideas and opinions such a free marketplace of ideas would permit, a sizeable number might not be as quick to agree. They may believe either that a consensus idea arrived at in the marketplace may be wrong or that a minority viewpoint may be incorrect or obnoxious or dangerous and therefore legitimately can and should be suppressed.

Nimmer, among others, responded to the criticism that truth will not always be the result of free marketplace forces by pointing out that such criticism "misses the point."[52] He noted that "Justice Holmes did not state that truth is to be found in the power of the thought to get itself accepted in the competition of the market. He said rather that this constitutes 'the best test' of truth."[53] As Nimmer said, "[w]hat is the alternative? It can only be acceptance of an idea by some individual or group narrower than that of the public at large. Thus the alternative to competition in the market must be some form of elitism. It seems hardly necessary to enlarge on the dangers of that path."[54]

Justice Holmes himself later responded to critics of a free marketplace who point out that allowing uninhibited free speech might protect a minority view that could prove "bad" or "false." Rather than government suppression, Holmes' solution was almost always the introduction of more speech. This approach was exemplified by Justice Brandeis in his concurring decision in *Whitney v. California*[55] in which he noted, "the fitting remedy for evil counsels is good ones. . . . If there be time to expose through discussion the falsehood and fallacies, to avert the evil by the process of education, the remedy to be applied is more speech, not enforced silence."[56] The reason is obvious for those who believe in free speech. That which the majority believes "bad" or "false" today, if allowed to be tested in the marketplace of ideas, may later prove to be the opposite. As Nimmer concludes, "[i]t is only through the process of testing by hearing more speech from others that a reliable judgment can be made as to the worth of the objectionable speech. This is the very essence of the enlightenment function" of free speech.[57]

Those who do not believe that the best test of truth is in the free marketplace of ideas—who wish to limit or prohibit speech rather than encourage more speech when they encounter ideas and opinions they consider dangerous or odious—often desire to regulate or legislate for what they believe to be the best of motives. Perhaps they see people doing "unacceptable" things and wish to discourage these activities by discouraging speech that promotes the behaviors. Alternatively, they may wish to regulate speech in the name of the afflicted or the weak. Unfortunately, these arguments are often raised in support of restricting or restraining advertising, public relations and other commercial speech.

Although the enlightenment function may be the primary rationale for free speech recognized by most scholars, it is not the only one. One of the better known alternative (if complementary) functions was advanced by Vincent Blasi who suggested that the primary value of free speech is to serve as a "checking function"[58] on the affairs of state. Free speech in this concept serves not so much as a means to test the truth of a multiplicity of views and opinions but as a counter balance to the power of government by ensuring that abuses of that power are restrained and exposed when they occur.

Alexander Meiklejohn proposed another, slightly different argument. In his viewpoint, freedom of speech is important because it allows intelligent choices by the electorate in a self-governing democracy.[59] Meiklejohn's ideas have been instrumental in formulating the concept that the First Amendment's primary purpose is to protect "political speech" from government regulation. "Its purpose," according to Meiklejohn, "is to give to every voting member of the body politic the fullest possible participation in the understanding of those problems with which the citizens of a self-governing society must deal."[60]

Even commentators who dispute the value of free speech as essential to democratic government or an enlightened society generally do not dispute that there are individual as well as societal benefits to free speech. Both as a way to vent frustration, rage or anger and as a means for self-expression, speech is an outlet for personal emotions that otherwise might lead to destructive acts or be repressed at psychological cost to the individual.

## The First Amendment in a Digital, New-Media Age: Emerging Issues

This introductory chapter gives the reader a brief overview of the development of First Amendment jurisprudence and an understanding of the major rationales for protection of speech and government attempts to breach that protection. Many of the issues and ideas discussed—including the categorization of different kinds of speech afforded different levels of First Amendment protection, court-created tests for laws and regulations of speech and non-content based restrictions on speech and expression— affect the regulation of advertising, public relations and other commercial speech discussed throughout the remainder of this book.

Not surprisingly, the advent of new media technologies has caused numerous collisions between First Amendment rights to free speech and government regulation thereof. For example, pornography is pornography whether it is viewed in print or electronically. But the nature of the Internet—a largely anonymous forum that often lacks the editorial safeguards and physical controls possible for traditional media materials—has inspired many individuals and bodies, including Congress, to seek ways to rein in this information dissemination beast. Sometimes these attempts bear implications for free speech.

Because the Internet provides easy, direct, computer access to words and images, production of online pornography was one of the first industries to successfully use online commerce. It also was one of the first industries to attract the attention of the public and lawmakers concerned about shielding children from inappropriate content.

Responding to public concerns about minors' access to pornography, Congress passed the 1996 Communications Decency Act (CDA),[61] which prohibited posting "indecent" or "patently offensive" materials in a public forum on the Internet. Free-speech advocates challenged the CDA as unconstitutional, and the Supreme Court of the United States ultimately agreed with many of their arguments. In July 1997, the Court affirmed a decision by a three-judge panel from the Eastern District of Pennsylvania, which held the CDA was too broad and therefore violated the First Amendment.[62]

The rise of new media technology as well as the increased use of other Web-based communication vehicles inevitably will create commercial-speech-related First Amendment issues that courts and media professionals will need to grapple with for years to come. Some of these issues are discussed in each of the remaining chapters. Wise and prudent advertising and public relations professionals might do well to not only make special note of this material, but be on perpetual lookout for new and, as of now, undreamed of First Amendment issues as they arise during the decades ahead.

# Chapter 2

# The Development of the Commercial Speech Doctrine

Distinct differences separate the legal challenges faced by advertising and public relations practitioners from those confronted by journalists and other communicators. Critics and commentators have suggested that the framers of the First Amendment intended its free-speech and press provisions to apply to debate and discussion of public issues, not advertising or other commercially oriented messages. They argue, therefore, that speech furthering the economic interests of the speaker can (and perhaps should) be subject to greater government regulation than "political speech."

Beginning with the first cases interpreting the constitutional protections of speech (discussed in the previous chapter), courts have accepted this general premise. Fortunately for advertising and public relations practitioners, courts also have determined that economically inspired speech is not devoid of all constitutional protection. This chapter looks at the development of this First Amendment body of law focusing on what courts typically refer to as "commercial speech."

## Development of Commercial Speech Jurisprudence

Clearly, most advertising of goods and services falls directly within the definition of "commercial speech." Less clear is whether marketing/public relations efforts by a profit-making corporation (e.g., a press release announcing a new product) fall within this definition. Advertising and public relations speech not directly focused on a for-profit organization's goods or services (e.g., a company's advertisement in the local newspaper publicly thanking its employees for community service efforts) finds itself in an even more ambiguous position vis-à-vis its relation to commercial speech. Advertising and public relations speech advancing a social issue or discussing important public problems, as well as speech by not-for-profit organizations, may not fit the definition of commercial speech at all.

# The History of Regulation of Commercial Speech from the Eighteenth to the Early Twentieth Centuries

Walking down the streets of Colonial Williamsburg, Virginia, or Old Sturbridge Village in Massachusetts or reading one of the newspapers these reconstructed communities of the late eighteenth and early nineteenth centuries produced, you might be struck by the virtual absence of advertising compared to the neon signs and commercial-filled mass media of a modern metropolis. This lack of advertising is no historic oversight.

In the days before the advent of regional or national mass-distribution of goods, residents of a community bought most items from local craftspeople, with the exception of a few relatively expensive products shipped by sea from England and the Continent. A window display, small painted sign, or, in larger communities, a classified-sized advertisement in the local weekly or monthly newspaper sufficed to inform a merchant's target market. By the end of the nineteenth century, however, first the railroads and then the mail-order business changed all that. Railroads made it possible for local stores to sell mass-produced goods shipped from sites perhaps hundreds of miles away. The mail-order catalog business meant that you need not depend only on your local tradesperson to make or purchase what you wanted.

Mass producers of items such as soap or cereal or wearing apparel depended at first only on local merchants to push their products. Soon, however, smart manufacturers saw the need for their own marketing and advertising campaigns to spur demand for particular brands and to build brand loyalty. Thus by the end of the nineteenth century, techniques of mass marketing and advertising began to catch up with the techniques for the mass production and distribution of goods, particularly the use of display advertising in rapidly expanding mass-circulation newspapers and magazines.

Until the development of advertising via the mass media, few manufacturers, retailers or consumers worried about the quality or the truthfulness of commercial speech. Strange as it seems in modern times, accustomed as we are to consumer watchdog groups and government regulatory agencies, most people in the nineteenth century followed the maxim of *caveat emptor* ("let the buyer beware"). Consumers depended on their proximity to the makers and sellers of goods to ensure quality control of the items they purchased. If the clientele found either the merchant's goods or services disappointing, they were sure to mention it the next time they saw the merchant in the street or stopped by the shop. Much of the commercial speech of the time communicated simple information such as store hours or featured items. Most people saw little advertising or product publicity of any kind as it would be defined today, and what little they did see generally was dismissed by all but the most gullible as inherently unbeliev-able, particularly because of the extravagant claims made for the benefits to be gained by selecting the touted products or services.

By the turn of the century, however, with mass media advertising and publicity becoming key determinants in purchasing behavior, both manu-facturers and consumers began to be more concerned with the truthfulness of the factual claims for products and services. These concerns led to the adoption of so-called "printer's ink" statutes at the state level. *Printer's Ink* magazine, a trade publication, had proposed a model statute in 1911. These statutes (discussed in more detail in later chapters) typically sub-jected those making false claims in their commercial speech to criminal prosecution, with a conviction punishable by a fine.

Congress created the Federal Trade Commission (FTC) in 1914. Its mandate was to ensure a level playing field in the competitive arena by pre-venting, among other things, "deceptive acts and practices."[1] Eventually, this included regulatory overview of commercial speech to ensure truthful, non-deceptive claims. The federal Food and Drug Administration (FDA) and the Bureau of Alcohol, Tobacco and Firearms (BATF) were created in the 1930s to regulate specialized products (e.g., medicines, health-care and beauty aids and controlled substances), including claims and other infor-mation manufacturers could put on container labels for these products. These government efforts to control commercial speech paralleled the development of self-regulatory schemes by various trade associations such as the Associated Advertising Clubs of America. These self-regulatory efforts depended largely on the use of moral suasion rather than penalizing offenders (such regulatory efforts will be discussed in more detail in later chapters).

From these early beginnings at the dawn of the twentieth century until World War II, federal and state efforts to regulate commercial speech con-tinued to grow, albeit in piecemeal fashion. Somewhat surprisingly, how-ever, despite this nearly half century of regulatory efforts, it was not until 1942 that attempts by government to limit commercial speech were chal-lenged as inherent violations of the Federal Constitution's guarantee of free speech. It took an eccentric individual entrepreneur to see the issue all the way through to the Supreme Court of the United States.

## The Commercial Speech "Exception" to the First Amendment: *Valentine v. Chrestensen*

The stage was set for the Court's initial foray into examining the constitu-tionality of commercial speech regulation by its decision in the 1939 case of *Schneider v. State (Town of Irvington)*.[2] Police arrested Clara Schneider, a Jehovah's Witness, for failing to obtain a permit before pros-elytizing her religious views door to door. The Court overturned her conviction on First Amendment speech and religion grounds but, in so doing, was careful to note that "[w]e are not to be taken as holding that commercial soliciting and canvassing may not be subjected to such regulation. . . ."[3] The Court seemed to suggest that rather than control commercial speech by a content-neutral, time-place-and-manner regulation, the community could legitimately discriminate against commercial speech based on the content of the message—the rationale being that commercial speech did not possess the same degree of First Amendment protection as other speech.

This apparent willingness by the Court to distinguish between regulation of commercial speech and other kinds of speech was borne out three year later in *Valentine v. Chrestensen*,[4] the first instance in which the Court decided the First Amendment issues in the case solely on the basis that the content of the speech in question was purely commercial speech.

F.J. Chrestensen was a small-time entrepreneur/showman who hit on the idea of rescuing a decommissioned United States Navy submarine from the scrap heap by purchasing it, refurbishing it and charging a small admission to tour the ship. After finally gaining permission from New York State officials to tie up at a pier in the East River (New York City officials had refused his initial request to use a city pier), Chrestensen was faced with the problem of how to attract visitors to his exhibition.

In New York City, it was virtually impossible for a small business to use conventional advertising to attract business. Because of scarcity and economies of scale, generally only large corporations or other organizations could either afford or need to reach the hundreds of thousands of readers, listeners and viewers the city's mass media served. A businessman like Chrestensen might have afforded a small advertisement or two to publicize his submarine tours, but unless he could spend thousands of advertising dollars to get his message across on a grand scale, his commercial speech was bound to be lost in the clutter of the other commercial messages vying for consumers' attention.

Having no large advertising budget at his disposal, Chrestensen turned instead to another traditional big-city publicity technique—handbills. Determining this to be a cheap (if less effective) means of reaching potential customers, Chrestensen created and had printed handbills that he distributed to passersby on the city's streets. Unfortunately for Chrestensen, this was in violation of the New York City Sanitary Code which said, in part, "No person shall . . . distribute . . . any handbill, circular . . . or other advertising matter whatsoever in or upon any street or public place . . . ."[5] The city ordinance made an exception, however, for "the lawful distribution of anything other than commercial and business advertising matter."[6]

The government interests were straightforward—protecting pedestrians from being accosted and perhaps impeded by street solicitors and preventing litter on city streets caused by the likelihood that those taking the handbills would throw them on the pavement. The countervailing interest of Chrestensen was equally clear—the freedom to advertise his submarine tour using a handbill containing legal, accurate and truthful speech.

After a number of unpleasant encounters with the police, Chrestensen, rather than face the continuing risk of arrest, chose instead to reprint his handbill with the commercial message (minus any mention of a tour fee) on one side and, as the Court later noted, "a protest against the action of the City Dock Department in refusing the respondent wharfage facilities at a city pier"[7] on the other. The police, seeing this as simply an effort by Chrestensen to get around the law by turning his commercial speech into a political protest, which the ordinance specifically allowed, again refused permission to distribute his reprinted handbill, although they conceded that distributing a circular with just the protest message would be legal under the city code.

At this point, Chrestensen turned to the federal courts, seeking a restraining order to stop the police from interfering with the distribution of his handbills. The district court found that the city ordinance indeed went too far and granted a permanent injunction against police enforcement of the disputed regulation.[8] The federal appeals court agreed, upholding the lower court's order in a divided opinion.[9]

The Supreme Court of the United States disagreed. The question, said the Court, is "whether the application of the ordinance to [Chrestensen's] activity was, in the circumstances, an unconstitutional abridgement of the freedom of the press and of speech."[10] While noting that previous decisions had "unequivocally held that the streets are proper places for the exercise of the freedom of communicating information and disseminating opinion and that . . . states and municipalities . . . may not unduly burden or proscribe its employment in these public thoroughfares . . . [W]e are equally clear that the Constitution imposes no such restraint on government as respects purely commercial advertising."[11] This clear rejection of "purely commercial advertising" as a category of speech protected by the Federal Constitution created what eventually became known as the "commercial-speech doctrine."[12] The Court did not return to evaluating the First Amendment status of pure commercial speech until more than three decades later with its decision in *Pittsburgh Press Co. v. Pittsburgh Commission on Human Relations*.[13]

## The "Exception" Begins to Narrow

The *Pittsburgh Press Co.* case is complex for a variety of reasons, not the least of which is that it requires the reader to think of by-gone times when newspapers like the *Pittsburgh Press* routinely ran classified advertising for employment under "HELP WANTED—MALE" and "HELP WANTED—FEMALE" columns. Typically, ads under the "MALE" heading sought lawyers, physicians and other professionals, whereas ads under the "FEMALE" heading were for public school teachers, nurses and office workers. The advertisements clearly implied that if you were female, you need not apply for jobs in the well-paid professions or for managerial positions in industry.

The general public gave little thought to such sex-based discrimination until these practices were challenged by civil rights laws passed by Congress in the mid-1960s. These federal statutes inspired state and local ordinances prohibiting sexual bias in the workplace, including the Human Relations Ordinance legislated by the city of Pittsburgh. The regulation prohibited hiring based on the job-seeker's sex, and made it unlawful "[f]or any person whether or not an employer, employment agency or labor organization, to aid . . . in the doing of any act declared to be an unlawful employment practice by this ordinance . . ." including publishing or circulating "any notice or advertisement relating to 'employment' or membership which indicates any discrimination because of . . . sex."[14]

In October 1969, the National Organization for Women filed a complaint with the Pittsburgh Commission on Human Relations charging that the *Pittsburgh Press* was in noncompliance with the ordinance. The Commission agreed and issued a cease-and-desist order instructing the newspaper to discontinue using the sex-based classification scheme. The newspaper's arguments that it simply was following the requests of advertisers and that the ordinance violated the newspaper's right to determine the layout and content of its advertising pages were specifically rejected. The *Pittsburgh Press* appealed the Commission's order to the local court of common pleas which upheld the order. On appeal, the Pennsylvania Commonwealth Court modified the order slightly but basically left it intact. The Pennsylvania Supreme Court refused to review the case and the newspaper appealed to the Supreme Court of the United States.

Conceding that protection of speech and press was paramount to a democracy, the Court nonetheless found that the city ordinance was not a significant infringement of the newspaper's economic well-being. Based on *Valentine*, the Court also found that the advertisements in question were "classic examples of commercial speech."[15] The newspaper had argued that, unlike *Valentine*, the commercial speech distinction was inapplicable in this case because the issue was the regulation of the editorial judgment of a newspaper rather than the control of commercial content or the actions of an advertiser. The Court rejected this argument, finding that decisions about placement of an advertisement failed to "lift the newspaper's actions from the category of commercial speech."[16]

The Court also rejected the newspaper's final argument that a distinction between commercial speech and other kinds of speech was inappropriate and should be abandoned. Saying this argument would be best left until a later day, the Court noted that the discriminatory advertising policy and contents of the advertisements in contention were "not only commercial activity but illegal commercial activity under the Ordinance."[17] The Count concluded that "[a]ny First Amendment interest which might be served by advertising an ordinary commercial proposal and which might arguably outweigh the government interest supporting the regulation is altogether absent when the commercial activity itself is illegal and the restriction on advertising is incidental to a valid limitation on economic activity."[18]

At first reading, the decision in *Pittsburgh Press* appeared to be a simple re-affirmation of the Court's commercial speech exception to the First Amendment. However, a more thorough analysis provided hope that the Court's blanket denial of constitutional protection for purely commercial speech was not as absolute as it had seemed. Rather than simply refusing to hear the case or dismissing the newspaper's First Amendment arguments out of hand, the Court was careful to base its decision on the notion that the commercial speech in question was for an illegal purpose and that the government's interests in regulation therefore outweighed the newspaper's speech interests. This opened the door ever so slightly to the idea that courts should scrutinize more carefully any government attempts to ban or in other ways regulate commercial speech for *legal* products or services.

This wedge in opening the way for at least some constitutional protection for commercial speech, and the unusual circumstances of the next important commercial speech case, *Bigelow v. Virginia*,[19] combined to create the first major breakthrough in the drive to place commercial speech within the ambit of the First Amendment.

The Court's decision in *Bigelow* emanated from a case involving an advertisement for an abortion referral service. Bigelow, the director and managing editor of his self-described "underground weekly newspaper," *The Virginia Weekly*,[20] published a display advertisement that read as follows:

UNWANTED PREGNANCY
LET US HELP YOU
Abortions are now legal in New York.
There are no residency requirements.
FOR IMMEDIATE PLACEMENT IN ACCREDITED
HOSPITALS AND CLINICS AT LOW COST
Contact
WOMEN'S PAVILION
515 Madison Avenue
New York, N.Y. 10022
or call any time
(212) 371–6670 or (212) 371–6650
AVAILABLE 7 DAYS A WEEK

STRICTLY CONFIDENTIAL.
We will make all arrangements for you
and help you with information and counseling.[21]

All of the information in the advertisement was true, including the legality of regulated abortions in New York State. Unfortunately for Bigelow, abortions were illegal at this time in his home state of Virginia as were, according to a Virginia statute, efforts of "any person by publication, lecture, advertisement, or by the sale or circulation of any publication, or in any other manner, [to] encourage or prompt the procuring of abortion or miscarriage . . . ."[22] The statute made such efforts a misdemeanor.

Bigelow was convicted of violating the statute and fined $500 ($350 of which was forgiven if he promised not to run similar advertisements in the future). The Supreme Court of Virginia upheld his conviction, specifically rejecting his First Amendment-based claim that the statute was unconstitutional. The Virginia court found that the speech in question was a "commercial advertisement" and therefore it could "constitutionally [be] prohibited by the state . . . [when] the advertising relates to the medical-health field."[23]

On appeal, the Supreme Court of the United States vacated Bigelow's conviction and returned the case to Virginia for further consideration without deciding on the merits of his First Amendment claims. It did so because of the decision in *Roe v. Wade*,[24] in which the Court—on a Federal Constitution-based, individual-privacy theory—limited a state's ability to regulate abortions. *Roe v. Wade* was decided soon after Bigelow's request for the Court to hear his case. The Supreme Court of Virginia reaffirmed its earlier opinion, upholding Bigelow's conviction on the basis that *Roe v. Wade* had not "mentioned the subject of abortion advertising."[25] Bigelow again appealed to the Supreme Court of the United States, and the high Court again reversed his conviction, this time on First Amendment grounds.

The Court began its opinion by noting that reliance on *Valentine* for the proposition that purely commercial speech is unprotected by the First Amendment is misplaced. "The fact that [*Valentine*] had the effect of banning a particular handbill does not mean that [it] is authority for the proposition that all statutes regulating commercial advertising are immune from constitutional challenge."[26] The Court said that although the classified advertisements in *Pittsburgh Press* were purely commercial speech, even they "would have received some degree of First Amendment protection if the commercial proposal had been legal."[27] The Court found that the advertisement in *Bigelow*

did more than simply propose a commercial transaction. It contained factual material of clear "public interest." Viewed in its entirety, the advertisement conveyed information of potential interest and value to a diverse audience—not only to readers possibly in need of the services offered, but also to those with a general curiosity about, or genuine interest in, the subject matter or the law of another State and its development, and to readers seeking reform in Virginia.[28]

It seems reasonable to believe that underlying the Court's decision in *Bigelow* was concern that Virginia's regulation of commercial speech for an abortion referral service was a none-too-subtle attempt to regulate a woman's constitutional right to seek an abortion. Support for this view comes from the language of the decision, including a disclaimer by the Court that "[w]e do not decide in this case the precise extent to which the First Amendment permits regulation of advertising that is related to activities the State may legitimately regulate or even prohibit."[29] Later in the opinion, the Court again noted that "[w]e need not decide here the extent to which constitutional protection is afforded commercial advertising under all circumstances and in the face of all kinds of regulation."[30]

However, the Court did find that "[t]o the extent that commercial activity is subject to regulation, the relationship of speech to that activity may be one factor among others, to be considered in weighing the First Amendment interest against the government interest alleged. Advertising is not thereby stripped of all First Amendment protection."[31] From now on, said the Court, "a court may not escape the task of assessing the First Amendment interest at stake and weighing it against the public interest allegedly served by the [government] regulation"[32] particularly if the commercial speech is not deceptive or fraudulent and it is related to a legal product or service.

Although *Bigelow* represented a significant step forward in overcoming the Court's 30-year acquiescence to government regulation of purely commercial speech, the decision failed to address a number of major issues. Although, after *Bigelow*, courts were required to balance speech interests against government regulatory interests, there was little discussion by the Court about how that balancing was to take place or how much weight should be assigned to either speech or government interests. (Remember that in other earlier cases, the Court placed a "heavy burden" on those who wish to regulate fully protected speech.) Nor was there discussion of the range of activities the Court had in mind when it noted that "the State may legitimately regulate or even prohibit"[33] advertising for some activities.

The Court also did not define the terms "deceptive" and "fraudulent" or the legality of a state limiting non-deceptive, legal advertising in its media for an activity or product illegal in another state (e.g., a New York statute banning advertising of an illegal abortion-referral service in Virginia). Finally, the Court did not indicate what the result might have been if Virginia's regulation had been aimed at an advertiser rather than at the newspaper or if potential consumers of the advertised service or product had any independent First Amendment rights to receive the information contained in the disputed advertising.

### *Virginia State Board of Pharmacy*: **The High-Water Mark for Protection of Commercial Speech**

It was this last issue that formed the basis for the Court's next decision, *Virginia State Board of Pharmacy v. Virginia Citizens Consumer Council, Inc.*,[34] still the high-water mark in the development of First Amendment protection for purely commercial speech. The Virginia State Board of Pharmacy is the agency empowered by the state to license and regulate pharmacists and the practice of pharmacy in Virginia. The Board had ruled that advertising the price of prescription drugs was inherently "unprofessional conduct"[35] and that such conduct could subject the pharmacist who violated this rule to sanctions, including license revocation. The Board's regulations were questioned neither by advertisers nor the media, but rather by a consumer group allegedly representing potential purchasers of prescription medicines. The council challenged the Board's anti-advertising rules on the somewhat novel thesis that consumers, who would benefit from information about prescription drug prices, had a First Amendment right to receive such information.

A three-judge district court weighed the state's stated interests in preventing abuse and deception in the practice of pharmacy against the speech-related arguments advanced by the plaintiff that price information could significantly reduce the costs of prescription medicines. Noting evidence that prices charged for the same drugs could vary as much as 600 percent from pharmacy to pharmacy, the court found that the consumer group's arguments carried greater weight and struck down the anti-advertising regulation on First Amendment grounds. The state pharmacy board appealed to the Supreme Court of the United States, arguing that Virginia's ban on advertising was a legitimate regulation of purely commercial speech.

The Court characterized the basic issue in this case as

> whether there is a First Amendment exception for "commercial speech". . . . Our pharmacist does not wish to editorialize on any subject, cultural philosophical or political. He does not wish to report any particularly newsworthy fact, or to make generalized observations even about commercial matters. The "idea" he wishes to communicate is simply this: "I will sell you the X prescription drug at the Y price." Our question, then is whether this communication is wholly outside the protection of the First Amendment.[36]

The Court said the answer was no.

The Court stressed four factors favoring disseminating commercial information about the price of prescription drugs over the government regulatory interests in banning such information. First, said the Court, the economic motivation behind the speech did not serve to disqualify it automatically from First Amendment protection. Second, the Court noted that "consumer's interest in the free flow of commercial information . . . may be as keen, if not keener by far, than his interest in the day's most urgent political debate."[37] This was especially true in this case, said the Court, because the poor and elderly represented by the plaintiff tend to spend a disproportionate amount of income on prescription drugs yet have little ability to comparison shop. The Court also found that striking down the ban on this form of commercial speech served to underlie the more general interest society has "in the free flow of commercial information."[38] Information of general public interest, like advertisements discussing the benefits of environmentally friendly products, would likely be protected from such government regulation and, the Court said, it could find little reason for not affording prescription-drug advertising similar status.

Finally, acknowledging that the American economic system is based on free enterprise, the Court concluded that the system, "no matter how tasteless and excessive it sometimes may seem is nonetheless [dependent on] dissemination of information as to who is producing and selling what product, for what reason, and at what price."[39] For it to work, said the Court, the system requires that "decisions, in the aggregate, be intelligent and well informed. To this end, the free flow of commercial information is indispensable."[40]

The Court accepted Virginia's arguments that prescription drug advertising could weaken the professionalism of licensed pharmacists but rejected banning advertising as a legitimate means for the state to accomplish its ends, noting the availability of many other regulations controlling the licensing and practices of the profession. Most such regulations would be permissible, said the Court, but adopting the one that relies "in large measure on the advantages of [keeping the public] in ignorance"[41] is not among them. "It is precisely this kind of choice, between the dangers of suppressing information, and the dangers of its misuse if it is freely available, that the First Amendment makes for us."[42]

In striking down the ban on prescription drug advertising, the Court added that it was not affording fully protected, First Amendment status to purely commercial speech. Legitimate time-place-and manner regulations would still be legal, said the Court, as would regulations restricting false, misleading or deceptive commercial speech. In an extensive footnote, the Court stated that because of the "hardiness" of commercial speech, and because the truth of the statements in such speech "may be more easily verifiable by its disseminator than, let us say, news reporting or political commentary," government could be granted greater leeway under the First Amendment to regulate purely commercial speech.[43]

> Since advertising is the *sine qua non* of commercial profits, there is lit-tle likelihood of its being chilled by proper regulation and foregone entirely. Attributes such as these, the greater objectivity and hardiness of commercial speech, may make it less necessary to tolerate inaccurate statement for fear of silencing the speaker. They may also make it appropriate to require that a commercial message appear in such a form or include such additional information, warnings and dis-claimers are necessary to prevent its being deceptive. They may also make inapplicable the prohibition against prior restraints.[44]

The Court concluded that none of these rationales for lawful regulation of purely commercial speech applied in this case. "What is at issue [here] is whether a State may completely suppress the dissemination of concededly truthful information about entirely lawful activity, fearful of that infor-mation's effect upon its disseminators and its recipients. . . . [W]e conclude that the answer . . . is in the negative."[45]

Despite the Court's reluctance to grant full First Amendment protection to pure commercial speech, the Court's change of focus in *Virginia State Board of Pharmacy* from protecting the rights of the speaker to protecting the needs and the rights of the audience to receive information gave hope to commercial-speech advocates that the commercial speech exception to the First Amendment was now limited to speech that touted an illegal product or activity or to commercial claims that could mislead or deceive the potential consumer. Under such a consumer-based approach, the gov-ernment would be hard pressed to deny readers and viewers the informa-tion they needed to make informed choices when deciding how to conduct their personal commercial transactions.

## The Supreme Court Begins to Retreat: *Bates et al. v. State Bar of Arizona*

Unfortunately, the euphoria generated by *Virginia State Board of Pharmacy* was almost immediately tempered by the reasoning of the Court in *Bates et al. v. State Bar of Arizona*[46] just one year later. John Bates and Van O'Steen, both attorneys practicing law in Phoenix, Arizona, formed a partnership to run a legal clinic to provide low-cost legal services for peo-ple of moderate income. It became apparent almost immediately that they would need to advertise to build a client base.

As part of this advertising, the partners decided they should include information about the fees charged for standard services such as uncontested divorces and simple personal bankruptcies. Advertising was expressly forbidden, however, by the rules covering the practice of law in Arizona administered by the state's bar association. When the two attorneys placed an advertisement in the *Arizona Republic*, the state bar president filed a complaint that eventually resulted in both Bates and O'Steen being suspended from the practice of law for one week. Both appealed their suspensions to the Arizona Supreme Court, arguing that the sanctions by the bar violated both antitrust and free-speech laws. The Arizona court upheld the suspensions and Bates and O'Steen appealed to the Supreme Court of the United States.

The Court dismissed contentions that the state bar rule violated federal antitrust provisions but found merit in the attorneys' First Amendment arguments. Citing *Virginia State Board of Pharmacy* for the proposition that commercial speech was at least somewhat protected by the First Amendment, the Court then turned its attention to the state's arguments that lawyer advertising was an exception to this rule or, in the alternative, that the particular advertising by Bates and O'Steen was inherently false and deceptive.

Ordinarily, said the Court, there is no need for a finding that a specific speaker's rights in fact have been violated before a court should strike down a law or regulation that suppresses speech as an infringement of the First Amendment. This, the Court said, "reflects the conclusion that the possible harm to society from allowing unprotected speech to go unpunished is outweighed by the possibility that protected speech will be muted."[47] In a case involving purely commercial speech, however, the Court noted that this overbreadth doctrine does not apply because there are "'commonsense differences' between commercial speech and other varieties [of speech]."[48]

One such difference, said the Court, is that because

> advertising is linked to commercial well-being, it seems unlikely that such speech is particularly susceptible to being crushed by overbroad regulations. Moreover, concerns for uncertainty in determining the scope of protection are reduced; the advertiser seeks to disseminate information about a product or service that he provides, and presumably he can determine more readily than others whether his speech is truthful and protected.[49]

The Court characterized the principal issue in *Bates* as "a narrow one"— whether "lawyers . . . may constitutionally advertise the prices at which certain routine services will be performed."[50] The state had argued that because the costs for legal services could only be determined on a case-by-case basis, advertising fixed prices was false and deceptive. The Court disagreed, holding that the state's total ban on lawyer advertising via the mass media (including advertising the price of standard services) was not permitted under the First Amendment but also noting that pure commercial speech still could be regulated in ways that fully protected speech cannot. For example, the Court explicitly stated that false, deceptive or misleading commercial speech could be restrained as could commercial speech about illegal products or transactions. Additionally, the Court noted that time-place-and-manner regulations could apply to commercial speech and that "the special problems of advertising on the electronic broadcast media . . . [could] warrant special considerations."[51]

The focus of the Court in *Bates*—"whether lawyers [i.e., the commercial speaker] . . . may constitutionally advertise"[52]—clearly indicated that the Court was no longer judging the constitutionality of laws regulating commercial speech by evaluating how much such laws infringe on the rights of the audience to receive commercial information. The Court could have characterized the issue in *Bates* as "whether consumers of legal services have a right to information about the prices of standard legal services," but chose not to do so. Although the Court indulged in some discussion of the need for informed decision making on the part of potential clients, *Bates* signaled the beginning of a continuing retreat from the *Virginia State Board of Pharmacy* audience-centered focus and a return to evaluating regulation of purely commercial speech by balancing the rights of the speaker—and not the receiver—against the interests of the government.

## Development of Modern Commercial Speech Regulation: *Central Hudson's* Four-Prong Test

In *Central Hudson Gas & Electric v. Public Service Commission*,[53] the Supreme Court attempted to resolve the confusion caused by its nearly four-decade-long, zigzag path through the world of commercial speech regulation by setting out a four-part test for judging the constitutionality of laws governing commercial speech.

The regulations challenged in *Central Hudson* banned advertising that promoted the use of electricity. Originally, the regulations had been promulgated by the state agency in charge of regulating utilities as a temporary response to an energy crisis in the early 1970s. The Public Service Commission (PSC) extended the advertising ban after the immediate crisis had passed, however, as a general conservation measure. The Commission admitted that prohibiting advertising was not a perfect remedy because it restricted electric power utilities from encouraging the most efficient uses of electric power and because the ban did not apply to alternative energy sources like oil or coal. Nonetheless, the Commission continued its ban, in part because it feared that allowing advertising would send "misleading signals"[54] to consumers that conservation of electric power was no longer an important energy conservation goal. Central Hudson Gas & Electric challenged the PSC's ban in state court, but its arguments that the ban violated the corporation's First Amendment rights received little sympathy. Central Hudson then appealed to the Supreme Court of the United States.

Citing *Virginia State Board of Pharmacy*, Justice Powell, writing for the majority, reiterated that the First Amendment protects commercial speech from unwarranted government regulation, but also noted the Court's decisions recognizing differences in constitutional protection between commercial speech and other kinds of speech. Therefore, he said, protection for commercial speech "turns on the nature both of the expression and of the government interests served by its regulation."[55]

According to Justice Powell, "[i]n commercial speech cases . . . a four-part analysis has developed."[56] First, said Justice Powell, the court needs to determine (a) if the speech in question is protected by the First Amendment at all. As examples of non-protected speech, Justice Powell noted that there was little constitutional value in commercial speech that promotes illegal activities or products or that contains statements that are false or which tend to mislead or deceive. If the speech in question falls into one of these categories, it fails the first part of the four-part test and the government may regulate as it sees fit. However, if the commercial speech the government intends to regulate does not fall into any of these categories, it is protected by the First Amendment and, said Justice Powell, "the government's power is more circumscribed."[57] Before regulating constitutionally protected commercial speech, said Justice Powell, the government must first show (b) that such regulation serves a "substantial" [not "compelling"] government purpose and, in addition, (c) that the actual manner in which the government proposes to regulate the speech directly aids the government in achieving its substantial purpose.[58] Finally, said the Court, the regulation must be (d) "narrowly tailored" to ensure that the regulation "is not more extensive than is necessary to further the [substantial government purpose.]"[59]

Applying its four-part test to the facts of *Central Hudson*, the Court first found that the Constitution protected the company's commercial speech because there was nothing illegal, false or deceptive about the commercial information the utility company was attempting to convey. Turning to the arguments of the state regulatory commission, the Court agreed that the state's interests in conserving natural resources and encouraging non-wasteful consumption of electric power were "substantial" government interests. The Court also accepted the Commission's arguments that the method chosen—regulating the utility's commercial speech—helped the state to realize its substantial interest in discouraging wasteful consumption of electric power. The Court based its finding on the premise that "there is an immediate connection between advertising and demand for electricity."[60]

However, the Court found that the actions by the state utility commission could not pass the fourth part of the test because the challenged regulations were overly broad. "The Commission's order," said the Court, "reaches all promotional advertising, regardless of the impact of the touted service on overall energy use."[61] The Court, noting that the utility company had argued that it would have informed consumers how to be more energy conscious if not for the advertising ban, held that "[t]o the extent that the Commission's order suppresses speech that in no way impairs the State's interest in energy conservation, [that] order violates the First and Fourteenth Amendments. . . ."[62] Justice Powell pointed out, however, that instead of a complete prohibition, the Court might accept alternative methods of regulating the utility company's commercial speech like restricting the format or limiting or requiring additional content.

Although the four-part *Central Hudson* test gained the approval of a majority of the Court as a cogent summation of the evolution of constitutional protection for purely commercial speech, several justices remained skeptical. Some felt that providing any constitutional protection for commercial speech extended the protective umbrella of the First Amendment to speech the authors of the First Amendment never meant to include. Others feared that such protection for commercial speech could water down protection for more important kinds of speech.

## The Court Applies the *Central Hudson* Test with Mixed Results

Chief among the critics of *Central Hudson* was Justice Rehnquist. He expressed some of his sharpest criticisms in his dissenting opinion in *Metromedia, Inc. v. San Diego*,[63] the first major commercial speech case to reach the Court after *Central Hudson*. *Metromedia* involved a challenge to the city of San Diego's municipal ordinance banning billboards and other outdoor advertising signs "to eliminate hazards to pedestrians and motorists"[64] and for general aesthetic reasons. A billboard company challenged the ordinance, arguing that the ordinance's exceptions for on-premise advertising of commercial names and/or services offered and for off-premise signs of a religious, historical or public-service nature were not sufficient to protect the commercial billboard company's free speech interests.

The Court struck down the city ordinance but the justices strenuously disagreed among themselves about how to apply the *Central Hudson* four-part test (Justice Rehnquist characterized the Court's collective opinions as "a virtual Tower of Babel").[65] Justice White and three other justices agreed that the city's regulatory scheme passed the *Central Hudson* test for legally regulating commercial speech, but they nonetheless disallowed the ordinance on the grounds that permitting on-premise advertising of commercial messages but disallowing noncommercial messages unconstitutionally discriminated against noncommercial speech. Justices Blackmun and Brennan agreed that the ordinance should be struck down, but on the grounds that it did not pass any part of the *Central Hudson* test. Chief Justice Burger and Justices Stevens and Rehnquist dissented in separate opinions, but each would have upheld the ordinance, agreeing that both the city's reasons for regulation and the means to accomplish its ends met the requirements of the *Central Hudson* test.

Similar internal divisions within the Court surfaced in a series of subsequent commercial speech cases raising constitutional questions in which shifting coalitions of justices alternately upheld and struck down government attempts to regulate commercial speech. For example, in *City Council v. Taxpayers for Vincent*,[66] the Court upheld a ban on signs that did not differentiate between commercial and noncommercial speech. Justices Brennan, Marshall and Blackmun dissented on the grounds that the majority had been much too deferential to the city's aesthetics arguments and had not carefully evaluated the competing speech interests. Justice Brennan would have required the city to at least demonstrate that it was engaged in a major, multi-method campaign to eradicate visual pollution and that banning signs was a necessary step in this campaign.

### Posadas de Puerto Rico Associates v. Tourism Company of Puerto Rico Foretells an Uncertain Future for So-Called "Vice Cases"

The elasticity of the *Central Hudson* test was best illustrated by the Court's decision in *Posadas de Puerto Rico Associates v. Tourism Company of Puerto Rico*.[67] The Puerto Rico legislature passed a statute legalizing casino gambling to encourage economic development of the island, but the statute specified that casinos would not "be permitted to advertise or otherwise offer their facilities to the public of Puerto Rico."[68] A later modification of the statute permitted advertising in "newspapers, magazines, radio, television or other publicity media outside Puerto Rico,"[69] even though such media might find their way into the hands of island residents.

Posadas de Puerto Rico Associates, a corporation operating the Condado Plaza Hotel and Casino, was fined and threatened with suspension of its gambling license for violating the advertising provisions of the statute by the Tourism Company of Puerto Rico, the agency delegated power by the commonwealth to regulate casinos. The corporation paid the fine under protest and asked the courts of Puerto Rico to judge the constitutionality of the statute. Although the courts agreed that the statute had been interpreted too broadly (apparently even imprinting the name of the casino on matchbook covers had been prohibited), they upheld the statute's prohibition of advertising in the mass media of Puerto Rico.

Justice Rehnquist, writing for a five-person majority, applied the *Central Hudson* test, but in a manner that seemed to diminish the commercial speech protection provided in that case. "The . . . commercial speech at issue here," said the Court, ". . . concerns a lawful activity and is not misleading or fraudulent, at least in the abstract. We must therefore proceed to the three remaining steps [of the test]. . . . The first of these . . . involves an assessment of the strength of the government's interest in restricting the speech."[70] The Court, without requiring the commonwealth to produce evidence justifying its conclusions, held that Puerto Rico had satisfied the second part of the *Central Hudson* four-part test, accepting the commonwealth's arguments that "casino gambling . . . would produce serious harmful effects on the health, safety and welfare of the Puerto Rican citizens, such as the disruption of moral and cultural patterns, the increase in local crime . . . and the infiltration of organized crime."[71] The Court added, "[w]e have no difficulty in concluding that the Puerto Rico Legislature's interest . . . [in the] welfare of its citizens constitutes a 'substantial' government interest."[72]

The Court characterized parts three and four of the *Central Hudson* test as requiring "a consideration of the 'fit' between the legislature's ends and means chosen to accomplish those ends."[73] Again without analysis, the Court accepted the commonwealth's "belief" that the "advertising of casino gambling aimed at the residents of Puerto Rico would serve to increase the demand for the product advertised."[74] The fourth part of the *Central Hudson* test proved no more of an obstacle. "We also think it clear beyond peradventure that the challenged statute and relations satisfy the fourth and last step . . . namely, whether the restrictions on commercial speech are no more extensive than necessary to serve the government's interest,"[75] the majority said. The Court noted that "[w]e think it is up to the legislature to decide whether or not such a 'counterspeech' policy would be as effective in reducing the demand for casino gambling as a restriction of advertising."[76]

Unlike other commercial speech cases that involved bans of commercial speech struck down on First Amendment grounds, the commercial speech in *Posadas* was not about a constitutionally protected activity like abortion or birth control. "In our view," said Justice Rehnquist, ". . . it is precisely because the government could have enacted a wholesale prohibition of the underlying conduct that it is permissible for the government to take the less intrusive step of allowing the conduct, but reducing the demand through restrictions on advertising."[77] The Court added that "[i]t would be . . . a strange constitutional doctrine which would concede to the legislature the authority to totally ban a product or activity but deny to the legislature the authority to forbid the stimulation of demand for the product or activity through advertising on behalf of those who would profit from such increased demand."[78]

If *Virginia State Board of Pharmacy* represents a high-water mark for the protection of commercial speech, *Posadas* may well be the opposite.

Since *Posadas*, the Court has continued to apply and further amplify the four-part *Central Hudson* test in a series of "pure" commercial speech cases. Unfortunately, the Court has lurched forward and backward, first finding increased First Amendment protection for commercial speech, then retreating from that position. The sum total of these cases has left the so-called commercial speech exception to the First Amendment intact and has done little to clarify the exact parameters and permissible extent of government regulation of commercial speech.

## SUNY v. Fox: The Court Diminishes the Fourth Prong of *Central Hudson*

In *Board of Trustees of State University of New York [SUNY] v. Fox*,[79] the Court stepped back from granting increased First Amendment protection for commercial speech. The case involved a Tupperware party in a college dorm room that ran afoul of a university policy against commercial solicitation in residence halls. A federal appeals court in the second circuit decided that the state's interests in maintaining an educational atmosphere in its residence halls, as well as safety considerations, met the "substantiality" requirement of the second part of the *Central Hudson* test. The appeals court, however, criticized the means chosen to achieve these interests and faulted the university for not choosing a method that was the least restrictive of the speech interests of the student plaintiffs.

The Supreme Court disagreed with this latter decision. Focusing on the fourth part of the *Central Hudson* test, the Court noted that

> [w]hile we have insisted that the free flow of commercial information is valuable enough to justify imposing on would-be regulators the costs of distinguishing . . . the harmless from the harmful, we have not gone so far as to impose upon them the burden of demonstrating that . . . the manner of restriction is absolutely the least severe that will achieve the desired end.[80]

The Court added, "[w]hat our decisions require is a 'fit' between the legislature's ends and the means chosen to accomplish those ends."[81]

This interpretation of the fourth part of the *Central Hudson* test was seen by many commentators as a significant diminution of First Amendment protection for commercial speech. Although requiring more than a rational reason for its regulation, the Court made it clear that if the government could demonstrate it had evaluated its options for regulation carefully, and presented evidence that it had adopted an option that was a reasonable means of accomplishing its legitimate ends, the Court would not require that the remedy chosen be the one least restrictive of speech.

A pair of cases in 1993, *City of Cincinnati v. Discovery Networks, Inc.*[82] and *Edenfield v. Fane*,[83] however, breathed new life into prongs three and four of the *Central Hudson* test. Discovery Network, Inc., a provider of "educational, recreational, and social programs to individuals,"[84] published a magazine touting its programs and distributed it via street news racks. Similarly, Harmon Publishing Co., a real-estate business, promoted its property listings by distributing free publications in news racks depicting and describing homes for sale. Both companies had sought and received permission to locate their news racks at approximately 40 sites in the Cincinnati area, but the city council rescinded this permission in a move the council described as an attempt to beautify the downtown streets as well as to make them safer for pedestrians and drivers. As applied, however, the removal order affected only the news racks of Discovery and Harmon, and not those of news publications. The council justified this discrimination on the theory that the non-news publications constituted commercial handbills and, therefore, legally could be regulated much more stringently than news publications.

Discovery Network and Harmon challenged the enforcement of the ordinance, claiming First Amendment violations along with due process concerns. City officials, although conceding that application of the ordinance to newspapers and news magazines would raise First Amendment problems, countered that the plaintiffs' speech was commercial in nature and, therefore, the city had greater license to regulate their speech because of the reduced First Amendment protection accorded commercial speech.

The federal trial court disagreed,[85] finding that the city had failed to demonstrate a reasonable fit between its desire for beauty and safety and its actions in banning the approximately 60 news racks owned by the plaintiffs. This lack of fit was especially noticeable, said the court, because the city had left in place the 1,500 to 2,000 street racks used by newspapers and news magazines.

On appeal, the sixth circuit characterized the only issue as "does Cincinnati's ordinance . . . prescribe a 'reasonable fit' between the ends asserted and the means chosen to advance them?"[86] The court found that it did not. Noting that the city was not concerned with the harm caused by the content of the publications but rather the "harms caused by the manner of delivering that speech,"[87] the appeals court agreed with the trial court that banning distribution of the publications by means of news racks was impermissible. Such actions, said the court, are not a "reasonable fit" between the city's interests and the "wide range of options open to the city to control the perceived ill effects of newsracks,"[88] including bolting the news racks to the sidewalk, establishing color and design standards for the racks and limiting the number of permits granted by employing a lottery-type system.

The Supreme Court of the United States accepted the city's appeal, observing that the "importance of the court of appeals decision, together with the dramatic growth in the use of newsracks throughout the country, prompted our grant of certiorari. . . ."[89] Writing for a six-person majority (Justice Blackman added a concurring opinion as well), Justice Stevens agreed with the Sixth Circuit's interpretation of the fourth prong of the *Central Hudson* test, holding that "[i]t was the city's burden to establish a 'reasonable fit' between its legitimate interests . . . and the means chosen to serve those interests."[90] The Court concluded, "[t]here is ample support in the record . . . that the city did not [meet the burden] we require."[91] Because, said the Court, "the city failed to address its recently developed concern about newsracks by regulating their size, shape, appearance, or number . . . it has not [as required by SUNY] 'carefully calculated' the costs and benefits associated with the burden on speech imposed by its prohibition."[92]

The Court briefly dismissed the city's contention that it could ban the specific street racks of the non-news-oriented companies on the theory that commercial speech is less protected by the First Amendment. The Court noted that

> the city contends that the fact that assertedly more valuable publications are allowed to use newsracks does not undermine its judgment that its aesthetic and safety interests are stronger than the interest in allowing commercial speakers to have similar access to the reading public. We cannot agree. In our view, the city's argument attaches more importance to the distinction between commercial and noncommercial speech than our cases warrant and seriously underestimates the value of commercial speech.[93]

The majority opinion traced the development of the commercial speech exception, beginning with *Valentine*, to demonstrate that the city had erred in believing that merely because the publications in question contained a high ratio of advertising to text, they should be exempted from normal constitutional protection. First, observing that "[s]ome ordinary newspapers try to maintain a ratio of 70 percent advertising to 30 percent editorial content,"[94] Justice Stevens pointed out that the Court's reasoning in earlier cases required the city to more strictly scrutinize the contents of the publications, noting that some of the material in question "is not what we have described as 'core' commercial speech."[95] The Court concluded that "[t]he regulation is not a permissible regulation of commercial speech, for on this record it is clear that the interests that Cincinnati has asserted are unrelated to any distinction between 'commercial handbills' and 'newspapers'."[96]

The Court also gave similar short shrift to the city's arguments that its ban was nothing more that a legitimate time-place-and-manner regulation. "[B]ecause the ban is predicated on the content of the publications distributed by the subject newsracks, it is not a valid . . . restriction of protected speech."[97] The Court concluded, "Cincinnati's categorical ban on the distribution, via newsrack, of 'commercial handbills' cannot be squared with the dictates of the First Amendment."[98]

Chief Justice Rehnquist disagreed that the city had been mistaken in believing that it could burden commercial speech to a greater degree than fully protected speech. "Based on the different levels of protection we have accorded commercial and noncommercial speech, we have previously said that localities may not favor commercial over noncommercial speech . . . . [B]efore today, we have never even suggested that the converse holds true . . . ."[99]

In *Edenfield*, decided only one month after *Discovery Network*, the Court went to work on prong three of *Central Hudson*, requiring the government to go beyond speculation and actually offer proof that its regulation serves the government's interests. Scott Fane, a certified public accountant, found himself at odds with the Florida Board of Accountancy which had created a rule forbidding the state's CPAs from engaging in in-person solicitation for new clients. Prior to relocating to Florida, Fane had owned an accounting practice in New Jersey, a state that allowed such solicitation.

Fane filed suit in the United States District Court for the Northern District of Florida,[100] asking the court for declaratory and injunctive relief to prevent the Board from enforcing its rule. A former chairman of the Florida Board testified that the rule was necessary to protect potential clients from unethical practices by the CPA community. In his testimony, the former chairman contended that accountants who solicit customers are "obviously in need of business, and may be willing to break the rules."[101]

The court disagreed with the Board's contention that a hungry accountant is necessarily a dishonest one. It issued summary judgment in favor of Fane and enjoined enforcement of the Florida Board of Accountancy's no in-person-solicitation rule. The federal Court of Appeals for the Eleventh Circuit affirmed the lower court ruling.[102]

The Supreme Court of the United States affirmed the two lower courts' decisions. Justice Kennedy, delivering the opinion for an eight-justice majority, focused on prong three of *Central Hudson*, stating the Florida Board had not satisfied the burden of proof that its rule "advance[s] the [government] interest asserted."[103] Addressing this burden, Justice Kennedy noted that "[t]his burden is not satisfied by mere speculation or conjecture; rather, a government body seeking to sustain a restriction on commercial speech must demonstrate that the harms it recites are real, and that its restriction will in fact alleviate them to a material degree."[104] Beyond abstract anecdotes and conjecture, the new interpretation offered by the majority in *Edenfield* apparently required *evidence* that the substantial interest articulated by the state was being met by the speech regulation in question.

Relying on analysis that seemed reminiscent of *Virginia State Board of Pharmacy*, the majority espoused the potential virtues associated with the robust communication of truthful, non-deceptive commercial speech. The majority contended that "[i]n the commercial context, solicitation may have considerable value. Unlike many other forms of commercial expression, solicitation allows direct and spontaneous communication between buyer and seller. . . . For the buyer, it provides an opportunity to explore in detail the way in which a particular product or service compares to its alternatives in the market."[105]

## Distinguishing Speech about Constitutionally Protected Activities/Products: *U.S. v. Edge Broadcasting Company*

In the midst of the celebration of the apparent resuscitation of the third and fourth parts of the *Central Hudson* test by the Court's holdings in *Discovery Network* and *Edenfield*, the Court handed down its opinion in *U.S. v. Edge Broadcasting Company*,[106] a case that, at the very least, made any celebration somewhat premature.

Edge Broadcasting Corporation is the license holder and operator of WMYK-FM, a radio station broadcasting from Elizabeth City, N.C. According to survey research, more than 90 percent of its listeners live over the border in the Hampton Roads, V.A. metropolitan area. The North Carolina station's legal problems arose when station management decided to boost advertising revenues by running commercials for the Virginia state lottery.

Unfortunately, for Edge Broadcasting, WMYK was shut out from cashing in on this lucrative source of revenue. A North Carolina statute made it a misdemeanor to participate in or advertise a lottery. What complicated matters even more was a federal statute[107] that specifically banned broadcasters like Edge Broadcasting from advertising lotteries in neighboring states if the state in which the station is licensed does not have a lottery. To avoid potentially unpleasant legal consequences, Edge Broadcasting sought to obtain a declaratory judgment in federal district court in the eastern district of Virginia that would hold the federal statute to be in violation of the broadcaster's First and Fourteenth Amendment rights.

The district court began its opinion by noting that the regulation of lotteries and lottery advertising by Congress was constitutionally permitted.[108] The court also agreed with the government that Congress had the right to regulate over-the-air broadcasts in ways it could not constitutionally regulate other media and that such regulation explicitly extended to disseminating information about lotteries.

Observing that because "content-based restrictions on noncommercial speech meet First Amendment standards 'only in the most extraordinary circumstances,'" the court said "this Court's task with respect to section 1304's application to noncommercial speech is rendered considerably easier by the government's statement . . . that [it] would not oppose a decree limiting application . . . to the realm of commercial speech . . . ."[109] The court expressly added, however, that the statutes in question "should not be read to prohibit [the station from broadcasting] noncommercial information about lotteries."[110]

The issue was not as clear for commercial information. In the proper circumstances, the court noted, the statutes could apply to commercial speech, reading the long list of cases beginning with *Valentine* to have plainly established that commercial speech is a lesser protected form of speech. "Nonetheless," the court continued, commercial speech "has been afforded significant First Amendment safeguards . . . ."[111] Chief among these, said the court, was the *Central Hudson* four-part test, which the court then applied to the government's interpretation of the regulation as related to Edge Broadcasting.

The court had little trouble deciding the lottery commercials were protected by the First Amendment because Virginia had "lawfully created" its lottery program and the information contained in the advertisements was neither false nor deceptive. The court, in turn, found that the government's overall interest in regulating commercial speech about lotteries was legitimately in "furtherance of fundamental interests of federalism enabling non-lottery states to discourage gambling."[112] The court gave short shrift to Edge Broadcasting's arguments that North Carolina's reasons for regulating gambling were outdated. As long as the state's ban on gambling is maintained, the court reasoned, "the federal government's interest in protecting the desires of non-lottery states . . . to limit lottery participation must still be termed 'substantial.'"[113]

The district court found, however, that both sections of the federal anti-lottery advertising statute ran afoul of the third prong of the *Central Hudson* test. The court found that the requirement that the challenged regulation directly advance an important government interest was not met by the statute's provisions because they were "ineffectual means of reducing lottery participation by North Carolina residents . . . because the . . . residents within the area of the [station's] signal receive most of their radio, newspaper and television communications from Virginia-based media."[114] Conversely, because so little of the station's listening audience resided in North Carolina, and because this audience was "exposed to significant lottery advertising on television" and print media emanating from Virginia, "sections 1304 and 1307 [of the federal statute], at most, have only a remote impact on Virginia lottery sales among North Carolina residents . . . ."[115]

Although the court faulted the statute for not meeting the "advance-an-important-government-interest" language of the third prong of *Central Hudson*, it found no problem with the method the government chose to achieve its purpose. In contrast to the trial court's handling of the ban on commercial news racks in *Discovery Network*, the trial court in *Edge Broadcasting* ruled that the government had satisfied the fourth part of the *Central Hudson* test, simply noting in passing that "[t]he statutory scheme [banning the lottery advertising completely] put in place by sections 1304 and 1307 is not unreasonable . . ."[116]

On appeal, the Fourth Circuit Court of Appeals upheld the trial court in a brief, unpublished opinion.[117] The government then petitioned the Supreme Court of the United States to hear its appeal, which was granted. Despite the government's urging to the contrary, the Court rejected the argument that commercial speech advocating or publicizing gambling was a vice-related activity and thus inherently within the power of government to control in any manner it chose. Instead, the Court elected to treat *Edge Broadcasting* as a normal commercial speech case requiring application of the four-part *Central Hudson* test.

Writing for the majority, Justice White noted that although for much of its long history "purely commercial advertising was not considered to implicate the constitutional protection of the First Amendment,"[118] beginning with *Virginia Board of Pharmacy*, such speech was at least somewhat protected. "Our decisions, however," continued the Court, "have recognized the 'common-sense' distinction between speech proposing a commercial transaction . . . and other varieties of speech."[119] Applying the *Central Hudson* test, the Court found that Edge Broadcasting's speech was truthful, for a lawful activity (in Virginia) and non-deceptive. It conversely found that the government had a substantial interest "in supporting the policy of non-lottery States, as well as not interfering with the policy of States that permit lotteries."[120]

The Court disagreed with the lower courts, however, that the government had been unable to meet the third part of the *Central Hudson* test. Characterizing the lower court holdings as failing to "not fully appreciate"[121] the government's interests, the Court observed that

> this question cannot be answered by limiting the inquiry to whether the government interest is directly advanced as applied to a single person or entity. Even if there were no advancement as applied in that manner . . . there would remain the matter of the regulation's general application to others. . . . This is not to say that the validity of the statute's application to Edge is an irrelevant inquiry, but that issue properly should be dealt with under the fourth factor of the *Central Hudson* test.[122]

There is "no doubt," said the Court,

that . . . Congress might have continued to ban all radio or television lottery advertisements. . . . This it did not do. Neither did it permit stations such as Edge, located in a non-lottery State, to carry lottery ads if their signals reached into a State that sponsors lotteries; similarly, it did not forbid stations in a lottery State such as Virginia from carrying lottery ads if their signals reached into an adjoining state.[123]

The Court held that "Congress surely knew that stations in one State could often be heard in another but expressly prevented each and every North Carolina station, including Edge, from carrying lottery ads. . . . This congressional policy of balancing the interests of lottery and non-lottery States is the substantial government interest that satisfies *Central Hudson*. . . ."[124]

Having concluded that the lower courts had incorrectly held that the government had not satisfied the third part of the *Central Hudson* test, however, did not end the case. "Left unresolved," said the Court, ". . . is the validity of applying the statutory restriction to Edge, an issue that we now address under the fourth *Central Hudson* factor."[125] The Court noted that this factor—"whether the regulation is more extensive than is necessary to serve the government interest"—was modified in *SUNY* to only "require a fit between the restriction and the government interest that is not necessarily perfect, but reasonable. This was also the approach in *Posadas*."[126]

It was not the approach of the majority in *Discovery Network*, however, decided only three months prior to *Edge Broadcasting*. Somewhat oddly, the Court in *Edge Broadcasting* never mentioned *Discovery Network*. In the prior case, the Court recognized a First Amendment mandate placing a burden on the government to "carefully calculate" the costs of its regulatory actions or run the risk of "underestimate[ing] the value of commercial speech."[127] The language of the majority opinion in *Edge Broadcasting* seems quite the opposite. "We have no doubt," said the Court,

> that the fit in this case was a reasonable one. Allowing [Edge Broadcasting] to carry lottery ads reaching over 90 percent of its listeners, all in Virginia, would surely enhance its revenues. But just as surely, because Edge's signals with lottery ads would be heard in the nine counties in North Carolina that its broadcasts reached, this would be in derogation of the substantial federal interest in supporting North Carolina's law . . .[128]

According to the Court, the deciding factor should be the relationship the regulation "bears to the general problem of accommodating the policies of both lottery and non-lottery states."[129] The Court concluded that as long as the government could demonstrate it had chosen a reasonable means to accomplish its ends, the burden of demonstrating the requirements for the fourth part of the *Central Hudson* four-part test had been met, even if a careful calculation might demonstrate alternative means were also feasible.

Justice Stevens, in dissent, was vehemently opposed to the majority's affirmation of the ban on the acceptance of lottery advertising by Edge Broadcasting. "Three months ago," he said, "this Court [in *Discovery Network*] reaffirmed that the proponents of a restriction on commercial speech bear the burden of demonstrating a 'reasonable fit' between the legislatures' goals and the means chosen to effectuate those goals."[130] To Justice Stevens, "suppressing truthful advertising regarding a neighboring State's lottery, an activity which is, of course, perfectly legal, is a patently unconstitutional means of effectuating the Government's asserted interest in protecting the policies of non-lottery states."[131] The government, concluded Justice Stevens, "has selected the most intrusive, and dangerous, form of regulation possible—a ban on truthful information regarding a lawful activity imposed for the purpose of manipulating, through ignorance, the consumer choices of some of its citizens. Unless justified by a truly substantial government interest, this extreme and extremely paternalistic, measure, surely cannot withstand scrutiny under the First Amendment."[132]

## The More Recent Cases

In 1987, the Coors Brewing Company filed an application with the Bureau of Alcohol, Tobacco and Firearms (BATF) for permission to print alcohol percentage contents on its beer container labels and in advertisements. Because these practices had been expressly forbidden by Section 205(e)(2) of the 1935 Federal Alcohol Administration Act (FAAA), the BATF rejected Coors' application.

Coors found a more receptive audience in the federal courts. Both the federal district court and the court of appeals agreed that the government had not met part three of the *Central Hudson* test. The government appealed to the Supreme Court. In *Rubin v. Coors Brewing Co.*,[133] counsel for the federal government advanced the theory that the law served a substantial government interest in preventing alcohol "strength wars" (a practice whereby producers of alcoholic beverages attempted to market their wares on the basis of higher alcohol content).

In the Supreme Court, the government argued that its interests could indeed be met because the FAAA provisions had the potential effect of deterring "a particular type of beer drinker—one who selects a beverage because of its high potency—from choosing beers solely for their alcohol content."[134] In the government's view, the Act satisfied prong three of *Central Hudson* by "restricting disclosure of information regarding a particular product characteristic ... [thereby] decreas[ing] the extent to which consumers will select the product on the basis of that characteristic."[135]

Understandably, Coors Brewing Company painted a different picture of the FAAA's provisions. First, Coors contended that the labeling restrictions failed part two of Central Hudson and did not constitute a substantial government interest because the law had not been created with the *intent* of preventing strength wars.

Coors also questioned the validity of the FAAA labeling provisions based on part three of *Central Hudson*. If the prohibition of alcohol content labeling truly advanced the government's interest of preventing strength wars, said Coors, why then did the law *require* wine and other distilled spirit manufacturers to provide the very same alcohol content disclosure on labels currently prohibited on beer labels?

Coors also argued that there was no longer a substantial interest in enforcing the 1935 Act based on "protecting the health, safety, and welfare of its citizens."[136] However, citing *Posadas*, the Court stated that "the prevention of misleading statements of alcohol content need not be the *exclusive* [emphasis added] government interest served by 205(e)(2)."[137]

The Court was much more sympathetic to Coors' prong three arguments, agreeing that "205(c)(2) cannot directly and materially advance [the government's] asserted interest because of the overall irrationality of the Government's regulatory scheme."[138] As evidence of this irrationality, the Court suggested that beer advertisements in the mass media that include statements of alcohol content were of potentially greater danger than product labels themselves, yet the Act only allowed an advertising ban for states that elected to do so. The Court also accepted Coors' argument that the lack of a level playing field between beer, wine and other distilled spirits in advertising and labeling regulations constituted proof that the government's stated interest was not being met by the law. Justice Thomas, writing for the Court, stated that "[i]f combating strength wars were the goal, we would assume that Congress would regulate disclosure of alcohol content for the strongest beverages as well as for the weakest ones."[139]

Beyond the victory for commercial speakers represented by the majority opinion in *Rubin*, the case also illustrates the growing sense of disquiet by some members of the Court about *Central Hudson*'s lack of deference to truthful, non-deceptive commercial speech. In his concurring opinion, Justice Stevens noted that suppression of any truthful commercial information "because of the perceived danger of that knowledge is an anathema to the Free Speech Clause."[140] He added, the possibility "that consumers should be misled or uninformed for their own protection . . . does not suffice to justify restrictions on protected speech in any context."[141]

Since *Rubin*, the Supreme Court has faced three additional cases involving so-called "vice" activities (e.g., gambling and consumption of alcohol and tobacco) and, in the process, added bite to prongs three and four of *Central Hudson*.

In the first, *44 Liquormart v. Rhode Island*,[142] the Court addressed constitutional challenges by two liquor retailers to the state's complete ban on non-point-of-sale alcohol price advertising. 44 Liquormart filed suit against the state after being cited and fined $400 for violating the state's price advertising ban. The retailer's ad pictured a number of items with explicit pricing information, as well as pictures of two different liquors accompanied by the word "WOW" (but no prices). Because price information accompanied many of the items in the advertisement, the Rhode Island Liquor Control administrator adjudged the word "WOW" to imply a discount price for the liquor as well.

After paying the fine, 44 Liquormart filed a suit in federal district court asking that the state law be overturned on First Amendment grounds. Citing multiple studies that called into question the link between alcohol advertising and alcohol abuse, the trial court concluded that the advertising ban did not satisfy the *Edenfield* requirement that a regulation materially advance the government's asserted interest.[143]

An appeals court reversed the lower court decision, forcing the liquor retailer to seek relief in the Supreme Court of the United States. In what would prove to be one of the most convoluted commercial speech decisions ever rendered by the Supreme Court, a shifting coalition of justices determined, among other things, that the Rhode Island alcohol price-advertising ban did indeed run afoul of First Amendment protections for commercial speech.

*44 Liquormart* is particularly important to those wishing to understand the current Court's stance on commercial speech because it illustrates the sharp differences between justices in their commercial speech considerations. Although all nine justices agreed that the Rhode Island law did not pass constitutional muster, their agreement ended with the judgment. The case featured an eight-part opinion written by Justice Stevens (with each part joined by different groups of justices), a three-part opinion penned by Justice Thomas, and a separate concurrence written by Justice O'Connor and joined by Chief Justice Rehnquist and Justices Souter and Breyer.

Specifically addressing the possibility that *Posadas* and *Edge Broadcasting* had created a subdivision of commercial speech for vice-related activities, Justice Stevens wrote that "[t]he respondents misread our precedent. Our decision last term striking down an alcohol-related advertising restriction [in *Rubin*] effectively rejected [a vice exception]."[144] Justice Stevens noted that "[f]urther consideration of [*Posadas*] persuades us that [it] should be rejected."[145]

Justice O'Connor's concurrence offered the most traditional *Central Hudson* analysis of the facts in the case, determining that Rhode Island failed to demonstrate a "reasonable fit" between the complete advertising ban and its asserted interest of curbing alcohol consumption.

Justice Thomas used his concurrence in *44 Liquormart* as a platform for advocating a return to the *Virginia State Board of Pharmacy* standard of viewing with strict scrutiny any attempt to silence truthful, non-deceptive commercial messages. "In cases such as this," said Justice Thomas, "in which the government's asserted interest is to keep legal users of a product or service ignorant in order to manipulate their choices in the marketplace, the balancing test adopted in *Central Hudson* . . . should not be applied."[146]

The principal opinion expressed some of the same unease with censoring truthful, non-deceptive commercial speech. Justice Stevens suggested that the Court should apply *Central Hudson* only in cases in which the regulation in question clearly attempts to protect consumers from false or deceptive commercial information. Conversely, according to Justice Stevens, any regulation not clearly designed to protect consumers from such messages should be treated with a greater presumption of unconstitutionality.

Three years later, in *Greater New Orleans Broadcasting Association v. United States*,[147] the Supreme Court once again granted review to a commercial speech case that challenged the constitutionality of Title 18 U.S.C. §1304 (the same federal statute in question in *Edge Broadcasting*) banning all broadcast advertising for gaming activities at privately owned casinos. A group of Louisiana broadcasters filed suit in federal district court seeking to have §1304 and its companion FCC regulations invalidated on First Amendment grounds.

Unlike *44 Liquormart*, the opinion in *Greater New Orleans* offered very little in the way of ambiguity. The justices unanimously agreed that §1304 and its companion FCC regulations could not be reconciled with First Amendment protections for commercial speech because they failed parts three and four of the *Central Hudson* test. Justice Stevens, writing for the Court, focused on the irrationality of §1304, noting that the government's "regulatory regime is so pierced by exemptions and inconsistencies that the Government cannot hope to exonerate it."[148] Specifically, the opinion dismissed the government's contention that the advertising ban would lower demand for the service. Indeed, said the Court, casino gambling advertising likely did little more than funnel hardcore gamblers to a particular casino rather than draw new customers into the gambling fold.

The most recent "vice" case occurred in *Lorillard Tobacco Company v. Reilly*.[149] In *Lorillard*, the tobacco corporation challenged a set of Massachusetts laws designed to protect children from exposure to tobacco advertising. Among the chief features of the law were prohibitions of billboard and other externally visible advertising within 1,000 feet of school grounds, as well as a prohibition of tobacco point-of-sale advertising less than 5 feet from the ground. The state had reasoned in passing the law that small children would be less likely to see advertisements were they above their eye level.

The Court ruled that the outdoor ban violated prong four of *Central Hudson*'s "not more extensive than necessary" clause. The Court found persuasive Lorillard's argument that the close proximity of schools in urban areas of the state would mean that the 1,000-foot rule effectively banned tobacco advertising in as much as 90 percent of the land area in some Massachusetts cities. The Court said this showed strong evidence that the regulations were more extensive than necessary and did "not demonstrate a careful calculation of the speech interests involved."[150]

Considering the 5-foot, point-of-sale rule, the Court engaged in a very brief but almost humorous dismissal of the regulation based on *Central Hudson* third and fourth prong grounds. Writing for the Court, Justice O'Connor said that "[t]he 5-foot rule does not seem to advance ... [the] goal [of curbing demand for tobacco products among children]. Not all children are less than 5 feet tall, and those who are certainly have the ability to look up and take in their surroundings."[151] The Court, in dismissing the notion that tobacco "is so special, so unlike any other object of regulation, that application of normal First Amendment principles should be suspended," noted that "[n]o such [vice] exemption exists."[152]

The Court's most recent commercial speech decision involved the atypical case of so-called "compelled speech" by producers for industry-wide promotional campaigns. In *Johanns v. Livestock Marketing Association*,[153] the plaintiff objected to paying a one-dollar assessment for each head of cattle required by the federal Beef Promotion and Research Act of 1985. The challenge to the statute focused on objections to the advertising of beef as a generic product as in the "Beef. It's What's for Dinner" campaign. The plaintiffs argued the promotion harmed their own efforts to promote their products as superior in quality and strongly objected to being required to pay for it.

Because the federal law mandated that all beef producers contribute to the promotional campaign, said the Court, the speech could be considered as government speech (despite being paid for by private parties) and therefore raised no First Amendment issues.

## Commercial Speech and Intrusiveness

Beginning with the Federal Trade Commission Act of 1914,[154] Congress has expressed clear concern over commercial communications directed both at competitors and potential customers. Unfortunately, unscrupulous sales and marketing practices have provided ample impetus for Congress and the states to pass subsequent consumer-oriented legislation. These laws, many of which are discussed elsewhere in this book, attempt to regulate how commercial entities communicate with their many publics, particularly prospective consumers.

In the early 1990s, the practice of communicating with prospective customers by telephoning them in their homes—commonly called telemarketing—captured lawmakers' attention. New telephone technologies had led to aggressive telemarketing techniques to which many consumers objected. In response, Congress passed the Telephone Consumer Protection Act (TCPA) of 1991[155] that requires telemarketers to follow a series of rules when soliciting prospective consumers in their homes via telephone.

The TCPA, which is administered by the Federal Communications Commission (FCC), requires a telemarketer to provide its name, the name of the organization it represents and a telephone number or address at which the sponsoring organization may be reached. The law also bars solicitation calls between 9 p.m. and 8 a.m.

Even with these requirements, citizens loudly and often protested the seemingly constant barrage of unwanted solicitation phone calls, many of which interrupted the dinner hour. The subsequent Telemarketing and Consumer Fraud and Abuse Prevention Act of 1994,[156] and the related Telemarketing Sales Rule,[157] adopted in 1995, represented additional attempts by Congress to regulate interstate telemarketing to deal with these complaints.

The boldest and most popular telemarketing legislation, at least from the consumers' perspective, occurred in 2003, when President George W. Bush signed into law the Do-Not-Call Implementation Act.[158] The Act amended the Telemarketing Sales Rule and called for the establishment of a national registry of home and personal wireless telephone numbers that are off limits to telemarketers' interstate sales solicitations. The resulting National Do Not Call Registry, or Do Not Call List, as it is also known, is a joint project of the FTC and the FCC; both agencies field complaints about telemarketers who violate the do-not-call rules. Sellers, defined as "any person or business who, in connection with a telemarketing transaction, provides, offers to provide, or arranges for others to provide goods or services to the customer in exchange for consideration,"[159] must be familiar with and follow the do-not-call rules or risk hefty fines of up to $11,000 per infraction.

To comply, sellers and telemarketers acting on behalf of sellers must subscribe to the National Do Not Call Registry, check it at least every 31 days, "scrub" registered telephone numbers from their call lists and refrain from calling those numbers. If a marketer has done business with a customer within the past 18 months or if a customer has given the seller permission, the marketer may contact the customer even if the customer's telephone number is on the registry. Several other types of calls are exempt from the prohibitions as well: charities, political organizations and groups conducting legitimate survey research may call numbers listed on the registry.

The Do-Not-Call Implementation Act may be one of the most popular pieces of legislation in the history of legislation. Millions of citizens have placed their telephone numbers on the registry, and public comment has been almost overwhelmingly favorable since the legislation was first conceived. But not everyone is enamored with the greater restrictions on telemarketing. National professional and trade associations whose members rely on telemarketing have challenged the Act as an unconstitutional restraint on speech.

Although the Supreme Court of the United States has not weighed in on the issue, several lower federal courts so far have upheld the Act's constitutionality. In 2004, for example, the United States Court of Appeals for the Tenth Circuit reversed a district court ruling that the regulations violated the First Amendment.[160] In that case, telemarketing companies and trade associations had challenged the regulations as being an unconstitutional restraint on free speech. The appellate court applied the *Central Hudson*[161] test (discussed earlier in this chapter) and determined the do-not-call registry "directly advances the government's interests by effectively blocking a significant number of the calls that cause the problems the government sought to address. It is narrowly tailored because its opt-in character ensures that it does not inhibit any speech directed at the home of a willing listener."[162]

Even prior to the federal Do-Not-Call statute, many states adopted their own versions of do-not-call legislation to regulate *intrastate* unsolicited telemarketing calls. These state laws work in concert with the federal Act (which regulates only *interstate* telemarketing). Prudent advertising and public relations professionals would be wise to check to see if such state regulations apply before initiating a telemarketing campaign. Several private entities, including the Direct Marketing Association, a private trade association that advocates for member institutions who have an interest in direct marketing, maintain a list of state do-not-call programs and contact information for each.[163]

Just as citizens have expressed disdain for unsolicited telephone marketing calls, many also have complained to Congress about the common practice of organizations sending unsolicited advertisements to fax machines. The Junk Fax Prevention Act of 2005[164] and newly enacted complementary FCC rules now generally prohibit sending unsolicited commercial messages to any fax machine (business or residential) without the recipient's prior express invitation or permission. To date, there have been no significant constitutional challenges to the Act.

The law provides that just as the do-not-call rules allow telemarketing calls to customers with whom an organization has an "established business relationship,"[165] the rules governing faxing allow the sending of unsolicited fax commercial messages to those with whom one is already doing business, provided that the customer has not declined to receive additional faxes. Fax commercial messages must contain specified notice and contact information on the faxed document that allow recipients to "opt-out" of any future faxes from the sender and must also detail the circumstances under which a request to "opt-out" complies with the Act.[166] Violators could face FCC fines of up to $11,000 per violation, and consumers who receive faxes in violation of the Act may seek a judicial remedy to recover any monetary losses resulting from unsolicited facsimiles.[167]

## What's So Different about Commercial Speech?

As we have seen, at times the Supreme Court of the United States has appeared to sympathize with those who wish to regulate commercial speech and at other times with those who desire it to be protected from such regulation. As we conclude this chapter, perhaps we need to address a basic question. What is it about this kind of speech that has produced this ambivalence?

Legal commentators Alex Kozinski and Stuart Banner[168] offer some interesting answers. The first is that pure commercial speech is not pure, i.e., it is motivated by monetary desire. Whether it is advertisers, advertising agencies, other corporate speakers or the media that carry the commercial messages, all have a profit-making motive for speaking. A second reason is the content of the speech. Much commercial speech is admittedly hyperbolic in nature, designed to influence and persuade the target market by appealing to psychological variables rather that providing straightforward information about the attributes of a product or service. These two reasons lead many critics of commercial speech to the conclusion that such speech is valueless and therefore not deserving of First Amendment protection.

Professors Ronald Collins and David Skover,[169] for example, have suggested that the statement that pure commercial speech contains no value is an objective statement of fact. As Kosinski and Banner point out, these critics of commercial speech make arguments like "people may think they prefer TV commercials to [the epic poem] *The Iliad*, but if they think harder they'll realize their original preference was wrong."[170]

Additionally, critics of commercial speech may argue that commercial speech is less deserving of First Amendment protection than other forms of speech because of characteristics inherent in the speech itself. For example, the Supreme Court in *Virginia State Board of Pharmacy* cited "common sense" differences between commercial and non-commercial speech as reasons for different levels of First Amendment protection. The Court noted that commercial speech is "verifiable" and therefore held to a higher standard than other forms of speech. Additionally, the Court found that commercial speech is a "more durable" type of speech because the speech is profit motivated and not as easily chilled by regulations as other forms of speech.[171]

In theory, each of these rationales for commercial speech regulation could be subject to verification. And even if true, it does not necessarily follow that they require a lesser degree of First Amendment protection for commercial speech. Courts, however, have almost universally accepted these rationales without question, as they have the judgment that commercial speech should be a form of less protected speech.

As Kozinski and Banner point out, however, there is no obvious inherent distinction between commercial and non-commercial speech in the wording of the First Amendment. In fact, the term "commercial speech" was not employed by the Court until the *Pittsburgh Press* case in 1973. The two commentators speculate that the reasons courts used the terms "advertising" and "soliciting" prior to this case is significant. "In *Valentine* [the first major case], . . . the Court wasn't facing a case about commercial speech; it was facing a case about advertising [a kind of business]."[172] They conclude that "[i]n 1942 . . . [*Valentine*] was easy not because the Court thought of commercial speech as a category of speech deserving no protection, but because the Court didn't treat the case as involving speech at all."[173]

Because courts have given their consent to the possibility of greater regulation of pure commercial speech does not mean that either regulators or legislators need to or should make such regulations and laws. Unfortunately for commercial speech advocates, lawmakers often have strong political motivations for doing so. Pure commercial speech may be the means by which consumers learn about the products and services they want and need, but most are ambivalent about the value of this speech, especially as compared to speech about important public issues. Many activists in political, environmental or social organizations go beyond mere ambivalence to argue that commercial speech is, at best, inconsequential and, at worst, evil in the sense that it promotes unwanted behavior or products and services harmful to the individual or the environment.

Not uncommonly, those who are active in promoting such causes believe so strongly in them that, to quote Justice Holmes, they fall into the category of those who see regulation of "expression of opinions . . . [as] perfectly logical. If you have no doubt of your premises or your power and want a certain result with all your heart you naturally express your wishes in law and sweep away all opposition."[174] With the bulk of the voting public indifferent, and with only groups of economically self-interested advertisers and media to represent the other side, legislators and regulators often can be persuaded that regulating or banning commercial speech is a cheap, politically expedient and easy way to tackle social ills.

## Commercial Speech Regulation in a Digital, New-Media Age: Emerging Issues

Although the history of constitutional protection for commercial speech often has resembled the health chart of a critically ill patient, the strengthening of prongs three and four of the *Central Hudson* test in the Court's most recent major decisions in this area, combined with the replacement of Chief Justice Rehnquist and Justice O'Connor with justices perhaps more sympathetic to commercial speech interests, provide hope that truthful, non-deceptive commercial speech is closer than ever to achieving full First Amendment protection.

Arguably, in any attempt to regulate commercial speech, the speech itself should be the focal point of a court's attention rather than the ways in which the messages are being communicated. Whether the intrusive nature of new media marketing and advertising techniques will put a crimp in the efforts to provide more constitutional protection for commercial speech, however, remains to be seen.

The problems associated with unsolicited commercial messages, whether by telephone, fax or Internet (discussed more fully in Chapter 10) have created emerging, troublesome jurisdictional issues with First Amendment implications. Jurisdiction refers to a court's authority to either adjudicate a particular type of dispute ("subject matter" jurisdiction) or to exercise authority over individuals or corporations ("personal" jurisdiction).

Personal jurisdiction is determined by several factors, the most significant of which is geography. Where one resides determines if a court has personal jurisdiction. For example, if you live in the state of Utopia, you can be hauled into court in Utopia, assuming you have broken a law or are involved in a lawsuit there. Personal jurisdiction also may be created by the type and volume of contacts established with a particular geographic location. For this to happen, you must have had at least "minimum contacts" with the other state. For instance, if you live and work in one state and do business with citizens of another state, that other state may be able to exercise personal jurisdiction over you if a lawsuit arises—minimum contact may have been established.

It may have occurred to you that jurisdiction is especially tricky where commercial speech, the First Amendment and new media are concerned. Today, communications and e-commerce occur not only across state lines but across international borders as well. The Internet presents many questions of jurisdiction, most of which are unsettled and are likely to remain so for some time.

Closer to home, some guidance may be found in domestic decisions handed down by courts in the United States. For example, it appears that simply posting a Web site with product information that could be accessed by people in other states will not necessarily subject the corporate Web site's sponsor to personal jurisdiction in those other states. On the other hand, if a corporate sponsor uses new media to actively promote, sell, advertise or otherwise target their products to residents of other states, the more likely it is to be subject to personal jurisdiction in those states.

A comprehensive discussion of international jurisdictional issues is beyond the scope of this text. But as a general rule, if one "purposely avails" oneself of the privilege of conducting business across state lines or international boundaries through commercial speech, the speaker may end up in court in foreign states or nations as well. In many such jurisdictions, the protections of commercial speech afforded by the First Amendment may be only a rumor.

# Chapter 3

# Public Interest Information as Commercial Speech

Chapter 2 traced the somewhat erratic course the Supreme Court of the United States has followed to create and implement "tests" that speakers, government regulators and lower courts should employ to gauge the degree of constitutional protection afforded commercial speech. While protecting non-commercial speech about public issues from regulation in all but truly unusual situations, the Court often has treated commercial speech as a First Amendment second-class citizen. In most circumstances, the Court has allowed regulation except when the government interest asserted as the basis for regulation is insubstantial or there are other means the government could employ that are less restrictive of speech and that reasonably enable the government to achieve its ends.

In so doing, however, the Court has held unequivocally that the mere fact that speakers have paid for the space or time to publish their speech does not automatically define such speech as "commercial speech" for First Amendment purposes. This differentiation between paid-for speech and true commercial speech has created a series of commercial-speech-related definitional issues discussed in this chapter. These are: (a) the degree of constitutional protection accorded paid-for speech that deals with matters of general public interest; (b) how courts define paid-for speech that contains a mixture of commercial and noncommercial messages or that may be commercial speech in disguise; (c) whether different categories of true commercial speech merit more or less constitutional protection; (d) how the second-class status of commercial speech interacts with other legal concepts like defamation or privacy; and (e) if there are special problems when the commercial speech involves political advertisements.

Although the answers to these commercial-speech-related questions obviously are significant to those in advertising, they are especially important to public relations practitioners, particularly because the Court has never dealt specifically with the constitutional status or definition of public relations speech. Public relations professionals should remember that many First Amendment-based protections of speech are predicated on the idea that the speech in question deserves protection because it is speech about important public issues. Although the public relations speech of most for-profit corporations is important to the speaker, it is by no means clear that courts and legislators also will treat such speech as important to the general public and therefore beyond the scope of laws and regulations that limit, or in other ways regulate, advertising and other commercial speech.

## Paid-For Public Interest Speech by Not-For-Profit Organizations

In *Valentine v. Chrestensen*,[1] the Court's initial foray into determining the constitutional limits on the regulation of commercial speech, the Court made no attempt to define the terms it used in determining New York City's legal right to ban handbills that advertised tours of Chrestensen's submarine. Chrestensen's disputed handbills did not contain any mention of an admission fee, but city authorities and the Court treated them as "commercial and business advertising matter"[2] forbidden by a municipal ordinance. The Court said that although citizens may use city streets to disseminate opinion, "[w]e are equally clear that the Constitution imposes no such restraint on government as respects purely commercial advertising."[3]

The Court noted that although New York City officials would have much less latitude to regulate the distribution of handbills that contained only public information or opinion, Chrestensen could not avoid regulation simply by adding a discussion of public issues if his speech still remained basically commercial in nature. In so doing, the Court's opinion foreshadowed two issues that continue to haunt commercial speech cases: the constitutional status of speech that takes the form of commercial speech but is not related to commercial activity, and the differences, if any, in the protection of that speech depending on the nature of the speaker.

Nearly two decades passed after *Valentine* before the Court again made a major pronouncement about the constitutionality of government regulations of commercial speech. It did so in its discussion of a variety of issues in *New York Times v. Sullivan*,[4] a 1964 case that made a major impact on libel law and the civil rights movement. In *Sullivan*, the Court carved out an important exception for what today are often called "advertorials" as well as for other forms of paid-for speech used by not-for-profit organizations to discuss matters of public interest.

The backdrop of the case was formed by the desegregation efforts led by Dr. Martin Luther King, Jr. in southern states in the late 1950s and early 1960s. On March 29, 1960, *The New York Times* carried a full-page advertisement entitled "Heed Their Rising Voices" that detailed what the advertisement called "the wave of terror" directed against the civil rights activities of Dr. King and other activists. Included as an example were charges that King and his followers had been threatened and arrested on trumped-up charges. The advertising copy, signed by 64 prominent Americans, included a request for monetary donation to help carry on the work of Dr. King.

The plaintiff in the libel suit was L.B. Sullivan, a Montgomery city commissioner whose duties included supervising the police department. Claiming that the statements in the advertisement about police misconduct libeled him, Sullivan brought suit against a number of African-American clergymen who had purchased the advertisement and against the *New York Times* for publishing it. An Alabama jury eventually awarded Sullivan $500,000—a verdict that eventually was appealed all the way to the Supreme Court of the United States.

All parties (and the Court) recognized that the fact that the allegedly libelous statements were published in an advertisement was an important factor in the case. The newspaper received $4,800 for running the advertisement purchased by a New York advertising agency. The manager of the department that determined acceptability of advertising material for *The New York Times* conceded that his department made no effort to check the information in the advertisement against news stories carried in the newspaper or to verify in other ways the statements contained in the advertisement. Arguing that the purchasers of the space were reputable, the newspaper's representative said that he had no reason to doubt their descriptions of the events that had occurred in Montgomery.

Relying on the wording of the Court's opinion in *Valentine*, Sullivan's attorney argued that the Court lacked jurisdiction even to hear the newspaper's appeal because there were no First Amendment issues present in the case. This argument was advanced on the premise that *Valentine* had determined that commercial advertisements had no special constitutional protection and that the speech in question in this case was admittedly in the form of a full-page advertisement.

The Court disagreed. Those relying on *Valentine*, said the Court, for the proposition that "the constitutional guarantees of freedom of speech and of the press are inapplicable here ... because the allegedly libelous statements were published as part of a paid, 'commercial' advertisement"[5] were guilty of misinterpreting the Court's intent. According to the Court, the crucial distinction was that its earlier holding was based on the conclusion that unlike the speech in the *Sullivan* case, the speech in *Valentine* was primarily purely commercial advertising.

The *Sullivan* Court said, "[t]he publication ... was not a 'commercial' advertisement in the sense in which the word was used in [*Valentine*]. It communicated information, expressed opinion, recited grievances, protested claimed abuses, and sought financial support on behalf of a movement whose existence and objectives are matters of the highest public interest and concern."[6]

Saying that failure to provide First Amendment protection would discourage others from buying or running what the opinion called "editorial advertisements,"[7] the Court noted that this result "might shut off an important outlet for the promulgation of information and ideas by persons who do not themselves have access to publishing facilities—who wish to exercise their freedom of speech even though they are not members of the press."[8] The Court concluded that "[t]o avoid placing such a handicap upon the freedoms of expression, we hold that if the allegedly libelous statements would otherwise be constitutionally protected from the present judgment, they do not forfeit that protection because they were published in the form of a paid advertisement."[9]

Definitional problems may occur whenever courts make distinctions in levels of protection for either classes of speakers or speech itself. Such problems occasionally have surfaced involving organizations fraudulently claiming to be not-for-profit or charitable in nature. Overall, however, since the *Sullivan* decision, there has been no serious challenge to its holding that "commercial" speech on matters of public interest by truly not-for-profit organizations is protected under the First Amendment, except in unusual circumstances.

## Paid-For Public Interest Speech by For-Profit Organizations

Roughly a decade after *New York Times v. Sullivan*, the Court returned to the subject of paid-for speech used to addresses public issues in *First National Bank of Boston v. Bellotti.*[10] Unlike *Sullivan*, this time, however, it was in the context of a case involving the government's efforts to regulate such speech by a profit-making corporation.

At issue was an attempt by the state of Massachusetts to enforce its statute limiting corporate expenditures "for the purpose of influencing the vote on referendum proposals...."[11] The statute prohibited banks, telephone companies, public utilities and most business corporations (and their officers) from spending money "for the purpose of ... influencing or affecting the vote on any question submitted to the voters, other than one materially affecting any of the property, business or assets of the corporation."[12] Another provision of the statute specified that no questions "submitted to the voters solely concerning the taxation of the income, property or transactions of individuals shall be deemed materially to affect the property business or assets of the corporation."[13]

First National Bank and other corporations challenged the statute as violating free speech when the corporations desired to purchase advertising space and time to express their opposition to a proposed state constitutional amendment authorizing the state to institute a graduated personal income tax. They were informed by the state's attorney general, Francis X.

Bellotti, that he would enforce the state's statutory prohibitions against such advertisements if the corporations persisted in their efforts to state their views via media advertising.

Because the penalties provided in the statute were severe (a fine of up to $50,000 for a corporation and/or a fine of up to $10,000 or imprisonment of up to one year or both for an officer or director of the corporation), First National Bank and its corporate allies sought a declaratory judgment—a sort of advisory opinion—to test the statute's constitutionality.

The state's highest court held the statute to be a valid limitation on the speech interests of the plaintiffs, finding that the First Amendment rights of corporations could constitutionally be "limited to issues that materially affect its business, property or assets."[14] It characterized the issue as whether a corporation's First Amendment rights were the equal of individuals and found as a matter of law that they were not. The state court noted that the statute did not prohibit speeches on the topic by corporate executives or statements to the press, internal newsletters, bulletins to stockholders or other typical corporate public relations activities so long as they did not involve contributions or "expenditure of corporate funds."[15]

On appeal, the Supreme Court of the United States made short work of the state's arguments. Refusing to frame the issue as the nature and extent of corporate First Amendment rights, the Court instead said, "[t]he proper question ... is not whether corporations 'have' First Amendment rights and, if so, whether they are co-extensive with those of natural persons. Instead, the question must be whether [the statute] abridges expression that the First Amendment was meant to protect. We hold that it does."[16]

The Court rejected arguments that allowing for-profit corporations to spend corporate assets to campaign against such referenda or to speak out on public issues would overwhelm the marketplace of ideas by drowning out other voices. There was no evidence of such a threat, said the Court, and there were other less drastic measures a state might take in order to alert its citizens about potential abuses of the marketplace of ideas, such as requiring advertisements placed by corporations to carry information identifying the source of the speech. In short, said the Court, when a for-profit corporation wishes to use advertising or other forms of paid-for speech to discuss matters of general public interest not connected with its commercial activities, such speech should receive the same degree of constitutional protection as speech from other sources.

Four years after *Bellotti*, the Court, in *Consolidated Edison Co. of New York, Inc. v. Public Service Commission of New York*,[17] reversed a lower court decision that had upheld a Commission policy banning the utility company's discussion of public issues in brochures and fliers included with monthly customer billings. The Commission's policy was based on the fact that the utility was a state-regulated monopoly and that ratepayers, characterized as a "captive audience,"[18] would not want to receive such information and commentary.

The Court disagreed. Citing *Bellotti*, Justice Powell reiterated that "the inherent worth of the speech in terms of its capacity for informing the public does not depend on the identity of its source."[19] Despite what Justice Blackmun (in dissent) called a "free ride"[20] for the utility company's propaganda at ratepayer expense, the majority held that such a total ban "strikes at the heart of the freedom to speak."[21] Amplifying its dislike of government arguments for differing levels of protection for speech based on the nature of the speaker, the Court noted, "the First Amendment's hostility to content-based regulation [dependent on the speaker] extends not only to restrictions on particular viewpoints, but also to prohibition of public discussion of an entire topic."[22] The Court also dismissed the public service commission's arguments involving the privacy interests of ratepayers, noting that any harm could be avoided "simply by transferring the bill from envelope to waste basket."[23]

The general euphoria that free-speech champions derived from the holdings in *Bellotti* and *Consolidated Edison* was dampened, however, by the subsequent opinion of the Court in *Austin v. Michigan Chamber of Commerce*,[24] a 1990 decision that appeared to shine a caution light on the Court's willingness to require the government to surmount a rigorous First Amendment challenge to government regulations in such cases. In *Austin*, the Court upheld government restrictions on a corporation's political speech for reasons similar to those struck down in *Bellotti* because, said the Court, the government had satisfied the definition of a compelling government interest.

Section 54(1) of the Michigan Campaign Act expressly prohibited corporations from contributing directly "to the nomination or election of a candidate."[25] The Act defined such contributions as "a payment, donation, loan, pledge, or promise of payment of money or anything of ascertainable monetary value . . ."[26] although it allowed corporations to spend money for such purposes if the money was maintained in a separate fund.

The Michigan Chamber of Commerce is a corporation established to encourage economic development and improve the state's business climate. Although not normally engaged in direct political support of candidates, the Chamber desired to buy advertising space in a local newspaper to support a candidate in a special election to fill a vacancy in the state legislature. The Chamber considered this candidate more pro-business than his opponent. Fearing that the campaign Act would prohibit such activity, the Chamber sought a declaratory judgment in federal district court that the statute should be unenforceable on First Amendment grounds.

Although the district court upheld the Act as a legitimate limitation on corporate activity[27] (the state statute was modeled in part on a similar federal statute), on appeal, the Sixth U.S. Circuit Court of Appeals ruled that the Michigan Campaign Act could not, for First Amendment reasons, apply to the Chamber because it was not a traditional corporation and was formed expressly to spread economic and political messages.[28] The federal appeals court found no compelling interest that would justify infringing the speech interests of the Chamber. On appeal by the state, the Supreme Court of the United States disagreed.

Although it was appropriate for the court of appeals to apply the compelling government interest test to this case, said the Court's majority, the lower court had erred in not recognizing that the state had met this requirement. The Court held that Michigan obviously was concerned with "the corrosive and distorting effects of immense aggregations of wealth that [were] accumulated with the help of the corporate form and that have little or no correlation to the public's support for the corporation's political ideas."[29]

The Court conceded both that the desire to support candidates for public office via advertising is speech that "constitute[s] 'political expression at the core of our electoral process and of the First Amendment freedoms,'" and that "[t]he mere fact that the Chamber is a corporation does not remove its speech from the ambit of the First Amendment."[30] However, said the Court, "the unique state-conferred corporate structure that facilitates the amassing of large treasuries warrants the limit in independent expenditures. Corporate wealth," continued the Court, "can unfairly influence elections when it is deployed in the form of independent expenditures.... We therefore hold that the State has articulated a sufficiently compelling rationale to support its restriction on independent expenditures...."[31]

The Court also rejected the argument that the Chamber was a not-for-profit corporation and therefore not subject to the statute. Citing earlier cases as precedent, the Court noted that the Chamber failed to meet the three criteria distinguishing not-for-profit corporations in terms of the campaign expenditure stature. "The first characteristic," said the Court, "[is] that the organization '[is] formed for the express purpose of promoting political ideas and cannot engage in business activities.'... [T]he second feature [is] the absence of 'shareholders or other persons affiliated so as to have a claim on its assets or earnings.' ... The final characteristic [is] the organization's independence from the influence of business corporations."[32] The Court concluded that "the Chamber does not possess the features that would compel the State to exempt it from restriction on independent political expenditures."[33]

In dissent, Justice Kennedy noted that in this situation involving the regulation of advertising constituting "a paradigm of political speech,"[34] the Court clearly "adopts a rule that allows Michigan to stifle the voices of some of the most respected groups in public life on subjects central to the integrity of our democratic system...."[35] Justice Kennedy continued,

[t]hose who thought that the First Amendment exists to protect all points of view in candidate elections will be disillusioned by the Court's opinion today; for that protection is given only to a preferred class of nonprofit corporate speakers: small, single-issue nonprofit corporations that pass the Court's own vague test for determining who are the favored participants in the electoral process.[36]

Justice Kennedy characterized the majority as demonstrating "hostility to the corporate form used by the speaker in this case,"[37] concluding that Michigan's "wholesale ban on corporate political speech"[38] could not be squared with the First Amendment.

The holding in *Austin* cast a pall over those who believed that the Court in *Bellotti* had recognized an almost absolute First Amendment protection for corporate speech about public issues. Nonetheless, it still seems safe to say that in most instances paid-for speech by for-profit corporations will be free from regulation if that speech discusses matters of general public interest and there is not a countervailing government interest of great importance.

Admittedly, corporate and other organizational paid-for speech on matters of public interest usually is of little concern to most advertising professionals who make their fortunes promoting the goods and services a corporation sells for profit. For public relations professionals, however, the continuing viability of full First Amendment protection for such speech is particularly important as it provides protection for an important weapon in the arsenal of public relations techniques for communicating organizational messages to important publics.

## Definitional Problems: Is It Commercial or Non-Commercial Speech?

It seems clear that, in most instances, the Court will treat speech by both not-for-profit and profit-making organizations as deserving full First Amendment protection when that speech addresses important matters of public policy unrelated to the economic interests of the organizations. This includes speech appearing in time or space purchased by organizations to disseminate their views. It is by no means as clear, however, how the courts or regulatory agencies will (or should) treat speech that, although not directly urging the purchase of goods or services, is, nonetheless, arguably commercial in nature.

This issue is particularly important to advertising and public relations professionals because those who advocate limitations on the speech of for-profit corporations may continue to press for greater regulation of such corporate speech on public policy grounds. If a corporation's speech is classified as commercial speech, there are a variety of legally acceptable means for regulating such speech that would be impermissible if the speech were fully protected under the First Amendment.

As discussed in Chapter 1, prior restraint in the form of bans or limitations is the least preferred remedy that courts and regulators may employ. However, there are other remedies, arguably less restrictive of speech, that have found favor with the Court and with lower courts particularly when involving commercial speech. In *Central Hudson*, Justice Powell, while decrying the complete ban on the utility company's advertising, suggested that other regulations on the "format and content"[39] of the advertisements might be acceptable. For instance, citing *Banzhaf v. FCC*,[40] Justice Powell noted that requiring the advertising to include "information about the relative efficiency and expense of [the utility company's] offered service, both under current conditions and for the foreseeable future"[41] would be preferable to the banning-of-speech remedy sought by the state's public service commission.

As calls for regulation of corporate paid-for speech have increased during the past two decades, critics of such speech have also suggested such measures as (a) limiting appeals especially targeting racial or ethnic groups (tobacco and liquor advertising); (b) requiring commercial speakers to include additional information representing other points of view, such as warning labels; and (c) restricting the design or graphic components of commercial speech presentations by banning cartoon characters or pictures of users of the product or service (so-called "tombstone ads").

Alternatively, regulation of paid-for speech might take the form of requirements, like those of the Federal Trade Commission, that the speaker bear the burden of demonstrating that the speech, if challenged, is neither false nor illegal nor deceptive. Additionally, such regulatory bodies have legally required speakers to back up factual claims with scientific data or results of rigorously conducted public opinion polls. Critics of corporate activity, including speech, clearly wish to have as broad a definition of commercial speech as possible so that almost all corporate speech could be subject to the restrictions noted above.

If speech designated as commercial speech continues to be accorded only second-class constitutional protection by the Supreme Court, it seems essential for the Court to draw a "bright line" that unambiguously provides a clear division between speech defined as commercial and speech classified as non-commercial (or, perhaps more to the point, speech that is fully protected and speech that is not). Despite numerous opportunities, the Court has failed to do so. What is worse, the Court itself continues to waiver in its handling of definitional issues related to commercial speech, depending on the nature and the facts of the case it is deciding.

For example, what is the First Amendment status of a cigarette company's advertisement questioning the validity of anti-smoking research claims; a press release by an automobile manufacturer touting the virtues of its new models; a magazine or brochure containing some information of general interest but obviously intended to promote the publisher's instructional programs, or a brewing company that prominently affixes its logo design on the side of a NASCAR racer? All of these examples are taken from real-life cases (some of which are discussed later), producing results that are confusing and often appear to be in direct conflict with each other over the issue of whether they fall within the definition of commercial speech.

The Court's failure to define commercial speech clearly has left regulators and lower courts to wrestle with definitional issues as best they can. Not surprisingly, the results have been mixed at best, with decisions and policies that are ambiguous and at times contradictory, and with many issues yet to be satisfactorily resolved.

It is difficult, and perhaps overly simplistic, to attempt to categorize the many changing and, at times, overlapping opinions and discussions by the members of the Court who have wrestled with the problem of whether speech the government wants to regulate should be defined as commercial speech. Nonetheless, an analysis of the Court's cases in which this question has been raised leads to the conclusion that the Court generally follows one of two conflicting definitions for determining if speech is within the ambit of the commercial speech exception to the First Amendment.

The formulation of commercial speech preferred by partisans of as little restriction of speech as possible is the narrow definition mentioned in the Court's first modern-day "purely commercial speech" case—*Pittsburgh Press*.[42] Reacting to the split in rationales and outcomes in the *Valentine* and *Sullivan* decisions, the Court attempted to position the gender-based, help-wanted ads at issue in *Pittsburgh Press* as more like those prohibited in *Valentine*. Characterizing the ads as "classic examples of commercial speech,"[43] the Court noted that the "critical feature" of the speech in question was that it "did no more than propose a commercial transaction."[44] The Court subsequently picked up this language in its decision in *Virginia State Board of Pharmacy*,[45] the case that stands as the high-water mark in the Court's meandering course toward ultimately establishing the level of First Amendment protection afforded commercial speech.

Before defining commercial speech, however, the Court in *Virginia State Board of Pharmacy* attempted to distinguish some examples of speech it considered not to be commercial speech. According to Justice Blackmun, writing for the majority, it would be improper to characterize all speech that is published in paid-for space or time as commercial speech, citing the civil-rights-related advertisement in *Sullivan*. Neither, said the Court, is speech automatically classified as commercial just because it appears in a medium that has a profit-making motive, citing cases involving bookstores and movies.

Also, the Court noted that speech soliciting financial contributions is not automatically commercial in nature even if paid for, again citing *Sullivan*. Finally, neither speech about subjects generally related to commerce (e.g., arguments for or against free trade) nor paid-for speech that simply communicates facts (e.g., the abortion clinic advertisements in *Bigelow*[46]) automatically makes the speech commercial.

Having discussed examples of what it did not consider commercial speech, the Court characterized the issue in *Virginia State Board of Pharmacy* as "whether speech which does 'no more than propose a commercial transaction' [citing *Pittsburgh Press*] . . . lacks all protection."[47] As discussed in Chapter 2, the Court then answered this question by holding that it did not.

A number of justices (e.g., Stevens and Blackmun) hostile to regulating commercial speech consistently used the narrow "commercial transaction" definition in subsequent opinions. Employing this definition, the Court in *SUNY*[48] (discussed in Chapter 2), noted that although speech involved in soliciting sales of Tupperware in college dormitories was commercial speech, it would be overly broad to encompass all "paid" speech within the definition of commercial speech. Expanding the definition beyond speech that "does no more than propose a commercial transaction,"[49] said the Court, would impermissibly define commercial speech occurring when, for example, payment is made for services like tutoring students, providing counseling sessions or offering advice on medical or legal matters.

Similarly, in *Discovery Network, Inc.*,[50] Justice Stevens rejected the city's contention that it could regulate the placement and number of news racks on city streets because of the difficulty in determining the differences between regular newspapers that are sold for profit and contain commercial messages and the commercial publications the city sought to control. Although not the deciding factor in the case, it is clear that at least some members of the majority in *Discovery Network, Inc.* rejected the city's reliance on language that first surfaced in *Bates*[51]—and was used again by the Court in the cases of *Friedman v. Rogers*[52] and *Central Hudson*[53]—that the correct method for determining if the speech in question is commercial speech is to evaluate the "economic motivation" for the speech rather than requiring the speech to contain elements of actual commercial transactions.

This alternative definition—"economic motivation" rather than "speech proposing a commercial transaction"—has found favor with a number of justices, however. For example, in *Dun & Bradstreet, Inc. v. Greenmoss Builders, Inc.*,[54] a credit reporting agency being sued for defamation argued it should receive First Amendment protection for its alleged defamatory statements. (Other constitutional issues involved in defamation commercial speech cases are discussed in Chapter 4.) The

Court held that such reliance was improper, in part because the credit report that falsely accused the plaintiff of bankruptcy was like commercial speech in that it was "solely motivated by the desire for profit, which, we have noted is a force less likely to be deterred than others."[55] The dissent vigorously challenged this formulation, arguing that economic motivation was too broad a term and that the "do no more than propose a commercial transaction"[56] language of *Pittsburgh Press* should be employed when defining commercial speech.

Perhaps the most notable use of the "economic motivation language" as the definition of commercial speech, however, appears in the majority decision in *Bolger v. Youngs Drug Products Corp.*,[57] a case in which the classification of the speech in question was one of the key issues confronting the Court. In *Bolger*, the Court followed the lead of Justice Powell's majority opinion in *Central Hudson*. In that case, the Court held that promotional advertising by the electric utility corporation was commercial speech, defined as "expression related solely to the economic interests of the speaker and its audience."[58]

In *Central Hudson*, Justice Powell expressly rejected the contentions of Justice Stevens (who filed an opinion concurring in the judgment) that the Court's use of "economic interests" as the basis for defining commercial speech would sweep more speech than was constitutionally permissible under the commercial-speech umbrella. Judging the utility company's speech to not be commercial speech, said Justice Powell, "would grant broad constitutional protection to any advertising that links a product to a current public debate. But many, if not most, products may be tied to public concerns . . . ."[59] Justice Powell, noting that in *Consolidated Edison* the Court provided utility companies with constitutional protection for their discussions of public issues, concluded, "[t]here is no reason for providing similar constitutional protection when such statements are made only in the context of commercial transactions."[60]

*Bolger* involved an alleged violation of a federal postal regulation prohibiting the mailing of "[a]ny unsolicited advertisement of matter . . . designed, adapted, or intended for preventing conception . . . ."[61] Postal officials' interpretation of the statute excluded from this ban any "unsolicited advertisements in which the mailer has no commercial interest."[62] Youngs Drug Products Corp. manufactured a variety of contraceptive devises, typically marketed through wholesalers who in turn would sell the products to pharmacists for eventual sales to the public. To stimulate demand, Youngs employed a number of marketing tactics including sending unsolicited direct-mail publications to the general public. Among these items were a multi-page flier promoting the company's entire inventory of products, circulars devoted only to marketing prophylactics and what the company characterized as "informational pamphlets" about the virtues of using prophylactics, especially those manufactured by Youngs.

When complaints reached postal authorities from customers concerned about receiving Youngs' direct-marketing materials, the postal service warned Youngs that continuing to mail such materials would violate the anti-mailing statute. Because violating the statute could include both criminal and civil penalties, the company sought relief in the federal courts in the form of a declaratory judgment, arguing that threats to apply the statute's provisions would interfere with Youngs' First Amendment rights. The lower courts held that all three direct-mail publications were examples of commercial speech, but held also that the government's arguments for banning the mailing of the publications were insufficient to withstand a First Amendment challenge based upon the *Central Hudson* four-part test.[63]

The Supreme Court agreed that the government had not been able to satisfy the *Central Hudson* four-part test, but also agreed, over Justice Stevens' objections, that all three types of marketing materials mailed by Youngs were examples of commercial speech. Noting that the Court had long recognized a "'common-sense' distinction"[64] between commercial and non-commercial speech and that the Court had also determined that commercial speech is only entitled to limited First Amendment protection, Justice Marshall characterized the Court's first task in *Bolger* as "determin[ing] the proper classification of the mailings at issue here. Appellee contends that his proposed mailings constitute 'fully protected' speech. . . . Appellants argue ... that the proposed mailings are all commercial speech."[65] The job of the Court, said Marshall, is to make sure "that speech deserving of greater constitutional protection is not inadvertently suppressed."[66]

The Court found that although most of the mailings in question "fall within the core notion of commercial speech—'speech which does no more than propose a commercial transaction,'"[67] the company's publications containing general information about the merits of prophylactics posed "a closer question."[68] In attempting to answer this close question, the Court began by observing that just because the publication was admittedly a direct-mail advertisement did not automatically classify it as commercial speech (citing *Sullivan*). Neither did the fact that the publications referred to the products manufactured by Youngs. In addition, the Court noted that economic motivation, by itself, would normally not be a sufficient determinant of the status of the publication (citing *Bigelow*).

But, the Court continued, "[t]he combination of all these characteristics ... provides strong support for the ... conclusion that the informational pamphlets are properly characterized as commercial speech. The mailings constitute commercial speech notwithstanding ... that they contain discussions of important issues . . . ."[69] The Court added, "[w]e have made clear that advertising which 'links a product to a current public debate' is not thereby entitled to the constitutional protection afforded noncommercial speech. A company has ... protections available to its direct comments on public issues, so there is no reason for providing similar constitutional protection when such statements are made in the context of commercial [speech]."[70]

In a footnote, Justice Marshall pointed out, however, that his three-part analysis was not meant to be a generalized test like the Court's four-prong *Central Hudson* test. The Court, said Marshall, does not "mean to suggest that each of the characteristics present in this case must necessarily be present in order for speech to be commercial. For example, we express no opinion as to whether reference to any particular product or service is a necessary element of commercial speech."[71]

## Lower Courts and Definitional Issues

Not surprisingly, lower courts and government agencies trying to interpret and apply the Court's varying definitions of commercial speech have produced a decidedly mixed bag of decisions and policy statements.

A number of courts have rejected government attempts to regulate speech based on judgments that the speech in question did not fall within the narrow "commercial transaction" definition of commercial speech. For example, in *Pan Am Corp. v. Delta Air Lines, Inc.,*[72] a federal district court rejected a request by a corporation in a bankruptcy proceeding that Standard & Poor's, a corporate credit analyzing and reporting agency, produce subpoenaed documents the corporation claimed it needed to establish its claims. The court based its decision, in part, on its characterization of Standard & Poor's analysis as fully protected speech under the First Amendment because the activities of and information produced by the agency were more analogous to a journalistic rather than a business function. Pan Am argued that Standard & Poor's should produce the material requested because the "market driven nature of the speech, and its objectively verifiable content"[73] should have categorized the speech as commercial speech and therefore "made heightened First Amendment protection unnecessary."[74]

Similarly, in *New York Public Interest Research Group v. Insurance Information Institute,*[75] the court dismissed the plaintiff's complaint on the basis that the speech in question was not commercial and therefore was fully protected. The public interest group had filed suit under New York false advertising laws claiming that ads alleging a crisis in health care caused by excessive malpractice lawsuits were misleading. In rejecting the suit, the court noted, "[t]he dividing line is ... clear. If, within a common sense reading, an advertisement is obviously intended to promote sales, it is commercial speech. If a public message or discussion is incorporated, it is still commercial speech. If, however, the advertisement is a direct comment on a public issue, unrelated to proposing any particular commercial transaction, it is protected."[76]

In *New York City v. American School Publications*,[77] a New York court[78] rejected claims that the defendant's magazine was commercial speech despite arguments by the plaintiff that much of the content of, and the motivation for, publishing the magazine were intended to market the defendant's school course offerings. The court based its decision on the rationale that it was the content of the speech rather than the intent of the speaker that should rule in a definitional argument. Citing *Pittsburgh Press* and *Sullivan*, the court noted that the defendant's speech should be fully protected if it "communicates information, expresses opinion, recites grievances, protests claimed abuses or solicits financial support on behalf of a movement whose existence and objective are matters of public concern...."[79]

Other courts have upheld government regulations based on a more expansive definition of commercial speech. In a decision that would appear to be a direct contradiction to the opinion in *American School*, a federal appeals court in Georgia, in *In re Domestic Air Transportation Antitrust Litigation*,[80] upheld an order issued in an antitrust dispute that required an airline's in-flight magazine to carry notice of the antitrust suit against the airline. The court reasoned that the publication was designed to further the company's economic interests even though most of the publication carried articles of general interest and there was little content that actually promoted the company. In *Abramson v. Gonzalez*,[81] the court recognized a definition of commercial speech broad enough to sanction a government regulation disallowing the use of the term "psychologist" by those lacking sufficient professional credentials, noting that the regulation was permissible because the speech related "solely to the economic interests of the speaker."[82]

In a 1977 case, a federal appeals court in *National Commission on Egg Nutrition v. FTC*[83] held that an advertisement claiming "there is no scientific evidence that eating eggs increases the risk of ... heart disease"[84] fit within the definition of commercial speech and thus was subject to government regulations involving potentially false or misleading advertising claims. According to the court, despite the language of the Supreme Court in *Pittsburgh Press* and *Virginia State Board of Pharmacy*, the definition of commercial speech "was not intended to be narrowly limited to the mere proposal of a commercial transaction but extend[s] to false claims as to the harmlessness of the advertiser's product asserted for the purpose of persuading members of the reading public to buy the product."[85] The case was not accepted for review by the Supreme Court.

An example that highlights the continuing disagreement over the proper definition of commercial speech involved the R.J. Reynolds Tobacco Company, a major cigarette manufacturer. The company ran a series of advertisements reporting on the results of a federally funded study of health risk factors called "MR FIT." According to the tobacco company, the results of the study, which tracked long-term health records of a large sample of regular citizens, demonstrated there was no evidence of the high correlation between smoking and various diseases claimed by anti-smoking forces. As the advertisement said, "[w]e at R.J. Reynolds do not claim this study proves that smoking doesn't cause heart disease ... [only] ... that the controversy over smoking and health remains an open one."[86]

Although the advertising copy contained no mention of a specific brand or any hint of a sales pitch, the Federal Trade Commission claimed jurisdiction over the advertisements on the basis that their real purpose was to induce people to continue smoking cigarettes and, therefore, constituted commercial speech that the FTC said was false or misleading. However, an administrative law judge threw out the complaint, holding that the advertisements were not commercial speech but rather editorial statements published as advertisements.[87] In rejecting the FTC's position, the judge found that deciding in favor of the government would make it virtually impossible for "any business firm ... [to] ever be able to publish an opinion in a newspaper or magazine ad on a controversial public issue which concerns one of its products without losing the full protection of the First Amendment and subjecting the firm and the ad to the Commission's jurisdiction."[88]

The FTC then overruled its administrative law judge (FTC procedures are discussed more fully in Chapter 10), on the basis that the judge had mishandled the classification of the advertisements as non-commercial speech.[89] Acknowledging that the FTC would lack jurisdiction to regulate the advertising if the speech were not commercial speech, the FTC concluded that the Supreme Court had not set forth a definitive test of that term. Therefore, said the FTC, it would be necessary in each individual case to evaluate the factors to be considered as found in the decisions by the Court and lower courts in relation to the facts of the case.

According to the FTC, among the factors to be considered were whether (a) the speech was published in paid-for time or space; (b) there was an economic motivation behind the speech; (c) the speech was designed to market or promote a product or service; and (d) the copy mentioned a particular product or service. Applying this formulation of the attributes of commercial speech to the advertisements by R.J. Reynolds, the agency concluded that the administrative law judge's decision was too hasty in that it failed to take these factors sufficiently into account. "A message that addresses health concerns that may be faced by purchasers or potential purchasers of the speaker's product," said the FTC, "may constitute commercial speech."[90] At this point, R.J. Reynolds decided to throw in the towel and signed a consent decree that did not admit any violation but contained an agreement not to misrepresent the data from the "MR FIT" study in future advertising.

## The Importance of the Definitional Issues

From an advertising or public relations point of view, if the Court continues to hold that commercial speech is entitled to only limited First Amendment protection, the narrow definition of commercial speech as "speech that does no more than propose a commercial transaction" is, by far, preferable. Unfortunately, the continuing viability of this definition as the one employed by future courts, legislatures and regulatory agencies is suspect.

The reasons for pessimism are simple: the Court's "commercial transaction" language has proven both unclear and inadequate. Perhaps this is because the Court, beginning in *Pittsburgh Press*, meant to use the term only as a "classic example" or as "the core meaning" of commercial speech rather than as the final comprehensive definition. It is unfortunately true (at least from the point of view of clarity and consistency in the law) that even those on the Court who defend this definition have not uniformly employed the "commercial transaction" definition in subsequent commercial speech cases.

The greatest reason for concern, however, is that the "commercial transaction" language just does not work. For example, it is reasonable to believe that (a) marketing press releases announcing and touting the virtues of a company's new product; (b) direct mail pieces that are "instructional" in nature but clearly require the purchase of a product for the instruction to be effective; (c) billboards depicting only a red bulldog with no other words or images (advertising Red Dog Beer); (d) broadcast advertisements featuring various physical feats of daring followed by the slogan "Just Do It" (a Nike commercial); or (e) letterhead stationery of physicians or attorneys claiming special skills will all be treated by courts and government regulatory agencies alike as commercial speech, despite the absence of any language proposing an actual commercial transaction. These examples are only a few of the myriad ways that profit-making organizations communicate in furtherance of their economic interests.

Although of academic interest, all this might be of little practical significance if no one were motivated to seek regulation of broadly defined commercial speech. Unfortunately for free-speech advocates, this is far from the case. Social engineers, government regulators, special interest representatives and a whole host of others who believe that the public needs protecting from its own freely made choices are often dismayed to find that, despite information campaigns and logical arguments to the contrary, some people simply persist in doing what others feel is bad for them. Whether it's smoking cigarettes, not wearing seat belts or eating trans-fat foods, there seem to be the recalcitrant few who will not fall in line with the prevailing winds from Vichy.

Other critics of commercial speech argue that for-profit corporations, particularly if large, are inherently dangerous unless kept in check and that restrictions on corporate speech are one of the few means of reining them in. Still others represent or claim to represent those (e.g., children or the mentally or physically impaired) characterized as inherently unable to make informed choices about corporate activities.

Some social activists are content to limit their efforts to moral suasion. Others, recognizing it would be difficult or perhaps impossible to regulate or ban the underlying corporate activity or product (e.g., Prohibition), have adopted the tactic of lobbying for governmentally imposed limits on speech by the "offending" corporation. Such efforts often seem to be a siren-like call for legislators and regulators who, by passing legislation or creating regulations, claim credit for attacking important social problems without spending any tax dollars or adding to government bureaucracy.

However, expansive efforts to regulate corporate speech may not succeed unless that speech falls under the definition of "commercial speech," as noted earlier, a lesser protected speech category. Therefore, those who wish to regulate will be doing their level best to say that most or all corporate speech activity should be classified as commercial speech. This clearly includes advertising, but also such marketing "speech activities" as billboards, ballpark signage, race-car sponsorship and a host of other promotional efforts. It seems inevitable that such efforts to sweep corporate speech into a regulatory framework will include marketing-oriented public relations corporate speech as well.

The question then becomes: how successful will these efforts be?

## The California Supreme Court Expands the Definition of Commercial Speech: *Kasky v. Nike*

For free-speech advocates, the California Supreme Court offered a most ominous answer to that question in the 2002 case of *Kasky v. Nike*.[91] The case originated in reaction to a late 1990s corporate-reputation campaign undertaken by Nike to answer critics of its overseas labor practices. Already the subject of numerous accusations by international labor rights advocacy groups that Nike engaged in so-called "sweatshop" labor practices, the company decided to respond aggressively to its critics after a negative critique of Nike's practices aired on the CBS newsmagazine *48 Hours*.

Nike began its reputation reclamation efforts by commissioning an audit of its corporate labor policies by Atlanta-based corporate consulting firm GoodWorks International, LLC. The choice of GoodWorks seemed a strategically wise move. The chairman of GoodWorks, Andrew Young, had been hailed throughout his life as a champion of human rights, most recently for his work as the United States' ambassador to the United

Nations. Young was best known, however, for being a close adviser and confidant of Dr. Martin Luther King, Jr. during the 1960s civil rights struggles.

Young made a 10-day trip to China, Indonesia and Vietnam, visiting 12 factories, including four that had been widely reported as being among the chief abusers of workers' rights. Upon his return, Young summarized his conclusions in a press release prepared by Nike with the statement, "[i]t is my sincere belief that NIKE is doing a good job in the application of its Code of Conduct. But NIKE can and should do better."[92] Young wrote that he found no evidence of illegal or unsafe working conditions at any of the factories he visited.

The press release marked Nike's opening salvo in a comprehensive public relations effort built around the GoodWorks report. Several days after the initial release, Nike purchased advertising space in various newspapers featuring headlines such as "Nike Passes Inspection—No Sweat." Andrew Young publicly defended Nike, writing letters to editors refuting attacks on Nike and questioning the motives of the corporation's critics. To quell the rising sense of unease about buying Nike products for college athletic teams, Nike Chief Executive Phil Knight penned letters to college athletics directors touting the GoodWorks study findings.

Response to the campaign predictably was mixed. Although some hailed Nike's audit as a step in the right direction, critics of the corporation denounced Nike's campaign as simply the latest effort by the company to pull the wool over the eyes of the public.

Any positive up-tick for Nike's image was short-lived. During the three months following the corporation's initial efforts, new allegations regarding both Nike and the GoodWorks report surfaced. Anita Chan, professor at the Australian National University's Contemporary China Center, wrote a letter to the editor of the *Journal of Commerce* stating that the GoodWorks report had erroneously listed her as an information resource. Additionally, Chan wrote that "Mr. Young's report is oblivious to the whole issue of worker safety" because it ignored the labor abuses that were taking place in Asian factories. Chan concluded, "[s]ending a sincere novice on a quick jaunt of Asia has the earmarks of a PR exercise. It appears that Mr. Young was taken for a ride."[93]

Additionally, still looming over Nike's head was the criticism that the corporation did not pay a living wage to its workers, a charge unanswered in the GoodWorks report and Nike's press statements. The company then issued a new release touting an additional Nike-commissioned study recently completed by a group of MBA students at Dartmouth University. The study determined that, contrary to the findings of the original *48 Hours* report, Nike workers in Vietnam and Indonesia were paid significantly higher than their countries' living wages. The critics answered the Dartmouth study less than three weeks later and, ironically, used Nike's own information against the corporation. The Transnational Resource and Action Center, a San Francisco-based corporate-responsibility advocacy group, released a leaked, year-old memo from an accounting firm study of one of Nike's Vietnam factories. The audit detailed a host of Nike's labor and safety violations ranging from allowing employees to work without protective clothing to requiring overtime for no extra pay. Nike acknowledged the accuracy of the report but noted that the year-old problems outlined in the audit had already been addressed.

Watching this public debate with interest was Californian Marc Kasky, a self-described environmentalist and community activist. Addressing Nike's corporate practices, Kasky later told a reporter from *The San Francisco Chronicle*, "I saw something that I thought was wrong, and I wanted to do something about it."[94] Kasky consulted attorney Alan Caplan (who had been an attorney of record in the lawsuit that eventually caused R.J. Reynolds Tobacco Company to shelve its Joe Camel advertising logo), inquiring about the feasibility of suing Nike for its recent public relations misstatements. Caplan suggested that Kasky invoke provisions of the state's Business and Professions Codes[95] which would allow him to file suit against Nike for false advertising and unfair trade practices as a "private attorney general" representing the people of the state.

Kasky filed suit in California Superior Court alleging four causes of action. Among other claims, the suit alleged that Nike had engaged in "unfair business practices within the meaning [of the law]" and that the company had violated the state's false advertising laws.[96] As remedies for Nike's alleged misdeeds, Kasky demanded that Nike engage in a court-supervised campaign to correct its misstatements and cease making false and misleading statements regarding its overseas labor practices. Kasky also demanded that Nike "disgorge all monies that it acquired by the alleged unlawful and unfair practices" in California.[97]

In reply, Nike challenged the constitutionality of the application of the Business and Professions Codes, relying on the First Amendment and portions of the California constitution. Specifically, Nike argued that its speech was noncommercial in nature and, therefore, not subject to California's false advertising and unfair competition laws. A superior court judge agreed and dismissed Kasky's case without leave to amend.[98] Kasky appealed this decision, but the California appeals court also dismissed Kasky's claim.[99]

Nike had won the first two rounds in the California court system, but its most serious challenge lay ahead. Kasky petitioned for review in the California Supreme Court, which reversed the appeals court decision.[100] Seizing on the federal Supreme Court's ambiguous definitions of commercial speech and the presumed false and deceptive elements of Nike's statements (even though made as part of a public relations campaign), the

*Kasky* majority determined that the facts in this case demanded a new and more comprehensive definition for commercial speech.

"We conclude," said the court, "that when a court must decide whether particular speech may be subjected to laws aimed at preventing false advertising or other forms of commercial deception, categorizing a particular statement as commercial or noncommercial speech requires consideration of three elements: *the speaker, the intended audience,* and *the content of the message.*"[101]

The court then applied its new definition of commercial speech to Nike's public relations campaign. Addressing the "speaker" element of the test, the court noted that "the first element—a commercial speaker—is satisfied because the speakers—Nike and its officers and directors—are engaged in commerce. Specifically, they manufacture, import, distribute, and sell consumer goods in the form of athletic shoes and apparel."[102] Next, addressing the "intended audience" portion of the test, the court said that "an intended commercial audience is also satisfied because Nike's letters to university presidents and directors of athletic departments were addressed directly to actual and potential purchasers of Nike's products."[103] The court also accepted the argument that "Nike's press releases and letters to newspaper editors, although addressed to the public generally, were also intended to reach and influence actual and potential purchasers of Nike's products."[104]

Finally, addressing the "content of the message" in Nike's campaign, the court said that factual statements "describing its own labor policies, the practices and working conditions in factories where its products are made, [t]he wages paid to the factories' employees ... the way they are treated, and whether the environmental conditions under which they work violate local health and safety laws"[105] all fall within the court's definitional conceptions of "commercial character" and "product references," thus satisfying the third part of the court's definition.

Summing up its analysis, the four-justice majority determined that Nike's public relations campaign did indeed amount to commercial speech and, therefore, was subject to a *Central Hudson* analysis. The case was sent back to the court of appeals to determine if Nike's statements were false. If so, the state's Business and Professions Codes would allow Kasky to claim damages on behalf of California's citizens.

Nike appealed to the Supreme Court of the United States, but after hearing oral arguments, the Court dismissed the case on procedural grounds and returned the case to the courts of California. Three months before a new trial date was set in California, Kasky and Nike issued a joint press release announcing a settlement in the case. According to the terms, Nike would commit $500,000 to maintain its overseas factories' worker-education programs and donate $1 million to the Fair Labor Association, an offshoot of the Clinton administration-created Apparel Industry Partnership.

Because of *Kasky*, and because of the broad reach of California's Business and Professions Codes, any for-profit corporation doing business in that state (even if not physically located there) may now assume that virtually all of its messages will fall within the state court's sweeping new definition of commercial speech. Potentially even more troubling to for-profit corporate communicators is that the *Kasky* commercial speech definition provides a roadmap for other states that may wish to revisit their own commercial speech definitions.

Perhaps the best illustration of *Kasky's* potential impact on future public relations practice is demonstrated by the advice published in the *Los Angeles Lawyer*, the local bar association's principal publication, to all attorneys representing corporate clients that do business in California. The article warned "when advising a business client on how to publicly address certain issues that the client considers noncommercial, practitioners should alert the client that the safest choice is silence."[106]

## Defamation and Commercial Speech: Constitutional Issues

Perhaps no better illustration of the problems caused by the failure of the Court to provide a precise definition of commercial speech exists than in the differences in outcomes that could occur in a lawsuit alleging harm to reputation. Much depends upon whether the libelous statements are classified as commercial or non-commercial speech.

A lawsuit for defamation of character typically arises in response to a false statement of fact about the plaintiff, published or disseminated in other ways to a third party by the defendant, causing harm to reputation. Such cases are examples of state-law-based, civil tort suits to permit recovery of monetary damages for harm to people or personal property (a more thorough analysis of commercial communication torts is found in later chapters).

Until *Sullivan* in 1964 (discussed earlier in this chapter), federal constitutional issues played almost no role in the resolution of such suits. However, in *Sullivan*, the Supreme Court was faced with a complex case, involving political speech, civil rights and editorial advertising that the Court felt demanded a First Amendment rule protecting false and defamatory speech directed against public officials in their official capacity. This rule was later extended to public figures in *Curtis Publishing Co. v. Butts*[107] and *A. P. v. Walker*,[108] and eventually to private plaintiffs in *Gertz v. Welch*.[109] Although the levels of constitutional protection differ, the underlying rationale for First Amendment protection of false and defamatory speech is the same: a commitment to encouraging "wide open discussion of public issues"[110] that could be chilled by overly stringent defamation laws.

Prior to *Sullivan*, state laws generally favored the plaintiff's cause in a defamation suit, holding the defendant to a strict standard for imposing liability. The holdings in *Sullivan* and *Butts* turned the tables almost 180 degrees, making it impossible for the plaintiff to win (if the plaintiff is a public person) unless the plaintiff can show actual malice—defined as whether the defendant either knew the defamatory statements were false or that the defendant entertained serious doubts about the truth of the statements before publishing them. *Gertz* extended this logic to private plaintiffs suing media defendants in matters of public interest, although only requiring that private plaintiffs in such situations prove that the defendant acted at least negligently.

Most corporations are extremely concerned about maintaining and protecting their good name within their business or professional communities. Therefore, they not only have reputations to defend but often are quick to do so. Corporations and other legally recognized organizations also can be guilty of issuing defamatory statements about individuals (e.g., a statement about reasons for employee termination) or other organizations (e.g., statements impugning the motives or activities of a competitor). For these reasons, it is not unusual to find defamation suits involving corporations and other organizations as either plaintiffs or defendants. In such situations, two competing First Amendment issues may intersect, perhaps violently.

The potential conflict is straightforward. Normally, if the plaintiff in a defamation suit is a public person, the defendant can count on constitutional protection for the speech in question unless the defendant knew the harmful speech was false or published with reckless disregard for the truth. If the plaintiff in such a suit is private, the defendant knows that the plaintiff must prove that the defendant was at least negligent. But what if the defamatory speech is also defined as commercial speech? In other situations, courts have decided that false or deceptive commercial speech merits no protection under the First Amendment and that even truthful, non-deceptive commercial speech is deserving of less protection than other kinds of speech. Should the defendant in a defamation-by-commercial-speech case benefit from the constitutional protections erected by the Court to the same degree as other defendants or are these First Amendment protections lost because the defamatory speech is commercial and therefore less protected?

The Court has obliquely recognized this conundrum but never directly addressed it. In *Bates*, the Court cited *Virginia State Board of Pharmacy* for the proposition that commercial speech should be differentiated from other speech in the context of advertising by attorneys and other professionals. "Since advertising is linked to commercial well being, it seems unlikely that such speech is particularly susceptible to being crushed by overbroad regulation.... [P]resumably [the advertiser] can determine

more readily than others whether his speech is truthful and protected."[111]
Similar sentiments surfaced in a footnote in *Central Hudson*.

In *Dun & Bradstreet, Inc. v. Greenmoss Builders*,[112] the Court was
faced with the appeal of a Vermont case involving a false credit report
harming the business reputation of a corporation. While the Court was
badly fragmented in its ruling, one of the rationales advanced by some
members of the Court for denying First Amendment protection to the
defendant's speech was that the speech in question did not address matters
of general interest or concern. This was true, said the Court, in part
because the credit reports were economically motivated and, therefore,
less like constitutionally protected commercial speech.

In *U.S. Healthcare Inc. v. Blue Cross of Greater Philadelphia*,[113] a federal court of appeals for the Third Circuit directly addressed the defama-
tion-in-the-context-of-commercial-speech issue. The case arose out of the
entry of U.S. Healthcare into the health insurance market which had been
dominated by the insurance programs provided by Blue Cross. The cornerstone of the new type of insurance plan was the concept of the health
maintenance organization (HMO) that provided savings in the costs of
medical insurance but required the participants in such plans to forego the
freedom to choose their own health-care providers. The HMO programs
became so popular that Blue Cross decided to mount an "aggressive and
provocative"[114] marketing campaign to convince both potential consumers and former customers that the more traditional insurance plans
offered by Blue Cross were preferable.

As part of this campaign, Blue Cross sponsored advertisements in newspapers and broadcast stations and sent direct mail circulars touting the
benefits of its insurance plans, "in particular, Personal Choice [a Blue
Cross preferred provider system] . . . at the expense of HMO products."[115]
The Blue Cross-sponsored advertisements, which did not mention U.S.
Healthcare, consisted of informational comparative advertising claims
(e.g., "I don't like those HMO heath plans. You get one doctor. No choice
of hospitals.")[116] and claims designed to appeal to the emotions (e.g., an
obviously saddened woman lamenting that "[t]he hospital my HMO sent
me to just wasn't enough. It's my fault.").[117] In a counter move, U.S.
Healthcare rolled out its own "responsive advertising campaign" to
"counteract the Blue Cross/Blue Shield message."[118] Like the Blue Cross
advertisements, the campaign consisted of informational and emotional
messages, although, unlike its competition, a number of U.S. Healthcare's
advertisements directly challenged Blue Cross and its Personal Choice plan
by name.

Not content simply to duel in the media, U.S. Healthcare also filed a
lawsuit charging, among other things, that the Blue Cross-sponsored
advertisements defamed U.S. Healthcare's products and its standing in the
community. Blue Cross responded with counter suits alleging similar

claims. Trying to sort out the various claims and counter-claims, the jury in the federal district court trial[119] eventually rejected all of the claims by Blue Cross but was unable to reach agreement on the claims by U.S. Healthcare. Before a new trial could begin, Blue Cross asked the court to rule that the First Amendment required a dismissal of U.S. Healthcare's libel claims. According to Blue Cross, because the Supreme Court of the United States had established that public persons defamed in a matter of public concern must show that the defendant knew the defamatory statements were false or was reckless about the truth of the statements, and because U.S. Healthcare could not meet this constitutionally imposed burden, the trial court should enter a judgment in favor of Blue Cross without the need for another trial. The district court agreed the constitutional standards did apply and granted the defendant's motion to terminate the libel claims.

On appeal, the court of appeals divided the advertisements into four categories, two of which, said the court, could give rise to a cause of action for defamation. Because the appeals court agreed with the trial court that at least some of the speech in the competing comparative advertisements could be defamatory, it also agreed that determining whether full First Amendment protections applied to the advertisements was essential in determining the outcome of the case. The appeals court disagreed with the lower court, however, on the issue of whether constitutional protections should apply, holding that the commercial speech in question was not entitled to the "heightened protection under the First Amendment"[120] merited by fully protected speech.

In reviewing the line of Supreme Court decisions involving defamation beginning with *Sullivan*, the appeals court found that principal factors underlying the balancing of speech vs. reputational interests were (a) the status of the plaintiff, and (b) the classification of the speech. Focusing on the latter of these two criteria, the court noted that the Supreme Court had established that commercial speech, although accorded some constitutional protection, nonetheless received "protection somewhat less extensive than that afforded 'noncommercial speech.'"[121] Therefore, noted the court, if the speech in question were truly commercial in nature, the First Amendment protections extended to other kinds of false and defamatory speech need not apply.

This was so, said the court, because allowing states greater latitude in regulating defamatory commercial speech would not inhibit such speech because the speaker, driven by economic considerations, would not be "deterred by proper regulation."[122] The court found that intolerance of false and defamatory statements of fact was justifiably higher in a situation in which commercial speakers were "uniquely qualified to evaluate the truthfulness of their speech"[123] because of their familiarity with both the goods and services they provide. On a more theoretical note, the court added that "requir[ing] a parity of constitutional protection for commercial and noncommercial speech alike could invite dilution, simply be a leveling process, of the force of the amendment's guarantee with respect to the latter kind of speech."[124]

The question that remained was whether any of the defamatory speech by either of the two health care insurers should be defined as commercial speech. Taking its definition from *Bolger,* the third circuit answered this question affirmatively, finding that the speech was in commercial form, was economically motivated and referred to specific products or services. In addition, because of the large financial interests involved on both sides, the court observed that "it would have to be a cold day before these corporations would be chilled from speaking about the comparative merits of their products."[125] Also, the court noted that a significant number of the advertisements had little or no true informational content but rather were emotional appeals designed to discourage participation in the competitor's programs.

Finally, the court rejected the arguments advanced by Blue Cross that its advertisements were part of an ongoing public controversy about health care systems and, therefore, deserving of heightened First Amendment protection. Quoting *Central Hudson,* the court noted that there was "[little] reason for providing constitutional protection when such statements are made only in the context of commercial transactions."[126]

The Supreme Court of the United States refused to accept the case on appeal, making *U.S. Healthcare* the only important decision on the issue of the constitutional protections accorded defamatory commercial speech to date. Although the circuit court's rationale has been criticized and the issue may still be decided differently by the Supreme Court, the decision stands as a warning sign for advertising and public relations practitioners that their speech may not be afforded heightened First Amendment protection if their organization is sued for defamation, particularly when that speech involves criticism of the commercial products or practices of the competition.

Although there are no major cases raising similar constitutional issues involving other communication-related torts (e.g., invasion of privacy or intentional infliction of emotional distress), there is no reason on the face of it to assume that courts would accord heightened First Amendment protection for commercial speech in cases raising such claims.

## Regulation of Paid-For Political Speech: Constitutional Issues

To bring this chapter full circle, we need to return to *New York Times v. Sullivan* and *First National Bank of Boston v. Bellotti* to examine the issues related to attempted government regulation of political speech. Both cases stand for the proposition that corporations and other organizations are free to spend money to publicize their views about issues of general public interest. Although corporate wealth could have the potential to make a substantial impact on the total amount of information available in the marketplace, said the Court in *Bellotti*, "the fact that advocacy may persuade the electorate is hardly a reason to suppress it ...."[127]

The vast majority of decisions in cases with fact patterns resembling *Bellotti* have been decided in favor of the paid-for speech interests. For example, in *C & C Plywood v. Hanson*,[128] a federal appeals court, citing *Bellotti*, struck down a Montana statute that banned corporate financial contributions in support of ballot issues. In *Let's Help Florida v. McCray*,[129] a federal appeals court[130] similarly held unconstitutional a Florida law limiting corporate contributions "[t]o any political committee in support of, or in opposition to, an issue to be voted on in a statewide election."[131]

However, advertising and public relations professionals involved in political campaign advertising should note that the rules may change considerably when financial contributions—including paying for political advertising and other forms of communication—are made to assist candidates for public office. For example, the Federal Elections Campaign Act[132] regulates the amount individuals and organizations may contribute directly to candidates for federal office and creates rigorous disclosure and reporting requirements for those making such contributions. Many states have passed similar statutes to regulate campaigns at the state level.[133]

The constitutionality of the federal Act was challenged in *Buckley v. Valeo*.[134] The Supreme Court ruled that restricting contributions to candidates was constitutional, although it struck down the provisions of the Act limiting the amounts candidates could spend and the total spent on behalf of a candidate by groups or organizations working independently of the candidate.

In *FEC v. National Conservative Political Action Committee*,[135] the Court invalidated limits on contributions by some kinds of independent political action committees (PACs), a method many corporations have employed to channel financial contributions in support of issues and candidates they favor. Subsequently, Congress passed the McCain-Feingold bill[136] which significantly regulates the raising and spending of so-called "soft money" by national political parties. The law also limits the activities of state political parties in soliciting and spending such funds for broadcast advertisements and for get-out-the-vote campaigns for federal, state and local candidates.

In addition, McCain-Feingold limits the use of corporate and union funds for broadcast messages within 60 days of a general election. The bill, signed into law by President Bush, withstood a later court challenge in *McConnell v. Federal Elections Commission*[137] and has significantly changed the face of political campaigns, although a variety of special-interest organizations nonetheless cleverly figured out ways to evade McCain-Feingold limitations (through so-called 527 groups) and spend considerable funds in attack advertisements during the Bush-Kerry presidential campaign.

In *Citizens United v. Federal Elections Commission*, decided as this book went to press,[138] the Supreme Court overruled two significant precedents in the areas of campaign finance and the regulation of paid-for speech by corporations. *Citizens United* involved the right of a corporation, formed as a non-profit organization, to air a documentary film about Senator Hillary Rodham Clinton entitled "Hillary: The Movie," and the right to air advertisements promoting the film during the presidential primary season.

The group filed suit in December 2007, asking the court to declare that certain sections of McCain-Feingold unconstitutional. Specifically they were concerned with Section 203, which prevented corporations (including non-profit advocacy organizations like Citizens United) and labor unions from financing campaign communications from their own treasury funds within 30 days before a primary or nominating convention, or within 60 days before a general election.

In a controversial 5 to 4 opinion, the Court held that the speech by Citizens United was the kind of political speech the First Amendment was designed to protect and, accordingly, that limits on independent expenditures by corporations or other speakers in support of candidates for office could not be prohibited. The Court rejected its earlier language in *McConnell* regarding campaign expenditures (McConnell primarily deals with spending limits related to political contributions and disclaimers required for paid-for speech).

The Court also overturned *Austin v. Michigan Chamber of Commerce* (discussed earlier in the chapter) that prohibited direct independent expenditures in support of candidates. In the process, the Court reinstituted the almost absolute First Amendment protection for corporate speech about public issues established in *Bellotti*.

The speech rights of corporate speakers remains a volatile issue, particularly in the areas of public issues and support of political candidates. Public relations and advertising professionals involved in political activities representing candidates or parties (or those who wish to support them), should make it their business to familiarize themselves with both federal and state regulations covering such campaign contributions on an ongoing basis.

## Public Interest Information and Commercial Speech in a Digital, New-Media Age: Emerging Issues

If, when and how the use of new media technologies or Web-based social networks might influence future courts in the rather murky areas of commercial speech law discussed in this chapter most likely will form the basis of law review articles and complicated court cases for years to come. For example, what is a blog that discusses new products or new political candidates in terms of the definition of commercial speech? How about "tweeting" by a movie celebrity who includes comments about a product or service, particularly if the celebrity is compensated for such endorsements?

It does seem a reasonable prediction that courts and regulators, seeking the defining term for characterizing commercial speech, will be inclined to adopt the more inclusive "economic motive" rather than the alternative "propose a commercial transaction." It is difficult to believe that those seeking to define and regulate such speech will not adopt the definition that those doing the commercial speaking have long recognized and, increasingly, are making a cornerstone of their marketing efforts through increased sales promotions and other similar non-media and new-media advertising, public relations and marketing communications techniques.

If this prediction becomes a reality, joining all or significant parts of a corporation's public relations functions with advertising and new-market communications efforts and then locating them all within the framework of an integrated marketing communications department—an increasingly seen corporate communications structure—becomes more problematic because of the tacit (if not overt) admission by the corporation that, by so doing, its public relations speech is speech made directly for economic motives. This issue is already a potentially troubling one for those corporate public relations departments which now within their corporate structure report to the marketing side of the corporation. However, until now, most of these can legitimately argue that this is a structural and not a functional relationship. Such arguments will be much more difficult to make, however, if function follows form.

Does this mean that all corporate speech will be subject to a commercial speech analysis? Those who want to regulate will certainly try to make that case, but it seems unlikely to be a winning one for speech about public issues as far removed from a corporation's business interests as First National Bank's anti-personal income tax stance, and perhaps even for speech more directly related to political candidates. In such situations, *Bellotti* probably is still good law.

The pro-regulation argument will be much more powerful if applied to corporate speech that touches even remotely on the direct interests of the corporation. In such cases, the experiences of R.J. Reynolds with the Federal Trade Commission and Nike in the courts of California may be just the first hints of the potential application of crippling commercial speech regulations and restrictions to corporate speech in all its varying forms—from paid advertising to in-house publications, speeches or legislative testimony.

It would appear that the safest strategy is to plan for a future in which any communication activities by a profit-making company (except news media or other mass communication companies) reasonably related to the company's products or services will likely be defined as commercial speech. If this proves true, for the time being, advertising and public relations professionals should be prepared for their commercial communications to meet the *Central Hudson* four-part test.

# Chapter 4

# Defamation, Product Disparagement and Related Torts

The First Amendment declares, "Congress shall make no law ... abridging the freedom of speech, or of the press. ..."[1] That sounds absolute. As we have seen in the discussion in the first three chapters, however, it is not. A business executive might criticize his or her local government, but had better not advocate its violent overthrow by creating a potential riot. A citizen is privileged to yell, "Go to hell!" (or worse) at a political rally, but not "Fire! Fire!" in a packed movie theater. Advertising agencies and business corporations have extensive liberty to print and broadcast messages promoting products and services, but not to make deceptive, false or unfair claims that might mislead the public.

The subjects of this chapter are defamation, product disparagement and related torts—areas in which the First Amendment plays only a limited role. The purpose of this chapter is not to provide a definitive treatment of these complex topics, but rather to suggest some of the legal dilemmas that advertising and public relations professionals might encounter while speaking with their publics or promoting goods and services. You will also see how the courts have reacted when forced to make tough choices in this area between either upholding freedom of expression or protecting an individual's, corporation's or product's reputation.

## Defamation

*Defamation* is one of the most common and most serious legal problems currently facing the mass communications industry. Although much defamation litigation arises out of newsgathering activities, defamation is of just as much concern to the public relations and advertising professions. Corporate, product, service and business reputations can be defamed in advertising or public relations messages as well as in other types of business communications.

On the other side of the equation, public relations specialists in particular have the responsibility to inform their clients about the possibly far-reaching consequences of bringing defamation suits; each court appearance or motion could expose their clients to further, potentially adverse coverage. Public relations practitioners should also help their clients understand that fair and accurate accounts of trials, legislative sessions and government actions and documents may be insulated from such suits. Thus, unfavorable and even damaging statements about their clients, in certain contexts, are protected speech under current defamation law.

## Background

From the time that caveman Urg smartly clubbed caveman Zog over the head after Zog criticized Urg's cave drawings as being "too post-modern," for eons and eons and millennia and millennia and centuries and centuries, people have been concerned about their reputations. Whether it's within their tribes, religious sects, social orders or local communities, members of such groups have been resolute in protecting their good names and personal standing.

For almost as long, the remedy for those who felt their reputations had been besmirched was to step outside and engage in fisticuffs or, if members of the aristocracy, engage in duels, often referred to as "affairs of honor." Eventually, in jolly old England, folks began to feel these remedies were somewhat inefficient in maintaining social order and so decided to bring these confrontations into the courtrooms rather than the town squares.

Thus over the centuries, the British developed the common law of defamation. Not surprisingly, when the British colonized the New World, they brought with them their common law, including law related to defamation. Equally not surprising, when the Colonists broke away to form a new country, they had plenty to do in creating a new nation without worrying about changing the common law, and so, British common law evolved into American common law. Today, the American and British laws of defamation resemble first cousins—many similarities, but some noticeable differences.

American common law is state-made law; there is no federal common law. Therefore, technically, there are 50 different sets of defamation laws in the United States. But, because of the way the law evolved, beginning with the original 13 states and then adopted state by state with each new addition to the union, the laws of defamation from Alaska to Wyoming look remarkably alike. That's why the discussion below is generally applicable to all jurisdictions, with a few variations around the edges (e.g., the effect of a retraction or length of time to bring a suit).

## Terminology

*Defamation* is commonly defined as statements that expose a person to hatred or contempt, lower that person in the esteem of friends and associates or hurt his or her business. Traditionally, printed defamation was referred to as *libel* and spoken defamation was called *slander*. In today's more complicated communications world, it might be better to think of libel as speech that is "fixed" rather than transitory. For example, is defamation that is broadcast libel or slander? If the offending statements came from a script or are on video recordings, they likely would be regarded as libelous. If they were ad-libs—spontaneous comments broadcast live—they would probably be classified as slander.

Because of its more long-lasting nature, courts have tended to regard libel as more serious than slander. Also, because virtually all defamation involving the mass media, including advertising and public relations, will most likely be treated as libel, the terms defamation and libel will generally be used interchangeably throughout the rest of this chapter to refer to the tort of defamation.

Although there have been criminal laws against defamation enacted by legislatures in every state, the overwhelming majority of libel and slander cases are handled as civil wrongs to be settled between individuals. This involves a branch of *tort* law—defined for our purposes as claims of harm to persons or personal property (e.g., automobile mishaps, determinations of negligence in medical malpractice cases and so forth). Criminal libel, in which the prosecuting attorney and the police get involved, is exceedingly rare. Those who lose a civil libel suit in court are not "found guilty" of libel, but are simply held *liable* for the injury caused by the libel.

Nearly every press release, news article or advertisement holds the potential for a libel suit. Although there have been a number of libel actions arising out of major advertising campaigns or momentous news stories originating in news releases, most libel suits are prompted by small messages that seem minor and are, for that reason, sometimes carelessly handled.

Libel suits are expensive, time-consuming and fatiguing for both sides. The person instigating the action (the plaintiff) seeks money damages to pay for restoring what he or she believes to be a sullied individual or business reputation. Judges and juries often are hard pressed to place precise dollar values on an individual's, organization's or product's reputation, much less on the depreciation caused by a libelous statement. As a result, libel suits often end in frustration for everyone concerned.

Many who bring suit for libel may be less interested in obtaining money than in moral vindication—in having some official organization, such as a court of law, put a stop to an unfair advertising campaign or in proclaiming to one and all that a wrong against them has been committed. Former Chief Justice Warren Burger and others have urged the government and the legal profession to develop mechanisms outside the judicial system for handling a share of civil disagreements. This search for what is called *alternative dispute resolution* has led to the creation of advertising review boards and other mediation services.[2]

For now, however, and probably for the near future, defamation questions are likely to be ultimately resolved in courts, and when plaintiffs win they are usually awarded a sum of money. This may seem a crude and inappropriate means to restore so intangible a thing as reputation, but it appears to have worked over time. If nothing else, payment of cold, hard cash translates the harm into a language everybody can understand.

## The Elements of Libel

Before a plaintiff can expect to win a libel suit, he or she must establish at the outset that (a) the offending defamatory statements have been made; (b) the offending statements have been published to at least one third party by the defendant (the one being sued, e.g., an advertising agency or public relations department); (c) the plaintiff has been identified in the statements; (d) the actions of the defendant are the true cause of the actual harm suffered by the plaintiff; (e) the plaintiff is entitled to be compensated by money damages for that harm; and (f) the defamatory statements appeared because the defendant has done all this with the required degree of fault established by law. Let's take a closer look at each of these points in turn.

## Defamation Defined

The plaintiff must show that the words, in fact, did have a defamatory meaning. Some words may be libelous *per se* (i.e., in and of themselves). *Swindler, cheat, blackmailer, prostitute, forger, tax-evader, crook, swine-flu carrier*—say these words about the next person who walks in the door (no matter who it turns out to be) and that person will have little trouble convincing a jury that the individual who has been so characterized is likely to be looked down upon by his or her fellow citizens.

Libel *per quod* means the words might appear to be perfectly innocent, but the way they are used makes them understood to be libelous by those familiar with the person who is the subject of the statement. Suppose the following item appears in a company newsletter for employees: "Mr. and Mrs. L.Q.C. Lamar III last week became the proud parents of twins." Upon reading this news, fellow employees might feel it appropriate to express their congratulations to the happy couple. The item is incorrect, however. The company publication misidentified the new parents. Have the Lamars been defamed? Quite possibly, if some readers knew that the couple married only a few months ago. In this situation, the knowledge the readers brought into their reading of the story—extrinsic circumstances— makes the item defamatory.

It also should be noted that the actual words themselves need not be false and clearly defamatory to be actionable nonetheless. In what is often called "libel by implication," courts have consistently held that if reasonable people exposed to the message draw a defamatory meaning from how the statements in the message relate to each other or from how an illustration suggests a meaning perhaps not intended by the communicator defendant, the message will be considered libelous even if, technically, each fact in the message is true. The statement, "John and Mary were seen entering the Smithville Hotel at 4 p.m. and then seen leaving four hours later smiling and hugging," could lead to a conclusion that is contrary to the actual truth that John and Mary had been a team in a dance competition held at the Smithville Hotel, won first prize and, as a result, split $10,000 in prize money.

Advertising and public relations professionals should develop the habit of carefully reviewing their communications for statements that possibly might be seen as defamatory before they are published. One method, often suggested by media lawyers, is to list every person and organization mentioned in the communication and note exactly what is being said about each. Finding and eliminating potentially libelous material in advance of publication is not only the best method for avoiding a possible lawsuit, but the mark of true professional communicators who know their business.

## Publication

The offending words must reach an audience, if only a small one. Person A may defame Person B in a confidential memo, for example, but Person B will not have a legitimate lawsuit for defamation unless Person A has shown the offending statements to at least one additional third party.

Technically, publication occurs the moment a third person has seen the communication. In *Dun & Bradstreet v. Greenmoss Builders, Inc.*,[3] the Supreme Court affirmed a substantial judgment against a credit reporting company for publicizing false and defamatory information, although only five copies of the credit report had been sent to the company's subscribers. In 1982, the Alton, Ill., *Telegraph* was hit with a $9.2 million libel judgment (enough to force the paper into bankruptcy, although the suit was eventually settled for $1.4 million) stemming from a note that never even got into the newspaper.[4] It was an internal memorandum written by two of the paper's reporters that accused a local contractor of having ties with a savings and loan institution that seemed, to the reporters at least, connected to organized crime. If communication circulates, publication has occurred.

Unlike these examples and unfortunately for the defendant, a plaintiff often has a relatively easy time demonstrating that publication has occurred because the defendant advertising agency or public relations department has disseminated the defamatory information to thousands, if not millions, of readers or viewers in network television advertising, press release material published in hundreds of news outlets or in campaigns on YouTube, Facebook or other social networking sites.

## Identification

If the audience, or even a tiny portion of it, believes that the defamatory statements refer to the plaintiff, then that person has been identified. Unfortunately, identification also is often made easy for the plaintiff by the defendant because of the emphasis on clearly identifying subjects inherent in the training of professional communicators. A plaintiff identified in a news release by name, age, title, place of business and hometown probably will have little difficulty convincing a jury that he or she is the subject of the defamatory comments.

Identification need not be by name, however. Veiled references may be enough for readers to know, or think they know, whom the story is about. Suppose, for example, a medical writer doing a story on liposuction for a local publication interviewed several of the 20 plastic and reconstructive surgeons in the area who perform this kind of medical procedure, as well as a number of former patients who underwent the surgery. The writer included comments from one, unidentified, former patient who, while generally satisfied with the results, had significant issues with what she believed to be a lack of communication between her surgeon's primary assistant (a former, head operating-room nurse) and herself that led to minor, post-operative complications.

This statement clearly could be harmful to the surgeon's reputation for providing competent medical care, but no surgeon was named in the story and the former patient was given a fictitious name. Is there sufficient identification of any surgeon in this story to single out one potential plaintiff? The answer, most likely, is yes. The average reader of the story probably would not know the identity of the unnamed surgeon, but it is very likely that every general practitioner who refers patients to surgeons for special procedures would know immediately which medical specialist employs a former, head operating-room nurse as his or her primary assistant (odds are great that there would not be two fitting this bill in the local area) and, therefore, which surgeon was the subject of the defamatory comments.

Identification of group members for libel purposes is more difficult. A statement such as "students at Siwash U. are deep into booze and drugs" may be hurtful to you if you are enrolled at Siwash University, but the courts would almost certainly decide that the student body is too large for any single member to be sufficiently identified by the statement. However, each member of a small group, traditionally about 25 members or fewer, may sue and be able to collect, even if he or she is not personally identified in a defamatory communication.

Two racy paragraphs from a 1952 book, *U.S.A. Confidential*, by Jack Lait and Lee Mortimer, illustrate this point. Breathlessly revealing "inside" information turned up in their travels, the two writers had this to say about employees in a chic, specialty store in Dallas:

He [Stanley Marcus, president of the Nieman-Marcus Company] may not know that some Nieman models are call girls—the top babes in town. The guy who escorts one feels in the same league with the playboys who take out [Las Vegas showgirls]. Price: a hundred bucks a night.

The sales girls are good, too—pretty, and often much cheaper—twenty bucks on the average. They're more fun, too, not as snooty as the models. We got this confidential, from a Dallas wolf.[5]

In the inevitable lawsuits that followed, the court found that the models—there were only nine of them—indeed had been identified. But 30 "sales girls," acting on behalf of the 382 then working at Nieman-Marcus, were not. The court held that this group was too large to permit individual identification.

Could the 30 "sales girls" sue as a group? The answer to the question is almost certainly no. This a good place to note who can be a plaintiff in a libel suit. The reason they could not sue is that the group of 30 is not recognized in the law as having legal standing. An individual obviously is so recognized. So, also, is any entity that is recognized as an individual in the eyes of the law, such as a company, partnership or other legal entity. By incorporating, the organization may act as an individual for such purposes as owning property, buying or selling goods and so forth, and it also means that such an entity can defend its reputation in a court of law. In the above example, both Mr. Marcus, as an individual, and the Nieman-Marcus Company, as an incorporated organization, could bring lawsuits for defamation and both would have the legal standing to do so.

## Causation

As in any tort, the plaintiff in a defamation suit must allege and prove that the actions of the defendant were the logical and proximate cause of the claimed injury. Often this is easily accomplished because the plaintiff is simply charging that the defendant published libelous statements seen by acquaintances who now think less of the plaintiff, or clients who have withdrawn their business or customers who are now former customers.

Other times, however, the causation factor is not so straightforward. For example, let's assume that a new restaurant, The Pickled Onion, has recently opened and has been doing good business in its first few months of operation. The food critic for the local entertainment Web site has finally gotten around to reviewing the new eating establishment and has given it a terrible review ("The steer my steak came from must have died of old age"). Subsequent to the review, the restaurant's business has begun to slowly decline. The owners of The Pickled Onion have filed suit, charging that the review damaged the restaurant's reputation and is the cause of the fall-off in business.

Most likely, the Web site's owners would argue that even if the statements in the published review about the quality of food at The Pickled Onion are libelous, the plaintiff cannot show that the loss of revenue has been caused solely by the actions of its food critic. Perhaps the restaurant's economic downturn was caused by the normal decline in patrons suffered by any new restaurant once the "initial tryers" have dined there once. Alternatively, it might be attributable to the worsening economic conditions in the local area, or maybe it's a seasonal slump. Perhaps it's some combination of all of these. Clearly, the owners of The Pickled Onion will have their work cut out for them to prove that the review was the sole, or even a contributing cause, of the loss in business.

## Compensation

Traditionally, a plaintiff seeking compensation for harm to reputation has been entitled to seek four different kinds of monetary awards: *nominal* damages, *special* damages, either *presumed* or *actual* damages (in some jurisdictions these two and special damages are sometimes lumped together into "general" or "compensatory" damages) and *punitive* (or "exemplary") damages. Let's look at each of these in turn.

Some may think it odd, but the general rule in American law is that a plaintiff has to be awarded something of value to win a lawsuit—the common law generally does not recognize moral victories. Therefore, a plaintiff not interested in seeking a large award, but interested in vindication of its good name, might simply seek a small or *nominal* damage award. Although inflation probably has increased the amount, traditionally, "$1.00" (and most likely attorney fees) was the typical language of such an award. Of course, it is also possible that, although a plaintiff actually was seeking millions for the supposed harm to reputation, a judge or jury found that even though the plaintiff technically had proven a case of libel, there had been no real harm done and, therefore, the plaintiff was not deserving of more than a nominal award of damages.

*Special* damages are often thought of as "out-of-pocket dollar loss." To obtain special damages, a plaintiff must produce evidence sufficient to prove that the libelous statements cost the plaintiff demonstrable monetary loss. In the example of the disputed restaurant review discussed above, most likely the plaintiff restaurant, if victorious in the suit, would be limited to special damages amounting to the provable loss of revenue attributable to the negative rating by the food critic.

The third category of damages, either *presumed* or *actual* damage, is one of the more unusual and, from the defendant's view, dangerous, aspects of defamation law. It developed over time in response to the situation in which a plaintiff was able to the show the first four elements of a case of defamation and logically claim that the plaintiff's acquaintances, therefore, thought less of the plaintiff as a result, but was incapable of placing a dollar value on how much damage had been done. Despite such lack of evidence, every judge and member of a jury trying such a defamation suit intuitively knew that they too would have lost something of real value if suffering loss of esteem in the eyes of their friends and acquaintances.

In reaction to this anomalous situation, the law eventually provided a category of damages, called presumed damages, that requires no proof of actual monetary loss on the part of the plaintiff. This means that a judge or jury may presume that harm occurred and award an amount of money presumed to compensate the plaintiff for that harm—an invitation for large damage awards for the plaintiff that many courts seem unable to resist. In *Gertz v. Robert Welch, Inc.*,[6] the Supreme Court limited this category of damages to actual damages in cases brought by private plaintiffs against media defendants when reporting matters of public interest. Although actual damages differ from presumed damages in that they require at least some evidence that the harm occurred, once established, judges or juries may award any amount of money thought necessary to compensate plaintiffs. The possibility of such mega-verdicts should be all the impetus needed for advertising and public relations professionals to take all possible precautions to avoid becoming embroiled in a libel suit.

*Punitive* damages are awarded not to compensate the plaintiff, but to punish the defendant. In that manner, they resemble a civil fine. In most parts of the world that recognize this category of damages, the defendant writes the check to the government. In American law, however, the defendant writes that check to the plaintiff as a kind of "extra bonus" for the harm suffered. Because they are meant to punish instead of compensate, punitive damages, generally, are awarded only when the defendant's actions are so outrageous that they offend the conscience of judges or juries. In a defamation suit, punitive damages might be awarded if the statements of the defendant were not only false and defamatory, but the defendant knew they were false when published and the statements were purposefully meant to harm the plaintiff. Like presumed damages, punitive damage awards can reach mega-amounts and are as dangerous, if not more so, to defendants.

## Falsity

Statements that are true may be injurious to reputation, but, most likely, would not be the subject of a successful suit for defamation. Therefore, one might think that to win a libel suit the plaintiff would need to prove that the statement is not only defamatory, but also false. This may not necessarily be correct.

An oddity of defamation law, brought over to the Colonies from English common law beginning in the late 1600s, is that truth or falsity made no difference. In the celebrated 1735 case of John Peter Zenger,[7] a newspaper publisher in colonial New York, however, an American jury determined that if the defamatory statements were true, the defendant would not be held liable for the harm to reputation. The way this verdict was worded, however, placed the responsibility for proving truth or falsity on the defendant, rather than the plaintiff.

Beginning in 1964, with the seminal case of *The New York Times v. Sullivan*[8] (mentioned in Chapter 2), the Supreme Court altered this allocation of burden for what were eventually called "public" persons, leaving the requirement that private plaintiffs need not show that the defamatory statements were false. Arguably, later decisions, beginning with *Gertz* changed the burden of proving falsity for private plaintiffs as well. In these subsequent decisions, however, the Court focused on "press and broadcast media."[9]

It remains an open question as to whether all advertising and public relations communications will be included in the definition of "media defendants." The prudent advertising and public relations professional, evaluating the potential of a defamation suit resulting from their communications, should, therefore, expect that he or she will need to prove that what was published is true.

## Defendant Fault

In addition to defamation, publication, identification, causation and compensation (and maybe falsity), the plaintiff bringing a libel suit must show that the defendant has acted with the degree of *fault* required by the law in permitting the offending material to be published or broadcast. The fault standard depends on whether the person or corporation bringing the suit is, in the eyes of the court, "private" or "public."

Current libel law is far more protective of private citizens or organizations. Historically, the fault standard in a defamation suit was the equivalent of "no fault." Called "strict liability," this unusual fault standard required plaintiffs only to show defamation, publication, identification, causation and compensation to carry their burden in a libel suit, and the defendant was strictly liable for the harm to reputation no matter how carefully the defendant had acted. This meant that even if the defamation was accidental (e.g. a made-up name for a character that actually turned out to be similar to the name of a real person) the defendant, unless having some other defense, paid the money.

Beginning with the decision in *Sullivan*, the fault standard changed for "public" persons.[10] *Gertz* changed the fault standard for private persons as well, at least when suing media defendants.[11] The new standard, although varying from state to state, is at least negligence. For example, a media defendant would not be held liable for an accidental mistake, but would be held liable for a negligent error like sloppy editing. However, there is no national standard for determining negligence in matters such as this and many courts may treat any mistake as evidence of negligence.

Some argue that advertising and public relations communications will be treated as media defendants requiring a negligence standard when sued by a private plaintiff. This, however, is only an argument. *Greenmoss Builders, Inc.*, discussed above, is an example of a large credit-reporting agency being treated by the Supreme Court as a non-media defendant in a defamation action. Similarly, it may well be the case that the at least some types of communications by advertising and public relations practitioners advancing the interests of clients or organizations will not be treated by the courts as emanating from media defendants and, therefore, such defendants still may be held to the traditional "strict liability" fault standard.

Advertising and public relations professionals, thus, may face the possibility of a defamation suit by a private plaintiff in which they will have to bear the burden of proving the truth of their statements. Additionally, they may be held to a fault standard that means they are strictly liable for any mistake, no matter how carefully they act. Prudent advertising and public relations professionals, therefore, should recognize the dangers inherent in not taking every precaution to avoid such suits.

Public persons—people who are decision makers in the affairs of government, celebrities or those who attempt to influence public issues—according to the law have less protection as plaintiffs in defamation actions. This is of importance to advertising and public relations professionals, as many business corporations, especially those with substantial advertising budgets and public relations departments, are likely to be classified, for defamation purposes, as public persons.

Public persons generally become public because they seek public attention. In seeking to become public, public persons, in a sense, should recognize that they are inviting commentary by the public on their actions. Some of that commentary may not be very pleasant. Courts consistently have held that the price of fame comes at the cost of protection of reputation. That is why public persons face a much tougher task in bringing a cause of action for defamation.

Public persons must show not only defamation, publication, identification, causation and compensation, but also that the offending message was false and published with a fault standard called *actual malice*—defined as the defendant deliberately published a lie or, alternatively, showed a reckless disregard for the truth in handling the communication. Such has been the letter and spirit of defamation law since 1964, when the Supreme Court handed down its far-reaching decision in *Sullivan*.

## The New York Times v. Sullivan

Because *Sullivan* represents a dramatic change in centuries-old law in defamation, it is worthwhile to take a moment to discuss this case. The controversy arose over a full-page advertisement that appeared in *The Times* on March 29, 1960, that attempted to raise money to support civil rights crusades in the South. The ad called attention to the leadership of a dynamic, young minister, Dr. Martin Luther King, Jr., who was leading the resistance to racial segregation policies in Montgomery, Al. The facsimile signatures of 64 celebrities, including Marlon Brando, Sidney Poitier and Eleanor Roosevelt, appeared in the advertisement indicating endorsement of the sentiments expressed.

The ad copy contained strong statements, many of which were later proven to be untrue, about the treatment accorded African-American leaders and their sympathizers. For example, the ad claimed that:

> In Montgomery, Alabama, after students sang "My Country, 'Tis of Thee," on the state capitol steps, their leaders were expelled from school, and truckloads of police armed with shotguns and tear gas ringed the Alabama State College campus. When the entire student body protested to state authorities by refusing to register, their dining hall was padlocked in an attempt to starve them into submission....
>
> Again and again Southern violators have answered Dr. King's peaceful protests with intimidation and violence. They have bombed his home, almost killing his wife and child. They have assaulted his person. They have arrested him seven times—for "speeding," "loitering," and similar "offenses." And now they have charged him with "perjury," a felony under which they could imprison him for ten years.[12]

These statements were embellished accounts of what actually transpired in Montgomery. There were no padlocks or tear gas, and King did not suffer the number of arrests suggested. When Montgomery city officials sued *The Times* saying they had been defamed, the newspaper, to its embarrassment, could not plead truth as a defense because it had not verified the assertions in the ad.

The first of what eventually turned out to be 11 lawsuits against the *Times* was filed by L.B. Sullivan, one of three elected city commissioners of Montgomery and the man responsible for overseeing the police department. At trial, the judge instructed the jury that the statements in the ad reflected adversely on the police department and its leaders and were libelous per se.[13] The jurors awarded Sullivan $500,000 in presumed and punitive damages. After this judgment was upheld by the Alabama Supreme Court,[14] the *Times* carried its appeal to the Supreme Court of the United States.

In a unanimous ruling, the Court reversed the judgment against *The Times* and, in the process, pronounced a new standard—*actual malice*—that public officials, criticized in their official capacity, would need to meet in order to win a suit for defamation.[15] Acknowledging that the newspaper may have been negligent in not checking for errors in the ad copy, the Court rejected the argument that the newspaper had published the errors intentionally and, therefore, the *Times* had not published with actual malice. The Court found that, in effect, the newspaper was attempting to do the job the press is supposed to do: discuss the public actions of public officials. Quoting John Stuart Mill's treatise *On Liberty* that "[e]ven a false statement may be deemed to make a valuable contribution to public debate ...",[16] the Court was emphatic in asserting that the right to criticize government should be protected so long as the criticism is genuinely meant and not laced with intentional lies.

The majority opinion, written by Justice William J. Brennan, noted, "[t]hus we consider this case against the background of a profound national commitment to the principle that debate on public issues should be uninhibited, robust, and wide open...."[17] To limit such criticism of government would diminish what the Court described as "the unfettered interchange of ideas for the bringing about of social changes desired by our people."[18] It also noted that Sullivan, a public official, was not helpless; he had the means to dish out criticism as well as take it. Public officials seek attention by running for office, the Court concluded, and heated attacks from the citizenry come with the territory.

Later decisions by the Court expanded the *Sullivan* doctrine to include public figures as well as public officials. In the eyes of the Court, public figures could be individuals who have achieved celebrity status either because of their involvement in public issues or because they have become famous through their exploits as entertainers, sports figures or newsmakers. Ralph Nader, Jay Leno, Britney Spears, Michael Jordan and Bill Gates come to mind.

Alternatively, individuals might become public figures in certain limited areas of interest if they are defamed as a result of their attempts to influence the outcome of a public controversy (e.g. legalization of marijuana or prayer in schools). Because they voluntarily stepped into the spotlight, they might be considered limited public figures for purposes of any libel action arising out of that particular controversy.

It is important to note that the term actual malice in the law of defamation does not refer to hatred or spite directed toward the plaintiff. Actual malice is malice toward the truth of the statement. The defendants in suits brought by public persons need only show that they neither knew that what they were publishing was false, nor seriously doubted what they were publishing was not true to defeat a claim of actual malice. A defendant who can legitimately say, "I don't know if what I published was true and I don't care" or "It could have been true—I didn't bother to check" has *not* acted with actual malice. Actual malice is hard to prove; as a result, most public officials and figures do not bring libel suits and those who do generally don't win.

Efforts to determine what advertising and public relations professionals believed before publishing controversial articles, advertisements or press releases have prompted libel lawyers to probe the communicators' "state of mind," as reflected in private conversations, internal memoranda, e-mail communications and social media messages.[19] Advertising and public relations professionals would be well advised to have a memorandum or e-mail record of responding affirmatively to superiors questioning the accuracy and validity of sources of information and to refrain from any asides or personal commentary that might suggest that they have doubts or disbeliefs about what they are about to publish.

## The Organization as a Public Figure

As with individuals, corporations, partnerships and other similar organizations may be classified for purposes of a libel suit as either public or private plaintiffs. In making this important determination, courts traditionally take into account the following factors:

1   *The size of an organization.* Martin Marietta Corp., a major manufacturer of aerospace and defense systems, was found to be a public figure on the strength of its being the 20th-largest defense contractor in the United States, and, therefore, in a position to influence the outcome of the issues in which it was involved.[20]

2   *The character and volume of an organization's marketing communications.* Not every organization that advertises or in other ways communicates with its publics is necessarily a public figure,[21] but organizations that attempt to influence events through advertising or other similar means are likely to yield their private-figure status. Evidence that an organization has advertised heavily may convince a court that it has ready access to the channels of communication, and that it can readily respond to negative statements about its activities.

3   *The history of an organization insofar as controversy is concerned.* If an organization has previously been involved in a public dispute (e.g., the controversy about how Nike Corporation manufactures its products), such participation may contribute to a decision to classify the organization as a public figure.[22]

4   *Whether an organization is engaged in a heavily regulated industry and whether the organization is publicly owned.* The actions of insurance companies, broadcast corporations and utility companies are tightly monitored and must be approved by regulatory agencies.[23] In

terms of defamation, such organizations would normally be treated as public figures.

It should be noted that financial institutions, such as savings and loan companies and banks, are usually classified separately where injurious falsehoods are concerned. Libeling a financial institution could even result in criminal prosecution. For example, the language of the Iowa Code, Section 528.89, states:

> Whoever maliciously or with intent to deceive makes, publishes, utters, repeats, or circulates any false report concerning any bank or trust company which imputes, or tends to impute, insolvency or unsound financial condition shall be fined not more than $5,000 or imprisoned more than five years in the penitentiary or by punishment by both such fine and imprisonment.[24]

## Affirmative Defenses

Once a libel plaintiff has made a *prima facie* case (i.e., established defamation, publication, identification and so forth), the other side must mount a defense. Called affirmative defenses, these traditional, common-law defenses have evolved over time to include *truth*, *conditional privilege*, *fair comment* and *opinion*.

*Truth* is now regarded as a complete defense, the rationale being that no individual or organization's reputation is greater than the truth that can be told about it. But truth is often hard to prove. In reality, it often boils down to one person's word against another's. Thus, one may know that something is true, but face enormous difficulty proving it before a judge and jury. Information sources who speak fearlessly while a news story or press release is being developed have been known to lose their nerve or their memories while under oath on the witness stand.

Absolute privilege is the freedom to discuss certain aspects of the public's business with impunity. For example, absolute privilege is conferred on members of Congress during debates and hearings. Society has determined that prosecuting attorneys, judges, mayors, city council and school board members or zoning commissioners, for example, should be able to comment fully and freely while performing official duties. If such individuals had to worry about speaking the absolute truth in everything they said, they might well become too inhibited to accomplish the public's business.

Those who report information stemming from someone who has absolute privilege enjoy a *conditional (or qualified) privilege*. Conditional privilege extends to reports of governmental documents as well. Journalists and other citizens can quote from privileged documents without fear of libel suits or criminal prosecutions so long as the published or broadcast accounts are full, fair and accurate. It should be noted, however, that a government news release may not be accorded a privilege.

Other common-law forms of privilege may apply, especially when commercial speech is concerned. First, a competitor is conditionally privileged to make boastful, embellished claims about its own products or services compared to those offered by the competition—even if it does not believe its own products or services are superior—so long as the comparison does not contain false assertions of fact.[25] This puffery, or exaggerated praise of one's own goods or services, is not considered defamatory, even if it is sharply critical of the competition, so long as the boasting is couched in general, nonspecific terms. Note, however, that if a claim states a product is superior, perhaps because the competition has employed substandard materials in its product, the statement has become specific (capable of being proved or disproved). The statement would no longer be covered by a qualified privilege because it would no longer be treated as puffery.[26]

Second, a defendant may have an interest privilege. This conditional privilege allows a reply to communications by others to serve one's own interests—in other words, to defend against the defamation of another, even if the reply itself may be defamatory. However, this does not mean that the response can be a knowing falsity or reflect a reckless disregard for the truth.[27] Deliberate, specific untruths constitute an abuse of privilege, and such statements will forfeit their protection.

*Fair comment* protects expression of opinions about things offered to the public for acceptance or rejection. A politician's record, a concert pianist's keyboard technique, an actor's stage presence, an architect's creativity or a restaurant's cuisine are all examples of acceptable targets of public discussion, even though such adverse criticisms might hurt the business or the professional reputation of the organization or individual.

In *Gertz*, the Supreme Court apparently created an additional affirmative defense for *opinion* statements. The Court commented, "We begin with the common ground. Under the First Amendment there is no such thing as a false idea. However pernicious an opinion may seem, we depend for its correction not on the conscience of judges and juries, but on the competition of other ideas."[28] Opinion statements are not susceptible to a truth or falsity test. "In our opinion, Acme's products are shoddily made," will most likely not be treated as an opinion statement by a court because it implies facts that can be proven or disproven. "Acme products are so bizarre they must have been made by Martians," most likely would be treated as opinion and, therefore, protected.

## Other Defenses

In addition to truth, conditional privilege, fair comment and opinion, there are secondary defenses, often called defenses in mitigation or incomplete defenses. One of these is *retraction*. A voluntary retraction can show good faith on the part of the communicator—an attempt to set the record straight and atone for a defamatory statement. For the court to find it persuasive, the retraction should be timely, prominent and complete. For example, if, in an angry political ad, your client mistakenly accuses a prominent businessman of tax evasion, your retraction should not say, "We are *sorry* that we said he is a tax dodger," but rather, "He is *not* guilty of tax evasion." Another secondary defense is to offer the offended persons the *right of reply*—to provide space to those who have been wronged, or think they have been, to tell their side of the story.

Neither a retraction nor a right of reply can be imposed. The courts recognize the rights of publishers to control the contents of their publications.[29] Corrections, retractions and rights of reply are all provided voluntarily, when they are provided at all. Secondary defenses do not allow the defendant to avoid a judgment, but they can lessen the blow of an adverse libel decision by reducing the amount of money a court might award.

## Who Is Liable?

In the eyes of the law, "tale bearers are as bad as tale makers."[30] Put another way, those who pass along a defamatory statement are as answerable in a court of law as those who originated it. For example, suppose a press release issued by a public relations agency quotes an outside expert as claiming that a competitor of your client has construction standards that are too low, resulting in the competitor's building of unsafe structures. Attributing the statement to the outside expert does not provide immunity for the public relations agency or the client. Similarly, the use of such qualifying terms as the *alleged* inside trader or the *reported* corporate embezzler also does not excuse the entity that made the statement.

Where defamation (and product disparagement and trade libel, discussed below) are concerned, each repetition of offending statements may be regarded as a separate publication for which damages may be recovered. Every person or organization with a hand in the publication of the statements could, in theory, be a defendant. Specifically, defendants can be categorized as:

1   *Primary publisher.* Advertising and public relations professionals, as well as reporters and editors, who actually prepare the harmful messages, clearly will be named as defendants in a defamation suit although in actual practice, the agency or organization for which they created the message will likely be the primary defendants in such a suit. In an agency situation, the client most likely also will be equally liable. The owner of a newspaper or television station carrying a

defamatory statement will be considered a primary publisher and thus held accountable for the message to the same extent as the original publishers. Everything that appears in print or on the air—including letters to the editor, advertising messages, news releases and other communications—becomes the responsibility of the publisher.

2   *Republisher.* Anyone who repeats or passes along a defamatory statement would be held accountable in the same was as a primary publisher, even if, in repeating the libel, the speaker makes it clear that the defamatory message is not believed. Note that this republication rule arguably is just as applicable to those who republish the information on a Facebook page, in a "tweet," on a blog or through another form of social media.

3   *Secondary publisher.* Those who help circulate the defamatory materials (e.g., the person who delivers the newspaper or an operator who plays the defamatory videotape or the owner of the bookstore) may also be held accountable, but only if they had knowledge, or should have had knowledge, of the defamatory content.

## Product Disparagement

While it is much like defamation, the tort of *product disparagement* involves injurious falsehoods that disparage the quality of a product or service but do not defame the company that provides and produces them.

### Terminology

The common law criteria for establishing product disparagement are: (a) the disparaging statement has been made; (b) the statement has been published to a third party by the defendant; (c) the statement is about a specific product or service; (d) the statement is the true cause of the actual harm suffered by the plaintiff; (e) the plaintiff is entitled to be compensated by money damages because the statement results in financial damage or is likely to do so; (f) the statement is false; and (g) the defendant acted with actual malice—meaning that the defendant knew the statement is untrue or entertained serious doubt that the statement is true. Thus actual malice, not mere negligence, must be shown in *all* product disparagement cases, not just those involving a public person as in defamation. The burden of showing falsity, similarly, is on the plaintiff.

### Product Disparagement vs. Defamation

Defamation and product disparagement represent concerns over somewhat different interests, but, at times, they may overlap. If a statement reflects merely on the quality of what the plaintiff is selling, it is product disparagement alone. If, however, it also alleges that the plaintiff is not honest, lacks integrity or is defrauding the public by selling something known to be defective, then the statement may also be defamatory.

Actions may be brought in the same lawsuit to cover both torts, so long as the damages are not duplicated. For example, in *Steaks Unlimited, Inc., v. Deaner,*[31] a charge of false advertising concerning the value of meat sold by the plaintiff was made by a local TV newscast. The court found both product disparagement and corporate defamation.

In recent years, many product disparagement claims, if they involve charges of false advertising, have been brought under the federal Lanham Act, which permits recovery for "any person who is or who believes he or she is likely to be damaged by a misrepresentation of the nature, characteristics, qualities, or geographic origin of his or her or another person's goods, services, or commercial activities."[32] The provisions of the Lanham Act are discussed more fully elsewhere in this book.

## Trade Libel

The term *trade libel* is an ancient one, coined to describe written defamations of the quality of commercial goods and services. Casting aspersions on the quality of goods and services was likened to personal defamation. In recent years, the expansion of the concept of product disparagement has left trade libel a rather narrow area. However, trade libel is different from product disparagement in several respects.

### Terminology

In trade libel: (a) special damages—pecuniary losses resulting from the offending statements—must be proved, and (b) under certain conditions, it is possible to obtain an injunction to stop the trade libel (e.g., in a continuing advertising campaign), whereas in product disparagement such speech cannot be enjoined. In some states, trade libel laws are referred to as "slander of goods" or "slander of title."

## Defamation, Product Disparagement and Trade Libel in a Digital, New-Media Age: Emerging Issues

The Supreme Court has not decided any major cases recently in the areas of defamation, product disparagement and trade libel, leaving the law to evolve at the state and lower federal court levels. Although the lower courts are generally applying the settled principles of defamation (discussed earlier in this chapter) to new media, they have begun to grapple with a number of difficult procedural issues related to unique aspects of Web-based and electronic communication.

Since Congress passed the Communications Decency Act (CDA) in 1996,[33] courts have been attempting to determine the extent of protection the Act provides for Web sites that publish false and defamatory material submitted by parties not connected with the site. Although the CDA's indecency restrictions designed to regulate pornographic material on the Internet were later found unconstitutional, other provisions of the Act remain in effect. Section 230 of the CDA (also known as Title V of the Telecommunications Act of 1996),[34] which shields Internet service providers (ISPs) from liability for content posted by others, arguably has been a terrific facilitator of online free speech. Section 230 is significant because it treats ISPs differently from, for example, newspaper publishers who also publish content provided by others.

Traditionally, those who publish defamatory statements may be responsible for harm that occurs if the statements prove to be false, even if those statements originate with a third party. This "republication rule" enables libel plaintiffs to sue both the originator of a defamatory statement and any subsequent publishers of the statement. Section 230, however, states that "[n]o provider or user of an interactive computer service shall be treated as the publisher or speaker or any information provided by another information content provider."[35] This means that ISPs who host but do not post Internet content may do so free of liability for what others post to the site.

For example, what is the extent of liability for the host site for defamatory material disseminated in an ad on Craigslist or a social networking site like Match.com? Most courts dealing with this issue have interpreted the statute as providing immunity from suit as long as those maintaining the site do not create or solicit the defamatory material.

Clearly, protection for the host site does not immunize the original contributor of the defamatory material, but what if the poster is anonymous or uses a pseudonym? Must the host Web site reveal information that would allow the aggrieved potential plaintiff to sue the originator of the libelous statements? Every court dealing with this issue has found at least some protection for such anonymous speech, but the procedural standards for when the ISP is obligated to reveal the source vary widely.

Some courts have established a relatively low-level, "good-faith" test, requiring only that the potential plaintiff state that the material is potentially defamatory and that the request to obtain the identity of the source has not been made for the purpose of annoyance or harassment. A number of states have passed so-called Anti-SLAPP (Strategic Lawsuit Against Public Participation) statutes to protect against such suits.[36] Other courts have raised relatively high hurdles to overcome before an ISP must yield such information about anonymous posters. Most of these latter tests require a potential plaintiff to provide ample evidence supporting the claim of defamation, and some courts even then will take the additional step of weighing and balancing the case for the plaintiff against the degree of First Amendment protection the court believes should attach to the anonymous speech.[37]

The catch to all this protection of anonymous ISP postings for advertising and public relations professionals is that this defamatory anonymous speech is often directed at their clients or organizations. Many of these cases have arisen in regard to postings on Web sites critical of companies, their products and/or their management.[38] Trying to address these negative comments by bringing suit against the critics may still be possible, but senior management should be informed that threatening legal action with hopes of stilling the voices of criticism may be a losing game, and it may even make the organization look ridiculous in the blog world. In such cases, more positive speech to counter the negative speech may be a more effective remedy.

Another procedural issue related to defamation involves jurisdiction—generally defined as what court has the power to make and enforce a judgment. In *Ehrenfeld v. Mahfouz*,[39] a federal court of appeals decision in New York enforcing a defamation judgment made by a court in England against a New York resident inspired the New York legislature to pass a so-called "libel tourism" law. The statute limits the enforceability of foreign judgments to those countries that have the same speech protections as guaranteed by our First Amendment. As this book is going to press, there are calls in Congress for similar legislation on a nationwide level.

Closer to home, jurisdictional issues have also arisen when conflicts arise between individuals or organizations in one state alleging defamation published by a Web-site defendant from another state. Courts remain split over whether to recognize jurisdiction over these out-of-state defendants. Advertising and public relations professionals should be aware, however, that the chances are not remote that they and their clients and organizations might have difficulty in bringing defamation-related suits in their home states against out-of-state defendants and, concomitantly, in a Catch-22-like situation, they may be held liable in out-of-state jurisdictions for statements made on a Web site that are accessed in locations far away.

## Products Liability

Products liability, as the name suggests, refers to the legal responsibility of manufacturers and sellers to compensate those suffering injury caused by defects in the goods that were purchased.

### Background

Manufacturers of faulty products throughout much of American legal history have often been held accountable for the harm caused by these products to those who purchased them. Historically, only the actual purchasers could recover damages for the harm; the public at large was not a factor. As one important 1852 New York appellate court opinion said:

> If A builds a wagon and sells it to B, who sells it to C, and C hires it to D, who in consequence of the gross negligence of A. in building the wagon is overturned and injured, D cannot recover damages against A, the builder. A's obligation to build the wagon faithfully arises solely out of his contract with B. The public [sic] have nothing to do with it. Misfortunes to third persons, not parties to the contract, would not be a natural and necessary consequence of the builder's negligence....[40]

However, this narrow interpretation was expanded greatly beginning early in the twentieth century. A leading case in this regard, *MacPherson v. Buick Motor Co.*,[41] involved the sale of an automobile to a retail dealer in New York. The dealer sold the automobile to MacPherson. While he was driving his new machine, a wheel came off causing the car to crash. MacPherson was thrown clear, but injured. The wheel later was proven to have been made of defective wood and its spokes had crumbled. The wheel was not manufactured by Buick, but rather by a subcontractor. MacPherson sued the automobile's manufacturer, Buick. Buick argued that its responsibility ended with the sale of the car to the dealer. Both the trial and appellate courts disagreed. In a ringing opinion, written by New York Court of Appeals Justice Benjamin Cardozo, the court held:

> If the nature of a thing is such that it is reasonably certain to place life and limb in peril when negligently made, it is then a thing of danger .... There must also be a knowledge that in the usual course of events the danger will be shared by others than the buyer. Such knowledge may often be inferred from the nature of the transaction.... We have put aside the notion that the duty to safeguard life and limb, when the consequences of negligence may be foreseen, grows out of contract and nothing else.[42]

The laws affecting liability for product-related injuries and damages have changed dramatically. The old notion of *caveat emptor* ("let the buyer beware") generally has been replaced by "strict liability" (i.e., liability even without the showing of negligence) in products liability cases. This strict liability philosophy is now in effect in most jurisdictions throughout the United States. As the *Restatement of Torts* explains it:

> ... the justification for the strict liability has been said to be that the seller, by marketing his product for use and consumption, has undertaken and assumed a special responsibility toward any member of the consuming public who may be injured by it; that the public has

the right to and does expect, in the case of products which it needs and for which it is forced to rely upon the seller, that reputable sellers will stand behind their goods; that public policy demands that the burden of accidental injuries caused by products intended for consumption be placed upon those who market them....[43]

Today, products liability cases can cover a variety of kinds of harm to various categories of persons connected to, or affected by, a product. Purchasers can sue, but so also can non-purchasing users, consumers and even bystanders who somehow have become affected (e.g., a passenger injured in a wreck caused by a manufacturing flaw in a vehicle). Besides the manufacturer, others who might be liable include the employees and subcontractors who helped design and build the product, the retailers who sold the product, the packagers who labeled the product and, perhaps, even advertising and public relations professionals who provided information about the product.

Products liability is one of the fastest growing areas of contemporary American law. More than a million claims for product-caused injuries are made each year, and more than half of these involve litigation.

Some critics believe that products liability litigation has moved too far too fast. They tell horror stories of seemingly bizarre court cases such as the $2.9 million award (later reduced) given in 1994 to a fast-food restaurant customer who was burned when the coffee she spilled on herself was thought to be unreasonably hot. Critics argue that allegedly outlandish verdicts such as this could destroy American business competitiveness. On the other side of this debate are those who defend products liability litigation as a means of recovery against what they regard as careless, profit-hungry manufacturers who flimflam the American public with dangerous products that should not be on the market.

## Commercial Speech Related to Product Liability

Historically, the mass media have been shielded from liability when publishing or broadcasting an advertising or other product-related message for a product that is somehow defective. Thus, an advertising or public relations professional employed by the mass media is similarly shielded.

This protective shield might not be available, however, if the advertising or marketing communications professionals employed by the media were the source of misinformation about the product or failed to inform about dangers of a product, resulting in harm to a consumer. An illustration can be found in the *Restatement of Torts*:

[Person] A manufactures automobiles. He advertises in newspapers and magazines that the glass in his cars is "shatterproof." B reads this advertising, and in reliance upon it purchases from a retail dealer an automobile manufactured by A. While B is driving the car, a stone thrown up by a passing truck strikes the windshield and shatters it, injuring B. A is subject to strict liability to B.[44]

Clearly if in the example above the employees in the advertising department of a newspaper simply accepted the ad placed by representatives of A, the automobile manufacturer, they would be shielded from liability for the defective windshield. However, if the "shatterproof" language originated from a newspaper's advertising staff, the newspaper might share liability.

This protection for the media and those employed by the media may not extend to advertising and public relations professionals not directly connected to the mass media. Vicarious liability (i.e., imposing responsibility on one person based on the actionable conduct of another because of a relationship between them) can involve individuals who simply provide information about products that prove harmful.

This is especially true of assurances about the quality or character of products, or about their fitness for the purpose for which they were bought. These statements might be construed as creating an "express warranty," a promise made about the goods by the seller—or his or her representative, such as an advertising agency—to induce the sale. Such promises often become a key part of the transaction. For example, a statement might describe a product as having "a one-year guarantee on parts and labor." The words *guarantee* or *warranty* might not even be used; an affirmation of benefits of using the product could be interpreted as an express warranty.

Note that warranties are based on facts, not opinions. High-flown sales rhetoric, so long as it remains the opinion of the seller or advertiser, does not constitute a warranty. As the Uniform Commercial Code puts it, "an affirmation merely of the value of the goods or a statement purporting to be merely the seller's opinion or commendation of the goods does not create a warranty."[45]

The lesson is clear. Prudent advertising and public relations professionals working for clients can head off many potential problems for themselves simply by submitting proofs of the advertising or other marketing communications copy to clients and obtaining their approval before the commercial message is published or broadcast. Marketing communications professionals employed by a product manufacturer cannot avail themselves of this protection, but it might be a wise career move to be able to demonstrate that the offending information disseminated by the communications professionals originated in some other part of the manufacturing organization.

## RICO, Mail Fraud and Product Liability Advertising: A Special Case

An ominous move in the late 1980s was the invocation of the federal Racketeer Influenced and Corrupt Organizations Act (RICO)[46] as a weapon against what was alleged to have been fraudulent advertising in a products liability context. Civil liability under RICO, which does not depend on a prior criminal conviction, allows the successful plaintiff to recover triple damages as well as attorney's fees. Many states have enacted RICO-type statutes as well.

The basic charge behind the RICO claims was that the advertiser committed acts of mail and wire fraud as part of an ongoing scheme to run false advertising in the media. The federal mail fraud statute prohibits "any scheme or artifice to defraud or for obtaining money or property by means of false or fraudulent pretenses, representations, or promises. . . ."[47] Therefore by reinvesting the income derived from the alleged mail and wire fraud activity, the advertiser was accused of perpetuating the false advertising scheme, which in turn increased sales—thus qualifying for a charge of racketeering.

In one such case, *In re Suzuki Samurai Products Liability Litigation*,[48] several disgruntled purchasers of Suzuki Samurai vehicles alleged that Suzuki advertising and public relations firms made false claims that the Samurai was "suitable and safe for on and off road use."[49] In fact, the vehicles allegedly tended to tip over on turns. The plaintiffs contended that the defendants, including the advertising and public relations professionals, used the mails in connection with these messages and reinvested the income derived from them.

The case was eventually dismissed; however, other cases have been allowed to go to trial. In one of these, a Pennsylvania court permitted consumers to sue the Ralston Purina Co.,[50] charging that the company's advertising falsely claimed that Purina Puppy Chow was helpful in preventing canine hip dysplasia, a disabling disorder caused by bone and cartilage degeneration. The class-action RICO lawsuit was ultimately settled, with Ralston creating a substantial fund providing for coupons offering cash discounts on subsequent purchases of its products. Cases such as this remain infrequent, but a major court victory against an advertiser in a RICO-inspired case might lead to a spate of products liability litigation in the future.

## Assumption of Risk and Foreseeability

Assumption of a foreseeable risk is a defense to products liability claims that has been widely recognized. If the victim of a product-related accident voluntarily decided to take on a known danger, the courts will normally expect the victim to bear responsibility for the consequences.

A number of lawsuits against tobacco companies have been decided on these grounds; smokers were aware of the possible consequences and continued to smoke anyway. Generally, if the consumer discovers the defect, is aware of the danger and proceeds accordingly, then recovery is unlikely. As a Nebraska court explained:

> In the law of products liability, misuse is use of a product in a way not reasonably foreseeable by the supplier or manufacturer, while assumption of risk is a user's willingness or consent to use a product which the user actually knows is defective and appreciates the danger resulting from such defect.[51]

For example, in *Maguire v. Pabst Brewing Co.*,[52] the plaintiff argued that advertising for Pabst Blue Ribbon beer was "an invitation to excess through exaltation of hedonistic tendencies over good judgment," specifically that that Pabst advertising produced "a danger to highway safety."[53] The Iowa Supreme Court rejected the argument.

## Product Liability in a Digital, New-Media Age: Emerging Issues

Early products liability cases were characterized by a strong tradition that business should be protected as much as possible from overly broad awards that could cripple American commerce. When they were challenged, the manufacturers fought back fiercely and with tenacity. For example, consider this internal, tobacco-industry memorandum for what it reveals about legal strategy and tactics:

> The aggressive posture we have taken regarding depositions and discovery in general continues to make these [products liability] cases extremely burdensome and expensive for plaintiffs' lawyers, particularly sole practitioners. To paraphrase General Patton, the way we won these cases was not by spending all of [RJR's, a tobacco company's] money, but by making that other son of a bitch spend all of his.[54]

Yet faulty and dangerous products do create legitimate victims and increasingly the courts and consumer protection agencies have befriended them. Thousands of products liability cases are filed each month, the victims represented by forceful trial lawyers determined to protect citizens' rights and punish corporate wrongdoing (and enrich themselves in the process). During the 1980s and early 1990s, the momentum began to swing toward the victims.

In the mid-1990s, however, following a decade or more of enormous jury awards, the country seemed ready to move back in the other direction.

The health care, medical, insurance and manufacturing communities flexed their considerable political muscle, putting pressure on Congress for changes in the laws affecting products liability. Tort reformists argued that American business was becoming intimidated by threats of malpractice and products liability litigation and, as a result, innovations were discouraged and products had become far more expensive than necessary. A bill designed to limit the kinds and amounts of damages that could be awarded to victims was defeated in 1994, but it proved to be the precursor of the ongoing momentum for drastic changes in the entire field of products liability law that continues to this day.

Even so, the complexities of modern society will certainly create new victims, and it is likely that products liability traditions will not ignore those who have been unfairly harmed. In this ongoing tug-of-war, advertising and public relations may well assume a larger role, particularly as new claims arise. For example, as manufacturers and retailers increasingly bypass the mass media through use of their own Web sites and social media, those who create and maintain these new media may find themselves more involved in lawsuits based on alleged product defects. Prudent advertising and public relations professionals will be wise to keep abreast of the latest developments in legal thinking related to what parties can be held liable in such cases.

# Chapter 5

# Invasion of Privacy

## False Light, Private Facts, Intrusion and Other Related Torts

In the twenty-first century, individuals find it increasingly difficult to live out their lives in peace. Our society bristles with computers, electronic eavesdropping devices, powerful telephoto lenses and a whole arsenal of other high-tech equipment capable of gathering, storing and retrieving personal and professional information about all of us.

If the federal government's databanks were linked together to combine income tax information with U.S. Census, Social Security and other data in the files, it would be quick and easy to compile a dossier of 20 pages or more on each man, woman and child in America, and no file would take more than a few seconds to locate. Commercial databanks possess salary, employment, credit, home-mortgage, healthcare and other personal information that may be even more sensitive. The mass media are capable of disseminating a great deal of information about us, including our physical likenesses, even if we might urgently wish them not to do so.

Although today's invasions of our personal privacy involve more than the mass media, it was the unrestrained, sensational press coverage of 130 years ago that prompted legal scholars to advocate the first privacy laws. The lurid era of yellow journalism in the late nineteenth century found reporters prying feverishly into the personal affairs of the rich and famous. An aristocratic Boston lawyer and businessman, Samuel Warren, was particularly offended by what he regarded as steamy, voracious press attention paid to the forthcoming wedding of his daughter.

Because no remedies were available under existing law to deal with such journalistic excesses, Warren declared that a different approach was needed. In collaboration with his former law partner, Louis Brandeis, Warren pounded out an angry, sweeping article for the *Harvard Law Review*.[1] They proposed that the legal system recognize a new principle, which they described as an individual's right to privacy:

> [t]he press is overstepping in every direction the obvious bounds of propriety and decency. Gossip is no longer the resource of the idle and of the vicious, but has become a trade, which is pursued with industry

as well as effrontery. . . . To occupy the indolent, column upon column is filled with idle gossip, which can only be procured by intrusion upon the domestic circle. The intensity and complexity of life, attending upon advancing civilization, have rendered necessary some retreat from the world, and man, under the refining influence of culture, has become more sensitive to the individual; but modern enterprise and invention have, through invasions upon his privacy, subjected him to mental pain and distress, far greater than could be inflicted by mere bodily injury.[2]

The courts and legislatures did not react immediately to provide citizens, in the Warren and Brandeis phrase, "some retreat from the world," but clearly the privacy thesis struck a responsive chord within the legal profession. Several privacy invasions were alleged in lawsuits, although a court would not allow the first recovery for damages until some 15 years later. Privacy law has been evolving, in fits and starts, ever since, responding—sometimes slowly, often inconsistently—to technological and social change.

Because of such inconsistency, noted legal scholar William Prosser proposed that most privacy issues could be categorized as belonging to one of four different types: (a) unreasonably placing an individual in a false light before the public; (b) unjustified publication of embarrassing private facts; (c) unreasonable intrusion on one's physical solitude; and (d) misappropriation of one's name, identity or likeness.[3] His suggested taxonomy proved to be just the ticket for making order out of chaos, and most legal scholars, state courts and legislatures subsequently adopted his four-part classification scheme.

Discussion of the basic elements of an invasion of privacy suit proves difficult because a plaintiff's case might involve any one of the four different types (e.g., proving a defendant committed an unreasonable act in an intrusion case versus demonstrating that a statement is not true in a false light case). Nonetheless, some issues are common across all categories. First, most courts make no distinction between oral speech and written or otherwise recorded communication. Additionally, the right to privacy is considered a personal right and therefore, generally cannot be enforced by family members or by the plaintiff's estate if the plaintiff is no longer living. For similar reasons, most jurisdictions have held that only individuals—and not corporations or other similar entities—may bring a cause of action for invasion of privacy because such organizations have no "feelings and sensibilities" of human beings (misappropriation, in some instances, being the exception to this rule).

This chapter discusses *false light*, *public disclosure of private, embarrassing facts* and *intrusion*. These three subcategories of the tort of invasion of privacy (generally defined as the wish to be left alone), are part of civil tort law defined in Chapter 4 as involving claims of harm to persons or personal property. The chapter concludes with a brief discussion of *infliction of emotional distress*, saving *misappropriation*, the subcategory of invasion of privacy perhaps of most concern to advertising and public relations professionals, for the next chapter.

## False Light

The tort of *false light* invasion of privacy involves portraying individuals as something they are not, and doing so in a way that ordinary persons find offensive. In some respects, false light privacy is much like defamation, a point we return to later. But there are important differences—enough of them to make false light, in the eyes of most courts, a separate matter entirely.

### Background

What might be considered among the first successful false light courtroom victories occurred in England in 1816. The winner was Lord Byron, one of the most colorful of all the English romantic poets. Angry because some-one had falsely attributed a mediocre poem to him—one he swore he had not written—Byron persuaded a British court to issue an order halting further publication and circulation of the poem.[4]

In the United States, false light evolved slowly from the beginnings of privacy law, which began in the early 1900s, but the tort sprang forth after a more than five-decade gestation period in the mid-1960s to become identified by most commentators as a separate subcategory of invasion of privacy. Today, most states have adopted some form of false light and courts in many of the remaining states have hinted that they may adopt the tort if presented with the appropriate case.

False light invasion of privacy has been severely criticized by many in the mass media and in the legal community as being so substantially like the tort of defamation that it should cease to be recognized as a separate cause of action. This line of thinking has recently led a number of states, including Florida,[5] Massachusetts,[6] Texas[7] and North Carolina,[8] to explicitly decline to recognize false light as cognizable by their courts. It is still too early to determine whether this is a trend that will continue.

### Terminology

The *Restatement of Torts* attempts to summarize the law in a general area. The *Restatement* defines *false light privacy* this way:

> One who gives publicity to a matter concerning another that places the other before the public in a false light is subject to liability to the other for invasion of his privacy, if

(a) the false light in which the other was placed would be highly offensive to a reasonable person, and

(b) the actor [perpetrator] had knowledge of or acted in reckless disregard as to the falsity of the publicized matter and the false light in which the other would be placed.[9]

## The Elements of False Light

Clearly, false light invasion of privacy resembles defamation of character (see Chapter 4). Similar to a suit for defamation, the plaintiff must first prove that (a) a false statement has been made that offends ordinary decency (but, unlike libel, not necessarily harmful to reputation); (b) the offending material must be shown to at least one other person by the defendant; (c) the plaintiff has been identified in the statements; (d) the actions of the defendant are the true cause of the actual harm suffered by the plaintiff (in this case, mental anguish rather than injury to reputation); (e) the plaintiff is entitled to be compensated by money damages for that harm; and (f) the defamatory statements appeared because the defendant has done all this with the required degree of fault established by law. Let's take a closer look at each of these points in turn.

## False Statements That Offend Ordinary Decency

The false light statement may not be defamatory—although it sometimes is—but it must be found offensive to a reasonable person. "Offensiveness" in defamation cases may not matter unless the statement hurts business—a condition not always easy to document. However, "offensiveness," in and of itself, can determine the outcome of a false light invasion of privacy lawsuit.

In 1947, when she was 10 years old, Eleanor Sue Leverton of Birmingham, Ala., was struck by a car, knocked down and nearly run over. As a woman bystander lifted the injured child from the pavement, a newspaper photographer, who happened to be nearby, shot a picture of the scene. His powerful, dramatic photograph was published the following morning in a Birmingham newspaper.

Nearly two years later, the *Saturday Evening Post* used that same picture—it had been purchased from a photo syndicate house—to illustrate a magazine article on pedestrian carelessness. The article was entitled "They Ask to Be Killed," and underneath Miss Leverton's photograph was this subheading: "Safety education in schools has reduced child accidents measurably, but unpredictable darting through traffic still takes a sobering toll." Beside the title was a box that read: "Do you invite massacre by your own carelessness? Here's how thousands have committed suicide by scorning laws that were passed to keep them alive."

Miss Leverton and her parents resented the implication that her misfortune was brought on by her own carelessness. Indeed, the Birmingham police concluded at the time that Miss Leverton's accident happened not because of her own carelessness, but because the motorist had run through a red light. The Levertons sued for an unwarranted invasion of their daughter's privacy and were awarded $5,000. The appeals court agreed that the judgment was appropriate: "The sum total of all this is that this particular plaintiff, the legitimate subject for publicity for one particular accident, now becomes a pictorial, frightful example of pedestrian carelessness. This, we think, exceeds the bounds of privilege."[10] In other words, Miss Leverton had been placed in a false and offensive light.

A wrong or misleading context alone, however, may not win a false light privacy suit if the conduct depicted is not found to be offensive. For example, consider the case of Clarence W. Arrington, whose photograph was used on the cover of *The New York Times* magazine in connection with a lengthy article entitled "The Black Middle Class: Making It."[11] The photograph, published without his consent, showed him walking down a Manhattan street wearing an expensive business suit, carrying a briefcase and, in general, looking prosperous.

Indeed, Arrington was doing well. He had earned an M.B.A. from Columbia University, and, at the time his photo was taken, was a financial analyst with General Motors. Still, he resented being associated with the *Times* magazine article, a harsh indictment of materialistic and status-conscious African-Americans who, the article contended, were becoming less and less concerned about the plight of their less fortunate African-American brothers and sisters.

Arrington sued the *Times*, claiming that he did not fit the theme of the article or the materialistic views of the persons who had been interviewed. He was placed in a false light, he argued, and, as a result, he was exposed to contempt and ridicule from his friends and suffered mental anguish. The trial court agreed, but the appeals court did not, holding that the *Times* article neither depicted him personally as being insensitive nor portrayed him in an offensive manner.[12]

Determining what is "highly offensive to a reasonable person" can be a vague and uncertain business, but it is in this arena that most false light privacy actions are fought. With few clear-cut guidelines to follow, judges and juries are given broad latitude to define what is "highly offensive," and the results are not always consistent or predictable.

## Publication

Like defamation, the offending words must reach an audience. Unlike defamation, most courts have held that the audience must be substantial in size. Technically, however, publication occurs the moment a third person has seen the communication.

Also like defamation, a false light plaintiff often has a relatively easy time demonstrating that publication has occurred. This is because the defendant advertising agency or public relations department has disseminated the false information to thousands, if not millions, of readers or viewers in network television advertising, press release material published in hundreds of news outlets or in campaigns on YouTube, Facebook or other social networking sites.

## Identification

The plaintiff in false light invasion of privacy cases faces virtually the same requirements to prove an audience, or even a tiny portion of it, believes that the statements refer to him or her, as does a libel plaintiff. Unfortunately, identification also is just as often made easy for the plaintiff by the defendant because of the emphasis on clearly identifying individuals inherent in the training of professional communicators.

Identification of group members for false light purposes is also identical. Like libel, each member of a small group, traditionally about 25 members or fewer, may sue and be able to collect, even if he or she is not personally identified in the false and shocking or outrageous communication. This a good place to note who can be a plaintiff in a false light suit because this is one area in which false light differs significantly from defamation.

The reason that individual members of a small group can sue is that each member of the group is recognized in the law as having legal standing. In defamation, so does any entity that is recognized as an individual in the eyes of the law, such as a company, partnership or other legal entity. These fictitious "individuals" generally cannot bring a cause of action for false light because, although they may have a reputation to defend for libel purposes, they cannot demonstrate they have suffered the mental anguish caused by the published false statement that is central to a plaintiff's case in proving false light invasion of privacy.

In an example cited in Chapter 4 involving defamation, it was noted that both the principal owner of a company and the corporation itself could bring separate suits to repair their respective reputations. In a false light invasion of privacy situation, however, Mr. Marcus (the principal owner) could sue as an individual, but the Neiman-Marcus Company, as an incorporated organization, could not bring such a lawsuit because it would lack the legal standing to do so.

## Causation

As in any tort, the plaintiff in a false light invasion of privacy suit must allege and prove that the actions of the defendant were the logical and proximate cause of the claimed injury. Often this is easily accomplished because the plaintiff is simply charging that he or she has suffered legitimate mental anguish when the defendant published false and outrageous statements seen by acquaintances or clients or customers.

Problems involving proving causation might arise when a plaintiff can be shown to be relatively unstable in general or is responding to a false statement that, in the opinion of a judge or jury, should not have caused mental anguish severe enough to warrant compensation. Also, if the false but not defamatory statement has been already widely circulated by others, the plaintiff may experience difficulty in convincing a jury that the defendant's repetition of the statement legitimately could be seen as causing the alleged harm to the plaintiff's mental well-being.

## Compensation   Nice Try, but No.

Although the devil is in the nuances differentiating the laws of false light from state to state, a plaintiff seeking compensation for harm to his or her mental well-being caused by an outrageous, false statement generally will be entitled to seek four different kinds of monetary awards: *nominal* damages, *special* damages, *actual* damages (in some jurisdictions, the second and third awards are sometimes combined and called "general" or "compensatory" damages) and *punitive* (or "exemplary") damages. Although these are discussed more thoroughly in Chapter 4, let's briefly look at each of these in turn.

The general rule in American law is that a plaintiff has to be awarded something of value to win a lawsuit—the common law generally does not recognize moral victories. Therefore, a plaintiff not interested in seeking a large award, but interested in proving to the world that the embarrassing or outrageous statements are false, might simply seek a small or *nominal* damage award. This is relatively rare, however, in false light cases. More typically, a plaintiff, actually seeking millions for the supposed mental anguish, is found by a judge or jury to have suffered no real harm and, therefore, not deserving of more than a nominal award of damages even though, technically, the plaintiff has proven all the elements of his or her false light case.

*Special* damages are often thought of as out-of-pocket dollar loss. To obtain special damages, a plaintiff must produce evidence sufficient to prove that the false and outrageous statements cost the plaintiff demonstrable monetary loss. Expenses for psychiatric care, counseling services or prescribed medications, as well as evidence of wages lost or other financial reverses because the plaintiff was too upset to function normally, are examples of special damages often claimed by plaintiffs in false light cases.

The third category of damages, *actual* damage, requires no proof of actual monetary loss on the part of the plaintiff, but often does require the plaintiff to demonstrate that the alleged mental anguish caused by the false and outrageous statements did, in fact, exist. In jurisdictions that ask for some evidence of mental anguish, plaintiffs seeking actual damages, in addition to their own testimony, typically introduce testimony from friends and medical and/or counseling professionals to meet this requirement.

If a judge or jury accepts that the harm has occurred, and the defendant has no additional defenses, money will be awarded to the plaintiff to compensate him or her based on the judge's or jury's estimation of the harm—an invitation for large damage awards for the plaintiff that many courts seem unable to resist. The possibility of such large verdicts should be all the impetus needed for advertising and public relations professionals to take all possible precautions to avoid becoming embroiled in a false light suit.

*Punitive* damages are awarded not to compensate the plaintiff, but to punish the defendant. Because they are meant to punish instead of compensate, punitive damages, generally, are awarded only when the defendant's actions are so outrageous that they offend the conscience of judges or juries. In a false light invasion of privacy suit, punitive damages might be awarded if the statements of the defendant were not only false, but the defendant both knew they were false when published and were purposefully meant to harm the plaintiff. Like actual damages, punitive damage awards can reach mega-amounts in invasion of privacy suits and are as dangerous, if not more so, to defendants.

## Defendant Fault

False light privacy, like defamation, requires that the offending publication resulted because the person who published the material meets the *fault* standard established by law. Although fault in tort law often is defined as an error in judgment or conduct (i.e., negligence, or any departure from normal care because of inattention, carelessness or incompetence), in false light invasion of privacy, the Supreme Court has decreed that the fault required is "actual malice" (i.e., the publication of a deliberate lie, or publishing with a reckless disregard as to whether the statement is true).

Actual malice is the fault standard required for public officials and public figures in defamation cases and, as discussed in Chapter 4, is a very difficult hurdle for such a plaintiff to overcome. In false light invasion of privacy suits, all plaintiffs must show actual malice regardless if they are public or private. Although one might conclude, therefore, that false light cases would be few and far between because of the extreme difficulty plaintiffs face in demonstrating actual malice in libel cases, for reasons discussed later in this chapter, proving actual malice in false light cases is often much easier because of the outrageous actions of defendants in publishing the complained of material.

## Time, Inc. v. Hill

The two criteria essential for winning a false light invasion of privacy suit are (a) that the false light in which the other person is placed would be highly offensive to a reasonable person, and (b) that the person who publicized the false and offensive information knew it was false at the time or acted in reckless disregard of whether the material was true. The latter criterion—the actual malice fault requirement—was first applied by the Supreme Court to false light invasion of privacy in 1967, in *Time, Inc., v. Hill*.[13] In this case, the first major invasion of privacy case ever ruled on by the Supreme Court, members of a quiet, private family had become the subject of intense and poorly handled mass media coverage because of the crush of events quite out of their control.

The case began with a jailbreak. In 1952, three convicts escaped from a maximum-security prison and, rather than head for the hills, slipped into the peaceful suburb of Whitemarsh, Pa., just outside Philadelphia. The three convicts, apparently selecting a private home at random, invaded the residence and held the owner, James Hill, and his wife and five children hostage for 19 hours.[14] The family members were not harmed or molested; in fact, they reported that they had been treated with courtesy despite the tenseness of the situation. Police, acting on a tip, found out about the hostages and surrounded the Hill home. When the convicts attempted to escape, two of the three were shot and killed in a gun battle with the police.

Early in the following year, a writer named Joseph Hayes published a novel about a family held hostage by three escaped convicts. Entitled *The Desperate Hours*,[15] the novel was inspired by the Hill family drama, although the author drew on other hostage situations as well. The book differed from actual events in several aspects. For one thing, the convict characters in the novel, far from being courteous, were mean and abusive, especially toward the daughter of the family. The upcoming publication of the book that was expected to become a bestseller, plus the trauma of the original experience and the subsequent intensive media attention surrounding the 19-hour standoff, prompted the Hill family to move to Connecticut where none of their new acquaintances knew of the hostage-related events.

The publication of the novel, however, was only the beginning. A short time later, Hayes decided to turn the book into a play. Drawing favorable attention from theatrical producers, the play was cast and then taken on the road to various cities on the east coast to ready it for possible production in New York City. After positive reviews in regional newspapers, the now definitely Broadway-bound play was scheduled to have its last out-of-town performances in Philadelphia.

At this juncture, editors at the country's leading news and photo magazine, *Life*, decided to do a piece about the play, but not just another run-of-the-mill, advance story on a Broadway-bound drama. Instead, *Life's* editors elected to dredge up the Hill family's ordeal and relate it to the fictional treatment depicted in *The Desperate Hours.*

"The play," the *Life* article exclaimed, "is a heart-stopping account of how a family rose to heroism in a crisis."[16] A series of photographs, taken both inside and outside the former Hill residence near Philadelphia, posed actors from the play illustrating scenes from the play. One photo depicted the son being roughed up by one of the convicts. Another photo, captioned "daring daughter," showed actors depicting the daughter in the play biting the hand of a convict, forcing him to drop a pistol on the floor, while still another photo was of the supposed father hurling the pistol out of a window. None of these things had happened to the Hill family.

The Hills had finally had enough, especially when it was announced that the play would become a major motion picture. A text and photo-illustrated article, clearly linking the Hills to the dramatized events, published in the one magazine that, at the time, was on every coffee table in every home and office in America, meant there was no place the Hills could live without seemingly forever being defined by the one trauma-causing event they had hoped to put behind them.

In their suit for invasion of privacy, the Hill's complaint was that the *Life* article placed them in a false light by implying that the fictionalized, sensationalized events shown in the photographs reflected their own experiences as hostages. The trial court jury[17] agreed that the magazine had been careless in linking the Hills to the play (at least in the photo captions) and found in their favor, as did the appeals court.[18] Eventually, the case made its way to the Supreme Court of the United States, with *Life* arguing that a constitutional issue—freedom of the press to discuss matters that are newsworthy—was involved.

The Court decided the case in the wake of its recent ruling in *New York Times v. Sullivan,*[19] which changed the fault standard in some defamation cases to actual malice (discussed in Chapter 4). The decision in *Hill* was a sweeping victory for freedom of the press. Although the connection between reporting on public events like the struggle for civil rights in Southern states that was at the heart of the *Sullivan* decision and an article about an upcoming play supposedly based on the Hill family's private ordeal struck some observers as tenuous, the Court made it nonetheless. Ruling in favor of *Life* magazine, the Court sent the case back for another trial, holding that the Hill family (and apparently all plaintiffs in future false light cases) could win only if actual malice could be proven.[20] *Life* magazine was careless, sloppy and negligent, perhaps, but its behavior clearly did not rise to the level of actual malice. At this point, the Hill family threw in the towel.

## Affirmative Defenses

Once a false light invasion of privacy plaintiff has made a *prima facie* case (established a false and outrageous statement, publication, identification and so forth), the other side must mount a defense. These affirmative defenses include *conditional privilege, opinion* and *consent*.

Those who report information stemming from someone who has absolute privilege enjoy a *conditional* (or *qualified*) *privilege* (this concept is discussed more fully in Chapter 4). Conditional privilege extends to reports of government documents as well. Journalists and other citizens may quote from privileged documents without fear of false light suits so long as the published or broadcast accounts are full, fair and accurate.

In *Gertz v. Robert Welch, Inc.* the Supreme Court apparently created an additional affirmative defense for *opinion* statements. The Court commented, "We begin with the common ground. Under the First Amendment there is no such thing as a false idea. However pernicious an opinion may seem, we depend for its correction not on the conscience of judges and juries, but on the competition of other ideas."[21] Opinion statements are truly opinion—not susceptible to a truth or falsity test—and, therefore, cannot be the basis of a false light case.

*Consent* is a third affirmative defense to a charge of false light. Although, technically, a defense to libel as well, few consent to have their good names tarnished. It might be the case, however, that individuals who expect to or find material published about them that makes them look better than they actually are, would initially agree to the publication. Remember that the Hill family was depicted falsely as behaving heroically in the face of danger. A signed, or in other ways documented, consent is almost always a foolproof affirmative defense to invasion of privacy suits unless the defendant has somehow gone beyond the scope of that consent.

## Other Defenses

In addition to *conditional privilege, opinion* and *consent*, there are secondary defenses, often called defenses in mitigation or incomplete defenses. One of these is *retraction*. As discussed in Chapter 4, a voluntary retraction can show good faith on the part of the communicator—an attempt to set the record straight and atone for a false statement. For the court to find it persuasive, the retraction should be timely, prominent and complete. Another secondary defense is to offer the offended people the *right of reply*—to provide space to those who have been wronged, or think they have been, to tell their side of the story.

Neither a retraction nor a right of reply can be imposed. The courts recognize the rights of communicators to control the contents of their communications. Corrections, retractions and rights of reply are all provided voluntarily, when they are provided at all. Secondary defenses do not allow the defendant to avoid a judgment, but they may reduce the amount of money a court might award.

## Subcategories of False Light

The subcategory of invasion of privacy called false light can, itself, be subdivided into three categories typically labeled as *embellishment, distortion* and *fictionalization*.[22] *Time, Inc. v. Hill* is an example of an embellishment case where the defendant has truthfully reported major facts about the plaintiff, but then has "embellished" the particulars by adding extra material to make it a better story. Let's look at each of these sub-subcategories in turn.

### Embellishment

In *Hill*, the Supreme Court held that all plaintiffs must show actual malice. As mentioned above, a plaintiff in a false light case often finds it easier to prove this fault standard than in a defamation suit. *Cantrell v. Forest City Publishing, Co.* is an example of a false light, *embellishment* case that demonstrates this principle.[23]

In 1967, the Silver Bridge across the Ohio River collapsed, killing 44 people, including Melvin Cantrell. The Cleveland *Plain Dealer* sent reporter Joseph Eszterhas and a photographer to the scene. Eszterhas, who subsequently went on to become a Hollywood writer well known for sleazy screenplays, including those for *Basic Instinct* and *Showgirls*, wrote several powerful, human-interest articles about the disaster. One of these award-winning pieces focused on the funeral of Mr. Cantrell and the impact of the tragedy on his family.

Five months later, Eszterhas was sent back to the Cantrell neighborhood in the Point Pleasant area to write a follow-up article. Eszterhas and a photographer visited the Cantrell home and talked with the Cantrell children, but Mrs. Margaret Cantrell, the widow, was not present. The article that Eszterhas developed from his revisit to Point Pleasant, later published in the Sunday magazine section of the *Plain Dealer*, emphasized the family's poverty-stricken condition. At one point, the text read:

> Margaret Cantrell will talk neither about what happened nor about how they are doing. She wears the same mask of non-expression she wore at the funeral. She is a proud woman. Her world has changed. She says that after it happened, the people in town offered to help them out with money and they refused to take it.[24]

Beyond the misleading impression that the reporter had personally interviewed Mrs. Cantrell, there were a number of other flaws in the piece. In particular, statements about the family's poverty were exaggerated. Mrs. Cantrell sued for false light invasion of privacy, alleging that the *Plain Dealer* article caused her family members to become objects of pity and that she and her son suffered mental distress, shame and humiliation.

The trial court awarded her $60,000 in damages, but the appeals court reversed.[25] The Supreme Court, however, agreed to review the case. In only the second invasion of privacy case to reach the Court, the Court ruled in favor of Mrs. Cantrell. "These were calculated falsehoods," the Court's opinion said of the *Plain Dealer* article, "and the jury was plainly justified in finding that Eszterhas had portrayed the Cantrells in a false light through knowing or reckless untruth."[26]

Another example of an embellishment, false light invasion of privacy decision was the case of baseball star Warren Spahn, who sued a company that published a fictitious biography of him. Entitled *The Warren Spahn Story*, the book was a highly flattering portrait of the famous left-handed pitcher who won more than 300 games and was a National League fan favorite for many years. The "biography" embellished Spahn's life in many ways, adding luster to his World War II record, for example, and including, as the trial court put it, "a host, a preponderant percentage, of factual errors, distortions and fanciful passages."[27] Spahn's stature as a public figure might allow for some latitude, the court conceded, but in this case "the findings of fact go far beyond the establishment of minor errors in an otherwise accurate biography."[28]

The lesson to be learned for advertising and public relations professionals is to not yield to the temptation to jazz up an ad, story or any other type of communication by adding a few extra, colorful comments or facts. The temptation is there because "we're not saying anything bad about somebody, so why would they object?" As these cases tell us, the plaintiffs may object not for what you said, but that you said anything at all—especially if you embellished the truth.

### Distortion

*Distortion*, false light privacy cases arise when the defendant, typically through visual or graphic means, allegedly "distorts" the personality of the plaintiff. Often this distortion is caused when the defendant uses a photo or illustration, originally intended for one purpose, to satisfy another. Both the Leverton case, involving the misuse of the photo of the child hit by the car to illustrate a subsequent story about careless pedestrians, and the Arrington case, where the photo of a young, prosperous male was used in an article about middle-class blacks turning their backs on their less fortunate brethren, are classic false light, distortion cases.

Unfortunately, such cases are numerous in legal annals. For example, the *Saturday Evening Post* provided what a court found to be a false and offensive context for a photograph it used to illustrate an article about taxicab drivers in Washington, D.C. Entitled "Never Give a Passenger an Even Break," the piece dwelled on what it said was the rude and conniving behavior of cabbies in the nation's capital, characterizing them as "ill-mannered, brazen, and contemptuous of their patrons. . . ." Accompanying the *Post* article was a photograph of a cab driver, Muriel Peay, who evidently was neither impolite, nor brazen. Peay sued and won on the claim that the article and photo had placed her in a false light.[29]

Another example is the case of Sue S. Crump, a coal miner in West Virginia, who, in 1977, agreed to be photographed to illustrate a newspaper article about women coal miners. Two years later, the same photograph was dug out of the files to illustrate a different article, this one about problems facing female coal miners. Entitled "Women Enter 'Man's' World," the article recounted various hazing incidents inflicted on female miners by their male counterparts. The article used as examples a Virginia woman miner who was physically attacked twice while underground, and a Wyoming woman miner who "was dangled off a 200-foot water tower accompanied by the suggestion that she quit her job. She did."

None of these incidents had happened to Ms. Crump, but when friends and associates began questioning her about them, she said the unfavorable attention prompted by the publication of her photograph in this different context caused her a great deal of embarrassment and humiliation.[30]

The lesson for communicators is clear. Advertising and public relations professionals should make certain that any photograph used to illustrate a story, brochure or Web site is used appropriately. For example, a public relations employee preparing an article for the company magazine about worker carelessness should not simply grab a file photo of employees working on the assembly line. This same admonition applies to an advertising agency art director who may be tempted to illustrate a public service TV spot about kids and handguns by using old file footage from a school playground video.

### Fictionalization

Fictitious, according to *Black's Law Dictionary*, is defined as: ". . . having the character of a fiction; pretended; . . . imaginary, not real. . . ."[31] *Fictionalization* false light, invasion of privacy involves enhancing a news article, book, play or film by inventing additional dialogue, thoughts, ideas or actions to characters portrayed as fictitious, but who, in fact, closely—perhaps too closely—resemble real people.

A classic example involved the case of *Bindrim v. Mitchell*.[32] In the course of writing her newest novel, Gwen Davis Mitchell, an author, asked to take part in something called nude encounter therapy. Dr. Paul Bindrim, a psychologist and leading exponent of this technique, agreed to her request, but stipulated that she should not write about the actual session she attended or identify Dr. Bindrim or his treatment center in any way.

The novelist promised to abide by these restrictions and, although including a fictional nude therapy group session in her novel, took pains to disguise the actual facts upon which it was based. Among other things, the writer coarsened the language of the group leader, described him in a manner that did not resemble Dr. Bindrim and changed both his academic credentials and the location of the session by placing it in a different state.

Dr. Bindrim, nonetheless, sued for false light, fictionalization invasion of privacy, claiming that, despite the changes, because of his celebrated status as the guru of nude encounter therapy, everyone reading the book would automatically think the alleged fictional character and situation were really about him and his practice. The court agreed that the measures adopted to disguise Bindrim were not only inadequate, but actually made him look worse than he actually was.

Those advertising and public relations professionals feeling especially creative need to remember that taking their frustrations out against former significant others, estranged family members, high-school principals or landlords that have cheated them out of their security deposits by thinly disguising them as antagonists in a piece of fiction should fight the feeling. It would be foolish to exact an ounce of revenge at the price of paying a pound's worth of damages to an aggrieved plaintiff.

## False Light in a Digital, New-Media Age: Emerging Issues

Whether the tort of false light invasion of privacy will survive much beyond the first decade of the twenty-first century is certainly a matter of some doubt. A recent trend for states either to rethink their adoption of false light, or to outright refuse to do so, coupled with decisions for defendants in many recent false light cases, does not bode well for those who advocate for false light as a separate cause of action from defamation or infliction of emotional distress.

Nonetheless, it still may be too early to plan the memorial service for a fallen tort. The majority of states still recognize some form of false light and the proliferation of social Web sites, filled with rumor and outright falsehoods, may yet provide the impetus for a renaissance of actions brought by the aggrieved subjects of such communications. Prudent advertising and public relations professionals, therefore, should continue to be vigilant that their messages live up to the traditional journalistic standards of truth and accuracy.

## Public Disclosure of Private, Embarrassing Facts

*Public disclosure of private, embarrassing facts* invasion of privacy involves portraying individuals truthfully and accurately, but, in the process, disclosing sensitive and embarrassing information about their private lives in a manner that other persons would find offensive if disclosed about them. Thus, it is the disclosure of the sensitive information that is shocking and outrageous.

If the disclosed information were false, clearly the plaintiff would bring a defamation suit or a false light case. In both of these torts, finding that the allegedly false statements were actually true would defeat the plaintiff's case. In contrast, the disclosed information in a private facts case, while true, is of such a highly private and embarrassing nature that making public such personal facts might persuade a judge or jury that those who disclosed this information have acted so outrageously that they should be made to pay the plaintiff money damages.

### Background

When Samuel D. Warren and Louis D. Brandeis wrote their famous *Harvard Law Review* article calling for the recognition of an individual's right to privacy, it was public disclosure of private, embarrassing facts they had in mind. "Gossip [even if true]," they wrote, "... has become a trade, which is pursued with industry as well as effrontery."[33]

Legal problems arising from the public disclosure of private facts are far more likely to involve news reporters and editors (i.e., journalists) than advertising and public relations professionals. However, it should be noted that several of the first lawsuits brought in this area were indeed prompted by public notices published as advertisements—one published in a newspaper, another posted prominently on a busy street, a third shouted from the highway—that certain debtors, identified by name, did not pay their debts, allegations that were as embarrassing in 1918, when such suits were first filed, as they might be today.

The tort of public disclosure of private, embarrassing facts really emerged in the mid-1960s to become identified by most commentators as a subcategory of invasion of privacy and recognized by courts as a separate cause of action. Today, most states have adopted some form of public disclosure of embarrassing facts, although several jurisdictions have limited its application in situations where plaintiffs are actually complaining about infliction of emotional distress that does not involve facts courts consider to be private (e.g., speech that publicly humiliates the plaintiff, but is of public interest). New York,[34] Virginia,[35] Indiana[36] and North Carolina[37] either have severely limited public disclosure of private facts cases or have declined to recognize the tort at all.

## Terminology

Embarrassing facts about an individual may be, and often are, safely publicized without violating a person's right to privacy. To create a cognizable case for public disclosure of private, embarrassing facts, two conditions must be met. First, a reasonable person would be offended by the disclosure and, second, the disclosure pertains to a purely private matter. If these conditions are met, then it is possible the disclosure would constitute an invasion of personal privacy.

According to the *Restatement of Torts*:

> One who gives publicity to a matter concerning the private life of another is subject to the other for invasion of his privacy, if the matter publicized is of a kind that
>
> (a)  would be highly offensive to a reasonable person, and
> (b)  is not of legitimate concern to the public.[38]

Disclosure of private information is one of the few media-related situations in which truth is not an absolute defense. The key phrases, again, are *highly offensive* and *legitimate public concern*.

Public relations professionals, especially, would do well to familiarize themselves with this aspect of privacy law. Public relations writers prepare publicity releases and other types of organizational communications on any number of topics and issues, and some of these messages could easily concern the public disclosure of private facts (e.g., explaining the complexities of a sensitive personnel decision, or backgrounding the issues in a heated proxy fight for control of a corporation). These and numerous other possible scenarios hold the potential for invasion of privacy suits.

Under current interpretations, unless the private facts disclosed are outrageously offensive and outside the broad realm of legitimate public interest, they may be publicized. Nonetheless, even if the law would eventually protect disclosure, the public relations professional and/or his or her organization or client might win in a court of law only to lose in the court of public opinion because the disclosure is considered beyond the bounds of ordinary decency.

## The Elements of Private, Embarrassing Facts

Like false light invasion of privacy, public disclosure of private, embarrassing facts resembles defamation. For a private facts case, the plaintiff must first show that (a) a statement has been made that discloses truthful, private, embarrassing facts and the disclosure of which offends ordinary decency; (b) the material must be shown to at least one other person by the defendant; (c) the plaintiff has been identified in the statements; (d) the actions of the defendant are the true cause of the actual harm suffered by the plaintiff (in this case, mental anguish); (e) the plaintiff is entitled to be compensated by money damages for that harm; and (f) the statements appeared because the defendant has done all this with the required degree of fault established by law. Let's take a closer look at each of these points in turn.

## Statement of Private, Embarrassing Facts

The statement containing highly embarrassing private facts must contain the kinds of information that reasonable people recognize as being so personal that public disclosure would be considered highly offensive. Thus disclosing information already in public records or giving publicity to matters that occur in public or in places where a potential plaintiff would not have a legitimate expectation of privacy (e.g., a place of business or event open to the public) would not give rise to a private facts cause of action.

"Offensiveness" in such cases often involves disclosing matters related to sexual practices or preferences, financial records or health or medical information. For example, on September 11, 1975, a deeply disturbed young woman named Sara Jane Moore approached President Gerald R. Ford as he was about to make a speech at Union Square in San Francisco. As President Ford was shaking hands with onlookers and well-wishers in the crowd, Ms. Moore edged her way toward the front of the spectators, brandishing a revolver. President Ford's secret service bodyguards failed to spot her, but Oliver W. Sipple, standing nearby, did see her. As she raised the pistol to fire, Sipple grabbed her arm causing the bullet to miss its mark, almost certainly saving the president's life. Sipple was hailed as a hero and, inevitably, subjected to massive local and national publicity.

Within hours, popular, local columnist Herb Caen published an item in his San Francisco *Chronicle* column suggesting that Sipple was homosexual.[39] An article the next day in the *Los Angeles Times,* theorized that President Ford's failure to promptly thank Sipple for his heroism was a direct result of Sipple's sexual orientation, and questions were raised in the gay community whether the White House was shunning Sipple because of his associations.[40]

From these articles, Sipple, who was, in fact, homosexual, said his parents, brothers and sisters learned for the first time of his sexual orientation. As a result, he said, he felt abandoned by his family and exposed to contempt and ridicule, causing him mental anguish, embarrassment and humiliation. Sipple sued the *Chronicle* for invasion of privacy because, he said, they published private, embarrassing information about his life. Sipple's membership in the local gay community was known in San Francisco. His concern was that the news of his sexual orientation was not known in the Midwest, where his parents and siblings lived.[41]

The court sided with the defendant news organization in the Sipple case because, the court said, the very public nature of the event would create legitimate news value in reporting the details about the person who saved the life of the President. Other courts, however, have held that displays of confidential autopsy photographs, [42] publishing a photograph of a nursing mother, [43] disclosing private information about medical health details, [44] publishing the name of a victim of child sexual abuse [45] and publicizing the name of an individual accused of failure to pay debts [46] do constitute publication of information that would be classified as highly embarrassing.

Clearly, determining what is "highly offensive to a reasonable person" can be a vague and uncertain business, but it is in this arena that most public disclosure of private, embarrassing facts actions are brought. Courts generally will disallow cases based on hypersensitive hurt feelings by insisting on an "ordinary decency" standard, but with few clear-cut guidelines to draw upon, judges and juries are given broad latitude to define what they consider private information that should be protected from disclosure, and the results are not always consistent or predictable.

## Publication

Publication must be attributable to actions by the defendant. Thus potential cases involving individuals active in social causes like AIDS prevention or anti-abortion campaigns or in which they have provided interviews to media outlets about aspects of their private lives likely would fail because plaintiffs would have little basis for complaining about additional disclosure of what once might otherwise have been considered private facts.

While technically publication occurs the moment a third person has seen the communication, like false light, the offending words must typically reach a broad audience, rather than just a few, to be actionable. Many jurisdictions refer to publication as giving "publicity" to the private, embarrassing information. Note, however, that a sizable minority of states has found the publication requirement satisfied in situations in which, for example, the offending information was made public to the plaintiff's co-workers or in other situations "when a special relationship exists between the plaintiff and the public to whom the information was disclosed." [47]

Like defamation, a private facts plaintiff often has a relatively easy time demonstrating that publication has occurred. This is because the defendant advertising agency or public relations department has disseminated the private, embarrassing information to thousands, if not millions, of readers or viewers in network television advertising, press release material published in hundreds of news outlets or in campaigns on YouTube, Facebook or other social networking sites.

## Identification

The plaintiff in a private, embarrassing facts privacy case must meet virtually the same requirements as a defamation or false light plaintiff to prove that an audience, or even a tiny portion of it, believes that the statements refer to him or her. Identification is often not difficult for the plaintiff because the defendant, as a professional communicator, has clearly identified the subjects in the communications.

Identification of group members for private, embarrassing facts purposes is identical to defamation and false light cases. A member of a small group, traditionally about 25 members or fewer, may sue and be able to collect, even if he or she is not personally identified in a shocking and outrageous communication. Like false light, the tort of public disclosure of private, embarrassing facts is limited to individuals because organizations cannot demonstrate they have suffered mental anguish about the published information.

## Causation

The plaintiff in a private, embarrassing facts privacy suit must allege and prove that the actions of the defendant were the logical and proximate cause of the claimed injury. Often this is easily accomplished because the plaintiff is simply charging that the he or she has understandably suffered mental anguish when the defendant outrageously disclosed private, embarrassing statements seen by acquaintances or clients or customers.

Problems involving proving causation might arise when a plaintiff is complaining about the disclosure of private, embarrassing facts, which, in the minds of a judge or jury, should not have caused mental anguish severe enough to warrant compensation. Also, if the private facts are already widely known by others, the plaintiff may experience difficulty in convincing a judge or jury that the defendant's disclosure of the statement legitimately could be seen as causing the additional alleged harm to the plaintiff's mental well-being.

## Compensation

A plaintiff seeking compensation for harm to his or her mental well-being resulting from disclosure of private, embarrassing facts generally will be entitled to seek four different kinds of monetary awards: *nominal* damages, *special* damages, *actual* damages (in some jurisdictions, the second and third awards are sometimes combined and called "general" or "compensatory" damages) and *punitive* (or "exemplary") damages. Although these are discussed more thoroughly in Chapter 4 and in the false light section above, let's revisit each of these in turn.

For a plaintiff to seek a small or *nominal* damage award is relatively rare in public disclosure of private, embarrassing facts cases. More typically, a plaintiff, actually seeking a large sum to compensate for the supposed mental anguish, is found by a judge or jury to have suffered no real harm and, therefore, not deserving of more than a nominal award of damages.

To obtain *special* damages, often thought of as "out-of-pocket dollar loss," plaintiffs must produce evidence sufficient to prove that the disclosure of the private, embarrassing facts cost the plaintiff a demonstrable monetary loss. Expenses for psychiatric care, counseling services or prescribed medications, as well as evidence of wages lost or other financial reverses because the plaintiff was too upset to function normally, are examples of special damages often claimed by plaintiffs in private, embarrassing facts cases.

The third category of damages, *actual* damage, requires no proof of actual monetary loss. However, the plaintiff must demonstrate that the alleged mental anguish caused by the outrageous disclosure does, in fact, exist. In jurisdictions that ask for some evidence of mental anguish, plaintiffs seeking actual damages typically, in addition to their own testimony, introduce testimony from friends and medical and/or counseling professionals about such psychic damages as "humiliation,"[48] "depression,"[49] "memory lapses"[50] or "insomnia"[51] to meet this requirement.

If a judge or jury accepts that the harm has occurred and the defendant has no additional defenses, money will be awarded to the plaintiff as compensation based on the judge or jury's estimation of the harm—an invitation for large damage awards for the plaintiff. The possibility of such large verdicts should be all the impetus needed for advertising and public relations professionals to take all possible precautions to avoid becoming embroiled in a private, embarrassing facts suit.

*Punitive* damages, generally, are awarded when the defendant's actions are so outrageous that they offend the conscience of judges or juries. In a private, embarrassing facts invasion of privacy suit, punitive damages might be awarded if the information was disclosed with a purposeful intent to harm the plaintiff or, as one court said, "a callous and conscious disregard" of the plaintiff's right to privacy. Like actual damages, punitive damage awards can reach mega-amounts in disclosure of private, embarrassing facts suits and are as dangerous, if not more so, to defendants.

## Defendant Fault

As with defamation and false light, private, embarrassing facts cases require the plaintiff to show the offending disclosure resulted because the person who published the material met the *fault* standard established by law. It is by no means clear, however, what that standard is.

A number of states have adopted standards that resemble a form of recklessness which requires a showing of knowing or reckless disregard for the offensive disclosure of information. Others have opted for an intentional standard, meaning that carelessness would not be sufficient. Unlike defamation and false light, even in those jurisdictions that have adopted stricter standards, generally there appears to be no differentiation between public and private plaintiffs in disclosure of private, embarrassing facts cases.

## Affirmative Defenses

Once a private, embarrassing facts privacy plaintiff has made a *prima facie* case (i.e., a statement containing sensitive private information, publication, identification and so forth), the other side must mount a defense. Affirmative defenses include *conditional privilege, consent* and, unlike defamation and false light privacy, *newsworthiness*.

Those who report information stemming from someone who has absolute privilege enjoy a *conditional* (or *qualified*) *privilege* (this concept is discussed more fully above and in Chapter 4). Conditional privilege extends to reports of government documents as well. Courts have consistently held that information in public records cannot be considered private. Journalists and other citizens can quote from privileged documents without fear of private, embarrassing facts suits so long as the published or broadcast accounts are full, fair and accurate.

The Supreme Court has created a constitutionally based privilege as well. The landmark case in this regard—the first time the Court acted on a private, embarrassing facts case—came in 1975, with *Cox Broadcasting v. Cohn*.[52] This invasion of privacy case arose when, during court proceedings involving a rape and murder case, a reporter from WSB-TV, the Cox-owned television station in Atlanta, asked the clerk for copies of the charges to check the accuracy of the details. The victim's name was listed in the documents and the journalist disclosed the young woman's name in his televised report that evening. The story was rebroadcast the following day.

Normally, only the victim in a disclosure of private information action can instigate a suit, but a Georgia law permitted close relatives of a rape victim to file the suit on her behalf. Additionally, Martin Cohn, the victim's father, brought suit against Cox Broadcasting, claiming that the disclosure of his daughter's name and other information invaded his privacy as well. After Georgia trial and appeals courts found in the plaintiff's favor, Cox Broadcasting appealed to the Supreme Court.

At issue was this: Could the news media be punished for publishing facts already on the public records of a court? In an 8–1 decision, the Court said no. As Justice White, writing for the majority, noted,

> We are reluctant to embark on a course that would make public records generally available to the media but forbid their publication if offensive to the sensibilities of the supposed reasonable man. Such a rule would make it very difficult for the media to inform citizens about the public business and yet stay within the law. The rule would invite timidity and self-censorship and very likely lead to the suppression of many items that would otherwise be published and that should be made available to the public.[53]

Some court records, such as juvenile proceedings, might not be open to the public. The Court's opinion in *Cox* avoided addressing any questions on the constitutionality of sealed court records. The thrust of the *Cox* holding was this: If the records are available to the public, then the mass media (or anyone else) cannot be restrained from publishing truthful articles based on them.

Essentially the same reasoning prevailed in another Court ruling— *The Florida Star v. B.J.F.*[54] This 1989 case also involved publication of a rape victim's name. A cub reporter for a Jacksonville weekly newspaper, leafing through the incident report prepared by officers in the Sheriff's Department based on their activities that day, ran across an item in which a woman had complained that she had been raped and robbed. The Jacksonville Sheriff's Department routinely made incident reports available to the press, but, normally, did not include the names of sexual assault victims. In this case there was a lapse—the full name of the rape victim was included and reported in the newspaper's story.

Obviously, the Sheriff's Department had carelessly included the rape victim's name in the report. Even so, there were signs in the pressroom where the report was made available that victims of sex crimes were not to be identified. There also was a Florida statute forbidding disclosure of a rape victim's name. Beyond that, *The Florida Star's* own editorial policy forbade the publication of a rape victim's identity.

The victim, subsequently referred to in court records as B.J.F., sued for private, embarrassing facts invasion of privacy, claiming that the publication caused her mental anguish, forced her to change her telephone number to avoid harassing phone messages and prompted her to seek psychiatric counseling. At trial, the judge found the newspaper to have been negligent, leaving it to the jury to determine the amount of damages. The jury awarded her $100,000.[55]

On appeal, the Florida high court affirmed the judgment.[56] However, the Supreme Court reversed, ruling that the newspaper should not be punished for publishing truthful information from an official source, even though the information was not part of a court proceeding and the information was obtained by mistake.

*Consent* is a second affirmative defense to a private embarrassing facts charge. Anyone who watches reality television programs or uses Facebook or views the YouTube Web site knows that it is not unusual for individuals who like the attention or simply don't care about revealing private information about themselves to post material that others might think would normally be the kinds of matters generally not discussed.

Consent can be either actual (e.g., expressed in a signed waiver) or implied. Implied consent often is found when plaintiffs have either engaged in conduct that points to acquiescence (listing a former employer as a credit reference) or participated in activities of a public nature (e.g., being a guest on a television talk show). As long as the defendant has a signed document or in other ways demonstrates consent, perhaps by showing that the plaintiff posted Web site information, consent is almost always a foolproof affirmative way to defuse a potential private, embarrassing facts case unless the defendant has somehow gone beyond the scope of that consent.

Because the information published by the defendant in a private, embarrassing facts case is true, not surprisingly, defendants often argue that publication was in the public interest because it was of legitimate *newsworthiness*, a third affirmative defense. The central purpose of the First Amendment, according to the distinguished scholar Alexander Meiklejohn,

> ... is to give to every voting member of the body politic the fullest possible participation in the understanding of those problems with which the citizens of a self-governing society must deal. ... Nor ... is freedom of the press confined to comment upon public affairs and those persons who have voluntarily sought the public spotlight ... the scope of the privilege thus extends to almost all reporting of recent events, even though it involves the publication of a purely private individual's name or likeness.[57]

Thus, the desire to keep information private is bound to collide with the right to disseminate information to the public. Over the years, much to the dismay of many who may not wish to see their affairs splashed on the front page or aired on the nightly news, courts have been quite liberal in defining public interest, not just as something people necessarily *should* read about, but as something they do read about, or anything in which people are interested.

Individuals who seek the public limelight, of course, are generally thought to deserve less protection when someone discloses private information about them than those individuals who prefer to live out their lives quietly. Private persons often find themselves drawn into an event that happens in a public place (an accident, as the victim of a crime or simply happening by chance to be present) that creates a newsworthy moment. The *Restatement of Torts* points out that even involuntary subjects may not always have their privacy protected:

> These persons [involuntary public figures] are regarded as properly subject to the public interest, and publishers are permitted to satisfy the curiosity of the public as to its heroes, leaders, villains and victims, and those who are closely associated with them. As in the case of the voluntary public figure, the authorized publicity is not limited to the event that itself arouses the public interest, and to some extent includes publicity given to facts about the individual that would otherwise be purely private.[58]

A South Carolina case, however, suggests that the public interest in a news story might take a back seat to protecting the privacy of an individual under certain circumstances. In a lengthy story dealing with teenage pregnancies, the *Greenville News* interviewed a male high school student who had been identified—by the unwed mother—as the father of her baby.

The young man said he had been led to believe he was talking to a data gatherer for a research study of teen pregnancies, not to a newspaper reporter, and that he had no idea his statements, including his identification by name and his admission that he fathered the child, would appear in the newspaper. When the newspaper printed the article, the young man sued. The newspaper argued that the information was newsworthy and of legitimate public concern. The South Carolina Supreme Court, however, determined that this was a matter for a jury to decide. The jury found the name of the father was not of great public concern and decided on a substantial judgment against the newspaper.[59]

## Subcategories of Private Facts

The subcategory of invasion of privacy called public disclosure of private, embarrassing facts can, itself, be subdivided into three categories typically labeled as *extent of intimacy vs. newsworthiness*, *passage of time* and *consent exceeded*.[60] The case of Oliver Sipple, outed by the media in examining the life of the man who likely saved the life of the President of the United States, is an example of an intimacy vs. newsworthiness case where the defendant truthfully reported major facts about the plaintiff, including the particulars of his sexual orientation, that Sipple would have preferred be kept from public knowledge. Let's look at each of these in sub-subcategories in turn.

## Extent of Intimacy vs. Newsworthiness

In making the determination on a case-by-case basis about who should win in the straightforward contest between the plaintiff's wish to keep certain intimate details of his or her life secret vs. the news media's determination that the public has a right to know such details, courts have taken into account such factors as the way the communication was presented, the nature of the information being publicized, the degree of intimacy such disclosure represents and the value of the disclosure—as measured in newsworthiness—to the general public. What often emerges, as Dean Prosser theorized some years ago, "is something in the nature of a 'mores test,' by which there will be liability only for publicity given to those things which the customs and ordinary views of the community will not tolerate."[61]

One of the saddest cases in this area, and one of the most often referred to in legal circles, is that of William James Sidis. Young Sidis was known far and wide for his mathematical prowess at an early age. By the time he was 11, he had already become an authority on the subject of four-dimensional bodies, and he lectured to distinguished mathematicians on that and other matters. At 16, and amid much public fanfare, he was graduated from Harvard College. However, Sidis' youthful genius did not prepare him for later life, and he never seemed comfortable as an adult. He lived as unobtrusively as possible and eventually became something of a recluse.

Twenty years later, the *New Yorker* magazine decided to develop a profile on Sidis, another in its series entitled "Where Are They Now?" The *New Yorker* writer found Sidis living in a hall bedroom in "Boston's shabby south end," and reported in great detail that: (a) his room was severely unkempt; (b) Sidis had developed a curious and hollow laugh; (c) he had suffered a nervous breakdown; (d) he regarded his former fame with contempt; (e) he was presently employed as an insignificant clerk, a position in which he would never use his astonishing mathematical gifts; (f) he maintained a bizarre collection of streetcar tokens; and (g) his consuming interest was now focused on the folklore of the Okamakammesset Native American tribe.[62]

As the court in the subsequent suit for disclosing private embarrassing facts would later point out:

> It is not contended that any of the matter printed [in the *New Yorker* profile] is untrue. Nor is the manner of the author unfriendly; Sidis today is described as having "a certain childlike charm." But the article is merciless in its dissection of intimate details of its subject's personal life, and this in company with elaborate accounts of Sidis's passion for privacy and the pitiable lengths to which he has gone in order to avoid public scrutiny. The work possesses great reader interest, for it is both amusing and instructive; but it may be fairly described as a ruthless exposure of a once public character, who has since sought and has now been deprived of the seclusion of private life.[63]

The *New Yorker* profile proved devastating to Sidis, and he sued the magazine for invading his privacy. However, the trial court found that the unfortunate Sidis, many years later, was still newsworthy and, somewhat reluctantly, found in favor of the *New Yorker*.

The court said,

> We express no comment on whether or not the news worthiness of the matter printed will always constitute a complete defense. Revelations may be so intimate and so unwarranted in view of the victim's position as to outrage the community's notions of decency. But when focused upon public characters, truthful comments upon dress, speech, habits, and the ordinary aspects of personality will usually not transgress this line. Regrettably or not, the misfortunes and frailties of neighbors and "public figures" are subjects of considerable interest and discussion to the rest of the population. And when such are the mores of the community, it would be unwise for a court to bar their expression in the newspapers, books, and magazines of the day.[64]

Apparently, the massive publicity about Sidis' childhood, which he may or may not have wanted even at the time, would continue to haunt him so long as audiences remembered him as a one-time celebrity.

Compare the outcome in *Sidis* with the result in *Barber v. Time*,[65] a case involving Dorothy Barber who suffered from a rare metabolic disease; although she ate constantly, she continued to lose weight. Eventually she was hospitalized for treatment.

The case was something of a medical curiosity, and several news media, including *Time* magazine, decided to do a piece about it. Bursting into her Kansas City hospital room, a news service photographer got a picture of Mrs. Barber, which, when it later appeared in *Time*, portrayed the unfortunate young woman in terms not unlike those that might be used to describe a freak: "Insatiable Eater Barber" read the caption accompanying the photograph. In the piece, she was referred to as "Starving Glutton" and "she eats for ten."

The publication of the article prompted Mrs. Barber to sue. The court agreed that, although the story might well be newsworthy, the specific identification of her by name and the way she and her medical problem were characterized were so odious as to represent an invasion of her privacy.[66] Barber won the case.

Although courts accord great deference to arguments by journalists that the newsworthiness of the disclosed sensitive information should outweigh individual privacy interests, such an argument may fall on deaf ears if made by advertising or public relations professionals. Prudent professionals would be wise to obtain documented consent for the disclosure of sensitive information rather than rely on arguments about the value of the disclosure.

## Passage of Time

Is there a point in which one's past can be safely buried? Does the law's concept of rehabilitation—as, for example, with convicts who, on being released from prison, are said to "have paid their debt to society "—apply to one's private life, once made public, or, as in the case of Mr. Sidis, discussed above, must they remain public forever? Again, the law is not clear.

For example, consider the case of Marvin Briscoe, who once hijacked a truck. He was subsequently arrested, convicted and served time in prison. Thereafter, as his lawyer subsequently noted, Briscoe "abandoned his life of shame and became entirely rehabilitated and thereafter lived an exemplary, virtuous, and honorable life . . . he has assumed a place in respectable society and made many friends who were not aware of the incident in his earlier life."[67]

But a magazine writer was aware of Briscoe's past and he used the unfortunate man's criminal example to illustrate an article entitled "The Big Business of Hijacking," which was later published by *Reader's Digest*. At one point, the article read: "Typical of many beginners, Marvin Briscoe and [another man] stole a 'valuable looking' truck in Danville, Ky., and then fought a gun battle with the local police, only to learn they had hijacked four bowling-pin spotters."[68]

Although the account was truthful, there was nothing in it to suggest that the incident had happened 11 years previously. Briscoe, who had since moved to California, found himself "scorned and abandoned" by his friends; his 11-year-old daughter learned of her father's conviction from the publication. He sued. The trial court decided Mr. Briscoe had no cause of action and effectively dismissed the case.[69]

On appeal, however, the California Supreme Court reversed this decision and sent the case back for trial. Briscoe's claim that he had been rehabilitated, the appeals court said, should be examined seriously by a jury:

> Ideally, his neighbors should recognize his present worth and forget his past life of shame. But men are not so divine as to forgive the past trespasses of others, and plaintiff therefore endeavored to reveal as little as possible of his past life. Yet, as if in some bizarre canyon of echoes, petitioner's past life pursues him through the pages of *Reader's Digest*, now published in 13 languages and distributed in 100 nations, with a circulation in California alone of almost 2,000,000 copies.[70]

In public disclosure of private, embarrassing facts, as in much else involving the First Amendment, courts generally presume that the balance is weighted in favor of free expression. The decision of the California appeals court in *Briscoe* warns, however, that public disclosures of delicate private facts can still carry grave consequences for the privacy interests of individuals. As the court noted,

> A publisher does have every reason to know, *before* publication, that identification of a man as a former criminal will be highly offensive to the individual involved. It does not require close reading of *Les Misérables*[71] or *The Scarlet Letter*[72] to know that men are haunted by the fear of disclosure of their past and destroyed by the exposure itself.[73]

Prudent advertising and public relations professionals should recognize that dredging up an occurrence that took place decades earlier, especially if it was not a criminal matter or otherwise reported in the public record, can have dangerous consequences. This is a good place to remind the reader that, for example, a now prominent and successful businessperson might be highly embarrassed by the revelation of his or her past childhood spent in impoverished circumstances, even though disclosure of the information was intended by the communicator to convey a positive statement about the level of achievement of the subject of the publication.

## Consent Exceeded

The courts explored this sub-subcategory in *Virgil v. Time Inc.*,[74] a 1975 case arising from a lively profile of a famed body surfer, Mike Virgil, as it appeared in *Sports Illustrated*. Described as the most fearless member of a daredevil band of surfers at The Wedge, dangerous waters near Newport Beach, Calif., Virgil was apparently as uninhibited on dry land as well as in the water.

During interviews with Curry Kirkpatrick of *Sports Illustrated*, Virgil spoke freely about his private life. He recalled that he had devoured insects and spiders, extinguished a lighted cigarette inside his mouth, won a bet by burning a hole through a dollar bill with a lighted cigarette while the dollar bill rested on the back of his hand, he had never learned to read, had thrown himself down a flight of stairs at a ski resort "to impress these chicks" and periodically contrived to injure himself by "... div[ing] off billboards or drop[ping] loads on myself so that I could collect unemployment compensation so that I could surf at The Wedge."[75]

Afterward, when a fact-checker from the magazine telephoned to verify these assertions, Virgil developed second thoughts about the article. Conceding that he could not stop the magazine from disclosing information about him it had learned from others, Virgil specifically asked *Sports Illustrated* not to print anything connected with his private life that he himself had told the writer. The magazine published the piece anyway, personal details and all, and Virgil sued for invasion of privacy.

Although he eventually lost his case because of a tortured reading of the California invasion privacy statute by a federal court (the judges in California had been out in the sun far too long), the lesson to be learned is plain. If an individual reveals personal, private information about himself or herself that could generally be considered highly embarrassing if given publicity, and, if prior to publication, the individual retracts permission to use the information that was obtained solely from that individual, prudent advertising and public relations professionals should respect that withdrawal of consent and not disclose the information.

## Disclosure of Private, Embarrassing Facts in a Digital, New-Media Age: Emerging Issues

Unlike false light, disclosure of private, embarrassing facts invasion of privacy cases seem on the verge of an explosive increase as technology makes it easier to obtain, process and disseminate information many still consider to be nobody else's business. In recent cases where the defendants have prevailed, the decisions often are based on a finding that the speech in question does not constitute private facts, either because the information is already known (e.g., *Smith v. NBC Universal, et al.*[76]) or because it comes from the public record (e.g., *Mendelson v. The Morning Call, Inc.*[77]).

Non-traditional media, however, have traveled into unexplored territory in private facts cases. For example, as more consumers use their computers for shopping or online financial transactions, the protection of consumer privacy is taking center stage (data privacy issues are discussed further in later chapters). Clearly it is illegal to use private information, such as Social Security numbers or credit card numbers, to perpetrate identity theft. To avoid becoming embroiled in such actions because of lax data protection, prudent advertising and public relations professionals should engage in the latest measures to protect an individual's personal information and encourage others within their organizations to do so as well.

Government regulators also have been keeping a wary eye on such practices as tracking consumer purchases based on Google searches, implanting "cookies" on personal computers or using information gained from users of social network sites for marketing purposes. Mining user profiles for information about personal and product preferences so that ads and other commercial messages can be specifically targeted may be crossing a personal privacy line.

President Obama's pick to head the Bureau of Consumer Protection at the Federal Trade Commission promises that his agency plans to be much more aggressive in protecting consumer privacy. He has hinted that the Bureau may consider requiring Web sites that collect personal data to first obtain the consent of the consumer, policies that are very different from current industry practices. If such policies are adopted, it would mean, for example, that sites could not as readily sell advertising based on specific information about consumer use. Seeking information from openly accessed Facebook or YouTube pages (which, surprisingly, seems to come as a surprise to some youthful users), on the other hand, raises no serious potential for disclosure of private, embarrassing facts suits.

What is the safest course of action? If, traditionally, the information would be considered private and is neither known, nor available in public records (it should be noted that all government information is not, by definition, public information), prudent advertising and public relations professionals should steer a wide course away from disclosure.

More recent privacy issues that just now are beginning to wend their way through both American and foreign legal systems involve the European Union's efforts to protect personal data that, to date, go much further in protecting such information from disclosure than in the U.S. While an extensive discussion of these issues, many of which are still being fleshed out, is beyond the scope of this chapter, wise and prudent advertising and public relations professionals need to be familiar with the laws protecting private data (and how that term is defined) in countries they obviously target via their Web sites and through other new media. They should then structure their messages and data-mining techniques accordingly.

## Intrusion

The next subject of this chapter is a brief mention of the tort of *intrusion* invasion of privacy. Often referred to as the "news gathering tort," intrusion invasion of privacy is of lesser concern to advertising and public relations professionals because they typically do not engage in the types of actions, such as the use of hidden video recorders or taping telephone conversations, that are often the subject of intrusion suits.

The intrusion tort does not focus on statements that have been published which place the plaintiff in a false (and sometimes defamatory) light or disclose sensitive, personal information, but rather on the *act* of gathering information. Thus, the elements of an intrusion claim differ markedly from the other subcategories of invasion of privacy.

*Background*

The history of the development of intrusion invasion of privacy parallels the subcategories of false light and public disclosure, maturing in the latter part of the twentieth century. Today, with the advent of sophisticated electronic recording devices and computer savvy experts, intrusion invasion of privacy is becoming one of the more common causes of action involving privacy suits. The vast majority of states currently recognize some form of intrusion as a separate tort.

*Terminology*

According to the *Restatement (Second) of Torts*, intrusion is defined as:

> One who intentionally intrudes, physically or otherwise, upon the solitude or seclusion of another or his private affairs or concerns, is subject to liability to the other for invasion of privacy, if the intrusion would be highly offensive to a reasonable person.[78]

## The Elements of Intrusion

To prevail in a suit for intrusion invasion of privacy, the plaintiff must first show that: (a) an intrusive act has been committed by the defendant that is highly offensive to a reasonable person; (b) the actions of the defendant are the true cause of the actual harm suffered by the plaintiff (in this case, mental anguish); (c) the plaintiff is entitled to be compensated by money damages for that harm; and (d) the intrusive action has been done by the defendant with the required degree of fault established by law.

## Subcategories of Intrusion

The tort of intrusion invasion of privacy traditionally has been subdivided into three categories: *surreptitious surveillance* (e.g., hidden recording devices or taping telephone conversations), *trespass* (e.g., entering onto property of another for information gathering purposes) and *consent exceeded* (i.e., situations in which the defendant has gone beyond the limits of the actual or implied consent of the plaintiff).[79] Let's look briefly at each of these in turn.

## Surreptitious Surveillance

*Surreptitious surveillance* is normally associated with the use of hidden recording devices, either visual or auditory. In analyzing potential liability for surreptitious surveillance intrusion, courts generally look at three factors: (a) the plaintiff's level of legitimate expectation to be free of un-consented-to, intrusive acts; (b) the openness of the defendant; and (c) the "hidden-ness" of the recording device.

Courts have held that the highest level of legitimate expectation to be free of unconsented-to, intrusive acts is in one's place of residence. At the other extreme, courts generally have held that people have almost no legitimate expectation to be free of such acts in public places. The contentious issues involving this factor often focus on the places in between (one's office, automobile, health club locker room and so forth).

For example, in the classic case of *Dietemann v. Time, Inc.*,[80] reporters posing as a patient and the patient's friend surreptitiously recorded the activities of an unlicensed medical practitioner in Dietemann's home in an effort to obtain evidence about his alleged unauthorized practice of medicine. The defendants were found liable for intrusion invasion of privacy based on these actions.

In contrast, in *Crow v. Crawford & Co*,[81] an employer surreptitiously videotaped the activities of a worker and members of his family in a public park. The court held that this was not an intrusive act, even though the taping took place in a "wooded and secluded" area, because of the lack of legitimate expectation to be free of such an intrusive act in a public place.

Advertising and public relations professionals should think not twice, but three times before engaging in audio recording, photographing or video taping individuals in places where those individuals have a reasonable expectation to be free from intrusive acts. Although the news media are often victorious in defending intrusive acts in the process of news gathering, advertising and public relations professionals, in most circumstances, would have a much more difficult time justifying such actions. Prudent advertising and public relations professionals should have a really good reason to engage in such activities even when the potential plaintiff is in a public place.

Recording telephone conversations poses additional risks because of federal and state regulations. Although some states allow telephone recording to take place if one party has knowledge of the taping, other states require both parties to be aware. The better course of action for advertising and public relations professionals would be to always obtain consent from all parties before recording a conversation.

## Trespass

*Trespass* intrusion invasion of privacy typically involves the unauthorized entry onto the private property of another. For example, in *Quinn Emanuel Urquhart Oliver & Hedges, LLP v. LaTorraca & Goettsch*,[82] a court held in favor of the plaintiff in a trespass invasion of privacy claim involving a comedian whose shtick was gaining admittance to events without buying a ticket. After being arrested on a complaint by the Academy

Awards, the plaintiff successfully sued the Academy for trespass because private investigators, hired by the Academy, eavesdropped on the plaintiff's conversations while in an area of the plaintiff's apartment complex clearly marked as a "no trespassing" zone.

Advertising and public relations professionals have the same rights to go onto private property as any other citizen. Public relations professionals, in particular, also should be alert to the fact that in situations where reporters are demanding entrance to an organization or a client's premises, members of the news media, generally, are afforded no more, no fewer rights to enter onto private property. Therefore, it is perfectly legitimate for organizations to deny the news media access to emergency rooms, corporate operating facilities or private events, for example, even if newsworthy activities have occurred.

It also may be possible to "trespass" to information. For example, in *Bilney v. Evening Star*,[83] a newspaper published confidential information about the academic records of the University of Maryland's basketball team. Although the intrusion claim was eventually dismissed because the reporters, themselves, did not ask for, or actually observe, confidential records, clearly those who, without authorization, had access to and provided these records to the reporters would likely have been liable for an intrusion invasion of privacy claim.

The lesson is clear. Advertising and public relations professionals who are not authorized to access sensitive health, personnel or personal information should neither surreptitiously obtain records of such information, nor employ or suggest to those who are authorized that they provide them with such records.

## Consent Exceeded

This sub-subcategory of invasion of privacy usually involves individuals who go beyond the plaintiff's actual or implied consent to tolerate acts that might otherwise be regarded as intrusive. The classic case is *LeMistral, Inc. v. Columbia Broadcasting System*[84] where television reporters, with cameras running, went into a prominent restaurant for a story related to health code violations. The court held that although the restaurant was open to the public as a place of public accommodation, the defendant had vitiated the restaurant's implied invitation to the public because the defendant had not intended to purchase the products and services offered there.

More recent cases often have dealt with paparazzi photographers stalking movie stars and other entertainers or reporters attempting to obtain photographs or video of events in quasi-public view. In 2006, California put into effect an expansion of its privacy law, popularly called the "Anti-Paparazzi Act."[85] The law provides for liability for trespass for the purposes of obtaining visual images or audio recordings and provides for significant money damages from those who violate its provisions. Perhaps of more interest to advertising and public relations professionals, it holds equally liable those who direct, solicit or induce others to engage in either physical or constructive invasion of privacy.

Advertising and public relations professionals should take heed. Although potential plaintiffs initially may have consented to have their privacy intruded upon, this does not provide *carte blanche* for actions that reasonable people would consider to be overstepping the boundaries of that consent.

## Intrusion Invasion of Privacy in a Digital, New-Media Age: Emerging Issues

As communication technology grows more sophisticated, so too does the use of that technology in committing what many may see as intrusive acts. Although it may be tempting for advertising and public relations professionals to secretly video or audio record recalcitrant employees, conferences with unruly clients or participants in special events, they should fight the feeling.

The same is true for soliciting a confederate to obtain information posted on an otherwise restricted-access Facebook page, snooping into an employee's private Twitter account or accessing others' personal e-mails. All of these activities might, under some circumstances, be considered outrageously intrusive unless advertising and public relations professionals have obtained knowing, demonstrable consent and have not gone beyond that consent in their actions.

## Infliction of Emotional Distress

The final subject of this chapter is a brief mention of the tort of *infliction of emotional distress*. The issue here refers to the ability of communications to damage one's psyche. In some respects, infliction of emotional distress is much like invasion of privacy. In others, it resembles defamation. In actual practice, lawsuits have been brought alleging all three—defamation of character, invasion of privacy and infliction of emotional distress—leaving it to the courts to sort out which torts, if any, might apply in a given situation.

### Background

Until the mid-twentieth century, the law generally shied away from protecting an individual's interest in emotional and mental tranquility. As late as the mid-1930s, the *Restatement of Torts* declared:

The interest in mental and emotional tranquility and, therefore, in freedom from mental and emotional disturbance is not, as a thing in itself, regarded as of sufficient importance to require others to refrain from conduct intended or recognizably likely to cause such disturbance.[86]

Beginning in the 1940s, however, courts began to recognize that sometimes mental distress can be so extreme as to bring on physical or mental illness, and a person intentionally subjecting another to such intense mental suffering can be found liable for the harm that results.

Today, the majority of states have adopted some form of this tort. Some states have incorporated infliction of emotional distress into their defamation or privacy laws, whereas others regard infliction of emotional distress as a separate wrong, particularly in situations where a public disclosure of private, embarrassing facts case is not appropriate because the facts, although of such a nature to cause mental distress, are not private.

### Terminology

Today the *Restatement (Second) of Torts* recognizes the tort of infliction of emotional distress. According to the *Restatement*:

One who by extreme or outrageous conduct intentionally or recklessly causes severe emotional distress to another is subject to liability

(a)  for such emotional distress, and

(b)  if bodily harm to the other results from it, for such bodily harm.[87]

## The Elements of Infliction of Emotional Distress

Before awarding a judgment in an infliction of emotional distress suit, a court must be satisfied that: (a) a statement has been made that offends ordinary decency; (b) the offending material must be shown to at least one other person by the defendant; (c) the plaintiff has been identified in the statement; (d) the actions of the defendant are the true cause of the actual harm suffered by the plaintiff (in this case, emotional distress); (e) the plaintiff is entitled to be compensated by money damages for that harm; and (f) the distressing statements appeared because the defendant has done all this with the required degree of fault established by law. Most jurisdictions recognize only intentional actions as the fault standard, but a growing number are also allowing a claim of negligent behavior in appropriate circumstances.

Because the elements of emotional distress resemble the elements of defamation if the statements are false and disclosure of private, embarrassing facts invasion of privacy if the statements are true, it would be redundant to discuss them in detail. Rather, a number of examples should be sufficient to illustrate these elements.

## Examples of Emotional Distress

Cases alleging infliction of emotional distress have been brought in situations involving excommunication from a church, religious harassment and religious shunning,[88] hounding for collection of an overdue bill,[89] a false report that the plaintiff was suffering from a fatal illness[90] and even an unexpected eviction notice.[91] In more recent years, a number of cases have arisen directly out of mass media-related situations, and thus in recent years infliction of emotional distress has become another tort affecting mass communications professionals.

The most famous case in this area, involving statements alleged to be false, was decided by the Supreme Court in *Hustler Magazine v. Falwell*.[92] The key players were the Rev. Jerry Falwell—a nationally known minister, commentator on public affairs and leader of The Moral Majority, a conservative action group—and Larry Flynt, publisher of the irreverent and often-raunchy magazine, *Hustler*.

The inside front cover of *Hustler's* November 1983 issue contained what the magazine referred to as a "parody" of a Campari Liquor advertisement featuring the name and picture of Mr. Falwell. Entitled "Jerry Falwell Talks About His First Time," the format resembled actual Campari ads in which celebrities recounted their "first times" of sampling the liquor. *Hustler* being *Hustler*, one may imagine what the rest of the ad contained. In tiny print at the bottom of the offending page was a disclaimer that read, "ad parody—not to be taken seriously."[93]

Falwell, however, did take it seriously, filing lawsuits for libel, invasion of privacy and intentional infliction of emotional distress. A Virginia judge summarily threw out the invasion of privacy claim and the trial jury found against Mr. Falwell on the libel allegation. But the jury did award Falwell a total of $200,000 on the intentional infliction of emotional distress claim.[94] The Federal Court of Appeals affirmed the judgment.[95]

The Supreme Court, however, reversed, holding that to punish a media defendant for its parody of a public figure such as Mr. Falwell could effectively silence political cartoonists, satirists and others who attempt to poke fun at public personalities, and curtail the free flow of ideas and opinions on matters of public interest and concern. The unanimous opinion, written by Chief Justice Rehnquist, conceded that the parody of Mr. Falwell was "offensive to him, and doubtless gross and repugnant in the eyes of most," but insisted that the members of the Court "have been particularly vigilant to ensure that individual expressions of ideas remain free from governmentally imposed sanctions. The First Amendment recognizes no such thing as a 'false' idea."[96]

Because of this, public officials and public figures—as defined in *Sullivan* and *Gertz* (see Chapter 4)—cannot win an intentional infliction of emotional distress lawsuit alleging false statements without showing actual malice. Early indications are that courts may hold private plaintiffs to a lesser standard in such cases in years to come, but this remains an open question.

Infliction of emotional distress cases that are complaining about true but distressing facts are equally difficult to win, especially if they involve a mass media defendant. For example, consider *Hood v. Naeter Brothers Publishing Co.*[97] *The Southwest Missourian*, a newspaper in Cape Girardeau, published the name and address, accurately taken from police reports, of Hood, an eyewitness to a liquor store robbery in which one person was killed. At the time, the suspects were still at large. Hood sued the newspaper, stating that as a result of the publication he had lived in constant fear, had to change his residence repeatedly and had had to submit to the care of a psychiatrist.

The information published by the newspaper was not injurious to reputation, it did not cast him in a false light and the court determined that the information disclosed about Hood were not private, embarrassing facts. Hood sued for infliction of emotional distress, claiming that the newspaper knew, or should have known, that his exposure as an eyewitness while the killers were still at large constituted outrageous behavior.

Both the trial court and the court of appeals ruled in favor of the newspaper. As the appeals court noted:

> The liability [for infliction of emotional distress] clearly does not extend to mere insults, indignities, threats, arrogancies, petty oppression, or other trivialities. The rough edges of our society are still in need of a good deal of filing down, and in the meantime plaintiffs must necessarily be expected and required to be hardened to a certain amount of rough language, and to occasional acts that are definitely inconsiderate and unkind.[98]

Cases of more relevance to advertising and public relations professionals include a former employee suing the defendant city agency personnel for statements made about the reason for his termination, a teacher complaining about her public treatment by school authorities during an investigation of violation of testing standards and harassing behavior by a mortgage company threatening home foreclosure. Either linking individuals to products or services they may abhor or providing information of a derogatory, if truthful, nature about individuals to the media may give rise to emotional distress cases as well as false light or private facts suits.

Although infliction of emotional distress cases are difficult to win against media defendants, advertising and public relations professionals should recognize that their communications may not always be treated by courts as meeting the definition of media. The Supreme Court and lower courts have consistently differentiated between media and non-media defendants and, just as consistently, provided less protection for non-media defendants.

## Infliction of Emotional Distress in a Digital, New-Media Age: Emerging Issues

Like false light and disclosure of private, embarrassing facts, the prognostication for the future of infliction of emotional distress lawsuits is for more of the same. Particularly because of the intemperate, if not vituperative, nature of many communications found on social networking sites, blogs and Web sites that invite users to post comments on points of interest of the day, outraged and aggrieved individuals who are the subjects of such communications may turn more and more to the courts to seek a remedy for the dissemination of information they argue has caused emotional distress. Public relations professionals, in particular, should be extremely vigilant to protect themselves and their organizations or clients from releasing the kinds of information or taking the kinds of actions related to their employees, competitors or critics that could provoke these types of lawsuits.

Commercial speakers should also beware of the increasing frequency of so-called "outrage" or copycat suits arising from claims of harm based on actions taken by plaintiffs encouraged by the media to engage in risky behaviors. For example, in *Strange v. Entercom Sacramento LLC*,[99] a radio station was assessed a more than $16 million damages award when a contestant in a station-sponsored contest later died after ingesting a lethal quantity of water.

Whether depicting drivers performing feats of daring-do in an automobile ad or sponsoring or conducting wacky promotional schemes, prudent advertising and public relations professionals should take steps to ensure that children or gullible adults are strongly discouraged from attempting to duplicate what they have seen and that they are not exposed to potential harm caused by participation in an event.

# Chapter 6

# Invasion of Privacy

## Misappropriation and Right of Publicity

This chapter focuses on the tort of *misappropriation* invasion of privacy and its offshoot, the right of publicity. Both involve the non-consented use of a person's name or likeness, often for commercial purposes. The cause of action differs somewhat depending upon whether the plaintiff is a private individual who is mentally anguished about the non-permitted use or a celebrity who wishes to be compensated when his or her name or likeness was used without permission.

## Misappropriation Background

When Warren and Brandeis were advancing their radical ideas for the *Harvard Law Review*[1] more than 100 years ago, they probably were not thinking in terms of misappropriation as a factor in their proposed right. Yet misappropriation cases were among the first to be presented as invasions of privacy. Over the years, such exploitation has become a major aspect of the ever-evolving laws of privacy and publicity.

The first attempts to recover monetary damages in misappropriation cases were not successful, although one plaintiff, an actress, was able to stop publication of a picture of her in a costume she thought to be scandalous.[2] Among the most famous of the early misappropriation cases was that of Abigail Roberson of Albany, N.Y., whose picture, published without her consent, appeared in 1902 on thousands of posters advertising Franklin Mills Flour. The attractive young woman, mortified at seeing pictures of her splashed across the city and with the accompanying copy describing her as "the flour of the family," brought suit for what she regarded as an invasion of privacy.

The New York Court of Appeals, in *Roberson v. Rochester Folding Box Co.*,[3] rejected the arguments that had been advanced by Warren and Brandeis and issued a majority opinion insisting that:

> ... an examination of the authorities leads us to the conclusion that the so-called "right of privacy" has not yet found an abiding place in our

jurisprudence, and, as we view it, the doctrine cannot now be incorporated without doing violence to settled principles of law by which
the profession and the public have long been guided.[4]

This ruling, allowing Miss Roberson no relief for what had clearly been
commercial exploitation of her physical appearance, touched off a
firestorm in the next session of the New York State legislature and, in 1903,
led to the passage of a statute making it both a criminal offense (a misdemeanor) and a civil wrong to make use of the name or likeness of an individual for "advertising purposes or for the purposes of trade" without first
obtaining written consent.[5] The new law permitted the person whose privacy had been invaded to seek monetary damages as well as an injunction
to halt further publication of the offensive material. This statute, which
later became part of the New York Civil Rights Law, was the first ever to
deal with the right of privacy, and it remains on the books to this day.

   The first common-law acceptance of the right of privacy came two years
after *Roberson* by the Georgia Supreme Court in 1904. An insurance company's advertising featured the name and picture of an Atlanta artist,
Paolo Pavesich. The ad copy also presented a testimonial, falsely attributed to him, as to the value of having a sound insurance portfolio. Pavesich
sued for $25,000 and won. The Georgia Supreme Court expressly rejected
the New York decision regarding Abigail Roberson and endorsed the earlier views of Warren and Brandeis:

> [t]he form and features of the plaintiff [Pavesich] are his own. The
> defendant insurance company and its agents had no more authority to
> display them in public for purposes of advertising . . . than they would
> have had to compel the plaintiff to place himself upon exhibition for
> this purpose.[6]

Once the misappropriation right of privacy was accepted in *Pavesich*,
most other jurisdictions—but by no means all—began to follow suit. For
example, a Washington court came down hard on an advertiser who used
a customer's name as an endorsement without permission: "Nothing so
exclusively belongs to a man or is so personal and valuable to him as his
name. . . . Others have no right to use it without his express consent, and
he has the right to go into any court at any time to enjoin or prohibit any
unauthorized use of it."[7] Today, the vast majority of states have adopted
some form of misappropriation and the right of publicity.

### Terminology

The *Restatement of Torts (Second)*, much referred to in this book, defines
misappropriation and the right of publicity as:

One who appropriates to his own use or benefit the name or likeness of another is subject to liability to the other for invasion of privacy.[8]

The key to understanding the tort of invasion of privacy by misappropriation is that it requires exploitation by another for purposes of trade or other benefit. The injury is personal.

## Elements of Misappropriation and the Right of Publicity

Although the specifics are defined somewhat differently from state to state, generally the individual hoping to present a solid case that he or she should be victorious in a misappropriation case must first demonstrate that: (a) statements that appropriate the plaintiff's identity or an identity licensed to or in other ways belonging to some other individual or organization bringing the lawsuit have been made; (b) the offending material has been shown to other persons by the defendant; (c) the plaintiff has been identified in the statements; (d) the actions of the defendant are the true cause of the actual harm suffered by the plaintiff; (e) the plaintiff is entitled to be compensated by money damages for that harm; and (f) the statements appeared because the defendant has done all this with the required degree of fault established by law. Let's take a closer look at each of these points in turn.

## Misappropriation Statement

The statement at the center of the misappropriation complaint must contain information about the plaintiff used in such a way that reasonable people would find offensive if it happened to them. Misappropriation in such cases often involves the use of a person's name, likeness or persona in a manner that offends, or in other ways upsets, the plaintiff.

Consider two hypothetical examples. First, Joe Piscoonyak works at Old Sandlapper Brewing Company and indeed consumes a substantial quantity of Old Sandlapper beer. Without his knowledge or consent, your photographer takes a photograph of Joe headed for the checkout stand in a local supermarket, his shopping cart filled with cartons of Old Sandlapper. The photograph is subsequently published as part of an advertisement and in a company promotional brochure. Although the photograph truthfully depicts his enthusiastic choice of brews, and despite the fact that he is an employee of the company, you have nevertheless invaded Joe's privacy by appropriating his likeness.

Second, Sally Sunshine's engagement picture, a splendid photographic portrait, is displayed without her knowledge and consent in the window of the photographer's studio as an example of the superior quality of work done by that studio. The work is indeed of admirable quality, yet Miss Sunshine's privacy similarly has been invaded.

These two hypothetical situations, and the thousands of actual cases that could be employed as real-life examples, should alert the reader to the care that should be exercised before using any public or private individual's name or likeness without permission, even if the use is by a not-for-profit organization. The reader should remember that the basis of a claim for invasion of privacy by misappropriation may not be because of concern about *what* was said or published, but rather that anything was said or published about the complainant *at all*. "Leave me alone" is the essence of this tort.

## Publication

While technically publication occurs the moment a third person has seen the communication, the offending message must typically reach a broad audience, rather than just a few, to be actionable. Many jurisdictions refer to publication as giving "publicity" to the misappropriated information.

Like defamation, a misappropriation invasion of privacy plaintiff often has a relatively easy time demonstrating that publication has occurred. This is because the defendant advertising agency or public relations department has disseminated the information to thousands, if not millions, of readers or viewers in network television advertising, press release material published in hundreds of news outlets or in campaigns on YouTube, Facebook or other social networking sites.

## Identification

The plaintiff in a misappropriation privacy case must meet virtually the same requirements as a defamation plaintiff to prove that an audience of concern to the plaintiff (e.g., fellow employees) believes that the statements are about him or her. Identification is often not difficult for the plaintiff because the defendant, as a professional communicator, has clearly identified the subjects in the communications.

The tort of misappropriation is limited to individuals if the claim involves a private person because organizations cannot demonstrate they have suffered mental anguish about the published information. However, if a celebrity has in some way conveyed the rights to the use of his or her name, likeness or persona to an organization, that organization can bring a misappropriation right of publicity claim for the loss of financial income attributable to the unauthorized use by the defendant.

## Causation

The plaintiffs in a misappropriation privacy suit must allege and prove that the actions of the defendant were the logical and proximate cause of the claimed injury. Often this is easily accomplished because the plaintiffs, if private citizens, are simply charging that they have understandably suffered mental anguish when the defendant outrageously misappropriated their names or likenesses and the results have been seen by acquaintances or clients or customers. Celebrity plaintiffs, similarly, may have an easy time if the misappropriation claim simply involves a complaint that their names have been linked to activities the celebrities find distasteful.

Problems proving causation might arise when private plaintiffs are complaining about the misuse of their identity in situations where, in the minds of a judge or jury, they have not suffered mental anguish severe enough to warrant compensation. Celebrities may experience difficulty in proving causation if their claims involve complaints of economic harm because they may find it difficult to provide evidence that the value of their endorsement appeal has declined or that they have been cheated out of potential income because of the actions of the defendant.

## Compensation

A private plaintiff seeking compensation for harm to his or her mental well-being resulting from misappropriation of his or her identity generally will be entitled to seek four different kinds of monetary awards. These are *nominal* damages, *special* damages, *actual* damages (in some jurisdictions, the second and third awards are sometimes combined and called "general" or "compensatory" damages) and *punitive* (or "exemplary") damages.

For a plaintiff to seek a small or *nominal* damage award is relatively rare in misappropriation cases. More typically, a private plaintiff, actually seeking a large sum to compensate for the supposed harm, is found by a judge or jury to have suffered no real harm and, therefore, not deserving of more than a nominal award of damages. The same is true for celebrities.

To obtain *special* damages, often thought of as "out-of-pocket dollar loss," plaintiffs must produce evidence sufficient to prove that the misappropriation of identity cost the plaintiff a demonstrable monetary loss. Expenses for psychiatric care, counseling services or prescribed medications, as well as evidence of wages lost or other financial reverses because the plaintiff was too upset to function normally, are examples of special damages often claimed by private plaintiffs. Celebrity plaintiffs, normally, are seeking reimbursement either for expenses linked to their mental anguish that are similar to a private plaintiff or for losses to their financial balance sheet (e.g., "I charge $10,000 for a product endorsement").

The third category of damages, *actual* damage, requires no proof of actual monetary loss. However, all plaintiffs must demonstrate that the alleged mental anguish caused by the misappropriation does, in fact, exist. In jurisdictions that ask for some evidence of mental anguish, plaintiffs seeking actual damages, typically, in addition to their own testimony, introduce testimony from friends and medical and/or counseling professionals about psychic damages. It should be noted that these damages are only available to a celebrity who is claiming mental anguish in addition to financial loss.

If a judge or jury accepts that the harm has occurred and the defendant has no additional defenses, money will be awarded to the plaintiff as compensation based on the judge or jury's estimation of the harm—an invitation for large damage awards for the plaintiff. The possibility of such large verdicts should be all the impetus needed for advertising and public relations professionals to take all possible precautions to avoid becoming embroiled in a misappropriation suit.

*Punitive* damages, generally, are awarded when the defendant's actions are so outrageous that they offend the conscience of judges or juries. In a private misappropriation invasion of privacy suit, punitive damages might be awarded if the misappropriation was done in a way that was considered outrageous and shocking (e.g., purposely linking the plaintiff to a controversial product). Punitive damages in celebrity misappropriation cases might be awarded either because the celebrity is linked to an outrageous activity, or has severely damaged the plaintiff's ability to capitalize on his or her own celebrity status. Like actual damages, punitive damage awards can reach mega-amounts in misappropriation suits and are as dangerous, if not more so, to defendants.

## Defendant Fault

Fault in tort law often is defined as an error in judgment or conduct, such as negligence or any departure from normal care because of inattention, carelessness or incompetence. However, in misappropriation invasion of privacy, the majority of states and state courts have decreed that the fault required is intentional or purposeful action, while others go further to mandate a fault standard that resembles common law malice (i.e., the taking of the name or likeness was an intentional act designed to harm the plaintiff).

## Affirmative Defenses

Once a misappropriation privacy plaintiff has made a *prima facie* case—a statement appropriating the name or likeness of another without consent, publication, identification and so forth—the other side must mount a defense. Affirmative defenses include *personal consent, property releases, incidental use, transformative use, satire, parody* and *newsworthiness.*

New York's ground-breaking Right of Privacy law says, in part:

> [a]ny person whose name, portrait or picture is used within this state for advertising purposes or for the purposes of trade without . . . written consent . . . may maintain an equitable action in the supreme court of this state against the person, firm or corporation so using his name, portrait or picture, to prevent and restrain the use thereof, and may also sue and recover damages for an injuries by reason of such use. . . .[9]

Experienced public relations practitioners and advertising professionals know the value of obtaining signed *personal consent* on release forms from their subjects and to ensure that those they hire to obtain or create information (e.g., a freelance videographer) obtain them as well. A photograph used purely for news reporting purposes does not require consent (this issue is discussed further later in this chapter). However, if the news organization reprints or sells the photo for later use in advertising or promotional materials, the newsworthiness defense might not apply, and some additional protection—in the form of a signed consent—may be necessary.

A photographer attempting to freelance a picture or a freelance writer seeking to market an article will find that a signed release to accompany the material will make it more marketable. An example of a tightly drawn sample model release is shown in Appendix D. Most professional photographers and writers routinely carry around pads of such blank release or consent forms to use as needed. Other, simpler versions of a release form may also be used; there is no single, uniform standardized release.

The consent form allows the person who is being used for commercial purposes to decide how much right of privacy to give up and on what terms. Even so, problems with consent can arise. The following are ways to avert some of them:

(a) The consent should be written. A number of states do not recognize oral agreements or handshakes where misappropriation lawsuits are concerned.
(b) It should be understandable to persons of average intelligence.
(c) The person giving the consent must be a competent adult. Minors—people under 18 years of age—cannot sign consent forms that are legally binding; a parent or guardian must sign the consent form on their behalf.

This latter point was sorely tested in prolonged litigation in New York by the actress Brooke Shields and her mother during the 1980s. At the age of

10, Ms. Shields posed semi-nude for a picture story that appeared in a Playboy Press book, *Sugar and Spice*. Her mother had signed the appropriate consent forms. Five years later, however, Ms. Shields, by then a promising young actress, had attained a measure of notoriety and the owner of the consent forms marketed the photos to other magazines, at least one of which published them with the caption "Brooke Shields Naked." Mrs. Shields sued and, in a complex series of trials, ultimately lost. The consent forms she had signed took away her and her daughter's rights to recovery.[10]

In some cases, the consent may become invalid. In a 1961 Louisiana case, a health spa owner obtained written consent to use photographs of a customer, Cole McAndrews, to illustrate the before-and-after effects of a rigorous exercise program. However, the health spa owner waited for 10 years before deciding to use the photos. During that time, the physical condition of McAndrews had deteriorated more than somewhat. He presumably resembled the "before" rather than the "after" photos. Thus, the health spa ads featuring his photos subjected him to a certain amount of embarrassment, and he sued. The trial judge was sympathetic, noting that, under the circumstances, the permission forms McAndrews had signed should have been renewed.[11]

If there is no consideration—something of value given in return for the consent—the consent can be withdrawn before the photographs are published. The consideration may be payment of as little as $1, or it may be something else of value. Without "valuable consideration," a consent form, as with other types of contracts, can be difficult to enforce.

Finally, if the photos are altered or the context in which they are used is materially changed from what the model thought it would be, the consent may not be binding. Retouching the photo, changing the background scene or using the photo to advertise one product when the model believed it to be another can effectively undermine a consent agreement. In an era when digital imaging makes it possible to alter photographs easily, this point becomes especially important.

The American Magazine Photographers Association offers its members this useful nuts-and-bolts advice:

1    Get a release whenever possible.
2    If you do not have a release, and if a person could be recognized by anyone, retouch the face and/or figure to eliminate all possibility of recognition when people might appear in: (a) paid ads; (b) promotional matter; or (c) any published use that could be deemed embarrassing or in incorrect context (no matter how remote).[12]

Similar to obtaining a release from individuals before using their name or likeness, it is also a good idea to obtain a *property release* from the owners of buildings and other real estate that might be used in photographs for advertising or other trade purposes. These owners do not have a "right of privacy" as such to be invaded by such photos, but courts have determined that there are property rights that cannot be unjustly exploited for commercial purposes. Property releases, signed by the owners or agents for the owners, may be needed for photographs of such places.

If the building is merely incidental or part of the background—a photograph of a street scene or other public gathering place—a property release probably is not necessary. Although most buildings in public places can be safely photographed and used in advertisements, there have been instances of successful claims that the photographs in an advertisement of an identifiable building in a public location constituted a legal infringement of the owner's property rights. Property rights can be and have been extended to owners of animals when the animals have been photographed for purposes of trade without the owner's consent. Again, specific consent forms signed by the owners should be obtained.[13]

As a general rule, use of names and likenesses in news contexts are protected, whereas use of names and likenesses in press releases, promotional materials and advertising messages may not be. Sometimes the distinctions are blurred. Professional football legend Joe Namath brought suit in 1976 against *Sports Illustrated* claiming that the use of his photograph, which had been on the magazine's cover, was actually intended as advertising and promotional materials to attract new readers. The New York Jets quarterback's claim was rejected when the court held that this was "*incidental use*" of his photograph to illustrate the "quality and content" of the publication and that this was a "necessary and logical extension" of the otherwise newsworthy photograph.[14]

If the photograph had been used in a manner to suggest that Namath was personally endorsing the magazine, however, the photograph would likely have been found to be misappropriation. The same reasoning applies to public relations messages, particularly in the preparation of employee publications.

Another factor to be considered in determining incidental use is whether the use of an individual's photo is sufficiently related to the commercial use as to constitute misappropriation. For example, a crowd shot to illustrate an advertisement may indeed have identifiable faces in it. If these faces are merely that—faces—and otherwise immaterial to the selling message, it is unlikely that a misappropriation action could be won by any of the individuals depicted in the photo. Again, it is the identity of the individual, not merely the incidental use of it, which must be appropriated. So long as these people are not shown as specifically endorsing the product in the ad, and so long as their presence is incidental to—and not directly supportive of—the selling message, an action for invasion of privacy would likely not succeed.

Recently, courts have begun dismissing misappropriation claims on the basis that the allegedly infringing use created a *"transformative"* work. In *Comedy III Productions Inc. v. Gary Saderup Inc.*,[15] the California Supreme Court, while upholding plaintiff's claim that use of images of The Three Stooges on T-shirts was actionable, noted that courts should balance the plaintiff's publicity interests against an "affirmative defense that the [disputed] work is protected by the First Amendment [if] it contains significant [artistic] transformative elements" that makes it a new creative effort.[16]

This was true for golfer Tiger Woods, who sued an artist for selling prints of a painting depicting past winners of a major golf tournament with Woods' likeness as the predominant image. A federal appeals court held that not only was the work of art a transformative creation protected under the First Amendment, but that the painting and prints artistically depicted historic events and the inclusion of Woods' image was an incidental use.[17] Note, however, that the use of the painting as an illustration in an advertisement for golf clubs might have produced a very different result.

Artistic "transformation" may be in the eyes of the beholder. Former hockey player Anthony "Tony Twist" Twistelli sued the creators of a comic book series after they gave his nickname to a character portrayed as a mafia don. The trial court in Missouri employed a "predominant use" test to find that the combination of the specific marketing of the comic books to hockey fans and admitting that the comic book character was named after Twistelli (both he and the character were considered toughguy "enforcers") were enough to demonstrate that the plaintiff's publicity rights had been violated. A jury award of $15 million was upheld on appeal, suggesting that perhaps comic books were not thought to merit an artistic transformative defense.[18]

The bottom line is that truly artistic or trivial uses of names or likenesses most likely will not constitute misappropriation or right of publicity invasion of privacy. Still, if there is any doubt about using a photograph showing a number of identifiable likenesses for commercial purposes, it may be a good idea to find another way to illustrate the concept. Either that or obtain consent to use the names and/or likenesses in this commercial context. Consent provides protection, but only if the consent is properly obtained and not exceeded.

Entertainers who make their living by performing impressions of celebrities in nightclubs or in media appearances generally are immune from right-of-publicity suits by the celebrities they imitate. This exception also protects late-night television comics, parachuting Elvis Presley look-alikes and satirists of contemporary social and political figures. It should be clear, however, that this defense of *satire* or *parody* would not hold up if these imitators use their talents to promote the commercial interests of others. Thus it would be perfectly acceptable, from a legal perspective, for the impressionist Rich Little to imitate the distinctive speaking voice of the actor John Wayne as part of Little's act, but not to perform such a vocal impersonation as part of a commercial to sell a particular brand of soft drink.

In addition, particularly in the case of impressionists who attempt to physically resemble a celebrity, the performer should take care not to create a performance that, in effect, duplicates all or a sizable portion of the original celebrity's act or to make use of symbols or images associated with the real celebrity in promoting the impressionist's performances.

Individuals cannot prevent publication of their names when they take part or become involved in the news or a public event. In matters "concerning *newsworthy* events or matters of public interest,"[19] the news media's right to inform the public will take precedence over an individual's right to privacy. A Kentucky resident, an innocent bystander at the scene of a brutal knife assault, sued when a local newspaper published a photograph of the incident. The Kentucky Supreme Court held that the man's privacy had not been unjustly violated:

> [t]he right of privacy is the right to live one's life in seclusion, without being subjected to unwarranted and undesired publicity. In short, it is the right to be left alone. . . . There are times, however, when one, whether willing or not, becomes an actor in an occurrence of public or general interest. When this takes place, he emerges from his seclusion, and it is not an invasion of his right or privacy to publish his photograph with an account of such occurrence.[20]

Thus, a name or photo of a person involved in a newsworthy situation may be used without that person's permission. This holds true despite the fact that most newspapers, magazines and broadcast stations are commercial enterprises attempting to make a profit. The primary consideration in newsworthiness is the attempt to inform the public about matters of general interest. The profit motive—that of selling newspapers or increasing audience share for advertising purposes—is regarded as secondary. The *Restatement of Torts (Second)* puts it this way:

> [t]he value of the plaintiff's name is not appropriated by mere mention of it, or by reference to it in connection with legitimate mention of his public activities. . . . The fact that the defendant is engaged in the business of publication, for example of a newspaper, out of which he makes a profit, is not enough to make the incidental publication a commercial use of the name or likeness.[21]

Much depends, however, on how the material is used. A photograph might be newsworthy in one context, but appropriation in another. For example, a Page 1 photograph of a victim of a hit-and-run driver would obviously be considered newsworthy. However, that same photo used in an advertisement to promote the newspaper's photographic talents as a reason to subscribe to the paper might well invade the victim's privacy.

Consider two other examples. First, a Sunday supplement news feature on spring styles, accompanied by photos of fashion models, would likely be newsworthy. The same photos in trade advertisements would not be protected. Second, a spectacular photograph taken in New York City's Times Square of a sailor kissing a nurse in celebration of the end of World War II could safely appear in *Life* magazine as being newsworthy. The same photo, reproduced and sold as a poster, would not.[22]

From the beginnings of privacy law, courts have recognized the conflict between an individual's desire for privacy and the public's concern about being informed. In the landmark *Pavesich* case, the Georgia Supreme Court held that it believed the right of privacy to be a natural right, recognized by "the law of nature."[23] But it also warned that enforcing an individual's right of privacy could "inevitably tend to curtail the liberty of speech and of the press," which, the court said, is also a natural right. "It will therefore be seen," the court predicted, "that the right of privacy must in some particulars yield to the right of speech and of the press."[24] This has proved to be the case.

Traditionally, the news media's most useful defense against invasion of privacy lawsuits has been the concept of "newsworthiness." But reports in the news media are very different, insofar as privacy laws are concerned, compared to advertising and public relations messages. Newsworthiness as a defense may be of little benefit whatsoever to an advertising agency or corporate public relations department threatened with a misappropriation invasion of privacy lawsuit.

## The Right of Publicity

Although misappropriation is designed to protect everyone, the *right of publicity* has evolved primarily to protect celebrities' hard-won fame—as reflected in their names, likenesses and voices—from unauthorized exploitation. The right of publicity has developed as an offshoot of a combination of misappropriation, the laws of unfair competition and protecting property rights as well. About half of the states expressly recognize the right of publicity by statute, while at least 14 others have accepted it as a part of the common law. In some states, the rights of privacy and publicity are merged to protect private citizens and celebrities alike under one common-law tort of "appropriation of name or likeness."[25]

The landmark ruling in right of publicity law is *Haelan Laboratories v. Topps Chewing Gum.*[26] This 1953 case involved major league baseball players who had consented to "an exclusive license" with a bubblegum company to publish their photographs on baseball cards. When a second company wanted to use some of the same players' photos, a lawsuit ensued. At issue was whether the players' rights to privacy could be assigned to a third party, the company with the license. The court of appeals held that the rights, under these circumstances, had economic value and could be protected as such. Judge Jerome Frank, in writing the opinion, described this unique characteristic as the "right of publicity."[27]

In numerous cases since that time, the right of publicity has become more clearly defined. Although much like misappropriation, it is different in a number of respects. In misappropriation, the nature of the damages is personal; it results in mental anguish, embarrassment, indignity or emotional distress. Celebrities have feelings too, of course, but in rights of publicity cases, the damage is largely economic. Not unlike copyright or patent law, the right of publicity allows these individuals to reap the rewards of their endeavors. The right of publicity often has less to do with emotional distress and more to do with protecting one's commercial interests as a celebrity.

The mass media and society have conferred celebrity status on vast numbers of people: film and TV stars, rock musicians, ballplayers, authors, fashion designers and a great many others. To these individuals, celebrity status has profound economic implications; unauthorized use of the names or images of the famous is, in effect, a form of thievery. Although police and prosecutors are unlikely to get involved in such cases, private attorneys can and do file lawsuits to protect their celebrity clients' interests.

This fast-moving area of the law, pursued with vigor by celebrities and their agents, has important consequences for advertisers, public relations specialists and promoters. The law is clear. Trading on the celebrity status of public people for commercial purposes without their express permission could prove to be a costly mistake that should never be made.

The right of privacy is essentially an individual matter, whereas the right of publicity is recognized in some jurisdictions as having a commercial life even after the death of the celebrity, unlike the right of privacy which is limited to living people.[28] Examples of such deceased celebrities who have achieved commercial life after death include John Wayne, Fred Astaire, Elvis Presley, Kurt Cobain and Michael Jackson. In the case of *Martin Luther King, Jr., Center for Social Change vs. American Heritage Products*,[29] the Georgia Supreme Court noted that a right of publicity survived the death of Dr. King even though he had never exploited his fame for commercial purposes during his lifetime.

## Celebrity Identification through Use of Name, Likeness or "Persona"

Increasingly, courts are willing to entertain claims based on the unauthorized use of a celebrity's likeness even where the person's image has not been used or might previously have been thought to be unrecognizable—in other words, a perception that the likeness is that of a Michael Jackson, a Muhammad Ali or a Vanna White. This reference by "persona," or that which brings to mind an individual even if no name or actual likeness is present, can encompass the protection of a nickname if the person associated with it can prove that someone else was using it for commercial gain, as the former University of Wisconsin and professional football star "Crazy Legs" Hirsch proved in a lawsuit against the maker of "Crazy Legs" pantyhose.[30]

Muhammad Ali, the former heavyweight-boxing champion, won an injunction to halt further publication in *Playgirl* magazine of a frontally nude black male sitting in a corner of a boxing ring. This was a drawing, not a photograph, but the face resembled that of Ali and the accompanying text referred to the figure as *The Greatest*—a term Ali had often used to describe himself in promoting boxing matches. In this context, the court held the nickname and likeness were indeed identified with Ali in the public mind and thus could be protected from unauthorized use.[31]

In some ways, such unauthorized use may be regarded as *deception*—akin to a violation of the Lanham Act that prohibits unfair competition (the Lanham Act,[32] as well as infringement on copyrighted material, is discussed at length in other chapters). In one such case, a court found that the likeness of a model used in promoting a video rental store looked enough like the actor and director Woody Allen to cause confusion in the minds of customers. The ad implied that Woody Allen was, in some fashion, involved with the video rental operation or endorsing it. Indeed, as New York's Chief Justice Motley wrote, the imitation in the advertising photograph was highly specific, portraying:

> a customer in a National Video Store, an individual in his forties, with a high forehead, tousled hair, and heavy black glasses ... his face, bearing an expression at once quizzical and somewhat smug, is leaning on his hand.... The features and pose are characteristic of the plaintiff. The staging of the photograph also evokes associations with plaintiff. Sitting on the counter are videotape cassettes of *Annie Hall* and *Bananas*, two of plaintiff's best-known films, as well as *Casablanca* and *The Maltese Falcon*. The latter two are Humphrey Bogart films of the 1940's associated with plaintiff primarily because of his play and film, "Play It Again, Sam," in which the spirit of Bogart appears to the character played by Allen and offers him romantic advice. In addition, the title "Play It Again, Sam" is a famous, although inaccurate, quotation from *Casablanca*.

> The individual in the advertisement is holding up a National Video V. I. P. Card, which apparently entitles the bearer to favorable terms on movie rentals. The woman behind the counter is smiling at the cus-

tomer and appears to be gasping in exaggerated excitement at the presence of a celebrity.[33]

Allen's objections, the court decided, were well founded. The comedian/film star/writer/director seemed to be personally offended. In Judge Motley's words, Allen, "to paraphrase Groucho Marx, wouldn't belong to any video club that would have him as a member."[34]

In *Onassis v. Christian Dior-New York, Inc.*,[35] a court found that an advertising photograph of a fictional wedding scene, where some of the guests were real celebrities, featured a model who too closely resembled Jacqueline Kennedy Onassis. She was able to get the advertisement stopped. Particularly hurtful to the defendant's case was the fact that the fashion photographer had specifically asked the modeling agency for a Jackie Kennedy look-alike. When photographed with the real-life celebrities, the model gave the advertisement a persuasive illusion of authenticity. Justice Edward J. Greenfield wrote:

> [d]efendants knew there was little or no likelihood that Mrs. Onassis would ever consent to be depicted in this kind of advertising campaign for Dior. She has asserted in her affidavit, and it is well known, that she has never permitted her name or picture to be used in connection with the promotion of commercial products. . . . [36]

The woman who had posed for the picture, a secretary named Barbara Reynolds, argued that she could not be prevented from using her own face. But the court held otherwise. "Where [the] use [of one's own face] is done in such a way as to be deceptive or promote confusion," the court said, "that use can be enjoined."[37]

To win a right of publicity case, a celebrity must convince a court that the defendant has benefited financially from the association with the celebrity. The association need not always be explicit. In *Cher v. Forum International, Ltd.*,[38] the singer won a substantial judgment on the basis of an interview article that was promoted as her personal endorsement of the magazine. The article, developed by a freelancer, was originally planned for *Us* magazine. Cher, who had stipulated before granting the interview that she wanted to approve any additional uses of the material, was unhappy with the way the interview had gone and requested the editors of *Us* not to use it. When the editors agreed, the freelancer then sold copies of the tape-recorded interview to *Forum* and to a supermarket tabloid, *The Star*.

*Forum* quickly used the tape to prepare a cover story about Cher and promoted the article with advertising that said, "[t]here are certain things that Cher won't tell *People* and would never tell *Us*."[39] The copy also urged audiences to "join Cher and *Forum's* hundreds of thousands of other adventurous readers today."[40] When Cher sued, the court agreed with her that the advertising copy could reasonably be interpreted as being Cher's personal endorsement of the magazine and thus a violation of her right of publicity.

Advertisers and other commercial speakers may violate a celebrity's right of publicity in ways other than unauthorized use of a name or likeness. A number of court decisions have held commercial speakers liable for damages in connection with the unauthorized use of a particular expression associated with the celebrity, a vocal sound-alike, a character created by the celebrity or even, in *Motschenbacher v. R.J. Reynolds Tobacco Co.*,[41] for unauthorized altering of the unusual decorations used by the owner of a racing car. The opinion noted:

> . . . plaintiff [Lothar Motschenbacher] has consistently "individualized" his [racing] cars to set them apart from those of other drivers and to make them more readily identifiable as his own. Since 1966, each of his cars his displayed a distinctive narrow white pinstripe appearing on no other car. This decoration has adorned the leading edges of the cars' bodies, which have uniformly been solid red. In addition, the white background for his racing number "11" has always been oval, in contrast to the circular background of all other cars.[42]

When these were altered slightly, and the cigarette brand name "Winston" was added to the markings of the car, the court found the driver's right of publicity had been violated.

In *Carson v. Here's Johnny Portable Toilets*,[43] the talk show host and comedian Johnny Carson objected to the phrase, "Here's Johnny!" as the name for a line of portable restrooms. Carson, who was not asking for monetary damages but instead to have the company adopt another name for its product, argued that he had been introduced for many years to the national television audience of the NBC "Tonight Show" with that phrase and that the public associated it with him. Additionally, Carson owned stock in a line of clothing that used "Here's Johnny!" in its advertising.

The manufacturer of the "Here's Johnny!" portable restrooms countered with the argument that "john" and "johnny" had been used by the public for years to describe restroom facilities, but admitted that he did indeed have Carson in mind when he named his business. In advertising the product, he referred to his company as "The World's Foremost Commodian." The majority of a divided court sided with Carson, holding that he had been unfairly capitalized upon—that the phrase had indeed become a part of his identity—and thus he should be permitted to control its use.

Another court determined that unique characters developed by actors can be protected—in this case the characters of Groucho, Chico and Harpo, creations of the Marx Brothers.[44] But the mere portrayal of a role does not give the actor publicity rights to it, as the heirs of Bela Lugosi learned when they attempted to control the character of Count Dracula that Lugosi played in a famous early 1930s movie. Tartly, the court noted that Lugosi did not have exclusive rights to Dracula any more than the actor Charlton Heston might have to Moses, a part he played in *The Ten Commandments*.[45] But note, however, that by the same token, depicting either Dracula or Moses as actually resembling either the actors Lugosi or Heston could result in a different outcome.

Bert Lahr, the comedian and film actor, and Bette Midler, the singer, among others, have been able to recover damages (in Ms. Midler's case, $400,000) for unauthorized imitations of their voices. Lahr, who played the part of the Cowardly Lion in the well-know film version of *The Wizard of Oz*, sued over an imitation of his voice in an advertisement. The court agreed with the actor, noting that the advertisement "had greater value because its audience believed it was listening to [Lahr]."[46]

In Ms. Midler's case, the advertising agency Young & Rubicam invited her to sing one of her hit recordings ("Do You Want to Dance?") in commercials for the Ford Motor Company. When she declined, the agency hired one of her former backup singers to imitate her voice, which she did, highly successfully. Ms. Midler sued, and the federal court found in her favor, commenting that "the human voice is one of the most palpable ways identity is manifested," and the unauthorized imitation was a violation of her right of publicity.[47] In a later case, a federal jury in Los Angeles found that a sound-alike commercial violated the publicity rights of Tom Waits and awarded the singer nearly $2.5 million in damages.[48]

There are those who would argue that in these and other decisions, the right of publicity, still in its relative youth, has already been stretched to the point that it could muzzle certain aspects of freedom of expression where advertising and promotion are concerned. Legal scholar Christopher Pesce warns, "[a]llowing celebrities to recover in cases where advertisers loosely imitate limited aspects of their 'personae' protects interests unworthy of the status of property, chills creative endeavor, and creates an unpredictable standard of recovery."[49]

Richard Kurnit, whose Manhattan law firm represents a number of publishers and advertising agencies, put it this way: "[t]he idea that entertainment properties are akin to explosives—if you hit someone you are strictly liable—is particularly frightening when you consider that publicity claims result in uncontrollable damage awards for emotional distress and punitive damages at the whim of a jury."[50]

## A First Amendment Threat?

Beyond the hazards posed by the right of publicity to creative people in the advertising and public relations fields, some First Amendment concerns have emerged as well. As noted above, a traditional defense in privacy cases—and, by extension, cases involving the right of publicity—has been newsworthiness. But a bizarre case, *Zacchini v. Scripps-Howard Broadcasting*,[51] blurred the distinction between commercial and noncommercial use and, in effect, changed the nature of misappropriation law.

Hugo Zacchini, billed as "the human cannonball," earned his living as an entertainer by allowing himself to be blasted from a huge cannon into a safety net some 200 feet away. His act, in its entirety, took only a few seconds. One evening, as Zacchini was about to perform in the Cleveland area, a TV news crew showed up and, over his protests, filmed the act (all 15 seconds of it) and showed the segment on the late evening news. Zacchini sued, claiming this showing violated his right of publicity and cost him thousands of dollars in lost revenue. Once his entire act had been shown on television, he argued, few people would be willing to pay money to watch him perform in person.

The TV station, for its part, argued that Zacchini's act had legitimate news value and that newscasts were securely protected by the First Amendment. Also, the station contended, the Zacchini segment represented only a tiny fraction of the newscast, and that the station did not realize any revenue, directly or indirectly, from reporting this particular news story. The Supreme Court of the United States ultimately agreed, but in a tortured 5–4 decision, sided with Zacchini anyway. In Justice White's opinion:

> [t]he broadcast of petitioner's [Zacchini's] entire performance, unlike the unauthorized use of another's name for purposes of trade or the incidental use of a name or picture by the press, goes to the heart of petitioner's ability to earn a living as an entertainer. Thus in this case, Ohio has recognized what may be the strongest case for a "right of publicity"—involving not the appropriation of an entertainer's reputation to enhance the attractiveness of a commercial product, but the appropriation of the very activity by which the entertainer acquired the reputation in the first place.[52]

The *Zacchini* decision, the first ruling ever by the Supreme Court of the United States in this sector of the law, could lead to further confusion in determining what is commercial exploitation and what is simply news. Some months after *Zacchini*, the ABC television network began to prepare a docudrama on the life of the celebrated actress Elizabeth Taylor. Ms. Taylor objected on the grounds that her life story was her own and that she might one day write her autobiography. A movie about her life now, she contended, might take away income that should be hers. Rather than risk a court suit, ABC decided to shelve the project.[53]

Because of the zany facts of the *Zacchini* case—few celebrities will find their total act being filmed for a newscast—it is unlikely that the case will have much in the way of direct influence on the rapidly emerging law of publicity. To the extent that it represents a judicial propensity to protect a celebrity's right of publicity, however, *Zacchini* might well be regarded as an important case.

## Misappropriation and the Right of Publicity in a Digital, New-Media Age: Emerging Issues

The dynamic growth of advertising, public relations and the mass media industry in recent years has given the concepts of misappropriation and right of publicity new status in the law of invasion of privacy. For example, mass media coverage, advertising, marketing campaigns and public relations messages have helped create thousands of celebrities, although many of them, obviously, may enjoy only a few fleeting moments of fame—think of American Idol contestants, someone doing something remarkably stupid on a YouTube site that receives millions of hits or reality television participants. No matter how brief, during their time in the spotlight, they understandably wish for some authority to protect their "professional personalities" from unauthorized exploitation.

To an ever-increasing degree, the courts seem inclined to grant that protection to them as well as to those plaintiffs who can legitimately demonstrate mental anguish as a result of defendants taking of their name or likeness. The number of cases of misappropriation, and especially the right of publicity, appears to be growing as the end of the first decade of the twenty-first century is reached, and the forecast is for more of the same. Simply put, the plaintiffs seem to be winning the cases they should win while losing those that involve more novel applications of privacy law.

For example, courts recently have found for the plaintiffs in cases involving the unconsented-to use of plaintiffs name or likeness (a) on a sex-oriented Web site that attributed a fictitious personal profile to the complainant;[54] (b) for continued use of a chef's name to promote a catering business after the chef had left the organization's employment;[55] (c) when an employer argued it maintained the rights to the names of former hosts of a radio program;[56] and (d) in the suit by a former NFL star who no longer wished to have his name attached to a trophy awarded by a sports group to the best college linebacker in the country.[57] Celebrities like Woody Allen concerned about his likeness being used by American Apparel to market clothing and Sam Keller, a former Arizona State University college football star, complaining that Electronic Arts and the NCAA had improperly used his likeness in a video game, are recent examples of right of publicity cases.[58] And note that the California Supreme Court, although rejecting a claim based on reuse of an actor's likeness on a coffee container label, added that the actor might have prevailed if the label had been redesigned or if the likeness has been used for marketing a different coffee company product.[59]

On the other hand, courts have found for the defendants in cases where

(a) the plaintiff was not considered to be a public figure (despite the plaintiff's rather exalted personal opinion to the contrary);[60]
(b) a rock band complained that the defendant's inclusion of a song attributed to them in a video game violated their rights of publicity;[61] and
(c) the Mars candy company displayed a giant M&M dressed (or rather undressed) like the plaintiff who has achieved some local celebrity status for his "Naked Cowboy" character (we don't make these up).[62]

In a much-watched case, *C.B.C. Distribution and Marketing, Inc. v. Major League Baseball Advanced Media, L.P.*,[63] Major League Baseball lost its attempt to limit the use of player names and stats by a fantasy baseball league though a misappropriation claim because, the courts said, the information was readily available in the news media and that prohibiting its use by the defendant, even for financial gain, would be in violation of the defendant's First Amendment rights. More recent cases pushing the new-media envelope include the football hall-of-famer Jim Brown[64] who sued the NFL claiming a computer-game avatar referred to him because it "played" the same position as Brown in his playing days, and numerous individuals suing for misappropriation because they appeared in the "Borat"[65] movies.

We have devoted an entire chapter to misappropriation and the right of publicity because this is the privacy tort most likely to trip up unwary advertising and public relations professionals. Clearly, the safest course of action for wise and prudent practitioners is to be sure that consent, either voluntarily given or purchased, has been obtained before using anyone's name, likeness or persona for any advertising or public relations purposes.

# Chapter 7

# Copyright

Copyright, trademarks and patents are typically grouped into an area of the law that has become known as *intellectual property*. Because copyright is an area of the law that has a substantial impact on advertising and public relations, this chapter deals exclusively with copyright law. The next chapter focuses on trademarks and includes a brief discussion of patents.

## Historical Background

American copyright law can be traced back to England and, specifically, the Statute of Anne[1] passed by Parliament in 1710 to recognize and protect the rights of authors. From the 1400s on, English printers and publishers were concerned about preventing competitors from pirating their works. These efforts culminated with the Act of Parliament that recognized the right of authors to ownership of their original works but, of interest for subsequent American copyright law, recognized such rights for only a limited amount of time (generally 14 years, with the possibility of renewal for an additional 14 years).

British law, including the law of copyright, formed the basis of American colonial law and it is, therefore, not surprising that when the framers of the United States Constitution drafted that document, they included authority for federal copyright law in Article I, Section 8 of the Constitution. This section gives Congress authority to grant a limited monopoly to "authors" that enables them to profit from their "writings" as an inducement for them to contribute to the "useful Arts."[2] Today, copyright protection by extension applies not only to authors, but to artists, photographers and others who produce original creative works.

Congress enacted the first federal copyright statute in 1790, one year after the Constitution was ratified and a year before the Bill of Rights took effect. The nineteenth century brought many revisions to the federal copyright scheme embodied in numerous revisions of the statute. What developed was a two-tiered system, with the federal statute protecting mainly published works and state common law governing unpublished works.

That system continued into the twentieth century with the revised 1909 law, which subsequently itself was revised on numerous occasions over the next six decades to accommodate new technologies and philosophies about what should be protected. In 1909, for example, radio had reached only an experimental stage. Computers, photocopy machines, compact disks, DVDs, MP3s, satellites and even television broadcasts were undreamed of. Under the 1909 law and its many revisions, copyright infringement was certainly possible, and creators definitely needed protection, but it was much more difficult than it is today to make unauthorized use of a person's creative work.

That all changed when, pushed by technological innovations, the Copyright Act of 1976 took effect and the pieces of what was once a colossal mess were assembled into some long-needed order. The 1976 Act, which is the basis for copyright protection today, brought significant changes; even the premises of the old and new statutes are at odds. As Kitch and Perlman noted, "[u]nder the old law, the starting principle was: the owner shall have the exclusive right to copy his copies. Under the new, the principle is: the owner shall have the exclusive right to exploit his work."[3] The new law clearly was designed to be an author-oriented statute that offers tremendous protection to the creators of original works of authorship.

## Creation of Copyright

Any attorney practicing copyright law can verify that one of the most common questions clients ask is: "What do I need to do to copyright this great idea I have?" Often, the "shocking" answer is: "Sorry. You can't copyright an idea; you can only copyright your expression of that idea."

A work cannot be copyrighted if it exists only in the mind of the creator; it is created under the current copyright statute "when it is fixed in a copy or phonorecord for the first time."[4] Once it is fixed in a tangible medium, the protection begins. When a work is developed over time, the portion that is fixed at a particular time is considered the work at that time. For instance, the copyrighted portion of this book at the time these words are being written on the word processor is everything written thus far to the end of this sentence. If a work is prepared in different versions, each version is a separate work for purposes of copyright. The first edition of this book is considered a separate work from the second edition and so on.

Probably the most important difference between the old and new copyright statutes is the point at which copyright protection begins. Under the 1909 federal statute, federal copyright protection generally could not be invoked until a work had been published with notice of copyright. There were a few exceptions to this rule, but unpublished works were basically protected only under state law, or what was known as *common-law copyright*. Common-law copyright certainly had some advantages, including perpetual protection for unpublished works, but with each state having its own common law, there was little uniformity.

The 1976 Copyright Law solved this problem easily: copyright exists automatically "in original works of authorship fixed in any tangible medium of expression, now known or later developed, from which they can be perceived, reproduced, or otherwise communicated, either directly or with the aid of a machine or device."[5] No registration is necessary. No publication is required. Not even a copyright notice has to be placed on the work for it to be copyrighted. The copyright exists automatically upon creation.

This is one of the most misunderstood aspects of copyright by advertising and public relations professionals who wish to make use of the creative works of others—a work is copyrighted the very second it is created in a tangible medium. Nothing could be simpler. No hocus-pocus, smoke and mirrors or other magic. Not even a government form to complete.

## "Fixing" an Idea

When does an idea become a work actually fixed in a medium? According to Section 101:

> A work is "fixed" in a tangible medium of expression when its embodiment in a copy or phonorecord, by or under authority of the author, is sufficiently permanent or stable to permit it to be perceived, reproduced, or otherwise communicated for a period of more than transitory duration. A work consisting of sounds, images, or both, that are being transmitted, is "fixed" for purposes of this title if a fixation of the work is being made simultaneously with its transmission.[6]

Suppose an enterprising skywriter composes a love poem in the sky to her fiancé during halftime of the Super Bowl. A few miles away, another romantic scribbles in the ocean sand the opening of a modernized version of the great film epic, *Beach Blanket Bingo*. Can these two original works of authorship be copyrighted? Both face a major obstacle—they are not yet fixed in a tangible medium of expression. Almost as soon as the love poem is written in the sky, it evaporates into thin air. Its transitory nature prevents it from being "fixed" for purposes of copyright. The same holds true for the film's opening sequence written in the sand because it ends up being washed away by the tide.

How does one "fix" these creative efforts? An easy way is to write them on a piece of paper or perhaps photograph or videotape them before they fade. But won't paper eventually deteriorate? Fixation does not require permanency; only that the medium be sufficiently permanent or stable to allow it to be perceived, copied or otherwise communicated for more than a transitory duration.

## Similar Ideas

Suppose two people have a similar idea and both express it in tangible terms. Can the one who first fixes the idea in a creative work prevent the other from profiting from his or her later efforts if the idea is the same but the creative efforts appear to be independent of each other?

In *Hoehling v. Universal City Studios, Inc.*,[7] a federal appellate court ruled that Universal had not infringed on the copyright of A.A. Hoehling's book, *Who Destroyed the Hindenburg?*, in a movie about the explosion of the German dirigible at Lakehurst, New Jersey, in 1937. The film was based on a book by Michael Mooney published in 1972, 10 years after Hoehling's work. Both books theorized that Eric Spehl, a disgruntled crew member who was among the 36 people killed in the disaster, had planted a bomb in one of the gas cells. Although the 1975 movie, which was a fictionalized account of the event, used a pseudonym for Spehl, its thesis about the cause of the tragedy was similar to that in Hoehling's book. (Investigators concluded that the airship blew up after static electricity ignited the hydrogen fuel, but speculation has always abounded about whether this was the actual cause.)

A federal district court judge issued a summary judgment in favor of the defendant, Universal City Studios, and a federal circuit court of appeals upheld the decision. According to the appeals court:

> [t]he protection afforded the copyright holder has never extended to history, be it documentary fact or explanatory hypothesis. The rationale for this doctrine is that the cause of knowledge is best served when history is the common property of all, and each generation remains free to draw upon the discoveries and insights of the past.[8]

Hoehling claimed there were other similarities, including random duplication of phrases and the chronology of the story, but the court saw no problem with such overlap.

A more recent example of idea versus expression of idea involved the 2007 copyright infringement lawsuit filed against Jessica Seinfeld, perhaps best known as the wife of comedian Jerry Seinfeld. The plaintiff, author Missy Chase Lapine, claimed that Seinfeld's book, *Deceptively Delicious: Simple Secrets to Get Your Kids Eating Good Food*, infringed her earlier-published cookbook, *The Sneaky Chef: Simple Strategies for Hiding Healthy Foods in Kids' Favorite Meals*. A federal judge dismissed the suit, finding that the works themselves, though based on similar ideas, were very different.[9]

## Protected Works

Under Section 102, copyright protection extends to "original works of authorship fixed in any tangible medium of expression, now known or later developed, from which they can be perceived, reproduced, or otherwise communicated, either directly or with the aid of a machine or device." This section enumerates seven categories under works of authorship: (a) literary works; (b) musical works, including any accompanying words; (c) dramatic works, including any accompanying music; (d) pantomimes and choreographic works; (e) pictorial, graphic and sculptural works; (f) motion pictures and other audiovisual works; and (g) sound recordings.[10]

Section 102(b) notes that copyright protection does not extend to "any idea, procedure, process, system, method of operation, concept, principle, or discovery, regardless of the form in which it is described, explained, illustrated, or embodied in such work."[11] As discussed in other chapters, some of these items may enjoy protection as trademarks, trade secrets or patents, but they cannot be copyrighted even though works in which they appear can be copyrighted.

In the case of compilations or derivative works, Section 103 specifies that only the material contributed by the author of a compilation or derivative work is granted new copyright protection; any preexisting material used in the derivative work or compilation does not gain additional protection, but maintains the same protection it had originally. In other words, you cannot expand the protection a work originally was granted by using it in another work such as a derivative work or compilation.

Section 101, which contains definitions of terms in the statute, defines a *compilation* as: ". . . a work formed by the collection and assembling of preexisting materials or of data that are selected, coordinated, or arranged in such a way that the resulting work as a whole constitutes an original work of authorship."[12] Compilations also include *collective works*, defined as: ". . . a work, such as a periodical issue, anthology, or encyclopedia, in which a number of contributions, constituting separate and independent works in themselves, are assembled into a collective whole."[13]

A *derivative work* is defined as:

> . . . a work based upon one or more preexisting works, such as a translation, musical arrangement, dramatization, fictionalization, motion picture version, sound recording, art reproduction, abridgment, condensation, or any other form in which a work may be recast, transformed, or adapted. A work consisting of editorial revisions, annotations, elaborations, or other modifications, which, as a whole, represent an original work of authorship, is a "derivative work."[14]

## Unprotected Works

People unfamiliar with the law wrongly assume that any creative work can be protected by copyright. Although the 1976 statute is broad, certain types of works do not fall under its wings. The most obvious example is a work that has not been fixed in a tangible medium. But, as discussed above, the Act also excludes "any idea, procedure, process, system, method of operation, concept, principle, or discovery."[15] Note, however, that although such works have no protection in and of themselves, *expressions* of them can be copyrighted. For example, a university professor who writes a textbook based on his ideas about advertising and public relations law cannot protect his ideas per se, but the expression of those ideas—a book—is copyrighted the moment it is created and put in a tangible medium.

Titles (e.g., "City of Angels"), names (e.g., Harry Potter), short phrases (e.g., "I'm Lovin It"), slogans (e.g., "The beer that made Milwaukee famous"), familiar symbols and designs (e.g., the Nike "swoosh") and mere listings of ingredients and contents cannot be copyrighted, although these may enjoy other forms of legal protection, such as trademarks. Four more categories of works that lack copyright protection include works by the U.S. Government, works of common information, works in the public domain and works consisting of basic facts.

## Government Works

The Copyright Act of 1976 generally prohibits the federal government from copyrighting works it creates. The major exception to this rule is that the government can acquire copyright for works it did not create. For example, U.S. postage stamp designs are copyrighted, as witnessed by the copyright notice in the margins of sheets and booklets, despite the fact that the U.S. Postal Service is a semiautonomous federal agency. Typically, the Postal Service contracts with freelance artists who design the stamps and then transfer the copyrights to the agency.

## Works of Common Information

Like works of the U.S. Government, works consisting wholly of common information having no original authorship such as standard calendars, weight and measure charts, rulers and so forth cannot be copyrighted. Note, however, that works that contain such information can be copyrighted even though the information cannot be. As an illustration, a calendar with pictures of herbs for each month could be copyrighted, but the copyright would extend only to the photographs and any other original work on the calendar, not the standard calendar itself.

## Works in the Public Domain

Under the 1909 law, copyright protection lasted for a maximum of two terms of 28 years each for a total of 56 years. Works copyrighted before changes made by the 1976 law took effect had the period of protection extended, but any work that was copyrighted prior to 1903 and any work whose copyright was not timely renewed no longer have protection. Thus, some works copyrighted as late as 1949 have gone into the public domain because no copyright renewal application was filed.

Once a work becomes public domain property, no royalties have to be paid and no permission needs to be sought from any owner before use. This is the reason that one can find such great prices on some old movies and television shows at the local Walmart or Kmart. Copyright owners simply did not bother at the time to renew the copyright. Before the advent of DVRs and especially cable and satellite television channels hungry for content, many copyright owners of such works believed there was no viable market for their productions after initial release.

## Facts

Facts alone are not eligible for copyright protection. The *expression* of facts, however, does enjoy protection. Thus, although news cannot be copyrighted, newscasts can be.

In *Miller v. Universal City Studios*,[16] a federal court of appeals overturned a district court decision that Universal had infringed the copyright of Gene Miller, a Pulitzer Prize-winning reporter for the *Miami Herald*, in a book entitled *83 Hours Till Dawn*. The non-fiction work focused on a young woman named Barbara Mackle who was rescued after being kidnapped and buried underground for five days in a box in which she could have survived for no more than a week. The trial court in *Miller* was impressed by the approximately 2,500 hours that the author said he had spent researching and writing the book: "To this court it doesn't square with reason or common sense to believe that Gene Miller would have undertaken the research required . . . if the author thought that upon completion of the book a movie producer or television network could simply come along and take the profits of the books and his research from him."[17]

Although there were several similarities between Miller's book and the script for Universal's docudrama, *The Longest Night*, including some of the same factual errors, the appellate court ordered a new trial on the ground that "the case was presented and argued to the jury on a false premise: that the labor of research by an author [unearthing the facts in the case] is protected by copyright."[18]

In 1991, the Supreme Court of the United States attempted to clarify the concept of "originality," which is closely linked to the facts-versus-compilation-of-facts distinction. In *Feist Publications, Inc. v. Rural Telephone Service Co.*,[19] the Court unanimously held that the white pages of a telephone directory could not be copyrighted. The case involved a telephone book publisher that used the names and telephone numbers from a competing telephone company's directory to compile its own area-wide telephone directories. The Court noted that, although the telephone company could claim copyright ownership in its directory as a whole, it could not prevent a competitor from using the elements of its compilation of names, towns and phone numbers to create the competitor's own directory. Facts are not copyrightable, the justices said, but the compilations of facts can generally be copyrighted.

The decision stressed that hard work or "sweat of the brow" is not enough; there must be originality of creative expression, which the Court characterized as the *sine qua non* of copyright. However, it should be noted that the *amount* of originality is not the test. "To be sure, the requisite level of creativity is extremely low; [but] even a slight amount will suffice,"[20] Justice O'Connor wrote for the Court.

## Who Owns the Copyright?

There is a world of difference between the treatment of copyright ownership under the 1909 statute and coexisting common law versus the treatment under the current Copyright Act of 1976. Under the old law, when an author, artist or other creator sold his or her copyright, the presumption was that all rights had been transferred unless rights were specifically reserved by the creator, usually in writing. For instance, an artist who sold his or her original painting to someone effectively transferred copyright ownership as well because the common law recognized that the sale of certain types of creative works invoked transfer of the copyright to the purchaser.

The presumption now works in the opposite direction. None of the exclusive rights (discussed later in this chapter), nor any subdivision of those rights, are legally transferred in the sale of a copyrighted work unless the transfer is in writing and signed by the original copyright owner or the owner's legal representative.

Under the current statute, the copyright is immediately vested in the original creator/author. If more than one creator (i.e., there is joint authorship), the copyright belongs to all of them. The creator or creators can, of course, transfer their rights, but the transfer of any exclusive rights must be in writing.

Oral agreements are sufficient for the transfer of nonexclusive rights. For example, a freelance artist could have a valid oral agreement with an advertising agency to create a series of drawings to be used in commercials for a life insurance company. At the same time, he or she could have an agreement with a magazine to do similar illustrations for a feature story. However, if the artist chose to transfer (a) an exclusive right, such as the sole right to reproduce the drawings; (b) a subdivided right, such as the right to reproduce the drawings in commercials; or (c) the right to produce a derivative work, such as a training film based on the drawings, such a transfer would need to be in writing for it to be binding.

## Ownership of Compilations and Derivative Works

Ownership becomes more complicated in compilations and derivative works. Remember that the key differences between a compilation and a derivative work are that (a) a compilation consists of pulling together separate works or pieces of works already created, whereas a derivative work can trace its origins to one previous work, and (b) the key creative element in a compilation is the way in which the preexisting works are compiled to create the whole (i.e., the new work), whereas the creative dimensions of a derivative work are basically independent of the previous work.

An anthology of poems by Robert Frost, which consists of poems previously published on their own, is an illustration of a compilation that is also a collective work. With certain exceptions, the owner—who is usually the creator—of an original work of authorship has exclusive rights that only he or she can exercise or authorize others to exercise. Thus the poet would normally own the copyright in his works, absent his assigning the rights to another party (his publisher, for example). If Frost did make such an assignment with five of his poems contained in the compilation, there would be three copyright holders in the work—the poet for most of the poems, the publisher for the five poems earlier obtained from Frost and the compiler of the final book, *Collected Works of Robert Frost*, for the ways the poems are arranged in the book, the typeface used in the printing of the work, any original commentary and so forth.

Prudent advertising and public relations professionals should recognize that in any one collective work like a movie or music recording, there may be a number of copyright owners. In the film, the director, the writer of the screenplay, the film editor and the creator of the original musical score may all have independent copyrights in the various elements that make up the finished product. Likewise in the music recording, the composer, lyricist and music arranger may all have separate ownership interests that need to be satisfied before the recording may be used.

The novel *Gone with the Wind* and its subsequent history provide an example of ownership of a derivative work. Margaret Mitchell's heirs, who inherited the rights to her novel after she was killed by an auto in 1949, nixed any sequels to the enormously popular book and movie for more than four decades. A series of sequels, including books and movies, probably would have brought in millions of dollars in royalties, but *Gone*

*With the Wind* devotees, dying to learn the fate of Rhett and Scarlett, had to wait until 1991 when agents representing the estate finally chose Alexandra Ripley to write *Scarlett: Tomorrow Is Another Day*. The 768-page sequel was published simultaneously in 40 countries, with excerpts appearing a month earlier in *Life* magazine. The television movie followed in 1994—all six hours plus commercials.

## Works Made for Hire

The sole exception to the rule of author-as-copyright-owner is a "work made for hire," which exists in two situations:

(a)  a work is prepared by an employee within the scope of his or her employment, or

(b)  a work is specially ordered or commissioned for use as a contribution to a collective work, as part of a motion picture or other audiovisual work, as a translation, as a supplementary work, as a compilation, as an instructional text, as a test, as answer material for a test, or as an atlas, if the parties expressly agree in a written instrument signed by them that the work shall be considered a work made for hire.[21]

In the case of a work made for hire, the employer is considered the author for purposes of copyright and automatically acquires all rights, exclusive and nonexclusive, unless the parties have signed an agreement to the contrary. Thus, the employer effectively attains the status of creator of the work.

For instance, a full-time copywriter for an advertising agency would have no rights to the copy he or she created for the agency. In contrast, a photo sold by a freelance photographer to a public relations firm for use in a press release normally would not be a work made for hire unless the photographer, who is contractually an independent contractor, had signed a contract specifically stating that the photo should be considered a work made for hire.

Suppose a public relations writer writes a novel about a fictional head of a public relations firm who solves major crime mysteries on the side. The book is written at home on the public relations professional's own time, but much of the inspiration comes from his or her observations at work. Is the novel a work made for hire? Clearly not; although the public relations professional may have gotten some ideas from interactions with his or her colleagues, the writing was completed outside the scope of employment. Serving as a source of inspiration alone is not enough for an employer of an individual to claim copyright. An employer-employee relationship must have existed in the context in which the work is created.

## Working with Freelancers

Freelancers create much of the copyrighted material existing today and work-made-for-hire principles play a major role in the copyright status of much of this creative output. Unfortunately, although the 1976 law defines dozens of terms, from an *anonymous work* to a *work made for hire*, it does not define *employer, employee* or *scope of his or her employment*. In 1989, however, the Supreme Court of the United States settled some perplexing questions regarding works made for hire by enunciating a clear principle for determining whether an individual is an "employee." In *Community for Creative Non-Violence v. Reid*, the Court unanimously held: "[t]o determine whether a work is for hire under the Act [Copyright Act of 1976], a court must first ascertain, using principles of general common law of agency, whether the work was prepared by an employer or an independent contractor. After making this determination, the court can apply the appropriate subsection of §101."[22]

The Court then indicated factors under the general common law of agency to be applied in determining whether the hired party is an employee or an independent contractor, including:

> ... the hiring party's right to control the manner and means by which the product is accomplished. Among the other factors relevant to this inquiry are the skill required; the source of the instrumentalities and tools; the location of the work; the duration of the relationship between the parties; whether the hiring party has the right to assign additional projects to the hired party; the extent of the hired party's discretion over when and how long to work; the method of payment; the hired party's role in hiring and paying assistants; whether the work is part of the regular business of the hiring party; whether the hiring party is in business; the provision of employee benefits; and the tax treatment of the hired party. . . . No one of these factors is determinative.[23]

*Community for Creative Non-Violence v. Reid* established the presumption that a work is not a work made for hire unless there is a written agreement to treat it as such. As the justices noted, the legislative history of the 1976 Act provides strong evidence that Congress meant to establish two mutually exclusive ways for a work to acquire work-made-for-hire status. The Court also pointed out that, "only enumerated categories of commissioned works may be accorded work for hire status . . . [and that the] . . . hiring party's right to control the product simply is not determinative."[24]

The Court specifically rejected an "actual control test" that the Community for Creative Non-Violence argued should be determinative. Under such a test, the hiring party could claim the copyright if it closely monitored the production of the work, but the Court said this approach "would impede Congress' paramount goal in revising the 1976 Act of enhancing predictability and certainty of copyright ownership."[25] The Court went on to note that "[b]ecause that test hinges on whether the hiring party has closely monitored the production process, the parties would not know until late in the process, if not until the work is completed, whether a work will ultimately fall within §101(1)."[26] Congress intended in the 1976 law that it must be clear who owns the copyright at the time a work is created, said the Court.

A 2001 case looked at the rights of individual copyright owners whose individual works were included in a collective work, namely specific editions of *The New York Times*, *Newsday* and *Sports Illustrated*. The issue, in *New York Times Company v. Tasini*,[27] concerned whether freelancers' copyrights in their individual articles were infringed when the articles were subsequently reproduced in electronic form without authorization. The freelancers had been compensated for the use of their works in print, but argued they were entitled to additional royalties for subsequent electronic uses such as inclusion in searchable CD-ROMs or databases. The Supreme Court found for the freelancers. Writing for the Court, Justice Ginsburg said:

> [i]f there is a demand for a freelance article standing alone or in a new collection, the Copyright Act allows the freelancer to benefit from that demand . . . It would scarcely "preserve the author's copyright in a contribution" as contemplated by Congress . . . if a newspaper or magazine publisher were permitted to reproduce or distribute copies of the author's contribution in isolation or within new collective works. . . .[28]

The practical effect of *Tasini* was to encourage organizations to seek all-encompassing releases from freelancers at the time of engagement. Freelancers, on the other hand, gained potential leverage to be used in negotiating fees and terms of use for their copyrighted contributions.

## Joint Authorship: An Alternative to Work for Hire?

Section 101 of the Copyright Act defines a *joint work* as "a work prepared by two or more authors with the intention that their contributions be merged into inseparable or independent parts of a unitary whole."[29] Unless there is a written agreement stating otherwise, joint authors are considered co-owners of the copyright in a work.

Joint authorship is certainly advantageous to the hiring party because a joint author has an undivided interest in the work, and, therefore, can make use of the work without seeking permission from the other joint owner or owners unless all the owners expressly agree in writing how the copyright ownership in the work is to be divided. Although *Community for Creative Non-Violence v. Reid* was a major victory for freelancers, it created a problem that one First Amendment expert characterized as "gratuitous joint-authorship claims of commissioning parties," because those hiring a freelancer would try to claim joint-author status based on their supervision of the production of the copyrighted work. He suggests this unintended consequence could be remedied if Congress enacted a statute banning such practices.[30] Under such a law, a freelancer would not become a joint author unless all parties agreed in writing in advance that the work was to be considered jointly authored.[31]

## The Copyright Owner's Exclusive Rights

Copyright laws give the copyright owner a series of exclusive rights the owner may sell, lease, give away or otherwise transfer as desired. Under Section 106, the copyright owner has the exclusive right:

(a) to reproduce the copyrighted work in copies or phonorecords;
(b) to prepare derivative works based upon the copyrighted work;
(c) to distribute copies or phonorecords of the copyrighted work to the public by sale or other transfer of ownership, or by rental, lease, or lending;
(d) in the case of literary, musical, dramatic, and choreographic works, pantomimes, and motion pictures and other audiovisual works, to perform the copyrighted work publicly; and
(e) in the case of literary, musical, dramatic, and choreographic works, pantomimes, and pictorial, graphic, or sculptural works, including the individual images of a motion picture or other audiovisual work, to display the copyrighted work publicly.[32]

Under certain limited conditions, a copyright owner who has transferred any of these exclusive rights to another may elect to terminate the transfer. Under Section 203, a copyright owner can terminate a grant of any exclusive or nonexclusive right after 35 years by notifying the individual or organization to whom the right was transferred.[33] This is an often-overlooked provision that can certainly work to the advantage of a copyright owner, especially when a work is slow in gaining popularity. This special termination of transfers provision applies neither to works made for hire, nor to grants to prepare specific derivative works.[34]

### Owning the Object Versus Owning the Copyright

In contemplating copyright ownership rights, it is necessary to distinguish between the actual work and the *copyright* in the original work. Ownership of a work, as opposed to ownership of the copyrights to a work, does not convey any copyrights. For example, if Jan Smurf purchases a DVD of Walt Disney's *Cinderella* at her local video store, she can play the disc to her heart's content in her own home, and even invite her friends for an evening of viewing on the big-screen television. However, she does not have the right to make a copy of the DVD or even to play it at a neighborhood fundraiser for the homeless. She does not even have the right to make her own edited version of the film.

In other words, purchasing the disc merely gave her the right to use it in the form in which it was intended to be used—nothing more. She could, of course, loan the DVD to a neighbor or even sell her copy to a stranger, just as she could with a book or other physical object. Her rights are strictly tangible; she has no intangible property rights.

## Moral Rights

One of the more controversial issues in the debate over whether the United States should join the Berne Convention (discussed later in this chapter) was Article 6bis that requires Convention members to protect the moral rights or *droit moral* of authors.[35] Although the United States does not recognize such rights to the same degree as its other Convention signees, the Visual Artists Rights Act (VARA),[36] adopted by the United States Congress in 1990, amended the Copyright Act to provide limited moral rights for the visual works of art created on or after June 1, 1991. These moral rights fall into two categories under VARA: attribution rights and integrity rights, both of which have been more broadly recognized in many other countries for some time.

Attribution rights involve the right to be credited as the author of a work and to prevent others from attributing a work to you that is essentially not your work. For example, both a publisher who, without consent, omitted the name of the primary author from a book and a magazine editor who falsely claimed an article was written by a well-known author to sell more copies or lend credibility to the magazine would be violating attribution rights.

Integrity rights basically involve "the right to object to distortion, other alteration of a work, or derogatory action prejudicial to the author's honor or reputation in relation to the work."[37] An example of the latter was a 1976 federal court of appeals decision to grant a preliminary injunction against the ABC Television Network on the ground that the copyright of the British comedy troupe known as Monty Python of "Monty Python's Flying Circus" fame was violated when the network extensively edited the troupe's programs, primarily to make room for commercials.[38] Although the comedy team had granted the British Broadcasting Corporation the right to license the programs overseas, that right did not include allowing licensees to significantly distort the programs.

## Public Performance Rights and Performance Licenses

Of the copyright owner's exclusive rights listed above, the right "to perform the copyrighted work publicly" is among the most misunderstood, particularly with regard to the public performance of music. Many businesses use music in communicating with customers to establish a mood or tone. Music frequently is featured in advertising, on Web sites, at special events, at sales meetings, in stores and during telephone contact with customers. Because these and other uses of music may implicate the public performance rights and result in possible copyright infringement, advertising and public relations practitioners should become familiar with public performance rights and understand when to seek permission prior to using copyrighted material.

Where recorded music is concerned, copyright law protects both the composer(s) of the musical work—those who wrote the music and/or any lyrics—as well as the sound recording itself. The musical work also is protected by the public performance right, which means anyone who wishes to publicly perform the work must obtain permission from the composer and/or lyricist. That's right; the band at a local watering spot "covering" a song they have learned without benefit of sheet music is infringing a copyrighted work.

As one might imagine, radio stations, bars and other businesses that rely on music would be quite busy if required to contact individual composers to secure licenses prior to playing music in their respective establishments—a ridiculously time-consuming and prohibitively expensive proposition. Fortunately for businesses and other entities wishing to publicly use copyrighted music, there is a mechanism—the performance license—that enables a potential user to avoid having to negotiate with individual copyright owners.

Performance licenses, typically acquired through performance rights societies, allow licensees to publicly perform music for which the society has acquired a nonexclusive right. The two primary licensing societies in the United States are the Association of Composers, Artists and Publishers (ASCAP) and Broadcast Music, Inc. (BMI).[39] Both organizations serve similar functions. ASCAP, founded in 1914, has a membership of more than 360,000 composers, authors and publishers and nonexclusive rights to more than 8 million musical compositions.[40] BMI, a nonprofit corporation formed in 1939, has about 400,000 writer and publisher affiliates, and holds nonexclusive rights to the public performance of more than 6.5 million musical compositions.[41] Both societies grant blanket licenses to broadcast stations and other entities so they can use any of the music licensed to the societies without having to obtain the permission of individual copyright owners.

Performance licensing is an efficient mechanism for collecting royalties because individual copyright owners are not faced with the onerous task of monitoring broadcast stations and performing venues around the country to catch copyright violators. Instead, the licensing society can handle this. The income from the fees garnered by each society is distributed, after a deduction for administrative expenses, to the copyright owners with whom the society has an agreement. Typically, the composer of a licensed song gets the same share of royalties as the publisher.

Performance licenses are often confused with two other types of licenses that apply to the use of music in movies or television shows: "synchronization" licenses and "master use" licenses. The use of music in film or video requires a synchronization license. A "sync" right allows the licensee to copy a musical recording onto the soundtrack of a film or other video production in synchronization with action so a single work is produced. Specialized agencies, such as the Harry Fox Agency, typically administer synchronization licenses on behalf of composers or those to whom copyrights have been transferred. If the music featured in the film or video (or commercial) is a *particular* sound recording of a musical work (not one produced especially for the film or video), a master use license is required. This gives the licensee the right to reproduce the "master" sound recording. Record companies that own sound recording copyrights usually administer master use licenses.

Broadcasters and film and television producers are not the only ones affected by licensing. In 1982, a federal court of appeals held that Gap clothing stores could be held liable for playing copyrighted music without a license when the company retransmitted radio station signals over speaker systems to customers in its stores. Generally, an office, store or other business (whether for-profit or nonprofit) does not have the right to rebroadcast radio signals because the station's blanket license covers only its original broadcast, not any other "public performance."

The key here is the retransmitting or amplification of a radio or television broadcast, as opposed to merely turning on the radio as background music in a business or workplace. The latter is allowed as a "homestyle exemption" under Section 110.[42] The homestyle exemption allows for televisions and radios carrying copyrighted programming to be played in commercial settings as long as (a) the receiving device is like that typically used in private homes; (b) there is no charge for seeing or hearing the broadcast; and (c) the transmission is not "retransmitted" to the public in any way.[43] Thus, the office worker who listens to his or her favorite country/western station at the office each day is not engaging in copyright infringement, but a metropolitan newspaper that, without consent, retransmits the music being played by a local top-rated radio station to the newspaper's 50 individual offices in its corporate headquarters is likely in violation.

To avoid liability, dozens of music services, such as Muzak, Super Radio and the Instore Satellite Network, offer audio services to stores and other public facilities. Most are delivered via satellite and are unscrambled. They cannot be broadcast without consent, however, which involves paying a monthly fee with the proceeds shared with owners of the copyrighted music, including composers and publishers.

It is no secret that ASCAP, BMI and other licensing societies routinely monitor radio and television stations and visit government-sponsored events, restaurants, bars, department stores and other public facilities to spot potential copyright infringers. Copyright violators are usually warned and threatened with a lawsuit if they do not halt infringement or obtain a performance or other appropriate license.

## Compulsory Licensing

One of the most controversial and complicated provisions of the Copyright Act of 1976 is Section 111, which provides a mechanism by which the management of a hotel, apartment complex or similar type of housing can retransmit the signals of local television and radio stations to the private lodgings of guests or residents. No direct charge may be made for the retransmitted signal and secondary transmission may not be accomplished by means of a cable system.[44] By paying a specified fee, a housing organization can make use of certain copyrighted works, such as songs or television signals, without obtaining consent from the copyright holder—hence the term "compulsory" licensing.

The primary beneficiaries of the royalties generated by compulsory licensing have been program syndicators, represented principally by the Motion Picture Association of America (MPAA). This group has typically gotten more than two thirds of the licensing revenue each year, but there are several other recipients, including the music industry (represented by ASCAP and BMI), professional and college sports associations and even National Public Radio (NPR).

## Copyright Duration

Assuming a creative work qualifies for copyright protection, it is important to keep in mind that the Constitution puts limits on the duration of such protection. Recall the language of Article 1, Section 8: "To promote the Progress of Science and useful Arts, by securing for limited Times to Authors . . . the exclusive Right to their respective Writings . . . ."[45] What is meant by "for limited Times" continues to be debated. Over the years, Congress has seen fit to extend the duration of copyright protection, granting authors increased protection and delaying the passage of works into the public domain.

With some exceptions, the 1976 law did not change copyright duration for works deemed protected prior to the new law taking effect. Under the old law, copyright lasted for 28 years and could be renewed for an additional 28 years for a possible total of 56 years. For these works, the 1976 law works the same way, but the length of the second (renewal) term is increased to 67 years. Thus, for works copyrighted before the 1976 law went into effect, the specific duration of protection depends on several factors, including whether the work was in its first term under the old law when the new law went into effect or whether the copyright had already been renewed when the new law went into effect.

The Copyright Act of 1976 is much more generous than the 1909 statute when it comes to duration, and even the 1976 Act has been amended to further increase the term of protection (the 1998 Sonny Bono Copyright Term Extension Act (CTEA) extended the original Act's copyright protection by 20 years).[46] Today, for the most part, works created under the 1976 Act are protected for the lifetime of the author, plus 70 years. That means that a 21-year-old songwriter who lives to be 91 will have the benefit of exclusive rights to his or her song for 70 years and the songwriter's heirs (assuming copyright has not been sold or otherwise transferred) will benefit an additional 70 years for a total of 140 years before the song goes into the public domain. The protection of a joint work (the songwriter contributed the music and a buddy wrote the lyrics) is measured by the lifetime plus 70 of the longest living contributor.

Works made for hire and anonymous or pseudonymous works are protected for 120 years from creation or 95 years from publication. Anonymous works are defined as works "of which no natural person is identified as author"; pseudonymous works are those on which "the author is identified under a fictitious name."[47]

## Copyright Notice

One of the most persistent myths about copyright, perhaps because the 1909 statutory requirements were so rigid, is that a copyright notice cannot be placed on a work unless the work has been officially registered. As noted earlier, this is not the case. The new law not only permits posting of the copyright notice on all works—registered and unregistered—but actually encourages this practice.

Under the 1909 law, published works that did not bear a copyright notice were lost forever in the twilight zone of the public domain. Copyright notice is still mandatory for works published before March 1, 1989, although failure to include the notice or giving an incorrect notice does not automatically negate the copyright, as it did under the 1909 law. Instead, the copyright owner is permitted to take certain steps, as provided in Sections 405 and 406 of the statute, to preserve the copyright. These steps include registering the work before it is published, before the omission took place or within five years after the error occurs, and making a reasonable effort to post a correct notice on all subsequent copies.[48]

Although not mandatory for works first published on or after March 1, 1989, a copyright notice is highly recommended. It gives the world notice that the work is protected, and provides useful information, including the copyright owner and year of publication, to anyone who may wish to seek permission to use the work. Providing the notice also prevents an individual or organization from claiming innocent infringement (discussed later in this chapter) as a defense to unauthorized use.

## Proper Notice

For purposes of notice, the copyright law divides works into two categories: visually perceptible copies ("copies from which the work can be visually perceived, either directly or with the aid of a machine or device"[49]) and phonorecords of sound recordings.[50] The distinction is important because the notices are different for the two.

For visually perceptible copies, the key three elements of notice are:

(a)  The symbol © ("C" encircled), the word *Copyright*, or the abbreviation *Copr.*
(b)  The year of first publication.
(c)  The name of the copyright owner.

Examples of a proper notice are:

(a)  © 2010 Roy L. Moore
(b)  Copyright 2010 Carmen Maye
(c)  Copr. 2010 Erik L. Collins

The first example is the one most recommended because it is the only form acceptable under the Universal Copyright Convention (UCC), of which the United States is a member. The UCC was founded in 1952 in Geneva, Switzerland, to bring international uniformity to copyright. If a work is unpublished, there is no mandatory form for notice because notice is not required, but a recommended form is: Unpublished work © 2010 Roy L. Moore.

## Placement of Notice

The Copyright Office has issued regulations that are quite specific, although flexible about where a copyright notice should be placed.[51] The statute says simply that for visually perceptible copies, "The notice shall be affixed to copies in such manner and location as to give reasonable notice of the claim of copyright."[52]

Congress delegated authority to prescribe regulations regarding notice to the Copyright Office in the same provision.[53] Examples of conforming positions of notice in the Copyright Office regulations for books are: (a) title page; (b) page immediately following the title page; (c) either side of front or back cover; or (d) first or last page of the main body of the work.[54] For *collective works* (defined earlier in this chapter), only one copyright notice needs to be given (i.e., it is not necessary, although permissible, for each separate and independent work to carry its own notice).

## Registration

Under the 1976 statute, a work is automatically copyrighted at the time it becomes tangibly fixed. The registration of a copyright, as opposed to its creation, is another matter. Although registration is no longer required for copyright protection,[55] there are major advantages to registration and the process is relatively simple. The advantages include:

(a)  public record of the copyright;
(b)  standing in court to file suit for infringement;
(c)  if made within five years of publication, *prima facie* evidence in court of the copyright's validity; and
(d)  if made within three months after publication or prior to infringement, the availability of statutory damages and attorney's fees.

Registration may be made at any time during the duration of the copyright by either mailing in a paper application form or by submitting an electronic application online. Registration must be made prior to filing suit for copyright infringement. As noted above, there are benefits to filing prior to or soon after infringement occurs, particularly in the assessment of damages. For works registered in timely fashion, the copyright owner may be entitled to statutory damages and attorney's fees. Failure to timely register requires the copyright owner to prove actual damages if litigation ensues.

Whether filing by mail or online, applicants must submit a completed application and a filing fee which, as of this writing, was $50.00 to $65.00 for paper filing (depending on the form used) and $35.00 for electronic filing. Payment may be made by check, by credit card or via a Copyright Office Deposit Account. Depending on the type of work being registered and the method of application, the applicant must deposit either electronic or hard copies of the work. Copies of published books, for example, must be sent in hard-copy form; unpublished manuscripts and certain other works, on the other hand, may be submitted electronically as long as they meet certain digital formatting and size requirements.

The new electronic system features a single form, Form CO, for copyright registration. Under the former system, different forms were required

(Form TX, VA, PA, etc.) for registration, depending on the type of work being registered. Although the older forms are still accepted for paper filing, the use of Form CO can now be used for both paper and electronic filing. Forms and more information are available on www.copyright.gov, the official Copyright Office Web site. The site also features an "eCO Tutorial" that helps explain the registration process.[56]

## Copyright Infringement

An *infringer* is defined as "[a]nyone who violates any of the exclusive rights of the copyright owner . . . or who imports copies or phonorecords into the United States in violation of section 602" ("Infringing importation of copies or phonorecords").[57] The Copyright Act of 1976 has considerable teeth for punishing infringers. Chapter 5 of the Act provides a wide variety of remedies, including civil and criminal penalties and injunctions. The 1989 revision, implementing the Berne Convention treaty, increased the penalties even more. The statute sends a clear message that copyright infringement does not pay.

The list of individuals and organizations who have been sued (many successfully) for copyright infringement are legion. As just two examples, in 2008 singer Avril Lavigne settled out of court with two songwriters who claimed in a lawsuit that Lavigne's hit "Girlfriend" was substantially similar to the songwriters' work, "I Wanna Be Your Boyfriend," recorded by the Rubinoos in 1978.[58] Two years earlier, a British firm, Shepperton Design Studios, and its president were ordered by a U.S. District Court judge to pay Lucasfilm Ltd. $20 million in damages for marketing unlicensed copies of helmets and costumes from the Star Wars films.[59]

And it needn't be just celebrities or major corporations. In 1984, the Roman Catholic Archdiocese of Chicago was found guilty of copyright infringement by a U.S. District Court jury and ordered to pay $3.2 million in damages for using copyrighted hymns without permission. The rights were owned by Dennis Fitzpatrick, a composer and president of F.E.L. Publications Ltd. of Los Angeles. The archdiocese unsuccessfully claimed that it had made an honest mistake and had not intentionally avoided paying royalties.[60] In 1989, Walt Disney Productions ordered the Very Important Babies Daycare Center in Hallandale, Fla., to remove paintings of Mickey and Minnie Mouse, Donald Duck and Goofy from its walls because of copyright infringement.[61] Note that although the characters are trademarks, their depictions in individual drawings were copyrighted.

In yet another example, Garrison Keillor, the star of National Public Radio's (NPR) "A Prairie Home Companion," sued the noncommercial network for copyright infringement after NPR included a Keillor speech in its catalog of cassettes offered for sale to the public. The tape contained Keillor's presentation to the National Press Club the year before, which was carried live on NPR. Keillor claimed he owned the rights to the recording, and that he had never granted NPR permission to tape and distribute it in its catalog. The two parties reached an out-of-court settlement, in which the radio network agreed to make available 400 cassettes of the speech free to anyone who requested one.[62]

Video piracy takes two basic forms: (a) unauthorized duplication and sale, in which a pirate acquires a master, makes duplicates and then sells them; and (b) "second generation" video piracy, in which a pirate forges copyright documents so it appears that he or she is the legitimate owner and then goes to another country and forces the rightful owner to prove its claim of title.[63] To stem the tide of pirated videos, more DVDs and digital materials are now being encoded with special codes that make copying difficult. For example, before Warner Brothers released the movie *Batman*, the studio marked each of the 4,000 prints distributed to theaters with a unique electronic code that would appear on any video copies so investigators could trace pirated copies to a specific source.[64] Warner Brothers, in coordination with the Motion Picture Association of America, announced a reward of $15,000 to anyone providing information that led to the arrest and conviction of anyone for pirating the movie and a $200 reward for each of the first 15 pirated copies turned in.[65]

## Contributory Infringement

Despite its best efforts, Congress left some gaps in the 1976 copyright law, many of which have been closed with various amendments enacted since the legislation originally passed. The most prominent gap, at least from the consumer perspective, was revealed in *Sony Corp. of America v. Universal City Studios, Inc.*[66]

The case developed when Universal Studios, Walt Disney Productions and other television production companies sued the Sony Corporation, the largest manufacturer of videocassette recorders (VCRs)[67] sold in the United States at that time, for contributory copyright infringement. The Supreme Court looked to patent law (discussed in Chapter 8) for help in defining contributory infringement:

> We recognize that there are substantial differences between the patent and copyright laws. But in both areas the contributory infringement doctrine is grounded on the recognition that adequate protection of a monopoly may require the courts to look beyond actual duplication of a device or publication to the products or activities that make such duplication possible.[68]

Thus, those who enable copyright infringement to occur may be liable for contributory infringement if their contribution advances infringement more so than legitimate, nonobjectionable ends. In *Sony*, the production companies claimed the Japanese firm marketed to the public the technology to infringe on copyrighted works they owned. This infringement occurred, according to the plaintiffs, when consumers used Sony's Betamax VCRs[69] to record copyrighted programs broadcast on local stations, specifically "time-shifting" (the Court characterized this practice as the principal use of a VCR by the average owner).

A U.S. District Court judge for the Central District of California ruled that recording of broadcasts carried on the public airwaves was a fair use of copyrighted works, and thus Sony could not be held liable as a contributory infringer even if such home recording were infringement. In a narrow decision that dealt only with Sony's liability for manufacturing and marketing the recorders, the Supreme Court agreed with the district court that the company was not guilty of contributory infringement. In a 5–4 opinion written by Justice Stevens, the Court concluded that home time-shifting was fair use:

> First, Sony demonstrated a significant likelihood that substantial numbers of copyright holders who license their works for broadcast on free television would not object to having their broadcasts time-shifted by private viewers. And second, respondents failed to demonstrate that time-shifting would cause any likelihood of nonminimal harm to the potential market for, or the value of, their copyrighted works. The Betamax is, therefore, capable of substantial noninfringing uses. Sony's sale of such equipment to the general public does not constitute contributory infringement of respondents' rights.[70]

The Court went on to note that there is no indication in the Copyright Act that Congress intended to make it unlawful for consumers to record programs for later viewing in the home or to prohibit the sale of recorders. "It may well be that Congress will take a fresh look at this new technology, just as it so often has examined other innovations in the past. But it is not our job to apply laws that have not yet been written."[71] After the decision, several bills were proposed in Congress to respond to the Court's holding, such as taxing recorders and blank tapes, but most legislators apparently felt the political fallout from such legislation would be too great.

The *Sony* decision, which barely attracted a majority of the justices, left many unanswered questions. Is videotaping at home an infringement? Although the Court said that home time-shifting was fair use, the fair use doctrine does not mention such use as permissible. Since *Sony*, new technology has raised similar questions, particularly with respect to home audio recording. For example, XM (now Sirius XM), the satellite radio service, for a time allowed current subscribers to keep copies of songs on special receivers.[72] Before that, the Rio MP3 music player gave rise to a lawsuit over whether copying audio files for "place-shifting" was fair use.[73] As technology has evolved, these cases and others have continued to raise *Sony*-like issues of direct and indirect copyright infringement.

## Proving Infringement

Under Section 501(a) of the current copyright statute, anyone who violates any of the exclusive rights of the copyright owner is an infringer, absent a legitimate defense. The statute provides a wide range of remedies from injunctions to criminal penalties. To prove infringement, a plaintiff must demonstrate that he or she owns the copyright to the infringed work and the defendant(s) copied the work. The latter involves proving the defendant(s) had access to the work and that the two works are substantially similar.

Proving ownership is usually not difficult because the owner simply has to produce sufficient evidence that he or she created the work or that the rights to the work were transferred to him or her. Registration is one way to establish this because it constitutes *prima facie* evidence of the validity of the copyright if registration is made prior to or within five years after publication.

Sometimes ownership may be in dispute, however, as illustrated in a 1990 decision by the Supreme Court involving the 1954 Alfred Hitchcock movie, *Rear Window*. In *Stewart v. Abend*,[74] the Supreme Court ruled 6–3 that actor James Stewart and the late film director Alfred Hitchcock had violated Sheldon Abend's copyright to *Rear Window* when they released the film in 1981 for television and in 1983 put it on videocassette and videodisc.

The complicated story began in 1942, when a short story entitled "It Had to Be Murder" by Cornell Woolrich appeared in *Dime Detective* magazine. In 1945, Woolrich sold only the movie rights to the story (and not the copyright itself) to the story to B.G. De Sylva Productions, with an agreement that De Sylva would have the same rights for the renewal period (which under the statute at that time was an additional 28 years). In 1953, De Sylva sold the movie rights to a production company owned by Stewart and Hitchcock, which made the story into the still highly popular classic film, *Rear Window*.[75]

When Woolrich died in 1968, he left his estate, including copyrights to his works, to Columbia University. Chase Manhattan Bank, the executor for Woolrich's estate, renewed the copyright and, in 1971, sold the renewed movie rights to "It Had to Be Murder" to Sheldon Abend, a literary agent.[76] In that same year, the movie was made available for television, and Abend informed Stewart, Hitchcock's estate and MCA, Inc. (which had released the film) that he would file suit for copyright infringement if the movie were distributed further. MCA ignored the warning and allowed the ABC Television Network to broadcast *Rear Window*.

In 1977, a Second Circuit U.S. Court of Appeals held that a company that had acquired derivative rights to a work still retained those rights even if the transfer of rights from the original work had expired.[77] MCA relied on that holding because *Rear Window* was a derivative work, and re-released the film in 1983 on videocassette and for cable television. Abend filed suit once again, this time in California. It was dismissed by a California district judge, but, on appeal, the Ninth Circuit reversed (disagreeing with the Second Circuit) and the Supreme Court upheld the reversal 6–3.

Writing for the majority, Justice O'Connor said the 1977 Second Circuit decision was wrong because the 1909 statute in effect at the time of the ruling provides that the original copyright to a work continues, if renewed, even if derivative rights have been granted. Thus, derivative rights expire when the original copyrights expire, and the owner of the original rights can prevent unauthorized use of the work. The Court was not sympathetic to the complaint by the defendants that "they will have to pay more for the use of works that they have employed in creating their own works. . . . [S]uch a result was contemplated by Congress and is consistent with the goals of the Copyright Act."[78] The decision affected hundreds of films and was estimated to cost the movie industry millions of dollars.[79]

Demonstrating access, the second major requirement for proving infringement, is usually a relatively simple matter, especially when a work has been widely distributed. But occasionally a defendant is able to prove lack of access. An example occurred in 1988, when rocker Mick Jagger successfully fought a copyright infringement suit against him for his hit song, "Just Another Night."[80] Reggae musician Patrick Alley claimed the chorus from Jagger's song had been lifted from a song Alley had recorded earlier. Alley claimed that Jagger had access to his song through a drummer who had played on both records, and that Jagger probably heard Alley's song when it was played on several smaller New York radio stations. Jagger denied he had heard the song, and a U.S. District Court jury in New York ruled in his favor after hearing testimony from the defendant that included him singing some of his lyrics.[81]

Substantial similarity is typically the key in proving an infringement case. Although it was rendered prior to enactment of the current copyright statute, a 1977 ruling by the Ninth Circuit has become a leading case on the criteria for evaluating substantial similarity. In *Sid and Marty Krofft Television Productions, Inc. v. McDonald's Corp.*,[82] the creators of the show "H.R. Pufnstuf" successfully claimed that McDonald's television commercials infringed on their copyright because the McDonaldland setting in the hamburger chain's ads and the characters portrayed in them were substantially similar to those in "H.R. Pufnstuf."

The court of appeals applied a two-prong test in reaching its conclusion. First, is there substantial similarity between the underlying general ideas of the two works? If the answer is "no," there is no infringement. If "yes," the second question is: is there substantial similarity in the manner of expression of the two works? If "yes," there is infringement. If no, the lawsuit fails. Both of these are questions of fact for a jury to determine (or for the judge in a bench trial).

A classic case of substantial similarity involved the highly popular movie, *Jaws*. In 1982, a federal district court in California found that the movie *Great White* was substantially similar to *Jaws* and, therefore, an infringement.[83] The similarities were quite striking, as the court noted, including similar characters (an English sea captain and a shark hunter who together track down a vicious shark), a similar plot and even opening and closing sequences that were virtually identical. The judge in the case felt that it was obvious that "the creators of *Great White* wished to be as closely connected with the plaintiff's motion picture *Jaws* as possible."[84] The producers of the infringing movie were ordered to pay damages, and an injunction was issued to further ban distribution of the film.

The similarities were also striking in a 1989 Seventh Circuit U.S. Court of Appeals decision involving greeting cards.[85] For two years, Ruolo designed distinctive greeting cards for Russ Berrie & Company under a contract granting the latter the exclusive right to produce and sell the cards in the "Feeling Sensitive" line. When the contract expired and Ruolo notified the company that it would not be renewed, Russ Berrie marketed a similar line of cards known as "Touching You." The appeals court upheld a jury decision awarding $4.3 million for Ruolo on the basis that the cards were substantially similar, including being designed for similar occasions and identical in size and layout.

This same "look and feel test" is often applied in determining infringement in computer software cases, although a seminal article on the issue concluded that, "while broad protection may be given by some courts to the structure, sequence and organization of a program, copyright law provides no general protection for the overall 'look and feel' of a computer program."[86]

## Remedies for Infringement: Injunctions, Impoundment and Disposition

Under Section 502 of the Copyright Act, federal courts can grant both temporary and permanent injunctions to prevent infringement once infringement has been proven. The permanent injunction against *Great White*, mentioned earlier, is an example of how this form of equitable relief can be effective. With the injunction, the movie could no longer be distributed, shown or sold anywhere in the United States.

Although injunctions are clearly a form of prior restraint (discussed in Chapter 1), the courts have indicated they are constitutionally permissible to prevent further infringement of intellectual property rights. A mere threatened infringement is usually not sufficient to warrant an injunction, but once infringement is proven, an injunction becomes a potent weapon available for the copyright owner. As with all injunctions, violations can subject a defendant to citation for contempt and fines as determined by the court.

Section 503 provides two other effective remedies—impoundment and disposition. Impoundment involves the government seizing potentially infringing materials or forcing a defendant to turn them over to the custody of the court until the case is decided. In its final decision, the court can also "order the destruction or other reasonable disposition of all copies or phonorecords" determined to violate copyright.[87] The federal courts rarely resort to these remedies, but they clearly have the authority to use them.

## Remedies for Infringement: Damages and Profits

The most common remedy for infringement is an award of damages. A copyright owner who files suit against an alleged infringer can opt at any time before the court issues its decision to claim either actual damages (along with any additional profits) or statutory damages, but he or she cannot recover both.

Under Section 504, an infringer can be liable for actual damages caused by the infringement, plus any profits attributable to the infringement. All the copyright owner needs to show at trial to establish the amount of profit is the infringer's gross revenue.[88] There is no limit on the amount of actual damages the copyright owner can recover, so long as there is sufficient evidence to demonstrate the extent of the harm suffered. As with all civil suits in federal courts, judges have a responsibility to ensure that awards are not excessive in light of the evidence presented at trial. However, the judge and jury have considerable discretion in determining what is reasonable.

The 1988 revision of the Copyright Act[89] and subsequent amendments substantially increased the amount of statutory damages available. If the copyright owner of an infringed work chooses statutory damages instead of actual damages and profits, he or she can obtain an award from $750 (minimum) to $30,000 (maximum) for each infringement of the work, depending on what the court considers an appropriate amount. If the copyright owner can prove that the infringement was willful, he or she can recover, at the court's discretion, up to $150,000 for each infringement.[90] However, if the infringer can convince the court that he or she was not aware and had no reason to believe that he or she was infringing (i.e., innocent infringement), the court can reduce the statutory damages to as low as $200.[91]

There is a "fair use" provision tucked away in Section 504, under which "an employer or agent of a nonprofit educational institution, library or archives acting within the scope of his or her employment . . ." cannot be held liable for statutory damages for infringement in reproducing a work if the person "believed and had reasonable grounds for believing that the use was a fair use."[92] A similar exception is made for public broadcasting employees who infringe by performing or reproducing a published, non-dramatic literary work.

## Other Remedies for Infringement

Under Section 505, a court can award court costs (i.e., the expenses involved in pursuing the litigation) and reasonable attorney's fees to whichever side wins.[93] These remedies are at the discretion of the judge. Finally, under certain circumstances, anyone who willfully infringes for commercial or private financial gain additionally can be fined up to $250,000 and/or imprisoned for a maximum of 5 years. Such willful actions include reproducing or distributing during any 180-day period at least 1,000 phonorecords or copies of one or more sound recordings,[94] or at least 65 copies of one or more motion pictures or other audiovisual works.[95]

The FBI is the primary police authority for enforcing the criminal provisions of the copyright statutes. The statutes also include a provision making it a federal crime to traffic in counterfeit labels for phonorecords and copies of motion pictures and other audiovisual works.[96]

## International Protection Against Copyright Infringement

Copyright owners are able to take criminal and civil action against infringers in other countries because of various international agreements the United States has signed and conventions treaties it has joined. However, there is no universal international copyright; instead, the treatment afforded works copyrighted in the United States differs considerably from country to country.

The most sweeping changes in international copyright have been wrought by the ongoing Berne Union for the Protection of Literary and Artistic Property (Berne Convention), which met first in Berlin in 1908 and most recently in Paris in 1971. The United States, however, did not join the convention until March 1, 1989, after 78 other nations were already members. The major impact of joining was that the United States must now treat the works copyrighted in other Berne Convention countries the same as it treats works of its own citizens, and member countries must offer at least the same protection for U.S. works as they do for those of their own citizens.[97]

On January 1, 1996, the International Agreement on Trade-Related Aspects on Intellectual Property Rights (TRIPS), which was part of the

General Agreement on Tariffs and Trade (GATT), took effect. The agreement, which affects all members of the World Trade Organization (WTO) including the United States, allows copyright protection to under certain conditions be automatically restored to works from other countries that had gone into the public domain in the United States. For example, this restoration of copyright applies to works from countries that had no copyright agreements with the United States at the time the work was published, or works that did not have the requisite copyright notice before the Berne Implementation Act removed that formality.[98]

Despite these international guidelines, international enforcement is difficult and piracy of copyrighted goods remains a huge problem for copyright owners. China is an example of a country that seems of two minds where protecting foreign copyrights is concerned. China is a signatory to the Berne Convention and has pledged to cooperate with the WTO's calls for it to honor its copyright-protection obligations. In reality, however, the International Intellectual Property Alliance maintains that global piracy causes significant economic losses to U.S. publishers, software manufacturers and motion picture producers.[99]

## Defenses to Infringement

There are four key defenses to copyright infringement, although the first one is technically not a defense, but a mitigation of damages: (a) *innocent infringement*, (b) *statute of limitations*, (c) *license*, and (d) *fair use* (including parody).

*Innocent infringement* occurs when a person uses a copyrighted work without consent on the good-faith assumption that the work is not copyrighted because it has been publicly distributed without a copyright notice. The innocent infringer must prove that he or she was misled by the omission of such notice. He or she can still be liable, at the court's discretion, for profits made from the infringement, although not liable for actual or statutory damages.

There are two major limitations to this "defense." First, an individual cannot claim innocent infringement in the case of works published after March 1, 1989—the effective date of the Berne Convention Implementation Act of 1988. The Berne Convention does not require a copyright notice on any works—published or unpublished—and thus effectively prohibits a claim of innocent infringement. Second, innocent infringement can only be claimed for published works, not for unpublished works, because a copyright notice was not required for unpublished works even before March 1, 1989.

According to Section 507, "No criminal proceeding shall be maintained ... unless it is commenced within 5 years after the cause of action arose,"[100] and "No civil action shall be maintained ... unless it is commenced within three years after the claim accrued."[101] If such actions are not initiated within that time, the *statute of limitations* imposes a complete bar, no matter how serious or extensive the infringement.

For example, an unscrupulous writer who uses another writer's chapter without consent in his or her book published in January 2010 could be sued anytime until January 2013 for the initial publication. However, if the unscrupulous writer continues to publish his or her book with the pirated chapter, he or she can still be held liable in February 2016 for a book he or she permitted to be sold in March 2005, although the initial infringement occurred more than three years previously. Thus, each publication, sale and so forth constitutes a separate and new infringement. Because the statute of limitations is relatively long, it is rarely used as a defense to either criminal or civil infringement.

The typical way in which a copyright is transferred is through a written contract granting a *license*. Therefore, a valid license is a strong defense to a charge of copyright infringement. The Copyright Office does not publish a model contract, but there are dozens of copyright and intellectual property handbooks—some geared to attorneys and others aimed at laypersons—that provide sample agreements. One such sample contract can be found in the Appendix to this book.

Section 205 of the 1976 Copyright Act allows, but does not require, parties to record transfer agreements in the Copyright Office.[102] With such a recording, the individual to whom a right or rights have been transferred gains some important legal advantages, including serving as constructive notice[103] of the terms of agreement to other parties to ward off or to answer a charge of copyright infringement.[104] Recording the transfer also provides a public record of the terms of the agreement and establishes priorities in the event of conflicting transfers.[105]

Recording of transfers must comply completely with the provisions in Section 205 and rules of the Copyright Office. A fee must also be paid for each document. All transfer documents are first checked by the Copyright Office to make sure they comply with the requirements and then they are cataloged for the public record.[106] Anyone can gain access to copies of the documents through the Copyright Office's online computer file or by using the equipment in the Copyright Card Catalog in the Library of Congress in Washington, D.C.[107]

*Fair use* is the most familiar defense to copyright infringement. In the authors' opinion, however, public relations and advertising professionals will rarely be able to raise a successful fair-use defense. However, because fair use is a significant component of copyright law and often one of the most misunderstood, it is worthy of some discussion here, despite its limited applicability to public relations and advertising efforts.

Congress included dozens of definitions in the Copyright Act of 1976, but *fair use* is deliberately not among them because the legislators had difficulty defining the concept, as indicated in a 1976 report of the House of Representatives Judiciary Committee:

> The claim that a defendant's acts constituted a fair use rather than an infringement has been raised as a defense in innumerable copyright actions over the years, and there is ample case law recognizing the existence of the doctrine and applying it. . . . Although the courts have considered and ruled upon the fair use doctrine over and over again, no real definition of the concept has ever emerged. Indeed, since the doctrine is an equitable rule of reason, no generally applicable definition is possible, and each case raising the question must be decided on its own facts.[108]

Congress chose instead to incorporate four criteria into Section 107 that had evolved from court cases attempting to determine fair use. In determining whether the use made of a work in a particular case is a "fair use," the factors to be considered include:

(a) the purpose and character of the use, including whether such use is of a commercial nature or is for nonprofit educational purposes;
(b) the nature of the copyrighted work;
(c) the amount and substantiality of the portion used in relation to the copyrighted work as a whole; and
(d) the effect of the use upon the potential market for or value of the copyrighted work.[109]

Section 107 mentions specific examples of purposes that can involve fair use, including "criticism, comment, news reporting, teaching (including multiple copies for classroom use), scholarship, or research."[110]

Congress chose to establish broad guidelines and trust the courts to determine, on a case-by-case basis, what is and is not fair use, and that is exactly what the courts have done. Hundreds of court decisions have dealt with fair use, under both the 1909 and 1976 statutes. Each of the four "fair-use factors" listed above is important, but none is, by itself, determinative. Instead, the courts evaluate each situation in light of all four and attempt to strike a balance among them.

For example, in the 1985 opinion in *Harper & Row v. Nation Enterprises*,[111] the Supreme Court held that *The Nation* magazine had infringed the copyright jointly owned by Harper & Row and Reader's Digest Association to the unpublished memoirs of former President Gerald Ford. In early 1977, shortly after he stepped down as president, Ford signed a contract with Harper & Row and Reader's Digest to publish his then-unwritten autobiography. Ford granted the two publishers the right to publish the manuscript in book form and as a serial ("first serial rights"). In 1979, they sold the exclusive right to excerpt 7,500 words from Ford's account of his pardon of former President Richard M. Nixon to *Time* magazine prior to publication. Subsequently, an unidentified source furnished the editor of *The Nation*, a monthly political commentary magazine, with a copy of the unpublished manuscript.

Before *Time* could publish its excerpt, *The Nation* carried a 2,250-word feature that included verbatim quotes from the original manuscript. According to the Court, these quotes comprised about 13 percent of the *Nation's* article and its editor neither made independent commentary nor did any independent research before publication because, as he admitted at trial, he wanted to scoop *Time*. *Time* decided not to publish its excerpt and refused to pay Harper & Row and Reader's Digest Association the remaining $12,500 of the $25,000 it had agreed to pay for prepublication rights. Harper & Row and Reader's Digest Association then filed suit for copyright infringement against *The Nation*.

Nation Enterprises argued fair use as a defense, which the Supreme Court ultimately rejected. The Court analyzed the case in light of each of the four factors, but paid particular attention to the fourth factor:

> In evaluating character and purpose [factor one] we cannot ignore *The Nation's* stated purpose of scooping the forthcoming hardcover and *Time* abstracts. *The Nation's* use had not merely the incidental effect but the intended purpose of supplanting the copyright holder's commercially valuable right of first publication. . . .[112]

On the third factor (amount and substantiality), the Court noted that, although "the words actually quoted were an insubstantial portion" of the book, *The Nation*, as the District Court said, "took what was essentially the heart of the book."[113] The Court cited *The Nation* editor's own testimony at trial as evidence that he selected the passages he ultimately published "precisely because they qualitatively embodied Ford's distinctive expression."[114]

On the last factor (effect of the use on the potential market), the Court was particularly critical of *The Nation's* action and its impact. Noting that this factor "is undoubtedly the single most important element of fair use," the majority pointed to the trial court's finding of an actual effect on the market, not simply a potential effect: ". . . *Time's* cancellation of its projected serialization and its refusal to pay the $12,500 were the direct result of the infringement . . . Rarely will a case of copyright infringement present such clear-cut evidence of actual damage."[115]

Another test case of fair use is of particular relevance to organizations that systematically photocopy and share subscription materials among employees. In 1992, in *American Geophysical Union v. Texaco*,[116] a federal district court judge ruled it was not fair use under Section 107 when a Texaco scientist made single copies of articles from the *Journal of Catalysis*.

According to the testimony at trial, Texaco scientists routinely had the company library make single copies of articles from journals to which the company subscribed. The advantages of this procedure include permitting the workers to keep easily referenced files in their desks or on their office shelves, eliminating the risks of errors when data were transcribed from articles and then taken back to a lab for research and making it possible for them to take articles home to read.

The trial-court judge held this was not fair use, and thus an infringement, because Texaco's use was for commercial gain, substantial portions of the works were copied and Texaco's use deprived the copyright holder of potential royalties.

The Second Circuit U.S. Court of Appeals, in an interlocutory appeal[117] from the district court, upheld the trial court's decision, but with somewhat different reasoning.[118] The appellate court held that three of the four fair-use factors, including the purpose and character of use (first factor) and the effect on potential market and value (fourth factor), favored the publisher. The majority opinion disagreed with a dissenting opinion filed by Circuit Judge Jacobs, who contended that the majority's ruling would require that an intellectual property lawyer be posted at each photocopy machine. As the majority saw it, all Texaco had to do in the specific circumstances of the case was to simply take advantage of existing licensing schemes or work out one on its own.

The court noted, "[w]e do not deal with the question of copying by an individual, for personal use in research or otherwise, recognizing that under fair use doctrine or the *de minimis* doctrine, such a practice by an individual might well not constitute an infringement."[119] The problem in this case was that Texaco had a policy of encouraging the photocopying— at least of single copies—by its scientists as a group, which meant there was the potential for hundreds of copies of articles being made, thereby presumably depriving the publishers of potential royalties.

Section 107 of the 1976 statute specifically mentions criticism, comment and news reporting as purposes that can be considered fair use. However, as the courts have made clear, these uses do not always enjoy protection in an infringement suit. For example, in May 1991, a federal district court judge in Atlanta awarded WSB-TV $108,000 plus attorneys' fees and court costs against TV News Clips for videotaping portions of the station's local newscasts and selling them to the public. The court also issued a permanent injunction barring the company from making any further copies of newscasts or offering them for sale.[120]

## Parody

On March 7, 1994, the Supreme Court handed down its decision in the long-awaited case of *Luther R. Campbell a.k.a. Luke Skyywalker v.*

*Acuff-Rose Music, Inc.*[121] involving the original song, "Oh, Pretty Woman," written by Roy Orbison and William Dees in 1964. Twenty-five years later, Luther R. Campbell wrote a song, "Pretty Woman," which was intended to satirize the original work.

Campbell asked Acuff-Rose Music, Inc., the copyright owner of the original song, for a license to use the song in a rap version by 2 Live Crew, but Acuff-Rose refused. 2 Live Crew recorded its version anyway on the album, "As Clean as They Wanna Be," which sold almost 250,000 copies in less than a year. In response, Acuff-Rose filed a copyright infringement suit in U.S. district court. The trial court granted a summary judgment for the defendants on the ground that the 2 Live Crew song was a parody of the original, and thus fair use under the Copyright Act of 1976. On appeal, the Sixth Circuit U.S. Court of Appeals reversed the trial court in a 2–1 decision, holding that the 2 Live Crew song's "blatantly commercial purpose . . . prevents this parody from being fair use."[122]

The Supreme Court invoked the four factors and came to a different conclusion. The Court noted that, on the first factor, parodies by definition must draw to some extent on the original work they are criticizing: ". . . For the purposes of Copyright law, the nub of the definitions, and the heart of any parodist's claim to quote from existing material, is the use of some elements of a prior author's composition to create a new one that, at least in part, comments on the author's works."[123]

The Supreme Court spent little time with the second factor, noting that this criterion had never been much help "in separating the fair use sheep from the infringing goats in a parody case." The Court differed substantially with the Court of Appeals on the third factor. However, the opinion noted that, although parodists cannot "skim the cream and get away scot free," the lower court "was insufficiently appreciative of parody's need for the recognizable sight or sound when it ruled 2 Live Crew's use unreasonable as a matter of law."

The Supreme Court could not make a final determination from the record on the fourth factor. It did, however, criticize the appellate court for applying the presumption that commercial use was unfair use on this factor. Parodies and the originals usually serve different markets, according to the justices. "We do not, of course, suggest that a parody may not harm the market at all, but when a lethal parody, like a scathing theater review, kills demand for the original, it does not produce a harm cognizable under the Copyright Act,"[124] the Court said. The key is whether the parody is acting as a substitute or as criticism. In reversing the judgment and remanding it back to the trial court, the Supreme Court held:

> It was error for the Court of Appeals to conclude that the commercial nature of 2 Live Crew's parody of "Oh Pretty Woman" rendered it presumptively unfair. No such evidentiary presumption is available to

address either the first factor, the character and purpose of the use, or the fourth, market harm, in determining whether a transformative use, such as parody, is a fair one. The court also erred in holding that 2 Live Crew had necessarily copied excessively from the Orbison original, considering the parodic purpose of the use.[125]

## Copyright in a Digital, New-Media Age: Emerging Issues

The quantity of information available over the Internet and the relative ease with which it can be acquired and transmitted has transformed how we live and do business. Articles, photographs, graphics and many other types of information are just a few clicks away; copying, downloading or sharing digital files is incredibly easy. Rather than thinking of the Internet as an information superhighway, one could be tempted to view it as an information super "buffet." Judging from the number of copyright infringement and lawsuits regarding online piracy, this view of the Internet as an all-you-can-eat smorgasbord of information appears to be quite common.

This is unfortunate. The problem is that the Internet provides many easy opportunities for copyright (and trademark) infringement. This means intellectual property owners who are "ripped off" online effectively lose the preferred position afforded to them by the law. Detecting infringement and identifying the culprits can be time-consuming and costly. Nonetheless intellectual property owners with the resources to do so are ramping up efforts to identify and pursue infringement lawsuits.[126] Congress has stepped up to the plate as well with specific legislation to define the scope of potential liability for copyright and trademark infringement arising from use of the Internet.

Because success in advertising and public relations necessarily involves assimilating existing information as well as creating new information, those who work in the fields should pay particular attention to copyright laws when using the Internet. Copyright law applies equally to Internet-based infringement. Several recent additional provisions supplement traditional laws by addressing online infringement per se.

The Digital Millennium Copyright Act (DMCA)[127] passed in 1998, increases penalties for copyright infringement on the Internet. It also addresses copyright infringement liability for ISPs. Like Section 230 of the Communications Decency Act (discussed in earlier chapters), which gives ISPs limited immunity from the legal harm caused by third-party posters, the DMCA "limits ISPs from copyright infringement liability for simply transmitting information over the Internet."[128] The DMCA, however, requires ISPs to remove online content when they have notice that the content may be infringing copyright or trademark protection. Note that ISPs that remove posted content later found to be non-infringing may not be sued for having removed it.

Most traditional copyright jurisprudence involves direct copyright infringement. As discussed earlier in this chapter, direct infringement occurs when one party copies, distributes, displays or otherwise abridges one of the "exclusive" rights afforded copyright owners.[129] For example, suppose a graphic designer downloads a copy of a photograph from the Internet for use in a print advertisement or company brochure. Unless the photograph is in the public domain or unless the designer obtains permission (i.e. a license from the owner of the copyright in the photo) the designer has just committed direct copyright infringement. The designer, or perhaps the designer's employer if the advertisement is a work for hire, will be liable for the infringement. As a second example, each time a college student, sitting in his or her dorm room, downloads a song for which he or she has not paid (or shares a paid-for song with someone else), a direct copyright infringement also has occurred.

Contributory infringement, also discussed earlier in this chapter, occurs when one party enables another to violate the copyrights of a third party. Contributory infringement is possible outside of cyberspace, but the Internet has proven to be fertile ground for lawsuits complaining of contributory infringement.

One of the most famous involved Napster, an online file-sharing service, that allowed computer users to share MP3 files among themselves. Recording industry giant A&M Records, Inc. sued Napster for, among other things, contributory copyright infringement.[130] The Ninth Circuit Court of Appeals affirmed a district court finding that Napster was guilty of contributory infringement,[131] and Napster entered bankruptcy proceedings soon thereafter.

In 2004, Metro-Goldwyn-Mayer Studios, Inc. and 27 other plaintiffs took similar action against Grokster, Ltd., another file-sharing service.[132] Grokster attempted to dodge claims of contributory infringement by arguing that, unlike Napster, it did not store copyrighted material on its own equipment; instead, Grokster argued, it merely made software that allowed computer users to communicate directly with each other and exchange files without using Grokster as a repository.

The lower federal courts agreed with Grokster, but the Supreme Court of the United States ultimately remanded the case, instructing the Ninth Circuit to reconsider in light of Grokster's business model, which primarily was based on the infringing uses of the company's software.[133] That focus, said the Court, distinguished Grokster from Sony Corporation, which had successfully defended itself against a contributory infringement suit in 1984 where the Court ruled that the Betamax, made by Sony and used by individuals to record movies and television shows for later playback, was also capable of "substantial noninfringing uses."[134] Because

Sony had not depended on or encouraged infringing activity, Sony was not liable for contributory infringement. Grokster, on the other hand, built its business model around illegal file sharing and actively encouraged the practice.

Advertising and public relations professionals also should note that even small amounts of copied material transmitted by e-mail, texting or tweeting can lead to copyright infringement suits. Wise and prudent practitioners, therefore, should be vigilant in their own practices and be alert to head off potential problems caused by others in their organizations or their clients' organizations who may not be aware of the dangers posed by improper attention being paid to avoiding the violation of the copyrights of others.

# Chapter 8

# Patents and Trademarks

Public relations and advertising professionals routinely encounter copyright issues. But in many organizations, patents (which relate to inventions) and trademarks (which identify goods) can play an important day-to-day role as well. That's why an understanding of these types of intellectual property is essential.

As with copyrights (discussed in Chapter 7), the constitutional origins of patents can be traced to Article I, Section 8, of the U.S. Constitution, which gives Congress the authority "[t]o promote the Progress of Science and useful Arts, by securing for limited Times to Authors and Inventors the exclusive Right to their respective Writings and Discoveries."[1] Whereas copyright law provides a limited monopoly—and therefore, an economic incentive—to those who produce original works of authorship, patent law provides a similar monopoly that allows inventors to profit from their innovations. Because of their clear origin in Article I, Section 8, patents and copyrights are regulated almost exclusively by federal statutes.

In contrast, trademarks involve both state and federal statutes, as well as common law. Federal trademark law arises out of the Constitution's "commerce" and "supremacy" clauses. The commerce clause, also in Article I, Section 8 of the U.S. Constitution, provides that Congress shall have the power "[t]o regulate Commerce with foreign Nations, and among the several States, and with the Indian Tribes. . . ."[2] This authority for Congress to regulate interstate ("among the several States") commerce has been interpreted broadly; one offshoot is federal trademark law, codified primarily in Title 15 of the United States Code (known as the "Lanham Act" or the "Trademark Act of 1946").[3]

The supremacy clause, in Article VI of the U.S. Constitution, gives federal law the right of preemption over state law. It provides, in part:

> This Constitution, and the Laws of the United States which shall be made in Pursuance thereof and all Treaties made, or which shall be made, under the Authority of the United States, shall be the supreme law of the Land; and the Judges in every State shall be bound thereby,

any Thing in the Constitution or Laws of any State to the Contrary not withstanding."[4]

As a result, trademarks may be registered and have protection under either state or federal statutes, the latter occurring if the mark is used in interstate commerce. State trademark laws, however, are not permitted to conflict with federal law.

## Patents

The U.S. Patent and Trademark Office (USPTO), which, as the name indicates, handles both patents and trademarks, is an agency in the Department of Commerce headed by the commissioner of patents and trademarks, an assistant secretary of commerce. Patents, trademarks and copyright are all forms of exclusive (i.e., monopolistic) control that owners, who can be individuals or companies, can exercise to ensure that others generally cannot market, use or sell the work, invention or mark without the owner's consent.

There are three basic types of patents: utility, plant and design. Patents on mechanical devices, electrical and electronic circuits, chemicals and similar items are known as *utility patents*.[5] *Plant patents* apply to the invention or asexual reproduction of a distinct new variety of a natural plant[6] and *design patents* are issued for new, original and ornamental designs.[7] In 1994, the U.S. Court of Appeals for the Federal Circuit, which hears all appeals from all decisions in patent infringement suits,[8] ruled that computer software could be patented, although mathematical formulas and algorithms cannot be. In *In re Alappat*, the court reasoned that software "creates a new machine, because a general purpose computer in effect becomes a special purpose computer once it is programmed."[9]

## Creation and Duration

Under the current law, patents generally are protected for a 20-year term, measured strictly from the filing date. In some cases, the 20-year period can be extended for a maximum of five years when marketing time was lost because of regulatory delay.[10] The 20-year period was chosen because it has been the standard of the rest of the industrialized world for some time. The law also creates a means by which a provisional application can be filed while the inventor prepares the regular application, which must be filed within one year.

Securing a patent is typically only the first step in the process. Before the invention can be marketed, approval from other federal and state agencies may be needed. For example, a new food or drug product would probably require a green light from the U.S. Food and Drug Administration.

Protecting a name under which the invention is to be sold would require compliance with provisions of trademark laws, and probably trademark registration at some point. Unlike trademark and copyright laws, patent law is incredibly complex and the process of obtaining a patent is expensive, time-consuming and complicated. Attorneys who handle patent applications must be specially admitted to the Patent Bar. The filing fee for registering a patent is $330–$850 (if the company has at least 500 employees), and the costs of a search, which may be necessary to establish the novelty of the invention, can add up to thousands of dollars more.

An inventor also may file a provisional patent application, under which the patent is protected from infringement for one year without having to demonstrate that the invention has already been built and used (a requirement for protection under traditional patent law). During the one-year interim, the inventor is given the opportunity to market the invention without fear of it being stolen.

## Patent Infringement

Because the stakes can be quite high, patent holders for popular inventions rigorously defend their rights even against small-time entrepreneurs and companies. Infringement of a patent can result in extensive damages, as illustrated in the infringement suit filed by Polaroid against Eastman Kodak over instant photography.[11] When the dust settled in 1986, Eastman Kodak was ordered to pay Polaroid more than $1 billion in damages and was prohibited from further sales of instant photo cameras, film and related products. The suit was based on patents granted to Polaroid in the 1970s.

Patents are generally granted on a first-come, first-served basis, and the race to the finish line can be intense when competitors battle. When two or more claimants apply separately for a patent on essentially similar inventions, the USPTO will hold an interference proceeding, complete with motions and testimony, to ascertain the rightful inventor.

## Trademarks

Under the Lanham Act, a trademark is defined as ". . . any word, name, symbol, or device, or any combination thereof adopted and used by a manufacturer or merchant to identify his or her goods or services."[12] Thus, a trademark can be a name, slogan, design or distinct sound so long as it identifies and distinguishes the trademarked goods or services from those of others. The key characteristics are identification and distinction. Classic examples are the Nike Corporation's use of the name Nike, the "swoosh" symbol that appears on Nike products and the slogan "Just do it."

Colors were recognized as potential trademarks in the 1995 Supreme Court decision *Qualitex Company v. Jacobson Products, Inc.*[13] A unanimous Court held that the Lanham Trademark Act of 1946 allows trademark registration of a color. The opinion, written by Justice Breyer, said that the special shade of green-gold used to identify dry cleaning press pads made by Qualitex had acquired the requisite "secondary meaning" under the Lanham Act. A color acquires secondary meaning when consumers strongly associate it with a particular product. Jacobson Products, a competitor to Qualitex, had challenged the trademark registration, unsuccessfully arguing that such registration would create uncertainty about what shades of color a competitor could use and that it was unworkable because of the limited supply of colors. Sounds, such as the roar of the MGM lion, have enjoyed trademark protection for some time, although registration for sounds is harder to come by. As with colors, sounds can attain trademark status only if they have acquired secondary meaning. In 1978, the Trademark Trial and Appeal Board recognized the combination of the musical notes "G, E, and C" used by the National Broadcasting Company as a valid trademark.[14] Harley-Davidson, Inc., which already owns the rights to the word *hog* for motorcycles, applied for a trademark on its engine sound in 1994, but several competitors, including Suzuki, Honda and Kawasaki, opposed the registration. After six years of litigation, and with no apparent end in sight, Harley-Davidson abandoned its sound trademark application in 2000.

## Service Marks

Service marks are essentially the same as trademarks, except that they identify the source of services rather than goods. Bank of America, for example, the name for the institution that provides banking and financial services, is a service mark, as is the red and blue stylized mark that appears on the company's checks, ATMs and brick-and-mortar banking centers. Other famous service marks include Hertz, Avis, Home Box Office, The Movie Channel, Citicorp and True Value. The distinction between trademarks and service marks is semantic; the law operates identically for both. To avoid repetition, the term *trademark* is used hereinafter to refer to both trademarks and service marks.

## Purpose

Trademarks are extremely important in advertising and public relations. Through the effective marketing and communication of its trademark, an owner can build invaluable market goodwill. Think about the value of trademarks such as Coca-Cola, McDonald's, IBM, Kodak, Xerox, Sony and Walt Disney—it is no wonder that trademark battles can be intense and drawn out, with large sums of money at stake.

The basic purpose of a trademark is to enable consumers to identify the origin of a product or service. Identifying the origin does not necessarily mean knowing the specific manufacturer, distributor or franchise—it simply indicates an association with a particular source. The idea is that the consumer should be able to have confidence that all goods with a specific trademark are associated with the owner of the mark.

For example, when a viewer sees a television commercial for Hershey's Kisses, it is reasonable for a person to assume that all Kisses come from Hershey's. That does not mean, however, that the consumer can assume that all candy bearing the Hershey's trademark is necessarily actually made by the same company, but simply that Hershey's has given its consent for, and presumably imposed its standards on, the distribution of the products under its name. In other words, trademarks provide some indication of quality assurance.

Coca-Cola, for example, has licensed its own line of clothing. Walt Disney licenses or produces thousands of products, including toys, movies, clothes, games and, of course, its own entertainment complexes throughout the world. Neither Disney nor Coca-Cola actually manufactures the goods bearing their names; instead, they have contracts with other firms granting permission for the use of their marks.

Trademarks, like patents and copyrights, can be sold and transferred by a written agreement or contract just as with other types of property. When corporations merge and large companies acquire smaller ones, the trademarks are often among the most valuable assets. Consumers rely heavily on brand names or trademarks in their decisions, which is why a company will pay hundreds of millions of dollars to acquire an already well-established trademark for a brand of candy bar, for example, rather than market a similar candy bar under a new trademark. The existing brand is a sure winner; a new name could be a huge risk.

## Creation

The USPTO handles both trademarks and patents, but trademark registration is much different and far less expensive than for patents. In fact, copyright and trademark registration involve quite similar processes, although they are administered by different federal agencies. The similarities, however, between trademarks and copyright end there. Unlike copyright and patents, trademarks do not derive their origin from the U.S. Constitution, although the authority of Congress to regulate trademarks and service marks comes from the Constitution—more specifically, the famous commerce clause referenced earlier in this chapter in note 2. Unlike copyrights and patents, which have limited duration, trademarks can last indefinitely as long as the owner continues to use and register the trademark and takes appropriate steps to ensure that infringers are prosecuted and that the mark does not go onto the public domain.

Trademarks are statutory creations of state and federal government. Before a trademark can be registered under federal law (i.e., the Lanham Act), the owner must either use the mark on goods that are shipped or sold in interstate or international commerce, or have a bona fide intention to use the mark in such commerce.[15] Trademarks that are not used or intended to be used in interstate and/or international commerce can be registered and protected only under state law. Because trademark laws vary considerably from state to state, state laws will not be discussed here. Prudent advertising and public relations professionals, however, should be aware of state trademark laws that might affect their or their clients' business.

## Trademark Infringement

Trademark infringement occurs generally in one of two ways. Either unscrupulous manufacturers produce "knockoff" items that improperly (and illegally) display legitimate trademarks owned by others, or a product displays a mark that is confusingly similar to another, similar product. If a street vendor offers to sell designer merchandise on the cheap, one can assume the goods are trademark-infringing knockoffs. This is clear trademark infringement with definite negative economic consequences for the owner of the trademark.

A second type of trademark infringement—based on a likelihood of consumer confusion—is less straightforward but may be equally detrimental to the trademark owner. Consumers are likely to be confused when similar marks appear on similar categories of goods. For example, a company that sells winter coats with the "Bobwhite" trademark probably would be concerned about someone else selling "Bobwhite" boots—consumers may reasonably think the boots are made by the coat people. This might give rise to a legitimate trademark infringement lawsuit because of the likelihood of confusion. Bobwhite Coats would likely have no legitimate complaint, however, about someone who sells "Bobwhite" birdseed. No reasonable consumer would confuse birdseed with coats, and such a lawsuit would likely be unsuccessful.

Even when a likelihood of confusion is slim, companies with valuable marks often are aggressive in discouraging *any* use of similar trademarks. In 1996, for example, some coffee companies who sell their products on the Internet got a warning from Sun Microsystems which owns the trademark "Java" for its computer programming language. Sun was concerned that its trademark was being infringed by the use of the term *java* in some of the coffee companies' Internet addresses. According to press reports, there was a bit of irony in that several of the companies had used Sun's Java language to create their own Web sites.[16]

Sometimes companies cease using their own legitimate trademarks even without the threat of litigation. Often, the decision to change or abandon a trademark is made because of public relations or related concerns. For example, the famous L'eggs package for women's hosiery is now history because the Sara Lee Corporation phased out the containers in 1992 in favor of cardboard packaging that is less taxing on the environment.

Trademarks also may be changed or even taken off the market at the behest or urging of government, or sometimes because of consumer perceptions. In 1991, the Kellogg Company changed the name of its Heartwise cereal to Fiberwise under pressure from the FDA, which has a policy of discouraging the use of *heart* in a brand name. In the same year, the U.S. Federal Trade Commission (FTC) rescinded its initial approval of Powermaster as a brand name for a beer with a higher-than-usual percentage of alcohol because the agency also has a policy of banning brand names of alcohol that promote the strength of the alcohol content.

The Procter & Gamble (P&G) Company redesigned its decades-old moon and stars trademark, including eliminating the curly hairs in the man's beard that look like the number "6." The company had filed lawsuits and repeatedly issued statements attempting to dispel rumors that P&G supported Satan because of the sixes that appeared in the symbol's beard. (The number 666 is mentioned in the *Book of Revelation* in connection with the devil.) The company has continued using the trademark in its revised form, but it also uses two newer symbols—a scriptlike Procter & Gamble and P&G.

## Registration

The registration process and protection under federal law for trademarks and service marks are the same. Among the changes wrought by the Trademark Revision Act of 1988 is that the use of the trademark is no longer necessary prior to registration. The trademark owner needs only to have a bona fide intention to use the mark. The law also cut the term of registration in half—from 20 years to 10 years.

Contrary to popular understanding, it is not necessary for a trademark to be registered to be protected but it certainly is a good idea. As with copyright, there are some important advantages to registration, including:

(a) providing *prima facie* evidence of first use of the mark in interstate commerce and the validity of the registration;
(b) permitting the owner to sue in federal court (U.S. District Court) for infringement;
(c) allowing lost profits, court costs, attorneys' fees, criminal penalties, and treble damages, in some cases, to be sought;
(d) serving as constructive notice of an ownership claim, preventing someone from claiming that the trademark was used because of a

good faith belief that no one else had claim to it. In other words, once the mark is registered, any potential user has an obligation to check the registry to ascertain that no one else owns the mark; and

(e) establishing a basis for foreign registration.

Registration is a fairly simple process. The owner files an application (online filing is available at www.uspto.gov), supplies a drawing of the mark, pays a filing fee for each class of goods or services for which the owner is applying and provides three specimens showing the actual use of the mark on goods or services if the mark already has been used in commerce. Filing fees for paper applications submitted by mail are $375. Online filing fee ranges from $275 to $325.

Once the USPTO has received the application materials, a trademark examining attorney must decide if the mark can actually be registered. Some registration attempts have been unsuccessful, such as the G. Anheuser-Busch Inc.'s failed effort with the mark "LA" for its low alcohol beer. The name "LA" was deemed merely descriptive, and thus lacking the requisite secondary meaning, or distinctiveness. According to the court, ". . . initials do not usually differ significantly in their trademark role from the description words that they represent . . . [and thus] . . . there is a heavy burden on a trademark claimant seeking to show an independent meaning of initials apart from the descriptive words which are their source."[17]

A registration refusal can be appealed to the Trademark Trial and Appeal Board, an administrative tribunal in the USPTO. Further refusal can be appealed to the federal courts. The Supreme Court of the United States has jurisdiction to hear further appeals, but rarely does so.

If approval is granted, the mark is published in the *Trademark Official Gazette*, a weekly bulletin from the USPTO. Anyone opposing the registration has 30 days after the publication to file a protest with the Trademark Trial and Appeal Board, which acts like a trial court. If there is no opposition, in about three months after publication, the registration then becomes official if the application was based on actual use in commerce. If the application is based on an intention to use the mark in commerce, the trademark owner has six months to either use the mark in commerce or request a six-month extension. As of January 1, 2010, there is a rebuttable presumption that if a trademark is not used for three years, it has been abandoned. Under a rebuttable presumption, the owner would have the burden of demonstrating that the trademark was in use in any subsequent infringement suit.

Once federal registration is issued by the USPTO, the owner must provide notice of registration by using (a) the ® symbol; (b) the phrase, Registered in U.S. Patent and Trademark Office; or (c) the abbreviation, Reg. U.S. Pat. & Tm. Off. These registration symbols cannot be used before registration. Prior to registration, an owner is free to use ™ or ℠ as symbols of a trademark and service mark, respectively, although he or she is not required to do so. Recall that, under the federal statute, registration is not required for trademark protection, although there are many advantages to registration.

Grounds on which marks can be excluded from registration include that the mark:

(a) disparages or falsely suggests a connection with people, organizations, beliefs, or national symbols, or brings them into contempt or disrepute;
(b) consists of or simulates the flag, coat of arms, or other insignia of the United States, a state, a city, or any foreign country;
(c) is immoral, deceptive, or scandalous;
(d) is the name, portrait, or signature of a living person unless he or she has given permission;
(e) is the name, portrait, or signature of a deceased U.S. president while his surviving spouse is alive unless the spouse has given consent;
(f) is so similar to a mark previously registered that it would be likely to confuse or deceive a reasonable person; and
(g) is simply descriptive or deceptively misdescriptive of the goods or services.

If an applicant can demonstrate that a mark already being used in commerce has become distinctive enough that the public now identifies the goods or services with the mark, it can be registered even if it is merely descriptive. For example, *World's Finest* is a registered trademark of World's Finest Chocolate, Inc.

Trademark registration is not restricted to commercial enterprises. Individuals, as well as nonprofit organizations, trade associations and other groups, can register trademarks. For example, the Society of Professional Journalists (SPJ) registered its name and logo—along with the name, Sigma Delta Chi—as trademarks in 1991. Trade names such as International Business Machines Corporation and Pepsi-Cola Bottling Company cannot be registered as trademarks under the federal statute, but the name associated with the product or service (i.e., International Business Machines, IBM, Pepsi-Cola and Pepsi) can be registered, and the corporation name can be filed and registered with the appropriate official (usually the Secretary of State) in each state.

Prudent advertising and public relations professionals should be familiar with the registration process because it can play a major role in determining the outcome of an infringement suit or a suit over ownership of the mark. A good start is the USPTO Web site, which features *Basic Facts About Trademarks*.[18] The International Trademark Association, a private organization in New York City, also distributes informative materials, as does the American Bar Association's Section on Intellectual Property Law.[19]

## Protecting a Trademark

The owners of popular trademarks such as Xerox, IBM, Kleenex and Kodak sometimes purchase ads in professional publications informing journalists and others that their names are registered trademarks and should be identified as such. Many famous former trademarks, such as cornflakes, linoleum, mimeograph, escalator and raisin bran, went into the public domain, and thus lost their protection as trademarks because they were abandoned or the owners did not aggressively fight infringers. Some companies send out press releases and buy ads in trade publications requesting that their trademarks be used as a proper adjective in connection with their products and services, and not as a verb. For example, one may use the search engine, Google, but should not "google" the search.

Advertisers are particularly irked when news stories and other communications mention trademarks without identifying them as such. *The Associated Press Stylebook and Briefing on Media Law* notes, in its "trademark" entry, "[i]n general, use a generic equivalent unless the trademark name is essential to the story."[20] The *Stylebook* also says that trademarks should be capitalized when they appear.

Some companies have a reputation for notifying newspapers, magazines and radio and television stations when they believe their trademarks have been used inappropriately. They do this because it is one way to demonstrate a strong effort to protect the marks in case an infringement occurs and they have to counter the claim from a defendant that the mark has become generic and thus no longer worthy of protection. Although a company would have no real basis for claiming infringement simply because a news or feature story made generic use of a trademark, the savvy advertiser and public relations professional should remind reporters, editors and other journalists from time to time that good journalistic practice dictates appropriate acknowledgment of trademarks. When registered slogans, names or symbols are used in an advertisement, press release or other publication, the registered trademark symbol or the ™ designation should be used, as appropriate to alert the world to the trademark's status.

## Remedies for Infringement

Thousands of battles have been fought about trademarks over the years for products ranging from apples to zippers. Trademark owners who discover trademark infringement have several options, ranging from friendly negotiation to intense litigation. Often, enforcement of trademark rights begins with a friendly (but firm) letter from the trademark owner's attorney pointing out the infringement and requesting that it cease immediately. If such a letter is ineffective, or if compensation is sought, the owner may ultimately turn to litigation in federal court. The traditional remedy for trademark infringement is injunctive relief. In other words, a court can require that an infringer take certain actions or cease taking certain actions. The Lanham Act gives courts power to grant injunctions in a variety of ways. Injunctive relief may include requiring the infringer to run corrective advertising and recall and destroy all goods bearing the infringing trademark.[21] In 2004, for example, Adidas America, Inc., the athletic-apparel maker famous for its three stripes, filed suit against Ralph Lauren Corp., complaining about a Polo jacket featuring sleeves with two stripes. Adidas requested that the court order the defendant to recall all the two-striped apparel and any related advertising materials so that it could be impounded and destroyed.

Sometimes a court will award monetary relief to a trademark owner. Monetary relief is not guaranteed in trademark litigation, but can be significant when awarded. The sum may include the defendant's profits, the cost for corrective advertising, attorney's fees, costs and triple the plaintiff's damages. In cases involving counterfeit goods, the Lanham Act allows for statutory damages of not less than $1,000 or more than $200,000 per counterfeit mark per type of goods.[22] If the counterfeit was willful, the statute allows the court to award up to $2 million per counterfeit per type of goods.[23]

## Trademarks and Parody

Although the Trademark Law Revision Act of 1988 permits a trademark owner to recover damages and get an injunction for product or service misrepresentation, the law only applies to commercial misrepresentation and not to political communication, editorial content or parodies.

An example of the latter is the case of *L.L. Bean, Inc. v. Drake Publishers, Inc.*[24] When Drake published a sex catalog parodying L.L. Bean's famous clothing catalog, L.L. Bean filed suit seeking an injunction against the parody, claiming that Drake's *Back-To-School-Sex-Catalog* violated Maine's anti-dilution statute. Such statutes are aimed at protecting trademarks and similar names from suffering disparagement, and thus having their commercial value chipped away through unauthorized use. The First Circuit U.S. Court of Appeals ruled that, because the sex catalog was noncommercial use, the anti-dilution statute could not be used to prohibit its publication because of First Amendment concerns.[25]

Note, however, if the sex catalog had been an attempt to actually market products rather than simply an artistic endeavor, and had it been published after the new Act took effect on November 16, 1989, the Court probably would have ruled in favor of L.L. Bean. Recall that Larry Flynt's notorious Campari parody about Jerry Falwell (discussed in Chapter 5) had First Amendment protection according to the Supreme Court of the United States. The manufacturer of Campari took no legal action against Flynt, but probably would have been unsuccessful anyway because the ad was editorial commentary, not commercial material.

## Trademarks in a Digital, New-Media Age: Emerging Issues

The Internet has spawned significant trademark legislation and litigation. The Federal Trademark Dilution Act of 1995 (FTDA)[26] gave trademark owners another means to pursue parties who use trademarks without permission. As noted at the outset of this chapter, a central concern of trademark law is to prevent a trademark from being used in such a way that it is likely to cause confusion among consumers as to the source of a good (or service, in the case of service marks). Even absent a likelihood of confusion, the FTDA allows owners of famous trademarks to pursue legal claims against others who disparage the mark or otherwise detract from the mark's distinctiveness.

An example of dilution that arose prior to the passage of the FTDA involved the sale of posters with the words "Enjoy Cocaine" in a typeface and colors that mimicked the Coca-Cola trademark. Coca-Cola Company obtained a court order prohibiting the sale of the posters. Similarly, food-service giant McDonald's Corporation also brought a successful dilution claim against a competing restaurant chain named McBagels, Inc. This type of use "blurs" or "tarnishes" the trademark's value and is specifically prohibited under the FTDA. Although the FTDA is a general statute that can apply outside of cyberspace, the Internet—particularly domain names—has given the statute a real workout over the last decade. An early case brought under the dilution Act was decided in 1998. In *Panavision International v. Toeppen*,[27] the makers of Panasonic products sued an individual who registered Internet domain names featuring famous trademarks and then attempted to sell them for profit. The defendant registered www.panavision.com,[28] preventing the internationally known electronics maker from registering this most obvious of domain names. The Ninth Circuit Court of Appeals affirmed the lower court's finding that the defendant had diluted the Panasonic mark by making it more difficult for potential customers to find the legitimate Panasonic Web site.[29]

Prior to 2006, it was unclear if a trademark owner claiming dilution under the FTDA had to prove the mark *actually* had been diluted or if the *potential* for dilution was sufficient to support a claim. In 2003, the Supreme Court of the United States decided *Moseley v. V Secret Catalogue, Inc.*,[30] and held that proof of actual dilution was required. In that case, lingerie seller Victoria's Secret unsuccessfully complained that

"Victor's Little Secret" (for a store selling adult-oriented merchandize, including lingerie) diluted the Victoria's Secret trademark. In its opinion, the Supreme Court said the fact that consumers may see the Victor's Little Secret mark and think of the more famous Victoria's Secret was not enough for dilution; proof of actual harm was required.[31]

Congress clarified its intent with the Trademark Dilution Revision Act of 2006,[32] effectively overturning *Moseley*. The revised Act provides that the likelihood of dilution, not actual dilution, is sufficient. It also attempts to define "blurring"[33] and "tarnishment"[34] and specifies that dilution claims must be based on one of these two grounds.

The conduct at issue in *Panasonic* is known as cybersquatting, a reference to the early Westward expansion of the United States, in which "squatters" inhabited parcels of land and then claimed them as their own. In 1999, Congress sought to protect the public from bad-faith, abusive registration of Internet domain names with the Anticybersquatting Consumer Protection Act (ACPA).[35] This Act allows owners of distinctive or famous trademarks to obtain injunctions against the misuse of their trademarks as well as damages from those who attempt to profit from the use of the trademark, at least if acting in bad faith.

Settling disputes over domain names does not always require litigation. A public–private partnership, Internet Corporation for Assigned Names and Numbers (ICANN), oversees the global registration of Internet domain names.[36] In 1999, ICANN adopted the Uniform Domain-Name Dispute Resolution Policy (UDRP) to help resolve domain-name disputes that allege abusive, bad-faith registration of a domain name. Disputes that do not include allegations of abuse or bad faith are not handled under the UDRP; these must be resolved through lawsuits or other negotiations.

Trademarks have considerable protection under both state and federal law, but trademark holders must take aggressive steps to ensure that their marks do not become diluted and risk going into the public domain. Prudent advertising and public relations professionals representing commercial and noncommercial enterprises should constantly monitor the use of their trademarks for possible infringement, while making sure that they treat the trademarks of others with appropriate respect.

# Chapter 9

# Other Ways to Protect "Ideas"

Once an idea is made public, it becomes "free as the air"[1]—that is unless the idea can qualify for protection under intellectual property law, other federal or state statutory laws or state common laws.

Intellectual property laws involving protection of patents, trademarks and copyrights discussed in the preceding chapters most often provide legal protection for "ideas" expressed in tangible forms, such as blueprints for devices, renderings of graphic logos or trade names, writings or other tangibly fixed artistic creative expressions. However, under appropriate circumstances, a variety of other legal remedies may come to the rescue of those who fear their ideas may be or have been commercially appropriated by others. Among these are laws dealing with the protection of trade secrets, the torts of misappropriation of intangible property interests and business schemes and the formation of contractual relationships related to creative expression.

## Trade Secrets

Trade secrets can take many forms including formulae, plans, processes, devices and compounds. Colonel Sanders' secret recipe for fried chicken or the original formula for the soft drink Coca-Cola come readily to mind. Other illustrations of this legal concept range from lists of ingredients or formulae for drugs to the maps of plans for acquisition of property to blueprints for expansion of an existing manufacturing plant. As an example of the wording of a typical state law, the Illinois Trade Secrets Act defines a trade secret as "information, including but not limited to, technical or non-technical data, a formula, pattern, compilation, program, device, method, technique, drawing, process, financial data. . . ."[2] Perhaps a more relevant example of a trade secret for advertising and public relations professionals would be an advertising/marketing communications campaign proposal for a potential client that the agency would not wish disclosed to a competing agency or the potential client's competitor.

According to the Uniform Trade Secrets Act,[3] the distinguishing characteristics of a protectable trade secret are: (a) the trade secret has commercial value by virtue of the fact that it gives the owner a business advantage over competitors who are not familiar with it; (b) the trade secret is known only to those individuals who are entitled to know it; and (c) those in possession of the trade secret have made reasonable efforts to protect it from detection.

In addition to the three-part test noted above, both federal and state laws generally require the alleged trade secret not only to contain some useful information, but also to contain an element of creativity "if merely because that which does not possess novelty is usually known; secrecy, in the context of trade secrets, thus implies at least minimal novelty."[4]

Under federal and state laws, a trade secret must be kept secret, particularly from competitors or potential competitors, to warrant protection. For example, North Carolina defines misappropriation of a trade secret as the "acquisition, disclosure, or use of a trade secret of another without express or implied authority or consent"[5] unless disclosed by someone who had authority to release the secret. Unauthorized disclosure of trade secrets may occur when an "insider" (e.g., an employee or prospective client) reveals the information to a competitor. To protect against such eventualities, organizations often require insiders to sign formal agreements imposing a duty of nondisclosure. Properly drawn, such contractual agreements generally are upheld by courts as a legitimate restriction on commercial speech.

Additionally, an organization may require a contractual agreement between itself and those employees with access to trade secrets promising not to accept future employment with competing companies or agencies for a reasonable period of time following departure from the original organization. The enforcement by the courts of such agreements (so-called "covenants not to compete") often depends on the reasonableness of the provisions of the employment contract as they relate to a particular employee challenging their application.

Courts, however, may also uphold sanctions for unauthorized disclosure of trade secrets in cases involving employees or business partners, even in the absence of any written agreement not to disclose. Such an implied duty of non-disclosure might arise in situations in which the courts find that the parties with access to the trade secret (e.g., partners in a firm) acted in such manner as to indicate that it was the expectation that the information not be disclosed.

For example, Pepsico successfully obtained a court injunction to prevent one of its former officers from assuming a position with Quaker Oats for six months after leaving his position and forever prevent him from disclosing trade secrets regarding the company's annual operating plan.[6] The annual plan included marketing strategies for Pepsico to position its AllSport drink to compete with Quaker's Gatorade.

Sometimes the disclosure of a trade secret may come not from an employee or business partner but from an "outsider." Obviously, stealing or engaging in criminally fraudulent activity to acquire trade secrets may well bring civil and criminal penalties. However, the methods employed to gain a competitive advantage by means of learning a rival's trade secrets need not rise to this level to be actionable. In *E.I. du Pont de Nemours & Co., Inc. v. Rolfe Christopher et al.*,[7] the defendants, who ran an aerial photography business, were found liable for illegally acquiring the plaintiff's trade secrets involving the building of a new chemical plant when they flew an airplane over the partially completed facility to photograph its construction in an attempt to discover du Pont's new manufacturing techniques.

Generally not actionable as illegal disclosures of trade secrets are disclosures that occur (a) without the recipient's awareness of the secret nature of the information (e.g., an innocent third party given or sold an idea by an unauthorized source); (b) as a result of deconstructing a product to determine its structure or ingredients; or (c) through legitimate use of freedom of information requests to a government office to obtain public documents (discussed in a later chapter).

Court-sanctioned remedies for appropriation of trade secrets may include injunctions, especially when (a) it is likely that a trade secret will be further disclosed if such a court order is not issued; (b) such disclosure likely would result in irreparable harm to the non-disclosing party; and (c) the information is still secret at the time the request for the injunction is made. More typically, those claiming disclosure of trade secrets may recover actual and/or punitive money damages to compensate for the harm done by the revelation of the information.

The Supreme Court of the United States has decided few cases directly involving trade secrets, probably because the lower federal courts generally are not involved in such cases unless they involve parties from two or more states ("diversity jurisdiction") or concern federal employees or federal law. Since 1974, the Court has decided only six cases focusing on trade secrets. In a 1974 case, *Kewanee Oil Co. v. Bicron Corp.*,[8] the Court held that Ohio's trade secret law may coexist with federal patent law. The Court noted, among other points, that the federal patent office policy of encouraging invention is not harmed by the existence of other incentives for invention like state trade secret statutes.

In 1986, in *Dow Chemical v. United States*[9] (a case based on the same facts as *E.I. du Pont de Nemours & Co., Inc. v. Rolfe Christopher et al.* discussed above), the Court held that the U.S. Environmental Protection Agency (EPA) was acting within its authority when it employed a commercial aerial photographer to take photographs from public airspace of a chemical plant after the company denied the EPA access for an onsite inspection. The Court said such observations were legitimate even though the company's competitors might be barred from such action under state trade secrets laws. The opinion noted that government agencies generally do not try to appropriate trade secrets from private enterprises and that state unfair competition laws do not define the Fourth Amendment's provision regarding unreasonable searches.

In *Ruckelshaus v. Monsanto Co.*,[10] the Court held that, under certain conditions, disclosure of a trade secret by a government agency could constitute a "taking" under the Fifth Amendment, particularly when such disclosures interferes with what the Court called "reasonable investment-backed expectations."[11] Without deciding whether there actually was a Fifth Amendment violation in the case, the Court said that trade secrets that enjoy protection under state law could constitute "property" for purposes of the Fifth Amendment, despite their intangible nature. The Court pointed out that the federal EPA had promised confidentiality in exchange for disclosure of the information to the Agency that the company had designated as trade secrets at the time of submission.

## Misappropriation of Intangible Property Interests

Advertising and public relations professionals are creative people. Creative people often look at a problem or situation and are struck with insights about how to resolve issues, improve on a company's performance or add to a corporation's intellectual property stock-in-trade. Unless these ideas can be tangibly fixed in so many versions as to make infringement of the idea impracticable or involve a character, design or other trademarkable concept, the tort of misappropriation of intangible property interests (and of business schemes discussed later in this chapter) may provide what little protection the law allows against those who "borrow" (some might say steal) and use others' creative ideas.

The principal question for disputants in a claim of misappropriation of intangible property is whether one party (a) appropriated another party's creative material that (b) was originally intended only for private use, and then (c) redistributed it to a broader public in order to make a profit. A classic example is a radio station with no news reporters that requires its announcers to simply "rip and read" slightly edited news stories taken directly from the local daily newspaper. The newspaper clearly expects many customers to buy individual copies of the paper, but does not appreciate these individual consumers (especially the radio station) then entering into competition with the newspaper by repackaging the creative efforts of the paper's reporting staff.[12]

The reader should note the difference between possible copyright infringement and a misappropriation of intangible property claim in the above example. If the radio station simply read the newspaper's reports over the air, the newspaper might have a violation of copyright case.

However, if the station makes minor changes in the wording of the newspaper's material and then uses it without permission, the newspaper's only remedy might be a lawsuit claiming misappropriation of intangible property.

In *Columbia Broadcasting System, Inc. v. Melody Recordings, Inc.*,[13] CBS complained that Melody Recordings engaged in the systematic process of re-recording records produced by the plaintiff and selling them under their own label. "What is involved in this case," said the court, "is the direct taking of the artistic and highly creative work of [CBS]. . . . Defendants have thus appropriated the unique product of CBS by re-recording its original records."[14] Characterizing the case as a classic misappropriation case, the court noted that:

> [t]he actionable unfairness of this practice inheres in a combination of factors—the substantial investment of time, labor, money and creative resources in the product by the plaintiff, the utilization of the actual product by the defendant, the misappropriation or use of the appropriated product by defendant in competition with plaintiff, and commercial damage to plaintiff.[15]

Similar examples have involved audio re-creation of ongoing sporting events and replication of clothing patterns.[16]

In addition to looking at the creative efforts of the plaintiff and the actions of the defendant in making use of the material to make a profit (usually with little effort to modify or change the original), courts recognizing the misappropriation tort also examine both the financial harm already suffered by the plaintiff and the probability that the plaintiff will be discouraged from continuing to produce the creative product if relief is not granted.

Remedies for misappropriation of intangible property interests usually involve money damages reflecting the amount lost by the plaintiff or gained by the defendant, although court orders (injunctive relief) ordering the defendant to stop the offending practices may be available in rare instances.

## Business Schemes

The term "business scheme" applies to ideas a creative individual dreams up (e.g., a new plot for an existing television show, a concept for a new movie or a new direction for an advertising or marketing campaign) and then attempts to sell to a client or producer. Like a work-for-hire under copyright law, the tort of misappropriation of a business scheme is not applicable to ideas suggested by regular, full-time employees of an organization who are paid to be creative as part of their normal, job-related requirements.

Because it not unusual for different individuals to think of similar creative concepts or for creative people to firmly believe that someone else has appropriated their good ideas (even in the face of evidence to the contrary), courts place a heavy burden on those seeking legal redress for misappropriation of business schemes.

Typically, a generic concept does not merit protection. "My idea is to have a television program about single women living in a big city and how they cope with modern life" might be a good idea, but most courts likely would find nothing so original or unique in such a concept that it could give rise to a successful suit for misappropriation of a business scheme if, after pitching the idea to a television network executive, subsequently a television network created a program with a similar theme. Even if the creative concept constitutes a genuinely break-though thought, evidence that another party independently also conceived of a similar notion might defeat such a lawsuit.

This does not mean that, for example, the entire concept of a new ad campaign must be reduced to storyboards or video spots before protection from piracy becomes available. State laws vary considerably, however, in the legal demands necessary to merit protection for ideas. States following the lead of the courts of New York tend to demand a showing of genuine novelty for an idea as a prerequisite for any protection. States following the lead of California courts, on the other hand, require only that an idea be of value and unique to another party.

In *Nadel v. Play-By-Play Toys & Novelties, Inc.,*[17] a New York-based federal court of appeals described the plaintiff as a "toy idea man. Toy companies regularly do business with independent inventors such as Nadel in order to develop and market new toy concepts as quickly as possible."[18] Nadel took the "eccentric mechanism" used in other toys "then on the market and placed the mechanism inside of a plush toy monkey skin to develop the prototype for a new table-top monkey toy. This plush toy figure sat upright, emitted sound, and spun when placed on a flat surface."[19]

Nadel met with representatives of Play-By-Play who "expressed interest in adapting the concept to a non-moving, plush Tasmanian Devil toy that Play-By-Play was already producing under license from Warner Bros."[20] When Play-By-Play subsequently introduced its "Tornado Taz" product at the New York Toy Fair, Nadel sued for misappropriation of a business scheme, claiming that, like his model, the defendants' toy "is a plush toy that emits sounds (including 'screaming,' 'laughing,' 'snarling,' and 'grunting'), sits upright, and spins by means of an internal eccentric vibration mechanism."[21]

In denying Nadel's allegations, Play-By-Play argued that "even if it did use Nadel's idea to develop 'Tornado Taz,' Nadel is not entitled to compensation because Nadel's concept was unoriginal and non-novel to the toy industry...."[22] A district court granted Play-By-Play's motion for summary judgment on the grounds that the plaintiff's "claims must ... fail for lack of novelty or originality because 'numerous toys containing the characteristics of [Nadel's] monkey were in existence prior to [the plaintiff's creation in] October 1996.'"[23]

The court of appeals noted that if Nadel's claim had been based on contract law, the plaintiff only needed to show that the toy mechanism idea was unknown to Play-By-Play. A misappropriation claim, on the other hand, "require[s] that the idea at issue be original and novel in absolute terms. This is so because unoriginal, known ideas have no value as property and the law does not protect against the use of that which is free and available to all."[24]

The California appeals court case of *Donahue v. Ziv Television Programs, Inc.*[25] demonstrates the alternative approach to the requirement of the novelty of the idea under dispute. According to the plaintiffs, "they conceived an idea for a television format which they entitled 'The Underwater Legion' [that was] submitted ... in written form, together with 12 story outlines, one screenplay and a proposed budget to defendant Ziv Television Programs, Inc."[26] Subsequently, the defendants (Ziv and Tors) produced "Sea Hunt" which, said the plaintiffs, "used, exploited and utilized plaintiffs' format and story outlines."[27]

The defendants denied that the idea for "Sea Hunt" was based on the plaintiffs' program format. The trial court found for the plaintiffs. On appeal, Ziv and Tors claimed that the idea underlying both the plaintiffs' concept and the program "Sea Hunt" had occurred to both parties independently and, therefore, the plaintiffs' material did not present a novel idea to the defendants.

The California court of appeals disagreed:

> An idea which can be the subject matter of a contract need not be novel or concrete. It may be valuable to the person to whom it is disclosed simply because the disclosure takes place at the right time. The success of 'Sea Hunt' tends to prove that somebody, whether it be plaintiffs or Tors, submitted a valuable idea to Ziv.[28]

The court noted that "[w]hether Ziv used plaintiffs' format or Tors' is another question, but certain evidence of similarities between some 'Sea Hunt' episodes and parts of the 12 outlines and the screenplay submitted by plaintiffs may have suggested to the jury that 'Sea Hunt' was based on plaintiffs' format."[29]

The court also noted that:

> [w]e do not imply that the outlines were protectable literary property or that there was any copying as to form or manner of expression. It is

just that there are enough similarities in basic plot ideas, themes, sequences and dramatic "gimmicks" that a jury might well have thought that plaintiffs' format and outlines had been submitted to Ziv as asserted by them and that it was their format which was the inspiration for "Sea Hunt," rather than Tors' alleged original idea. It appears to us that a jury could easily find that the format of "Sea Hunt" is quite similar.[30]

## Contracts as a Means for the Protection of Ideas

When someone mentions the word "law" in casual conversation, those within earshot might immediately think of a recently received parking ticket or the FCC's reaction to a nationally televised "wardrobe malfunction" during Super Bowl halftime or perhaps a television crime-show like *Law & Order*. We interface with massive amounts of "public" law every day, so it is not surprising that when the average American thinks of the "law," he or she thinks of law created within a legislative chamber or courtroom.

In fact, however, all of the thousands of volumes of codes, regulations and court opinions make up a mere fraction of the complex organism that is American law. Much of the legal system consists of little bits of "private" law, more commonly known as contracts.

It is useful and indeed relatively accurate to think of a contract as a kind of private statute that defines the behaviors, risks and obligations of the parties who have entered into it. The contract could be immensely complex, such as an agreement governing the exchange of billions of dollars for the construction of a new metropolitan airport. More commonly, though, it may be as simple as a customer in a local grocery store signing a credit card slip to purchase a six-pack of Miller High Life.

Each of the millions of credit sale transactions that occurs every day is a contract, or an enactment of private law, that defines the performances of the parties to the transaction: the credit card company (who has agreed to pay the retailer), the cardholder (who signs the slip and agrees to pay the credit card company at a certain time each month and at a certain interest rate) and the retailer (who performs the store's obligation by surrendering the six-pack to the purchaser).

Contractual arrangements are not limited to sales of goods. They literally may be used to define the boundaries of almost any relationship among bargaining parties, from employment and procurement of services, to the present context of protecting personal intellectual enterprise from exploitation by others. To understand how contract law might enter into the protection of ideas and creative expression, it is beneficial to first understand the basic components of contract law.

## The "Bargained-For Exchange"

Classical contract law is based on the concept that two sophisticated parties capable of exercising free will may enter into a private agreement that, if valid, will take its place alongside statutes and regulations as enforceable law. If one party to the contract fails to perform as promised (called a "breach"), the other party may then call upon public institutions such as courts to enforce a remedy against the breaching party. Courts, because they offer similar deference to private law as they do to statutory or regulatory law, may enforce a variety of remedies, ranging from awarding money damages to requiring the breaching party to live up to the letter of the contract, called "specific performance."

In simple terms, a valid contract requires a bargained-for exchange: one party makes an offer in the form of a promise to perform an act, and the other party has a right to accept the offer, either through a return promise or by performing an act. Each party's return promise or performance is referred to as "consideration" for the other person's promise or performance. To be enforceable as a contract, all promises must be supported by consideration of actual value.

To illustrate the concepts of offer, acceptance and consideration, consider the age-old practice of the neighborhood teen who makes extra money by mowing lawns. He approaches his neighbor and promises to mow the neighbor's lawn promptly that afternoon for a payment of $20. The neighbor happily accepts the teen's offer.

In this situation, the boy made an offer to perform a service that was accepted by the neighbor's return promise to make a payment of $20 when the job was completed satisfactorily. Each promise served as consideration for the other. On its face, this situation represents a valid, enforceable contract. If the boy cut the grass to the exact terms of the agreement but was not paid, the teen could be reasonably assured that a court would enforce a judgment for breach of contract against the non-paying neighbor.

Changing the scenario slightly, however, might create different results. If the boy had gone to the neighbor's house and offered to mow the lawn for free but then did not follow through with his promise, the neighbor could not expect to win a judgment against the teen for breach of contract because a court would likely say "no consideration = no contract."

Consideration may not be based on the performance of some past act. This becomes an important concept when we return to the discussion of protection of novel ideas.[31] For example, in our scenario, if the teen were feeling charitable, went to an elderly neighbor's house and cut the grass "just to be nice," the neighbor's subsequent promise to reward the teen with $20 would not create an enforceable contract at law if the promise slipped the elderly neighbor's mind. The teen's *past* act of mowing the lawn would not serve as consideration for the neighbor's promise to pay him. With these basic concepts in hand, it becomes somewhat easier to understand the dilemma that faces independent creative advertising consultants or starving aspiring sit-com scriptwriters.

Creative mass communicators who have chosen not to work in a corporate or organizational setting should give serious thought to protecting their creative efforts through any and all available means. If an idea has taken shape into an expressible form, the most obvious avenue of protection is to tangibly fix the expression so that it becomes subject to federal copyright law. When the idea is still just an idea, however, and thus not yet copyrightable, a confidentiality or non-disclosure contract may be the best available means of protection for the creator. Such a contract might provide a way to prohibit someone from appropriating the creative communicator's idea or even disclosing the idea in any context unless the communicator was compensated for its use.

The confidentiality/non-disclosure contract seems like a great idea on its surface, especially after the other party dutifully signs it. But what protection does such an agreement really provide? The answer is not as clear-cut as one might think.

Imagine that our hypothetical aspiring scriptwriter has approached a major network with an idea for a situation comedy. The network's creative team agrees to meet with the writer. At the appointed hour, the author pitches a great idea for a new sit-com: "a show about nothing." The writer describes a group of friends who are the primary characters on the proposed show and then outlines some of the situations in which the characters could be placed. Further ideas are suggested regarding ancillary characters who would be ideal comically inspired antagonists for the hypothetical show's main character.

The network representative tells the scriptwriter that the idea is great and that the network will "be in touch" regarding the possibility of collaborating on a pilot. No one from the network, however, ever does get back in touch. Some months later, while flipping through the channels one evening, the scriptwriter sees what appears to be an almost identical show—a show that goes on to become one of the most successful situation comedies in the history of television.

Any redress of this grievance for the writer? Even if the scriptwriter had hired an attorney to draft a non-disclosure/confidentiality contract to protect the ideas *prior* to pitching the idea (the wiser course of action), the question of whether a *pre*-disclosure agreement would be binding on the parties presents a difficult question. In this scenario, the scriptwriter makes an offer to share an idea with the network in exchange for the promise that the network will not appropriate the idea for its own use without properly compensating the writer. The terms of the agreement are direct, complete and unambiguous—seemingly setting the foundation for an enforceable contract that the writer may use as a basis for legal action when the show appears at the top of the Nielsen ratings without the writer having received credit or compensation for the show's creation.

Unfortunately, problems with consideration might invalidate the scriptwriter's hypothetical pre-disclosure contract. Recalling discussion of the underlying theory for copyright protection in Chapter 7, copyrighted material derives value as property from the concept that the creative expression in question has moved *beyond* the idea stage of development and has been tangibly fixed in some way. To state this concept in the negative, ideas that have *not* been tangibly fixed and have *not* developed beyond the "mere idea" stage are outside the protection of federal copyright laws.

Our scriptwriter's idea for a sit-com has not been tangibly fixed (there were no scripts or character sketches) and thus could not have been copyrighted because, according to federal copyright law, ideas have *no* value. Because consideration *must* possess some actual value, the contract proposed by the scriptwriter and accepted by the network arguably may not have been supported by adequate consideration, making the contract unenforceable at law.

Some courts might hold that "novel" ideas possess intrinsic value and thus can serve as valid consideration in a confidentiality/non-disclosure contract. More often, however, the communicator simply must place blind faith in the party sitting across the table unless the creative material is so tangibly fixed as to be copyrightable.

Even assuming that a court would find such a contract enforceable, the scriptwriter would still face a daunting task in securing a judgment for breach of that contract. Because the idea was not tangibly fixed by the scriptwriter prior to the meeting with the network creative team, the subsequent use of the idea by the network boils down to a "he said/she said" fight, in which the writer will claim the idea, and the network will dispute that claim.

If the non-disclosure contract were presented and accepted *after* the disclosure of the sit-com idea, courts would give very short shrift to the writer's argument that the contract is enforceable. As noted above, consideration cannot be valid if offered in exchange for a past act, as the lawn-mowing example illustrated. Therefore, the network's promise was without valid consideration and thus unenforceable at law.

## Other Remedies

The text of the previous section was peppered with the phrase "at law" when it characterized the nature of a breach of contract lawsuit. That phrase did not appear accidentally. Contracts provide remedies for aggrieved parties "at law," and generally allow recovery for a classification of damages referred to as "expectation damages." Expectation damages are generally money damages that place a party injured by a breach of contract in the position in which he or she could have reasonably expected to have been if the contract had been fulfilled, as if both parties had performed their respective contractual obligations. Because of the consideration problems with the non-disclosure/confidentiality contracts mentioned above, the scriptwriter might have difficulty recovering at law because courts would have difficulty finding that a contract did, in fact, exist.

There are other types of remedies in civil actions, however, called actions in *equity* that may allow a plaintiff to recover damages when an action at law may not. The term "law" implies a more rigid, by-the-book view of legal principles. The term "equity" invokes principles of justice and fairness that underlie the stated law. One such principle in equity is a concept referred to as a "contract implied in law," formerly called a "quasi-contract" and often referred to in lay terms as "unjust enrichment." The theory behind an implied-in-law contract is that a party has conferred a benefit upon another party but has not been justly compensated. If certain conditions are met, the scriptwriter in our hypothetical case may be able to sue to recover the "market value" of the new sit-com idea unjustly retained by the network.

One federal court case, *Phillips v. Avis, Inc.*,[32] has addressed the potential applicability of equitable principles to the protection of ideas. In this case, entrepreneurs Frances and Peter Phillips approached several rental car companies pitching an idea to offer customers tape-recorded street directions. After considerable negotiation between Avis and the Phillips failed to result in a contractual agreement between the parties—although the parties progressed in their negotiations to the point of discussing the amount of compensation should Avis decide to use the Phillips' Drive Time USA service—news leaked that Avis planned to offer a direction service using the Northstar™ system via cellular telephones and vehicle-tracking technology.

The Phillips sued Avis, claiming misappropriation of a trade secret, unfair competition, misappropriation of an idea and breach of an implied contract. The United States District Court for the Northern District of Illinois rendered summary judgment for Avis on the first three claims. The court rejected the Phillips' contract implied-in-fact theory, stating that the lack of novelty and originality made the ideas presented to Avis worthless. Thus, said the court, Avis was not unjustly enriched by anything of value retained from its negotiations with the Phillips.[33]

However, the District Court did allow the possibility that the Phillips might be able to recover on another, closely related equitable theory based on a contract implied in *fact*. A contract implied in fact exists when "the conduct of the parties . . . [allows a court] to infer the terms of a contract."[34] In this case, wrote the court, it was relatively obvious that the

Phillips would not have disclosed their idea to Avis had the corporation not offered assurances of compensation should the idea be used. "The Phillips did not present Drive Time USA to Avis as a gift; this was a business proposition. Indeed, by inviting the Phillips to their offices and allowing them to present their idea, Avis consented to the contract [implied in fact]."[35]

Avis argued that the contract could not exist because the Phillips' idea represented no valuable consideration. In the context of an implied-in-fact contractual theory, the court rejected Avis' argument, stating that the Phillips' idea was indeed valuable because it was "novel to the *seller*" (i.e., that the Phillips were offering something to Avis that they considered quite valuable, even if copyright or other statutory law perceived the idea differently).[36] Unfortunately for further clarification of the law, after Avis' motion for summary judgment on the Phillips' implied contract claim was denied, the case proceeded no further—presumably the parties settled out of court—leaving unanswered the question of whether ideas may be protected based on a contract implied in fact theory.

## Promissory Restitution as a Possible Basis for Recovery

Let's go back to our sit-com scriptwriter example. Even if the promise to compensate the writer for the proposed program concept had been made by the network *after* the disclosure of the idea, an action in equity might be available based on a concept that might be referred to as "promissory restitution" or the "material benefit rule."[37] Promissory restitution actions, a hybrid of contract law and equitable actions, may allow a plaintiff to recover the value of an unjustly retained benefit in situations in which the benefiting party makes a promise to compensate *after* the benefit is conferred. Application of promissory restitution principles to protection of ideas is highly speculative, but such a theory does offer one more potential avenue for a creative communicator wishing to protect ideas and business schemes from appropriation.

## Other Ways to Protect Ideas in a Digital, New-Media Age: Emerging Issues

To remove as much speculation from the equation as possible, a creative communicator should understand that the most sure-fire method of protecting ideas is to reduce them to a tangible enough form that they merit the protection of federal copyright or trademark laws. When this is impossible, the other methods discussed in this chapter may be all that are available.

In a relatively easy-to-enter, new-media world, it is likely that the courts will see an upsurge in cases alleging the stealing of trade secrets as insiders with access to private information make it available in Web-based communications. Whether for personal gain or as a means of striking out against a current or former employer, disclosures by anonymous Web site posters of company secrets increasingly poses potential problems for those wishing to maintain secrecy about product formulas, new business plans or potential advertising or public relations campaigns.

In addition, the practice of sending unsolicited e-mail messages to organizations proposing ideas and product suggestions will likely resort in an uptick of cases involving disgruntled individuals convinced that a company has relied on their suggestions if the organization actually begins to produce products or take other steps that resemble the business schemes suggested in the unasked for messages. Prudent advertising and public relations professionals might be wise to increase efforts to guard against disclosure of trade secrets by creating or strengthening existing policies and procedures designed to inhibit such disclosures by employees and other insiders within their organizations and to discourage discussions between company employees and those who have contributed unsolicited ideas that could be considered trade secrets.

For similar reasons, when many users seem to have the unwarranted belief that information found on the Web is free of copyright or trademark protection, it may not be surprising to find an increase in incidents of misappropriation of intangible property. While perhaps it is understandable that individuals may think little about the dangers of rewriting or repackaging information obtained from the Internet, prudent advertising and public relations professionals should be vigilant in protecting their own intellectual efforts and in not misusing the protected works of others.

The trend in the law of appropriation of business schemes seems to be favoring the California approach which requires only that the "novelty element" of a business scheme be novel to the organization that appropriates that scheme. This is particularly true in cases in which no specific form of contract exists and the uniqueness of the idea can be viewed as a substitute for the "consideration" (or thing of value) usually required to find the formation of a valid agreement between the two parties.

To avoid the charge of appropriation of a business scheme, agencies and other entities dealing in intellectual material are beginning to erect and maintain rigid barriers between their creative departments and the individuals within the organization to whom unsolicited creative ideas are directed. In addition, organizations should require an individual submitting unsolicited ideas which might constitute a business scheme to immediately sign an agreement specifying that any payments or other compensation that might be forthcoming are at the discretion of the purchasing organization.

# Chapter 10

# The Federal Trade Commission, the Food and Drug Administration and the Securities and Exchange Commission

Consider the following hypothetical.

"ChrispChips Lite" is the latest entry in the potato chip industry and your agency's client. The creative folks have put together an entire theme of "ChrispChips Lite" as the perfect snack for consumers who prefer Miller Lite or Bud Lite. Besides mentioning the two beer brands, the ad copy contains words and phrases like "The greatest new taste in chips with a new and different flavor" and "Wholesome," "Crunchier," and "The chip preferred two to one by those good-time people who are too Wise to eat a tired old chip that just Lay's there."

The agency head has turned to you for your opinion of all this. The facts are that (a) there have been no consumer studies and no clinical testing done on the product; (b) the product is not lower in calories but simply lighter in weight and color than regular potato chips; (c) no agreement to link the product to either Miller or Anheuser-Busch products has been reached; and (d) it really is not technically a new product because your client company is simply repackaging one of its old brands.

Earlier chapters discussed laws that allow competitors and individuals to bring suits against commercial speakers whose speech is alleged to be harmful to personal or property interests. You probably have already spotted potential court cases involving product disparagement and trademark infringement claims in the facts of the hypothetical. These laws, however, provide just some of the weapons available to those who wish to police commercial speech.

The advertising copy in our hypothetical example refers to statements about the quality, alleged consumer preference and the health benefits of the product—all highly questionable. Congress and state legislatures have created numerous government regulatory agencies with the power to make and enforce rules governing commercial enterprises and their business practices, including commercial speech, to deal with these kinds of issues.

## The Federal Trade Commission

Although a veritable alphabet soup of federal and state agencies exists to regulate specific categories of commercial speech (e.g., the Bureau of Alcohol, Tobacco and Firearms), the Federal Trade Commission (FTC) remains the agency most involved on a day-to-day basis in regulating the totality of commercial speech. This agency, established at the beginning of the last century, originally was given power to regulate unfair trade practices between and among business competitors. Eventually, Congress expanded its role to investigate and remedy a variety of marketplace abuses—including false or deceptive commercial speech.

## History and Jurisdiction of the FTC in Relation to Commercial Speech

The FTC traces its roots to the growth of monopolistic practices in industries like petroleum production, meat packing and cigarette and steel manufacturing beginning in the early 1880s. Even in those times—the heyday of laissez-faire, ungoverned, free-market economic policy—many in the business community urged the federal government to combat these anticompetitive practices that, it was feared, could result in a few powerful interests gaining control over the free marketplace of goods and services.

In response, Congress passed the Sherman Antitrust Act of 1890[1] to curb these abuses by the trusts and cartels. Although an important first step, the law proved ineffective in combating the major ills associated with economic monopolies. Continuing abuses led to demands that the federal government enact further legislation and set up a mechanism for ensuring that its provisions be enforced. To answer these demands, Congress passed the Federal Trade Commission Act in 1914.[2] The Act specified that, "[u]nfair methods of competition in commerce are hereby declared unlawful."[3] It focused on maintaining a competitive marketplace for business and industry but contained little of direct concern to consumers. The Act further created the FTC, consisting of five commissioners and support staff, to oversee the enforcement of the Act by promulgating rules and regulations ultimately enforceable by civil lawsuits in federal courts.

A major modification of the Act, with direct significance to those engaged in commercial speech, occurred when Congress passed the Wheeler-Lea Amendment in 1938.[4] The addition of the words *unfair or deceptive acts or practices in commerce* in the amended law gave the FTC authority for the first time to protect consumers by taking action against those who attempt to deceive the public about the nature or quality of their products, malign their competitors and/or engage in unfair competitive practices. Such practices specifically included false or deceptive advertising or other commercial messages.

## The FTC Today

The basic structure of the FTC remains the same as originally established by the 1914 Act. The president, with the advice and consent of the Senate, appoints five commission members. No more than three members may be from the same political party. Each commissioner is appointed to a seven-year term and may be reappointed to additional terms. To ensure both continuity and a minimum of partisanship, FTC members serve staggered terms to avoid a complete turnover in personnel at any one time. The President appoints one member to chair the FTC.

Originally staffed by a small number of employees transferred from other government agencies, today the FTC boasts an expanded staff that encompasses numerous offices and bureaus including public information, general counsel, administrative law judges and compliance and litigation divisions. Of particular significance to commercial speech interests is the Bureau of Consumer Protection that contains within it the National Advertising Division. This department investigates and enforces FTC regulations in cases of alleged deceptive or unfair commercial speech. The FTC also maintains 11 offices across the country to spot and deal with problems at the regional level.

The FTC provides guidance to commercial speakers through a variety of communications and publications such as industry guides, informal responses to inquiries and detailed advisory opinions issued when a commercial speaker wishes to determine in advance if proposed commercial messages meet FTC standards. FTC guidelines and publications can be obtained on written request or from the agency's Web site and should be sought in advance by commercial speakers who have questions or doubts about the legality of their proposed commercial messages.

Cases arise when the FTC receives requests from consumers, competitors or Congress to investigate an alleged violation of law or FTC regulation. Commissioners or their staff also may note possible violations on their own initiative. FTC staff members, usually from the Bureau of Consumer Protection, determine whether further procedures seem merited. If the investigators' conclusion is affirmative, the FTC typically sends an informal request for more information to the party under investigation. Should this request be ignored, or if the staff believes the information provided is either non-responsive or inadequate to meet the request, the investigators usually seek authority from the FTC for a more formal investigation.

Congress has granted the FTC sweeping subpoena power to obtain data and other relevant information from parties under investigation. The courts have held that the FTC may use its power to demand information before launching lawsuits or other more formal judicial proceedings even if there is only mere suspicion that a party may be in violation of a law or regulation. After the staff completes its investigation, a formal report is forwarded to the FTC suggesting what next steps need to be taken, if any. Should the conclusion be that a legitimate complaint exists, the FTC may then authorize formal enforcement proceedings.

Typically, parties resolve such complaints through use of a consent order whereby the offending party, often without admitting any violation of the law, agrees to stop the actions challenged by the FTC. The wording of such a consent order often is open to negotiation with the FTC so as to avoid damaging publicity. If no agreement is reached, however, the FTC possesses broad authority to seek other remedies to enforce its orders. These and other possible actions by the FTC are discussed in more detail later in this chapter.

A dispute between the FTC and a party under investigation that cannot be settled by negotiation often results in a hearing before an FTC administrative law judge (ALJ), who adjudicates the issue. Either the FTC staff or the other party may appeal an ALJ's ruling to the full Commission. Even if the decision is not appealed, the FTC on its own may elect to overrule its ALJ. The FTC's final ruling can be challenged in the federal courts of appeal and, if accepted, ultimately in the Supreme Court of the United States.

## The FTC's Regulation of False or Deceptive Commercial Speech

Until the 1970s, few gave much thought to the constitutionality of the FTC's regulations covering commercial speech, especially after the Supreme Court's decision in *Valentine v. Chrestensen*[5] that purely commercial speech merited no First Amendment protection. However, with the development of limited constitutional protection for such speech beginning with *Pittsburgh Press Co. v. Pittsburgh Commission on Human Relations*,[6] critics of the FTC began to question both its jurisdiction and its rulings on First Amendment grounds.

These issues were resolved in the FTC's favor by the Court's opinion in *Virginia State Board of Pharmacy v. Virginia Citizens Consumer Council*.[7] Justice Blackmun, while according commercial speech shelter under the umbrella of the First Amendment, also noted that "we . . . do not hold that it can never be regulated in any way."[8] Categories of commercial speech specifically mentioned as candidates for regulation included *untruthful speech,* which the Court defined as "false or misleading."[9] The Court added that "obviously, much commercial speech is not provably false, or even wholly false, but only deceptive or misleading. We foresee no obstacle to a State's dealing effectively with this problem."[10]

Although *Virginia State Board of Pharmacy* did not end challenges to the FTC's rulings on First Amendment grounds in lower courts, the

Supreme Court has refused to hear such cases. The C[...]
reiterated its support for the constitutionality of th[...]
regulate commercial speech in a number of decisions,[...]
*v. American Mini Theatres, Inc.,*[11] in which the Court o[...]
FTC's "power . . . to restrain misleading, as well as false[...]
labels and advertisements has long been recognized."[12]

At the heart of the FTC's activities involving commercia[...]
attempts to eliminate speech considered "deceptive or m[...]ading."
Section 5 of the Federal Trade Commission Act (15 U.S.C. §45—the FTC's
basic enabling legislation) provides that the FTC shall be empowered to
prevent "unfair or deceptive acts or practices in or affecting commerce."[13]
Included in such "acts or practices" are what Section 12 of the Act calls
"[disseminating] or . . . causing to be disseminated . . . any false advertisement"[14] involving the wide range of products and services covered in the
Act. By *false advertisement*, the Act means:

> an advertisement . . . which is misleading in a material respect; and in
> determining whether an advertisement is misleading, there shall be
> taken into account (among other things) not only representations
> made or suggested by statement, word, design, device, sound, or any
> combination thereof, but also the extent to which the advertisement
> fails to reveal facts material in the light of such representations or
> material with respect to consequences which may result from the use
> of the commodity to which the advertisement relates under the condi-
> tions prescribed in said advertisement, or under such conditions as are
> customary or usual.[15]

Although the language of the statute refers to *advertising*, the FTC's jurisdiction presumably extends to all forms of communication, including
brochures, direct mail publications, press releases and so forth, if used for
publicity or marketing purposes. This broad definition of advertising has
been used by courts in other areas of the law as well. For example, in *Levitt
Corporation v. Levitt*,[16] a federal court of appeals in the second circuit[17]
upheld a lower court's injunctive order prohibiting the defendant from
issuing press releases and other materials in a trademark infringement
claim. Similarly, in *Smith-Victor Corporation v. Sylvania Electric
Products, Inc.,*[18] a federal district court[19] found the defendant guilty of a
product disparagement violation in which the offending speech was disseminated by both advertisements and press releases.

## False and Deceptive Defined

It is important to note that, under the statute's definition, the determination of whether commercial speech is *false* is based on the perception or

possible perception of the commercial message by the receiver of the message. The FTC's definition of *false* is quite broad. It includes statements or other commercial-speech content (including pictures, graphic depictions or sound) that, although not technically false, reasonably might mislead the receiver of the message. If the reader or listener could reasonably interpret the message to receive a false impression or in other ways be deceived by the message, the message will be considered false. Thus, it will not avail a speaker to argue that actually no false statement appears in the advertisement or other communication. Commercial speakers should also note that the "reasonableness" requirement applies to the belief that a commercial speech claim makes a promise of performance and not to whether anybody should have believed the claim.

This broad definition includes sins of omission as well. Therefore, it is equally unavailing for the commercial speaker to avoid liability for false and deceptive speech by including only statements that are true (and that the receiver interprets correctly) if there is any significant information left out of the original message. This is particularly true if including the omitted information could change the receiver's evaluation of the claim by casting it in a negative or different light. For example, in *Chrysler Corp. v. FTC*,[20] the FTC found that advertisements claiming superior gas mileage for Chrysler products equipped with six-cylinder engines were deceptive because the ads failed to note that the same models with eight-cylinder engines were less fuel-efficient than similar models made by other manufacturers.

The FTC established its current definition of a *deceptive* act or practice in a policy statement in 1983.[21] Subsequently ratified by the FTC in *In re Cliffdale Assocs., Inc.*,[22] the statement defines such practices as messages that contain: (a) a representation, practice, or omission likely to mislead consumers; (b) content that consumers are interpreting reasonably under the circumstances; and (c) a material representation that could influence a consumer's decision with respect to the purchase of a product.[23]

The FTC defines a *material claim* as a statement or omission of a statement that is "likely to affect a consumer's choice of or conduct regarding a product or service."[24] Such statements or omissions "pertain to the central characteristics of the products or services being marketed, such as their performance, quality, cost or purpose."[25] The FTC is concerned with the likelihood that the average consumer might rely on a claim and suffer possible detriment. Therefore, the FTC may take action even without proof that a consumer actually has so relied and suffered actual harm. Representations involving material claims can be either express or implied. Express verbal claims—"Contains No Alcohol" or "Swiss-Made Watch"—that prove false almost certainly will be judged by the FTC to be deceptive. Similarly, the FTC will find visual messages deceptive if expressly promising more than the product or service can deliver.

Merely listing every complaint filed by the FTC against a business for deceptive advertising during the last 10 years would probably take as much space as a chapter in this book. As the Rosdens note in their epic multi-volume work *The Law of Advertising*, statements challenged as factually untrue have ranged from:

> [m]erchandise . . . called "antique" without justification, and "bonded" when it was not bonded . . . [to] goods [that] were "fireproof" when they were only fire-resistant . . . goods [that] were "handmade" when they were not . . . [to claims] that meat products were"'kosher" when they were not; that goods were made of "leather" when they were not . . . that merchandise was "shock-proof," "skid proof," "waterproof" when it was not and was merely shock-resistant, skid-resistant, or water-resistant. Other goods were called "natural" in circumstances that did not permit the use of that appellation; or they were called "rayon" when they consisted of a different textile. Other merchandise has been called "safe" when it was demonstrably unsafe [footnotes omitted].[26]

In a contest between a commercial speaker and the FTC, the government nearly always wins, although occasionally a business may achieve a partial victory. Traditionally, the courts defer to the FTC because the agency has the necessary expertise to make such decisions.

A quartet of examples from the mid-to-late 1990s illustrates the FTC's approach. In late 1996, the FTC announced that Van Den Bergh Foods Co., one of the largest marketers of margarines in the United States, had signed a consent order agreeing to halt its national advertising campaign for Promise margarine that used the slogan "Get Heart Smart" and included heart-shaped pats of Promise on food items. Under a consent order, the FTC agrees to take no further action against a business if the company agrees to immediately halt the activity. The FTC alleged the ads implied that using Promise helped cut the risk of heart disease and that the ads made false claims regarding low fat. According to the FTC, Van Den Bergh had not adequately substantiated its claims.[27]

In *In re Häagen-Dazs Company*,[28] the FTC issued its final order in a settlement with the company in which the ice cream manufacturer agreed to immediately halt advertising claims that its frozen yogurt was "low fat" and "98% fat free" and that its frozen yogurt bars had only 100 calories and one gram of fat. The ads included a disclaimer in small type noting that the claims were for frozen yogurt and sorbet combinations. The FTC claimed only two of the nine frozen yogurt flavors actually had three grams of fat or less per serving and thus were low fat as defined by the Food and Drug Administration. Some of the flavors made by Häagen-Dazs had as many as 12 grams of fat, and three had as many as 230 calories.[29]

In yet another example, the FTC filed a complaint against Third Option Laboratories, Inc. for claiming that its drink called "Jogging in a Jug" acted "like a natural solvent for the body, cleaning crystal deposits that are the base of clogged arteries and arthritis."[30] In a $480,000 settlement, the company agreed to stop making false or unsubstantiated claims for any food, drug or dietary supplement and to notify its distributors and consumers who ordered the drink directly from the company about the settlement.[31]

As a final example, in mid-1995, the Federal Communications Commission (FCC), with the blessing of the FTC, issued a set of revised administrative regulations that clamped down considerably on slamming by long-distance phone carriers. This practice, by which an individual's preferred long-distance carrier is switched without that person's knowledge, had drawn extensive complaints from both consumers and some of the carriers, particularly AT&T, which had by far the largest share of the market. Most of the complaints centered on the manner in which companies attracted new customers through contests and other promotions in which the consumer signs a form such as a prize entry or a simulated check that is really an authorization to switch carriers. One of the provisions of the revised rules required the carrier to provide a separate form for the authorization rather than combining an authorization form with another form such as a contest entry.[32]

Implied deceptive commercial speech claims usually involve a combination of true statements or visual representations that could cause deception because of the implications the recipient takes away from the overall message. One advertising technique determined by the FTC to be potentially deceptive involves descriptions of characteristics or properties of a product that are truthful, but that have little to do with the product's actual intended use.

For example, assume that to demonstrate the superiority of brand "X" paper towels, an advertising campaign features a single sheet of the product that has been dunked in water. The advertisement then shows the towel supporting the weight of an apple while two sheets of the competition's brand disintegrate under a similar weight. The FTC might find such a demonstration deceptive if the advertising claims focus on the greater absorbency of brand "X" compared to its competitor's products because there is no actual evidence that brand "X" is superior to its competition when it came to absorbing liquids—the logical (and misleading) interpretation the FTC might feel the average consumer would take away from the advertisement's strength test.

Although the FTC provides no specific guidelines for what evidence is necessary to prove how those receiving the information interpret such "representations," it has held (in *In re International Harvester Co.*[33]) that some omissions of fact are acceptable as long as the omitted facts concern "a subject upon which the seller has simply said nothing, in circumstances that do not give any particular meaning to his silence."[34] What the FTC called "pure omissions" are not actionable because they are not omissions that "presumptively or generally reflect a deliberate act on the part of the seller,"[35] and therefore the FTC finds no reason to seek sanctions against the speaker. Any other approach to analyzing the effects of omitted information, said the FTC, would expand the definition of a deceptive act "virtually beyond limits,"[36] given the almost infinite range of possible consumer misinterpretations based on missing information.

The FTC has determined that the speaker may not argue that a consumer should have been smart enough *not* to have relied on the claims made in the commercial message. According to the FTC, the test hinges upon whether a consumer's interpretation of the message, broadly speaking, is reasonable. Reasonableness, says the FTC, is determined by an analysis of the totality of the message. However, the FTC has held that reasonableness does not extent to interpretations of a message that are silly or bizarre, or to claims that would be inherently unbelievable to the average viewer or listener. If consumers reasonably can interpret the message in two ways (one deceptive and one not), the FTC generally will categorize the speech as deceptive.

Commercial claims directed to more vulnerable members of the audience (e.g., children, older adults and those suffering from illness) may be judged deceptive based on the likelihood that the members of that segment of the audience might be deceived. Thus, (a) claims that a toy oven "Means You Can Bake Bread Just Like Your Mom and Dad"; (b) advertisements not disclosing that more parts are needed to equal what the child sees in an advertisement; or (c) failure to mention that calling 900-numbers creates phone charges could run afoul of the FTC's prohibitions on deceptive claims (although no reasonable, normally functioning adult would likely be deceived by such claims).

In almost all cases, straightforward express claims will be considered "material" and contain the potential for deception on their face. In less straightforward situations, the FTC may rely on consumer research to determine such things as the nature and extent of the deception, the importance of the claim to the decision to purchase or use the product or the reasonableness of interpretation. Research techniques favored by the FTC include public opinion polls, focus groups and content analyses.

## Deception by Visual Simulation

Perhaps the most notable instance of visual deception eventually led to the case of *FTC v. Colgate-Palmolive*.[37] Colgate-Palmolive, makers of Rapid Shave™, produced a commercial that gave the appearance the shaving cream was so good at softening beards for easy shaves, it could literally soften sandpaper. To demonstrate this softening power, the company simulated the process because, the company said, real sandpaper did not show up well on television. The FTC filed a complaint against Colgate-Palmolive alleging that the ads were false and deceptive because the type of sandpaper used in the commercials required about 80 minutes of soaking to soften, a fact not disclosed in the advertising, Additionally, the commercials did not use sandpaper, but instead used a mock-up of Plexiglas and sand. A hearing examiner dismissed the complaint on the ground that neither misrepresentation was a material misrepresentation that would mislead consumers.[38] The FTC overruled the hearing examiner, holding that the company had misrepresented the moisturizing abilities of the shaving cream because it could not shave sandpaper within the time implied by the commercials. The FTC also held that the Plexiglas ploy was a separate deceptive act and issued an order forbidding the future use of undisclosed simulations in TV commercials.

The Supreme Court agreed with the FTC and rejected Colgate-Palmolive's argument that such simulations were really no different from the practice of substituting a scoop of mashed potatoes for what appears to be ice cream in a commercial, which the FTC had permitted. According to the Court:

> [w]e do not understand this difficulty [making a distinction between the two practices]. In the ice cream case, the mashed potato prop is not being used for additional proof of the product claim, while the purpose of the Rapid Shave commercial is to give the viewer objective proof of the claim made. If in the ice cream hypothetical the focus of the commercial becomes the undisclosed potato prop and the viewer is invited, explicitly or by implication, to see for himself the truth of the claims about the ice cream's rich texture and full color, and perhaps compare it to a "rival product," then the commercial has become similar to the one now before us. Clearly, however, a commercial which depicts happy actors delightedly eating ice cream that is in fact mashed potatoes or drinking a product appearing to be coffee but which is in fact some other substance is not covered by the present order.[39]

*In re Campbell Soup Co.*,[40] the FTC held that the addition of glass marbles to a saucepan of Campbell soup created deception by visual simulation. The vat of soup, shown bubbling merrily on a stove (marbles and all), formed the visual centerpiece of a television commercial. The advertisement, said the Commission, misrepresented "the quantity or abundance of solid ingredients in a can of Campbell's soup [and] therefore the aforesaid advertisements are false, misleading, and deceptive."[41] Campbell Soup Company argued that the added marbles did nothing more than make the soup appear as it would if observed by a consumer when cooking the soup at home. Nonetheless, the company agreed to cease running the disputed commercial.

## Unfair Commercial Speech

The FTC's working definitions of *unfair* and *deceptive* commercial speech have varied over time and with the political and economic philosophies of FTC members. In the early 1980s, Congress took away the FTC's authority to deal with unfair advertising or other commercial speech. From then until 1994, the FTC was funded from year to year, in part because of the controversy over the regulation of unfair commercial speech. The Agency was finally reauthorized after an agreement between the House and the Senate that the FTC could not regulate an "unfair" act or practice unless it "causes or is likely to cause substantial injury to consumers that is not reasonably avoidable by consumers themselves and not outweighed by countervailing benefits to consumers or to competition,"[42] or promotes activities contrary to public policy or exploits vulnerable populations. This is a tough standard to meet, and there continue to be fewer complaints filed by the FTC for unfair commercial speech (especially commercial speech that is truthful) than for deceptive commercial speech.

But examples do exist. As one illustration, a study in 1993 by the U.S. Centers for Disease Control and Prevention (CDC) in Atlanta, found that the three most heavily advertised brands of cigarettes—Marlboro, Camels and Newport—controlled 86 percent of the market share for smokers ages 12 to 18, compared with only 33 percent of the U.S. market share overall (Marlboro had 60 percent while Camels and Newport each had 13 percent).[43] According to the CDC survey, three million adolescents were smoking one billion packs of cigarettes each year.[44]

In response, FTC staff recommended the ban of ads for Camel cigarettes that included the character "Old Joe" or "Joe Camel." Studies allegedly showed that even young children associated the character with Camels.[45] Within three years after Joe appeared, said the complaint, the illegal sale of Camels to children under 18 reportedly rose from $6 million to a whopping $476 million a year.[46]

The FTC then launched a much-heralded investigation of the "Joe Camel" advertising campaign. R.J. Reynolds Tobacco Company had spent $42.9 million in major market advertising for Camels the previous year.[47] In June of the same year, the FTC formally announced it was ending the investigation, saying there was no evidence to support claims that children were lured to smoke by the campaign, thus accepting the arguments of the tobacco industry. However, after a series of setbacks in court cases brought against the tobacco industry by anti-smoking groups and the publication of the results of more studies, the FTC announced that it planned to reverse its earlier decision and issue a complaint against R.J. Reynolds for unfair advertising for its Joe Camel ads. The company subsequently abandoned its jaunty dromedary spokesman.

Other issues noted by the Rosdens that have triggered the FTC's unfairness jurisdiction include: (a) falsely suggesting a product is being offered at a reduced price; (b) not revealing additional charges beyond the advertised price; (c) advertising goods as "free" when there actually are hidden costs or requirements; and (d) "adverting prices as wholesale or factory prices when they are not."[48] The FTC may also treat changes in the ingredients, elements or terms of products or services as creating unfairness concerns unless commercial speakers first modify their marketing messages to alert potential consumers about these changes.[49]

The difficulty in defining an unfair commercial speech act or practice that will withstand a First Amendment challenge has severely limited the applicability of this concept in commercial speech situations. The concept of "unfairness" is also controversial because it implies that commercial speech that is neither false nor deceptive can nonetheless be subject to sanction by the FTC.

## The FTC's Requirements for Prior Substantiation

By far, the most common complaints about false or deceptive commercial speech focus on the failure of the touted products or services to live up to the claims made for them. To discourage such practices, the FTC requires commercial speakers to be ready to provide evidence that all of the material claims made in their commercial speech have been substantiated in advance.

This policy was originated in the FTC's 1972 decision in *In re Pfizer Inc.*[50] In advertising for a sunburn remedy called "Un-Burn," Pfizer claimed that its product "anesthetizes nerves in sensitive sunburned skin," and that it "relieves pain fast."[51] A complaint to the FTC resulted in an action for issuance of a cease-and-desist order on the basis that Pfizer had failed to back up its claims with "well-controlled scientific studies or tests prior to the making of such statements."[52] Although the FTC eventually dropped its investigation of Pfizer, it informally adopted a prior substantiation rule on the basis that a "consumer . . . cannot make the necessary tests or investigations to determine whether the . . . claims made for a product are true."[53]

The FTC, noting the unequal status between those making product claims and those potentially using those products, added that "it is more rational, and imposes far less cost on society, to require a manufacturer to confirm his affirmative product claims rather than impose . . . [that] burden upon each individual consumer to test, investigate, or experiment for himself. . . ."[54]

The FTC upheld and refined its prior substantiation rules in a series of subsequent cases. By 1976, just three years after *Pfizer*, the FTC, in *In re National Commission on Egg Nutrition*,[55] could describe its rules requiring "substantiation" of product claims as established policy. The FTC explained that, "[t]he justification for such a requirement is . . . [that] consumers are likely to assume that when a product claim is advanced which is in theory subject to objective verification, the party making [the claim] possesses a reasonable basis for so doing. . . ."[56] The FTC concluded that consumers have a right to expect that "advertising claims couched in objective terms are not merely statements of unsubstantiated opinion."[57]

The 1984 Policy Statement on Advertising Substantiation[58] codified these decisions. The policy expressly stated that those seeing or hearing claims of a factual nature about a product can reasonably expect that such claims are based on objective evidence. If advertisers refer to specific tests or experiments, consumers should legitimately expect that claims based on these tests have been substantiated to the degree claimed in the message.

When the FTC says prior substantiation, it means *prior* substantiation. To inhibit commercial speakers from gambling on the mere possibility that their claims may later be substantiated, the FTC holds that the burden of proof rests with those making commercial speech claims to demonstrate that the claims have been substantiated prior to publication.[59] This means that the FTC may act to regulate commercial speech when there is a complaint about an objective material claim made for a product or service even if it eventually turns out that the speech contains no demonstrably false statement of fact.

For example, a claim that a product increases the speed of operation by 30 percent compared to a competing product's performance might lead to FTC action if the claimant cannot show evidence to substantiate those claims prior to publicizing the product. This despite the fact that subsequent research conducted after the claims were challenged might prove the statements to have been true.[60]

Not all claims require the same degree of prior substantiation. The FTC requires the highest levels of proof for statements that readers or viewers reasonably interpret as based on specific evidence for objective claims. Such claims may include wording like "four clinical trials" or "the results of two surveys reveal." For example, in *Pfizer*, the FTC noted that the company's testing "consisting of injections of [the drug] benzocaine could not indicate the probable anesthetic effect of a topical [on the skin] application of this substance."[61] The FTC concluded that Pfizer's commercials were unacceptable because they implied clinical trials supporting the claims made for pain relief although the company, in fact, "did not conduct adequate and well-controlled scientific studies or tests prior to marketing Un-Burn to substantiate the efficacy claims made for Un-Burn."[62] Similarly, the use of such terms as "scientific proof" and "lab-tested evidence," although not establishing the amount or specific level of proof, normally must be substantiated by the kinds of evidence those terms would imply to the reasonable consumer.

Commercial speech that sets specific performance standards—"Lasts Twice as Long as Any Other Leading Brand" or "Gets 30 mpg at Highway Speeds"—requires prior substantiation that demonstrates the accuracy of these claims. The case of *Firestone Tire & Rubber Co. v. FTC*[63] illustrates this heightened prior substantiation requirement for specific claims. Firestone asserted that its "wide oval" tires stopped "25% quicker" than other tires. Finding these claims raised a safety issue, the FTC ordered the company to stop advertising such claims unless and until they could be substantiated.

Often, however, the offending commercial speech does not expressly or by implication refer to specific levels or standards of substantiation. In these instances, the FTC sets the prior substantiation requirements for an objectively testable claim at a "reasonableness" level, based on the legitimate expectations of the consumer. Although the FTC has not established a "bright-line test" to determine reasonableness of prior substantiation in such cases, analysis of the evidence used by the speaker in arriving at the claims and the potential harm to consumers relying on these claims normally will be factors contributing to the FTC's evaluation. For example, claims for health-related products likely will call for more exacting "reasonable" prior substantiation than claims for another kind of product because of the physical risks posed for the unwary consumer.

Reasonable prior substantiation might also involve analyzing the practices of comparable companies or evidence of industry-wide standards. For example, objective claims for a medical product might be compared to a testing-within-the industry standard (e.g., three scientifically controlled tests) if the FTC determines the existence of generally accepted standards established by the medical community for such products. However, if a product is widely used, and consumers themselves could easily verify objective claims, the FTC normally will not require submission of evidence of industry-wide tests to demonstrate the reasonableness of a claim. The FTC also will give great weight to the findings of other agencies (e.g., the Bureau of Alcohol, Tobacco and Firearms or the Food and Drug Administration) in accepting the reasonableness of commercial speakers' objective claims.

Balancing the costs of regulation against the benefits such regulation might bring to the consumer may also be considered by the FTC in evaluating the reasonableness of an objective claim. Setting reasonableness standards at too high a level might discourage the introduction of beneficial new products and services into the marketplace. Recognizing that, because of the inductive logic of scientific testing, critics could almost always argue "we need one more study," the FTC normally tempers its requirements for prior substantiation by employing an *ad-hoc*, cost-benefit analysis. Factors in the balancing process might include an evaluation of the likelihood that additional testing could change the evidence supporting the claim, the cost and time needed to conduct such additional tests and the degree of risk to the consumer if the objective claims turned out to be false.

## "Puffing": A Special Prior Substantiation Problem

Although objective claims create the problem of evaluating the reasonable prior substantiation of such claims, other kinds of statements about a product or service—"It's the Best," "There's No Other One for You," or "No Competing Brand Comes Close"—have forced the FTC to create a workable definition of just what constitutes a nonobjective (or "puffing") statement. *Puffing* has been defined as commercial speech "that is not deceptive [because] no one would rely on its exaggerated claims."[64]

Typically, the FTC and courts are more likely to find a claim to be puffing if the statements in the commercial speech refer to a product or service taken as a whole rather than to any specific attributes of the product or service. The statement "It's a Great Truck" would be more likely treated as simple puffery than would the statement "It Gets Great Gas Mileage." Adding the statement "It Gets 5 Miles More Per Gallon at Highway Speeds" would almost certainly turn the statement into an objective claim requiring prior substantiation.

Thus, for example, in *In re Dannon Milk Products, Inc.*,[65] the FTC held that a description of yogurt as one of nature's perfect foods constituted more than puffery because it stated an objective fact about a product's nutritional attributes.

Employing similar reasoning, the FTC and courts usually treat a company's general comparative advertising claims of superiority for its product or service as puffery but tend to require prior substantiation for specific comparative statements about individual characteristics of its products or services because they are objective claims.

The FTC also looks at a claim to determine whether it can be factually verified. Some statements ("You'll Just Feel More Assured Wearing Acme Shoes") are opinion statements and almost always treated as puffery. However, if the statement appears to be based on factual information ("If You Could See the Results of the Studies I've Seen, You'd Agree That Acme Shoes Are Better"), the statement might be treated as expressing fact. The reader should note that simply placing an "I believe . . ." or "In my opinion . . ." in front of a fact statement will not turn that statement into an opinion statement and therefore free of a prior-substantiation requirement.

Perhaps the most troubling element of its puffing-versus-fact standard from the commercial speaker's point of view is the FTC's definition of an *average consumer* standard. The FTC's (and the courts') evaluation of the intelligence the "average consumer" displays often differs sharply from the estimations held by commercial speakers.

In *In re Matter of Better Living, Inc.*,[66] the court agreed with the FTC that the statement that the company guaranteed "the world's lowest price"[67] was a claim of objective fact (and not puffery) requiring substantiation, despite arguments to the contrary that no reasonable consumer could be misled or deceived by such statements. Similarly, in *Gillette Co. v. Wilkinson Sword, Inc.*,[68] the court found that "smoothest, most comfortable shave possible" was "a performance claim for one of the most important characteristics of the product being sold,"[69] although it is open to question whether the "average consumer" would be that easily fooled by such a claim.

The frequent use of the term *new*—as in "New and Improved"—in commercial claims has led the FTC to issue a special policy statement concerning the use of that term. Describing a product or service on the market for more than six months as *new* will be considered questionable unless the product or service provider is conducting a test-marketing campaign. The FTC has indicated that, in such a situation, it will enforce its six-month policy only after the product or service is introduced into the marketplace in final form.

## The FTC Substantiation Standards for Commercial Claims about Health and Beauty Products

Based on a pattern of recurring complaints by consumers and consumer groups, the FTC generally looks with special scrutiny at complaints about commercial claims for health-care products because of the potential for immediate, serious physical harm such products could cause.

After years of extensive hearings and litigation, the FTC established a requirement that commercial claims for medicines or personal-care products based directly or indirectly on clinical or scientific evidence must be substantiated by a minimum of two independent clinical trials. The FTC created this standard because it felt that consumers would likely be deceived by claims allegedly based on "clinical studies," believing such procedures had been conducted "scientifically." Also, the FTC reasoned the average consumer would be unable to independently evaluate such claims.

For example, in *In re Thompson Medical Co.*,[70] the company marketing Aspercreme™ claimed that using its topical skin product reduced aches and pains attributed to arthritis as well as, if not better than, ingesting regular aspirin. Unfortunately for Thompson, these claims were not based on evidence the FTC considered scientifically valid. The FTC ordered the manufacturer to stop making any claims about the pain-relieving qualities of Aspercreme unless it conducted "at least two adequate and well-con-trolled, double-blinded clinical studies"[71] that met what the FTC felt were the standards of accepted scientific research.

In instances involving nonspecific claims for healthcare products, the FTC generally has been content with only one clinical trial. These are rare, however, and usually involve claims about either attributes of a product not considered potentially harmful or involving physical properties that can be measured by instrumentation.

To meet FTC substantiation requirements, clinical tests and trials nor-mally must be conducted by qualified independent investigators following an acceptable plan of research. At a minimum, this research plan should be specified in advance of the actual clinical trials and should establish sam-ple sizes, statistical tests and levels of significance that experts in the field recognize as appropriate.

As might be expected, numerous differences in interpretation have arisen between the FTC and commercial speakers over the definitions and implementation of requirements for approved clinical test procedures. Generally, the FTC requires that investigators in different clinical trials be different researchers and operate independently of each other. In *Thompson*, the FTC affirmed that, "[t]he personnel who administer the test should also be experienced, as well as properly trained and instructed in using the measures involved in the clinical trial."[72] The FTC has also held that when comparing two products, clinical test procedures should normally include the use of a placebo or its equivalent as a control.

Because it is possible for two products to prove virtually identical in everyday use but to differ when measured by statistical tests, the FTC usu-ally requires claims of superiority for one of the products to be based on both empirical and practical, real-world differences. The FTC also may permit claims that rely on chemical or laboratory test results in lieu of clin-ical trials if the testing procedures prove acceptable within the scientific community. If the commercial speech about a product also involves claims about freedom from unpleasant side effects ("And It Doesn't Upset Your Stomach"), the FTC normally requires such claims to be substantiated in the same manner as primary claims.

## The FTC and Games of Chance

Although the terms are often used interchangeably by commercial speak-ers, the FTC makes sharp distinctions between and among *lotteries, con-tests, games of chance, drawings* and *sweepstakes*. Lotteries, unless permitted by statute and conducted by a government agency, are banned by law in most states. Generally, a contest is treated as an illegal lottery if contestants must pay money or take any other kind of action that could be considered to be payment of "consideration," including, in some states, the purchase of a product or service. In addition, a contest risks being judged a lottery if the contestant can win by chance alone, rather than by demonstrating any special skill, and the winners are awarded prizes of economic value.

The FTC is concerned that commercial speech about legal contests, drawings, sweepstakes and other such promotional techniques creates a risk of deception for potential consumers. In an attempt to minimize this risk, the FTC publishes specific guidelines for disclosure of information that apply to games of chance when used by commercial speakers promoting the sale of either food items or gasoline.[73] Those representing these industries would be wise to be in contact with the FTC before creating such contests. The FTC also has used its general supervisory powers to challenge the use of contests and other similar techniques when employed by commercial speakers to promote products or services in other industries.

Although a comprehensive discussion of the wide range of rules covering such techniques is beyond the scope of this chapter, it would be prudent for a commercial speaker contemplating use of a promotional contest to, at a minimum, include clearly written and displayed information in all promotional material about (a) the true chances of winning any prize of value; (b) a description of all prizes (including their value); and (c) the number of prizes to be awarded. Also, the rules and conditions (including any deadlines) for entering the contest or sweepstakes should be publicized, as should information about who is eligible to be a contestant.

## FTC Regulation of Testimonials and Endorsements

Concerns about the use of endorsements and testimonials by celebrities or other non-company spokespersons to promote products and services caused the FTC to develop a separate policy statement regulating such practices. The *FTC Guides Concerning Use of Endorsements and Testimonials in Advertising*[74] states that an endorsement is "any advertising message (including verbal statements, demonstrations, or depictions of the name, signature, likeness, or other identifying personal characteristics of an individual or the name or seal of an organization) which message consumers are likely to believe reflects the opinions, beliefs, findings or experience of a party other than the sponsoring advertiser."[75]

Generally, the FTC has held that endorsement statements must meet the same substantiation requirements as other material claims. In *In re Cliffdale Associates, Inc.*,[76] the advertiser of the Ball-Matic Gas Saver Valve claimed that the product was "the most significant automotive breakthrough in the last 10 years,"[77] and produced several advertisements with testimonials by alleged users of the product claiming that the valve gave them substantial improvement in miles per gallon of gasoline. The FTC challenged the accuracy of these and other claims for the product. In response, Cliffdale

Associates Inc. tried to argue that because the consumers providing the testimonials legitimately believed that they had obtained improved gas mileage, no other proof was necessary to justify the claims.

The FTC would have none of it. "[C]onsumer tests and testimonials," said the FTC, "are not a recognized way of testing fuel economy."[78] It went on to note that, "irrespective of the veracity of the individual consumer testimonials, use of the testimonials to make underlying claims that were false and deceptive was, itself, deceptive."[79]

In its policy statement, the FTC describes typical examples of endorsements to help commercial speakers understand and follow its guidelines. For example, if a celebrity has been a long-term spokesperson for a company or product, the use of the celebrity in commercial speech normally would not constitute an endorsement because consumers likely recognize the celebrity is speaking on behalf of the company and not a specific product or service. However, if a company employs a popular sports figure or entertainer with no long-term association with a company as part of the company's marketing campaign for a product, the FTC may consider that to be an endorsement, even if the celebrity never actually makes any overt testimonial statements.

Similarly, the FTC may consider statements by critics or reviewers favorable to a product or service that are subsequently used by a company in commercial messages to be endorsements because of the possible confusion in the mind of the consumer about which are the critics' views and which are the company's.

Companies that use celebrities to endorse their products or services must be able to demonstrate that the endorsements are both genuine and accurate in all important details. For example, in *In re Cooga Mooga, Inc.*,[80] the FTC held that statements by singer Pat Boone and members of his family endorsing "Acne-Statin," an anti-acne skin product, were false and deceptive. The commercials claimed, among other things, that Boone's daughters had used the product and that it produced satisfactory results. In finding that most of the health claims for the product were false or exaggerated, the FTC also noted that not all of Boone's daughters had used the medication and that the implication that all had done so constituted an additional untrue claim.

The use of a celebrity endorser must be limited to the time that the celebrity actually uses the product or service. Statements to the effect that a celebrity "drives the Terraplane Z6" would constitute false and deceptive claims if the celebrity either never or no longer drives this automobile. The reader should also remember that those employing the celebrity endorser may be liable for engaging in illegal practices in a Lanham Act cause of action (discussed in Chapter 10).

Regardless of whether the providers of a testimonial are celebrities or individuals portrayed as typical consumers, the claims they make must reflect what the average consumer would experience in normal usage of the product or service. This means that although the endorser may truthfully testify that he or she experienced a phenomenal response or improvement after using a product or service, such claims may be considered deceptive if scientific or statistical evidence reveals such experiences to be significantly different from what the typical user of the product or service might find.

One method of possibly avoiding the need to substantiate an endorsement claim is the use of a disclaimer statement. The FTC's guidelines indicate that such a disclaimer—stating the more typical performance record of the product or service and phrasing and displaying it in such a manner as to be readily understood by the listener or viewer—may be sufficient to satisfy the FTC's requirements for non-deceptive commercial speech. However, simply stating that the endorsement claim "may not be typical" or other similarly worded general disclaimers normally are not sufficient. The reader also should note that the more extravagant the claim, the less likely the FTC will accept a simple disclaimer to avoid a charge of deceptive commercial speech.

In addition to celebrities and individuals portrayed as average citizens, commercial speakers often employ professionals described as experts to recommend the speaker's product or service. Not surprisingly, the FTC guidelines on testimonials and endorsements make special provision for such endorsers because of the tendency for consumers to believe such experts and their greater capacity to deceive consumers. A commercial speaker employing an expert should be able to demonstrate the expert actually has evaluated the product or service and has done so in a manner "as extensive as someone with the same degree of expertise would normally need to conduct in order to support the conclusions presented in the endorsement."[81] When the endorsement contains claims that the product or service is the equal of, or better than, a competitor, the expert endorser similarly must also have evaluated the competitor's product or service.

A claim made by an expert must be based on the standards employed by the industry involved or by other experts in the field. Similarly, the credentials of the expert providing the endorsement must demonstrate that the expert is qualified to provide such testimonial endorsement. For example, it would be inappropriate to use a medical doctor in an advertisement endorsing a product if that product is outside the medical specialty of the physician. In *In re Cooper*,[82] the former astronaut Gordon Cooper, a stakeholder in a company that manufactured and sold the "G-R Gas Saver Valve," appeared in the company's advertising wearing what appeared to be his space suit, touting the virtues of the product. Cooper was billed as an expert engineer who had performed tests of the valve in his "independent engineering laboratory."[83] The FTC, although not questioning

Cooper's credentials as an astronaut with NASA, ordered the company to cease and desist using Cooper as an endorser of the valve in the company's commercial efforts because he was unqualified to serve as an expert in evaluating and recommending automobile products, despite his scientific and engineering expertise.

FTC guidelines do not prohibit an expert in one field from endorsing a product in another if the endorsement is merely a personal rather than a professional endorsement and the endorsement meets the other requirements for testimonials discussed earlier. When a group or organization supplies the testimonial statement, the FTC requires that the statement reflect the overall consensus of its members. Such groups or organizations must have performed the appropriate tests or in other ways evaluated the product or service in question if the commercial message states or suggests that they have done so. For example, in *Niresk Industries, Inc. v. FTC*,[84] the FTC ordered the company to stop advertising that its products were endorsed by *Good Housekeeping* magazine's "Seal of Approval," when, in fact, that organization had not endorsed them.

Commercial speakers should beware of employing statements published by consumer groups that claim to objectively test products or services even if the quotes are true and accurate. Such consumer organizations jealously guard their reputations as independent evaluators and may resort to legal action to prevent the appearance of an endorsement.

## The FTC and Retail Sales

Unlike commercial speech by manufacturers or service providers, commercial speech by retailers usually involves claims about the conditions of the sales situation, including special sales, low prices or unusual merchandising practices. The FTC, recognizing that such commercial speech can be equally as deceptive to the average consumer as claims for products or services, publishes an extensive set of rules governing retail sales. Although a comprehensive review of these rules is beyond the scope of this chapter, a brief overview of the FTC's efforts in this area may serve to alert retail commercial speakers to the need to familiarize themselves with regulations affecting their activities.

One of the FTC's greatest concerns is potentially deceptive claims involving the pricing of goods and services. The FTC publishes its *Guides Against Deceptive Pricing*[85] to provide retail commercial speakers with guidance in this area. Some of the regulations covered in these and other guidelines involve specific rules describing when speakers legitimately may claim that an item is reduced in price from its "usual" or "regular" price. To meet FTC requirements, such sales claims must be based on a comparison with the normal price charged for the item or, if no specific dollar amount or percentage of savings is mentioned, the sale price must be low enough to constitute what the average consumer reasonably would consider a legitimate savings.

If a commercial speaker claims that its prices are lower than its competitions' prices or are at manufacturer or wholesale prices, the FTC normally requires such claims to be based on legitimate comparisons with its nearby competitors' normal pricing policies or the usual manufacturers' or wholesalers' prices.

Other FTC guidelines for retailers cover practices such as using the terms *"Introductory Sale"* or *"Buy One, Get One Free"* or *"Free Gift,"* as well as prohibitions on so-called "bait-and-switch advertising." This latter term is defined by the FTC as "an alluring but insincere offer to sell a product or service . . . [for the purpose of switching] consumers from [the advertised item] to . . . something else, usually at a higher price or on a basis more advantageous to the advertiser."[86] Retail commercial speech practices involving mail-order sales and sales of such items as household furniture, electronics, jewelry and luggage are addressed by specific industry standards. Readers of this text who engage in commercial speech involving these and related practices should obtain guidelines from the FTC before making any retail commercial claims.

The FTC also monitors and regulates aspects of commercial speech involving offers of credit extended by retailers to consumers under provisions of the federal Truth-in-Lending Act.[87] The Act, which covers all those who advertise or offer consumer credit, regardless of whether they are actual creditors, calls for non-deceptive commercial speech about the conditions to be met, the actual credit rate the consumer can expect to receive, how any finance charge is computed and other pertinent information. The Act also covers offers of lease agreements and requires similar disclosures of terms, conditions and so forth. The reader engaged in commercial speech involving offers of consumer credit is urged to be in contact with the FTC for guidance to avoid running afoul of its regulations in this area.

## The FTC and CAN-SPAM

The Internet has evolved into a global information infrastructure with far-reaching implications for business and commercial speech. The body of law that applies to the Internet is sometimes called "cyberspace law," but with a few exceptions, laws that apply in other contexts apply to cyberspace as well. The tort of defamation (discussed in Chapter 4) is defamation, whether it is published online or in a traditional print newspaper. But as we shall see, the structure of the Internet prompted Congress to pass special laws that, for example, apply to Internet service providers (ISPs) which host but do not control Web site postings. Thus, the Internet and other communications technologies are governed both by long-established legal principles and newer statutory provisions enacted by Congress in response to challenges raised by these technologies.

Recently, consumers and Congress have turned their attention to electronic mail (e-mail). Jurisdictional issues concerning the Internet make the regulation of electronic mail and other Web-based communications challenging, to say the least. That, however, has not prevented Congress from trying to get a handle on annoying online marketing practices that have grown along with the Internet.

Anyone who checks his or her e-mail for business-related or personal messages only to discover multiple unsolicited and unwanted marketing solicitations likely can relate to the frustration engendered by "spamming," defined as the practice of sending unwanted e-mail to unsuspecting e-mail users that is often misleading and obnoxious (and sometimes for illegal purposes or pornographic in nature as well). In 2003, President Bush signed the Controlling the Assault of Non-Solicited Pornography and Marketing Act (CAN-SPAM Act)[88] to address the problem of deceptive or fraudulent commercial e-mail. The CAN-SPAM Act became effective January 1, 2004, and created a single set of rules designed to apply nationwide to commercial e-mails. The Act specifically preempts state laws regulating the use of electronic mail.

The CAN-SPAM Act is enforced by the Federal Trade Commission (FTC) and other federal and state agencies that have jurisdiction over specific organizations. The Act provides for criminal sanctions enforceable by the United States Department of Justice (DOJ), and allows companies that provide Internet access to sue those who violate the Act. The DOJ has made several high-profile arrests of professional spammers who are alleged to have sent billions of spam messages in violation of CAN-SPAM.[89] It is important to note that the CAN-SPAM Act does not ban unsolicited commercial e-mail. Rather, it establishes requirements for those who send such e-mail, spells out potential penalties for violators and allows consumers to demand that e-mailers stop sending spam.[90]

Some observers suggest the CAN-SPAM Act may have had the unintended consequence of actually increasing the volume of spam e-mails by giving commercial e-mailers clear instructions for allowable e-mail behavior, thereby emboldening them to "spam away." Skeptics of the law's actual effectiveness also note that the FTC lacks the resources to aggressively enforce CAN-SPAM, a limitation that gives the law more bark than bite. Proponents of CAN-SPAM, nonetheless, applaud the effort and point to the availability of a private right of action the Act gives to Internet service providers and others seeking to hold violators accountable. Whether the law and its related criminal sanctions, in reality, will effectively curtail or eliminate spamming remains to be seen.

The relative anonymity of the Internet makes it difficult to know who is sending, receiving and viewing what. This presents particular problems for those concerned about shielding children from inappropriate messages. The CAN-SPAM Act addresses some of these concerns, and several states—Michigan and Utah, among the most notable—have also passed laws designed to keep adult-oriented computer content away from children.[91] These laws have been drafted to avoid conflict or overlap with CAN-SPAM. Prudent marketing and public relations professionals who attempt to reach children by computer should understand both CAN-SPAM and any state laws that may apply.[92]

## Enforcing FTC Regulations: Corrective Orders

Without the ability to enforce its rules and regulations, the FTC's function would be limited to advisory status. The Federal Trade Commission Act provides the FTC with the power to "issue and cause to be served on such person, partnership, or corporation [in violation of the law] an order requiring such person, partnership, or corporation to cease and desist from using such method of competition or such act or practice."[93] These "cease-and-desist" orders may be imposed by the FTC itself without resorting to the courts for enforcement.

A cease-and-desist order, directed against a party the FTC believes is engaging in false or deceptive commercial speech, is an action of last resort. As discussed earlier, almost without exception such an order comes only after a series of negotiations during the investigatory phase of the FTC's preliminary inquiry. Only if the FTC and the commercial speaker cannot agree on an informal alternative course of action to resolve their disagreements will the FTC initiate a more formal complaint procedure.

The overwhelming bulk of cases are settled, usually as a result of a negotiated, signed consent decree. By agreeing to discontinue the challenged practice, the commercial speaker can avoid the potentially negative publicity of litigation and need not admit wrongdoing.

Given the normally short shelf life of most commercial speech, such a remedy often satisfies all parties. However, commercial speakers may object to signing such a consent decree if they feel it is unjustified or would seriously interfere either with an ongoing or a planned commercial campaign. In that eventuality, typically the next step after issuance of a formal complaint is a hearing before an administrative law judge (ALJ). The ALJ is empowered to obtain evidence through subpoena and, in many respects, the hearing is like a trial. At its termination, the judge must render a decision within 90 days. The ALJ may decide that a cease-and-desist order be entered, some other remedy is called for or may decide in favor of the party charged with violating the regulation and dismiss the complaint.

If the judge decides that a cease-and-desist order should be issued and the FTC is in accord with that judgment, the party against whom the order is issued must file a compliance report within 60 days, spelling out a compliance plan. If the FTC disagrees with the ALJ, it may elect to over-rule the decision and impose its own sanctions. Rather than comply with the FTC, the party against whom an order is entered may then elect to appeal the FTC's actions in the federal appeals court system.

In its simplest form, the purpose of a cease-and-desist decree is to remedy the problem by ordering the offending commercial speaker to stop. However, the FTC is not limited to such a remedy if, in its opinion, additional steps are needed to correct the existing problem or to prevent similar problems from recurring. In such instances, the FTC may issue a broad order that covers commercial speech for other products or services produced by the offending company as well as for claims already found to be false or deceptive.

These so-called "fencing-in" orders, extending to commercial speech about other products or services the offending organization provides, are the FTC's method of attempting to ensure that the company does not make deceptive claims in future commercial speech. Fencing-in cease-and-desist orders may apply to some or all of the products or services a company provides, or they may be applied to some or all of the claims made for a particular product or service. Normally the FTC only expands its cease-and-desist order to fence in a commercial speaker in circumstances in which there is evidence that the offending speaker has both a history of deceptive commercial speech claims and when there is a future "likelihood of . . . committing the sort of unfair practice"[94] complained of in the present case.

In more extreme cases, the FTC may ban future commercial speech about a product or service unless affirmative disclosures accompany the speech. Perhaps the best-known example of such an affirmative disclosure order is the agreement reached by the FTC with cigarette manufacturers to include the Surgeon General's warning label in all commercial speech about their products.[95]

When the FTC finds a pattern of long and persistent publication of false and deceptive speech, it may also take the additional step of requiring a commercial speaker to publish corrective information. Although the line between affirmative disclosure and corrective information is not well drawn, the triggering mechanism for FTC action appears to be (a) the longevity of the party's advertising or other commercial speech campaign; (b) the nature and extent of the claims the FTC finds to be false and deceptive; and (c) the hypothesized continuing effects the prior speech might have on the decisions by consumers in the future.

In one of the more notable corrective commercial speech cases, *Warner-Lambert Co. v. FTC*,[96] a federal appeals court upheld the FTC's directive to require corrective information in future advertisements for Listerine. The claim that Listerine somehow could prevent colds and related symptoms had been a part of the product's advertising and marketing campaigns for decades. The FTC's remedy was to require Warner-Lambert to insert information clearly refuting such claims in each future advertisement until the company had spent as much money correcting its advertising as it had spent on all its advertising during the preceding 20 years—approximately $10 million. The court of appeals agreed with the FTC that such a drastic remedy was justified on the basis that the "deceptive advertisement[s] . . . played a substantial role in creating or reinforcing in the public's mind a false and material belief which lives on after the false advertising ceases."[97]

## The FTC and the Courts

In addition to its own sanctions, the FTC can turn to the courts to remedy false or deceptive commercial speech claims. For example, the FTC may seek a temporary court order to halt an immediate violation of the law. Although the normal standard for imposition of such an order is a finding that a violation will cause immediate and irreparable harm, at least one court has held that deference by the judiciary to rulings by the FTC means that the FTC need only meet a general-public-interest standard. A court-ordered temporary injunction could become permanent if the court finds that the public would best be served by following this course of action.[98]

When a cease-and-desist order has been ignored or disobeyed, the FTC likely will seek a civil-law remedy from the courts by invoking Section 45(m) of the Federal Trade Commission Act.[99] This section permits a court to impose stiff financial penalties for each day the defendant is in violation of the order. For example, in *United States v. Readers Digest Association*,[100] the court assessed a 10-cent penalty for each simulated sweepstakes check the publication had disseminated. Unfortunately for *Readers Digest*, the total number of checks reached more than 17 million, resulting in a fine of $1,750,000.

The reader should also note that the FTC similarly may prevail in civil suits involving commercial speech claims against manufacturers of products or providers of services who are not the subjects of specific FTC cease-and-desist orders but who nonetheless should be aware that their commercial speech claims are in violation of such orders issued to prohibit similar claims by their competitors.

If the situation warrants, the FTC may ask a court to find a commercial speaker guilty of a criminal misdemeanor. Typically, this would involve cases of commercial speech claims for medicines or health-related products when an average consumer, believing in the claims for the product, could be seriously harmed and the offending party has ignored earlier warnings or orders by the FTC.

Not surprisingly, the use and reach of the FTC's remedial powers comprises a substantial percentage of the disputes between the FTC and commercial speakers. Much of this litigation has come from challenges to the scope of cease-and-desist orders. Although generally victorious, sometimes the courts have found the FTC guilty of overreaching.

For example, in *Chrysler Corp. v. FTC*,[101] the FTC ordered the automobile manufacturer to not only cease potentially deceptive claims for the fuel efficiency of its products but to avoid misrepresenting the results of any tests or other research in its future advertising. A federal court of appeals in the District of Columbia approved the general order, but found that the FTC had over-reached to the extent of the order limiting discussion of tests and research results.[102] The court noted that such a prohibition was "potentially limitless,"[103] that Chrysler's infractions "were unintentional and non-continuing" and that the offending speech had appeared in only "two out of a campaign of fourteen advertisements. . . ."[104]

Similarly, in *ITT Continental Baking Co. v. FTC*,[105] a federal appeals court struck down the FTC's limitations on the company's comparative advertising claims as overbroad, in large measure because the company's statements about the nutritional value of its products were found to be accurate in 11 of the 12 cases discussed. In *American Medical Association v. FTC*,[106] a federal court of appeals in the second circuit modified the FTC's cease-and-desist order directed against the AMA by limiting it to a simple requirement that the association add the words "respondent reasonably believes" to its medical advertising.[107]

At times, courts may disagree with the scope of the FTC's orders when the offending commercial speaker has already discontinued the disputed practices prior to the FTC's investigation and issuance of the cease-and-desist mandate. However, if the cessation occurs after an investigation is initiated, courts generally are reluctant to overturn or modify FTC rulings.

## The FTC and Commercial Speakers: Who Is Liable for What?

The FTC's regulations and enforcement procedures apply both to independent commercial speakers, such as advertising or public relations agencies, and to the original manufacturers or providers of the products or services for which allegedly false and deceptive claims are made. The FTC typically excuses independent agencies from liability for violations of the law if the agencies can demonstrate good-faith efforts to ensure that the claims made for their clients' goods and services are truthful. The criteria for these good-faith efforts usually can be satisfied if an agency has reasonably relied on information supplied by the client and if the agency has no cause to believe that such information is untrue or deceptive.

However, advertising or public relations agencies can be held vicariously liable as defendants in product liability suits, especially when a product harms a consumer, and directly liable for false, misleading or deceptive commercial speech created for clients. In *Standard Oil v. FTC,*[108] the FTC issued its cease-and-desist order against both the oil company and its advertising agency Batten, Barton, Durstine & Osborn, Inc. for broadcasting the company's "F-310" commercials. A federal court of appeals upheld the FTC's decision. As the court noted:

> BBD&O contends the Commission acted improperly in holding it liable under section 5. The standard of care to be exercised by an advertising agency in determining what express and implied representations are contained in an ad and in assessing the truth or falsity of those representations increases in direct relation to the advertising agency's participation in the commercial project. [citations omitted] The degree of its participation is measured by a number of factors including the agency's role in writing and editing the text of the ad, its work in creating and designing the graphic or audio-visual material, its research and analysis of public opinions and attitudes, and its selection of the appropriate audience for the advertising message. Precisely these factors were weighed in reaching the conclusion that BBD&O knew or should have known of the deceptive nature of the F-310 advertising.[109]

The two factors considered by the FTC and the courts in determining whether an agency will be held liable are whether the agency "knew or should have known of the deceptive nature" of the commercial speech and the degree to which the agency participated in the creation and display of the message. The second factor is probably weighed more in the determination. An agency with actual knowledge of an attempt by a client to deceive the public (or which it could have known about if it had acted in a reasonable matter by exercising appropriate diligence) will have a difficult time convincing the FTC and the courts that the agency should not be held jointly liable with the advertiser. Active participation by the agency in the creative process is strong evidence that the agency had actual or constructive knowledge of the deception.

Agencies are liable if the claims made in the commercial speech questioned by the FTC are the product of the creative efforts of the agency, regardless of whether such claims are express or implied. Agencies also have an affirmative duty to modify commercial claims if the agencies acquire new information about the products or services from their clients or other sources. This duty extends to being in compliance with FTC regulations or orders directed against their competitors. The FTC generally presupposes that an agency is responsible for the claims made for a product or service and therefore carefully scrutinizes arguments made by an agency that it had no reason to question whether the information supplied by the agency's clients was false or deceptive.

If an agency is held liable, it can be subjected to the same remedies as its client. Of particular concern have been attempts by the FTC, some successful and some not, to extend its "fencing-in" requirements to all of the commercial speech an agency creates for all of the products and services of any and all clients the agency represents. Agencies may also be liable for fines up to $10,000 per day for each violation of an FTC cease-and-desist order.

## The FTC in a Digital, New-Media Age: Emerging Issues

Because the degree of zeal the federal government displays in aggressively policing commercial speech depends, in large measure, on the "regulatory climate" of Washington, D.C., during the "Bush years" that began the twenty-first century, the FTC was not pushed to engage in either overly strict enforcement or expansive interpretation of federal agency regulations of commercial speech. The advent of the Obama administration, however, may signal a change in such a hands-off approach.

The most prudent course of action for those engaged in commercial speech is to be familiar with the guidelines, regulations and cases interpreting federal policies before making claims for products or services or statements about financial matters and to keep a weather eye out for the actions of those federal regulatory agencies with oversight of the interests of the commercial speaker. As noted earlier, federal regulatory agencies routinely produce a number of publications discussing their current and proposed policies and often answer specific questions as well.

In determining the likelihood that speech claims will attract regulatory agency attention, commercial speakers should be especially careful if they direct commercial claims toward a vulnerable target audience, such as children, the elderly or the infirm, or if the speech appeals to the audience based on claims related to concern for the environment, health issues or some other aspect of physical well-being. Similarly, speakers would be wise to be wary of claims that are almost sure to raise the ire of competing companies (e.g., comparative or negative claims), consumer or special-interest groups opposed to the product or service or potential investors in new or existing company securities offerings.

For example, the FTC has been unusually aggressive in raising and investigating complaints about commercial claims involving so-called "green" issues. In its *Guides for the Use of Environmental Marketing Claims*,[110] the FTC provides guidelines for "environmental claims ... about ... the attributes of a product or package in connection with the sale ... or marketing of such product or package" to individuals and commercial enterprises.[111] The FTC is especially concerned with the use of such terms as *recyclable*, *biodegradable* and *environmentally friendly* and has created guidelines that detail the degree of prior substantiation for such claims.

The FTC also has recently paid particular attention to weight reduction and other diet claims related to drugs, special foods or vitamins. The agency is especially critical of such claims as:

1   Consumers who use the advertised product can lose two pounds or more per week (over four or more weeks) without reducing caloric intake or increasing their physical activity;
2   Consumers who use the advertised product can lose substantial weight while still enjoying unlimited amounts of high calorie foods;
3   The advertised product will cause permanent weight loss even when the user stops using the product;
4   The advertised product will cause substantial weight loss through the blockage of absorption of fat or calories.[112]

The FTC appears to be equally concerned with commercial messages presented by experts or "typical" consumers acting as spokespeople. As an example of the Obama administration's potentially more sympathetic stance to federal regulation, the FTC is considering changing the language contained in the "Guide Concerning the Use of Endorsements and Testimonials in Advertising." As the FTC has explained, the guide does not create law, but it does explain the way the FTC will interpret the law and much of our understanding of what is acceptable comes from the language contained therein. If implemented, the changes primarily would impact the use of disclaimers to accompany true endorsement claims that do not reflect the average experience, and on the types of endorsements companies can receive from new media sources like blogs and message boards.

The changes would close what currently the FTC may see as a "safe harbor" for disclaimers that do no more than say "results not typical" or "individual results may vary." The new language would state that individual testimonials will "likely" be interpreted as representing that the endorser's experience is representative of the average experience. If the testimonial does not represent the average experience, then the advertiser "should clearly and conspicuously disclose the generally expected performance in the depicted circumstances."

Changes that have already been implemented expand the requirements of disclosure of material connections with regard to new media technology. The FTC has provided several examples of endorsement or praise that appear in new media that need to be disclosed to avoid being labeled misleading, and has established that the commercial speaker would be responsible for false or misleading claims made by a Web-based representative.

These are not new ideas. What is new is a series of specific examples outlining new media scenarios. In one example, a company pays a person to blog about a product. The FTC states in the example that the company is liable for any false or misleading statements made by the blogger, including a failure by the blogger to disclose that he or she was paid for endorsements.

In another example, the FTC discusses a video game blogger who receives a free copy of a gaming system from the manufacturer for review. The FTC states that readers would be unlikely to know that the blogger received the product for free, and that this knowledge could affect the credibility they attach to the endorsement and, therefore, disclosure is required. Additionally, the FTC requires that an employee of a product-producing company who participates in a message board relating to the company's industry must disclose his or her status of employment because such knowledge would likely affect the credibility of the employee's endorsement.

It is important to note that these changes may greatly affect the techniques companies use to market themselves via new media. Prudent advertising and public relations professionals should stay abreast of developments regarding regulations of such new marketing methods.

Clearly, electronic marketing—whether by phone, fax or e-mail—is fraught with potential legal problems. But even having successfully navigated the legal requirements for electronic commercial speech messages and converted a prospective consumer into an actual customer does not mean a commercial speaker can rest easy, particularly if the customer shops online.

Although electronic commerce has developed more slowly than some predicted, by the end of the first decade of the twenty-first century, Web-based commerce comprised more than five percent of all United States retail sales (estimated at about $116 billion in 2007) and is clearly a key component for many businesses. Advertising dollars once earmarked for "traditional" media outlets—television, newspaper, radio and outdoor—increasingly are being diverted to the Internet. Even for organizations that do not emphasize sales or marketing, the Internet is a vital public relations communication tool with great potential impact on key constituents. Successful organizations today simply must have an Internet presence; the world-wide Web may not be ignored.

As more consumers use their computers for shopping or online financial transactions, the protection of consumer privacy is taking center stage. Since 2005, a number of large companies have reported breaches that may have placed consumers' personal information into the hands of identity thieves. For example, the data collection company ChoicePoint revealed that identity thieves had swiped personal information for almost 150,000 consumers, at least 750 of whom reported being the victims of identity theft.[113] Banks, universities and other organizations also have reported the loss or theft of personal information about consumers, including Social Security numbers and other important sensitive information.

In response, many states have adopted laws to protect consumers' personal information.[114] Before Congress turned its attention to safeguarding customer data, most attempts to address this problem at the federal level originated with the FTC. Section 5 of the Federal Trade Commission Act gives that agency the power to condemn "unfair or deceptive acts or practices."[115] The FTC uses this power to regulate a broad range of business behaviors including consumer privacy violations. FTC actions to date generally have dealt with companies' failure to implement adequate safety measures protective of consumers' personal information.

One of the most notable involved BJ's Wholesale Club, which, according to the FTC, engaged in an unfair trade practice by failing to secure customers' sensitive information embedded in the magnetic strip on the back of credit cards.[116] The club settled with the FTC and agreed to establish and maintain a "comprehensive information security program that includes administrative, technical and physical safeguards."[117]

In November 2007, the FTC published its so-called "Red Flags Rule," requiring that banks, savings and loans organizations and credit unions, as well as businesses and institutions that extend credit to consumers like auto dealers and cable companies, develop specific methods for identifying and detecting signs of possible identity theft. Originally scheduled to go into effect in 2008, the "Red Flags Rule" is now set for implementation late in 2010 to allow those with objections to the proposed rule to make their comments known.

Such "red flags" might include "unusual account activity, fraud alerts on a consumer report, or attempted use of suspicious account application documents. The program must also describe appropriate responses that would prevent and mitigate the crime and detail a plan to update the program."[118] The programs "must be managed by the Board of Directors or senior employees of the financial institution or creditor, include appropriate staff training, and provide for oversight of any service providers,"[119] words of importance to public relations professionals working in such organizations.

The ill-gotten gain attained from identity theft almost guarantees that this type of criminal activity will persist. It also ensures that well-established laws, such as Section 5 of the FTC Act, and new laws, such as the "Red Flags Rule," will continue to evolve in response.

## The Food and Drug Administration

Although the Federal Trade Commission is the agency that exercises the most pervasive, day-to-day regulation of commercial speech, numerous government agencies, commissions and boards retain limited jurisdiction over commercial speech dealing with specific products or services. One prominent example is the Food and Drug Administration (FDA).

## The History of the FDA and Its Jurisdiction Over Commercial Speech

The FDA is part of the larger U.S. Department of Health and Human Services. Headquartered in the Washington, D.C., area, the FDA employs more than 7,000 people in Washington and in 10 regional offices across the country. Its missions include: (a) approving new drugs, medical devices and certain food additives for safety and, in some cases, effectiveness; (b) setting standards for foods and the labeling of foods and then ensuring via testing that such foods meet these standards; (c) inspecting sites where drugs, cosmetics, medical devices and foods are produced to ensure these products meet the FDA's public safety standards; and (d) issuing public warnings or taking legal action when unsafe products threaten the public welfare. The FDA's professional staff consists mainly of biologists, chemists, nutritionists, pharmacologists, attorneys and other compliance personnel and consumer-affairs officers.

Although its name might imply a wider jurisdiction, for the most part the FDA's direct interest in commercial speech is limited to regulating information about the contents and safety of drugs available only by prescription when advertised or promoted through the mass media or direct marketing to consumers. The Federal Food, Drug and Cosmetic Act[120] defines a *prescription drug* as a drug "not safe for [human] use except under the supervision of a licensed practitioner"[121] because of potential harm to the consumer either as the result of its use or from employing the methods necessary for its use. Any new drug may be defined as a "prescription drug" following the FDA's policy of labeling all such products as initially needing "the professional supervision of a practitioner licensed by law to administer such drug[s]"[122] unless the Agency is satisfied that the new drug can be safely introduced and sold over the counter without this requirement.

The FDA's jurisdiction over prescription drug-related commercial speech emanates, in part, from its original grant of power to regulate "labels and any written, printed or graphic matter (1) upon any article [drug] or any of its containers or wrappers, or (2) accompanying such article."[123] Although the statute does not specifically define what is meant by "printed or graphic matter . . . accompanying such [an] article," the FDA and the courts have treated this language as authorizing broad authority over commercial messages that are part of a promotional campaign, including retail sales promotion materials and direct mail pieces.

The FDA's authority to regulate commercial speech was made more explicit by a series of amendments to the Food, Drug and Cosmetic Act, beginning in the 1960s, that specifically gave the FDA jurisdiction over commercial speech involving prescription drugs, reserving the power to regulate nonprescription drug commercial speech to the FTC.

Usually the FDA will treat commercial speech as falling within its regulatory authority if the prescription drug information is disseminated through broadcast or print commercials or through public relations activities aimed at the mass media. FDA jurisdiction over non-media promotional techniques is neither expressly defined nor directly suggested by the statute. However, in *Nature Food Centres, Inc., v. U.S.*,[124] a series of lectures touting the alleged virtues of a dietary supplement was permitted to be entered as evidence on the question of whether the supplement was mislabeled.

In *U.S. v. Articles of Drug, etc.*,[125] and *U.S. v. Guardian Chemical Corp.*,[126] courts held that printed brochures and pamphlets need not directly accompany a drug to be considered part of the drug's "label" and therefore are subject to FDA regulation. Similarly, in *U.S. v. Diapulse Mfg. Corp. of America*,[127] the court ruled that the sending of reprints of medical journal articles constituted "labels" accompanying a medical device. However, despite these rulings, marketing campaigns carried out by direct personal contact with physicians or public relations tactics such as news conferences announcing the creation or availability of new drugs may not be within the FDA's regulatory reach.

Although the FDA retains jurisdiction over the content of the labeling of over-the-counter drugs, cosmetics and foodstuffs, Sections 5 and 12 of the Federal Trade Commission Act give the FTC regulatory power over commercial mass media advertising and other forms of non-label commercial speech involving these products.

Although normally the FTC will follow its own guidelines for regulation of over-the-counter drugs, cosmetics and foodstuffs, including requirements for prior substantiation and appropriate clinical trials, the two agencies usually work closely together in determining what will be considered false or deceptive commercial speech. For example, the FDA publishes guidelines that specify appropriate requirements for the labels of products falling under its jurisdiction. These include uses and levels of effectiveness for many over-the-counter medications and health claims related to food. The FTC will normally take these specifications into account in determining its regulations of commercial speech in the media involving such products.

## FDA Content-Based Regulation of Prescription Drug Commercial Speech

The specific regulations promulgated and enforced with respect to the content of commercial speech within the FDA's jurisdiction are primarily designed to ensure consumer safety. Such content-based regulation would appear to be constitutional under *Virginia State Board of Pharmacy* (discussed earlier) if the commercial speech in question falls within the speech the Supreme Court of the United States defines as "false or misleading." As the Court noted, "[o]bviously, much commercial speech is not provably false, or even wholly false, but only deceptive or misleading. We foresee no obstacle to a State's dealing effectively with this problem."[128]

FDA regulations normally require that a detailed list of the ingredients appear in a prominent and readable manner within a prescription drug advertisement or other commercial speech. Additionally, the message must indicate the percentage of each ingredient and the list of ingredients must follow the same order as found on the prescription drug's label.

Beginning in the early 1960s, the FDA also mandated that commercial advertising must contain the prescription drug's generic name each time the brand name of the product is mentioned. As might be imagined, the requirement that the generic name accompany the brand name proved to be a pain for copywriters and designers attempting to use advertisements, brochures and other communication vehicles. The regulation eventually was challenged in federal court by the pharmaceutical industry in *Abbott Laboratories v. Celebrezze*.[129] The case was eventually settled when the FDA agreed to modify its requirements. The generic name now needs to appear in conjunction with the brand name when the brand name is "featured" in the advertisement but not when subsequently appearing in body copy on the same page of the advertisement. However, the generic name must be included with the brand name in statements specifying benefits of the drug or detailing side effects.

FDA regulations also require that generic drug names be visually or aurally prominent and must be located close to the brand name in the text of the advertisement. Typically, this may be accomplished by placing the generic name in brackets after the brand name or by adding such wording as ". . . a brand of (generic name)." The regulations also specify that the generic name must be set in type that is at least half the size of the brand name.

## FDA Requirements for a "True Summary" of Side Effects and Effectiveness

The Food, Drug and Cosmetic Act mandates that each commercial message promoting a prescription drug include a "summary" of specified information about its safety and effectiveness.[130] FDA regulations specify that the information within this summary must reflect the wording accepted by the FDA for the drug's package labeling, including a description of all the specific side effects and "contraindications" that could result from taking the drug as well as any warnings or cautions for its use.[131]

The regulations prescribe that the requirements for a truthful summary apply to the entire advertisement. "[U]ntrue or misleading information in [one part] of the advertisement" cannot be corrected by inclusion of correct information in another.[132] However, even if part of the advertisement "would make the advertisement false or misleading by reason of the [omission] of appropriate qualification," the overall advertisement still will be in compliance if a "prominent reference [is included] of a more complete discussion of such qualification or information."[133]

The requirements for information about effectiveness and side effects are limited to information about the purposes for which the drug is intended and as promoted in the commercial message. The FDA does not require an advertisement for a prescription drug that promotes a specific use for the drug to contain statements of side effects or effectiveness for all the other possible purposes for which a drug might be adopted or recommended by the medical or pharmaceutical communities. However, the FDA has ruled that it is impermissible to group a number of side effects or contraindications together under one general warning unless the language of the warning conforms with the FDA's previously approved language. Also, specific information about possible side effects must be included for each "contraindication" or claim.

Commercial speakers need beware inadvertently suggesting uses for drugs not given prior approval by the FDA for fear the commercial claims may cause the drug to be reclassified as a "new drug." Uses for a drug "generally recognized as safe and effective among experts qualified by scientific training and experience to evaluate the safety and effectiveness"[134] will not be seen as creating a "new drug" so long as well-conducted clinical evaluations or documentation in medical literature provide evidence the drug meets FDA requirements.

FDA regulations detailing the kinds of information or omissions of information the agency might find to be false or misleading are extensive. Clearly, commercial speech about prescription drugs will be judged false and deceptive if it (a) fails to indicate possible side effects; (b) exaggerates the effectiveness of a drug compared to its drawbacks; (c) neglects to specify the negative effects of long-term usage; (d) contains "a representation . . . that a drug is better, more effective, [or] useful in a broader range of conditions or patients" than can be justified by at least two appropriate clinical trials;[135] or (e) claims that a drug is safer than a competitor's product without appropriate scientific evidence.

Additionally, a number of FDA regulations specifying the kinds of commercial speech claims the agency might find false or deceptive concern the inappropriate use of statistical tests, sample sizes and levels of statistical significance. Examples include statements such as "pooling data from various insignificant or dissimilar studies"[136] in such a way as to incorrectly suggest statistical significance, erroneously using a statistical finding of "'no significant difference' . . . to deny or conceal . . . real clinical difference,"[137] or employing "reports or statements represented to be statistical analyses . . . that are inconsistent with or violate the established principles of statistical theory."[138]

A third general category of potentially misleading statements involves misrepresentations about the subjects taking part in clinical trials. For example, it is false and deceptive to include "normal individuals without disclosing that [they] are normal"[139] unless the drug is marketed to such individuals. Similarly, commercial messages that fail to disclose the potential side effects of a drug when administered to a "selected class" of subjects for whom the drug is actually intended would likely draw the FDA's fire. So too would claims for a drug's effectiveness when the test data are "derived with dosages different from those recommended in approved or permitted labeling,"[140] or when they "represent or suggest that drug dosages properly recommended for use in the treatment of certain classes of patients . . . are safe and effective for the treatment of other classes of patients [e.g., children] . . . when such is not the case."[141]

A fourth category of deceptive statements involves inclusion or reference to literature that either is false or could be construed in a misleading way. For example, commercial speakers should be careful not to publish testimonials about a drug's effectiveness that exceed the product's actual tested effectiveness or that have been made questionable by scientific studies published more recently than those cited in the testimonials. Additionally, commercial statements may run afoul of FDA regulation if they tout a drug's effectiveness that could be attributed to either a combination of drugs or to the psychological "placebo effect" of taking any medication.[142]

The FDA also might find problems with the manner in which commercial information is presented. For example, false or misleading statements may arise from a failure "to present information relating to side effects . . . with [appropriate] prominence and readability . . . taking into account . . . [such] factors as typography, layout, contrast headlines . . . [and] white space. . . ."[143] Similar concerns also could arise in broadcast advertisements.

The FDA has recognized a number of limited exceptions to its "brief summary" requirements for prescription drugs. Commercial speech that simply "reminds" providers or consumers of a drug by mentioning its name and/or the costs of such a drug need not provide information on side effects, contraindications or ingredients. Similarly, advertisements for sale of drugs in bulk to be repackaged or relabeled and advertisements intended for drugs used as ingredients of medications pharmacists create for their clientele are exempt as long as the advertisements do not contain claims for a drug's safety or effectiveness.[144]

A more general exception to the "brief summary requirements" for commercial speech about prescription drugs was created by the FDA to encourage dissemination of information about new drugs or new uses for existing drugs through scientific colloquia and professional conferences. Even when a new drug has not officially passed FDA standards, the agency will usually permit information about the existence and properties of the drug to be communicated in these forums, so long as such meetings are conducted under the auspices of disinterested parties, such as scientific societies or universities, and the information presented is factually correct and balanced. However, although there has been little litigation on this issue to date, the FDA may not be as willing to forego its information requirements for new drugs if the information is communicated by means of manufacturer-sponsored conventions, press conferences, news releases or other public relations techniques.

## Enforcement of FDA Prescription Drug Advertising Regulations

Although the FDA's enabling legislation provides for a number of legal remedies by which the agency may enforce its regulations of prescription drug-related commercial speech, for the most part these remedies remain weapons for threatening legal action rather than for actual use. The mere threat of legal action has proven to be a virtual guarantee the offending party will voluntarily take the steps necessary to bring the criticized commercial speech within FDA guidelines.

The Food, Drug and Cosmetic Act provides the FDA with the power to seek injunctive relief, seize offending products and seek criminal penalties for advertising of prescription drugs the FDA believes have been "misbranded."[145] Short of these drastic remedies, the offending party must notify physicians or others to whom the commercial speech has been addressed when the information or omission of information the FDA feels is a problem is corrected and it then must become part of the drug manufacturer's commercial message.

## FDA in a Digital, New-Media Age: Emerging Issues

The FDA is likely to be even more aggressive in scrutinizing claims by "alternative" remedies for accomplishing weight loss, increased stamina or the maintenance of general well-being. This also may extend to programs like diet plans or exercise regimes.

It is also possible that the FDA will take a second look at its requirements for the advertising and marketing of prescription drugs with an eye to requiring even more disclosure of limitations and side effects. In addition, Congress may extend the jurisdiction of the FDA to products like tobacco that arguably contain substances that could cause health-related problems.

Wise and prudent advertising and public relations professionals should stay up to date with the latest pronouncements by the FDA if they deal with products that could fall under its jurisdiction. They should also be alert to continuing efforts by Congress to give the FDA greater latitude in regulating "vice-like" products based on health related issues.

## The Securities and Exchange Commission

The Securities and Exchange Commission (SEC), which oversees the regulation of stock markets as well as the companies and investors that trade securities in these markets, is of vital concern to large segments of both the advertising and public relations communities.

## The History of the SEC and Its Jurisdiction over Commercial Speech

The SEC traces its origins to early attempts at regulating the buying and selling of securities, beginning in the late 1880s. Prior to that time, a recurring cycle of financial good times invariably yielding to a period of economic chaos and a major depression created a pattern of boom-or-bust that eventually brought calls for reform of the nation's economic system. Initial efforts at regulation at both the federal and state levels proved ineffective, however. Finally, the financial crises that led to the Great Depression in the early 1930s provided the impetus for real reform. These efforts began with passage of the Securities Act of 1933[146] and the Securities Exchange Act of 1934.[147] The latter Act established the SEC and charged it with the responsibility of ensuring that timely, complete and truthful information be made available to the public about publicly traded securities.

Until the 1960s, the SEC largely went about its business of enforcing existing regulations involving disclosure of information. However, revisions of the Securities Exchange Act in 1964,[148] coupled with a greater willingness by the SEC's staff to initiate investigations of investment companies, set the SEC on a collision course with many existing business practices throughout the 1960s and 1970s. This eventually led to a number of further reforms in financial marketplace activities. Although the 1980s brought a lessening in the SEC's aggressiveness, the events surrounding the collapse of the Enron Corporation and revelations of other corporate improprieties at the beginning of this century inspired Congress to pass tough new financial accountability laws and reinvigorated the SEC as a major player in maintaining the stability of the securities market today.[149]

The Commission itself is composed of five commissioners, appointed for five-year terms by the President with the concurrence of the Senate. One of these appointees is selected by the President to chair the SEC. To reduce partisanship, no more than three commissioners may be members of the same political party. Headquartered in Washington, D.C., the SEC maintains eight regional offices across the country. The SEC's professional staff includes securities analysts, accountants, attorneys and various regulatory and enforcement personnel. The SEC's activities are segmented into divisions. The most important for commercial speakers is the Division of Corporation Finance. This division, among other duties, oversees corporate registration statements, annual and quarterly reports and other corporate financial communication activities.

## SEC Regulation of First-Time or Additional New Offerings of Securities

According to the SEC, the primary purposes of the 1933 Securities Act were to "provide investors with material financial and other information" and "to prohibit misrepresentation, deceit, and other fraudulent acts and practices in the sale of securities generally. . . ."[150] The Supreme Court, in *Ernst and Ernst v. Hochfelder*,[151] characterized the purpose of the statute as providing "full disclosure of material information concerning public offerings . . . to protect investors against fraud and, through the imposition of specified civil liabilities, to promote ethical standards of honesty and fair dealing."[152]

The Act's definition of a *security* includes "any note, stock, treasury stock, bond, . . . certificate of interest or participation in any profit-sharing agreement, . . . investment contract, . . . certificate of deposit for a security, fractional undivided interest in oil, gas, or other mineral rights, or, in general, any interest in an instrument commonly known as a 'security' . . . or guarantee of, or warrant or right to subscribe to or purchase any of the foregoing. . . ."[153]

With the exceptions of offerings sold completely within one state (and therefore subject to state rather than federal regulation) and those for small amounts, generally less than $500,000, Section 5 of the Act specifies that before a security can be offered for sale, a "registration statement" must be formally filed with the SEC. Prior to the filing of this statement of registration, the law mandates that no press releases, news conferences, mass media advertising or sales promotions issued with the intent or effect of encouraging the sale of the company's securities are permitted. For this reason, commercial speakers must be extremely wary of disseminating any information that the SEC might interpret as promoting the sale of new securities, including disseminating information about the price of new securities or claims for the safety or benefits of investing.

After the required registration statement is filed with the SEC, the Securities Act requires a 20-day waiting period, during which the party offering the securities for sale may communicate limited information about the issuance of the securities. Typically, this is done by means of a formal preliminary "prospectus." No actual purchase offers can be accepted until the waiting period expires. The preliminary prospectus must conform to the format and contain the copious detailed information specifically called for by the Act to meet SEC approval. The Securities Act provides an exception to its no-advertising policy during the formal waiting period for "tombstone advertisements," so called because their appearance is strictly curtailed by the SEC's rules. Such advertisements are generally restricted to a straightforward presentation of information about the price of a security, who is offering it for sale and how it may be purchased.[154]

Disregard of the no-promotional-activities strictures in the Securities Act by commercial speakers can lead to unfortunate results. In *S.E.C. Arvida Corporation*,[155] a press release, issued by the brokerage firm Loeb, Rhoades & Co., touted the virtues of the stock offered by a new company, the Arvida Corporation. The release described the company's financial stability and the extensiveness of its land holdings. Unfortunately for Arvida, the news release was issued and distributed to the nation's leading financial publications before the formal processes mandated by the Act had been completed, causing the SEC to determine that the requirements for a formal registration statement had been breached.

In a companion action, *In re Carl M. Loeb, Rhoades & Co.*,[156] the SEC challenged the issuance of a press release as a violation of Section 5 of the Securities Act on the basis that it had "set in motion the processes of distribution . . . by arousing and stimulating investor and dealer interest in Arvida securities."[157] Loeb, Rhoades argued that the news release was exactly that—news—and therefore could not be grounds for a Section 5 violation. The SEC disagreed, holding that "astute public relations activities" had created the "news," and that this was "precisely the evil which the Securities Act seeks to prevent."[158]

The court concluded that, "[a]lthough it appears that defendants acted in good faith . . . and although [they] continue to deny [liability] . . . nevertheless the Court finds that defendants violated Section 5(c) of the Securities Act"[159] and ordered the parties not to offer common shares of Arvida unless a registration statement was filed with the SEC and all other agency requirements met.

## SEC Regulation of the National Securities Marketplace

Congress passed the Securities Exchange Act of 1934 to regulate the ongoing trading of securities after the first-time offering for sale in stock exchanges and by brokers. Like the Securities Act, the Securities Exchange Act's basic purpose is to ensure that investors are assured of full disclosure of all timely and pertinent information necessary to make a reasoned and informed decision about selling or purchasing a security. A second purpose is to prevent "any manipulative or deceptive device or contrivance"[160] that could lead to fraud in the securities market, including false or deceptive advertising or other commercial speech.

To provide potential investors with the accurate and truthful financial information they need, the SEC enforces the Securities Exchange Act's requirements for full disclosure by requiring companies offering their stock for sale to the public, in a stock market or through a broker, to provide periodic reports that detail the state of the company, its future plans and other similar financial information.

Every publicly traded company, except for small or intrastate corporations, must keep a registration statement on file with the SEC that provides information similar to the statement required under the Securities Act. In addition, they are required to file an annual comprehensive report (Form 10-K), quarterly updates and various other reports as needed to meet the SEC's regulations for timely disclosure of new information about a company's financial status. This information includes changes in senior management or board of directors, initiation of bankruptcy proceedings or any other "material" event.

Congress broadened normal reporting requirements with its passage of the Williams Act in 1968.[161] The Act mandated that a company proposing to take control of another company by acquiring a majority of outstanding shares from current stockholders (a so-called "tender offer") must disclose (a) detailed information to the SEC, the target company and current shareholders about the take-over company; (b) the reasons behind the tender offer; and (c) what the purchaser plans to do with the acquired company. If such disclosure is not complete, or if the SEC finds the information provided either false or misleading, the SEC can initiate legal action to ensure compliance.

Because tender offers often are made via the mass media or other publicity techniques, public relations and advertising professionals should be aware of SEC rulings about what constitutes the actual commencement of an official tender order. Otherwise, making statements in advertisements or other forms of publicity that the SEC might consider as sufficient to create such an order could trigger requirements that the tender offeror submit the requisite copious financial information on appropriate forms and within specified time limits or risk legal sanction by the SEC.

Under SEC Rule 14(d) of the Act, for example, publicity about the possible or impending purchase of another company has been held to create a tender offer if it is published in newspaper advertisements or disseminated to security holders or investors by other means. If such publicity is interpreted as creating a tender offer, Section 14(e) of the Act mandates that the communication must include everything from the identity of the bidder to a statement that stockholder lists are being used to reach securities holders. Also, the communication must include the expiration date of the offer, the degree to which the offer will result in control of the target company by the bidder and how securities holders may obtain information from the bidder.

## SEC Regulation of False or Deceptive Commercial Speech

The SEC's enabling legislation and regulations demand that commercial speech involving securities must be truthful, non-deceptive and comprehensive. The SEC's interpretation of Rule 14(a) that broadly defines deceptive information involving tender offers was upheld in *Gillette Company v. RB Partners*.[162] In that case, a chart in a newspaper advertisement was judged to misrepresent the conditions of the offer even though all of the information presented was true. The problem, said the SEC, was that the design of the chart made it appear that foreign parties predominated in the group seeking to make the offer when such was not the case.

Like the FTC, the SEC looks with especial disfavor on statements that could mislead potential consumers or investors in the ultimate decision to purchase. In the selling and buying of securities, such deceptive statements might include speculative or untruthful information about (a) changes in senior management of a corporation; (b) potential mergers or takeovers; (c) revenues or profits; (d) significant new markets; or (e) plans for new securities offerings. Omission of information in corporate public statements that could deceive investors in any of the ways noted above raises equally problematic issues for corporate communicators.

Allegedly deceptive statements can be disseminated in press releases, speeches before public bodies, media interviews or company publications. If a misstatement occurs, the company (and its public relations counsel) must publicly correct the error or risk liability. Such affirmative action is also required if statements initially true have been made false by changes in the company or in the marketplace. There is no affirmative duty, however, to correct the misstatements of outside third parties (e.g., market analysts or financial reporters) if the company had no hand in preparing or distributing the allegedly deceptive information.

The extent of the SEC's reach in regulating commercial speech involving tender offers and proxy solicitations is exemplified by the case of *Long Island Lighting Company (LILCO) v. Barbash*.[163] In *LILCO*, a coalition of politicians and activists initiated a proxy fight to change the utility's board of directors and forestall the construction of a nuclear power plant. As part of this campaign, those opposed to the current operation of the utility purchased a newspaper advertisement urging stockholders to vote for replacing management and in favor of turning the utility into a municipally run company.

The utility, challenging the advertisement as false and misleading, sought an injunction to prohibit "solicitation" of the company's shareholders "until the claimed false and misleading statements had been corrected" and information to that effect had been filed with the SEC.[164] The company argued that the purpose of the advertisement was to "influence the exercise of proxies by LILCO shareholders," and that the statements were "false and misleading in numerous respects relating to alleged advantages for ratepayers . . . ."[165]

A federal district court judge dismissed the complaint, holding that the SEC's rules about the permissible use and content of commercial speech involving proxy solicitations did not apply because the advertisement in question was not specifically directed toward shareholders.[166] The judge also noted significant First Amendment concerns because "[a]llowing injunctive relief on the ground that the advertisement constitutes an improper proxy solicitation would pervert the legitimate protective function of the regulation into an unconstitutional licensing of political speech."[167]

A federal court of appeals, however, overruled the trial court, holding that the SEC's rule could apply even when there was no direct appeal to shareholders.[168] The rules apply, said the appeals court, "not only to direct requests to furnish, revoke or withhold proxies, but also to communications which may indirectly accomplish such a result or constitute a step in a chain of communications designed ultimately to accomplish such a result."[169] According to the court, "[d]etermination in every case is whether the challenged communication, seen in the totality of circumstances, is 'reasonably calculated' to influence the shareholders' votes."[170]

Noting that SEC rules require that "solicitations in the form of 'speeches, press releases, and television scripts' be filed with the SEC,"[171] the court agreed with the SEC's brief in favor of LILCO's position that "it would 'permit easy evasion of the proxy rules' to exempt all general and indirect communications to shareholders,"[172] including the advertisement in question, even if the information it contained also concerned matters of general public interest.

*Securities and Exchange Commission v. Texas Gulf Sulphur Co.*[173] illustrates the problems that public relations and advertising professionals face in determining (a) the kinds of information a company can and should make public if that information could impact the trading of its securities; (b) when that information should be released; and (c) the ramifications of either carelessness or deliberate deception in the information-dissemination process.

The case began in the early 1960s when Texas Gulf Sulphur's geophysical surveys revealed the possibility of significant deposits of copper, zinc and other valuable ores in land owned by the company in eastern Canada. Testing at the site confirmed the high probability that a valuable strike had been located. This information was kept strictly confidential so that Texas Gulf Sulphur could acquire additional lands adjoining its holdings. Further chemical testing convinced the company's scientists and senior management that, if anything, the initial estimates of the worth of the discovery significantly underestimated its value.

Approximately six months later, with most of its land acquisition complete, the company again began to drill into the ore to obtain additional samples. During this time, a number of Texas Gulf Sulphur's management officials (and people alleged to have received tips from these officials about the value of the discovery) purchased significant amounts of the company's stock. In addition, the company issued stock options to its highest paid employees, several of whom knew about the findings revealed by the analysis of the samples from the Canadian site.

With exploratory drilling underway, rumors of a potentially valuable discovery by Texas Gulf Sulphur began to circulate in the financial community. Concerned that the company's strategic and tactical plans for announcing the findings could be compromised, the company, with the help of a public relations consultant, drafted a press statement that was released to major daily newspapers. The statement announced that, although a strike had been made and early results appeared favorable, the rumors of a major discovery exaggerated "the scale of operations and mention plans and statistics . . . that are without factual basis. . . ." According to the release, "[t]he work done to date [on the Canadian site] has not been sufficient to reach definite conclusions and any statement as to size and grade of ore would be premature and possibly misleading."[174]

In the SEC's opinion, the statements made or implied in Texas Gulf Sulphur's press release about the potential value of the ore, as well as the omission of information known to the company but not included in the release, involved "material" facts. This satisfied the legal requirement, specified by the Securities Exchange Act, that before a company's commercial speech can be challenged under Rule 10(b)(5)[175] as fraudulent it must contain information that allegedly could have influenced investors or shareholders to purchase, dispose of or fail to trade in a company's stock (or how to vote in a proxy dispute).

Although the extent of actual detriment to potential investors and shareholders who might have either not purchased additional shares or prematurely disposed of their stock in the company based on the information contained in the press release was questioned by both the federal district court and the federal appeals court that subsequently heard the case on an appeal by the company, both courts concluded that the SEC and aggrieved investors and shareholders had sufficient evidence to pursue suits that eventually cost the company hundreds of thousands of dollars and much negative publicity.

*Texas Gulf Sulphur* illustrates a number of important issues for those engaged in communication activities involving securities transactions or proxy issues. The courts noted that there was nothing wrong with withholding information about the potential value of the discovery until additional land purchases were completed. However, Texas Gulf Sulphur had an affirmative duty to disclose the information promptly once the acquisitions were completed and drilling had resumed or it would risk violating the SEC's rules requiring timely disclosure of material information.

Although the courts found that the company had partly satisfied the requirement for timely disclosure, they also found that the SEC's rules mandating that the dissemination of material information be made so as to give the information wide distribution had been violated. In defending themselves against accusations of fraud, several of Texas Gulf Sulphur's corporate officials involved in the case argued that the information about the strike was already public, based on limited publication by Canadian media. The court gave short shrift to this argument, finding that, "rumors and casual disclosure through Canadian media, especially in view of the [earlier] 'gloomy' . . . release denying the rumors. . . hardly sufficed to inform traders on American [stock] exchanges. . . ."[176]

Although ultimately not a factor in the outcome, the efforts of the company's outside public relations counsel in drafting the fraudulent press release also could have subjected the public relations agency to legal liability if a court determined that the agency either knew or should have known that false or misleading material statements of fact were being disseminated. Additionally, although the courts held that Texas Gulf Sulphur had no duty to correct speculation or misstatements made by the financial press to which the company made no contribution, such a duty could arise if misinformation began to circulate based on the company's own statements unless the company's clearly articulated message was simply misquoted or misunderstood by the media.

Finally, although the SEC and the courts focused on the content of the communication and not its form, it seems likely that Texas Gulf Sulphur would have been found equally liable for disseminating misleading information if the information had been conveyed by an internal newsletter, in-person briefing, news conference, quarterly or annual report, company Web site or other public relations tactic, so long as there was evidence that the information was "material" and that investors or shareholders learned of it and relied on it to their detriment.

## Insider Trading

Yet another issue of importance to advertising and public relations professionals illustrated in the *Texas Gulf Sulphur* case is the possibility of violating a fiduciary relationship through "insider trading" or "tipping."[177] The primary duty of those who oversee the management of a corporation is to represent the best interests of the company's shareholders. Thus, using nonpublic information about a company's financial status to trade in a company's securities or engage in stock option plans without first publicly disclosing such information might constitute a breach of fiduciary responsibility that could subject the company and individual officials—including those who manage the company's communication efforts—to legal liabilities.

Similarly, "tipping off" confidants or financial consultants about nonpublic material information that could influence trading in a company's securities may constitute a violation of fiduciary trust. As the appeals court in *Texas Gulf Sulphur* noted, the SEC's regulations are "also applicable to one possessing the information who may not be strictly termed an 'insider' within the meaning of [the Act]. Thus anyone in possession of material inside information must either disclose it to the investing public or, if disabled from disclosing to protect a corporate confidence . . . must abstain from trading in or recommending the securities concerned. . . ." [178]

Clearly, such requirements apply to public relations or advertising counsel. Violations of the anti-tipping rules could subject both those who pass along the information and those who profit from it to legal sanctions. For example, the court in *Texas Gulf Sulphur* concluded that, "all transactions in TGS stock or [stock option] calls by individuals apprised of the drilling results . . . were made in violation of [SEC] Rule 10(b)(5)." [179]

Perhaps the best-known incident involving communication professionals and insider trading involved Anthony Franco, who, at the time of the incident, was president of the Public Relations Society of America (PRSA). According to the SEC, Franco was guilty of a violation of fiduciary trust for allegedly purchasing stock in a company to which he was a consultant, based on insider information that the company would soon be acquired by another corporation. Although formally admitting no wrong doing, Franco eventually resigned the PRSA presidency and pledged not to act on insider information in the future.

The Franco incident raises yet another concern for those engaged in commercial speech. Even when not officially acting as an agent or consultant to a company, and therefore technically with no fiduciary responsibility to its shareholders, advertising and public relations professionals may learn of material information about a company's financial status. The SEC and the courts have held in a number of instances that there is a duty for these "market" insiders, as well as for those actually inside the company, to divulge such information or forego trading in the securities to avoid the risk of being found in violation of Rule 10(b)(5).

In *Carpenter v. U.S.*,[180] the Supreme Court refused to overturn a finding that fraud had been committed by a financial columnist for the *Wall Street Journal* who was convicted of using information learned "on the street" for his own gain and for tipping off investors in advance about companies he would tout or condemn in his column. Although the columnist was judged not to possess any fiduciary relationship to the companies mentioned in his column or to the market, he nonetheless was held liable under SEC rules prohibiting fraud.

## Enforcement of SEC Regulations

Congress has given the SEC power to seek civil and criminal remedies for violations of the securities laws and regulations. In addition, the courts have interpreted the securities laws as providing private citizens with the right to go to court to seek money damages from companies and individuals who have, through omission or misrepresentation of material information, induced the investors to buy or sell securities to their disadvantage.

The *Texas Gulf Sulphur* case provides illustrations of how these sanctions may be imposed. After finding that the press release downplaying the magnitude of the ore deposit discovery could mislead stockholders and investors (and that actions by the company's senior officials and their friends acting on their tips constituted illegal insider trading), the federal appeals court turned its attention to establishing liability and assessing damages. The court found that, contrary to the lower court's opinion, Texas Gulf Sulphur could be subjected to an injunction sought by the SEC to desist from future insider trading. The court remanded the case to the district court for further action on this issue.

Similarly, the appeals court sent back for further proceedings the assessment of liability for the company officials who had violated Rule 10(b)(5) either by insider trading or by exercising stock options during the period before full public disclosure was made. The court also opened the door to later civil suits by stockholders and traders who could demonstrate that they had been materially misled by the fraudulent activities of both the company and its managers.

In a series of subsequent cases, the lower courts decreed that the individuals within the company who had purchased stock based on insider information would be forced to disgorge their profits from such purchases and enjoined from future insider trading practices. Although it was judged that the company could be the subject of the injunction sought by the SEC if there were evidence of continuing or probable future wrongdoing, more troubling for the company was the filing of more than 100 civil lawsuits by disgruntled investors against the company and its management. Depending on how the value of the shares traded based on the misrepresentation by the company was determined, at one point the damages claims against the company ranged from roughly $80 million to as much as $390 million—a figure more than the total worth of the company.

The lessons to be learned for advertising and public relations professionals are clear. Prudent professionals should be extremely careful in counseling senior management about the needs for a company's broad and timely disclosure of securities information as well as to create a system of checks and balances within the department or agency by instituting a "disclosure compliance program."[181] Such programs could help forestall the risk of inadvertently publishing information or running afoul of other provisions of the securities laws that could lead to violations of SEC regulations and possibly subject the company or client to crippling lawsuits.

Additionally, advertising and public relations professionals should be wary of trading in securities based on material information they acquire by virtue of their status as company or marketplace insiders as well as passing along tips about such information to friends or brokers. It would be wise to pursue such efforts only after seeking sound investment advice from financial consultants knowledgeable about the most up-to-date rulings by the SEC regarding the obligations and legal liabilities of those who engage in such trading practices.

## The SEC in a Digital, New-Media Age: Emerging Issues

Not surprisingly, considering the recent shenanigans by members of the financial community, the SEC appears to be stressing the breadth and timeliness of disclosure of information. Simply posting information on a company Web site, for example, may not meet the SEC's requirements for wide distribution of important securities news.

The degree of scrutiny of information deemed by the SEC to possibly violate its strict no-promotional-efforts policies perhaps is exemplified in the agency's suggestion that a personal interview with the founders of the Internet search company Google, serendipitously published in *Playboy* magazine in the summer of 2004 just prior to the company going public, might give cause for SEC sanctions. Although no penalties eventually were imposed, the SEC's actions were a clear indication of the aggressive nature of SEC investigators in regulating commercial speech during the time of an original securities offering, efforts that will only redouble in years to come.

As an overall rule, speakers should satisfy themselves that a reasonable segment of the audience will not misperceive the claims in a commercial message and that the absence of information will not create material errors of omission. If claims could be misconstrued, those creating such claims should evaluate the language of any disclaimers used to avoid liability to ensure that these disclaimers are effective from the point of view of the target consumer.

Additionally, commercial speakers would be wise to continually keep in mind the harm an investigation by a federal regulatory agency could have not only on the life of a particular commercial campaign, but on the long-term reputations of both the product or service and the organizations responsible for creating the problematic commercial message.

# Chapter 11

# Other Federal and State Regulation of Commercial Speech

Corporate communicators who successfully wend their way through the tangled maze of federal regulations have avoided only a portion of the potential legal pitfalls of their profession. In addition to federal regulations and a 60-year body of common law pertaining to commercial speech (discussed in earlier chapters), corporate communicators must be equally aware of numerous obligations and responsibilities defined by federal and state statutory laws as well as industry-specific regulatory agencies. This chapter discusses the unfair-competition provisions of the federal Lanham Act and other specific statutes and agencies concerned with commercial speech. Additionally, the chapter explores some common elements of state unfair competition and false advertising laws that should be of particular interest to corporate communicators.

## The Lanham Act

In 1946, Congress passed the Lanham Act[1] (named after Representative Fritz C. Lanham) that substantially revised the Trademark Act of 1905.[2] The Lanham Act, also known as the Trademark Protection Act of 1946, provides a means for registration and protection of trademarks and remedies for the disparagement of products and services. Section 43(a) of the Act says that, "any person who believes that he or she is or is likely to be damaged by such [a disparaging] act" can sue for damages.[3]

With the 1988 passage of the Trademark Law Revision Act and subsequent revision in 1992,[4] the second purpose of the Act, *regulation of false and deceptive advertising*, became much more explicit. In part, the revised Act not only protects trademarks but also now includes causes of action for "any false designation of origin, false or misleading description of fact, or false or misleading representation of fact."[5] The phrasing, "any person who believes that he or she is or is likely to be damaged by such act," remains the same in the revised Act, but the statute defines *any person* as including "any State, instrumentality of a State or employee of a State or instrumentality of a State acting in his or her official capacity."[6]

In 1993, the Third Circuit U.S. Court of Appeals, in a case involving lawsuits brought by consumers for ads promoting premium gasoline and rust inhibitors for automobiles, said the intent of Congress in approving the revised Act was not to provide a remedy for consumers. The court noted that the wording including "a consumer" was originally proposed to be included in the Act, but was dropped from the final draft.[7]

Exclusion of consumers from bringing suits under the Lanham Act underscores a substantial difference between the Act's provisions and more traditional remedies for false advertising. Although the Lanham Act's false advertising provisions do seek to protect consumers from the potential harms of marketplace confusion, the Act's core function is much more aligned with its intellectual property roots—preserving a fair market for those endeavoring to engage in commerce.

Remedies for a Lanham Act plaintiff (e.g., a business competitor) are generally divided into three categories: (a) injunctive relief; (b) market (actual) financial damages; and (c) court-ordered corrective advertising. The first, injunctive relief, only requires that a plaintiff show consumer confusion and "likelihood of damage" resulting from defendant's deceptive advertising. No actual proof of harm, such as documentation of lost sales or consumer confusion, is necessary for injunctive relief.

When a Lanham Act plaintiff seeks financial damages or asks the court to order corrective advertising, however, the burden of proof generally increases to require a showing that the defendant's false or deceptive advertising materially affected the plaintiff's bottom line or customer base in a negative way. Courts have generally required plaintiffs to offer compelling expert testimony and independent consumer research that provide a causal link between the competitor's campaign and actual consumer confusion.

The interpretation of the Lanham Act's false advertising provisions is by no means settled, however, as two more recent federal appellate court decisions illustrate. The first, *Balance Dynamics Corp. v. Schmitt Industries, Inc.*,[8] addressed the "likelihood [of harm] versus actuality" distinction. Balance Dynamics filed a lawsuit against the defendant Schmitt for implying in direct correspondence with corporations in the machining industry that Balance Dynamics' industrial products would soon run afoul of the federal Environmental Protection Agency's ban on ozone-depleting substances. In its correspondence to corporations, Schmitt Industries suggested that, unlike its competitors, including Balance Dynamics, Schmitt Industries offered a line of quality, ozone-friendly replacements for that technology.

Balance Dynamics took exception to this communication and eventually filed suit in federal district court. The plaintiff claimed no actual damage as a result of Schmitt Industries' allegedly deceptive campaign, but instead requested that it be compensated by the defendant for "damage control" efforts (i.e., funds to cover Balance Dynamics' own corrective measures). The district court, determining that the plaintiff had not provided evidence of a single consumer who was confused by Schmitt Industries' communications, ruled in favor of the defendant.[9]

The Sixth Circuit Court of Appeals vacated the decision and remanded to the district court for further proceedings. The appeals court noted that, based on its own analysis of Lanham Act false advertising claims, plaintiffs seeking "damage control" compensation do not need to show evidence of actual harm or consumer confusion. This relaxation of proof burden for Lanham Act plaintiffs should serve as a warning for any corporation or agency engaging in comparative advertising. *Balance Dynamics* is also worthy of note because the "advertising" in question was not advertising at all; rather, it was direct correspondence with actual and potential consumers of the two corporations' products. Just as with the common law of commercial speech, courts seem to possess varying definitions of "advertising," creating additional uncertainty for corporate communicators.

The uncertainty surrounding Lanham Act unfair competition litigation increased in subsequent cases. In *Pizza Hut v. Papa John's International, Inc.*,[10] decided by the Fifth Circuit Court of Appeals, the pendulum seemingly swung back toward an approach that was more defendant-friendly. After Papa John's began to make a dent in Pizza Hut's market share with its "Better Ingredients. Better Pizza" slogan and a series of comparative advertisements touting the superiority and freshness of Papa John's dough and tomato sauce, Pizza Hut filed a Lanham Act lawsuit in federal district court. Although offering no actual proof of the claim, Pizza Hut successfully argued that the combination of Papa John's new slogan and comparative advertising related to the production of the corporations' pizza crusts and sauce constituted false or deceptive statements of fact likely to confuse consumers. The court ordered Papa John's to immediately cease using its "Better Ingredients. Better Pizza," slogan which the corporation had spent millions of dollars printing on its boxes and other promotional materials, as well as awarding Pizza Hut a settlement of almost a half million dollars.[11]

The case was reversed on appeal in the Fifth Circuit. The court determined that Papa John's slogan, taken by itself, was not a quantifiable material statement of fact (i.e., puffery) and was therefore not actionable under Lanham Act provisions. In combination with the dough and sauce advertisements, however, the appeals court agreed with the lower court that "Better Ingredients. Better Pizza" acquired a new meaning that was indeed deceptive. The appeals court deviated from the lower court, however, in determining that Pizza Hut did need to present evidence that consumers' pizza-buying decisions had been and likely would continue to be affected by the deceptive campaign and slogan. On this ground, the court overturned the lower court's decision. This case left some legal observers scratching their heads because the court seemingly suggested that it cannot be assumed that consumers make their food-consumption decisions based on taste and quality.

The future of Lanham Act unfair competition jurisprudence remains unsettled. As *Pizza Hut* and *Balance Dynamics* illustrate, federal district and circuit courts continue to wrestle with fault standards for the various Lanham Act remedies, and, at a more elemental level, have not completely disposed of the question of what constitutes an "advertisement" under the Act's provisions. This latter uncertainty mirrors the California Supreme Court's determination in *Kasky v. Nike*[12] (discussed in Chapter 3) that Nike's non-advertising public relations efforts could be characterized as regulable commercial speech.

## Regulation of Commercial Speech and the Federal Fair Housing Act

The Federal Fair Housing Act of 1968[13] makes it illegal to discriminate in the sale or rental of housing. Section 804(c) of the Act also "prohibits the making, printing, and publishing of advertisements [or other commercial speech] which state a preference, limitation or discrimination on the basis of race, color, religion, sex, handicap, familial status or national origin."[14] The prohibition applies to publishers, such as newspapers and directories, as well as to people and entities who place real estate advertisements.

Practices that have run afoul of provisions of this statute, or of the regulations promulgated by the Department of Housing and Urban Development (HUD), the federal agency charged with enforcing fair housing laws, include (a) exclusively employing white models in photographs or illustrations accompanying advertisements depicting potential clients in marketing campaigns for housing developments; (b) showing only adult couples in brochures describing rental property; or (c) specifying preferences for gender ("males preferred") or religion ("a Christian community") in advertising copy. Classified advertisements by individuals seeking roommates are exceptions.

Advertising and public relations professionals should be alert to possible trouble when using terms such as *exclusive* or *private, mature* or *adult, no children* or *couples preferred* (or *only*), and *only kosher meals served* or *close to (named denominational) church* in commercial speech related to the sale or rental of housing properties. Exceptions are recognized for commercial speech related to housing that is specifically designed for the elderly or the physically challenged or is restricted to members of a religious sect, although such speech cannot discriminate by race or other characteristics unrelated to the specific exemption.

HUD's expansive interpretation of the Federal Fair Housing Act's regulation of discriminatory commercial speech has been ratified by the courts.

In *Ragin v. The New York Times*,[15] a second circuit federal court of appeals in New York disagreed with the trial court and upheld the viability of a discrimination claim based on the failure to use minorities as models in housing advertisements. The plaintiffs had claimed the ads indicated a preference for whites as purchasers or renters in certain neighborhoods and rental complexes. Finding that such evidence might cause a jury to conclude that *The New York Times* had violated the Fair Housing Act's provisions, the court remanded the case for further consideration. The Supreme Court of the United States elected not to hear the newspaper's appeal.

## Regulation of Commercial Speech by Other Federal Laws and Agencies

Simply listing the federal statutes and regulations governing commercial speech, in addition to those involving the FTC, the FDA and the SEC (discussed in the preceding chapter), could take up much of the rest of this book. For example, there are more than 800 federal statutes affecting commercial speech about everything from atomic energy to Woodsy Owl, including burial of veterans, currency usage in advertising, eavesdropping devices, foods from avocados to watermelons, use of insignias of the Girl Scouts and the Olympics, railroads, the Swiss Federation coat of arms and water hyacinths (transportation thereof). In addition, more than 4,000 federal regulations cover these subjects in more detail, as well as specify procedural and technical requirements for satisfying these regulations. Prudent advertising and public relations professionals would be wise to review the list of these laws and regulations to determine which pertain to their commercial speech efforts.

Nonetheless, there are a number of subjects covered by federal statutes and regulations that deserve brief special mention because of the problems they might cause for significant numbers of those engaged in commercial speech. These include commercial speech about employment, banking, billboards and alcoholic beverages.

## Employment Issues

Various civil rights statutes make discrimination by race, age and other characteristics illegal in employment practices. These same strictures often apply to commercial speech publicizing these subjects. The Civil Rights Act of 1964[16] forbids employment notices that appear to discriminate by race or sex and gives those harmed by such advertising the right to file civil suits seeking money damages both against those who place the notices and, in some cases, against those who publish them.

For example, in *Hailes v. United Air Lines*,[17] a federal appeals court upheld a claim that an employment notice seeking women for flight attendant positions had reasonably been interpreted by a man as discouraging his application for such a position. In *Pittsburgh Press v. Pittsburgh Commission on Human Relations*[18] (discussed in Chapter 2), the Supreme Court of the United States found that the newspaper's help-wanted advertisements, segregated by male and female headings, were not protected by the First Amendment. Congress enacted similar restrictions against discrimination by age in the Age Discrimination in Employment Act of 1967[19] and against physical and mental disabilities in the Americans with Disabilities Act of 1990.[20]

Complaints about discrimination involving these characteristics are often generated by use of such terms in commercial speech employment notices as *young, recent college graduate* or *able-bodied*. Advertising and public relations professionals should also be alert to terms like *junior assistant, first-time* or *beginner* in describing the position level that is the subject of the commercial speech.

Even potentially more dangerous for those engaged in commercial speech about employment opportunities are the sections of federal laws banning activities indicating "any preference . . . based on race," including advertising and other publicity. Until *Ragin* (discussed earlier), most authorities had agreed with the logic of the court in *Housing Opportunities Made Equal v. Cincinnati Enquirer, Inc.*[21] that civil rights claims should be limited to statements constituting a "campaign of discrimination," or indicating a "preference, limitation, or discrimination based on race, color . . . or national origin . . . ."[22] The expansive interpretation by the federal court in *Ragin*, holding that the use of models lacking racial diversity could constitute discrimination, should be a warning signal for advertising and public relations professionals to take a second look at common practices or thoughtless actions that could be considered discriminatory, particularly when viewed through the eyes of groups that historically have experienced the effects of discrimination.

## Financial Issues

Advertising and public relations related to the banking industry are closely regulated by a variety of federal agencies. Both the Federal Reserve System and the Federal Deposit Insurance Corporation set policies for the operation of member banks and financial institutions, including regulations involving commercial speech. Similarly, the Federal Home Loan Bank Board regulates the commercial speech of federal thrift institutions, while the National Credit Union Administration oversees federal credit unions.

Each federal agency's concerns with commercial speech arise primarily with enforcement of various provisions of the federal "Truth In Lending Act,"[23] which regulates commercial speech involving offers of consumer credit. Both regulatory agencies and the courts have broadly defined commercial speech under the Act, including, for example, media advertising, direct mail solicitations and messages accompanying loan applications or checking account statements. The Act forbids commercial speech designed to encourage offers of credit that are not of a "usual and customary" nature, such as offers of low interest that actually are unavailable to the average consumer.[24]

The statute also requires commercial speakers to include "disclosures" in a "clear and conspicuous" manner about actual finance charges and other charges not specified in the finance program (e.g., membership fees and annual percentage rates) if the subject of the speech is the offer of a credit card or charge plan that entails continuing offers of credit at a specified interest rate. Terms that may "trigger" these disclosure requirements include promotional come-ons like *six months at no interest and then a small monthly charge* or *no money down* or *easy credit terms available.*[25]

Those engaged in commercial speech involving financial institutions also should be aware of the provisions of the Federal Consumer Leasing Act,[26] that regulates the offering of leases on personal property (e.g., automobiles), and the antidiscrimination provisions of the Equal Credit Opportunity Act[27] and the Federal Deposit Insurance Corporation,[28] which make it illegal to deny credit or provide loans based on such characteristics as race, gender or age.

## Outdoor Advertising Issues

Although most laws regulating outdoor advertising are state laws, several federal statutes and regulations—notably the Federal Highway Act[29] and the Highway Beautification Act[30]—limit the location and size of billboards along federal highways. Because billboards and other signage often run afoul of community or environmental groups on aesthetic grounds, there have been frequent efforts to limit or ban such signs either by zoning regulations or laws forbidding all outdoor advertising. Objections to such laws and regulations based on a First Amendment rationale have met with mixed results.

In *Metromedia, Inc. v. City of San Diego*[31] (discussed in Chapter 2), the Supreme Court of the United States rendered a mixed opinion regarding the constitutionality of the city's efforts to limit billboards for safety and aesthetic reasons. The Court held that efforts to limit otherwise protected commercial speech must serve an important government purpose and be no more extensive than necessary to carry out the government's legitimate interests. As more outdoor advertising signs are erected, complete with eye-catching graphics and high definition, electronic displays that move and change, the question of whether purely aesthetic reasons will suffice for governments constitutionally to ban or limit billboards is yet to be determined.

## Alcoholic Beverage Issues

Unlike billboard advertising, commercial speech involving alcoholic beverages has historically been the subject of extensive federal and state regulations. Because of the controversial nature of the effects of drinking alcoholic beverages, regulations involving its production, consumption and promotion date back two centuries. Although a complete discussion of the myriad laws and rules regulating commercial speech about alcohol is beyond the scope of this text, advertising and public relations professionals involved with these products should be aware of the more significant federal statutes and Bureau of Alcohol, Tobacco and Firearms (BATF) regulations that impact the promotion of alcoholic beverages.[32]

Now the BATFE (the word "Explosives" was added to the agency's name under the Homeland Security Act), the Bureau generally requires that all commercial speech about alcoholic beverages contain information that includes (a) required government warnings about the effects of consumption; (b) the company that has produced the product and paid for the speech; and (c) whether the beverage is considered to be a malt beverage, wine or distilled spirit. Prohibited statements include disparagement of a competitor's products, claims of a health or medicinal nature and messages considered false, misleading or indecent.

In addition, the Bureau strictly regulates such marketing activities as cooperative advertising schemes and the purchase of advertising in publications produced by retailers. It also has interpreted an Internal Revenue Service ruling as prohibiting the use of athletes in distilled liquor commercial speech and limits their use in wine or beer promotions.

Because the federal government acquired unique control over alcohol through the passage of the twenty-first Amendment,[33] the status of the constitutional protection for commercial speech involving intoxicating beverages is somewhat muddled. Although the *Central Hudson*[34] four-part test (discussed in Chapter 2) normally would be applicable to such commercial speech, those wishing to regulate speech promoting alcoholic beverages typically argue that, by definition, the government's interest in regulating such speech outweighs the First Amendment interests of the commercial speaker. For a time in the early to mid 1990s, these anti-alcohol speech arguments often were found persuasive by courts hearing such cases. However, since the Supreme Court's decisions in *Rubin v. Coors Brewing Co.*,[35] *44 Liquormart v. Rhode Island*[36] and a number of so-called "vice activity" cases subsequently decided by the Court, such arguments have largely fallen on deaf ears.

## Overview of State Regulation of Commercial Speech

Because of the federal Constitutional First Amendment issues inherent in government attempts to restrict commercial speech as well as the prominence of federal regulatory agencies like the FTC and SEC, many of those working in advertising or public relations lose sight of the role that state statutes and regulations play in the overall regulation of commercial speech. However, in the same way that much of the law that impacts our everyday existence is found at the state level, state regulation of commercial speech is both comprehensive and extensive.

With the California Supreme Court's 2002 decision in *Kasky* (discussed in Chapter 3), state efforts to regulate false and deceptive corporate messages have taken center stage. Although it is too early to predict if *Kasky* will mark an emerging trend of even greater state involvement in advertising and business practices, the case does serve as a stern warning to all for-profit corporate communicators that they should be just as intimately acquainted with state statutes, court decisions and state regulatory agencies regarding their communication practices as they are with federal statutes and regulations.

Many of these laws and regulations are discussed in other parts of this text. However, a number of state statutes and administrative regulations deserve special mention here because of their impact on advertising and public relations professionals and because they parallel the federal regulations discussed in this and the preceding chapter.

## False, Unfair or Deceptive Commercial Speech: The State Approach

Beginning in the early 1900s, states tried to regulate the negative effects of wildly extravagant advertising claims by passing so-called "Printers' Ink" statutes. These efforts largely proved ineffective, however, because they neither allowed consumers or competitors to bring private causes of action nor established effective state agencies or commissions to oversee and enforce the law. Instead, most of these early state laws left to local prosecutors the option of instigating criminal proceedings against those accused of violating commercial speech statutes—a process that proved cumbersome because of the long and detailed procedures necessary to carry out criminal investigations and prosecutions.[37]

Therefore, it was not surprising that federal regulation, either by federal laws or federal agency rules, became the method of choice by those who wished to regulate commercial speech. The development of federal statutes and regulations, however, did not mean that states surrendered complete control of commercial speech to the federal government. Today, all 50 states have their versions of "mini" Federal Trade Commission/ Lanham Acts that prohibit various deceptive commercial speech practices, although generally without the provisions for separate regulatory commissions or agencies. In addition, numerous state statutes, common laws and administrative rules regulate many specific products, occupations and services, either co-extensively with federal law or in addition to federal regulation.

Sorting out exactly who has jurisdiction in a commercial speech case, or whether and in what circumstances both the federal and state legal systems can each have a hand in regulating a commercial speaker's efforts, creates the kinds of problems that form the bases of final exams in law schools. Generally, federal law prevails if Congress either has exclusive jurisdiction conferred on it by the Constitution (e.g., the power to determine the copyright status of an original creative work) or if a federal statute specifically or implicitly is meant to reserve regulation for the federal government, such as various federal statutes regulating over-the-air broadcasting.

In those areas in which both the federal government and a state may regulate commercial speech, the federal rules will exclusively apply if the state regulation conflicts with an express federal statutory provision. Although conflicts of a jurisdictional nature might help a defendant in the procedural development of a lawsuit claiming injury suffered because of false or deceptive commercial speech, perhaps the wisest course of action for advertising and public relations professionals is to be familiar with both state and federal regulations, assume that both apply and act accordingly.

Most state statutes mimicking the Federal Trade Commission/Lanham Acts' provisions regulating false, unfair or deceptive commercial speech allow competitors to pursue private lawsuits in state courts in addition to suits brought under the appropriate federal statutes. Some states have even gone a step beyond allowance of private causes of action. California's Business and Professions Codes,[38] for example, allow any Californian (like Marc Kasky) to file an unfair competition lawsuit on behalf of the state's citizens. Unlike other states, however, the creation in California of a "private attorney general" allows an unfair competition plaintiff to recover damages even though he or she was not personally damaged by the unfair practices.

The allowance of private actions reflects the historical antecedents of much of state regulation of commercial speech in English common law focusing on stopping one manufacturer from "passing off" his or her goods as the product of another. Often called "unfair competition" or "palming off," these statutes almost always come into play when speech negligently or intentionally misrepresents a product in ways that have a tendency to cause confusion on the part of a potential consumer.[39]

State statutes against "passing off" generally require a complainant to show that the defendant has actively and directly engaged in some action designed to mislead. Interestingly, although such efforts may run afoul of other state laws, using "trade dress" (distinctive design or packaging) that resembles another product is usually not considered "passing off." Similarly, removing a label from one's own product or simply failing to label a product generally do not invoke the provisions of state anti-"passing off" statutes.

In addition to laws and regulations prohibiting "passing off," a significant number of states today have either modified existing statutes or passed additional laws to permit private lawsuits by consumers and, in some instances, competitors. These statutes, often referred to as "consumer protection" or "consumer fraud prevention" acts, usually are based on claims of harm other than "passing off" that allegedly result from detrimental reliance on false, unfair or deceptive commercial speech. A number of states also permit the filing of class-action suits by consumers in such cases. In many states, these consumer-oriented statutes authorize the state's attorney general or other state officials to bring suits to prevent false or deceptive commercial speech practices as either representatives of consumers, competitors or on their own initiative.

Variations in these laws from state to state make it difficult to summarize them in any meaningful manner. For example, some states require that suits can only be brought by those somehow directly connected with defendants (sometimes referred to as "privity of contract"), either by being in actual competition with the defendants or by being a recipient of their false or deceptive commercial speech. Other states permit suits by those only indirectly related to, or affected by, the defendant's disputed commercial speech practices as well. Wise advertising and public relations professionals should both take note and seek interpretation of the applicable statutes in the states in which they practice to minimize unpleasant legal encounters with disgruntled state officials, consumers or competitors.

Perhaps not surprisingly, many state courts, faced with adjudicating cases under state laws prohibiting false, unfair or deceptive commercial speech, look to the interpretations of the FTC or the federal courts for guidance in defining these terms so as not to produce a jumble of confusing and possibly conflicting decisions. Similarly, state courts often take their cue for determination of "unfairness" from cases involving interpretation of FTC regulations. For example, numerous state courts follow the lead of the Supreme Court of the United States in *F.T.C. v. Sperry & Hutchinson*.[40] In this case, the Court approved a definition of *unfairness* that looked at the extent of harm to those relying on commercial speech claims that are either offensive to public policy or in violation of some legal definition of immoral activity.

Although federal regulatory agency and commission interpretations are influential when it comes to the definition of terms, state courts typically do not incorporate federal policy requirements (e.g., the FTC's prior-substantiation doctrine) into the substantive language of state mini-FTC/Lanham Act statutes.

## State Remedies for False, Deceptive or Unfair Commercial Speech: "Passing Off"

Remedies provided by state statutes for those harmed by false, deceptive or unfair commercial speech include the possibility of injunctive relief (a court order), money damages for actual or statutorily defined harm and/or court costs and attorney fees. (The possibility of remedies in state law for other kinds of injuries from false or deceptive commercial speech is discussed elsewhere in earlier chapters.)

Injunctions or court orders prohibiting or limiting commercial speech are inherently suspect because of First Amendment issues. However, these concerns may be overcome in situations in which states have approved statutes that make "passing off" goods a criminal offense. In such cases, the normal requirements for injunctive relief typically would apply (i.e., the threat of irreparable injury and the unavailability of other remedies that might prove effective to provide the relief sought by the plaintiff). Court orders in other circumstances may be available if directed at general business practices so as to prohibit a defendant from linking its product or service to those provided by the plaintiff.[41]

Although it is common to compensate any plaintiff who can demonstrate injury caused by the actions of the defendant with money damages, this remedy is frequently unavailable in cases in which plaintiffs are alleging harm amounting to "passing off" of products or services based on false or deceptive commercial speech. The problem lies in the difficulty of establishing the causal relationship between the defendant's actions and the plaintiff's claimed economic losses. Almost all states require evidence that either the economic loss by the plaintiff or the monetary gain by the defendant could not have been caused by anything other than the defendant's false or deceptive commercial speech. Short of providing testimony by individuals that they had been deceived into making their purchasing decisions solely by the defendant's bogus commercial claims, the burden of convincing a court to award damages in a "passing off" case often is too difficult for plaintiffs to meet.

Most state courts have the power to award plaintiffs' attorney fees and other financial costs associated with bringing a cause of action against the defendant. The possibility of such often substantial awards, coupled with the possibility of injunctive relief, frequently provide a strong deterrent for those guilty of using commercial speech to pass off a product or service as that of another. This should be sufficient to caution the prudent public relations or advertising professional to avoid the possibility of such practices.

## Four Examples of State Regulation of Commercial Speech

To fully discuss the statutes, rules and regulations that control commercial speech in each state would require an additional chapter for each state. Although many of these state regulatory schemes look similar because they mirror their federal counterparts, almost every state statute or rule is worded slightly differently from those of its neighbors, creating nuances requiring state-by-state legal interpretations of how such laws apply.

Four examples of commercial speech regulation at the state level involving controversial, tightly controlled or currently socially relevant products or services that are also regulated by the federal government (and discussed in this and the preceding chapter) are discussed next to illustrate the breadth and complexity of such state regulatory efforts.

## State Regulation of Environmental Advertising

During the past two decades, environmental issues, ranging from a diminishing ozone layer to reports of the accumulating garbage in dumps and landfills and the resulting problem of what to do with this increasing waste, have served as the basis for extensive public debate and discussion. Partially in response to these problems, environmental activists and others have pushed for the adoption of environmentally friendly policies by providers of products and services.

Fortunately, many companies have found that significant numbers of consumers are more prone to purchase items if they are publicized as environmentally safe. Additionally, consumers can be persuaded to recycle containers (as long as doing so is not too expensive or inconvenient) and they will participate in programs to reuse or recycle packaging materials. These findings have led companies to provide environmentally friendly products and services and to make such efforts part of their advertising and public relations campaigns as well.

Using the environmental angle as a means to promote a product or service can create negative legal repercussions, however, if the dissemination of information about environmentally friendly practices does not comport with state statutes that spell out how and in what circumstances such claims may be made. Even neighboring states may differ considerably on how they regulate commercial speech regarding environmental issues including, for example, the legal definitions of such key terms used to describe a product as *environmentally friendly* or *recyclable*.

Compounding the issue is the inability of states to agree on a common set of standards or procedures for solving environmental problems. This has led to confusion in the enforcement of regulations regarding environmental issues and the packaging and advertising of a product. For example, the bottom of most plastic containers features a triangle of recycling arrows with a number in the middle. This number refers to the ingredients in that type of plastic and also provides a grouping number for workers sorting the containers so that they can ascertain which plastics can be melted together for recycling. However, not all states recycle all types of plastic. The result is that in Oregon, for example, marketing a detergent as bottled in a recyclable container may be truthful and non-deceptive, whereas an identical advertisement in Tennessee for the same product in the same container with the same environmental claim might be judged as an example of deceptive commercial speech.

Concerns about such commercial speech-related environmental issues have inspired a number of states to prepare guidelines for companies that wish to tout the environmental benefits of their products or services. For example, Minnesota's guidelines state that:

1 Marketers should be wary of tie-ins with environmental groups because their long-term aims may not be compatible;
2 Marketers should distinguish between green claims for products and those for packaging;
3 Marketers should not make an environmental claim unless the claim covers all their products; and
4 Marketers should avoid generalizations and half-truths in claims.[42]

Because such efforts are fairly new, state statutes and rules involving commercial speech and environmental issues are still awaiting final enactment or interpretation by the courts in many states adopting such regulations. Perhaps the safest policy for advertising and public relations professionals is to double-check the current status of environmental regulations in the states in which marketing or other communication campaigns are planned to confirm that contemplated commercial speech claims involving environmental issues do not run the risk of being judged as false or deceptive. Corporate communicators can rest assured that environmental activists will have already done their homework.

## State Regulation of Securities Advertising

Mention was made in the preceding chapter that the origin of the SEC could be found in early attempts to regulate commercial speech at the state level under so-called "Blue Sky" laws. The term *blue sky* came from the get-rich-quick schemes of fraudulent promoters whose "speculative schemes . . . have no more basis than so many feet of blue sky."[43] Many times, the only information consumers received about securities came from a promoter's commercial speech. Because investments and securities are, for the most part, intangible products, promoters found it easy to twist information, omit some information or otherwise deceive gullible buyers all too ready to believe claims of easy money to be made through investments.

Eventually, state "Blue Sky" laws were enacted to provide at least some protection for consumers from the more outrageous examples of fraudulent or deceptive commercial speech practices involving securities. Today, although federal regulation of commercial speech about the offering or trading of securities overshadows efforts at the state level, "Blue Sky" laws still substantially impact the commercial speech practices of advertising and public relations professionals.

Although in the past, individual state "Blue Sky" laws varied considerably, most such regulatory schemes involved one or more of three methods for preventing false or deceptive commercial speech related to offering or trading securities. These were: (a) creating a regulatory scheme to regulate who can deal in securities; (b) requiring registration for those who sell or offer securities within a state; and (c) requiring that securities be registered before being offered to the public. As may be imagined, determining which state had adopted any of the three methods and exactly how each was interpreted by an individual state became extremely taxing for commercial speakers engaged in communicating on a regional or national level. Recognizing this difficulty, and to "avoid the complexities involved in satisfying the varying requirements of several states when offering securities for sale,"[44] the model Uniform Securities Act was developed in 1956.[45]

The Act, which provides for variations on all three methods mentioned above, gives states a pattern from which to mold and shape their individual approaches to securities regulation. The popularity of the Act "resulted in its adoption in some form in most jurisdictions."[46]

Advertising and public relations practitioners should note that although most states now base their statutes regulating securities-related commercial speech on Section 403 of the Uniform Securities Act, there still remain individual variations in state law that need to be understood before disseminating securities information in a particular state. For example, some states, including Alaska, Colorado, Montana, North Dakota and Washington, require a filed notification five days prior to the publication of any commercial speech regarding securities.

Other states may also require prior notification, but the filing deadlines differ from state to state. In addition, the steps to be followed in each state during this filing period may vary considerably. In Alaska, for example, the law requires that a copy of the material to be distributed must be submitted for approval. In Montana, the five-day filing period is often waived. In Washington, the five-day filing period does not apply to all types of commercial speech, such as reports to shareholders, tombstone advertising without photographs or illustrations as well as some other kinds of sales literature.

Many states also address unfair practices in the insurance industry in much the same fashion. States that have articulated separate unfair competition laws (UCL) for insurers operating within their borders generally cite as a rationale for these laws the high potential for confusion in insurance policy "fine print" (e.g., "term" versus "whole-life" insurance, denial of coverage under certain conditions, deductible and premium structures, etc.). Additionally, because insurance companies also often provide consumers with avenues of investment (e.g., annuities), state unfair competition laws pertaining to insurance often bear remarkable similarity to legislation regulating their securities counter-parts.

Advertising and public relations practitioners should be alert to these nuances in state law before engaging in securities or insurance-related commercial speech practices, or risk unpleasant legal sanctions.

## Lotteries, Sweepstakes and Games of Chance

A few states, including Nevada and New Jersey, have legalized casino-style gambling. Significantly more states allow supervised betting on sporting events. Some states have begun to get in on the action by creating state-run lotteries. In all cases, however, gambling is a highly controlled activity with detailed state laws specifying who can own or run gambling establishments, how wagers are placed or lottery tickets purchased and so forth.

It is common for providers of products and services to use contests such as sweepstakes or other games of chance as a marketing technique. For example, offering incentives in advertising or as part of marketing special events attracts potential consumers by suggesting that the possibility of a prize may accompany a purchase. The focus of the commercial speech is not on a benefit of the product or service, but rather on the possible gain the purchaser might realize by winning a contest. Advertising and public relations professionals must be extremely careful about how such contests are presented, or legal action by state regulatory agencies could quickly put an end to the game.

All 50 states prohibit private lotteries. However, many types of contests, sweepstakes and other promotional devices may be legal if they follow the rules established by individual state legislatures. As discussed in the pre-ceding chapter, three key elements help determine if a promotional device is a lottery: (a) if there is "consideration" or an effort made on the part of the consumer (e.g., buying a product or traveling to a destination to pick up a contest application); (b) if a prize is awarded; and (c) if winning is based on chance as opposed to a demonstration of at least some level of skill. If a proposed promotion or contest contains these elements, an advertising or public relations professional would be wise to seek advice from competent legal counsel before proceeding with the commercial campaign.

Like commercial speech about environmental issues and the offering or selling of securities, definitions of key terms in commercial speech about promotions vary from state to state and between the various states and the federal government. Some of these terms include *promotional device, chance, prize* and *consideration*. Additionally, most states have specific statutes or rules regulating games of chance. For example, Arkansas and Alabama allow promotional contests as long as the chances of winning or the prizes awarded do not depend on the payment of money or purchase of products by contest participants. Virginia has specific instructions about the information that must be disclosed to conduct a promotional contest, including the number of prizes to be awarded, odds of winning and the retail value of the prizes. Nevada prohibits gasoline and other motor-vehicle fuel dealers and sellers from sponsoring games of chance or contests as a means of promotion.

Although contests, sweepstakes and games of chance are popular promotional and advertising tools, advertising and public relations professionals should be familiar with the regulations imposed on such contests in each state where their commercial speech may be disseminated and should tailor their messages accordingly.

## Commercial Speech about Alcoholic Beverages

As noted earlier, manufacture and sale of alcoholic beverages historically have raised important social issues as illustrated by the enactment and ultimate failure of Prohibition in the 1920s. State laws regulating commercial speech about alcoholic beverages differ widely because of many factors, including the drinking age recognized by the state, rules about the sales of alcohol and statutes punishing drinking and driving.

At present, Alaska and Nevada are the only states that do not have restrictions on commercial speech involving alcoholic beverages. Eighteen states handle the sale and distribution of alcohol within their borders with the exception of bars and restaurants. The remaining states allow alcoholic beverages to be sold by private enterprises, but under control by state commissions or agencies. Although for the most part state regulations parallel federal regulations, details of such regulatory schemes vary widely. Advertising and public relations professionals involved in disseminating commercial speech about alcoholic beverages might consider obtaining a copy of the *Code of Responsible Practices for Beverage Alcohol Advertising and Marketing* published by the Distilled Spirits Council of the United States.[47]

## Other Federal and State Regulation of Commercial Speech in a Digital, New-Media Age: Emerging Issues

The rapid diffusion in the past two decades of personal communication technology and Internet access has created myriad opportunities for organizations wishing to extend their communicative reach. Electronic communication via computers, cellular telephony and other portable devices now allow such organizations to vastly expand their potential audiences, often at a fraction of the cost of communicating through other channels.

For example, a so-called "e-business" with a fee of less than $100 to register a domain name and a small team of well-trained programmers may forego the high overhead costs of building and maintaining bricks-and-mortar outlets for its goods, opting instead for a Web-based, virtual storefront. On one Web site, customers may browse and purchase the e-business's merchandise, find comparisons of the company's wares to its competitors' products, read information about the organization and be exposed to the marketing and branding efforts that the corporation has woven into its Web presence. One Web site can contain most of the core functions of the e-business—sales support, marketing and public relations. To generate more traffic on its e-business Web site, a corporate marketing department might choose to send mass electronic mailings to current and potential customers for pennies on the dollar compared to traditional, direct-mail marketing efforts.

Of course, this hypothetical business model is highly oversimplified, but the virtues of electronic commerce now dominate discussions in classrooms and boardrooms everywhere. Although entrepreneurs may see the goldmine that exists in harnessing the power of the Web and new communication technologies for profit-making ventures, e-corporate communicators who fail to understand the implications of state laws such as unfair competition statutes may well find the goldmine envisioned quickly morphing into a minefield.

For example, several states, including Louisiana, Washington, California and Vermont, have crafted their unfair competition laws to include information delivered by electronic means, including the Web and electronic mail. Such state unfair competition laws generally do not demand a defendant corporation be a state resident, often requiring only that the corporation's messages be received by that state's residents.

In the past, such provisions were of concern for only the largest of corporations. Smaller businesses, unable to afford the high advertising rates of regional or national mass media, generally limited their advertising and promotional efforts to local audiences. With a reasonable degree of certainty, based on circulation data and broadcast ratings, businesses "knew" and could control the scope of the audience they were reaching.

Web and electronic mail communications have drastically altered this landscape. By employing a Web site to communicate with consumers, corporations cede their ability to limit the boundaries of their communication to a particular geographic area or to a particular demographic. In exchange for potentially reaching millions of people, corporations with Web sites bear the concomitant burden of being liable for an exponential explosion of potential suits brought by plaintiffs in different jurisdictions, invoking different state laws.

Likewise, corporations engaging in mass electronic mailings for marketing purposes, especially if e-mail addresses have been purchased from external sources, cannot divine the final destination of their e-mail communication when employing such ubiquitous domain names as Hotmail.com™, whose users just as likely live in Duluth, Ga. as Duluth, Minn.

In a state like California, in which private attorneys general are not required to show personal harm to recover damages in an unfair competition or false advertising suits, the collision of modern communication technology and such state laws creates an extremely treacherous terrain for corporate communicators. If corporations wish to maintain a robust Web presence, they also must commit to maintaining the legal expertise necessary to help them navigate this dangerous landscape successfully.

Add together federal and state regulations, rules and statutes that range from the national FTC Act to state laws regulating commercial speech about everything from automobiles to zoological parks and it is clear that even prudent advertising and public relations practitioners face formidable challenges in safely fulfilling their professional obligations in the decades ahead. Although the task may appear daunting, only the irresponsible practitioner would respond by claiming "it's all just too complicated" and trust only to luck to avoid legal entanglements. The appropriate way to meet these challenges is to check the applicable state and federal laws and regulations so practitioners can identify when it is necessary to seek the advice of legal counsel. This knowledge should sharply reduce the chances of accidentally running afoul of legal restrictions on commercial speech that could injure organizations, clients and professional careers.

# Chapter 12

# Access to Information, Free Press/Fair Trial, Journalist Privilege and Other Issues Related to News Gathering/Dissemination

Although the principal focus of this book is on the laws and regulations affecting commercial speech, readers should also be aware of a number of legal issues related to the news-gathering and disseminating process facing the print, broadcast and online journalists with whom they share the marketplace of ideas.

Among these issues are the arguments for and against conducting public business "in the sunshine" by allowing access to public records and meeting places, the inevitable tensions involved in protecting the freedom of journalists to fully and accurately report on the criminal and civil law processes while at the same time ensuring that those parties actually involved in a case are afforded the right to the fair and unbiased judicial proceeding that the Constitution promises and whether to grant journalists a constitutional or statutory "privilege" to withhold information from law enforcement, legislative and judicial authorities.

The reader should note that this chapter is purposely written from the perspective of the news journalist because the issues discussed most directly impact the newsgathering process. However, these issues have implications for public relations practitioners and, to a lesser extent, advertising professionals as well. These are noted in the chapter where appropriate.

## Freedom of Information and Access to Places

Although the Supreme Court of the United States has expanded a right of access to trials and other criminal proceedings (discussed later in this chapter), it seems safe to say that the First Amendment provides no general right of access except for situations where public access—often represented by journalists—has been both the rule historically and adds legitimacy to the situation. In *Pell v. Procunier*[1] and *Saxbe v. The Washington Post*,[2] for example, the Court specifically rejected claims that journalists have a special right to gain access to prisons and other government facilities, holding that the mass media have no greater right of access than the average citizen.

Lower federal and state courts have followed the Court's lead, ruling in almost every instance that journalists have no superior access rights than those afforded the general public to enter property, gain entrance to crime scenes or be admitted to meetings. In practice, the public relations staffs of most government agencies often (and arguably should) try to accommodate the requests of journalists to gain access if their presence does not interfere significantly with the department's operations.

What is true for access to physical places is also true for access to records and other information. With the exception of some categories of material related to criminal proceedings, particularly evidence or supporting matter introduced in open court, the courts consistently have held that the mass media have no greater right of access to records and documents than do members of the general public.

Just because the First Amendment has not been interpreted as providing a special right of access for journalists and the public, however, does not mean that the reasons for allowing access to records and places are without merit. To accomplish by statute what could not be achieved by constitutional interpretation, Congress passed the Freedom of Information Act (FOIA) in 1966,[3] supplemented by the 1974 Privacy Act[4] and the Electronic Freedom of Information Act Amendments adopted in 1996.[5] These laws provide a qualified right of access to information maintained in the files of federal agencies. All 50 states have now followed suit with their own freedom of information (FOI) laws to provide a statutory right of access to state records.

FOI laws are not only for journalists. Knowledgeable advertising and public relations practitioners often can find valuable information, such as who got a government contract, business dealings by competitors or data about consumer behavior, from Census and other government sources obtained through the strategic use of freedom of information requests.

The federal FOIA mandates that all federal executive departments and federal regulatory agencies disclose how and from whom their records may be obtained by the public for viewing and/or photocopying. According to the Act, the term "agency" includes "[a]ny executive department, military department, Government corporation, Government controlled corporation, or other establishment in the executive branch of the government. . . ."[6] The federal FOIA also applies to federal regulatory "agencies" (e.g., FTC, FDA or BATFE). Government information covered by the Act includes—but is not limited to—(a) printed records or printouts of computer files; (b) photographs, illustrations and graphs/charts; and (c) electronically recorded information including data stored in electronic databases. As the people to whom a freedom of information inquiry often is made or referred, the public relations professionals in government organizations should make themselves intimately familiar with both federal and applicable state FOI statutes.

The federal FOIA covers information in the possession of, and controlled by, a government agency. Disputes, sometimes leading to legal challenges, have arisen about the definitions of "possession" and "control." If the records sought were created by agency personnel and remain within the agency that created them, both requirements likely will be satisfied. Grayer areas involve records created by outside contractors or technically no longer under the jurisdiction of the agency to which the FOI request is made.

The statute specifies that (a) all final court opinions and orders related to agency matters; (b) policy statements; and (c) interpretations of regulations, documents and records about agency actions or proposed actions that are not exempted from disclosure by the nine specific exceptions in the Act must be made available for public inspection. Even if some parts of a document might be exempted, the Act requires the government agency producing the document to make a reasonable effort to ensure that the non-exempted portions are provided to members of the public seeking the information.

## Exemptions to the Federal FOIA

The first exemption to the requirements of disclosure in the Act is material designated by an executive order to be kept secret in the interests of national defense or foreign policy. This has proven in practice to be a rather large exception because Congress and the courts have given great deference to the executive branch in determining what is classified. The current test is simply whether disclosure could reasonably be expected to endanger national security. Not only can the government maintain a document as classified under the national security/foreign policy exemption, but it can even reclassify a document formerly in the public domain as secret after an FOIA request has been made.

The second exemption is for information that is related solely to the internal personnel rules and practices of an agency. The third is for documents already exempted by other federal statutes.

The fourth exemption to the federal FOIA is for trade secrets or commercial and financial information that are considered to be privileged or confidential. This exemption gave rise to a decision by the Supreme Court of the United States of significance to corporate public relations professionals. The Court held that the federal FOIA permits but does not require an agency to withhold documents that arguably fall within one of the exemptions.

The case of *Chrysler Corp. v. Brown*[7] involved a request for information about Chrysler Corporation's affirmative action policies. This information had been provided to the U.S. Department of Labor by Chrysler under federal statutory provisions requiring such submissions from any company with multiple contracts with the federal government. Before the information could be made public, Chrysler sought an injunction in a federal district court in Delaware to block its release. The trial court granted the injunction, but this decision was overturned by the Court on the basis that the FOIA does not provide for private action by a company to prevent disclosures. Today, acting under executive order, federal agencies routinely notify organizations if information they have supplied is to be released to the public. Organizations are permitted a 10-day period to protest such release and, if necessary, to seek injunctive relief in federal district courts to stop the information from being divulged.

Exemption five to the federal FOIA protects inter-agency and intra-agency memoranda or letters from public disclosure. This exemption has been interpreted as protecting working papers and other documents produced as part of an agency's ongoing decision-making process as well as the "work-product" of government attorneys normally protected as privileged communications under rules of legal civil procedure.

Exemption six, which protects personnel, medical and other similar government files containing information of a normally private nature about specific individuals, has produced much controversy and litigation. For example, a federal appellate court sided with an agency decision to deny FOIA disclosure to requests for information about the citizenship status of foreign nationals. Another federal court, on the other hand, allowed *The New York Times* access to the last seconds of recorded conversations among the seven crew members of the space shuttle *Challenger* before the space craft exploded, killing all aboard.[8]

Exemption seven has also seen its share of litigation and controversy. With the continuing emphasis on the reporting of crime news by American news media, the exemption created by the federal FOIA for records or other documents compiled for law enforcement purposes frequently is challenged when law enforcement officials decline to provide journalists with information about criminals or criminal investigations. Government agencies wishing to classify information related to law enforcement must demonstrate either that disclosure could reasonably be expected to interfere with enforcement procedures or deprive a person of a right to a fair trial. Also, exemption seven often affords protection for information constituting an unwarranted invasion of privacy, identifying a confidential source, revealing law enforcement techniques or endangering the life or physical safety of an individual.

The eighth exemption, permitting classification of information related to the examination, operation or condition of a financial institution, and exemption nine, concerning documentation of geological and geophysical investigations, have produced little litigation.

State FOI laws typically parallel their federal counterpart, complete with exemptions for law enforcement documents, confidential business data and individual privacy interests. Although a comprehensive discussion of these state statutes is beyond the scope of this text, those interested in learning more about a state's FOIA are advised to access the Web site of the individual state's press association for the wording of and advice about how to employ the Act.

Although procedures for requesting information vary, most FOI Acts, including the federal statute, require that (a) those requesting information submit a written request for specific records, although visiting the agency and asking the FOI officer politely to see a record sometimes works; (b) the government agency must provide the desired records within a specified time period or explain why the information is being withheld; and (c) the government normally be permitted to charge a nominal fee for compiling and photocopying documents, although the fee may be waived upon request.

## Open Meeting Laws

All states have passed statutes mandating open meetings of public bodies such as city commissions, state regulatory agencies, school boards and so forth. Most of these so-called "sunshine laws" also provide for closed-door sessions when officials are discussing such things as legal matters, property acquisition and individual personnel issues, although no official business may be finalized or final votes taken behind closed doors. Access to federal government agency meetings is provided by the "Government in the Sunshine Act" of 1977[9] that provides rights and exemptions similar to state laws.

Notification of public meetings must be posted to give enough time for the public to attend. Although emergency meetings are allowed, the emergency must be genuine. "Informal" meetings, such as cocktail parties, backyard barbecues or early-morning breakfasts (where lawmakers "just happen" to get together), tend to be treated as public meetings by open-meeting statutes and are therefore subject to the same requirements as regular meetings.

## Freedom of Information and Access to Places in a Digital, New-Media Age: Emerging Issues

Cases involving challenges to government actions denying requests for information or access to meetings or locations continue to clog the court dockets at both the federal and state levels. Whether it involves recent issues like the scope of disclosure of documents filed with a court or media access to state-supported college and secondary school sporting events, apparently the efforts of those in public office or employed by a government agency to prevent disclosure of public information or limit access by the public to public events or places are never ending.

Those responding to freedom of information requests should note that attempts to hide information created or maintained in Web sites, e-mails or other new media technologies most likely will be futile. Court decisions to date tend to treat "documents" alike whether in new media or old when it comes to FOIA inquiries.

It is the belief of the authors that wise and prudent public relations professionals practicing in government offices might do well to keep in mind the motto stated in the United States Department of Defense's public affairs policy, "maximum disclosure, minimum delay"[10] when it comes to FOI or sunshine requests by the public, and especially the media, if they wish actually to accomplish good relations with the public. They also should to continue to educate those who head such government agencies and offices about FOI requirements.

## Free Press/Fair Trail Issues

Imagine you recently asked one of your friends, a part-time reporter for a local daily newspaper in your area, to give you a ride to get your car at the repair shop. She agreed, but added, "I hope you don't mind if we make just one brief stop while I meet with a man at a restaurant—it's on our way." The reporter explained she hoped to obtain information from the source— local mobster Harry "The Mule" Smith—to be used as the basis for a story about illegal drug dealing.

Assume that authorities subsequently acquired enough information from undercover police investigations to focus on Harry as being a likely kingpin in drug trafficking in your city and obtained an arrest warrant to detain him. City police found Harry walking down the street, handcuffed him, threw him into a squad car, took him downtown and booked him. Nobody read him his rights (the so-called *Miranda*[11] warning), nobody offered to allow a phone call to an attorney, in fact, nobody got to see Harry for three days because the police kept him locked in the basement of the jail, seated in a straight-backed chair with the light from a 500-watt bulb shining in his eyes while teams of brawny police officers constantly interrogated him.

Harry finally cracked under the strain and confessed, not only to drug dealing but to the murder of two rival mobsters. He told police that they could find the evidence they needed, including a still-smoking revolver with bullets matching those found in one of the victims, a blood-stained knife covered with Harry's fingerprints and a diary in Harry's handwriting revealing how he planned his foul deeds, all buried under the old oak tree in his backyard. The police rushed to Harry's house and, sure enough, dug up all the evidence Harry said would be there. Police Chief O'Malley, at the urging of his public relations counsel, then stepped forward at a specially called press conference and announced to the world that Harry had been caught, confessed to the crimes, the police had uncovered all of the evidence and that "obviously we have caught the bum that did it. He's guilty as sin."

By now, most if not all of you probably have wanted to raise objections about the police conduct described in this hypothetical situation. You most likely have seen enough television programs about law enforcement and the judicial process to feel that courts would never allow the police to operate in this high-handed fashion and hope to make the charges stick.

Much of the evidence gathered by the police in this example likely would be inadmissible in court because the judge, in order to ensure Harry a fair trial, would employ the so-called "exclusionary rule" to keep it out. This rule of evidence, along with other rules to keep potentially prejudicial information from the jury (e.g., a prior criminal record) have been developed by courts and approved by the Supreme Court of the United States as methods to ensure that police and prosecutors, in the process of enforcing the criminal law, do not violate the rights of those charged with a crime. This means that police and prosecutors know that evidence that could be useful, and perhaps decisive, in proving the guilt of the criminally accused may be excluded from consideration by a jury unless the law enforcement officials play by the rules.

The rules work because police and prosecutors measure their success in how many bad guys are apprehended, convicted and removed as threats to society. It is doubtful that any modern-day law enforcement agency would operate the way the police did in our hypothetical scenario. But if it did, or in a more likely occurrence, if the police simply make a mistake in the enforcement process, the courts have the responsibility and the power (the "exclusionary rule") to prevent the jury from being prejudiced by learning about the tainted evidence. Unfortunately from the perspective of the court, no such power exists to prevent *potential* jurors from learning about the tainted evidence by reading or hearing about it in their local and national media.

Remember the press conference conducted by the police chief in our scenario? He not only spoke in detail about the evidence, but conclusively stated the guilt of the accused. The newspapers and television stations serving the area would be sure to report this as news—it might even be the lead story. Assume that on returning to your residence at the end of the day, you picked up your mail but then put it aside to get a snack before dinner while watching an evening local television news show. The program leads with a full report of the details of the police chief's press conference. Now, having been exposed to news about Harry's confession, police discovery of murder weapons and the police chief's conclusions about Harry's guilt, you open your mail and discover that you have been chosen for jury duty.

See the problem? If you were selected for the jury pool in Harry's upcoming trial, you would have been exposed to pre-trial publicity about evidence potentially prejudicial to Harry's case that you most likely would not have learned about as a juror in the courtroom. Because of this prior knowledge, you might ask to be excused from jury duty or be challenged by one of the parties to the case. But what if almost everyone in town has been exposed to the prejudicial information? How can Harry (or Martha Stewart or Michael Vick, to name just two real-life examples) be assured of a fair and unbiased trial by his peers in these circumstances?

At the heart of the "free press/fair trial" issue is this conflict—the courts' responsibility to ensure the criminally accused and, to a lesser degree, the people (represented by the prosecutor) the right to a fair and unbiased trial on the one hand, and the responsibility of the mass media to accurately and comprehensively report the news and to carry out this task free from unwarranted government interference, on the other.

## Free Press/Fair Trial: The Courts Get Involved

For much of the nation's history, this conflict was only theoretical. The media disseminated what they wanted and if the rights of the criminally accused were diminished, it was just too bad. But as concerns about protection of civil liberties increased during the 1950s, courts became more and more worried about the prejudicial publicity problem. Things came to a head with the Supreme Court's decision in *Sheppard v. Maxwell*.[12] Dr. Sheppard, an osteopathic surgeon, was charged with murder in the slaying of his wife. Sheppard claimed an intruder had invaded their home, knocked him unconscious and killed Mrs. Sheppard, but police soon made Sheppard their number one suspect.

In what today would likely be called a "media circus," the newspapers covering the case employed sensational headlines suggesting his guilt, officials made public statements of a similar nature prior to trial and the news media were given almost free rein inside and outside the courtroom during the trial. Found guilty and sent to prison, Sheppard pursued the appeal of his conviction all the way to the Supreme Court. In a landmark decision, the Court overturned Sheppard's conviction and ordered a new trial on the basis that the trial judge failed to "fulfill his duty to protect [Sheppard] from the inherently prejudicial publicity which saturated the community and to control disruptive influences in the courtroom."[13]

Many of the Court's suggestions for trial courts to use as remedies for alleviating potential bias are familiar to most readers today. These include (a) a delay of trial or other proceedings; (b) change of venue; (c) maintaining order inside the courtroom; (d) intensive screening of potential jurors to root out bias; (e) instructions to the jury to avoid reading or viewing the news media while the case proceeds; and, in more extreme cases, (f) sequestering the jury for the length of the trial. With these tools at a judge's disposal, once the jury pool is chosen arguably there should be little reason to worry about prejudicial publicity reaching the jury unless the judge fails to do his or her duty. Unfortunately, the remedies that are most effective in minimizing bias require the judge to have control over the jury members. These measures are largely ineffective in preventing *pre*-trial prejudicial publicity from reaching *potential* jurors.

This conundrum—trial court judges charged by the Supreme Court with minimizing prejudicial publicity or risk having their cases overturned on appeal, yet being unable to effectively use the remedies for prevention suggested by the Court—led to the first great confrontation between the legal system and the press over the issue of free press/fair trial: the use of prior restraints or so-called "gag orders."

## Use of Prior Restraint to Ensure Fair Trials

Charged by the Supreme Court with the responsibility for mitigating the effects of prejudicial pre-trial publicity, but lacking effective means to carry out this responsibility, beginning in the late 1960s a few trial courts began to experiment with restraining orders directed at the press. These orders, placed on news media representatives in the early stages of a criminal case, usually allowed the press to be present at pre-trial hearings or other proceedings and to obtain information from law enforcement officials but mandated that the press not publicize certain kinds of potentially prejudicial information. Journalists violating such orders ran the substantial risk of being found in contempt of court and made to pay fines and/or spend time in jail.

The effectiveness of these court orders, quickly dubbed "gag rules" by the news media, made their use attractive to other judges and the number of courts across the country employing these court orders in some form quickly snowballed. Because these court orders also undeniably were examples of government agencies employing prior restraint (as discussed in Chapter 1, the most constitutionally suspect method of government abridgement of speech), it was only a matter of time before a challenge to their use arrived at the door of the Supreme Court.

The case that presented the Court with the opportunity to speak about the legitimacy of the use of such restraints was *Nebraska Press Association v. Stuart*,[14] an appeal of a decision by the Nebraska Supreme Court. The sensational facts of the case included the murder of all six members of a family living in the small town of Sutherland, Nebraska (population 850). Police almost immediately suspected Erwin Simants, who turned himself in to authorities the next day. Because mass murder was not a common occurrence in Nebraska, the case garnered widespread attention from both regional and national print and broadcast media.

After three days of constant media attention, both Simants' attorney and the county prosecutor asked a county court judge to issue an order prohibiting the media from divulging "news which would make difficult, if not impossible, the impaneling of an impartial jury and tend to prevent a fair trial."[15] The judge granted the motion that "prohibited everyone in attendance from 'releasing or authorizing the release for public dissemination in any form or manner whatsoever any testimony given or evidence adduced. . . .' "[16]

After a preliminary hearing, Simants was bound over for trial to the state district court presided over by Judge Hugh Stuart. Various journalist organizations, including the Nebraska Press Association representing the state's newspapers, as well as individual newspapers and broadcast stations asked Judge Stuart to lift the restraining order issued by the county court.

Finding that there was "a clear and present danger that pre-trial publicity could impinge upon the defendant's right to a fair trial,"[17] the judge refused the request to lift the restraint on publication but modified the county court's original order to reflect the Nebraska Bar-Press Guidelines. These guidelines for disseminating information had been adopted earlier by print and broadcast media associations in cooperation with various law enforcement personnel and judicial officers. The Nebraska Bar-Press Guidelines, like those that had been adopted by many other states, suggested that in criminal cases it would be inappropriate to report information about a suspect's confession or other admissions, the results of physical tests that might be inadmissible in court (e.g., a lie-detector test), opinions by officials about guilt or innocence and other statements that might inflame or influence potential jurors to which the actual jury members hearing the case might not be exposed.

Although the Nebraska Press Association had participated in the drafting of these guidelines, it, along with other news media representatives, appealed to the Nebraska Supreme Court asking that the restraining order be overturned on the premise that making voluntary guidelines mandatory violated free speech/press rights. When the Nebraska high court refused, the press association took its appeal to the Supreme Court of the United States.

Characterizing the "problems presented by this case [as] almost as old as the Republic,"[18] Chief Justice Burger, writing for the majority (all nine justices agreed on the outcome), traced problems of prejudicial publicity surrounding criminal proceedings back to the trial of Aaron Burr for treason in 1807. The Chief Justice noted that even back then, Chief Justice Marshall had expressed concern about the problems in selecting an unbiased jury and he observed that the "speed of communication and the pervasiveness of the modern news media have exacerbated these problems."[19] Nonetheless, the Court concluded that such sensational cases "are relatively rare, and we have held in other cases that trials have been fair in spite of widespread publicity."[20]

Observing the existence of a number of other measures to minimize the effects of prejudicial publicity including changing the venue (location) of the trial, delaying the proceedings, interrogating potential jurors to determine bias, instructing jurors as to how they should view the evidence in a case, restraining participants in the case (e.g., lawyers, defendants, witnesses) from discussing it with the news media, regulating the activities of the media in the courtroom and sequestering the jury, the Court overturned the ruling by the Nebraska Supreme Court and struck down the restraining order on First Amendment grounds.

In so holding, however, the Court did not rule out the limited use of judicial restraining orders in future cases. Instead, the Court created a three-part test for determining the constitutionality of such restraints of the media. First, said the Court, the judge issuing a restraining order directed against the press must be able to show a clear record of "intense and pervasive"[21] news coverage that demonstrates prejudicial pre-trial publicity has occurred, is likely to continue and that such "publicity might impair the defendant's right to a fair trial."[22] The second part of the test requires the judge to demonstrate on the record that he or she has investigated the feasibility of employing one or more of the alternatives to prior restraint noted above, but has found that no other method or methods would be sufficient to protect the defendant's right to a fair trial.

Part three of the test relates to "the probable efficacy of prior restraint on publication as a workable method of protecting [the defendant's] right[s]."[23] Noting that, as a practical matter, a court must have jurisdiction over the parties involved in a case if its orders are not to be ignored, the Court pointed out that in a sensational case (e.g., the O.J. Simpson murder trial) it would be of little avail for a judge to issue a restraining order that could apply only to local or regional media but not control the coverage of the case by national media.

From the point of view of the news media, the results of the *Nebraska Press Association* case produced two important results, one good and one bad. The good news was that, although not prohibiting so-called gag rules completely, the Court's three-prong test signaled a clear message to lower courts seeking to enforce such rules that it was extremely unlikely the constitutionality of such prior-restraint orders directed against the news media would be sustained on appeal. This has proven to be the case.

Note, however, that the Court explicitly suggested that such restraints would be justifiable if imposed on other participants in the case, including public relations professionals representing clients involved in the litigation. The reader is cautioned not to trifle with or ignore a court order. The savvy public relations practitioner would be wise to follow such orders to the letter in releasing information to the public and, if in doubt, consult with the court before speaking and advise clients about their responsibilities to do likewise.

The bad news for the news media in *Nebraska Press Association* was contained in language in the Court's majority opinion that seemed to view with approval the Nebraska Supreme Court's suggestion that closing the preliminary hearing and other pre-trial proceedings to the public, including the news media, was an acceptable alternative to prior restraint.[24] Soon, trial courts, discouraged by the Court in *Nebraska Press Association* from using gag rules except in rare circumstances, began to deny the press and public access to pre-trial judicial hearings and other proceedings. It was only a matter of time before closing the courtroom doors, and thus denying to the public the ability to scrutinize the workings of the judicial process, also was challenged in the courts as a violation of the Constitution.

## Closing the Courtroom to Ensure Fair Trials

The case presenting this opportunity was *Gannett Co. v. DePasquale.*[25] One day, Wayne Clapp and two of his buddies went fishing on Seneca Lake in upstate New York. Only his buddies returned. Police, alerted to Clapp's disappearance by his family, found his bullet-riddled boat and surmised that Clapp had met a violent end. Newspapers in the area, including one owned by Gannett Co., reported the story of Clapp's apparent death and the apprehension of the two suspects in Michigan several days later. The stories included details about the case against the suspects, including statements made by them to police, and the discovery of a supposed murder weapon. As the case against them developed, both defendants moved to suppress various pieces of evidence, including much of the information they had given to police, on the grounds "that those statements had been given involuntarily. They also sought to suppress physical evidence seized as fruits of the allegedly involuntary confessions,"[26] specifically, the revolver said to have been involved in the alleged killing.

At the pre-trial suppression-of-evidence hearing before Judge Daniel A. DePasquale, defendants' attorneys asked that the press be barred from the proceedings based on the already significant adverse publicity about the case and the possibility of a threat to the fair-trial rights of the accused if the press were allowed to report on evidence that later might be excluded at trial. Neither the prosecution nor representatives of the media opposed the motion to close although a reporter for the Gannett newspaper was present in the courtroom. Judge DePasquale granted the defendants' request and closed the hearing to the public.

When Gannett's attorneys later objected to the closure, Judge DePasquale, although noting that the press had a limited constitutional right of access, refused to lift the closure order on the basis that allowing the press to report on the outcome of a hearing to suppress evidence "would pose a 'reasonable probability of prejudice to these defendants' ... [and] ruled that the interest of the press and the public was outweighed in this case by the defendants' right to a fair trial."[27] When the New York Court of Appeals upheld Judge DePasquale's ruling, Gannett took its case to the Supreme Court.

The Court's majority opinion rejected First Amendment arguments in favor of overturning Judge DePasquale's closure order because media representatives had been present when the order was issued and had failed to object at that time, a subsequent hearing had been granted to the newspaper company in which to argue for openness and the closure order was "only temporary. Once the danger of prejudice had dissipated, a transcript of the suppression hearing was made available."[28] Chief Justice Burger, in a concurring opinion, specifically noted that a First Amendment-based claim of access was inapplicable in this case because *Gannett* involved a pre-trial proceeding unknown at the time the First Amendment was adopted.

Based on *Gannett*, lower courts across the country increased their use of closure as a means of ensuring defendants a fair trial. This movement finally culminated in *Richmond Newspapers, Inc. v. Virginia*,[29] in which a judge closed an actual criminal trial. This set the stage for a second chance for First Amendment-based arguments in favor of public access to judicial proceedings.

The case involved the fourth trial of a defendant accused of murdering a hotel manager. His conviction in the first trial was reversed on appeal because a blood-stained shirt was improperly introduced as evidence. A second trial ended when a juror was forced to retire and no alternate was available. The third trial was aborted when it was discovered that a prospective juror had read about the earlier attempts to try the defendant, including the bloody-shirt evidence, and informed other jurors about these efforts.

At the beginning of trial four, defense counsel, citing the possibility of prejudicial publicity, asked the judge to close the proceedings to the press and public. When neither the prosecution nor the journalists present objected, the judge cleared the courtroom "of all parties except the witnesses when they testify."[30] At a subsequent hearing, requested by the Richmond Newspapers, Inc. to protest closure, the trial judge refused to vacate his order (finding the criminal defendant's arguments about the number of trials to date and the smallness of the community persuasive) and the trial continued with the press and public barred. The defendant was eventually found not guilty of murder. The Virginia Supreme Court upheld the validity of the trial court's closure order and Richmond Newspapers, Inc. took its case to the Supreme Court of the United States.

Although the Court was fragmented in deciding on an overall rationale for its decision (Chief Justice Burger's opinion was joined by only two other justices and no other opinion represented the views of more than two justices), seven justices agreed that the lower court's order should be overturned on First Amendment grounds. The Chief Justice's opinion began by observing that "this precise issue . . . has not previously been before this Court. . . . [H]ere for the first time the Court is asked to decide whether a criminal *trial* itself may be closed to the public upon the unopposed request of a defendant [absent] any demonstration that closure is required to protect the defendant's superior right to a fair trial . . ." (italics added).[31]

Tracing the origins of a tradition of openness for such trials to before the Norman conquest of England in 1066, Chief Justice Burger noted that this tradition had been brought over to the English colonies in America and had become part of the American legal system. Based on this evidence, the Chief Justice concluded "[f]rom this unbroken, uncontradicted history, supported by reasons as valid today as in centuries past, . . . a presumption of openness inheres in the very nature of a criminal trial under our system of justice."[32]

Despite this presumption, Virginia officials argued that no explicit provision of the Constitution guarantees that the press and public should be permitted access to all criminal trials. Although agreeing in principle, the Chief Justice found that "[i]n guaranteeing freedoms such as those of speech and press, the First Amendment can be read as protecting the right of everyone to attend trials . . . . '[T]he First Amendment goes beyond protection of the press and the self-expression of individuals to prohibit government from limiting the stock of information from which members of the public may draw.'"[33]

Although not providing a general right of access, Chief Justice Burger held that "[t]he right of access to places traditionally open to the public, as criminal trials have long been, may be seen as assured by the amalgam of the First Amendment guarantees of speech and press; and their affinity to the right of assembly is not without relevance."[34] The Chief Justice concluded that despite the failure of the Constitution to enumerate a guarantee of access, "the right to attend criminal trials is implicit in the guarantees of the First Amendment; without the freedom to attend such trials, which people have exercised for centuries, important aspects of freedom of speech and 'of the press could be eviscerated.'"[35]

Although the Chief Justice, in fashioning a limited First Amendment-based right of access, was careful to maintain the distinction between pretrial proceedings and actual criminal trials, the limitation almost immediately began to suffer erosion. In *Globe Newspaper v. Norfolk County Superior Court*,[36] the Court struck down a state law mandating closing of trials involving victims of sexual offenses under the age of 18 on the basis that the law permitted no judicial discretion. Such a law, said the

Court, could not be squared with the constitutional presumption of openness of criminal proceedings.

In *Press Enterprise Co. v. Riverside County Superior Court*,[37] the Court held that jury selection was so integral to the criminal trial process and was so intimately related to the actual trial that it too was presumptively open to the press and public despite arguments that, in addition to prejudicial pre-trial publicity, potential jurors and witnesses might be intimidated or embarrassed by media reports.

In a later case with the same name, often referred to as *Press-Enterprise II*,[38] the Court was presented with the rather unusual situation of a pre-trial preliminary hearing that continued for 41 days in a case involving a nurse charged with multiple murders of patients under his care. Unlike a typical preliminary hearing, which generally lasts no more than a day or two, the proceedings in *Press-Enterprise II* involved presentation of extensive medical and scientific evidence as well as testimonial evidence from the defendant's co-workers which was then subjected to searching cross-examination by the defendant's legal counsel.

At the beginning of the proceedings, the defendant asked that the preliminary hearing be closed. The trial judge granted the motion, which was unopposed, on the basis that "closure was necessary because the case had attracted national publicity and 'only one side may get reported in the media.'"[39] At the end of the preliminary hearing, Press-Enterprise asked that the transcript of the proceedings be made public, but the judge denied the request. The appeal of the closure and sealing of the transcript was taken to the California Supreme Court which upheld the lower court. The Supreme Court of the United States subsequently overturned the lower court's decisions on First Amendment grounds.

The Court recognized the lower courts' concerns about ensuring the defendant's rights to a fair trial and that its own rulings in earlier cases might be construed as to deny First Amendment claims of access to pre-trial proceedings. However, said the Court, despite the fact that the closure order involved a pre-trial proceeding, "the First Amendment question cannot be resolved solely on the label we give the event, i.e., 'trial' or otherwise, particularly where the preliminary hearing functions much like a full-scale trial."[40] Instead, said the Court, a possible constitutional right of access must be based on "two complementary considerations. First, . . . we have considered whether the place and process have *historically* been open to the press and general public" (italics added).[41] The Court added, "[we have also] traditionally considered whether public access plays a significant *positive role* in the functioning of the particular process in question" (italics added).[42]

Finding that although in California proceedings like grand jury deliberations had not been open to public scrutiny, "there has been a tradition of accessibility to preliminary hearings of the type conducted in [this case]."[43]

In fact, noted the Court, "[f]rom [the case of Aaron] Burr until the present day, the near uniform practice of state and federal courts has been to conduct preliminary hearing in open court."[44]

Although some states historically have allowed preliminary hearings to be closed on occasion, the Court observed that "even in these States the proceedings are presumptively open to the public and are closed only for cause shown."[45] Based on its decisions in *Richmond Newspapers* and *Press-Enterprise I* that public access "is essential to the proper functioning of the criminal justice system,"[46] the Court held that, when conducted like those in California, "preliminary hearings are sufficiently like a trial to justify the same conclusion."[47]

After the series of cases ending in *Press-Enterprise II*, lower courts apparently got the message that closing criminal court proceedings to minimize prejudicial publicity should not be the method of choice except in unusual situations. Lower courts, therefore, have increasingly turned to delay, change of venue and especially to the use of gag rules on police and trial participants to prevent them from talking to the press. Although there have been no significant cases for the Court to expand on its rulings in this area, it seems a safe bet that there is little enthusiasm on the part of the current members of the Court for narrowing the trend to openness recognized for criminal proceedings.

There remains the question, however, of whether this trend will be extended to provide a constitutional right of access to civil proceedings. Although most civil trials are routinely open to the public, lower courts, at least for the time being, still retain a greater ability to deny access if they so choose. Arguably, however, the benefits of public access to criminal proceedings articulated by the Court in cases ranging from *Richmond Newspapers* to *Press-Enterprise II* should adhere to civil proceedings with equal validity.

## Cameras in the Courtroom: A Special Access Problem

In 1927, Charles Lindbergh captured the imagination of the world when he flew his airplane, the *Spirit of St. Louis*, solo between New York and Paris. He returned to the United States a hero and his fame increased as he toured the country, and then foreign nations as well, with his bride, Anne Morrow Lindbergh. Tragically, their lives were shattered in 1934 when their infant son was kidnapped and later killed. The details of the kidnapping, the arrest of a suspect, Bruno Hauptmann, and his subsequent trial for murder created a news media frenzy, so much so that the American Bar Association was moved to adopt Canon 35 of its code of legal ethics which banned broadcast coverage as well as still photography in courtrooms.

This prohibition of cameras and microphones in the courtroom continued to be enforced for more than four decades. Beginning in the late 1970s, however, recognizing that modern technology had reduced the intrusiveness of broadcasting and photography, the courts began to slowly experiment with allowing photographers and electronic journalists access to pre-trial and trial proceedings. In *Chandler v. Florida*[48] in 1981, the Supreme Court held that it was not an inherent abridgement of a defendant's rights to a fair trial to allow cameras and microphones in the courtroom. However, the Court did not find a blanket right of access for such mechanical devices, leaving it to lower courts to establish rules and guidelines for allowing or prohibiting their presence.

Today, with the advent of truTV (formerly Court TV) on many cable systems and the nationwide televising of high-profile trials like those of William Kennedy Smith (acquitted of a charge of rape) and O.J. Simpson (found not guilty of killing his former wife and an acquaintance), the presence of cameras in the courtroom has become commonplace.

The O.J. Simpson case, however, illustrates not only the benefits but the perils of extensive coverage by the electronic media, both inside and outside the courtroom. Although presenting an accurate portrayal of a major criminal trial (at least in California) with all its moments of great drama as well as the much more common hours of routine legal procedure, the Simpson pre-trial and trial proceedings also were rife with public bickering and posturing by lawyers for both sides. Network and cable television carried live coverage of the innumerable problems that arose with selecting and keeping jury members, determining the validity of DNA evidence after extensive legal wrangling and the relevance of taped interviews indicating racial bias by one of the prosecution's star witnesses: all in a case involving a defendant many in the public believed from the start was guilty as charged.

The resulting dismay with the Simpson proceedings and the legal process in general voiced by members of the viewing public on call-in talk shows, letters-to-the-editor and public opinion polls, produced calls for renewed prohibitions on cameras in the courtroom by members of the legal profession concerned both with the image of the judicial system and the effects of the telecasts on participants in subsequent criminal proceedings.

## Susan Smith: A Case Study

Perhaps nowhere was the negative fallout from the coverage of the Simpson trial as well as the ongoing tensions between the courts and the mass media demonstrated more dramatically than in the events surrounding Susan Smith, a 22-year-old South Carolina mother charged with the drowning deaths of her two young sons. Although the murder of children by a parent is not considered as newsworthy in America as it once was, the events surrounding the Smith case, including Smith's story that her

BURN!

children had been abducted by an African-American man, her tearful requests that her children be returned broadcast on network television and then the startling revelation that all of this was a lie and that she herself had steered her automobile into a lake near her home with her two children strapped in their car seats, ensured that the subsequent proceedings to determine her fate—there was no doubt of her guilt—would be a major media event.

Recognizing the high probability of possible pre-trial publicity (although Smith's hometown, Union, S.C., has a population of about 10,000, a total of only 40,000 people live in all of Union County), police initially were extremely cautious about giving out information during their investigations but eventually did release the news that Smith had confessed to the crimes and permitted the news media to view the crime scene.

While all this was transpiring, the pre-trial proceedings, including evidence hearings and jury selection, were moving forward. And so were the preparations for covering the trial by the major television networks, syndicated tabloid news programs and local and regional television stations from Charlotte, N.C., to Atlanta. As the trial date neared, the broadcast media commandeered much of the rental property in the town to house its personnel, built a fortress-like system of make-shift broadcasting booths on risers stretching the length of one city block in front of the Union County courthouse and incessantly interviewed Union residents brave enough to venture downtown about their opinions of the possible penalty Susan Smith should face.

Perhaps this build-up of media presence caused a last-minute decision by the trial judge to grant the Susan Smith defense team's request to ban all electronic and photographic equipment from the courtroom despite the fact that extensive modifications of the courtroom requested by the judge to facilitate the electronic media had already been completed. The judge cited the possible reluctance of witnesses to testify truthfully if their testimony were shown on television as the principal reason for his decision. But it is fair to speculate, given that everyone in the small town would almost immediately be aware of such testimony, that he was more concerned with losing control of the proceedings and risk becoming another Judge Lance Ito (the trial judge in the O.J. Simpson case, criticized for his performance and satirized on widely viewed late-night television shows).

Because the admittance of electronic media and photographic cameras in the courtroom, by statute, is left to the discretion of a trial judge in South Carolina, the judge's exclusion of electronic media in this case could not be appealed. As a result, the reporting of the trial was left entirely to print media and to the broadcasts of renderings by courtroom artists.

Until the memory of the O.J. Simpson trial fades (not to mention the subsequent cases involving Kobe Bryant, Michael Jackson and Martha Stewart), courts and legal commentators may continue to regard requests to broadcast criminal proceedings and expansive interpretations of journalist privilege with suspicion. The negative media-related results of the Susan Smith trial should serve as a sobering reminder of the fragile nature of the free-speech protections for journalists when they try to protect the identity of their sources, despite state shield laws, or when they seek access to courtrooms to report on the criminal or civil law processes.

## Free Press/Fair Trial in a Digital, New-Media Age: Emerging Issues

Protecting the freedom of journalists to fully and accurately report on criminal and civil law processes while ensuring fair trials continues to be a major issue in mass media law involving journalists. It is important for advertising and public relations professionals to understand the problems journalists face in doing their job and, where ethical and appropriate, join them in fighting attempts to restrict freedom of the press in such situations, particularly in an era of closed and sometimes secret hearings and trials dealing with alleged terrorists since 9/11.

## Journalist Privilege

Remember your hypothetical friend, the part-time reporter for a local daily newspaper in your area, who was giving you a ride to get your car at the repair shop but needed to make one brief stop at a restaurant to interview Harry "The Mule" Smith for a story about illegal drug dealing? This was fine with you and, rather than waiting outside in her car, you accompanied the reporter to the interview, sitting quietly in a corner of the tavern's back room, sipping a cold brew, while the reporter interviewed the source. The reporter told the source that you were "just another reporter."

During the course of the interview, the source unexpectedly described not only how illegal drugs are brought into the county, but allowed the reporter to take pictures of a demonstration (with no faces shown) of how easily a parcel of these drugs could be divided into small packages designed for sale to school children. Before doing so, however, Harry asked for and received a promise from the reporter that everything connected with the interview was "off the record" and that the reporter would never reveal where, how or from whom the information was obtained.

The reporter's subsequent story, published as a page-one exposé, caught the attention of a state grand jury investigating illegal drug dealing. The grand jury then asked that a subpoena be issued to the reporter, ordering her to appear to testify as to the source of the information about drug sales and to provide any other information that might assist the grand jury in its investigations. The reporter has so far refused to testify, and, as a result, risks being found in contempt of court, a position that could land her in jail and/or require her to pay criminal or civil fines.

It is just this kind of scenario that has created a demand by many in the journalist community for the recognition of a "journalist privilege" to withhold information requested by a court, grand jury or government commission or committee. Being granted a privilege in the law usually means that the person accorded the privilege is excused from following normal legal rules except under certain specific instances or, more rarely, is excused from complying with such requirements in all circumstances. The recognition of a journalist privilege would permit a reporter to refuse to disclose information an average citizen normally would be obliged to surrender.

## Practical Reasons for Recognition of a Journalist Privilege

The arguments for granting a journalist the privilege to withhold information from government authorities are based both on the practical difficulties faced by a reporter in gathering information without such legal protection and the possibility that, in the absence of such a journalist privilege, information with important implications for public policy might never reach readers or viewers.

In an era of general public distrust of government and big business, it should come as no surprise that, for reasons ranging from the honorable to the most mean-spirited self-interest, many people with information about possible wrongdoing or malfeasance in office are reluctant to reveal that information to government authorities. Whether they fear retaliation on the job, physical harm to themselves or their families, prosecution for criminal activity or just unwanted involvement in an uncomfortable situation, people "in the know" often will not complain or publicly blow the whistle.

They may confide in a journalist, however, with the idea that the journalist, in making the information public, can set the wheels of reform in motion. Often the price of that information is a promise by the reporter never to reveal anything that could lead to the source of the information.

The ability and legal right of the reporter to make and keep such a pledge of confidentiality is an important weapon in the arsenal of journalists to ensure the news media effectively fulfill their function as a community watchdog. That important societal role would be made much more difficult if a journalist were forced to reveal the source of the information. Not only would the journalist lose an important and reliable informant in the current as well as in subsequent investigations (and bear the moral responsibility of possibly placing that source in jeopardy), but it is likely that other potential sources would be reluctant to divulge information to the news media if they believed their confidences also might be disclosed.

Additionally, reporters argue, the watchdog role of the news media could be subverted by turning reporters into de facto agents of the government by routinely subpoenaing journalists to appear before legislative or judicial bodies and forcing them to reveal with whom they had spoken and the subject matter of such conversations. As a reporter who refused to provide information to a grand jury in Ohio explained, "I believe reporters should not be used by our society as cops. If I cooperated [with the grand jury request], it would shatter the credibility of all reporters. If I cooperated, any sources looking at me—past, present or future—would wonder, 'Can I trust her?'"[49]

An issue of even greater concern is the harm caused by the failure of the reporter to acquire the information when confidences cannot be kept between reporter and source. Although it is true the reporter's job becomes more difficult if confidential sources are afraid or unwilling to provide information without a guarantee of confidentiality, the fact remains that journalists still will be able to produce a product at the end of the day, albeit perhaps an inferior one. For that reason, many supporters of a journalist privilege argue that actually it is the public that most benefits from the recognition of such a privilege.

This argument is buttressed by the numerous instances of wrongdoing that have come to light only through the collaborative efforts between confidential sources and investigative reporters. Examples range from the Watergate investigations of the early 1970s that eventually resulted in the resignation of President Richard M. Nixon to revelations of illegal or unethical behavior in the 1990s by state legislators and other officials in New York, South Carolina, Virginia and elsewhere to disclosures about the possible use of steroids by professional baseball players in 2005 that led to congressional hearings and a crackdown on drug use by Major League Baseball.

## Objections to Recognition of a Journalist Privilege

With so many arguments in its favor, the reader might assume that the acceptance of a journalist privilege at the state and federal levels has become commonplace. Such an assumption would be in error. Although it is true that the majority of states have provided some kind of privilege either by statute or court decision and that a number of federal appeals courts have interpreted the Supreme Court of the United States' rulings on this subject as recognizing a qualified First Amendment-based privilege, strong countervailing arguments against a privilege for journalists have served to limit—and in some instances defeat—efforts to recognize or create such a privilege.

One argument centers on the bedrock principle in the American legal system, that every person who possesses information that could assist in the administration of justice must come forward and provide that information if so required by law. Courts, grand juries and other investigative government bodies could hardly function if people were free to flout this principle. Failure to provide such information, or to do so untruthfully, usually constitutes a serious criminal offense.

Because acquiring the most accurate and comprehensive information possible is so vital to the administration of justice, and because those who wish to exert a privilege not to provide testimonial evidence often possess information that would materially aid the search for truth, it is no wonder that the rule has developed that "*all privileges of exemption from this duty* [to testify] *are exceptional* and are therefore to be discountenanced."[50]

Yet some privileges do exist. The privilege to be free from self-incrimination is recognized as a fundamental liberty and enshrined in the provisions of the federal Constitution. Reaching far back into our antecedents in the English legal system, American common law today continues to recognize that privileged communications exist in the interactions between husband and wife; attorney and client; physician and patient; and priest (or other member of the clergy) and penitent. Although the extent and nature of each of these privileged situations varies, if the relationships satisfy the definitions specified by law, the confidences shared in these relationships remain privileged and may not be subjected to judicial or investigative scrutiny.

Each of these privileged relationships is based on a societal view that says we consider that other values (e.g., family harmony, the ablest legal representation or the health of the body and the soul) are of more importance than acquisition of the information that could be obtained by revealing the confidences shared in each of these relationships.

The reader should not lose sight, however, of the tremendous assistance obtaining such information would provide to those charged with ascertaining truth and administering justice. That's why many in the legal system resist creating any new privileges in the law to protect the confidences shared in other relationships. Journalists are by no means alone in requesting that privilege be extended to them. Spiritual advisers, school counselors, social workers and individuals in a wide variety of other occupations and professions advance similar arguments. Faced with these demands, it should come as little surprise that courts and legislatures show marked reluctance to opening the door even slightly to recognize additional privileges beyond those long recognized by the Constitution or the common law.

Journalists face other formidable obstacles in obtaining widespread acceptance of a privilege to protect their sources of information. Although credentialing or accrediting procedures often serve to officially designate those eligible to practice in specific professions or occupations, no such procedures exist to certify who is and who is not a journalist. In fact, most journalists actively resist the notion of any such licensing scheme, arguing that such a system would be a violation of the First Amendment. Extending privilege to journalists, therefore, presents difficult definitional problems. Such issues often arise when a journalist privilege is asserted by such individuals as a freelance writer, an academic preparing a scholarly manuscript, a documentary filmmaker or a blogger.

Another problem relates to the rationale usually advanced for protecting those relationships already recognized by the law. The extension of privilege in such situations generally protects the nonprofessional party in the relationship. For example, the confidentiality of the relationship between an attorney and client is meant to ensure that a client may speak openly and candidly to his or her legal representative without fear that the attorney subsequently will be forced to reveal these confidences. A privileged situation normally comes into existence the moment the professional nature of the relationship is established, as opposed to a casual conversation at a social gathering, for example. If, however, clients do not object to revealing the contents of a privileged conversation, attorneys normally will not be exempted from providing information to a court or other legal body by claiming their own privilege.

Those in favor of recognition of a journalist privilege suggest that, unlike other relationships, the privilege should protect the journalist (e.g., the professional) and not the source. According to this argument, journalists should be able to make the decision as to whether a privileged situation exists, the nature and extent of the privilege and decide to withhold information or reveal it, at times irrespective of the wishes of the source.

Yet another problem with the recognition of a journalist privilege is the skepticism of many jurists and others in the legal community about the need for such a privilege. These critics argue that promises of confidentiality may be too easily given and that there is little hard evidence that the flow of important information to the public would be seriously lessened if sources, instead of talking to journalists about wrongdoing, simply reported it to the proper authorities.

Additionally, because the shielding of sources often prevents law enforcement officials from identifying individuals who themselves have committed an illegal or unethical act (e.g., the hypothetical drug dealer who provided information to the reporter in the scenario that began this discussion of journalist privilege), many in the legal community worry about a privilege that permits journalists to rise above the law by ignoring their civic responsibility to immediately report criminal activity or malfeasance in office. As Justice White noted in the seminal Supreme Court decision in this area, "we cannot seriously entertain the notion that [a privilege should exist] on the theory that it is better to write about crime than to do something about it,"[51] including providing timely information to investigators or courts.

## Journalist Privilege: Legal Issues

Many supporters of a privilege for journalists not to testify in legal proceedings ground their advocacy in the language of the First Amendment. Although admitting that requiring journalists to provide information to legal authorities is not a direct, content-based "abridgment" of speech, these advocates argue that the inhibition of sources, the threat to journalist integrity and the resulting restriction on the free flow of information of importance to the public raise significant First Amendment issues.

By no means, however, is there unanimous support for a First Amendment rationale as the basis for a privilege, even by those who are strong supporters of the general concept. Those who object to a constitutionally based privilege do so because, they argue, such a position requires an interpretation of the First Amendment to provide one level of constitutional protection for "typical" individuals and a second, higher level for "journalists," a position these critics find untenable.

To understand this better, we need to return to our hypothetical example that began this discussion of journalist privilege. Remember that you accompanied your friend, the reporter, while she interviewed a source in a restaurant. Her subsequent story was based on information provided only after the reporter promised the identity of the informant would remain confidential. A grand jury later subpoenaed the reporter and ordered her to reveal the source of her article. Assume, for the moment, that the reporter argued that she had a First Amendment privilege to withhold that information, and further assume that a court upheld her argument, ruling that she did not have to testify.

As you may imagine, the court's action has upset the members of the grand jury who are charged with the duty of investigating drug trafficking and now feel stymied in this search by the refusal of the journalist to provide relevant, material information. A quick-witted member of the grand jury, however, has an idea. "Does anyone else know to whom the reporter spoke and maybe what was said?" he asks. Suddenly, all eyes are looking directly at *you*!

Wondering how in the world you got involved in an investigation of illegal drugs, you call your reporter friend, asking how she avoided testifying. She tells you that the court accepted the argument that she has a First Amendment-based journalist privilege not to testify and suggests you try a similar approach.

See the problem?

Unless you happen to have a press card or can convince the court that somehow you also should be treated as a journalist, it is extremely unlikely the court will grant you a similar privilege not to testify, despite the fact that you only saw and heard exactly what the reporter did. Those who are concerned by what, to them, seem contradictory outcomes in such a case usually argue that the Constitution does not provide the basis for a journalist privilege because the First Amendment should be interpreted as protecting every individual equally and, therefore, cannot be "twisted" into differentiating journalists from non-journalists.

Those in favor of a journalist privilege, but who reject a First Amendment-based rationale, generally instead opt for achieving their objective by statutory means on a state-by-state basis, urging legislatures to pass so-called "shield laws." Shield laws are seldom drafted in such a way as to create an absolute privilege for journalists to refuse to testify in all cases. Instead, most create a qualified privilege that provides protection for reporters under most circumstances, but can be overcome if the government body seeking information from the reporter can justify its request by meeting the requirements established in the statute.

## *Branzburg v. Hayes*: The Supreme Court and Journalist Privilege

The idea that journalists should be granted a legal privilege to withhold information gained popular support within the news media community by the late 1960s. A number of states passed so-called shield laws recognizing a journalist privilege. Many of these laws then became the subject of court challenges when judges and grand juries nonetheless required reporters to reveal sources or face punishment for contempt of a lawful order. In many of these cases, as well as in cases in the federal courts, reporters argued that in addition to any statutory protection, the First Amendment should be construed as conferring constitutional protection. Thus the stage was set for the Supreme Court of the United States to hear a case focusing on the extent, if any, of a First Amendment-based journalist privilege.

The opportunity presented itself in *Branzburg v. Hayes*,[52] a consolidated appeal of three cases involving reporter privilege, two from state supreme courts and one from the federal court of appeals for the ninth circuit. The facts of the first case involving Branzburg, a reporter for the *Louisville* (Ky.) *Courier Journal*, paralleled those in our opening scenario. The reporter, working on a story about drug dealing, promised confidentiality to his informants whom he had observed and photographed synthesizing hashish from marijuana. Subpoenaed by a county grand jury investigating illegal drug sales, Branzburg refused to reveal the names of the persons he had observed. A second story resulted in another subpoena, but this time the reporter refused to appear before the grand jury at all. In each instance, Branzburg's attorneys, in addition to the practical arguments in favor of recognizing a privilege for journalists, argued that there were three legal bases why the reporter should not be forced to testify: the First Amendment, Kentucky's state constitutional protections of speech and the state's shield law.

Ultimately, the Kentucky Supreme Court rejected all of these arguments, holding that the First Amendment did not provide a federal constitutional shield and that nothing in the state constitution could be construed as creating a privilege for journalists. The Kentucky court further held that Kentucky's shield law provided "a newsman the privilege of refusing to divulge the identity of an informant"[53] but added that "the statute did not permit a reporter to refuse to testify about events [the reporter] had observed personally. . . ."[54] Branzburg then took his appeal to the Supreme Court of the United States.

The second case in the *Branzburg* trilogy, *In re Pappas*, involved a reporter working for a New Bedford, Mass., television station. Pappas was permitted to enter and report from inside the local headquarters of the radical Black Panthers group during a period of social unrest on the condition that he not "disclose anything he saw or heard inside . . . except an anticipated police raid. . . ."[55] The raid never materialized and Pappas never prepared a story. Nonetheless, a county grand jury summoned him to appear and to tell all he had learned by being inside the headquarters. Pappas refused, citing both the state and federal constitutional protections of speech (Massachusetts had no shield law).

On appeal, the Supreme Judicial Court of Massachusetts upheld a lower court's decision ordering the requested information be provided, noting that a privilege to avoid testifying in Massachusetts was "limited" and that "[t]he principle that the public 'has a right to every man's evidence'" was the general rule recognized by the state.[56] The state high court also concluded that the federal Constitution provided no privilege to avoid testifying in such circumstances. Like Branzburg, Pappas appealed this latter ruling to the Supreme Court.

*U.S. v. Caldwell*, the third of the three cases on appeal, involved a reporter for *The New York Times* who also was covering the activities of radical groups, including the Black Panthers. A federal grand jury in California, investigating the causes of recent civil unrest in that state, subpoenaed Caldwell, ordering him to bring with him "notes and tape recordings of interviews . . . reflecting statements made for publication by officers and spokesmen for the Black Panther Party. . . ."[57] Although the order to produce materials was eventually withdrawn, Caldwell was still subpoenaed to personally appear before the grand jury to testify about his knowledge of possible criminal activity. Caldwell refused, citing the First Amendment.

A federal district court then ordered the reporter to be jailed for contempt of court, but the ninth circuit reversed that decision, holding that the First Amendment provided a qualified constitutional privilege for newsgathering. Faced with state court decisions denying the existence of a First Amendment-based journalist privilege in Kentucky and Massachusetts and a federal appeals court holding to the contrary in the states covered by the federal ninth circuit, the Supreme Court consolidated the three cases for consideration of a constitutional privilege.

Those hoping that the Court's decision in *Branzburg* would provide a definitive answer as to whether the First Amendment provides a privilege for journalists, however, were to be disappointed. In a divided opinion, the Court upheld the orders directed against the three journalists but, at the same time, appeared to hold that there was at least some First Amendment-based protection for reporters to protect their sources from forced disclosure.

Justice White, in an opinion joined by Chief Justice Burger and Justices Blackmun and Rehnquist, strongly rejected the notion of constitutional privilege. "We do not question the significance of free speech . . . [n]or is it suggested that news gathering does not qualify for First Amendment protection. . . . But these cases involve no intrusions upon speech . . . no prior restraint or restriction on what the press may publish, and no express or implied command that the press publish what it prefers to withhold."[58] In addition, wrote Justice White, there is

> [n]o exaction or tax for the privilege of publishing, and no penalty, civil or criminal, related to the content of published material is at issue here. The use of confidential sources by the press is not forbidden or restricted. . . . The sole issue before us is the obligation of reporters to respond to grand jury subpoenas as other citizens do and to answer questions relevant to an investigation into the commission of crime.[59]

Noting that the First Amendment had been interpreted as permitting "incidental burdening" of the press in enforcing other laws and that the press was not free to invade privacy, defame, ignore laws applicable to others or to gain special access to records, meetings or places,[60] "[i]t is thus not surprising," said Justice White, "that the great weight of authority is that newsmen are not exempt from the normal duty of appearing before a grand jury and answering questions relevant to a criminal investigation."[61] Justice White added that "[u]ntil now, the only testimonial privilege for unofficial witnesses . . . in the Federal Constitution is the Fifth Amendment privilege against compelled self-incrimination. We are asked to create another by interpreting the First Amendment to grant newsmen a testimonial privilege that other citizens do not enjoy. This we decline to do."[62]

The reasons for this disinclination, explained Justice White, included (a) the law's historic dislike of privilege in general; (b) a concern that extending a privilege to journalists could inhibit law enforcement officials and courts from investigating criminal activity; (c) the possibility that informants themselves could escape criminal liability; and (d) skepticism about the dire results predicted by reporters for the news-gathering process if such a privilege were not extended. The Court also envisioned problems in determining to whom such a constitutional privilege should be extended, "a questionable procedure in light of the traditional doctrine that liberty of the press is the right of the lonely pamphleteer who uses carbon paper or a mimeograph just as much as of the large metropolitan publisher who utilizes the latest photocomposition methods."[63] Justice White indicated as well that states and the federal government were free to establish journalist privilege by statute or other means if they so chose.

In contrast to the opinion authored by Justice White, the four justices in dissent found a First Amendment-based privilege for journalists that, in effect, mirrored the holding of the federal court of appeals in *Caldwell*. Justice Stewart, writing for two other justices (Justice Douglas filed his own dissenting opinion), argued that the reasons for a constitutional privilege were compelling enough to warrant recognizing a privilege to protect journalists and their sources in most circumstances. Such a privilege was qualified, however, meaning that it could be overcome if the court or other government agency seeking to compel the reporter's testimony could demonstrate the information sought was highly relevant, could be obtained from no other source and was essential to a substantial government interest. This became the so-called *Branzburg* three-part test. Clearly, however, the Constitution, according to Justice Stewart, places the burden of meeting this three-prong test on the government. Unless the government can show such evidence, said Justice Stewart, a journalist has a First Amendment privilege to refuse to testify.

With four justices in *Branzburg* firmly committed to the position that the First Amendment does not provide a privilege for journalists and four others just as convinced that it does, all eyes turned to the swing vote of Justice Powell. Unfortunately for those seeking a decision that would settle this issue once and for all, Justice Powell contributed an opinion that seemed to come down squarely in the middle. He concurred with Justice White's opinion that a First Amendment-based privilege would be inapplicable in cases in which the journalists had actually witnessed criminal activity. On the other hand, Justice Powell seemed to find at least some constitutional basis for according journalists privilege in other (unspecified) situations, noting that "[t]his Court does not hold that newsmen . . . are without constitutional rights with respect to the gathering of news or in safeguarding their sources."[64]

The upshot of Justice Powell's enigmatic opinion is that, today, those who argue the First Amendment provides no privilege for journalists cite *Branzburg* as authority for their position, and those who argue that indeed there is such constitutional protection also cite *Branzburg* as upholding their view. As the reader may imagine, lower federal and state courts have been confused when encountering such arguments and, predictably, some have recognized a First Amendment privilege whereas others have not. The majority of courts that have recognized some form of journalist privilege usually have adopted the *Branzburg* minority's three-prong test, although they "often have applied it in a manner resulting in a requirement that the journalist testify."[65]

In a case with serious ramifications for journalists, and of interest to public relations practitioners as well, the Supreme Court of the United States has upheld a breach of contract-like claim by a source against a Minnesota newspaper that revealed his identity after promising him it would not do so. That case, *Cohen v. Cowles Media Co.*,[66] would appear to place journalists who promise confidentiality in the unfortunate position of facing contempt of court citations, involving possible jail terms and/or fines, if they do not reveal information when called to testify, and the possibility of payment of substantial money damages to the now-named aggrieved source if they do.

## Susan Smith Again

In the sensational Susan Smith trial (discussed earlier in this chapter), the trial judge feared that it might be difficult to obtain an unbiased jury to decide her sentence from among the residents of the county given the media frenzy accompanying this case. Rather than attempting to gag the media, the judge instead, following the options suggested in *Nebraska Press Association*, issued a restraining order prohibiting any public discussion of the case by the prosecution's staff, defense attorneys, all potential witnesses, police and any others who might have access to or knowledge of evidence that might be at issue in the proceedings.

Despite these efforts, Twyla Decker, a reporter for *The State* newspaper in Columbia, S.C., obtained information for a story that was subsequently published in the newspaper about the defendant's psychiatric profile both during and after the commission of the crime. Believing that the person revealing this information to the reporter might have been covered by his restraining order, the judge ordered the reporter to reveal the name of her source. Decker refused, citing South Carolina's recently enacted shield law[67] and free-speech protections guaranteed by the state and federal constitutions. The South Carolina shield law was modeled after the three-part test of *Branzburg* and was generally regarded as an example of a statute providing strong protection for the news media.

The trial judge ruled, however, that the shield law was inapplicable or, in the alternative, that the test for the government agency seeking to overcome the provisions of the shield law (i.e., information that is highly relevant, incapable of being provided by an alternative source and needed by the government to establish its case) had been satisfied. Finding little merit in the reporter's arguments of constitutional protection, the judge ordered Ms. Decker to either turn over the information or face going to jail on charges of criminal contempt of court.

On appeal, the South Carolina Supreme Court upheld the lower court.[68] When he received the high court's ruling, however, the trial judge stayed his decision about the fate of the newspaper reporter until the Susan Smith sentencing trial was completed. Susan Smith eventually was found guilty of the crimes as charged, but the jury unanimously voted to send her to prison for life rather than impose the death penalty, one of several options under South Carolina law. At the conclusion of the trial, the trial judge elected not to send *The State*'s newspaper reporter to jail for disobeying his pre-trial disclosure order.

## Journalist Privilege in a Digital, New-Media Age: Emerging Issues

At the state court level, journalists and the news media continue to lose some and win some privilege cases. On the negative side, the *Alton (Illinois) Telegram*[69] was denied a privilege to prevent revealing information about the identity of a writer of a letter-to-the-editor; a New Hampshire court[70] reached a similar conclusion. On a more positive note, an Oregon court[71] found that privilege extended to those invited to comment on the news but who did so anonymously and a Montana court[72] decided similarly in a parallel case in that state.

These last two cases point to a major privilege issue likely to be the source of much litigation in years to come. With the advent of news organizations publishing on Web sites that solicit and publish opinions of viewers often unedited, the issue focuses on the legal ability to protect the sources of this commentary, who have posted anonymously, from disclosure to those who believe the comments have libeled them or invaded their privacy or some other similar grievance.

Because the Communications Decency Act (discussed in earlier chapters) generally protects the sponsor of the Web site, the original poster of the message may be the only target available to outraged potential plaintiffs. One may imagine their increased anger upon finding that the Web site is attempting to exert a privilege to protect the anonymity of the sources of the comments, which in effect bars the potential plaintiffs from bringing suit at all. To date, courts in different states have employed a range of different rationales in determining if potential plaintiffs will be able to discover the sources of anonymous comments. How other lower courts and, perhaps, ultimately the Supreme Court will deal with this issue will be interesting to observe, particularly for public relations professionals looking to engage in reputation management for an organization damaged by such anonymous speakers.

Another major emerging issue in journalist privilege is the potential passage of a federal shield law. To date, more than half of the states have adopted some form of shield law, although these laws vary considerably in terms of who and what is protected and when such protection is provided. It appears that such shield laws will withstand challenge unless they interfere with the constitutional right of individuals accused of crimes to obtain evidence to defend themselves.

As this is written, however, there is as yet no federal shield law. The bill creating such a privilege at the federal level is under discussion in both the House and the Senate. President Obama has promised to sign such a bill into law should it make its way out of the Congress. Perhaps he will have done so by the time you are reading this chapter. Advertising and public relations professionals, unfortunately, largely have been on the sidelines in the fight to pass a federal shield law. If such efforts are still needed when you read this, the authors strongly urge support in the form of friend-of-court briefs and public messages explaining the purposes of, and the need for, such a law.

Other major issues of recent contention in claims-of-privilege cases have involved (a) subpoenas directed at broadcast "outtakes"; (b) how thorough a court or other government entity must be in exhausting all other avenues to obtain information before establishing that the reporter is the sole source; and (c) the remedies legally available to a court if privilege is asserted by the journalist in a libel trial to protect the source of the allegedly libelous statements.

Public relations professionals dealing with the news media in situations in which they request that the information provided is on a confidential basis should be aware that despite a pledge of secrecy, a journalist may be placed under tremendous pressure to reveal the source of his or her information. The prudent public relations professional, therefore, would be well advised not to provide confidential information to the news media if such provision is conditioned on a promise that the journalist will not reveal the source.

# Appendix A: The Constitution of the United States

September 17, 1787

We the People of the United States, in Order to form a more perfect Union, establish Justice, insure domestic Tranquility, provide for the common defense, promote the general Welfare, and secure the Blessings of Liberty to ourselves and our Posterity, do ordain and establish this Constitution for the United States of America.

## Article One

**Section 1.** All legislative Powers herein granted shall be vested in a Congress of the United States, which shall consist of a Senate and House of Representatives.

**Section 2.** The House of Representatives shall be composed of Members chosen every second Year by the People of the several States, and the Electors in each State shall have the Qualifications requisite for Electors of the most numerous Branch of the State Legislature.

No Person shall be a Representative who shall not have attained to the Age of twenty five Years, and been seven Years a Citizen of the United States, and who shall not, when elected, be an Inhabitant of that State in which he shall be chosen.

Representatives and direct Taxes shall be apportioned among the several States which may be included within this Union, according to their respective Numbers, which shall be determined by adding to the whole Number of free Persons, including those bound to Service for a Term of Years, and excluding Indians not taxed, three fifths of all other Persons. The actual Enumeration shall be made within three Years after the first Meeting of the Congress of the United States, and within every subsequent Term of ten Years, in such Manner as they shall by Law direct. The Number of Representatives shall not exceed one for every thirty Thousand, but each State shall have at Least one Representative; and until such enumeration shall be made, the State of New Hampshire shall be entitled to choose three, Massachusetts eight, Rhode Island and Providence Plantations one, Connecticut five, New York six, New Jersey four, Pennsylvania eight, Delaware one, Maryland six, Virginia ten, North Carolina five, South Carolina five, and Georgia three.

When vacancies happen in the Representation from any State, the Executive Authority thereof shall issue Writs of Election to fill such Vacancies.

The House of Representatives shall choose their Speaker and other Officers; and shall have the sole Power of Impeachment.

**Section 3.** The Senate of the United States shall be composed of two Senators from each State, chosen by the Legislature thereof for six Years; and each Senator shall have one Vote.

Immediately after they shall be assembled in Consequence of the first Election, they shall be divided as equally as may be into three Classes. The Seats of the Senators of the first Class shall be vacated at the Expiration of the second Year, of the second Class at the Expiration of the fourth Year, and of the third Class at the Expiration of the sixth Year, so that one third may be chosen every second Year; and if Vacancies happen by Resignation, or otherwise, during the Recess of the Legislature of any State, the Executive thereof may make temporary Appointments until the next Meeting of the Legislature, which shall then fill such Vacancies.

No Person shall be a Senator who shall not have attained to the Age of thirty Years, and been nine Years a Citizen of the United States, and who shall not, when elected, be an Inhabitant of that State for which he shall be chosen.

The Vice President of the United States shall be President of the Senate, but shall have no Vote, unless they be equally divided.

The Senate shall choose their other Officers, and also a President pro tempore, in the Absence of the Vice President, or when he shall exercise the Office of President of the United States.

The Senate shall have the sole Power to try all Impeachments. When sitting for that Purpose, they shall be on Oath or Affirmation. When the President of the United States is tried, the Chief Justice shall preside: And no Person shall be convicted without the Concurrence of two thirds of the Members present.

Judgment in Cases of Impeachment shall not extend further than to removal from Office, and disqualification to hold and enjoy any Office of honor, Trust or Profit under the United States: but the Party convicted shall nevertheless be liable and subject to Indictment, Trial, Judgment and Punishment, according to Law.

**Section 4.** The Times, Places and Manner of holding Elections for Senators and Representatives, shall be prescribed in each State by the Legislature thereof; but the Congress may at any time by Law make or alter such Regulations, except as to the Places of choosing Senators.

The Congress shall assemble at least once in every Year, and such Meeting shall be on the first Monday in December, unless they shall by Law appoint a different Day.

**Section 5.** Each House shall be the Judge of the Elections, Returns and Qualifications of its own Members, and a Majority of each shall constitute a Quorum to do Business; but a smaller Number may adjourn from day to day, and may be authorized to compel the Attendance of absent Members, in such Manner, and under such Penalties as each House may provide.

Each House may determine the Rules of its Proceedings, punish its Members for disorderly Behavior, and, with the Concurrence of two thirds, expel a Member.

Each House shall keep a Journal of its Proceedings, and from time to time publish the same, excepting such Parts as may in their Judgment require Secrecy; and the Yeas and Nays of the Members of either House on any question shall, at the Desire of one fifth of those Present, be entered on the Journal.

Neither House, during the Session of Congress, shall, without the Consent of the other, adjourn for more than three days, nor to any other Place than that in which the two Houses shall be sitting.

**Section 6.** The Senators and Representatives shall receive a Compensation for their Services, to be ascertained by Law, and paid out of the Treasury of the United States. They shall in all Cases, except Treason, Felony and Breach of the Peace, be privileged from Arrest during their Attendance at the Session of their respective Houses, and in going to and returning from the same; and for any Speech or Debate in either House, they shall not be questioned in any other Place.

No Senator or Representative shall, during the Time for which he was elected, be appointed to any civil Office under the Authority of the United States, which shall have been created, or the Emoluments whereof shall have been increased during such time; and no Person holding any Office under the United States, shall be a Member of either House during his Continuance in Office.

**Section 7.** All Bills for raising Revenue shall originate in the House of Representatives; but the Senate may propose or concur with Amendments as on other Bills.

Every Bill which shall have passed the House of Representatives and the Senate, shall, before it become a Law, be presented to the President of the United States: If he approve he shall sign it, but if not he shall return it, with his Objections to that House in which it shall have originated, who shall enter the Objections at large on their Journal, and proceed to reconsider it. If after such Reconsideration two thirds of that House shall agree to pass the Bill, it shall be sent, together with the Objections, to the other House, by which it shall likewise be reconsidered, and if approved by two thirds of that House, it shall become a Law. But in all such Cases the Votes of both Houses shall be determined by yeas and Nays, and the Names of the Persons voting for and against the Bill shall be entered on the Journal of each House respectively. If any Bill shall not be returned by the President within ten Days (Sundays excepted) after it shall have been presented to him, the Same shall be a Law, in like Manner as if he had signed it, unless the Congress by their Adjournment prevent its Return, in which Case it shall not be a Law.

Every Order, Resolution, or Vote to which the Concurrence of the Senate and House of Representatives may be necessary (except on a question of Adjournment) shall be presented to the President of the United States; and before the Same shall take Effect, shall be approved by him, or being disapproved by him, shall be repassed by two thirds of the Senate and House of Representatives, according to the Rules and Limitations prescribed in the Case of a Bill.

**Section 8.** The Congress shall have Power To lay and collect Taxes, Duties, Imposts and Excises, to pay the Debts and provide for the common Defense and general Welfare of the United States; but all Duties, Imposts and Excises shall be uniform throughout the United States;

To borrow Money on the credit of the United States;

To regulate Commerce with foreign Nations, and among the several States, and with the Indian Tribes;

To establish an uniform Rule of Naturalization, and uniform Laws on the subject of Bankruptcies throughout the United States;

To coin Money, regulate the Value thereof, and of foreign Coin, and fix the Standard of Weights and Measures;

To provide for the Punishment of counterfeiting the Securities and current Coin of the United States;

To establish Post Offices and post Roads;

To promote the Progress of Science and useful Arts, by securing for limited Times to Authors and Inventors the exclusive Right to their respective Writings and Discoveries;

To constitute Tribunals inferior to the Supreme Court;

To define and punish Piracies and Felonies committed on the high Seas, and Offences against the Law of Nations;

To declare War, grant Letters of Marque and Reprisal, and make Rules concerning Captures on Land and Water;

To raise and support Armies, but no Appropriation of Money to that Use shall be for a longer Term than two Years;

To provide and maintain a Navy;

To make Rules for the Government and Regulation of the land and naval Forces;

To provide for calling forth the Militia to execute the Laws of the Union, suppress Insurrections and repel Invasions;

To provide for organizing, arming, and disciplining, the Militia, and for governing such Part of them as may be employed in the Service of the United States, reserving to the States respectively, the Appointment of the Officers, and the Authority of training the Militia according to the discipline prescribed by Congress;

To exercise exclusive Legislation in all Cases whatsoever, over such District (not exceeding ten Miles square) as may, by Cession of particular States, and the Acceptance of Congress, become the Seat of the Government of the United States, and to exercise like Authority over all Places purchased by the Consent of the Legislature of the State in which the Same shall be, for the Erection of Forts, Magazines, Arsenals, dock-Yards, and other needful Buildings; And

To make all Laws which shall be necessary and proper for carrying into Execution the foregoing Powers, and all other Powers vested by this Constitution in the Government of the United States, or in any Department or Officer thereof.

**Section 9.** The Migration or Importation of such Persons as any of the States now existing shall think proper to admit, shall not be prohibited by the Congress prior to the Year one thousand eight hundred and eight, but a Tax or duty may be imposed on such Importation, not exceeding ten dollars for each Person.

Privilege of the Writ of Habeas Corpus shall not be suspended, unless when in Cases of Rebellion or Invasion the public Safety may require it.

No Bill of Attainder or ex post facto Law shall be passed.

No Capitation, or other direct, Tax shall be laid, unless in Proportion to the Census or enumeration herein before directed to be taken.

No Tax or Duty shall be laid on Articles exported from any State.

No Preference shall be given by any Regulation of Commerce or Revenue to the Ports of one State over those of another; nor shall Vessels bound to, or from, one State, be obliged to enter, clear, or pay Duties in another.

No Money shall be drawn from the Treasury, but in Consequence of Appropriations made by Law; and a regular Statement and Account of the Receipts and Expenditures of all public Money shall be published from time to time.

No Title of Nobility shall be granted by the United States: And no Person holding any Office of Profit or Trust under them, shall, without the Consent of the Congress, accept of any present, Emolument, Office, or Title, of any kind whatever, from any King, Prince, or foreign State.

**Section 10.** No State shall enter into any Treaty, Alliance, or Confederation; grant Letters of Marque and Reprisal; coin Money; emit Bills of Credit; make any Thing but gold and silver Coin a Tender in Payment of Debts; pass any Bill of Attainder, ex post facto Law, or Law impairing the Obligation of Contracts, or grant any Title of Nobility.

No State shall, without the Consent of the Congress, lay any Imposts or Duties on Imports or Exports, except what may be absolutely necessary for executing it's inspection Laws: and the net Produce of all Duties and Imposts, laid by any State on Imports or Exports, shall be for the Use of the Treasury of the United States; and all such Laws shall be subject to the Revision and Control of the Congress.

No State shall, without the Consent of Congress, lay any Duty of Tonnage, keep Troops, or Ships of War in time of Peace, enter into any Agreement or Compact with another State, or with a foreign Power, or engage in War, unless actually invaded, or in such imminent Danger as will not admit of delay.

## Article Two

**Section 1.** The executive Power shall be vested in a President of the United States of America. He shall hold his Office during the Term of four Years, and, together with the Vice President, chosen for the same Term, be elected, as follows:

Each State shall appoint, in such Manner as the Legislature thereof may direct, a Number of Electors, equal to the whole Number of Senators and Representatives to which the State may be entitled in the Congress: but no Senator or Representative, or Person holding an Office of Trust or Profit under the United States, shall be appointed an Elector.

The Electors shall meet in their respective States, and vote by Ballot for two Persons, of whom one at least shall not be an Inhabitant of the same State with themselves. And they shall make a List of all the Persons voted for, and of the Number of Votes for each; which List they shall sign and certify, and transmit sealed to the Seat of the Government of the United States, directed to the President of the Senate. The President of the Senate shall, in the Presence of the Senate and House of Representatives, open all the Certificates, and the Votes shall then be counted. The Person having the greatest Number of Votes shall be the President, if such Number be a Majority of the whole Number of Electors appointed; and if there be more than one who have such Majority, and have an equal Number of Votes, then the House of Representatives shall immediately choose by Ballot one of them for President; and if no Person have a Majority, then from the five highest on the List the said House shall in like Manner choose the President. But in choosing the President, the Votes shall be taken by States, the Representation from each State having one Vote; A quorum for this purpose shall consist of a Member or Members from two thirds of the States, and a Majority of all the States shall be necessary to a Choice. In every Case, after the Choice of the President, the Person having the greatest Number of Votes of the Electors shall be the Vice President. But if there should remain two or more who have equal Votes, the Senate shall choose from them by Ballot the Vice President.

The Congress may determine the Time of choosing the Electors, and the Day on which they shall give their Votes; which Day shall be the same throughout the United States.

No Person except a natural born Citizen, or a Citizen of the United States, at the time of the Adoption of this Constitution, shall be eligible to the Office of President; neither shall any Person be eligible to that Office who shall not have attained to the Age of thirty five Years, and been fourteen Years a Resident within the United States.

In Case of the Removal of the President from Office, or of his Death, Resignation, or Inability to discharge the Powers and Duties of the said Office, the Same shall devolve on the Vice President, and the Congress may by Law provide for the Case of Removal, Death, Resignation or Inability, both of the President and Vice President, declaring what Officer shall then act as President, and such Officer shall act accordingly, until the Disability be removed, or a President shall be elected.

The President shall, at stated Times, receive for his Services, a Compensation, which shall neither be increased nor diminished during the Period for which he shall have been elected, and he shall not receive within that Period any other Emolument from the United States, or any of them.

Before he enter on the Execution of his Office, he shall take the following Oath or Affirmation: "I do solemnly swear (or affirm) that I will faithfully execute the Office of President of the United States, and will to the best of my Ability, preserve, protect and defend the Constitution of the United States."

**Section 2.** The President shall be Commander in Chief of the Army and Navy of the United States, and of the Militia of the several States, when called into the actual Service of the United States; he may require the Opinion, in writing, of the principal Officer in each of the executive Departments, upon any Subject relating to the Duties of their respective Offices, and he shall have Power to grant Reprieves and Pardons for Offences against the United States, except in Cases of Impeachment.

He shall have Power, by and with the Advice and Consent of the Senate, to make Treaties, provided two thirds of the Senators present concur; and he shall nominate, and by and with the Advice and Consent of the Senate, shall appoint Ambassadors, other public Ministers and Consuls, Judges of the supreme Court, and all other Officers of the United States, whose Appointments are not herein otherwise provided for, and which shall be established by Law: but the Congress may by Law vest the Appointment of such inferior Officers, as they think proper, in the President alone, in the Courts of Law, or in the Heads of Departments.

The President shall have Power to fill up all Vacancies that may happen during the Recess of the Senate, by granting Commissions which shall expire at the End of their next Session.

**Section 3.** He shall from time to time give to the Congress Information of the State of the Union, and recommend to their Consideration such Measures as he shall judge necessary and expedient; he may, on extraordinary Occasions, convene both Houses, or either of them, and in Case of Disagreement between them, with Respect to the Time of Adjournment, he may adjourn them to such Time as he shall think proper; he shall receive Ambassadors and other public Ministers; he shall take Care that the Laws be faithfully executed, and shall Commission all the Officers of the United States.

**Section 4.** The President, Vice President and all civil Officers of the United States, shall be removed from Office on Impeachment for, and Conviction of, Treason, Bribery, or other high Crimes and Misdemeanors.

## Article Three

**Section 1.** The judicial Power of the United States shall be vested in one Supreme Court, and in such inferior Courts as the Congress may from time to time ordain and establish. The Judges, both of the supreme and inferior Courts, shall hold their Offices during good Behavior, and shall, at stated Times, receive for their Services a Compensation, which shall not be diminished during their Continuance in Office.

**Section 2.** The judicial Power shall extend to all Cases, in Law and Equity, arising under this Constitution, the Laws of the United States, and Treaties made, or which shall be made, under their Authority; to all Cases affecting Ambassadors, other public Ministers and Consuls; to all Cases of admiralty and maritime Jurisdiction; to Controversies to which the United States shall be a Party; to Controversies between two or more States; between a State and Citizens of another State, between Citizens of different States, between Citizens of the same State claiming Lands under Grants of different States, and between a State, or the Citizens thereof, and foreign States, Citizens or Subjects.

In all Cases affecting Ambassadors, other public Ministers and Consuls, and those in which a State shall be Party, the Supreme Court shall have original Jurisdiction. In all the other Cases before mentioned, the Supreme Court shall have appellate Jurisdiction, both as to Law and Fact, with such Exceptions, and under such Regulations as the Congress shall make.

The Trial of all Crimes, except in Cases of Impeachment, shall be by Jury; and such Trial shall be held in the State where the said Crimes shall have been committed; but when not committed within any State, the Trial shall be at such Place or Places as the Congress may by Law have directed.

**Section 3.** Treason against the United States, shall consist only in levying War against them, or in adhering to their Enemies, giving them Aid and Comfort. No Person shall be convicted of Treason unless on the Testimony of two Witnesses to the same overt Act, or on Confession in open Court.

The Congress shall have Power to declare the Punishment of Treason, but no Attainder of Treason shall work Corruption of Blood, or Forfeiture except during the Life of the Person attainted.

## Article Four

**Section 1.** Full Faith and Credit shall be given in each State to the public Acts, Records, and judicial Proceedings of every other State. And the Congress may by general Laws prescribe the Manner in which such Acts, Records and Proceedings shall be proved, and the Effect thereof.

**Section 2.** The Citizens of each State shall be entitled to all Privileges and Immunities of Citizens in the several States.

A Person charged in any State with Treason, Felony, or other Crime, who shall flee from Justice, and be found in another State, shall on Demand of the executive Authority of the State from which he fled, be delivered up, to be removed to the State having Jurisdiction of the Crime.

No Person held to Service or Labor in one State, under the Laws thereof, escaping into another, shall, in Consequence of any Law or Regulation therein, be discharged from such Service or Labor, but shall be delivered up on Claim of the Party to whom such Service or Labor may be due.

**Section 3.** New States may be admitted by the Congress into this Union; but no new State shall be formed or erected within the Jurisdiction of any other State; nor any State be formed by the Junction of two or more States, or Parts of States, without the Consent of the Legislatures of the States concerned as well as of the Congress.

The Congress shall have Power to dispose of and make all needful Rules and Regulations respecting the Territory or other Property belonging to the United States; and nothing in this Constitution shall be so construed as to Prejudice any Claims of the United States, or of any particular State.

**Section 4.** The United States shall guarantee to every State in this Union a Republican Form of Government, and shall protect each of them against

Invasion; and on Application of the Legislature, or of the Executive (when the Legislature cannot be convened), against domestic Violence.

## Article Five

The Congress, whenever two thirds of both Houses shall deem it necessary, shall propose Amendments to this Constitution, or, on the Application of the Legislatures of two thirds of the several States, shall call a Convention for proposing Amendments, which, in either Case, shall be valid to all Intents and Purposes, as Part of this Constitution, when ratified by the Legislatures of three fourths of the several States, or by Conventions in three fourths thereof, as the one or the other Mode of Ratification may be proposed by the Congress; Provided that no Amendment which may be made prior to the Year One thousand eight hundred and eight shall in any Manner affect the first and fourth Clauses in the Ninth Section of the first Article; and that no State, without its Consent, shall be deprived of its equal Suffrage in the Senate.

## Article Six

All Debts contracted and Engagements entered into, before the Adoption of this Constitution, shall be as valid against the United States under this Constitution, as under the Confederation.

This Constitution, and the Laws of the United States which shall be made in Pursuance thereof; and all Treaties made, or which shall be made, under the Authority of the United States, shall be the supreme Law of the Land; and the Judges in every State shall be bound thereby, any Thing in the Constitution or Laws of any State to the Contrary notwithstanding.

The Senators and Representatives before mentioned, and the Members of the several State Legislatures, and all executive and judicial Officers, both of the United States and of the several States, shall be bound by Oath or Affirmation, to support this Constitution; but no religious Test shall ever be required as a Qualification to any Office or public Trust under the United States.

## Article Seven

The Ratification of the Conventions of nine States, shall be sufficient for the Establishment of this Constitution between the States so ratifying the same.

Done in Convention by the Unanimous Consent of the States present the Seventeenth Day of September in the Year of our Lord one thousand seven hundred and Eighty seven and of the Independence of the United States of America the Twelfth In witness whereof

We have hereunto subscribed our Names,
GEO. WASHINGTON—President and deputy from Virginia

**New Hampshire**
John Langdon
Nicholas Gilman

**Massachusetts**
Nathaniel Gorham
Rufus King

**Connecticut**
Wm Saml Johnson
Roger Sherman

**New York**
Alexander Hamilton

**New Jersey**
Wil. Livingston
David Brearley
Wm Patterson
Jona. Dayton

**Pennsylvania**
B Franklin
Thomas Mifflin
Robt Morris
Geo Clymer
Thos Fitzsimons
Jared Ingersoll
James Wilson
Gouv. Morris

**Delaware**
Geo Read
Gunning Bedford Jun.
John Dickinson
Richard Bassett
Jaco. Broom

**Maryland**
James McHenry
Dan of St Tho Jenifer
Danl Carroll

**Virginia**
John Blair
James Madison Jr.

**North Carolina**
Wm Blount
Richd Dobbs Spaight
Hu Williamson

**South Carolina**
J. Rutledge
Charles Cotesworth Pinckney
Charles Pinckney
Pierce Butler

**Georgia**
William Few
Abr Baldwin

*Attest*
William Jackson

## Amendments to the Constitution of the United States

*Note: The first ten Amendments (the Bill of Rights) were ratified effective December 15, 1791.*

### Amendment One

Congress shall make no law respecting an establishment of religion, or prohibiting the free exercise thereof; or abridging the freedom of speech, or of the press; or the right of the people peaceably to assemble, and to petition the Government for a redress of grievances.

### Amendment Two

A well regulated Militia, being necessary to the security of a free State, the right of the people to keep and bear Arms, shall not be infringed.

### Amendment Three

No Soldier shall, in time of peace be quartered in any house, without the consent of the Owner, nor in time of war, but in a manner to be prescribed by law.

### Amendment Four

The right of the people to be secure in their persons, houses, papers, and effects, against unreasonable searches and seizures, shall not be violated, and no Warrants shall issue, but upon probable cause, supported by Oath or affirmation, and particularly describing the place to be searched, and the persons or things to be seized.

### Amendment Five

No person shall be held to answer for a capital, or otherwise infamous crime, unless on a presentment or indictment of a Grand Jury, except in cases arising in the land or naval forces, or in the Militia, when in actual service in time of War or public danger; nor shall any person be subject for the same offence to be twice put in jeopardy of life or limb; nor shall be compelled in any criminal case to be a witness against himself, nor be deprived of life, liberty, or property, without due process of law; nor shall private property be taken for public use, without just compensation.

### Amendment Six

In all criminal prosecutions, the accused shall enjoy the right to a speedy and public trial, by an impartial jury of the State and district wherein the crime shall have been committed, which district shall have been previously ascertained by law, and to be informed of the nature and cause of the accusation; to be confronted with the witnesses against him; to have compulsory process for obtaining witnesses in his favor, and to have the Assistance of Counsel for his defense.

### Amendment Seven

In Suits at common law, where the value in controversy shall exceed twenty dollars, the right of trial by jury shall be preserved, and no fact tried by a jury, shall be otherwise re-examined in any Court of the United States, than according to the rules of the common law.

### Amendment Eight

Excessive bail shall not be required, nor excessive fines imposed, nor cruel and unusual punishments inflicted.

### Amendment Nine

The enumeration in the Constitution, of certain rights, shall not be construed to deny or disparage others retained by the people.

### Amendment Ten

The powers not delegated to the United States by the Constitution, nor prohibited by it to the States, are reserved to the States respectively, or to the people.

### Amendment Eleven

February 7, 1795
*Note: Article III, section 2, of the Constitution was modified by Amendment 11.*

The Judicial power of the United States shall not be construed to extend to any suit in law or equity, commenced or prosecuted against one of the United States by Citizens of another State, or by Citizens or Subjects of any Foreign State.

### Amendment Twelve

June 15, 1804
*Note: A portion of Article II, section 1 of the Constitution was superseded by Amendment 12.*

The Electors shall meet in their respective states and vote by ballot for President and Vice-President, one of whom, at least, shall not be an inhabitant of the same state with themselves; they shall name in their ballots the person voted for as President, and in distinct ballots the person voted for as Vice-President, and they shall make distinct lists of all persons voted for as President, and of all persons voted for as Vice-President, and of the number of votes for each, which lists they shall sign and certify, and transmit sealed to the seat of the government of the United States, directed to the President of the Senate; the President of the Senate shall, in the presence of the Senate and House of Representatives, open all the certificates and the votes shall then be counted; The person having the greatest number of votes for President, shall be the President, if such number be a majority of the whole number of Electors appointed; and if no person have such majority, then from the persons having the highest numbers not exceeding three on the list of those voted for as President, the House of Representatives shall choose immediately, by ballot, the President. But in choosing the President, the votes shall be taken by states, the representation from each state having one vote; a quorum for this purpose shall consist of a member or members from two-thirds of the states, and a majority of all the states shall be necessary to a choice. [And if the House of Representatives shall not choose a President whenever the right of choice shall devolve upon them, before the fourth day of March next following, then the Vice-President shall act as President, as in case of the death or other constitutional disability of the President.]* The person having the greatest number of votes as Vice-President, shall be the Vice-President, if such number be a majority of the whole number of Electors appointed, and if no person have a majority, then from the two highest numbers on the list, the Senate shall choose the Vice-President; a quorum for the purpose shall consist of two-thirds of the whole number of Senators, and a majority of the whole number shall be necessary to a choice. But no person constitutionally ineligible to the office of President shall be eligible to that of Vice-President of the United States.

*Superseded by section 3 of Amendment 20.

### Amendment Thirteen

December 6, 1865
*Note: A portion of Article IV, section 2, of the Constitution was superseded by Amendment 13.*

**Section 1.** Neither slavery nor involuntary servitude, except as a punishment for crime whereof the party shall have been duly convicted, shall exist within the United States, or any place subject to their jurisdiction.

**Section 2.** Congress shall have power to enforce this article by appropriate legislation.

### Amendment Fourteen

July 9, 1868
*Note: Article I, section 2, of the Constitution was modified by section 2 of Amendment 14.*

**Section 1.** All persons born or naturalized in the United States, and subject to the jurisdiction thereof, are citizens of the United States and of the State wherein they reside. No State shall make or enforce any law which shall abridge the privileges or immunities of citizens of the United States; nor shall any State deprive any person of life, liberty, or property, without due process of law; nor deny to any person within its jurisdiction the equal protection of the laws.

**Section 2.** Representatives shall be apportioned among the several States according to their respective numbers, counting the whole number of persons in each State, excluding Indians not taxed. But when the right to vote at any election for the choice of electors for President and Vice-President of the United States, Representatives in Congress, the Executive and Judicial officers of a State, or the members of the Legislature thereof, is denied to any of the male inhabitants of such State, being twenty-one years of age,* and citizens of the United States, or in any way abridged, except for participation in rebellion, or other crime, the basis of representation therein shall be reduced in the proportion which the number of such male citizens shall bear to the whole number of male citizens twenty-one years of age in such State.

Section 3. No person shall be a Senator or Representative in Congress, or elector of President and Vice-President, or hold any office, civil or military, under the United States, or under any State, who, having previously taken an oath, as a member of Congress, or as an officer of the United States, or as a member of any State legislature, or as an executive or judicial officer of any State, to support the Constitution of the United States, shall have engaged in insurrection or rebellion against the same, or given aid or comfort to the enemies thereof. But Congress may by a vote of two-thirds of each House, remove such disability.

Section 4. The validity of the public debt of the United States, authorized by law, including debts incurred for payment of pensions and bounties for services in suppressing insurrection or rebellion, shall not be questioned. But neither the United States nor any State shall assume or pay any debt or obligation incurred in aid of insurrection or rebellion against the United States, or any claim for the loss or emancipation of any slave; but all such debts, obligations and claims shall be held illegal and void.

Section 5. The Congress shall have the power to enforce, by appropriate legislation, the provisions of this article.

*Changed by section 1 of Amendment 26.

### Amendment Fifteen

February 3, 1870

Section 1. The right of citizens of the United States to vote shall not be denied or abridged by the United States or by any State on account of race, color, or previous condition of servitude.

Section 2. The Congress shall have the power to enforce this article by appropriate legislation.

### Amendment Sixteen

February 3, 1913
Note: Article I, section 9, of the Constitution was modified by Amendment 16.

The Congress shall have power to lay and collect taxes on incomes, from whatever source derived, without apportionment among the several States, and without regard to any census or enumeration.

## Amendment Seventeen

April 8, 1913
*Note: Article I, section 3, of the Constitution was modified by Amendment 17.*

The Senate of the United States shall be composed of two Senators from each State, elected by the people thereof, for six years; and each Senator shall have one vote. The electors in each State shall have the qualifications requisite for electors of the most numerous branch of the State legislatures.

When vacancies happen in the representation of any State in the Senate, the executive authority of such State shall issue writs of election to fill such vacancies: Provided, That the legislature of any State may empower the executive thereof to make temporary appointments until the people fill the vacancies by election as the legislature may direct.

This amendment shall not be so construed as to affect the election or term of any Senator chosen before it becomes valid as part of the Constitution.

## Amendment Eighteen

January 16, 1919
*Note: Amendment 18 was repealed by Amendment 21.*

**Section 1.** After one year from the ratification of this article the manufacture, sale, or transportation of intoxicating liquors within, the importation thereof into, or the exportation thereof from the United States and all territory subject to the jurisdiction thereof for beverage purposes is hereby prohibited.

**Section 2.** The Congress and the several States shall have concurrent power to enforce this article by appropriate legislation.

**Section 3.** This article shall be inoperative unless it shall have been ratified as an amendment to the Constitution by the legislatures of the several States, as provided in the Constitution, within seven years from the date of the submission hereof to the States by the Congress.

## Amendment Nineteen

August 18, 1920
The right of citizens of the United States to vote shall not be denied or abridged by the United States or by any State on account of sex.

Congress shall have power to enforce this article by appropriate legislation.

### Amendment Twenty

January 23, 1933
*Note: Article I, section 4, of the Constitution was modified by section 2 of this Amendment. In addition, a portion of Amendment 12 was superseded by section 3.*

**Section 1.** The terms of the President and the Vice President shall end at noon on the 20th day of January, and the terms of Senators and Representatives at noon on the 3d day of January, of the years in which such terms would have ended if this article had not been ratified; and the terms of their successors shall then begin.

**Section 2.** The Congress shall assemble at least once in every year, and such meeting shall begin at noon on the 3d day of January, unless they shall by law appoint a different day.

**Section 3.** If, at the time fixed for the beginning of the term of the President, the President elect shall have died, the Vice President elect shall become President. If a President shall not have been chosen before the time fixed for the beginning of his term, or if the President elect shall have failed to qualify, then the Vice President elect shall act as President until a President shall have qualified; and the Congress may by law provide for the case wherein neither a President elect nor a Vice President shall have qualified, declaring who shall then act as President, or the manner in which one who is to act shall be selected, and such person shall act accordingly until a President or Vice President shall have qualified.

**Section 4.** The Congress may by law provide for the case of the death of any of the persons from whom the House of Representatives may choose a President whenever the right of choice shall have devolved upon them, and for the case of the death of any of the persons from whom the Senate may choose a Vice President whenever the right of choice shall have devolved upon them.

**Section 5.** Sections 1 and 2 shall take effect on the 15th day of October following the ratification of this article.

**Section 6.** This article shall be inoperative unless it shall have been ratified as an amendment to the Constitution by the legislatures of three-fourths of the several States within seven years from the date of its submission.

## Amendment Twenty-One

December 5, 1933

Section 1. The eighteenth article of amendment to the Constitution of the United States is hereby repealed.

Section 2. The transportation or importation into any State, Territory, or Possession of the United States for delivery or use therein of intoxicating liquors, in violation of the laws thereof, is hereby prohibited.

Section 3. This article shall be inoperative unless it shall have been ratified as an amendment to the Constitution by conventions in the several States, as provided in the Constitution, within seven years from the date of the submission hereof to the States by the Congress.

## Amendment Twenty-Two

February 27, 1951

Section 1. No person shall be elected to the office of the President more than twice, and no person who has held the office of President, or acted as President, for more than two years of a term to which some other person was elected President shall be elected to the office of President more than once. But this Article shall not apply to any person holding the office of President when this Article was proposed by Congress, and shall not prevent any person who may be holding the office of President, or acting as President, during the term within which this Article becomes operative from holding the office of President or acting as President during the remainder of such term.

Section 2. This article shall be inoperative unless it shall have been ratified as an amendment to the Constitution by the legislatures of three-fourths of the several States within seven years from the date of its submission to the States by the Congress.

## Amendment Twenty-Three

March 29, 1961

Section 1. The District constituting the seat of Government of the United States shall appoint in such manner as Congress may direct:
    A number of electors of President and Vice President equal to the whole number of Senators and Representatives in Congress to which the District would be entitled if it were a State, but in no event more than the least

populous State; they shall be in addition to those appointed by the States, but they shall be considered, for the purposes of the election of President and Vice President, to be electors appointed by a State; and they shall meet in the District and perform such duties as provided by the twelfth article of amendment.

**Section 2.** The Congress shall have power to enforce this article by appropriate legislation.

## Amendment Twenty-Four

January 23, 1964

**Section 1.** The right of citizens of the United States to vote in any primary or other election for President or Vice President, for electors for President or Vice President, or for Senator or Representative in Congress, shall not be denied or abridged by the United States or any State by reason of failure to pay poll tax or other tax.

**Section 2.** The Congress shall have power to enforce this article by appropriate legislation.

## Amendment Twenty-Five

February 10, 1967
*Note: Article II, section 1, of the Constitution was affected by the 25th amendment.*

**Section 1.** In case of the removal of the President from office or of his death or resignation, the Vice President shall become President.

**Section 2.** Whenever there is a vacancy in the office of the Vice President, the President shall nominate a Vice President who shall take office upon confirmation by a majority vote of both Houses of Congress.

**Section 3.** Whenever the President transmits to the President pro tempore of the Senate and the Speaker of the House of Representatives his written declaration that he is unable to discharge the powers and duties of his office, and until he transmits to them a written declaration to the contrary, such powers and duties shall be discharged by the Vice President as Acting President.

**Section 4.** Whenever the Vice President and a majority of either the principal officers of the executive departments or of such other body as Congress may by law provide, transmit to the President pro tempore of the Senate and the Speaker of the House of Representatives their written declaration that the President is unable to discharge the powers and duties of his office, the Vice President shall immediately assume the powers and duties of the office as Acting President.

Thereafter, when the President transmits to the President pro tempore of the Senate and the Speaker of the House of Representatives his written declaration that no inability exists, he shall resume the powers and duties of his office unless the Vice President and a majority of either the principal officers of the executive department or of such other body as Congress may by law provide, transmit within four days to the President pro tempore of the Senate and the Speaker of the House of Representatives their written declaration that the President is unable to discharge the powers and duties of his office. Thereupon Congress shall decide the issue, assembling within forty-eight hours for that purpose if not in session. If the Congress, within twenty-one days after receipt of the latter written declaration, or, if Congress is not in session, within twenty-one days after Congress is required to assemble, determines by two-thirds vote of both Houses that the President is unable to discharge the powers and duties of his office, the Vice President shall continue to discharge the same as Acting President; otherwise, the President shall resume the powers and duties of his office.

## Amendment Twenty-Six

July 1, 1971
*Note: Amendment 14, section 2, of the Constitution was modified by section 1 of the 26th amendment.*

**Section 1.** The right of citizens of the United States, who are eighteen years of age or older, to vote shall not be denied or abridged by the United States or by any State on account of age.

**Section 2.** The Congress shall have power to enforce this article by appropriate legislation.

## Amendment Twenty-Seven

May 7, 1992
No law, varying the compensation for the services of the Senators and Representatives, shall take effect, until an election of representatives shall have intervened.

# Appendix B: The United States Court System

# The United States Court System

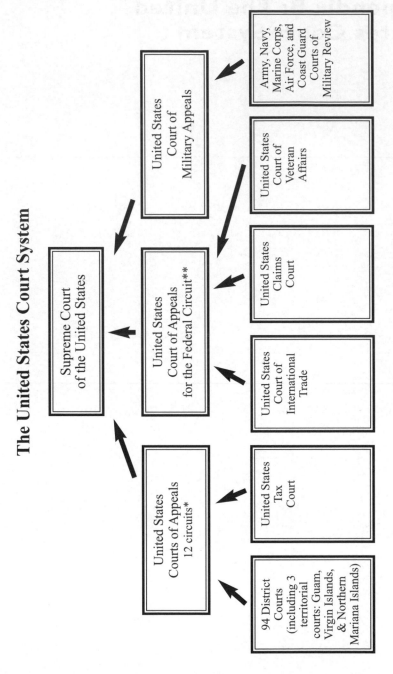

* The 12 original Courts of Appeals also review cases from a number of federal agencies.

** The Court of Appeals for the Federal Circuit also receives cases from the International Trade Commission, the Merit Systems Protection Board, the Patent and Trademark Office, and the Board of Contract Appeals.

# Appendix C: Professional Codes of Ethics

# Appendix C.1: Public Relations Society of America (PRSA) Code of Ethics

http://www.prsa.org/AboutPRSA/Ethics/CodeEnglish/

## Preamble

Public Relations Society of America Member Code of Ethics 2000
- Professional Values
- Principles of Conduct
- Commitment and Compliance

This Code applies to PRSA members. The Code is designed to be a useful guide for PRSA members as they carry out their ethical responsibilities. This document is designed to anticipate and accommodate, by precedent, ethical challenges that may arise. The scenarios outlined in the Code provision are actual examples of misconduct. More will be added as experience with the Code occurs.

The Public Relations Society of America (PRSA) is committed to ethical practices. The level of public trust PRSA members seek, as we serve the public good, means we have taken on a special obligation to operate ethically.

The value of member reputation depends upon the ethical conduct of everyone affiliated with the Public Relations Society of America. Each of us sets an example for each other—as well as other professionals—by our pursuit of excellence with powerful standards of performance, professionalism, and ethical conduct.

Emphasis on enforcement of the Code has been eliminated. But, the PRSA Board of Directors retains the right to bar from membership or expel from the Society any individual who has been or is sanctioned by a government agency or convicted in a court of law of an action that is in violation of this Code.

Ethical practice is the most important obligation of a PRSA member. We view the Member Code of Ethics as a model for other professions, organizations, and professionals.

## PRSA Member Statement of Professional Values

This statement presents the core values of PRSA members and, more broadly, of the public relations profession. These values provide the foundation for the Member Code of Ethics and set the industry standard for the professional practice of public relations. These values are the fundamental beliefs that guide our behaviors and decision-making process. We believe our professional values are vital to the integrity of the profession as a whole.

### Advocacy

We serve the public interest by acting as responsible advocates for those we represent. We provide a voice in the marketplace of ideas, facts, and viewpoints to aid informed public debate.

### Honesty

We adhere to the highest standards of accuracy and truth in advancing the interests of those we represent and in communicating with the public.

### Expertise

We acquire and responsibly use specialized knowledge and experience. We advance the profession through continued professional development, research, and education. We build mutual understanding, credibility, and relationships among a wide array of institutions and audiences.

### Independence

We provide objective counsel to those we represent. We are accountable for our actions.

### Loyalty

We are faithful to those we represent, while honoring our obligation to serve the public interest.

### Fairness

We deal fairly with clients, employers, competitors, peers, vendors, the media, and the general public. We respect all opinions and support the right of free expression.

## PRSA Code Provisions

### Free Flow of Information

Core Principle Protecting and advancing the free flow of accurate and truthful information is essential to serving the public interest and contributing to informed decision making in a democratic society.

### Intent:

To maintain the integrity of relationships with the media, government officials, and the public.

To aid informed decision-making.

### Guidelines:

A member shall:

Preserve the integrity of the process of communication.

Be honest and accurate in all communications.

Act promptly to correct erroneous communications for which the practitioner is responsible.

Preserve the free flow of unprejudiced information when giving or receiving gifts by ensuring that gifts are nominal, legal, and infrequent.

### Examples of Improper Conduct under this Provision:

A member representing a ski manufacturer gives a pair of expensive racing skis to a sports magazine columnist, to influence the columnist to write favorable articles about the product.

A member entertains a government official beyond legal limits and/or in violation of government reporting requirements.

### Competition

Core Principle Promoting healthy and fair competition among professionals preserves an ethical climate while fostering a robust business environment.

### Intent:

To promote respect and fair competition among public relations professionals.

To serve the public interest by providing the widest choice of practitioner options.

*Guidelines:*

A member shall:

Follow ethical hiring practices designed to respect free and open competition without deliberately undermining a competitor.

Preserve intellectual property rights in the marketplace.

*Examples of Improper Conduct under This Provision:*

A member employed by a "client organization" shares helpful information with a counseling firm that is competing with others for the organization's business.

A member spreads malicious and unfounded rumors about a competitor in order to alienate the competitor's clients and employees in a ploy to recruit people and business.

## Disclosure of Information

Core Principle Open communication fosters informed decision making in a democratic society.

*Intent:*

To build trust with the public by revealing all information needed for responsible decision making.

*Guidelines:*

A member shall:

Be honest and accurate in all communications.

Act promptly to correct erroneous communications for which the member is responsible.

Investigate the truthfulness and accuracy of information released on behalf of those represented.

Reveal the sponsors for causes and interests represented.

Disclose financial interest (such as stock ownership) in a client's organization.

Avoid deceptive practices.

*Examples of Improper Conduct under This Provision:*

Front groups: A member implements "grass roots" campaigns or letter-writing campaigns to legislators on behalf of undisclosed interest groups.

Lying by omission: A practitioner for a corporation knowingly fails to release financial information, giving a misleading impression of the corporation's performance.

A member discovers inaccurate information disseminated via a Web site or media kit and does not correct the information.

A member deceives the public by employing people to pose as volunteers to speak at public hearings and participate in "grass roots" campaigns.

### Safeguarding Confidences

Core Principle Client trust requires appropriate protection of confidential and private information.

### Intent:

To protect the privacy rights of clients, organizations, and individuals by safeguarding confidential information.

### Guidelines:

A member shall: Safeguard the confidences and privacy rights of present, former, and prospective clients and employees.

Protect privileged, confidential, or insider information gained from a client or organization.

Immediately advise an appropriate authority if a member discovers that confidential information is being divulged by an employee of a client company or organization.

### Examples of Improper Conduct under This Provision:

A member changes jobs, takes confidential information, and uses that information in the new position to the detriment of the former employer.

A member intentionally leaks proprietary information to the detriment of some other party.

### Conflicts of Interest

Core Principle Avoiding real, potential or perceived conflicts of interest builds the trust of clients, employers, and the publics.

### Intent:

To earn trust and mutual respect with clients or employers.

To build trust with the public by avoiding or ending situations that put one's personal or professional interests in conflict with society's interests.

*Guidelines:*

A member shall:

Act in the best interests of the client or employer, even subordinating the member's personal interests.

Avoid actions and circumstances that may appear to compromise good business judgment or create a conflict between personal and professional interests.

Disclose promptly any existing or potential conflict of interest to affected clients or organizations.

Encourage clients and customers to determine if a conflict exists after notifying all affected parties.

*Examples of Improper Conduct under This Provision:*

The member fails to disclose that he or she has a strong financial interest in a client's chief competitor.

The member represents a "competitor company" or a "conflicting interest" without informing a prospective client.

## Enhancing the Profession

Core Principle Public relations professionals work constantly to strengthen the public's trust in the profession.

*Intent:*

To build respect and credibility with the public for the profession of public relations.

To improve, adapt and expand professional practices.

*Guidelines:*

A member shall: Acknowledge that there is an obligation to protect and enhance the profession.

Keep informed and educated about practices in the profession to ensure ethical conduct.

Actively pursue personal professional development.

Decline representation of clients or organizations that urge or require actions contrary to this Code.

Accurately define what public relations activities can accomplish.

Counsel subordinates in proper ethical decision making.

Require that subordinates adhere to the ethical requirements of the Code.

Report ethical violations, whether committed by PRSA members or not, to the appropriate authority.

*Examples of Improper Conduct under This Provision:*

A PRSA member declares publicly that a product the client sells is safe, without disclosing evidence to the contrary.

A member initially assigns some questionable client work to a nonmember practitioner to avoid the ethical obligation of PRSA membership.

Reprinted with Permission

# Appendix C.2: The American Association of Advertising Agencies (AAAA) Standards of Practice

http://www2.aaaa.org/about/association/pages/standardsofpractice.aspx

## Standards of Practice

*(First adopted October 16, 1924; most recently revised September 18, 1990)*

We hold that a responsibility of advertising agencies is to be a constructive force in business.

We hold that, to discharge this responsibility, advertising agencies must recognize an obligation, not only to their clients, but to the public, the media they employ, and to each other. As a business, the advertising agency must operate within the framework of competition. It is recognized that keen and vigorous competition, honestly conducted, is necessary to the growth and the health of American business. However, unethical competitive practices in the advertising agency business lead to financial waste, dilution of service, diversion of manpower, loss of prestige, and tend to weaken public confidence both in advertisements and in the institution of advertising.

We hold that the advertising agency should compete on merit and not by attempts at discrediting or disparaging a competitor agency, or its work, directly or by inference, or by circulating harmful rumors about another agency, or by making unwarranted claims of particular skill in judging or prejudging advertising copy.

To these ends, the American Association of Advertising Agencies has adopted the following Creative Code as being in the best interests of the public, the advertisers, the media, and the agencies themselves. The AAAA believes the Code's provisions serve as a guide to the kind of agency conduct that experience has shown to be wise, foresighted, and constructive. In accepting membership, an agency agrees to follow it.

## Creative Code

We, the members of the American Association of Advertising Agencies, in addition to supporting and obeying the laws and legal regulations pertaining to advertising, undertake to extend and broaden the application of high ethical standards. Specifically, we will not knowingly create advertising that contains:

a)  *False or misleading statements or exaggerations, visual or verbal*

b)  *Testimonials that do not reflect the real opinion of the individual(s) involved*

c)  *Price claims that are misleading*

d)  *Claims insufficiently supported or that distort the true meaning or practicable application of statements made by professional or scientific authority*

e)  *Statements, suggestions, or pictures offensive to public decency or minority segments of the population.*

We recognize that there are areas that are subject to honestly different interpretations and judgment. Nevertheless, we agree not to recommend to an advertiser, and to discourage the use of, advertising that is in poor or questionable taste or that is deliberately irritating through aural or visual content or presentation.

Comparative advertising shall be governed by the same standards of truthfulness, claim substantiation, tastefulness, etc., as apply to other types of advertising.

These Standards of Practice of the American Association of Advertising Agencies come from the belief that sound and ethical practice is good business. Confidence and respect are indispensable to success in a business embracing the many intangibles of agency service and involving relationships so dependent upon good faith.

Clear and willful violations of these Standards of Practice may be referred to the Board of Directors of the American Association of Advertising Agencies for appropriate action, including possible annulment of membership as provided by Article IV, Section 5, of the Constitution and By-Laws.

Reprinted with Permission

# Appendix C.3: The Outdoor Advertising Association of America (OAAA) Code of Industry Principles

http://www.oaaa.org/about/industrycode.aspx
In addition to adhering to external laws and regulations, the members of the Outdoor Advertising Association of America (OAAA) have adopted a set of voluntary industry principles. The OAAA endorses this Code and encourages its members to operate in conformance with these principles.

## Observe Highest Free Speech Standards

- We support the First Amendment right of advertisers to promote legal products and services, however, we also support the right of outdoor advertising companies to reject advertising that is misleading, offensive, or otherwise incompatible with individual community standards, and in particular, we reject the posting of obscene words or pictorial content.

## Protect the Children

- We are careful to place outdoor advertisements for products illegal for sale to minors on advertising displays that are a reasonable distance from the public places where children most frequently congregate.
- We are committed to a program that establishes exclusionary zones that prohibit stationary advertisements of products illegal for sale to minors that are intended to be read from, at least 500 feet of, elementary and secondary schools, public playgrounds, and established places of worship.
- We support reasonable limits on the total number of outdoor advertising displays in a market that may carry messages about products that are illegal for sale to minors.
- We seek to maintain broad diversification of customers that advertise using outdoor advertising.

## Support Worthy Public Causes

- We are committed to providing pro bono public service messages to promote worthy community causes.
- We advocate the use of outdoor advertising for political, editorial, public service, and other noncommercial messages.

## Provide an Effective, Attractive Medium for Advertisers

- We are committed to providing value and service to advertisers in communities nationwide.
- We are committed to maintaining and improving the quality, appearance, and safety of outdoor advertising structures and locations.
- We encourage the use of new technologies to continuously improve the service provided to advertisers and the information provided to the public.
- We are committed to excellence in the ads we exhibit because outdoor advertising provides the most public "art gallery" there is.

## Respect the Environment

- We are committed to environmental stewardship.
- We encourage environmentally friendly business practices for the reduction of waste, improvement of energy efficiency, and use of recyclable materials.

## Provide Effective and Safe Digital Billboards

- We are committed to ensuring that the commercial and noncommercial messages disseminated on standard-size digital billboards will be static messages and the content shall not include animated, flashing, scrolling, intermittent or full-motion video elements (outside established entertainment areas).
- We are committed to ensuring that the ambient light conditions associated with standard-size digital billboards are monitored by a light sensing device at all times and that display brightness will be appropriately adjusted as ambient light levels change.

## Uphold Billboard Industry Self-Regulation

- We support billboard advertising as a business use to be erected in commercial and industrial areas.

- We support new billboard locations in unzoned commercial and industrial areas only where there is business activity.
- We oppose the construction of stacked bulletins (i.e., two 14' x 48' faces or larger facing in the same direction)
- We oppose the construction of new billboards on truly scenic segments of highways outside of commercial and industrial areas.
- We oppose illegal cutting, and are committed to reasonable control and maintenance of vegetation surrounding billboards.
- We support the expeditious removal of illegally erected billboards without compensation; OAAA member companies are encouraged to inform responsible authorities if they become aware that illegal billboards are being erected.

## Protect Billboard Industry Rights

- We support the right of outdoor advertising companies to maintain lawfully erected billboards.
- We support laws that assure just compensation for removal of legal billboards.

Reprinted with Permission

# Appendix C.4: Better Business Bureau (BBB) Code of Advertising

http://www.bbb.org/us/code-of-advertising/

These basic advertising standards are issued for the guidance of advertisers, advertising agencies and advertising media.

It is not possible to cover fully the wide variety of advertising practices by specific standards in a code of this type which is designed to apply to the offering of all goods and services. Where the Better Business Bureau has developed specific industry advertising codes, it is recommended that industry members adhere to them. If specific questions arise which are not covered or involve advertising directed to children, it is recommended that *Do's and Don'ts in Advertising* (a comprehensive two volume loose-leaf compendium published by the Council of Better Business Bureaus) be consulted. Advertisers, agencies and media should also be sure that they are in compliance with local, state and federal laws and regulations governing advertising.

Adherence to the provisions of this Code will be a significant contribution toward effective self-regulation in the public interest.

## Basic Principles

1. The primary responsibility for truthful and non-deceptive advertising rests with the advertiser. Advertisers should be prepared to substantiate any claims or offers made before publication or broadcast and, upon request, present such substantiation promptly to the advertising medium or the Better Business Bureau.
2. Advertisements which are untrue, misleading, deceptive, fraudulent, falsely disparaging of competitors, or insincere offers to sell, shall not be used.
3. An advertisement as a whole may be misleading although every sentence separately considered is literally true. Misrepresentation may result not only from direct statements but by omitting or obscuring a material fact.

## I. Comparative Price, Value and Savings Claims

Advertisers may offer a price reduction or saving by comparing their selling price with:

a.   their own former selling price,

b.   the current selling price of identical merchandise sold by others in the market area, or

c.   The current selling price of comparable merchandise sold by the advertiser or by others in the market area. When any one of these comparisons is made in advertising. The claim should be based on the following criteria *and* the advertising should make clear to which of the above the comparative price or savings claim relates.

### a. Comparison with Own Former Selling Price

1.   The former price should be the actual price at which the advertiser has been currently offering (see below (2)) the merchandise immediately preceding the sale, on a regular basis, and for a reasonably substantial period of time.

2.   Offering prices, as distinguished from actual former selling prices, have frequently been used as a comparative to deceptively imply a saving. In the event few or no sales were made at the advertised comparative price, the advertiser should make sure that the higher price does not exceed the advertiser's usual and customary retail markup for similar merchandise, not an inflated or exaggerated price, and is one at which the merchandise was openly and actively offered for sale, for a reasonably substantial period of time, in the recent, regular course of business, honestly and in good faith.

3.   Descriptive terminology often used by advertisers includes: "regularly," "was," "you save $_____," and "originally." If the word "originally" is used and the original price is not the last previous price, that fact should be disclosed by stating the last previous price, or that intermediate markdowns have been taken, e.g., "originally $400, formerly $300, now $250"; "originally $400, intermediate markdowns taken, now $250."

### b. Comparison with Current Price of Identical Merchandise Sold by Others

1.   The comparative price should not exceed the price at which representative principal retail outlets in the market area have been selling the identical merchandise immediately preceding the advertiser's offer, on a regular basis and for a reasonably substantial period of time. Such comparisons should be substantiated by the advertiser immediately prior to making any advertised comparisons.

2. Descriptive terminology often used by advertisers includes: "selling elsewhere at $_____." (Refers to market area cited in (1) above.)

### c. Comparison with Current Price of Comparable Merchandise Sold by the Advertiser or by Others

1. The comparative price should not exceed the price at which the advertiser or representative principal retail outlets in the market area have been selling the comparable merchandise immediately preceding the advertiser's sale, on a regular basis and for a reasonably substantial period of time. Such comparisons should be substantiated by the advertiser immediately prior to making any advertised comparisons.
2. In all such cases, the advertiser should make certain that comparable merchandise is similar in all respects and of at least like grade and quality.
3. Descriptive terminology often used by advertisers includes: "comparable value," "compares with merchandise selling at $," "equal to merchandise selling for $_____."

### d. List Prices

"List price," "manufacturer's list price," "reference price," "suggested retail price," and similar terms have been used deceptively to state or imply a saving which was not, in fact, the case. A list price may be advertised as a comparative to the advertised sales price only to the extent that it is the actual selling price currently charged by the advertiser or by representative principal retailers in the market area where the claim is made.

Such a comparison should be substantiated by the advertiser immediately prior to making any advertised comparison.

### e. "Imperfects," "Irregulars," "Seconds"

No comparative price should be used in connection with an imperfect, irregular or second article unless it is accompanied by a clear and conspicuous disclosure that such comparative price applies to the price of the article, if perfect. The comparative price advertised should be based on (1) the price currently charged by the advertiser for the article without defects, or (2) the price currently charged by representative principal retailers in the trade area for the article without defects, and the advertisement should disclose which basis of comparison is being used.

## f. "Factory to You," "Factory Direct," "Wholesaler," "Wholesale Prices"

The terms "factory to you," "factory direct," "wholesaler," "wholesale prices" and others of similar import have been the subject of great abuse in advertising. They imply a significant saving from the actual price at which identical merchandise is currently being offered by representative principal retailers in the market area, or where identical merchandise is not being offered, from comparable values in the market area. Such terms should not be used unless the implied savings can be substantiated and the terms meet all of the requirements below.

1.  The terms "factory to you," "direct from maker," "factory outlet" and the like should not be used unless all advertised merchandise is actually manufactured by the advertiser or in factories owned or controlled by the advertiser.
2.  The terms "wholesaler," "wholesale outlet," "distributor" and the like should not be used unless the advertiser actually owns and operates or directly and absolutely controls a wholesale or distribution facility which primarily sells products to retailers for resale.
3.  The terms "wholesale price," "at cost" and the like should not be used unless they are the current prices which retailers usually and customarily pay when they buy such merchandise for resale.

## g. Sales

1.  The unqualified term "sale" may be used in advertising only if there is a significant reduction from the advertiser's usual and customary price of the merchandise offered and the sale is for a limited period of time. If the sale exceeds thirty days advertisers should be prepared to substantiate that the offering is indeed a valid reduction and has not become their regular price.
2.  Time limit sales should be rigidly observed. For example, merchandise offered in a "one-day sale," "three-day sale," "this week only," sale should be taken off "sale" and revert to the regular price immediately following expiration of the stated time.
3.  Introductory sales should be limited to a stated time period, and the selling price should be increased to the advertised regular price immediately following termination of the stated period.
4.  Price predictions advertisers may currently advertise future increases in their own prices on a subsequent date provided that they do, in fact, increase the price to the stated amount on that date and maintain it for a reasonably substantial period of time thereafter.

## h. "Emergency" or "Distress" Sales

Emergency or distress sales, including but not limited to bankruptcy, liquidation and going out of business sales, should not be advertised unless the stated or implied reason is a fact, should be limited to a stated period of time, and should offer only such merchandise as is affected by the emergency. "Selling out," "closing out sale," and similar terms should not be used unless the concern so advertising is actually going out of business. The unqualified term "liquidation sale" means that the advertiser's entire business is in the process of actually being liquidated prior to actual closing. Advertisers should conform with the requirements of applicable local, state and federal laws.

## i. "Up to" Savings Claims

Savings or price reduction claims covering a group of items with a range of savings should state both the minimum and maximum savings without undue or misleading display of the maximum. The number of items available at the maximum savings should comprise a significant percentage, typically 10%, of all the items in the offering, unless local or state law requires otherwise.

## J. Lowest Price, Underselling Claims

Despite an advertiser's best efforts to ascertain competitive prices, the rapidity with which prices fluctuate and the difficulty of determining prices of all sellers at all times preclude an absolute knowledge of the truth of generalized underselling/lowest price claims. Advertisers should have proper substantiation for all claims prior to dissemination; unverifiable underselling claims should be avoided.

## k. Price Equaling, Meeting Competitors' Prices

Advertisements which set out company policy of matching or bettering competitors' prices may be used, provided the terms of the offer are specific and in good faith and provided the terms of the offer are not unrealistic or unreasonable. Advertisers should be aware that such claims can create an implicit obligation to adjust prices generally for specific merchandise upon a showing that the advertiser's price for that merchandise is not as low as or lower than a competitor's, in order to preserve the accuracy of the advertised claims.

An advertisement which expresses a policy of matching or bettering competitors' prices should conspicuously and fully disclose any material and significant conditions which apply and specify what evidence a consumer must present to take advantage of the offer. Such evidence should not place an unrealistic or unreasonable burden on the consumer.

## 2. "Free"

a.  The word "free" may be used in advertising whenever the advertiser is offering an unconditional gift. If receipt of the "free" merchandise or service is conditional on a purchase:
    - the advertiser must disclose this condition clearly and conspicuously together with the "free" offer (not by placing an asterisk or symbol next to "free" and referring to the condition(s) in a footnote);
    - the normal price of the merchandise or service to be purchased must not have been increased nor its quantity or quality reduced; and
    - The "free" offer must be temporary; otherwise, it would become a continuous combination offer, no part of which is free.
b.  In a negotiated sale no "free" offer of another product or service should be made where:
    1.  the product or service to be purchased usually is sold at a price arrived at through bargaining, rather than at a regular price; or
    2.  There may be a regular price but other material factors such as quantity, quality or size are arrived at through bargaining.

## 3. "Cents-off" Sales

The principles stated in the standard dealing with "free" should be followed in the advertising of "cents-off" sales.

## 4. Trade-in Allowances

Any advertised trade-in allowance should be an amount deducted from the advertiser's current selling price without a trade-in. That selling price must be clearly disclosed in the advertisement. It is misleading to offer a fixed and arbitrary allowance regardless of the size, type, age, condition, or value of the article traded in, for the purpose of disguising the true retail price or creating the false impression that a reduced price or a special price is obtainable only by such trade-in.

## 5. Credit

Whenever a specific credit term is advertised, it should be available to all respondents unless qualified as to respondents' credit acceptability. All credit terms must be clearly and conspicuously disclosed in the advertisement, as required by the federal Truth in Lending Act and applicable state laws.

The Truth in Lending Act and Regulation Z which implements the Act, as well as Regulation M which covers consumer leasing, contain important provisions that affect any advertising to aid or promote the extension of consumer credit and should be carefully reviewed by every advertiser.

### a. Open-end credit

The requirements for advertising open-end credit under Regulation Z are complex. Therefore, advertisers are advised to consult Section 226.16 of the Regulation for details on terms triggering disclosure, prescribed terminology and information that must be disclosed.

### b. Closed-end credit

Advertisers are advised to consult Section 226.24 of Regulation Z for details of closed-end credit advertising. If an advertisement of closed-end credit contains any of the following triggering terms, three specific disclosures must also be stated, clearly and conspicuously. The *triggering* terms are:
1. the amount or percentage of any down payment;
2. the number of payments or period of repayment; (3) the amount of any payment, expressed either as a percentage or as a dollar amount; or
3. The amount of any finance charge. The three *disclosures* are:
   1. the amount or percentage of the down payment;
   2. the terms of repayment; and
   3. The "annual percentage rate," using that term spelled out in full. If the rate may be increased after consummation of the credit transaction, that fact must be disclosed.

### c. "Easy Credit," "Liberal Terms"

The terms "easy credit," "easy credit terms," "liberal terms," "easy pay plan" and other similar phrases relate to credit worthiness as well as to the terms of sale and credit repayment, and should be used only when:
1. consumer credit is extended to persons whose ability to pay or credit rating is below typical standards of credit worthiness;
2. the finance charges and annual percentage rate do not exceed those charged to persons whose credit rating has been determined and who meet generally accepted standards of credit worthiness;
3. the down payment is as low and the period of repayment of the same duration as in consumer credit extensions to those of previously determined credit worthiness; and

4.  The debtor is dealt with fairly on all conditions of the transaction including the consequences of a delayed or missed payment.

### d. "No Credit Rejected"

The words "no credit rejected" or words of similar import should not be used unless true, since they imply that consumer credit will be extended to anyone regardless of the person's credit worthiness or financial ability to pay.

## 6. Extra Charges

Whenever a price is mentioned in advertising, any extra charges should also be disclosed in immediate conjunction with the price (e.g., delivery, installation, assembly, excise tax, postage and handling).

## 7. Bait Advertising and Selling

A.  "bait" offer is an alluring but insincere offer to sell a product or service which the advertiser does not intend to sell. Its purpose is to switch consumers from buying the advertised merchandise or service, in order to sell something else, usually at a higher price or on a basis more advantageous to the advertiser.

B.  No advertisement should be published unless it is a bona fide offer to sell the advertised merchandise or service.

C.  The advertising should not create a false impression about the product or service being offered in order to lay the foundation for a later "switch" to other, more expensive products or services, or products of a lesser quality at the same price.

D.  Subsequent full disclosure by the advertiser of all other facts about the advertised article does not preclude the existence of a bait scheme.

E.  An advertiser should not use nor permit the use of the following bait scheme practices: refusing to show or demonstrate the advertised merchandise or service;
   - disparaging the advertised merchandise or service, its warranty, availability, services and parts, credit terms, etc.;
   - selling the advertised merchandise or service and thereafter "unselling" the customer to make a switch to other merchandise or service; refusing to take orders for the advertised merchandise or service or to deliver it within a reasonable time; demonstrating or showing a defective sample of the advertised merchandise; or, having a sales compensation plan designed to penalize salespersons who sell the advertised merchandise or service.

F.  An advertiser should have on hand a sufficient quantity of advertised merchandise to meet reasonably anticipated demands, unless the advertisement discloses the number of items available or states "while supplies last." If items are available only at certain branches, their specific locations should be disclosed. The use of "rainchecks" is no justification for inadequate estimates of reasonably anticipated demand.

G. Actual sales of the advertised merchandise or service may not preclude the existence of a bait scheme since this may be merely an attempt to create an aura of legitimacy. A key factor in determining the existence of "bait" is the number of times the merchandise or service was advertised compared to the number of actual sales of the merchandise or service.

## 8. Warranties (or Guarantees)

A. When the term "warranty" (or "guarantee") is used in product advertising, the following disclosure should be made clearly and prominently: a statement that the complete details of the warranty can be seen at the advertiser's store prior to sale, or in the case of mail or telephone order sales, are available free on written request.

B. (1) "satisfaction guarantee," "money back guarantee," "free trial offer," or similar representations should be used in advertising only if the seller or manufacturer refunds the full purchase price of the advertised product at the purchaser's request.
(2) When "satisfaction guarantee" or similar representations are used in advertising, any material limitations or conditions that apply to the guarantee should be clearly and prominently disclosed.

C. When the term "lifetime," "life" or similar representations are used in advertising to describe the duration of the warranty or guarantee, the advertisement should clearly and prominently disclose the life to which the representation refers.

D. Sellers or manufacturers should advertise that a product is warranted or guaranteed only if the seller or manufacturer promptly and fully performs its obligations under the warranty or guarantee.

E. Advertisers should make certain that any advertising of warranties complies with the Consumer Products Warranty Act, effective July 4, 1975, relevant Federal Trade Commission requirements and any applicable state and local laws.

## 9. Layout and Illustrations

The composition and layout of advertisements should be such as to minimize the possibility of misunderstanding by the reader. For example, prices, illustrations, or descriptions should not be so placed in an advertisement as to give the impression that the price or terms of featured merchandise apply to other merchandise in the advertisement when such is not the fact. An advertisement should not be used which features merchandise at a price or terms boldly displayed, together with illustrations of higher-priced merchandise, so arranged as to give the impression that the lower price or more favorable terms apply to the other merchandise, when such is not the fact.

## 10. Asterisks

An asterisk may be used to impart additional information about a word or term which is not in itself inherently deceptive. The asterisk or other reference symbol should not be used as a means of contradicting or substantially changing the meaning of any advertising statement. Information referenced by asterisks should be clearly and prominently disclosed.

## 11. Abbreviations

Commonly known abbreviations may be used in advertising. However, abbreviations not generally known to or understood by the general public should be avoided.

For example, "deliv. extra" is understood to mean that there is an extra charge for delivery of the merchandise. "New Battery, $25 W.T.," is not generally understood to mean "with trade-in."

## 12. Use or Condition Disclosures

### A. Used, Secondhand, etc.

A product previously used by a consumer should be clearly and conspicuously described as such, e.g., "used," "secondhand," "pre-owned," "repossessed," "rebuilt," "reconditioned."

### B. Rebuilt, Reconditioned

1. The term "rebuilt" should be used only to describe products that have been completely disassembled, reconstructed, repaired and refinished, including replacement of parts.
2. The term "reconditioned" should be used only to describe products that have received such repairs, adjustments or finishing as were necessary to put the product in satisfactory condition without rebuilding.

### C. "As Is"

When merchandise is offered on an "as is" basis, i.e., in the condition in which it is displayed at the place of sale, the words "as is" should be indicated in any advertising and on the bill of sale. An advertiser also may describe the condition of the merchandise if so desired.

### D.  Second, Irregular, Imperfect

If merchandise is defective or rejected by the manufacturer because it falls below specifications, it should be advertised by terms such as "second," "irregular," or "imperfect."

### E.  "Discontinued"

Merchandise should not be described as "discontinued," "discontinued model," or by words of similar import unless the manufacturer has, in fact, discontinued its manufacture, or the retail advertiser will discontinue offering it entirely after clearance of existing inventories. If discontinuance is only by the retailer, the advertising should indicate that fact, e.g., "we are discontinuing stocking these items."

## 13.  Superiority Claims—Comparatives—Disparagement

A.  Truthful comparisons using factual information may help consumers make informed buying decisions, provided:
1.  all representations are consistent with the general rules and prohibitions against false and deceptive advertising;
2.  all comparisons that claim or imply, unqualifiedly, superiority to competitive products or services are not based on a selected or limited list of characteristics in which the advertiser excels while ignoring those in which the competitors excel;
3.  the advertisement clearly discloses any material or significant limitations of the comparison; and
4.  The advertiser can substantiate all claims made.
B.  Advertising which deceptively or falsely disparages a competitor or competing products or services should not be used.

## 14.  Superlative Claims-Puffery

Superlative statements, like other advertising claims, are objective (factual) or subjective (puffery):
*   Objective claims relate to tangible qualities and performance values of a product or service which can be measured against accepted standards or tests. As statements of fact, such claims can be proved or disproved and the advertiser should possess substantiation.
*   Subjective claims are expressions of opinion or personal evaluation of

the intangible qualities of a product or service. Individual opinions, statements of corporate pride and promises may sometimes be considered puffery and not subject to test of their truth and accuracy. Subjective superlatives which tend to mislead should be avoided.

## 15. Testimonials and Endorsements

In general, advertising which uses testimonials or endorsements is likely to mislead or confuse if:

- it is not genuine and does not actually represent the current opinion of the endorser;
- it is not quoted in its entirety, thereby altering its overall meaning and impact;
- it contains representations or statements which would be misleading if otherwise used in advertising;
- while literally true, it creates deceptive implications;
- the endorser is not competent or sufficiently qualified to express an opinion concerning the quality of the product or service being advertised or the results likely to be achieved by its use;
- it is not clearly stated that the endorser, associated with some well-known and highly-regarded institution, is speaking only in a personal capacity, and not on behalf of such an institution, if such be the fact;
- broad claims are made as to endorsements or approval by indefinitely large or vague groups, e.g., "the homeowners of America," "the doctors of America";
- an endorser has a pecuniary interest in the company whose product or service is endorsed and this is not made known in the advertisement.

Advertisers should consult Federal Trade Commission Guides on Testimonials and Endorsements for detailed guidance.

## 16. Rebate

The terms "rebate," "cash rebate," or similar terms may be used only when payment of money will be made by the retailer or manufacturer to a purchaser after the sale, and the advertising should make clear who is making the payment.

## 17. Company Name or Trade Style

No words should be used in a company name or trade style which would mislead the public either directly or by implication. For example, the words "factory" or "manufacturer" should not be used in a company name unless the advertiser actually owns and operates or directly and absolutely controls the manufacturing facility that produces the advertised products. Similarly, the term "wholesale" or "wholesaler" should not be used in a company name unless the advertiser actually owns and operates or directly and absolutely controls a wholesale or distribution facility which primarily sells products to retailers for resale.

## 18. Contests and Games of Chance

a.  If contests are used, the advertiser should publish clear, complete and concise rules and provide competent impartial judges to determine the winners.
b.  No contest, drawing or other game of chance that involves the three elements of prize, chance and consideration should be conducted since it constitutes a lottery and is in violation of federal statutes.
c.  The Federal Trade Commission has rendered various decisions on contests and games of chance relating to disclosure of the number of prizes to be awarded and the odds of winning each prize, and issued a trade regulation rule for games of chance in the food retailing and gasoline industries. Advertisers should make certain any contest conforms to FTC requirements as well as any applicable local and state laws.

## 19. Claimed Results

Claims as to energy savings, performance, safety, efficacy, results, etc. which will be obtained by or realized from a particular product or service should be based on recent and competent scientific, engineering or other objective data.

## 20. Unassembled Merchandise

When advertised merchandise requires partial or complete assembly by the purchaser, the advertising should disclose that fact, e.g., "unassembled," "partial assembly required."

# Appendix C.5  Children's Advertising Review Unit (CARU) of the National Advertising Division of the Council of Better Business Bureaus Self-Regulatory Guidelines

http://www.caru.org/guidelines/guidelines.pdf

Self-Regulatory Program for Children's Advertising

## Core Principles

The following Core Principles apply to all practices covered by the self-regulatory program.

1. Advertisers have special responsibilities when advertising to children or collecting data from children online. They should take into account the limited knowledge, experience, sophistication and maturity of the audience to which the message is directed. They should recognize that younger children have a limited capacity to evaluate the credibility of information, may not understand the persuasive intent of advertising, and may not even understand that they are being subject to advertising.
2. Advertising should be neither deceptive nor unfair, as these terms are applied under the Federal Trade Commission Act, to the children to whom it is directed.
3. Advertisers should have adequate substantiation for objective advertising claims, as those claims are reasonably interpreted by the children to whom they are directed.
4. Advertising should not stimulate children's unreasonable expectations about product quality or performance.
5. Products and content inappropriate for children should not be advertised directly to them.
6. Advertisers should avoid social stereotyping and appeals to prejudice, and are encouraged to incorporate minority and other groups in advertisements and to present positive role models whenever possible.
7. Advertisers are encouraged to capitalize on the potential of advertising to serve an educational role and influence positive personal qualities and behaviors in children, *e.g.*, being honest and respectful of others, taking safety precautions, engaging in physical activity.

8.  Although there are many influences that affect a child's personal and social development, it remains the prime responsibility of the parents to provide guidance for children. Advertisers should contribute to this parent-child relationship in a constructive manner.

Reprinted with Permission

# Appendix C.6: Direct Marketing Association's (DMA) Guidelines for Ethical Business Practice

http://www.dmaresponsibility.org/guidelines/

## The Terms of the Offer

### HONESTY AND CLARITY OF OFFER

*Article #1*

All offers should be clear, honest, and complete so that the consumer may know the exact nature of what is being offered, the price, the terms of payment (including all extra charges) and the commitment involved in the placing of an order. Before publication of an offer, marketers should be prepared to substantiate any claims or offers made. Advertisements or specific claims that are untrue, misleading, deceptive, or fraudulent should not be used.

### ACCURACY AND CONSISTENCY

*Article #2*

Simple and consistent statements or representations of all the essential points of the offer should appear in the promotional material. The overall impression of an offer should not be contradicted by individual statements, representations, or disclaimers.

### CLARITY OF REPRESENTATIONS

*Article #3*

Representations which, by their size, placement, duration, or other characteristics are unlikely to be noticed or are difficult to understand should not be used if they are material to the offer.

## ACTUAL CONDITIONS

### Article #4

All descriptions, promises, and claims of limitation should be in accordance with actual conditions, situations, and circumstances existing at the time of the promotion.

## DISPARAGEMENT

### Article #5

Disparagement of any person or group on grounds addressed by federal or state laws that prohibit discrimination is unacceptable.

## DECENCY

### Article #6

Solicitations should not be sent to consumers who have indicated to the marketer that they consider those solicitations to be vulgar, immoral, profane, pornographic, or offensive in any way and who do not want to receive them.

## PHOTOGRAPHS AND ART WORK

### Article #7

Photographs, illustrations, artwork, and the situations they describe should be accurate portrayals and current reproductions of the products, services, or other subjects they represent.

## DISCLOSURE OF SPONSOR AND INTENT

### Article #8

All marketing contacts should disclose the name of the sponsor and each purpose of the contact. No one should make offers or solicitations in the guise of one purpose when the intent is a different purpose regardless of the marketing channel used.

## ACCESSIBILITY

### Article #9

Every offer should clearly identify the marketer's name and street address or telephone number, or both, at which the individual may obtain service and exercise their marketing preferences. If an offer is made online, the marketer should provide its name, an Internet-based contact mechanism, and a street address. For e-mail solicitations, marketers should comply with Article #38 (Commercial Solicitations Online). For telephone and mobile solicitations, marketers should comply with Articles #54–56 to provide adequate notice to consumers to allow them to exercise their marketing preferences.

### SOLICITATION IN THE GUISE OF AN INVOICE OR GOVERNMENTAL NOTIFICATION

#### Article #10

Offers that are likely to be mistaken for bills, invoices, or notices from public utilities or governmental agencies should not be used.

### POSTAGE, SHIPPING, OR HANDLING CHARGES

#### Article #11

Postage, shipping, or handling charges, if any, should bear a reasonable relationship to actual costs incurred.
   [. . .]

## Marketing to Children

### MARKETING TO CHILDREN

#### Article #13

Offers and the manner in which they are presented that are suitable for adults only should not be made to children. In determining the suitability of a communication with children online, via wireless devices such as a mobile phone or in any other medium, marketers should predetermine whether the use of the child's data for marketing purposes or the sending of marketing material to the child is permitted under federal law, such as the Children's Online Privacy Protection Act (COPPA), or state law. Where marketing to children is permitted by law, marketers should ensure the marketing is suitable for the child taking into account the age range, knowledge, sophistication, and maturity of their intended audience.

### PARENTAL RESPONSIBILITY AND CHOICE

#### Article #14

Marketers should provide notice and an opportunity to opt out of the marketing process so that parents have the ability to limit the collection, use, and disclosure of their children's names, addresses, or other personally identifiable information.

## INFORMATION FROM OR ABOUT CHILDREN

### Article #15

Marketers should take into account the age range, knowledge, sophistication, and maturity of children when collecting information from them. Marketers should limit the collection, use, and dissemination of information collected from or about children to information required for the promotion, sale, and delivery of goods and services, provision of customer services, conducting market research, and engaging in other appropriate marketing activities.

Marketers should effectively explain that the information is being requested for marketing purposes. Information not appropriate for marketing purposes should not be collected.

Upon request from a parent, marketers should promptly provide the source and general nature of information maintained about a child. Marketers should implement strict security measures to ensure against unauthorized access, alteration, or dissemination of the data collected from or about children, and should provide information regarding such measures upon request to the parent or guardian of the minor.

## MARKETING ONLINE TO CHILDREN UNDER 13 YEARS OF AGE

### Article #16

Marketers should not knowingly collect personally identifiable information online or via wireless handsets or devices from a child under 13 without prior parental consent or direct parental notification of the nature and intended use of such information, and shall provide an opportunity for the parent to prevent such use and participation in the activity. Online and wireless/mobile contact information should only be used to directly respond to an activity initiated by a child and not to recontact a child for other purposes without prior parental consent. However, a marketer may contact and get information from a child for the purpose of obtaining parental consent.

Marketers should not knowingly collect, without prior parental consent, personally identifiable information online or via a wireless handset or device from children that would permit any offline contact with the child.

Marketers should not knowingly distribute to third parties, without prior parental consent, information collected from a child that would permit any contact with that child.

Marketers should take reasonable steps to prevent the online publication or posting of information that would allow a third party to contact a child offline unless the marketer has prior parental consent.

Marketers should not entice a child to divulge personally identifiable information by the prospect of a special game, prize, or other offer.

Marketers should not make a child's access to website or mobile content contingent on the collection of personally identifiable information. Only online contact information used to enhance the interactivity of the site is permitted.

The following assumptions underlie these online guidelines:

When a marketer directs a site at a certain age group, it can expect that the visitors to that site are in that age range, and

When a marketer asks the age of the child, the marketer can assume the answer to be truthful.

## Special Offers and Claims

### USE OF THE WORD "FREE" AND OTHER SIMILAR REPRESENTATIONS

*Article #17*

A product or service that is offered without cost or obligation to the recipient may be unqualifiedly described as "free."

If a product or service is offered as "free," all qualifications and conditions should be clearly and conspicuously disclosed, in close conjunction with the use of the term "free" or other similar phrase. When the term "free" or other similar representations are made (for example, 2-for-1, half-price, or 1-cent offers), the product or service required to be purchased should not have been increased in price or decreased in quality or quantity.

### PRICE COMPARISONS

*Article #18*

Price comparisons, including those between a marketer's current price and a former, future, or suggested price, or between a marketer's price and the price of a competitor's comparable product, should be fair and accurate.

In each case of comparison to a former, manufacturer's suggested, or competitor's comparable product price, recent substantial sales should have been made at that price in the same trade area.

For comparisons with a future price, there should be a reasonable expectation that the new price will be charged in the foreseeable future.

## GUARANTEES

### Article #19

If a product or service is offered with a guarantee or a warranty, either the terms and conditions should be set forth in full in the promotion, or the promotion should state how the consumer may obtain a copy. The guarantee should clearly state the name and address of the guarantor and the duration of the guarantee.

Any requests for repair, replacement, or refund under the terms of a guarantee or warranty should be honored promptly. In an unqualified offer of refund, repair, or replacement, the customer's preference should prevail.

## USE OF TEST OR SURVEY DATA

### Article #20

All test or survey data referred to in advertising should be valid and reliable as to source and methodology, and should support the specific claim for which it is cited. Advertising claims should not distort test or survey results or take them out of context.

## TESTIMONIALS AND ENDORSEMENTS

### Article #21

Testimonials and endorsements should be used only if they are:
a. Authorized by the person quoted
b. Genuine and related to the experience of the person giving them both at the time made and at the time of the promotion and
c. Not taken out of context so as to distort the endorser's opinion or experience with the product.

# Sweepstakes

## USE OF THE TERM "SWEEPSTAKES"

### Article #22

Sweepstakes are promotional devices by which items of value (prizes) are awarded to participants by chance without the promoter's requiring the participants to render something of value (consideration) to be eligible to participate. The co-existence of all three elements—prize, chance and consideration—in the same promotion constitutes a lottery. It is illegal for any private enterprise to run a lottery without specific governmental authorization.

When skill replaces chance, the promotion becomes a skill contest. When gifts (premiums or other items of value) are given to all participants independent of the element of chance, the promotion is not a sweepstakes. Promotions that are not sweepstakes should not be held out as such.

Only those promotional devices that satisfy the definition stated above should be called or held out to be a sweepstakes.

## No Purchase Option

### Article #23

Promotions should clearly state that no purchase is required to win sweepstakes prizes. They should not represent that those who make a purchase or otherwise render consideration with their entry will have a better chance of winning or will be eligible to win more or larger prizes than those who do not make a purchase or otherwise render consideration. The method for entering without ordering should be easy to find, read, and understand. When response devices used only for entering the sweepstakes are provided, they should be as easy to find as those utilized for ordering the product or service.

## Chances of Winning

### Article #24

No sweepstakes promotion, or any of its parts, should represent that a recipient or entrant has won a prize or that any entry stands a greater chance of winning a prize than any other entry when this is not the case. Winners should be selected in a manner that ensures fair application of the laws of chance.

## Prizes

### Article #25

Sweepstakes prizes should be advertised in a manner that is clear, honest, and complete so that the consumer may know the exact nature of what is being offered. For prizes paid over time, the annual payment schedule and number of years should be clearly disclosed.

Photographs, illustrations, artwork, and the situations they represent should be accurate portrayals of the prizes listed in the promotion.

No award or prize should be held forth directly or by implication as having substantial monetary value if it is of nominal worth. The value of a non-cash prize should be stated at regular retail value, whether actual cost to the sponsor is greater or less.

All prizes should be awarded and delivered without cost to the participant. If there are certain conditions under which a prize or prizes will not be awarded, that fact should be disclosed in a manner that is easy to find, read, and understand.

## PREMIUMS

### Article #26

Premiums should be advertised in a manner that is clear, honest, and complete so that the consumer may know the exact nature of what is being offered.

A premium, gift or item should not be called or held out to be a "prize" if it is offered to every recipient of or participant in a promotion. If all participants will receive a premium, gift, or item, that fact should be clearly disclosed.

## DISCLOSURE OF RULES

### Article #27

All terms and conditions of the sweepstakes, including entry procedures and rules, should be easy to find, read, and understand. Disclosures set out in the rules section concerning no purchase option, prizes, and chances of winning should not contradict the overall impression created by the promotion.

The following should be set forth clearly in the rules:

No purchase of the advertised product or service is required in order to win a prize

A purchase will not improve the chances of winning

Procedures for entry

If applicable, disclosure that a facsimile of the entry blank or other alternate means (such as a 3" × 5" card) may be used to enter the sweepstakes

The termination date for eligibility in the sweepstakes. The termination date should specify whether it is a date of mailing or receipt of entry deadline

The number, retail value (of non-cash prizes), and complete description of all prizes offered, and whether cash may be awarded instead of merchandise. If a cash prize is to be awarded by installment payments, that fact should be clearly disclosed, along with the nature and timing of the payments

The estimated odds of winning each prize. If the odds depend upon the number of entries, the stated odds should be based on an estimate of the number of entries

The method by which winners will be selected

The geographic area covered by the sweepstakes and those areas in which the offer is void

All eligibility requirements, if any

Approximate dates when winners will be selected and notified

Publicity rights regarding the use of winner's name

Taxes are the responsibility of the winner

Provision of a mailing address to allow consumers to receive a list of winners of prizes over $25.00 in value

[. . .]

## Online Marketing

### ONLINE INFORMATION

#### Article #38

This Article addresses the collection of personally identifiable information by websites for online marketing and the collection and use of information for online behavioral advertising purposes, as defined in the Glossary of Terms.

*General Notice to Online Visitors*

If your organization operates an online site and/or is engaged in online behavioral advertising, you should make your information practices available to visitors in a prominent place on your website's home page or in a place on your website that is easily accessible from the home page. The notice about information practices on your website should be easy to find, read, and understand. Visitors should be able to comprehend the scope of the notice and how they can exercise their choices regarding use of personally identifiable information or information used for online behavioral advertising purposes. The notice should be available prior to or at the time personally identifiable information or information used for online behavioral advertising purposes is collected.

Your organization and its postal address, and the website(s) to which the notice applies, should be identified so visitors know who is responsible for the website. You also should provide specific contact information so visitors can contact your organization for service or information.

If your organization collects personally identifiable information from visitors and/or collects information from non-affiliate websites for online behavioral advertising purposes, your notice should include:

The nature of the information collected online for marketing purposes, and the types of uses you make of such information, including uses for online behavioral advertising purposes;

The use(s) of such information, including whether you transfer information to third parties for use by them for their own marketing or online behavioral advertising purposes and the mechanism by which consumers can exercise choice not to have such information transferred;

Whether personally identifiable information is collected by, used by, or transferred to agents (entities working on your behalf) as part of the business activities related to the visitor's actions on the site, including to fulfill orders or to provide information or requested services;

Whether you use cookies or other passive means of information collection, and whether such information collected is for internal purposes or transferred to third parties for marketing purposes, including online behavioral advertising purposes;

What procedures your organization has put in place for accountability and enforcement purposes; and

That your organization maintains appropriate physical, electronic, and administrative safeguards to protect information collected online.

In addition, marketers should refer to Article #32 (Personal Data) specifically to assure that marketing data are used only for marketing purposes.

### Third-Party Notice for Online Behavioral Advertising

When information is collected from or used on a website for online behavioral advertising purposes, visitors should be provided with notice (easy to find, read and understand) about the third party's policies for online behavioral advertising. Third parties, as defined in the Glossary of Terms, should provide notice in one of the following ways:

- through a clear, meaningful, and prominent link described in or proximate to the advertisement delivered on the Web page where information is collected;
- on DMA's approved website(s), such as DMAchoice.org or another comprehensive industry-developed website(s), that is linked from the disclosure that describes the fact that information is being collected for online behavioral advertising purposes;
- on the web page where the information is collected if there is an arrangement with the website operator for the provision of such notice;
- if agreed to by the operator of the website(s) on its web page disclosing notice and choice regarding information collected for online behavioral advertising purposes.

## Consumer Choice for Third-Party Online Behavioral Advertising

A third party should provide consumers with the ability to exercise choice with respect to the collection and use of information for online behavioral advertising purposes or the transfer of such information to a non-affiliate for such purposes. Such choice should be available through the notice options as detailed above.

## Material Changes to Existing Policies

If your organization's policy changes materially with respect to the sharing of personally identifiable information with third parties including but not limited to changes for online behavioral advertising purposes, you should update your policy and give consumers conspicuous notice to that effect, offering an opportunity for individuals to select their preferences. Prior to making a materially different use of information collected from an individual for online behavioral advertising purposes, and before notice of your organization's policy change is given, organizations should obtain informed consent to such a new marketing use from the consumer.

## Honoring Choice

You should honor a website visitor's choice regarding use and transfer of personally identifiable information made in accordance with your stated policy. If you have promised to honor the visitor's choice for a specific time period, and if that time period subsequently expires, then you should provide that visitor with a new notice and choice. You should provide choices online. You may also offer choice options by mail or telephone.

## Providing Access

You should honor any representations made in your online policy notice regarding access.

## Information Security

Your organization should maintain appropriate physical, technical and administrative safeguards and use appropriate security technologies and methods to protect information collected or used online, and to guard against unauthorized access, alteration, or dissemination of personally identifiable information during transfer and storage. Your procedures should require that employees and agents of your organization who have access to personally identifiable information use and disclose that information only in a lawful and authorized manner. Organizations should retain information that is collected and used for online behavioral advertising purposes only for as long as necessary to fulfill a legitimate business need, or as required by law.

### Visitors under 13 Years of Age

If your organization has a site directed to children under the age of 13 or collects personally identifiable information from visitors known to be under 13 years of age, your website should take the additional steps required by the *Marketing to Children* Articles of the *Guidelines for Ethical Business Practice* and inform visitors that your disclosures and practices are subject to compliance with the Children's Online Privacy Protection Act ("COPPA"). In addition, an organization should not engage in online behavioral advertising directed to children where it has actual knowledge that the children are under the age of 13, unless compliant with COPPA and these Guidelines.

### Health and Financial Information

Entities should not collect and use financial account numbers, Social Security numbers, pharmaceutical prescriptions, or medical records about a specific individual for online behavioral advertising purposes without prior express consent and unless compliant with the Health Insurance Portability & Accountability Act ("HIPPA") and these Guidelines.

### Accountability

There should be a meaningful, timely, and effective procedure through which your organization can demonstrate adherence to your stated online information practices. Such a procedure may include: (1) self or third-party verification and monitoring, (2) complaint resolution, and (3) education and outreach. This can be accomplished by an independent auditor, public self-certification, a third-party privacy seal program, a licensing program, and/or membership in a trade, professional or other membership association with a self-regulatory program.

### Service Provider Treatment of Online Behavioral Advertising Information

A service provider, as defined in the Glossary of Terms, should not collect and use information for online behavioral advertising purposes without consent and should provide an easy-to-use ongoing means to withdraw consent to the collection and use of that information for online behavioral advertising purposes.

In addition, a service provider should take the following steps regarding information collected and used for online behavioral advertising purposes:

1. Alter, anonymize, or randomize (e.g., through "hashing" or substantial redaction) any personally identifiable information or unique identifier in order to prevent the information from being reconstructed into its original form in the ordinary course of business.
2. Disclose in the notice described above the circumstances in which information is collected and used for online behavioral advertising purposes.
3. Take reasonable steps to protect the non-identifiable nature of information if and when it is distributed to non-affiliates, including not disclosing the algorithm or other mechanism used for anonymizing or randomizing the information, and obtaining satisfactory written assurance that such non-affiliates will not attempt to re-construct the information and will use or disclose the anonymized information only for purposes of online behavioral advertising or other uses as specified to users. This assurance will be considered satisfied if a non-affiliate does not have any independent right to use the information for its own purposes under a written contract.
4. Take reasonable steps to ensure that any non-affiliate that receives anonymized information will itself ensure that any other non-affiliate to which such information is disclosed agrees to the restrictions and conditions set forth in this subsection. This obligation is also considered satisfied if a non-affiliate does not have any independent right to use the data for its own purposes under a written contract.

## Glossary of Terms

**Ad Delivery**    means the delivery of online advertisements or advertising-related services using ad reporting data. Ad delivery does not include the collection and use of ad reporting data when such data are used to deliver advertisements to a computer or device based on the preferences or interests inferred from information collected over time and across non-affiliate sites because this type of collection and use is covered by the definition of online behavioral advertising.

**Ad Reporting**    refers to the logging of page views on a website(s) or the collection or use of other information about a browser, operating system, domain name, clickstream within a site, date and time of the viewing of the Web page or advertisement, and related information for purposes including but not limited to: statistical reporting in connection with the activity on a website(s); Web analytics and analysis for improved marketing and better site design; and logging the number and type of advertisements served on a particular website(s).

**Affiliate**    refers to an entity that controls, is controlled by, or is under common control with, another entity.

**Consent**    means an individual's action in response to a clear, meaningful and prominent notice regarding the collection and use of data for online behavioral advertising purposes. Informed consent is based on information provided to an individual that allows them to select their preferences, prior express consent means consent required from an individual prior to any marketing communication from the marketer or others.

**Contextual Advertising**    Advertising based on a consumer's current visit to a Web page or search query. Online behavioral advertising, as defined in this Article's Glossary of Terms, does not include contextual advertising.

**Control**    of an entity means that one entity (1) is under significant common ownership or operational control of the other entity, or (2) has the power to exercise a controlling influence over the management or policies of the other entity. In addition, for an entity to be under the control of another entity and thus be treated as a first party under these principles, the entity must adhere to online behavioral advertising policies that are not materially inconsistent with the other entity's policies.

**First Party**    is the entity that is the owner of the website, or those of its affiliates, and has control over the website with which the consumer interacts.

**Online Behavioral Advertising**    means the collection of information from a particular computer or device regarding Web viewing behaviors over time and across non-affiliate websites for the purpose of using such information to predict user preferences or interests to deliver advertising to that computer or device based on the preferences or interests inferred from such Web viewing behaviors. Online behavioral advertising does not include the activities of first parties, ad delivery or ad reporting, or contextual advertising (i.e. advertising based on the content of the Web page being visited, a consumer's current visit to a Web page, or a search query). The activities of search engines fall within the scope of online behavioral advertising to the extent that they include collection of data regarding Web viewing behaviors over time and across non-affiliate websites in order to deliver advertising to that computer or device based on the preferences or interests inferred from such Web viewing behaviors.

*Personally Identifiable Information and Non-Personally Identifiable*

**Information**    for purposes of this Article, personally identifiable information refers to name, address, or other information that identifies a specific individual; non-personally identifiable information (non-PII) refers to information, such as a computer's IP address, that does not tie the information to a specific individual. Non-personally identifiable information collected by third parties from websites for online behavioral advertising should be combined with personally identifiable information collected about an individual for marketing purposes only with that individual's consent, unless the individual was provided with notice and choice with respect to such potential combination at the time the non-personally identifiable information was collected and did not opt out.

**Service Provider**    refers to an organization that collects and uses information from all or substantially all URLs traversed by a Web browser across websites for purposes of online behavioral advertising. Examples of service providers in this context are internet access service providers and providers of desktop applications software such as Web browser "tool bars."

**Third Party**    an entity is a third party to the extent that it engages in online behavioral advertising on a non-affiliate's website.

## MOBILE SERVICE COMMERCIAL MESSAGE SOLICITATIONS (MSCMS) DELIVERED TO A WIRELESS DEVICE

### Article #39

A Mobile Service Commercial Message (MSCM) is a commercial electronic mail message that is transmitted directly to a wireless device that is utilized by a subscriber of a commercial mobile service. Marketers sending MSCMs messages should obtain prior express consent from recipients and should abide by CAN-SPAM, the Federal Communications Commission's Wireless Email Rule, DMA Guidelines for Online & Mobile Marketing, and any additional federal and state regulations.

## COMMERCIAL SOLICITATIONS ONLINE

### Article #40

Marketers may send commercial solicitations online [with the exception of Mobile Service Commercial Messages (MSCMs), refer to Article #39] under the following circumstances:

- The solicitations are sent to the marketers' own customers, or
- Individuals have given their affirmative consent to the marketer to receive solicitations online, or
- Individuals did not opt out after the marketer has given notice of the opportunity to opt out from solicitations online, or
- The marketer has received assurance from the third party list provider that the individuals whose e-mail addresses appear on that list:

- have already provided affirmative consent to receive solicitations online, or
- have already received notice of the opportunity to have their e-mail addresses removed and have not opted out, and
- The individual is not on the marketer's in-house suppression list

Within each e-mail solicitation, marketers should furnish individuals with a notice and an Internet-based mechanism they can use to:

Request that the marketer not send them future e-mail solicitations and Request that the marketer not rent, sell, or exchange their e-mail addresses for online solicitation purposes

If individuals request that their names be removed from the marketer's in-house online suppression list, then the marketer may not rent, sell, or exchange their e-mail addresses with third parties for solicitation purposes.

The above requests should be honored within 10 business days, and the marketer's opt-out mechanism should be active for at least 30 days from the date of the e-mail solicitation.

Only those marketers that rent, sell, or exchange information need to provide notice of a mechanism to opt out of information transfer to third-party marketers.

Marketers should process commercial e-mail lists obtained from third parties using DMA's E-Mail Preference Service suppression file. E-MPS need not be used on one's own *customer* lists, or when individuals have given affirmative consent to the marketer directly.

Solicitations sent via e-mail should disclose the marketer's identity and street address. The subject and "from" lines should be clear, honest, and not misleading, and the subject line should reflect the actual content of the message so that recipients understand that the e-mail is an advertisement. The header information should be accurate. A marketer should also provide specific contact information at which the individual can obtain service or information.

## E-MAIL AUTHENTICATION

### Article #41

Marketers that use e-mail for communication and transaction purposes should adopt and use identification and authentication protocols.

## USE OF SOFTWARE OR OTHER SIMILAR TECHNOLOGY INSTALLED ON A COMPUTER OR SIMILAR DEVICE

### Article #42

Marketers should not install, have installed, or use, software or other similar technology on a computer or similar device that initiates deceptive practices or interferes with a user's expectation of the functionality of the computer and its programs. Such practices include, but are not limited to, software or other similar technology that:

Takes control of a computer (e.g., relaying spam and viruses, modem hijacking, denial of service attacks, or endless loop pop-up advertisements)

Deceptively modifies or deceptively disables security or browser settings or

Prevents the user's efforts to disable or uninstall the software or other similar technology

Anyone that offers software or other similar technology that is installed on a computer or similar device for marketing purposes should:

Give the computer user clear and conspicuous notice and choice at the point of joining a service or before the software or other similar technology begins operating on the user's computer, including notice of significant effects* of having the software or other similar technology installed

Give the user an easy means to uninstall the software or other similar technology and/or disable all functionality

Give an easily accessible link to your privacy policy and

Give clear identification of the software or other similar technology's name and company information, and the ability for the user to contact that company

Determination of whether there are significant effects includes, for example:

* Whether pop-up advertisements appear that are unexpected by the consumer

* Whether there are changes to the computer's home page or tool bar

* Whether there are any changes to settings in security software, such as a firewall, to permit the software to communicate with the marketer or the company deploying the software, or

* Whether there are any other operational results that would inhibit the user's expected functionality

Cookies or other passive means of data collection, including Web beacons, are not governed by this Guideline. Article #38 provides guidance regarding cookies and other passive means of data collection.

## ONLINE REFERRAL MARKETING

### Article #43

Online referral marketing is a technique marketers use to get new marketing leads. Typically, the online marketer:

1. Encourages an individual to forward a marketing piece on to another individual (personally identifiable information is not collected), or

2. Asks an individual to provide the marketer with personally identifiable information about another individual so the marketer may contact that person directly

This guideline relates only to the second type of online referral marketing above, where personal information about a prospect is given to the marketer.

A marketer should not use personally identifiable information about a prospect provided online by another individual unless:

The marketer has first clearly disclosed to the referring individual the intended uses of the information

The marketer has disclosed to the referring individual that their own contact information will be provided to those they have referred to the marketer

The marketer discloses to the referred person the fact that their contact information was obtained from another individual. The marketer should make the referring person's information available in the first e-mail communication to the prospect. Or, the marketer can tell the prospect how to get the referring person's contact information at no cost and

The marketer provides, in the first and any subsequent e-mail communications, the ability to remove the referred person's name from future contact

Marketers should not contact referred individuals who are on their in-house email suppression lists, and should not sell, rent, share, transfer, or exchange a referred e-mail address unless they receive prior permission from the referred person to do so.

In addition, marketers who send Mobile Service Commercial Messages (MSCMs) to an email address on an Internet domain of a wireless network should comply with Article #39.

## E-MAIL APPENDING TO CONSUMER RECORDS

### Article #44

Definition of e-mail address appending: E-mail address appending is the process of adding a consumer's e-mail address to that consumer's record. The e-mail address is obtained by matching those records from the marketer's database against a third-party database to produce a corresponding e-mail address.

A marketer should append a consumer's e-mail address to its database only when the consumer gives a marketer permission to add his or her e-mail address to the marketer's database; or

1. There is an established business relationship with that consumer either online or offline, and

2. The data used in the append process are from sources that provided notice and choice regarding the acceptance of receiving third-party e-mail offers and where the consumer did not opt out, and

3. Reasonable efforts are taken to ensure the appending of accurate e-mail addresses to the corresponding consumer records

Marketers should not send e-mails to appended e-mail addresses that are on their in-house e-mail suppression files. Marketers should not send Mobile Service Commercial Messages (MSCMs) to appended e-mail addresses that belong to wireless handsets or devices unless the recipient has provided prior express authorization to receive such messages from the sender. A marketer should not sell, rent, transfer, or exchange an appended e-mail address of a consumer unless it first offers notice and choice to the consumer. All messages to an e-mail appended address should include a notice and choice to continue to communicate via e-mail.

Marketers should have in place appropriate record-keeping systems to ensure compliance with these guidelines.

## Telephone Marketing to Landline and Wireless Devices

### REASONABLE HOURS

#### Article #45

Telephone contacts, whether to a landline or wireless handset or device, should be made during reasonable hours as specified by federal and state laws and regulations.

### TAPING OF CONVERSATIONS

#### Article #46

Taping of telephone conversations by telephone marketers should only be conducted with notice to or consent of all parties, or the use of a beeping device, as required by applicable federal and state laws and regulations.

### RESTRICTED CONTACTS

#### Article #47

A marketer should not knowingly call or send a voice solicitation message to a consumer who has an unlisted or unpublished telephone number except in instances where that specific number was provided by the consumer to that marketer for that purpose. A marketer should maintain an in-house Do-Not-Call list and refrain from calling numbers for solicitation purposes that are on the marketer's in-house Do-Not-Call list.

A marketer should not knowingly call a wireless device, except in instances where the recipient has provided prior express consent to receive such calls from that marketer.

Prior to contacting a landline or wireless device, marketers should use applicable federal and DMA Wireless Suppression Files or another comprehensive wireless suppression service. Such suppression files should assist marketers in determining whether or not they are contacting a wireless device, including landline numbers that have been ported to wireless handsets or devices.

A marketer should use DMA's Telephone Preference Service as required in Article #31 and must use the federal Do-Not-Call registry and state Do-Not-Call lists when applicable prior to using any outbound calling list. Telemarketing calls may be made to landline telephones, where the telemarketer has an established business relationship with the individuals even if the individual is on the national registry. An established business relationship is defined as those persons with whom the marketer has had a transaction/received a payment within the last 18 months or those persons who have inquired about the marketer's products/services within the last 3 months. (Note: State laws may vary. DMA's website at: www.thedma.org/government/donotcall-lists.shtml attempts to provide current information on state Do-Not-Call lists.) Consumers who have provided informed, written permission to the marketer do not need to be suppressed by any Do-Not-Call list. Individuals can add or remove themselves from company-specific Do-Not-Call lists either orally or in writing.

Marketers should not use randomly or sequentially generated numbers in sales or marketing solicitations.

## CALLER-ID/AUTOMATIC NUMBER IDENTIFICATION REQUIREMENTS

### Article #48

Marketers engaging in telemarketing to landline and wireless telephone numbers should generate caller identification information, including:

A telephone number for the seller, service bureau, or customer service department that the consumer can call back during normal business hours to ask questions and/or to request not to receive future calls by making a do-not-call request, and

Whenever the technology is available from the marketer's telecommunications carrier, the name of the seller on whose behalf the call is placed or service bureau making the call.

Marketers should not block transmission of caller identification or transmit a false name or telephone number.

Telephone marketers using automatic number identification (ANI) should not rent, sell, transfer, or exchange, without customer consent, landline telephone numbers gained from ANI, except where a prior business relationship exists for the sale of directly related goods or services. With regard to mobile telephone numbers, marketers should abide by Articles #31 and #35.

## USE OF AUTOMATED DIALING EQUIPMENT

### Article #49

Marketers using automated dialing equipment should allow 15 seconds or four rings before disconnecting an unanswered call.

Marketers should connect calls to live representatives within two seconds of the consumer's completed greeting (except in cases where a prerecorded marketing message is used, in accordance with Article #55). If the connection does not occur within the two-second period, then the call is considered abandoned whether or not the call is eventually connected.

For any abandoned calls, the marketer should play a prerecorded identification message that includes the seller's name and telephone number, states the purpose of the call, and provides a telephone number at which the consumer can request not to receive future marketing calls.

Repeated abandoned or "hang up" calls to consumers' residential telephone numbers should be minimized. In no case should calls be abandoned more than:

> Three percent of answered calls, measured over the duration of a single calling campaign, if the campaign is less than 30 days, or separately over each successive 30-day period or portion of that period during which the campaign continues (unless a more restrictive state law applies), or
>
> Twice to the same telephone number within a 48-hour time period.

Marketers should only use automated dialing equipment that allows the telephone to immediately release the line when the called party terminates the connection.

When using any automated dialing equipment to reach a multi-line location, whether for business-to-consumer or business-to-business marketing, the equipment should release each line used before connecting to another.

Companies that manufacture and/or sell automated dialing equipment should design the software with the goal of minimizing abandoned calls to consumers. The software should be delivered to the user set as close to 0% as possible. Manufacturers should distribute these Guidelines for Automated Dialing Equipment to purchasers of dialing equipment and recommend that they be followed.

The dialers' software should be capable of generating a report that permits the user of the equipment to substantiate compliance with the guideline.

*Glossary of Terms Used*

**Automated Dialing Equipment**   any system or device that initiates outgoing call attempts from a predetermined list of phone numbers, based on a computerized pacing algorithm.

**Abandoned Call**   a call placed by automated dialing equipment to a consumer which when answered by the consumer, (1) breaks the connection because no live agent is available to speak to the consumer, or (2) no live agent is available to speak to the consumer within 2 seconds of the consumer's completed greeting.

**Abandonment Rate**   the number of abandoned calls over a 30-day period divided by the total number of calls that are answered by a live consumer. Calls that are not answered by a live consumer do not count in the calculation of the abandonment rate.

**Campaign**   refers to an offer of same good or service for the same seller. As long as the same good or service is being offered by the same seller, the offer is part of a single campaign, regardless of whether there are changes in the terms of the offer or the wording of any marketing material, including any telemarketing script, used to convey the offer. This definition applies to Article 48 only and is based on the FTC's definition of a "campaign" for purposes of calculating the abandonment rate.

**Report**   reportable information that should be made available which contains key points, including the percentage of abandoned calls.

**Telemarketing**   a telephone call, prerecorded message or text message placed to a landline or wireless number for the purpose of promoting, advertising, marketing or offering goods or services.

## USE OF PRERECORDED VOICE MESSAGING

### *Article #50*

Marketers who use prerecorded voice messaging should not automatically terminate calls or provide misleading or inaccurate information when a live consumer answers the telephone. Marketers should only use prerecorded voice messaging to sell good or services if they have first obtained the call recipient's prior express written agreement to receive prerecorded messages. In obtaining the consumer's written agreement, a marketer should observe the following:

Before obtaining the consumer's informed consent, the marketer should clearly and conspicuously disclose that the purpose of the agreement is to allow the marketer to make prerecorded message calls to the consumer.

The written agreement should evidence the consumer's informed consent to receive prerecorded calls by or on behalf of the specific marketer

The marketer should not require that the consumer agree to receive prerecorded calls as a condition of purchasing any good or service.

The agreement should include the consumer's telephone number and signature.

Marketers may obtain the written agreement electronically in accordance with applicable laws such as the E-Sign Act.

Marketers should begin making the initial disclosures as specified under Article #52 within two seconds of the call recipient's completed greeting.

Immediately following the initial disclosures, marketers should provide an opt-out mechanism that the call recipient can use to be placed on the company's do-not-call list. The type of mechanism that the marketer should provide depends on whether the call can be answered by a live person or by an automated device. If the marketer is able to determine whether a prerecorded call has been answered by a live person or an automated device, the marketer should tailor the prerecorded message to include the appropriate opt-out mechanism (either option 1 or 2 below):

(1)  If the call is answered by a live person, then the marketer should provide an automated interactive voice and/or keypress-activated opt-out mechanism that the recipient can use to make an opt-out request. The mechanism should be available for use at any time during the message.

(2)  If the call is answered by an answering machine or voicemail system, then the prerecorded message should provide a toll-free telephone number that the recipient can call to make an opt-out request at any time during the telemarketing campaign. The telephone number provided should connect directly to an automated interactive voice and/or keypress-activated opt-out mechanism. Consumers should be able to call at any time of the day, and on any day, during the duration of the campaign.

If the marketer is not able to determine whether a prerecorded call has been answered by a live person or an automated device, the prerecorded message should include both options 1 and 2.

The interactive voice and/or keypress-activated opt-out mechanism – regardless of whether the prerecorded call can be answered by a live person or automated answering device – should have the following features:

The opt-out mechanism should automatically add the number called to the entity's company-specific do-not-call list; and

The opt-out mechanism should immediately disconnect the call once the opt-out request is made.

Marketers may use prerecorded messages that provide information, but do not induce the purchase of goods or services, without first obtaining written consent and without providing an opt-out mechanism. Such calls should promptly disclose the identity of the caller at the outset of the call and provide a telephone number sometime during the call.

## USE OF TELEPHONE FACSIMILE MACHINES

### *Article #51*

Unless there is an established business relationship, or unless prior permission has been granted, advertisements, offers and solicitations, whether sent to a consumer or a business, should not be transmitted to a facsimile machine, including computer fax machines. An established business relationship in the fax context is defined as a prior or existing relationship based on a voluntary, two-way communication between the sender and recipient of the fax. Such communication includes a purchase, transaction, inquiry, or application for or about goods or services offered by the sender. For business relationships formed after July 9, 2005, the fax number must be provided voluntarily by the recipient to the sender, or be made available voluntarily by the recipient in a directory, advertisement, or Internet site.

Each permitted transmission to a fax machine must clearly contain on the first page:

> the date and time the transmission is sent;
> the identity of the sender which is registered as a business with a state;
> the telephone number of the sender or the sending machine; and

a clear and conspicuous opt-out notice.

The opt-out notice should:

> clearly state that the recipient may opt out of any future faxes and provide clear instructions for doing so;
> provide a domestic telephone number and fax number for recipients to transmit an opt-out request; and
> unless the telephone or fax number is toll-free, a cost-free mechanism to submit an opt-out request.

Senders must accept opt-out requests at any time.

Opt-out requests must be honored in 30 days, or sooner if feasible. An opt-out request terminates permission to send future faxes based only on an established business relationship.

## PROMOTIONS FOR RESPONSE BY TOLL-FREE AND PAY-PER-CALL NUMBERS

### *Article #52*

Promotions for response by 800 or other toll-free numbers should be used only when there is no charge to the consumer for the call itself and when there is no transfer from a toll-free number to a pay call.

Promotions for response by using 900 numbers or any other type of pay-per-call programs should clearly and conspicuously disclose all charges for the call. A preamble at the beginning of the 900 or other pay-per-call should include the nature of the service or program, charge per minute, and the total estimated charge for the call, as well as the name, address, and telephone number of the sponsor. The caller should be given the option to disconnect the call at any time during the preamble without incurring any charge. The 900 number or other pay-per-call should only use equipment that ceases accumulating time and charges immediately upon disconnection by the caller.

## DISCLOSURE AND TACTICS

### Article #53

Marketers should make the following initial disclosures promptly:
> The identity of the seller or charitable organization on behalf of which the call is made;
> That the purpose of the call is to sell goods or services or to solicit a charitable contribution;
> The nature of the goods or services offered during the call (if applicable); and
> If a prize promotion is offered, that no purchase or payment is necessary to be able to win a prize or participate in a prize promotion and that any purchase or payment will not increase the person's chances of winning.

Prior to asking consumers for payment authorization, telephone marketers should disclose the cost of the merchandise or service and all terms and conditions, including payment plans, whether or not there is a no refund or a no cancellation policy in place, limitations, and the amount or existence of any extra charges such as shipping and handling and insurance. At no time should high pressure tactics be utilized.

### Mobile Marketing

Please refer to the Glossary of Terms at the end of this section for the complete definitions of key concepts and terms used within this section.

## OBTAINING CONSENT TO CONTACT MOBILE DEVICES

### Article #54

Marketers should obtain prior express consent from existing and prospective customers before sending mobile marketing to a wireless device. A marketer should be able to demonstrate that the recipients knowingly and affirmatively consented. Consent may be obtained orally, in writing or electronically.

## PROVIDING NOTICE ABOUT MOBILE MARKETING PRACTICES

### Article #55

Marketers that send or intend to send mobile messages should publish an easily accessible notice of their practices (which includes but is not limited to a notice in their respective privacy policies) with regard to mobile marketing. The notice must include sufficient information to allow individuals to make an informed choice about their interaction with the marketer. This should include, at minimum, any applicable terms and conditions, details of the marketer's information handling practices and clear directions about how to unsubscribe.

The notice should be easy to find, read and understand, and should comply with existing DMA Guidelines. Of particular note, mobile marketers should review and comply with the Terms of the Offer (Articles #1–6, #8, #9), Advance Consent Marketing (Article #12), Special Offers & Claims (Articles #17–21), and Sweepstakes (Articles #22–27).

## MOBILE OPT-OUT REQUESTS

### Article #56

Every mobile marketing message sent must include a simple and easy-to-use mechanism through which the individual can opt out of receiving future mobile marketing messages. Where possible, the opt-out mechanism provided should allow the recipient to opt out via reply text message.

Where individuals respond to a marketer indicating that they do not wish to receive future mobile marketing messages (e.g. an individual replies "STOP"), the marketer should honor the request. Mobile opt-out requests should be honored within 10 days of being received and in accordance with Article #31.

## SPONSORSHIP OR AFFILIATE MOBILE MARKETING

### Article #57

A marketer may include an affiliate or sponsorship message within a mobile marketing communication, providing that the recipient has provided prior express consent to receive mobile marketing communications from that marketer and that it is clear from the mobile marketing communication that the message has been sent by that marketer and not by the sponsor. A marketer should also comply with Article #8—Disclosure of Sponsor and Intent.

## LOCATION-BASED MOBILE MARKETING

### Article #58

Marketers sending location-based mobile marketing messages to recipients should adhere to Articles #54–56. In addition, marketers should inform individuals how location information will be used, disclosed and protected so that the individual may make an informed decision about whether or not to use the service or consent to the receipt of such communications. Location-based information must not be shared with third-party marketers unless the individual has given prior express consent for the disclosure.

## MOBILE SUBSCRIPTION SERVICES AND PREMIUM-RATE MOBILE SERVICES

### Article #59

Mobile subscription services and mobile premium-rate products and/or services should be offered and delivered in accordance with DMA Guidelines, in particular the Terms of the Offer (Articles #1–6, #8, #9), Advance Consent Marketing (Article #12), Marketing to Children (Article #13–16), Special Offers & Claims (Articles #17–21) and Sweepstakes (Articles #22–27). All advertising and marketing for mobile subscription services or premium-rate mobile products/services should clearly define the service offered and outline the terms and conditions of the offer in accordance with these articles. Mobile subscription services or premium-rate mobile services should not be supplied unless the recipient has actively requested to receive the specific service to be supplied. Further, prior express consent should be obtained from a recipient prior to supplying additional or separate mobile subscription services and premium-rate mobile services at a subsequent date.

In accordance with Articles #12 and #48, and prior to sending or charging recipients for mobile subscription services and/or premium-rate mobile products/services, marketers should:

- provide the individual with an opportunity to see or hear the terms and conditions relating to the subscription service, including:
  - the cost per unit or the total cost of the subscription or premium-rate service;
  - the term of the subscription or premium-rate service;
  - the frequency of the subscription or premium-rate service;
  - payment intervals;
  - how to terminate the subscription or premium-rate service including any terms and conditions that apply to such termination.
- obtain prior express consent from recipients to receive and be charged for said subscriptions, products and/or services;

- inform recipients in the initial offer and in renewal reminders of their right to cancel their participation in the plan, and include contact information within the initial and renewal messages that allows the recipient to directly contact them;
- provide renewal reminders at the frequency specified in the initial offer;
- promptly honor requests for refunds due upon a consumer's cancellation of the plan;
- abide by Articles #13–16 and #48, and take reasonable precautions and implement adequate technical accountability and authentication measures to ascertain that
  (a) the mobile phone number or email address provided indeed belongs to the intended recipient of the subscriptions, products or services, and
  (b) periodically, and not less than once a month, include contact information within the mobile subscription service message or premium-rate mobile service message that allows the individual to directly contact the marketer.

### Glossary of Terms Used

**Individuals**    refers to the recipients or potential recipients of mobile marketing communications. For purposes of opting out (refer to Article #56), individuals refers to the number(s) and/or electronic address(es) of the wireless device(s) used by the recipients.

**Location-Based Services**    marketing text message targeted to a recipient dependent on their location, by a handset or user's physical location.

**Mobile Marketing**    refers to a sales and promotion technique in which promotional materials are delivered to a wireless phone or device. It can include both 'direct mobile marketing' (i.e. marketing communications targeted, sent or "pushed" to a wireless handset or device, such as marketing text messages) and 'indirect mobile marketing' (i.e. marketing that can be accessed or "pulled" by an individual via a wireless handset or device such as a mobile enabled website). Examples include the sending of SMS, MMS or WAP push messages, Bluetooth messaging and other interrupt based marketing to wireless devices.

**Mobile Service Commercial Message (MSCM)**    a commercial electronic message that is transmitted directly to a wireless device that is utilized by a subscriber of commercial mobile service.

**Multi-Media Messaging Services (MMS)**    an extension of a the Short Message Service Technology that permits the marketer to send marketing messages to a wireless handset that include multimedia objects such as images, audio and video.

**Mobile Subscription Service** a service that is provided periodically or on an ongoing basis that is delivered to an individual via a wireless handset or device. This includes free services and paid subscription services.

**Premium Rate Mobile Services** a service that is provided in a single instance, periodically or on an ongoing basis that is delivered to an individual via a wireless handset or device whereby the recipient pays a rate that exceeds the standard tariff to either receive or send a mobile message.

**Prior Express Consent** refers to affirmative, express and informed consent. A marketer should be able to demonstrate that recipients knowingly and affirmatively consented to be contacted on their wireless devices by that marketer for any purposes. Consent may be obtained orally, in writing or electronically. The notice to obtain consent should include a clear and conspicuous disclosure and require an active step on the part of the recipient to demonstrate that he/she agrees to receive the communication and/or product or service. This consent may be obtained via any channel. A pre-checked box, for example, would not suffice as an adequate means for obtaining consent.

**Recipient** any natural or legal person or business that receives a mobile marketing communication.

**Short Message Service (SMS)** a marketing message sent as a text message.

**Text message** a brief electronic message sent between mobile phones, containing text composed by the sender, usually input via a lettering system on a cell phone's numeric keypad.

**Wireless Application Protocol (WAP)** Refers to a secure specification that allows users to access information instantly via handheld wireless devices such as mobile phones, pagers, two-way radios, smartphones and communicators.

**Wireless** Refers to telecommunications in which electromagnetic waves (rather than some form of wire) carry the signal over part or all of the communication path.

**Wireless Handset** Umbrella term for devices, typically with keys to input data, that are mobile and can be operated by hand. Examples are mobile phones, pagers, two-way radios, smartphones and communicators.

## FUNDRAISING

### Article #60

In addition to compliance with these guidelines, fundraisers and other charitable solicitors should, whenever requested by donors or potential donors, provide financial information regarding use of funds.

## LAWS, CODES, AND REGULATIONS

### *Article #61*

Direct marketers should operate in accordance with laws and regulations of the United States Postal Service, the Federal Trade Commission, the Federal Communications Commission, the Federal Reserve Board, and other applicable federal, state, and local laws governing advertising, marketing practices, and the transaction of business.

Reprinted with Permission

# Appendix C.7: Society of Professional Journalists (SPJ) Code of Ethics

http://www.spj.org/ethicscode.asp

## Preamble

Members of the Society of Professional Journalists believe that public enlightenment is the forerunner of justice and the foundation of democracy. The duty of the journalist is to further those ends by seeking truth and providing a fair and comprehensive account of events and issues. Conscientious journalists from all media and specialties strive to serve the public with thoroughness and honesty. Professional integrity is the cornerstone of a journalist's credibility. Members of the Society share a dedication to ethical behavior and adopt this code to declare the Society's principles and standards of practice.

## Seek Truth and Report It

Journalists should be honest, fair and courageous in gathering, reporting and interpreting information.

Journalists should:

— Test the accuracy of information from all sources and exercise care to avoid inadvertent error. Deliberate distortion is never permissible.
— Diligently seek out subjects of news stories to give them the opportunity to respond to allegations of wrongdoing.
— Identify sources whenever feasible. The public is entitled to as much information as possible on sources' reliability.
— Always question sources' motives before promising anonymity. Clarify conditions attached to any promise made in exchange for information. Keep promises.
— Make certain that headlines, news teases and promotional material, photos, video, audio, graphics, sound bites and quotations do not misrepresent. They should not oversimplify or highlight incidents out of context.

— Never distort the content of news photos or video. Image enhancement for technical clarity is always permissible. Label montages and photo illustrations.
— Avoid misleading re-enactments or staged news events. If re-enactment is necessary to tell a story, label it.
— Avoid undercover or other surreptitious methods of gathering information except when traditional open methods will not yield information vital to the public. Use of such methods should be explained as part of the story.
— Never plagiarize.
— Tell the story of the diversity and magnitude of the human experience boldly, even when it is unpopular to do so.
— Examine their own cultural values and avoid imposing those values on others.
— Avoid stereotyping by race, gender, age, religion, ethnicity, geography, sexual orientation, disability, physical appearance or social status.
— Support the open exchange of views, even views they find repugnant.
— Give voice to the voiceless; official and unofficial sources of information can be equally valid.
— Distinguish between advocacy and news reporting. Analysis and commentary should be labeled and not misrepresent fact or context.
— Distinguish news from advertising and shun hybrids that blur the lines between the two.
— Recognize a special obligation to ensure that the public's business is conducted in the open and that government records are open to inspection.

## Minimize Harm

Ethical journalists treat sources, subjects and colleagues as human beings deserving of respect.
  Journalists should:

— Show compassion for those who may be affected adversely by news coverage. Use special sensitivity when dealing with children and inexperienced sources or subjects.
— Be sensitive when seeking or using interviews or photographs of those affected by tragedy or grief.
— Recognize that gathering and reporting information may cause harm or discomfort. Pursuit of the news is not a license for arrogance.
— Recognize that private people have a greater right to control information about themselves than do public officials and others who seek power, influence or attention. Only an overriding public need can justify intrusion into anyone's privacy.

— Show good taste. Avoid pandering to lurid curiosity.
— Be cautious about identifying juvenile suspects or victims of sex crimes.
— Be judicious about naming criminal suspects before the formal filing of charges.
— Balance a criminal suspect's fair trial rights with the public's right to be informed.

## Act Independently

Journalists should be free of obligation to any interest other than the public's right to know.
  Journalists should:

— Avoid conflicts of interest, real or perceived.
— Remain free of associations and activities that may compromise integrity or damage credibility.
— Refuse gifts, favors, fees, free travel and special treatment, and shun secondary employment, political involvement, public office and service in community organizations if they compromise journalistic integrity.
— Disclose unavoidable conflicts.
— Be vigilant and courageous about holding those with power accountable.
— Deny favored treatment to advertisers and special interests and resist their pressure to influence news coverage.
— Be wary of sources offering information for favors or money; avoid bidding for news.

## Be Accountable

Journalists are accountable to their readers, listeners, viewers and each other.
  Journalists should:

— Clarify and explain news coverage and invite dialogue with the public over journalistic conduct.
— Encourage the public to voice grievances against the news media.
— Admit mistakes and correct them promptly.
— Expose unethical practices of journalists and the news media.
— Abide by the same high standards to which they hold others.

*The SPJ Code of Ethics is voluntarily embraced by thousands of writers, editors and other news professionals. The present version of the code was adopted by the 1996 SPJ National Convention, after months of study and debate among the Society's members.*

# Appendix C.8: Radio Television Digital News Association

http://www.rtdna.org/pages/media_items/code-of-ethics-and-profes-sional-conduct48.php

Code of Ethics and Professional Conduct

## Preamble

Professional electronic journalists should operate as trustees of the public, seek the truth, report it fairly and with integrity and independence, and stand accountable for their actions.

*Public Trust:*   Professional electronic journalists should recognize that their first obligation is to the public.

   Professional electronic journalists should:
* Understand that any commitment other than service to the public undermines trust and credibility.
* Recognize that service in the public interest creates an obligation to reflect the diversity of the community and guard against oversimplification of issues or events.
* Provide a full range of information to enable the public to make enlightened decisions.
* Fight to ensure that the public's business is conducted in public.

*Truth:*   Professional electronic journalists should pursue truth aggressively and present the news accurately, in context, and as completely as possible.

Professional electronic journalists should:
* Continuously seek the truth.
* Resist distortions that obscure the importance of events.
* Clearly disclose the origin of information and label all material provided by outsiders.

Professional electronic journalists should not:

- Report anything known to be false.
- Manipulate images or sounds in any way that is misleading.
- Plagiarize.
- Present images or sounds that are reenacted without informing the public.

*Fairness*    Professional electronic journalists should present the news fairly and impartially, placing primary value on significance and relevance. Professional electronic journalists should:
- Treat all subjects of news coverage with respect and dignity, showing particular compassion to victims of crime or tragedy.
- Exercise special care when children are involved in a story and give children greater privacy protection than adults.
- Seek to understand the diversity of their community and inform the public without bias or stereotype.
- Present a diversity of expressions, opinions, and ideas in context.
- Present analytical reporting based on professional perspective, not personal bias.
- Respect the right to a fair trial.

*Integrity:*    Professional electronic journalists should present the news with integrity and decency, avoiding real or perceived conflicts of interest, and respect the dignity and intelligence of the audience as well as the subjects of news.
   Professional electronic journalists should:
- Identify sources whenever possible. Confidential sources should be used only when it is clearly in the public interest to gather or convey important information or when a person providing information might be harmed. Journalists should keep all commitments to protect a confidential source.
- Clearly label opinion and commentary.
- Guard against extended coverage of events or individuals that fails to significantly advance a story, place the event in context, or add to the public knowledge.
- Refrain from contacting participants in violent situations while the situation is in progress.
- Use technological tools with skill and thoughtfulness, avoiding techniques that skew facts, distort reality, or sensationalize events.
- Use surreptitious newsgathering techniques, including hidden cameras or microphones, only if there is no other way to obtain stories of significant public importance and only if the technique is explained to the audience.
- Disseminate the private transmissions of other news organizations only with permission.

Professional electronic journalists should not:
- Pay news sources who have a vested interest in a story.
- Accept gifts, favors, or compensation from those who might seek to influence coverage.
- Engage in activities that may compromise their integrity or independence.

*Independence:*   Professional electronic journalists should defend the independence of all journalists from those seeking influence or control over news content.

Professional electronic journalists should:
- Gather and report news without fear or favor, and vigorously resist undue influence from any outside forces, including advertisers, sources, story subjects, powerful individuals, and special interest groups.
- Resist those who would seek to buy or politically influence news content or who would seek to intimidate those who gather and disseminate the news.
- Determine news content solely through editorial judgment and not as the result of outside influence.
- Resist any self-interest or peer pressure that might erode journalistic duty and service to the public.
- Recognize that sponsorship of the news will not be used in any way to determine, restrict, or manipulate content.
- Refuse to allow the interests of ownership or management to influence news judgment and content inappropriately.
- Defend the rights of the free press for all journalists, recognizing that any professional or government licensing of journalists is a violation of that freedom.

*Accountability:*   Professional electronic journalists should recognize that they are accountable for their actions to the public, the profession, and themselves.

Professional electronic journalists should:
- Actively encourage adherence to these standards by all journalists and their employers.
- Respond to public concerns. Investigate complaints and correct errors promptly and with as much prominence as the original report.
- Explain journalistic processes to the public, especially when practices spark questions or controversy.
- Recognize that professional electronic journalists are duty-bound to conduct themselves ethically.
- Refrain from ordering or encouraging courses of action that would force employees to commit an unethical act.

- Carefully listen to employees who raise ethical objections and create environments in which such objections and discussions are encouraged.
- Seek support for and provide opportunities to train employees in ethical decision-making.

In meeting its responsibility to the profession of electronic journalism, RTDNA has created this code to identify important issues, to serve as a guide for its members, to facilitate self-scrutiny, and to shape future debate.

Adopted at RTNDA2000 in Minneapolis September 14, 2000.

Reprinted with Permission

# Appendix D: Sample Model Release Forms

## ADULT MODEL RELEASE

For valuable consideration received, I hereby grant to _____ ("Photographer") the absolute and irrevocable right and unrestricted permission, in respect of photographic portraits or pictures that he/she has taken of me or in which I may be included with others, to copyright the same, in his/her own name or otherwise; to use, re-use, publish, and re-publish the same in whole or in part, individually or in conjunction with other photographs, and in conjunction with any printed matter, in any and all media now or hereafter known, and for any purpose whatever, for illustration, promotion, art, editorial, advertising and trade, or any other purpose whatsoever without restriction as to alteration; and to use my name in connection therewith if he/she so chooses.

I hereby release and discharge Photographer from any and all claims and demands arising out of or in connection with the use of photographs, including without limitation any and all claims for libel or invasion of privacy.

This authorization and release shall also inure to the benefit of the heirs, legal representatives, licensees, and assigns of the Photographer, as well as the person(s) for whom he/she took the photographs.

I am of full age and have the right to contract in my own name. I have read the foregoing and fully understand the contents thereof. This release shall be binding upon me and my heirs, legal representatives, and assigns.

_____          _____
Date                                                          Name

                                                              _____

                                                              _____
                                                              Address

_____
Witness

## MINOR MODEL RELEASE

In consideration of the engagement as a model of the minor named below, and for other good and valuable consideration herein acknowledged as received, upon the terms hereinafter stated, I hereby grant to _____ ("Photographer"), his/her legal representative and assigns, those for whom Photographer is acting, and those acting with his/her authority and permission, the absolute right and permission to copyright and use, re-use, publish, and re-publish photographic portraits or pictures of the minor or in which the minor may be included, in whole or in part, or composite or distorted in character or form, without restriction as to changes or alterations from time to time, in conjunction with the minor's own or a fictitious name, or reproductions thereof in color or otherwise, made through any medium at his/her studios or elsewhere, and in any and all media now or hereafter known, for art, advertising, trade, or any other purpose whatsoever. I also consent to the use of any printed matter in conjunction therewith.

I hereby waive any right that I or the minor may have to inspect or approve the finished product or products or the advertising copy or printed matter that may be used in connection therewith or the use to which it may be applied.

I hereby release, discharge, and agree to save harmless Photographer, his/her legal representatives or assigns, and all persons acting under his/her permission or authority or those for whom he/she is acting, from any liability by virtue of any blurring, distortion, alteration, optical illusion, or use in composite form, whether intentional or otherwise, that may occur or be produced in the taking of said picture or in any subsequent processing thereof, as well as any publication thereof, including without limitation any claims for libel or invasion of privacy.

I hereby warrant that I am of full age and have every right to contract for the minor in the above regard. I state further that I have read the above authorization, release, and agreement, prior to its execution, and that I am fully familiar with the contents thereof. This release shall be binding upon me and my heirs, legal representatives, and assigns.

_____
Date

_____
Minor's Name

_____
Father/Mother/Guardian

_____
Minor's Address

_____
Address

_____
Witness

# Appendix E: Sample Copyright Agreements

## Sample Exclusive Copyright Agreement

___[John Doe]_____ (hereinafter "Licensor") is the author and owner of the rights of __[Photograph A]_____ (hereinafter the "Work"). ____[Jane Roe]_____ (hereinafter "Licensee") intends to acquire the right to use the Work as specified in this agreement (hereinafter "the Agreement").

1.  LICENSEE PUBLICATION. The Work will appear in _____[Great Photos in Sports]_____.

2.  GRANT OF RIGHTS. Licensor grants to Licensee and Licensee's successors and assigns, the exclusive right to reproduce and distribute the Work, in all foreign-language versions of the Work, in all media now known or later devised, and in promotional materials published and distributed in conjunction with the Work.

3.  FEES. Licensee shall pay Licensor a fee of ____[$X,XXX.XX]_____ as full payment for all rights granted. Payment shall be made upon execution of this Agreement or in other manner agreed to by the Parties.

4.  CREDIT AND SAMPLES. All versions of the Work shall attribute the Work to Licensor by including the following statement conspicuously displayed: By ___[John Doe]_____. Licensee shall have discretion over any additional, accompanying attribution or credit to accompany the Work.

Upon publication, Licensee shall furnish ___X___ copies of the Work to Licensor.

5.  REPRESENTATIONS AND WARRANTIES. Licensor warrants that he/she has the right to grant permission for the uses of the Work and the Work does not infringe the rights of any third parties.

6.  MISCELLANEOUS. This Agreement may not be amended except in a written document signed by both parties. The Parties agree that any court proceedings related to this Agreement shall be held in the exclusive jurisdiction of either the state or federal courts located in __[Your State, USA]_____.

This Agreement expresses the complete understanding of the parties with respect to the subject matter and supersedes all prior representations and understandings.

LICENSOR : _____
                        Name                                    Date

LICENSEE: _____
                        Name                                    Date

Sample Non-Exclusive Copyright Agreement

___[John Doe]_____ (hereinafter "Licensor") is the author and owner of the rights of __[Photograph A]_____ (hereinafter the "Work"). ____[Jane Roe]_____ (hereinafter "Licensee") intends to acquire the right to use the Work as specified in this agreement (hereinafter "the Agreement").

1. LICENSEE PUBLICATION. The Work will appear in a book entitled _____[Great Photos in
Sports]_____.

2. GRANT OF RIGHTS. Licensor grants to Licensee, and Licensee's successors and assigns, the non-exclusive right to reproduce and distribute the Work in _____[Great Photos in Sports] _____ and in printed and online advertising materials that specifically promote the sale of _____[Great Photos in Sports] _____. All other rights are reserved to the Licensor.

3. FEES. Licensee shall pay Licensor a fee of ____[$X,XXX.XX]_____ as full payment for all rights granted. Payment shall be made upon execution of this Agreement or in other manner agreed to by the Parties.

4. CREDIT AND SAMPLES. All versions of the Work shall attribute the Work to Licensor by including the following statement conspicuously displayed: Photo by ___[John Doe]_____. Licensee shall have discretion over any additional, accompanying attribution or credit to accompany the Work.

Upon publication, Licensee shall furnish ___X___ copies of the Work to Licensor.

5. REPRESENTATIONS AND WARRANTIES. Licensor warrants that he/she has the right to grant permission for the uses of the Work and the Work does not infringe the rights of any third parties.

6. MISCELLANEOUS. This Agreement may not be amended except in a written document signed by both parties. The Parties agree that any court proceedings related to this Agreement shall be held in the exclusive jurisdiction of either the state or federal courts located in __[Your State, USA]_____.

This Agreement expresses the complete understanding of the parties with respect to the subject matter and supersedes all prior representations and understandings.

LICENSOR:   _____
            Name                        Date

LICENSEE:   _____
            Name                        Date

# Notes

## 1 The First Amendment

1 U.S. CONST. amend. I.
2 *New York Times v. Sullivan*, 376 U.S. 254, 270 (1964).
3 R. Bork, *Neutral Principles and Some First Amendment Problems*, 47 IND. L.J. 1, 20 (1971).
4 D. M. Rabban, *The First Amendment in its Forgotten Years*, 90 YALE L.J. 514 (1981).
5 *Barron v. Mayor of Baltimore*, 32 U.S. (7 Pet.) 243 (1833).
6 *See*, e.g., F. J. TURNER, THE FRONTIER IN AMERICAN HISTORY (Henry Holt Co., New York, 1935).
7 C. 30, tit. 1, §3, 40 Stat. 217, 219 (comp. new st. 1917, §1012c).
8 *Schenck v. U.S.*, 249 U.S. 47 (1919).
9 *Abrams v. U.S.*, 250 U.S. 616 (1919).
10 *Schenck*, 249 U.S. at 52.
11 *Id.*
12 *Abrams*, 250 U.S. at 630 (Holmes, J., dissenting).
13 *See*, e.g., Criminal Anarchy Statute, N.Y. PENAL LAWS §160,161 (1909), originally enacted 1902.
14 *Gitlow v. New York*, 268 U.S. 652 (1925).
15 *Near v. Minnesota*, 283 U.S. 697 (1931).
16 *Dennis v. U.S.*, 341 U.S. 494 (1951).
17 *Yates v. U.S.*, 354 U.S. 298 (1957).
18 *Dennis*, 341 U.S. at 511.
19 *Id.*
20 *Brandenburg v. Ohio*, 395 U.S. 444 (1969).
21 *Id.* at 447.
22 *New York Times v. U.S.*, 403 U.S. 713 (1971).
23 *Id.*, quoting *Bantam Books Inc. v. Sullivan*, 372 U.S. 58, 70 (1963).
24 M. B. NIMMER, NIMMER ON FREEDOM OF SPEECH: A TREATISE ON THE FIRST AMENDMENT, §2.05 [B] 2–29 (Matthew Bender, 1988).
25 *Schenck*, 249 U.S. at 52.
26 NIMMER at §2.05 [B] 2–29. *See*, e.g., *Marsh v. Alabama*, 326 U.S. 501 (1946).
27 *Id.*, quoting *Greer v. Spock*, 424 U.S. 828 (1976).
28 NIMMER at §2.03, 2–15.
29 U.S. CONST. amend. XIV.
30 *Gitlow*, 268 U.S. 652.
31 *Whitney v. California*, 274 U.S. 357, 377 (1927).

32  *See*, e.g., *Shaw v. Hunt*, 519 U.S. 804 (1996).
33  *Barenblatt v. U.S.*, 360 U.S. 109 (1959).
34  *Id*. at 126.
35  NIMMER at §2.02 2–9.
36  44 Stat. 1162 (1927).
37  47 U.S.C. §151 (1934).
38  48 Stat. 1064 (1934) 47 U.S.C.A. §151 et seq.
39  *Nat'l. Broadcasting Co. v. U.S.*, and *C.B.S. v U.S.*, 319 U.S. 190 (1943).
40  *Miller v. California*, 413 U.S. 15 (1973).
41  *Id*.
42  *Texas v. Johnson*, 491 U.S. 997 (1989).
43  *Barnes v. Glen Theatre*, 501 U.S. 560, 111 S. Ct. 2456 (1991).
44  NIMMER at §1.02 [A], 1–7.
45  *Id*., quoting *Whitney v. California*, 274 U.S. 357, 375 (1927).
46  NIMMER at §1.02 [A], 1–7.
47  J. MILTON, AREOPAGITICA (Harlan Davidson, Wheeling, Ill., 1987).
48  J.S. MILL, ON LIBERTY, 1–8 (Cambridge University Press, New York, 1989).
49  NIMMER at §1.02 [A], 1–7.
50  *Abrams*, 250 U.S. at 630 (Holmes, J., dissenting).
51  *Id*.
52  NIMMER at §1.02 [B], 1–12.
53  *Id*., citing *Abrams*, 250 U.S. at 630 (Holmes, J., dissenting).
54  NIMMER at §1.02 [B], 1–12.
55  *Whitney*, 274 U.S. at 375 (Brandeis, J., concurring)
56  *Id*.
57  NIMMER at §1.02 [G], 1–42.
58  *Id*. at 1.02[I], 1–47, quoting V. Blasi, *The Checking Value in First Amendment Theory*, AM. B. FOUND. RES. J. (1977) 521.
59  NIMMER at §1.02 [H], 1–44.
60  *Id*., at 1–45, quoting A. MEIKLEJOHN, POLITICAL FREEDOM: THE CONSTITUTIONAL POWERS OF THE PEOPLE 75 (Oxford University Press, New York, 1965).
61  Title V of the Telecommunications Act of 1996, Pub. L. No. 104–104, 110 Stat. 56 (1996).
62  929 F. Supp. 824 (E.D. Pa. 1996).

## 2  The Development of the Commercial Speech Doctrine

1  FEDERAL TRADE COMMISSION, A GUIDE TO THE FEDERAL TRADE COMMISSION (1992).
2  *Schneider v. State*, 308 U.S. 147 (1939).
3  *Id*. at 165.
4  *Valentine v. Chrestensen*, 316 U.S. 52 (1942).
5  §318 of the N.Y.C. SANITARY CODE.
6  *Valentine*, 316 at 53 n. 1.
7  *Id*.
8  *Chrestensen v. Valentine*, 34 F. Supp. 596 (S.D.N.Y. 1940), *aff'd*, 122 F.2d 511 (2d Cir. 1941), *overruled*, 316 U.S. 52 (1942).
9  *Chrestensen v. Valentine*, 122 F.2d 511 (2d Cir. 1941), *overruled by* 316 U.S. 52 (1942).
10  *Valentine*, 316 U.S. at 54.
11  *Id*.

12 *See*, e.g., *Pittsburgh Press Co. v. Pittsburgh Commission on Human Relations et al.*, 413 U.S. 376 (1973).
13 *Pittsburgh Press*, 413 U.S. 376.
14 *Bigelow v. Virginia*, 421 U.S. 809 (1975).
15 *Pittsburgh Press*, 413 U.S. at 385.
16 *Id.* at 387.
17 *Id.* at 388.
18 *Id.* at 389.
19 *Bigelow v. Virginia*, 421 U.S. 809 (1975).
20 *Id.* at 811 n. 1.
21 *Id.* at 812.
22 *Id.* at 812, quoting VA. CODE ANN. §18.1–63 (1960).
23 *Id.* at 814, quoting 213 Va. 193–195, 191 S.E. 2d at 174–176.
24 *Roe v. Wade*, 410 U.S. 113 (1973).
25 *Bigelow*, 421 U.S. at 815.
26 *Id.* at 818.
27 *Id.* at 821.
28 *Id.* at 822.
29 *Id.* at 825.
30 *Id.*
31 *Id.* at 826.
32 *Id.*
33 *Id.* at 825.
34 *Va. State Bd. of Pharmacy v. Va. Citizens Consumer Council*, 425 U.S. 748 (1976).
35 *Id.* at 749.
36 *Id.* at 761.
37 *Id.* at 763.
38 *Id.*
39 *Id.* at 765.
40 *Id.*
41 *Id.* at 769.
42 *Id.* at 770.
43 *Id.* at 772 n. 1.
44 *Id.* at 772 n. 24.
45 *Id.* at 773.
46 *Bates v. State Bar of Arizona*, 433 U.S. 350 (1977).
47 *Id.* at 380.
48 *Id.* at 381.
49 *Id.*
50 *Id.* at 366–367.
51 *Id.* at 384.
52 *Id.* at 367.
53 *Central Hudson Gas & Elec. v. Public Serv. Comm'n*, 447 U.S. 557 (1980).
54 *Id.* at 560.
55 *Id.* at 563.
56 *Id.* at 566.
57 *Id.* at 564.
58 *Id.* at 599.
59 *Id.* at 569.
60 *Id.*
61 *Id.* at 570.

62  *Id.*
63  *Metromedia, Inc. v. City of San Diego*, 453 U.S. 490 (1981).
64  *Id.* at 493.
65  *Id.* at 543.
66  *Members of City Council v. Taxpayers for Vincent*, 466 U.S. 789 (1984).
67  *Posadas de Puerto Rico Assocs. v. Tourism Co.*, 478 U.S. 328 (1986).
68  *Id.* at 332.
69  *Id.*
70  *Id.* at 340.
71  *Id.* at 341.
72  *Id.*
73  *Id.*
74  *Id.* at 342.
75  *Id.* at 343.
76  *Id.* at 344.
77  *Id.* at 346.
78  *Id.*
79  *Bd. of Trustees St. Univ. of N.Y. v. Fox*, 492 U.S. 469 (1989).
80  *Id.* at 480.
81  *Id.*
82  *City of Cincinnati v. Discovery Network, Inc.*, 507 U.S. 410 (1993).
83  *Edenfield v. Fane*, 507 U.S. 761 (1993).
84  *City of Cincinnati v. Discovery Network, Inc.*, 507 U.S. 410 (1993).
85  *Discovery Network, Inc. v. City of Cincinnati*, 1990 S.D. Ohio 90–00437.
86  *Discovery Network, Inc. v. City of Cincinnati*, 946 F.2d 464, 468 (1991).
87  *Id.* at 471.
88  *Id.* at 472–473.
89  *Discovery Network*, 507 U.S. at 415.
90  *Id.* at 416.
91  *Id.*
92  *Id.* at 417.
93  *Id.* at 419.
94  *Id.* at 420 n. 16.
95  *Id.* at 423.
96  *Id.* at 430.
97  *Id.*
98  *Id.* at 431.
99  *Id.* at 443.
100 *Fane v. Edenfield*, 1990 U.S. Dist. LEXIS 18829 (N.D. Fla. Sep. 13, 1990).
101 *Edenfield*, 507 U.S. at 765.
102 *Fane v. Edenfield*, 945 F.2d 1514 (11th Cir. 1991).
103 *Edenfield*, 507 U.S. at 767.
104 *Id.* at 770–771.
105 *Id.* at 776.
106 *United States v. Edge Broadcasting Co.*, 509 U.S. 418 (1993).
107 18 U.S.C. §§1304 & 1307.
108 *Edge Broadcasting Co. v. United States*, 732 F. Supp. 633, 637 (E.D. Va. 1990).
109 *Id.*
110 *Id.* at 638.
111 *Id.*

112  *Id.*
113  *Id.* at 639.
114  *Id.*
115  *Id.* at 641.
116  *Id.* at 642.
117  *Edge Broadcasting Co. v. United States*, 5 F.3d 59 (4th Cir. 1992).
118  *Edge*, 509 U.S. at 426.
119  *Id.*, citing *Ohralik v. Ohio State Bar Ass'n*, 436 U.S. 447, 455–456 (1978).
120  *Id.* at 426.
121  *Id.* at 428.
122  *Id.* at 427.
123  *Id.* at 428.
124  *Id.*
125  *Id.* at 429.
126  *Id.*
127  *Discovery Network*, 507 U.S. at 419.
128  *Edge*, 509 U.S. at 429.
129  *Id.* at 430.
130  *Id.* at 436.
131  *Id.* at 437.
132  *Id.* at 439.
133  *Rubin v. Coors Brewing Co.*, 514 U.S. 476 (1995).
134  *Id.* at 484.
135  *Id.*
136  *Id.* at 485.
137  *Id.* at 484–485.
138  *Id.* at 488.
139  *Id.*
140  *Id.* at 497 (Stevens, J., concurring).
141  *Id.*
142  *44 Liquormart, Inc. & People's Super Liquor Stores, Inc. v. Rhode Is. & Rhode Is. Liquor Stores Ass'n*, 517 U.S. 484 (1996).
143  *44 Liquormart v. Racine*, 829 F. Supp. 543 (D.R.I., 1993).
144  *44 Liquormart*, 517 U.S. at 513.
145  *Id.* at 488.
146  *Id.* at 518.
147  *Greater New Orleans Broad. Ass'n, Inc. v. United States*, 527 U.S. 173 (1999).
148  *Id.* at 190.
149  *Lorillard Tobacco Co. v. Reilly*, 533 U.S. 525 (2001).
150  *Id.* at 562.
151  *Id.* at 566.
152  *Id.* at 586.
153  *Johanns v. Livestock Marketing Ass'n*, 544 U.S. 550 (2005).
154  15 U.S.C. §§41 *et seq.*
155  16 C.F.R. Part 310.
156  15 U.S.C. §§1601 *et seq.*
157  *National Do-Not-Call Registry*, https://www.donotcall.gov/FAQ/FAQBusiness.aspx#definitions (last visited July 20, 2007).
158  *Mainstream Marketing Services, Inc. v. FTC*, 355 F.3d 1228 (10th Cir. 2004).
159  447 U.S. 557 (1980).

160  *Mainstream Marketing Services, Inc. v. FTC* at 1238.
161  http://www.the-dma.org/government/donotcalllists.shtml.
162  47 U.S.C. §609 *et seq.*
163  *Id.*
164  FEDERAL COMMUNICATIONS COMMISSION, FAX ADVERTISING: WHAT YOU NEED TO KNOW, http://www.fcc.gov/cgb/consumerfacts/unwantedfaxes.html.
165  Kelly L. Frey *et al.*, *Don't Call, Email, Fax: The Consumer Advertising Labyrinth*, 43 (Apr.) TENN. B.J. 22.
166  A. Kozinski and S. Banner, *Who's Afraid of Commercial Speech?*, 76 VA. L. REV. 627 (1990).
167  R. Collins and D. Skover, *Commerce and Communication*, 71 TEX L. REV. 697 (1993).
168  A. Kozinski and S. Banner, *The Anti-History and Pre-History of Commercial Speech*, 71 TEX L. REV. 747.
169  *Virginia State Bd. of Pharmacy v. Virginia Citizens Consumer Council, Inc.*, 425 U.S. 748, 771 n. 24 (1976).
170  A. Kozinski and S. Banner, *The Anti-History and Pre-History of Commercial Speech*, 71 TEX L. REV. 747, at 757.
171  *Id.* at 758.
172  *Abrams v. U.S.*, 250 U.S. 616 at 630 (1919), (Justice Holmes, dissenting).
173  15 U.S.C. §§41 *et seq.*
174  Pub. L. 102–243, Dec. 20, 1991, 705 Stat. 2394, amending Title II of the Communications Act of 1934, 47 U.S.C. §§201 *et seq.*

## 3  Public Interest Information as Commercial Speech

1   *Valentine v. Chrestensen*, 316 U.S. 52 (1942).
2   *Id.* at 53.
3   *Id.* at 54.
4   *New York Times Co. v. Sullivan*, 376 U.S. 254 (1964).
5   *Id.* at 265.
6   *Id.* at 266.
7   *Id.*
8   *Id.*
9   *Id.*
10  *First National Bank of Boston v. Bellotti*, 435 U.S. 765 (1978).
11  *Id.* at 767.
12  *Id.* at 768.
13  *Id.*
14  *Id.* at 767.
15  *Id.* at 793.
16  *Id.* at 776.
17  *Consolidated Edison Co. v. Public Service Comm'n*, 447 U.S. 530 (1980).
18  *Id.* at 533.
19  *Id.*
20  *Id.*
21  *Id.* at 535.
22  *Id.* at 537.
23  *Id.* at 542.
24  *Austin v. Michigan St. Chamber of Commerce*, 494 U.S. 652 (1990).
25  *Id.* at 655.
26  *Id.*

27 *Michigan State Chamber of Commerce v. Austin*, 643 F. Supp. 397 (D. Mich., 1986).
28 *Michigan State Chamber of Commerce v. Austin*, 856 F.2d 783 (6th Cir. 1988).
29 *Austin*, 494 U.S. at 660.
30 *Id.* at 657; citing *Buckley v. Valeo*, 424 U.S. 39,96 (1976); quoting *Williams v. Rhodes*, 393 U.S. 23 (1968).
31 *Id.* at 657.
32 *Id.* at 660.
33 *Id.* at 662–664.
34 *Id.* at 664.
35 *Id.* at 698.
36 *Id.* at 700.
37 *Id.* at 713.
38 *Id.*
39 *Central Hudson Gas & Elec. v. Public Service Comm'n*, 447 U.S. 557, 571 (1980).
40 *Banzhaf v. FCC*, 405 F.2d 1082 (1968).
41 *Central Hudson*, 447 U.S. at 571 citing *Banzhaf*, 405 F.2d 1082.
42 *Pittsburgh Press Co. v. Human Rel. Comm'n*, 413 U.S. 376 (1973).
43 *Id.* at 385.
44 *Id.*
45 *Va. State Bd. of Pharmacy v. Va. Citizens Consumer Council*, 425 U.S. 748 (1976).
46 *Bigelow v. Virginia*, 421 U.S. 809 (1974).
47 *Virginia Pharmacy*, 425 U.S. at 762; citing *Pittsburgh Press*, 413 U.S. at 385; *Chaplinsky v. New Hampshire*, 315 U.S. 568, 572 (1942); *Roth v. United States*, 354 U.S. 476, 84 (1957).
48 *Board of Trustees, State Univ. of N.Y. v. Fox*, 492 U.S. 469 (1989).
49 *Pittsburgh Press*, 413 U.S. at 385.
50 *City of Cincinnati v. Discovery Network, Inc.*, 507 U.S. 410 (1993).
51 *Bates v. State Bar of Ariz.*, 433 U.S. 350 (1977).
52 *Friedman v. Rogers*, 440 U.S. 1 (1979).
53 *Central Hudson*, 447 U.S. 557.
54 *Dun & Bradstreet, Inc. v. Greenmoss Builders*, 472 U.S. 749 (1985).
55 *Id.* at 762.
56 *Id.* at 790, quoting *Pittsburgh Press*, 413 U.S. at 385.
57 *Bolger v. Youngs Drug Products Corp.*, 463 U.S. 60 (1983).
58 *Central Hudson*, 447 U.S. at 561.
59 *Id.* at 563 n. 5.
60 *Bolger*, 463 U.S. at 68.
61 *Id.* at 61.
62 *Id.* at 62.
63 *Youngs Drug Prods. Corp. v. Bolger*, 526 F. Supp. 823 (D.D.C., 1981)
64 *Ohralik v. Ohio State Bar Association*, 436 U.S. 447, 455–456 (1978).
65 *Bolger*, 463 U.S. at 65.
66 *Id.* at 66.
67 *Virginia Pharmacy*, 425 U.S. at 762; citing *Pittsburgh Press*, 413 U.S. at 385.
68 *Bolger*, 463 U.S. at 66.
69 *Id.* at 67.
70 *Id.*
71 *Id.* at n. 14.

72  *Pan Am Corp. v. Delta Air Lines (In re Pan Am Corp.)*, 161 B.R. 577 (S.D.N.Y., 1993)

73  *Id.* at 583.

74  *Id.*

75  *New York Public Interest Research Group v. Insurance Information Institute*, 531 N.Y.S.2d 1002 (N.Y. Misc., 1988).

76  *Id.* at 1011.

77  *New York City v. American School Publications*, 505 N.Y.S.2d 599 (July 31, 1986).

78  *New York City v. American School Publications*, 119 A.D.2d 13 (N.Y. App. Div. 1986).

79  *American School Publications*, 505 N.Y.S.2d at 603.

80  *In re Domestic Air Transportation Antitrust Litigation*, 141 F.R.D. 534 (N.D. Ga. 1992).

81  *Abramson v. Gonzalez*, 949 F.2d 1567 (11th Cir. 1992).

82  *Id.* at 1574, citing *Central Hudson*, 447 U.S. at 561.

83  *National Comm'n on Egg Nutrition v. F.T.C.*, 570 F.2d 157 (7th Cir. 1978).

84  *Id.* at 159.

85  *Id.* at 163.

86  *In re R. J. Reynolds Tobacco Co.*, [1983–1987] Trade Reg. Rep. (CCH) ¶ 22, 385 at 23, 467 (Aug. 6, 1986) *rev'd* Trade Reg. Rep. (CCH) ¶ 22, 522 at 22, 180 (April 11, 1988), *stay denied*, Trade Reg. Rep. (CCH) ¶22, 549 at 22, 231 (June 3, 1988).

87  *Id.*

88  *Id.*

89  *Id.*

90  *Id.*

91  *Kasky v. Nike, Inc.*, 119 Cal. Rptr. 2d 296 (Cal. 2002).

92  Press Release, Vada O. Manager, *NIKE Responds to Ambassador Young's Report on the NIKE Code of Conduct* (Jun. 24, 1997) (on file with PR Newswire).

93  Letter from Anita Chan, Professor, Contemporary China Centre, Australian National University, to Editor, *Journal of Commerce* 8A (Jul. 25, 1997) (on file with *Journal of Commerce*).

94  Steve Rubenstein, *S.F. Man Changes from Customer to Adversary*, SAN FRANCISCO CHRONICLE, May 3, 2002, at A6.

95  CAL. BUS. & PROF. CODE §§17200–17204; CAL. BUS. & PROF. CODE §17500; CAL. BUS. & PROF. CODE §17535.

96  *Kasky v. Nike, Inc.*, 93 Cal. Rptr. 2d 854, 857 (Cal. Ct. App. 1st Cir. 2000), *rev'd and rem'd*, 119 Cal. 4th 296 (2002).

97  *Kasky*, 119 Cal. Rptr. 2d at 302.

98  *Kasky*, 93 Cal. Rptr. 2d 854.

99  *Id.*

100  *Kasky*, 119 Cal. Rptr. 2d 296.

101  *Id.* at 311.

102  *Id.* at 313.

103  *Id.* at 313–314.

104  *Id.* at 314.

105  *Id.*

106  Jonathan A. Loeb and Jeffrey A. Sklar, *Practice Tips: The California Supreme Court's New Test for Commercial Speech*, 25 L.A. LAWYER 13, 13 (2002).

107  *Curtis Pub. Co. v. Butts*, 388 U.S. 130 (1967).

108 *Id.*
109 *Gertz v. Welch*, 418 U.S. 323 (1974).
110 *Sullivan*, 376 U.S. at 270.
111 *Bates*, 433 U.S. at 381.
112 *Dun & Bradstreet*, 472 U.S. 749.
113 *U.S. Healthcare, Inc. v. Blue Cross of Greater Philadelphia*, 898 F.2d 914 (3d Cir. 1990).
114 *Id.* at 918.
115 *Id.*
116 *Id.*
117 *Id.* at 919.
118 *Id.*
119 *U.S. Healthcare, Inc. v. Blue Cross of Greater Philadelphia*, 1988 U.S. Dist. LEXIS 1832 (E.D. Pa., 1988).
120 *U.S. Healthcare*, 898 F.2d at 920.
121 *Id.* at 932.
122 *Id.*
123 *Id.* at 934.
124 *Ohralik*, 436 U.S. at 456.
125 *U.S. Healthcare*, 898 F.2d at 935.
126 *Id.*
127 *Bellotti*, 435 U.S. at 791.
128 *C & C Plywood v. Hanson*, 583 F.2d 421 (9th Cir. 1978).
129 *Let's Help Florida v. McCray*, 621 F.2d 195 (5th Cir. 1980).
130 *Id.*
131 *Id.* at 197.
132 2 U.S.C. §441 (a) 1988.
133 To date, some 27 states have done so.
134 *Buckley v. Valeo*, 424 U.S. 1 (1976).
135 *FEC v. National Conservative Political Action Committee*, 470 U.S. 480 (1985).
136 Bipartisan Campaign Finance Act of 1997, S. 25, 105 Cong. (1997) (enacted).
137 *McConnell v. Federal Election Commission*, 540 U.S. 93 (1993).
138 Supreme Court docket 08–205 on appeal from *Citizens United v. Federal Election Commission* 530 F. Supp. 2d 274, 275 (2008).

## 4 Defamation, Product Disparagement and Related Torts

1 U.S. CONST. amend. I.
2 Alex S. Jones, *Iowa Experiment Offers Arbitration for Settling Libel Disputes Out of Court*, N.Y. TIMES, May 4, 1987.
3 *Dun & Bradstreet v. Greenmoss Builders, Inc.*, 472 U.S. 749 (1985).
4 *Paper Loses $9.2 Million Libel Suit*, N.Y. TIMES, Sec. 1, Part 2, at 29 (July 20, 1980).
5 *Nieman-Marcus v. Lait*, 13 F.R.D. 311.
6 *Gertz v. Robert Welch, Inc.*, 418 U.S. 323, 349 (1974).
7 JAMES ALEXANDER, ED. S. N. KATZ, A BRIEF NARRATIVE OF THE CASE AND TRIAL OF JOHN PETER ZENGER, PRINTER OF THE NEW YORK WEEKLY JOURNAL, John Harvard library (Belknap Press of Harvard University Press, Cambridge, Mass., 1972).
8 *New York Times v. Sullivan*, 376 U.S. 254 (1964).
9 *Gertz v. Robert Welch, Inc.*, 418 U.S. 323, 349 (1974).

10 *New York Times Co. v. Sullivan*, 376 U.S. 254 (1964).
11 *Gertz v. Robert Welch, Inc.*, 418 U.S. 323, 349 (1974).
12 *New York Times Co. v. Sullivan*, 376 U.S. 254, 257–258 (1964).
13 *Id.* at 262.
14 *New York Times Co. v. Sullivan*, 273 Ala. 646, 679 (1962).
15 *New York Times Co. v. Sullivan*, 376 U.S. 254, 280 (1964).
16 *Id.* at 279.
17 *Id.* at 270.
18 Id. at 269, quoting *Roth v. United States*, 354 U.S. 476, 484 (1957).
19 *Tavoulareas v. Piro*, 93 F.R.D. 35, 41 (D.D.C. 1981)
20 *Martin Marietta Corp. v. Evening Star Newspaper Co.*, 417 F. Supp., 956; also, KENNETH A. PLEVAN & MIRIAM L. SIROKY, ADVERTISING COMPLIANCE HANDBOOK (2d ed. 1991) at 513–546 (New York, Practising Law Institute, 1991).
21 *Golden Bear Distributing System v. Chase Revel, Inc.*, 708 F.2d 944, 952 (5th Circ. 1983).
22 *Steaks Unlimited v. Deaner*, 623 F.2d 264, 274 (3d Cir.1980); PLEVAN & SIROKY, ADVERTISING COMPLIANCE HANDBOOK, at 519.
23 *Coronado Credit Union v. KOAT Television, Inc.*, 99 N.M. 233 (1982); PLEVAN & SIROKY, ADVERTISING COMPLIANCE HANDBOOK, at 518.
24 IOWA CODE §528.29.
25 AMERICAN LAW INSTITUTE, RESTATEMENT OF THE LAW OF TORTS (2d ed.), Sec. 649 (American Law Institute Publishers, St. Paul, Minn., 1975).
26 *Id.*, Sec. 650A.
27 PLEVAN & SIROKY, ADVERTISING COMPLIANCE HANDBOOK, at 533.
28 *Gertz v. Welch*, 418 U.S. 323, 339–340 (1974).
29 *See* especially *Miami Herald v. Tornillo*, 418 U.S. 241.
30 Richard Sheridan as quoted in *Missner v. Clifford*, 2009 WL 2525007.
31 *Steaks Unlimited, Inc. v. Deaner*, 468 F. Supp. 779 (D.C. Pa. 1979).
32 15 U.S.C.A. §1125
33 47 U.S.C. §230
34 47 U.S.C. §230 (c)(1).
35 *Id.*
36 See for example CAL. CIV. PROC. §425.16, MINN. STAT. §541.02, GA. CODE §9–11–11.1, MCKINNEY'S CIVIL RIGHTS LAW §70-a.
37 See *Doe v. Cahill*, 884 A.2d 451 (Del. 2005) and *Dendrite International v. Doe*, 775 A.2d 756 (N.J. App. Div. 2001).
38 See *Ecommerce Innovations, LLC v. Does*, 2008 W.L. 5082292 (D. Ariz. Nov. 26, 2008) and *Krinsky v. Doe 6*, 159 Cal. App. 4th 1154, 72 Cal. Rptr. 3d 231 (Cal. Ct. App. 2008).
39 *Ehrenfeld v. Mahfouz*, 489 F.3d 542 (2d Cir. 2007).
40 *Thomas v. Winchester*, 6 New York 397 (1852).
41 *MacPherson v. Buick Motor Co.*, 217 N.Y. 382, 111 N.E. 1050 (1916).
42 *Id.*
43 AMERICAN LAW INSTITUTE, RESTATEMENT OF THE LAW OF TORTS (2d ed.), 402A (1965).
44 *Id.*
45 U.C.C. §2–313 (2).
46 Racketeer Influenced and Corrupt Organizations Act, Pub. L. No. 91–452.
47 *Id.*, §901(a), 84 Stat. 941 (1970).
48 BRUCE P. KELLER & TIFFANY D. TRUNKO, CONSUMER USE OF RICO TO

CHALLENGE FALSE ADVERTISING CLAIMS (American Law Institute Publishers, St. Paul, Minn., 1991).

49  *Id.*

50  *Bauder v. Ralston Purina Co.*, 1989 WL 143283 (E.D. Pa.); interview with Elkan Katz, attorney for Bauder, December 30, 1994.

51  *Rahmig v. Mosely Machinery Co.*, 226 Neb. 423, 412 N.W.2d (1987).

52  Quoted in Janet R. Pritchett, *Texas Supreme Court Refuses to Impose a Duty to Warn of Alcoholism Upon Beverage Alcohol Manufacturers*, 22 TEX. TECH L. REV. 937 (1991).

53  *Id.*

54  Quoted in *Haines v. Liggett Group, Inc.*, 814 F. Supp. 414 (424 F. Supp. D.N.J. 1993); reprinted in Richard A. Daynard, *The Third Wave of Tobacco Products Liability Cases*, TRIAL (November 1994) at 34.

## 5  Invasion of Privacy: False Light, Private Facts, Intrusion and Other Related Torts

1   Samuel Warren & Louis Brandeis, *The Right to Privacy*, 4 HARV. L. REV. 193 (1890).

2   *Id.* at 196.

3   William L. Prosser, *Privacy*, 48 CAL. L. REV. 383 (1960).

4   *Id.* at 398.

5   *Jews for Jesus, Inc. v. Rapp*, 997 So. 2d 1098 (Fla. 2008).

6   *Ayash v. Dana-Farber Cancer Institute*, 443 Mass. 367 (2005).

7   *Cain v. Hearst Corp.*, 878 S.W.2d 577 (Tex., 1994).

8   *Renwick v. News & Observer Pub. Co.*, 310 N.C. 312 (1984).

9   AMERICAN LAW INSTITUTE, RESTATEMENT OF THE LAW OF TORTS (2d ed.), §649 (American Law Institute Publishers, St. Paul, Minn., 1975).

10  *Leverton et al. v. Curtis Publishing Co.*, 192 F.2d 974 (1951).

11  William Brashler, *The Black Middle Class: Making It*, N.Y. TIMES MAGAZINE, Dec. 3, 1978, 147–148.

12  *Arrington v. New York Times*, 5 Media L. Rep. 2581 (1980).

13  *Time, Inc., v. Hill*, 385 U.S. 374 (1974).

14  *Id.*

15  *Id.*

16  *Id.*

17  *Hill v. Hayes*, 18 A.D.2d 485 (N.Y.A.D. 1963).

18  *Hill v. Hayes*, 15 N.Y.2d 986 (N.Y. 1965).

19  *New York Times v. Sullivan*, 376 U.S. 254 (1964).

20  *Time, Inc., v. Hill*, 385 U.S. 374 (1974).

21  *Gertz v. Robert Welch, Inc.*, 418 U.S. 323, 339–340 (1974).

22  PRACTISING LAW INSTITUTE, COMMUNICATIONS LAW, Vol. 1, 526 (Practising Law Institute, New York, 2005).

23  *Cantrell v. Forest City Publishing Co.*, 419 U.S. 245 (1974).

24  *Id.*

25  *Cantrell v. Forest City Publishing Co.*, 484 F.2d 150.

26  *Cantrell v. Forest City Publishing Co.*, 419 U.S. at 253.

27  *Spahn v. Julian Messner*, 221 N.E.2d 543, 545 (1966).

28  *Id.*

29  *Peay v. Curtis Publishing Co.*, 28 F. Supp. 305 (1948).

30  *Crump v. Beckley Newspapers Inc.*, 320 S.E.2d 70 (1984).

31  BLACK'S LAW DICTIONARY (West Group, St. Paul, Minn., 6th ed. 1990).

32  *Bindrim v. Mitchell*, 92 Cal. App. 3d 61(Cal. App. 1979).
33  4 HARV. L. REV. at 196 (1890).
34  *Wojtowicz v. Delacorte Press*, 43 N.Y.2d 858 (1978).
35  *WJLA-TV v. Levin*, 264 Va. 140 (2002).
36  *Doe v. Methodist Hosp.*, 690 N.E.2d 681 (1997).
37  *Hall v. Post*, 323 N.C. 259 (1988).
38  RESTATEMENT (SECOND) OF TORTS, §652D.
39  *Sipple v. Chronicle Publishing Co.*, 154 Cal. App. 3d 1040 (1984).
40  *Id.*
41  *Id.*
42  *Reid v. Pierce County*, 136 Wash. 2d 195 (1998).
43  RESTATEMENT (SECOND) OF TORTS §652D, illus. 10 (1977).
44  *Horn v. Patton*, 291 Ala. 701 (1973).
45  *M.G. v. Time Warner, Inc.*, 89 Cal. App. 4th 623 (2001).
46  *Trammell v. Citizens News Co.*, 285 Ky. 539 (1941).
47  *McSurely v. McClellan*, 753 F.2d 88, 112 (D.C. Cir. 1985).
48  *Id.* at 109 (D.C. Cir. 1985).
49  *Diaz v. Oakland Tribune, Inc.*, 139 Cal. App. 3d 118 (1983).
50  *Id.*
51  *Id.*
52  *Cox Broadcasting Co. v. Cohn*, 420 U.S. 469 (1975).
53  *Id.* at 496.
54  *The Florida Star v. B.J.F.*, 491 U.S. 524 (1989).
55  *Id.* at 529.
56  *Florida Star v. B.J.F.*, 499 So. 2d 883 (Fla. App. 1 Dist., 1986).
57  Quoted in GEORGE C. CHRISTIE & JAMES E. MEEKS, CASES AND MATERIALS ON THE LAW OF TORTS (Gale Cengage, Florence, Ky., 2d ed. 1990) at 1116.
58  RESTATEMENT (SECOND) OF TORTS §652D.
59  *Hawkins v. Multimedia*, 344 S.E.2d 145 (1986).
60  PRACTISING LAW INSTITUTE, COMMUNICATIONS LAW, Vol. 1, 524 (Practising Law Institute, New York, 2005).
61  William L. Prosser, *Privacy*, 48 CAL. L. REV. 383, 397 (1960).
62  *Sidis v. F-R Publishing Corp.*, 113 F.2d 806 (1940).
63  *Id.* at 807–808.
64  *Id.* at 809.
65  *Barber v. Time, Inc.*, 159 S.W.2d (1942).
66  *Id.*
67  *Briscoe v. Reader's Digest Association*, 483 P.2d 34 (1971). Overruled 2004.
68  *Id.*
69  *Id.*
70  *Id.* at 41–42.
71  VICTOR HUGO, LES MISERABLES (Hurst & Blackett, London, 1862).
72  NATHANIEL HAWTHORNE, THE SCARLET LETTER (Ticknor & Fields, Boston, Mass., 1850).
73  *Briscoe v. Reader's Digest Association*, 483 P.2d at 44 n. 18 (1971).
74  *Virgil v. Time, Inc.*, 527 F.2d 1122 (1975).
75  *Id.* at 1124 n. 1.
76  *Smith v. NBC Universal, et al.* 524 F. Supp. 2d 315 (S.D.N.Y. 2007).
77  *Mendelson v. The Morning Call, Inc.*, 2007 Pa. Dist. & Cnty. Dec. LEXIS 256 (C.P. Leh. Sept. 4, 2007).
78  RESTATEMENT (SECOND) OF TORTS §652B (1977).

79 See for example, COMMUNICATIONS LAW IN A DIGITAL AGE, Vol. 3, 286 (Practising Law Institute, 2008).
80 *Dietemann v. Time, Inc.*, 449 F.2d 245 (9th Cir. 1971).
81 *Crow v. Crawford and Co.*, 259 S.W.3d 104 (2008).
82 *Quinn Emanuel Urquhart Oliver & Hedges, LLP v. LaTorraca & Goettsch*, 2006 Cal. App. Unpub. LEXIS 1706, 34 Med. L. Rptr. 1453 (2006).
83 *Bilney v. Evening Star*, 43 Md. App. 560, 406 A.2d 652 (1979).
84 *LeMistral, Inc. v. Columbia Broadcasting System*, 61 A.D.2d 491 (1978).
85 CAL. CIV. CODE §1708.8 (2006).
86 RESTATEMENT (FIRST) OF TORTS §46, cmt. c (1934).
87 RESTATEMENT (SECOND) OF TORTS §46 (1965).
88 *Bear v. Reformed Mennonite Church*, 462 Pa. 330, 342 A.2d 105 (1975).
89 *Ford Motor Credit Co. v. Sheehan*, 373 So. 2d 956 (1979).
90 *Chuy v. Philadelphia Eagles Football Club*, 595 F.2d 1265 (3rd cir. 1979).
91 *Meiter v. Cavenaugh*, 40 Colo. App. 454 (1978).
92 *Hustler Magazine v. Falwell*, 485 U.S. 46 (1988).
93 *Id.* at 48.
94 *Id.* at 49.
95 *Falwell v. Flynt*, 797 F.2d 1270 (1986).
96 *Hustler Magazine v. Falwell*, 485 U.S. at 51 (1988).
97 *Hood v. Naeter Brothers Publishing Co.*, 562 S.W.2d 770 (1970).
98 *Id.* at 771.
99 *Strange v. Entercom Sacramento LLC*, Case no. 07AS00377 (Cal. Super. Ct. Sacramento County, 2009).

## 6 Invasion of Privacy: Misappropriation and Right of Publicity

1 As later scholarship has noted, however, Warren's daughter was only 7 years old at the time. In *Demystifying a Landmark Citation*, 13 SUFFOLK U.L. REV. 875, Professor Jerome Barron suggests that Warren was in fact angry at press criticism of his father-in-law, Thomas Bayard, Sr., who had been a U.S. Senator and a member of President Grover Cleveland's cabinet.
2 Samuel Warren & Louis Brandeis, *The Right to Privacy*, 4 HARV. L. REV. 193 (1890).
3 *Roberson v. Rochester Folding Box Co.*, 171 N.Y. 538, 556 (1902).
4 *Id.*
5 N.Y. CLS CIV. R. §§50–51.
6 *Pavesich v. New England Life Ins. Co.*, 50 S.E. 68, 79 (1905).
7 *State v. Hinkle*, 131 Wash. 86, 93 (1924).
8 AMERICAN LAW INSTITUTE, RESTATEMENT OF THE LAW OF TORTS (2d ed.), Sec. 652d (American Law Institute Publishers, St. Paul, Minn., 1975).
9 Quoted in an excellent discussion of privacy in GEORGE C. CHRISTIE & JAMES E. MEEKS, CASES AND MATERIALS ON THE LAW OF TORTS (Gale Cengage, Farmington Hills, Mich., 1990) at 1088ff.
10 *Shields v. Gross*, 563 F. Supp. 1253 (D.N.Y. 1983).
11 *McAndrews v. Roy*, 131 So. 2d 256 (La. Ct. App., 1961).
12 MICHAEL HERON, STOCK PHOTOGRAPHY HANDBOOK (American Society of Media Photographers, 2d ed. 1990), at 123–139.
13 *Id.* at 127.
14 *Namath v. Sports Illustrated*, 48 A.D.2d 487 (N.Y. App. Div. 1975).
15 *Comedy III Productions, Inc. v. Gary Saderup, Inc.*, 25 Cal. 4th 387 (2001).
16 *Id.* at 407.

17  *ETW Corp. v. Jireh Publ'g, Inc.*, 332 F.3d 915 (6th Cir. 2003).
18  *Doe v. McFarlane*, 207 S.W.3d 52 (Mo. App. E.D. 2006).
19  *Allen v. National Video, Inc.*, 610 F. Supp. 612 (S.D.N.Y. 1985).
20  *Jones v. Herald Post Co.*, 18 S.W.2d 972, 973 (Ky. 1929).
21  RESTATEMENT (SECOND) OF TORTS, §652D.
22  *Mendonsa v. Time Inc.*, 678 F. Supp. 967 (D.R.I. 1988).
23  *Pavesich v. New England Life Ins. Co.*, 50 S.E. at 69.
24  *Id.* at 74.
25  Christopher Pesce, *The Likeness Monster: Should the Right of Publicity Protect Against Imitation?*, 65 N.Y.U. L. REV. 782, 782 (1990).
26  *Haelan Laboratories v. Topps Chewing Gum*, 202 F.2d 866 (2d Cir. 1953); cert. denied, 346 U.S. 816 (1953).
27  *Id.* at 868.
28  There is some dispute on this point. William L. Prosser, in HANDBOOK OF THE LAW OF TORTS (4th ed. 1971), found slim evidence to suggest the possibility of descendability (a 1945 Arizona case, *Reed v. Real Detective Pub. Co.*, 63 Ariz. 294), but as he noted, "there is no common law right of action for a publication concerning one who is already dead."
29  *Martin Luther King, Jr., Center for Social Change, Inc. v. American Heritage Products, Inc.*, 250 Ga. 135 (1982).
30  *Hirsch v. S. C. Johnson & Son*, 90 Wis. 2d 379 (1979).
31  *Ali v. Playgirl*, 447 F. Supp. 723 (S.D.N.Y. 1978).
32  Lanham Act (15 U.S.C. §1051–1127).
33  *Allen v. National Video, Inc.*, 610 F. Supp. 612 (S.D.N.Y. 1985).
34  *Id.* at 617.
35  *Onassis v. Christian Dior-New York, Inc.*, 122 Misc. 2d 603 (N.Y. Misc., 1984).
36  *Id.* at 605.
37  *Id.* at 612.
38  *Cher v. Forum International*, 692 F.2d 634 (9th Cir. 1982).
39  *Id.* at 638.
40  *Id.* at 639.
41  *The Motschenbacher v. R. J. Reynolds Tobacco Co.*, 498 F.2d 821 (9th Cir. 1974).
42  *Id.* at 822.
43  *Carson v. Here's Johnny Portable Toilets*, 698 F.2d 831 (6th Cir. 1983).
44  *Groucho Marx Prods., Inc. v. Day & Night Co.*, 523 F. Supp. 485, 491 (S.D.N.Y. 1981).
45  *Lugosi v. Universal Pictures*, 25 Cal. 3rd 813 (1979), as reported by PLEVAN & SIROKY, ADVERTISING COMPLIANCE HANDBOOK, at 557.
46  *Lahr v. Adell Chemical Co.*, 300 F.2d 256 (1st Cir. 1962).
47  *Midler v. Ford Motor Co.*, 849 F.2d 460 (9th Cir. 1988).
48  Paul Feldman, *Tom Waits Wins $2 ½ Million in Voice-Theft Suit*, L.A. TIMES, May 9, 1990, Metro; Part-B, Metro Desk.
49  Pesce, *Likeness Monster*, supra n. 25, at 818.
50  Richard Kurnit, *Right of Publicity*, ENT. & SPORT LAW. 4, 3 (Winter/Spring 1986), at 15.
51  *Zacchini v. Scripps-Howard Broadcasting Co.*, 433 U.S. 562 (1977).
52  *Id.* at 576.
53  Tamar Lewin, *Whose Life Is It, Anyway? It's Hard to Tell*, N.Y. TIMES, Nov. 21, 1982; RALPH L. HOLSINGER, MEDIA LAW (McGraw-Hill, New York, c.1991) at 231.

54  *Doe v. Friendfinder Network, Inc.*, 540 F. Supp. 2d 288 (D.N.H. 2008).
55  *Lewis v. Marriot Int'l*, 527 F. Supp. 2d 422 (E.D. Pa., Dec. 20, 2007).
56  *Amigo Broad. v. Spanish Broad. Sys., Inc.*, 521 F.3d 472 (5th Cir. 2008).
57  *Butkus v. Downtown Athletic Club of Orlando, Inc.*, 2008 W.L. 2485524 (C.D. Cal., March 31, 2008).
58  C. J. Hughes, *For $5 Million, Woody Allen Agrees to Drop Lawsuit*, N.Y. TIMES, May 19, 2009; *Samuel Michael Keller v. Electronic Arts Inc. et al.*, CV 09–1967 (N.D. Cal 2009).
59  *Christoff v. Nestle USA, Inc.*, 213 P.3d 132 (Cal. 2009).
60  *Ji v. Bose Corp.*, 526 F. Supp. 2d 349 (D. Mass. 2008).
61  *The Romantics v. Activision Publishing Inc.*, 532 F. Supp. 2d 884 (E.D. Mich. 2008).
62  *Burck v. Mars, Inc. et al.*, 2008 W.L. 2557427 (S.D.N.Y. 2008).
63  *C.B.C. Distribution & Marketing, Inc. v. Major League Baseball Advanced Media*, L.P., 505 F.3d 818 (8th Cir. 2007).
64  Katie Thomas, *Retired NFL Player Jim Brown Loses Lawsuit Against Video Game Publisher*, N.Y. TIMES, Sept. 29, 2009.
65  Jay Reeves, *Borat Wins Court Case Against Etiquette Teacher*, HUFFINGTON POST, Jan. 19, 2008.

## 7  Copyright

1  Statute of Anne (1710), *Primary Sources on Copyright* (1450–1900), eds L. Bently & M. Kretschmer, www.copyrighthistory.org (last visited January 6, 2010).
2  U.S. CONST art. I, §8.
3  EDMUND KITCH & HARVEY PERLMAN, LEGAL REGULATION OF THE COMPETITIVE PROCESS 622 (Foundation Press, New York, 1979).
4  17 U.S.C. §101 (1996).
5  17 U.S.C. §102 (a) (1996).
6  *Id.*
7  *Hoehling v. Universal City Studios, Inc.*, 618 F.2d 927, 6 Med. L. Rptr. 1053 (2d Cir. 1980); *cert. denied*, 449 U.S. 841 (1980).
8  *Id.*
9  *Lapine v. Seinfeld*, 2009 U.S. Dist. LEXIS 82304; 92 U.S.P.Q.2d (BNA) 1428; Copyright L. Rep. (CCH) P29, 828.
10  17 U.S.C. §102 (1996).
11  *Id.*
12  17 U.S.C. §101 (1996).
13  *Id.*
14  *Id.*
15  17 U.S.C. §102 (1996).
16  *Miller v. Universal Studios, Inc.*, 650 F.2d 1365, 7 Med. L. Rptr. 1735 (5th Cir. 1981).
17  *Miller v. Universal Studios, Inc.*, 460 F. Supp. 984 (S.D. Fla. 1978).
18  *Id.*
19  *Feist Publications, Inc. v. Rural Telephone Service Co.*, 499 U.S. 340, 111 S. Ct. 1282 (1991).
20  *Id.*
21  17 U.S.C. §101.
22  *Community for Creative Non-Violence v. Reid*, 490 U.S. 730, 109 S. Ct. 2166, 104 L. Ed. 2d 811, 16 Med. L. Rptr. 1769 (1989).

23  *Id.*
24  *Id.*
25  *Id.*
26  *Id.*
27  *New York Times Co., Inc. v. Tasini,* 533 U.S. 483 (2001).
28  *Id.*
29  17 U.S.C. § 101 (1996).
30  Kent Middleton, *Freelance Photographers and Publishers: The Need for a Contract to Establish Joint Authorship in Commissioned Works.* Paper presented to the Association for Education in Journalism and Mass Communication Southeast Regional Colloquium, Orlando, Florida, April 1991, at 23.
31  *Id.*
32  17 U.S.C. § 106 (1996).
33  See http://www.copyright.gov.
34  17 U.S.C. § 203(b)(1) (1996).
35  U.S. Copyright Office, *The United States Joins the Berne Union* (Circular 93a) (1989) at 3.
36  Pub. L. No. 101–650, tit. VI, 104 Stat. 5089, 5128–33 (1990).
37  *Id.*
38  *Gilliam v. American Broadcasting Cos., Inc.* 538 F.2d 14 (2d Cir. 1976).
39  Another licensing agency is SESAC, Inc. (which was one known as the Society of European State Authors and Composers), but ASCAP and BMI dominate the field.
40  See *Buffalo Broadcasting Co., Inc. v. American Society of Composers, Authors and Publishers,* 744 F.2d 917 (2d Cir. 1984); *cert. denied,* 469 U.S. 121, 105 S. Ct. 1181, 84 L. Ed. 2d 329 (1985).
41  *Id.*
42  The Fairness in Music Licensing Act (FIMLA), part of the Sonny Bono Copyright Term Extension Act referenced in note 46, is codified at Pub. L. No. 105–298, 112 Stat. 2830, title II.
43  Pub. L. No. 105–298, 112 Stat. 2830, title II.
44  17 U.S.C. 111 (a)(1) (1996).
45  U.S. CONST. art. 1, § 8.
46  Copyright Term Extension Act (CTEA), Pub. L. 105–298, § 102(b) and (d), 112 Stat. 2827–2828.
47  17 U.S.C. § 101 (1996).
48  17 U.S.C. §§ 405 and 406 (1996).
49  17 U.S.C. § 401(a) (1996).
50  17 U.S.C. § 402(a) (1996).
51  See C.F.R. § 201.20 for the complete regulations. They also are reprinted in Circular 96–Section 201.20 (Methods of Affixation and Positions of the Copyright Notice on Various Types of Works") (1006) of the Copyright Office and summarized in Circular 3 ("Copyright Notice") (1996) at 4–5 of the Copyright Office.
52  17 U.S.C. § 401(c) (1996).
53  *Id.*
54  See C.F.R. § 201(df) and U.S. Copyright Office, COPYRIGHT NOTICE (Circular 3) (1996), at 4.
55  Public Law 103–307, enacted on June 26, 1992, made even renewal registration optional by automatically extending the duration of copyright obtained between January 1, 1964, and December 21, 1977, to an additional 47-year

period. No registration renewal needs to be filed for this extension. There are some advantages to renewal registration, however. See U.S. Copyright Office, Renewal of Copyright (Circular 61) (1995) at 2.

56  See http://www.copyright.gov.

57  17 U.S.C. §501(a) (1996).

58  Mariana McConnell, *Lavigne Settles in Copyright Infringement Lawsuit*, http://www.cinemablend.com/music/Lavigne-Settles-in-Copyright-Infringement-Lawsuit-8229.html (last visited January 6, 2010).

59  Business Wire, *Lucasfilm Ltd. Wins Major Copyright Infringement Lawsuit Against Star Wars Stormtrooper Pirate*, http://findarticles.com/p/articles/mi_m0EIN/is_2006_Oct_11/ai_n27041843 (last visited January 6, 2010).

60  *Chicago Catholics Lose Copyright Case*, ("National Digest" section), ATLANTA JOURNAL (wire reports), April 20, 1984, at A1, col. 1.

61  *Before You Wish Upon a Star, Better Check the Copyright*, ("People" section), Lexington (Ky.) HERALD-LEADER (wire services), May 1, 1989, at A12, col. 1.

62  *Garrison Keillor Settles Suit with National Public Radio*, ("People" section), CINCINNATI POST, June 24, 1988, at A2, col. 3.

63  John Maatta & Lorin Brennan, *Comments on International Video Piracy— A Review of the Problem and Some Potential Solutions*, 10 HASTINGS COMM. & ENT. L.J. 1081 (1987–1988).

64  Joseph, *"Batman" Takes on Those Villainous Video Purloiners*, Lexington (Ky.) HERALD-LEADER (Orlando Sentinel), Aug. 18, 1989. At B10, col. 1.

65  *Id.*

66  *Sony Corp. of America v. Universal City Studios, Inc.*, 465 U.S. 1112, 104 S. Ct. 1619, 80 L. Ed. 2d 1480 (1984).

67  At the time of the Court's decision, these devices were called videotape recorders or VTRs, but the terminology changed to videocassette recorders (VCRs).

68  *Sony Corp. of America v. Universal City Studios, Inc.*, 464 U.S. 417, 442.

69  Betamax VCRs used the Beta format, which ultimately lost out to the VHS format; but at the time of the suit, Beta was the dominant format. Even Sony abandoned Beta for VHS in VCRs for home use.

70  *Sony Corp. of America v. Universal City Studios, Inc.*

71  *Id.*

72  See *Atlantic Recording Corp. v. XM Satellite Radio, Inc.*, 2007 WL 136186 (S.D.N.Y. July 17, 2006) (No. 06 Civ. 3733).

73  See *RIAA v. Diamond Multimedia Sys., Inc.*, 180 F.3d 1072 (9th Cir. 1999).

74  *Stewart v. Abend*, 495 U.S. 201, 110 S. Ct. 1750, 109 L. Ed. 2d 184 (1990).

75  *See* EPSTEIN, *Court Ruling Could Pull Classic Videos from Shelves*, Lexington (Ky.) HERALD-LEADER (Knight-Ridder News Service), April 25, 1990, at A1, col. 1.

76  *Id.*

77  *Rohauer v. Killiam Shows*, 551 F.2d 484 (2d Cir. 1977); *cert. denied*, 431 U.S. 949 (1977).

78  *Stewart v. Abend.*

79  *See Epstein, supra.*

80  See *Jagger Gets Satisfaction in Lawsuit over Song*, Lexington (Ky.), HERALD-LEADER (Associated Press), April 27, 1988, at A22, col. 3.

81  *Id.*

82  *Sid and Marty Krofft Television Productions, Inc. v. McDonald's Corp.*, 562 F.2d 1157 (9th Cir. 1977).

83  *Universal City Studios, Inc. v. Film Ventures International, Inc.* 543 F. Supp. 1134 (C.D. Calif. 1982).

84  *Id.*

85  *Ruolo v. Russ Berrie & Co.*, 886 F.2d 931 (7th Cir. 1989).

86  Ronald Abramson, *"Look and Feel" of Computer Software*, CASE AND COMMENT (Jan.–Feb. 1990) at 3.

87  17 U.S.C. §503(b) (1996).

88  17 U.S.C. §504(b) (1996).

89  Pub. L. No. 100–568, 102 Stat. 2853, 2860 (1988).

90  The amounts prior to the October 31, 1988, enactment of the new law were $250 and $10,000, respectively.

91  17 U.S.C. §504(c)(2) (1996).

92  *Id.*

93  17 U.S.C. §505 (1996).

94  See 17 U.S.C. §506 (1996) and 18 U.S.C. §2319(b)(1)(A) (1996).

95  18 U.S.C. §2319(b)(b)(B) (1996).

96  18 U.S.C. §2318 (1996).

97  See U.S. Copyright Office, *International Copyright Relations* (Circular 38a) (1996) for a complete list of countries having copyright agreements with the United States.

98  See U.S. Copyright Office, *Copyright Amendments Contained in the Uruguay Round Agreements Act* (URAA) (Circular 38a) (1995).

99  *IIPA Statement on USTR's Decisions in its 2009 Special 301 Review Affecting Copyright Protection Enforcement Around the World*, April 30, 2009. Available at http://www.iipa.com/pdf/IIPAStatementonUSTRs2009 Special301Decisions043009.pdf(last visited January 8, 2009).

100  17 U.S.C. §507(a) (1996).

101  17 U.S.C. §507(b) (1996).

102  17 U.S.C. §205 (1996).

103  *Constructive notice* is a legal term implying or imputing that the public has been notified in the eyes of the law by being provided a means for learning such information. In other words, by recording the agreement in the Copyright Office, the transferor and transferee have met any public notice requirements because anyone who examined the copies of the documents in the Copyright Office would know the terms of the agreement. This is in contrast to *actual notice*, in which the parties have formally provided other parties with actual copies of the documents.

104  *See* 17 U.S.C. §205(c)(1)–(2) (1996).

105  *See* 17 U.S.C. §205(d) and (e) (1996).

106  See U.S. Copyright Office, *Recordation of Transfers and Other Documents* (Circular 12) (1996), at 4.

107  *Id.*

108  H.R. Rep. No. 94–1476, 94th Cong., 2d Sess. 65 (1976). Excerpts are reproduced in U.S. Copyright Office, *Reproduction of Copyrighted Works by Educators and Librarians* (Circular 21) (1995), at 8–9

109  17 U.S.C. §107 (1996).

110  *Id.*

111  *Harper & Row Publishers, Inc. and The Reader's Digest Association, Inc. v. Nation Enterprises*, 471 U.S. 539, 105 S. Ct. 2218, 88 L. Ed. 2d 588, 11 Med. L. Rptr. 1969 (1985).

112  *Id.*

113  *Id.*

114 *Id.*
115 *Id.*
116 *American Geophysical Union v. Texaco*, 85 Cov. 3446, 802 F. Supp. 1 (S.D.N.Y. 1992).
117 Under the Federal Interlocutory Appeals Act, 28 U.S.C. §1292 (b), a U.S. Court of Appeals can review any interlocutory order (an interim order pending final disposition of the controversy) in a civil case if the district court judge states in the decision that there is a controlling question of law on which there is apparent disagreement in the courts. The judge in this case had issued such an order so the appellate court could make the final determination.
118 *American Geophysical Union v. Texaco*, 37 F.3d 881, 32 U.S.P.Q.2d 1545 (2d Cir. 1992).
119 *American Geophysical Union v. Texaco*, 60 F.3d 913 (2d Cir. 1995).
120 *Court Clips Wings of Atlanta Video Clipping Service*, BROADCASTING (June 10, 1991) at 63, 65.
121 *Luther R. Campbell a.k.a. Luke Skyywalker v. Acuff-Rose Music, Inc.*, 510 U.S. 569 (1994).
122 *Luther R. Campbell a.k.a. Luke Skyywalker v. Acuff-Rose Music, Inc.*, 972 F.2d 1429; 1992 U.S. App. LEXIS 18761; 23 U.S.P.Q.2d (BNA) 1817; Copy. L. Rep. (CCH) P26, 966.
123 *Id.*
124 *Id.*
125 *Id.*
126 The Recording Industry Association of America (RIAA) and the Motion Picture Association of America, for example, have initiated hundreds of copyright infringement lawsuits. The RIAA is especially focused on illegal file sharing and trafficking on college campuses.
127 Pub. L. 105–3–4, Oct. 28, 1998, 112 Stat 2860.
128 *Id.*
129 17 U.S.C. §§101 *et seq.*
130 *A & M Records, Inc. v. Napster, Inc.*, 114 F. Supp. 2d 896 (N.D. Cal. 2000).
131 *Id.*
132 259 F. Supp. 2d 1029 (C.D. Cal. 2003).
133 125 S. Ct. 2764 (2005).
134 464 U.S. 417 at 456.

## 8 Patents and Trademarks

1 U.S. CONST. art. I, §8.
2 Id.
3 15 U.S.C. §1051 *et seq.*
4 U.S. CONST. art. VI.
5 *See* 35 U.S.C. §101.
6 *See* 35 U.S.C. §161.
7 *See* 35 U.S.C. §171.
8 All patent infringement suits must be brought in U.S. District Court. Other federal courts and state courts have no jurisdiction. Appeals from a U.S. District Court are then heard exclusively by the U.S. Court of Appeals for the Federal Circuit. Upon a *writ of certiorari*, a discretionary writ, the U.S. Supreme Court can, if it so chooses, hear any appeals from the Federal Circuit.
9 *In re Alappat*, 33 F.3d 1526, 13 U.S.P.Q.2d 1545 (Fed. Cir. 1994).

10  Pub. L. No. 98–417 (1984) and Pub. L. No. 100–670 (1988) had granted such an extension for drugs, but the 1989 Act broadened the extension to include patents for other inventions and discoveries.

11  *Polaroid v. Eastman Kodak*, 789 F.2d 1556, 229 U.S.P.Q. 561 (Fed. Cir. 1986); *cert. denied*, 479 U.S. 850.

12  15 U.S.C. §1051.

13  *Qualitex Company v. Jacobson Products, Inc.*, 514 U.S. 159, 115 S. Ct. 1300, 131 L.Ed.2d 248 (1995).

14  *In re General Electric Co.*, 199 U.S.P.Q. 560 (T.T.A.B. 1978).

15  http://www.uspto.gov/trademarks/basics/index.jsp (last visited Dec. 8, 2009).

16  *See Java Can Get You in Hot Water*, Lexington (Ky.), HERALD-LEADER, June 15, 1996, at A11, col. 1.

17  *G. Heileman Brewing Co., Inc. v. Anheuser-Busch, Inc.*, Nos. 88–1223, 88–1309, 88–1310 (April 26, 1989); *see LA Law*, 75 A.B.A. J. 92 (Aug. 1989).

18  http://www.uspto.gov/trademarks/basics/index.jsp (last visited Dec. 8, 2009).

19  AMERICAN BAR ASSOCIATION, WHAT IS A TRADEMARK? (1995).

20  *ASSOCIATED PRESS 2008 STYLEBOOK AND BRIEFING ON MEDIA LAW* (D. Christian *et al.* eds., The Associated Press, New York, 2009).

21  15 U.S.C. §116(a).

22  15 U.S.C. §117(c).

23  *Id.*

24  *L.L. Bean, Inc. v. Drake Publishers, Inc.*, 811 F.2d 26, 13 Med. L. Rptr. 2009 (1st Cir. 1987).

25  *Id.*

26  15 U.S.C. §1125(c).

27  *Panavision Intern., L.P. v. Toeppen*, 938 F. Supp. 616 (C.D. Cal. 1996).

28  The corresponding web site showed a photograph of Pana, Illinois.

29  141 F.3d 1316 (9th Cir. 1998).

30  *Moseley v. V Secret Catalogue, Inc.*, 537 U.S. 418 (2003).

31  *Id.*

32  Pub. L. No. 109–312, Oct. 6, 2006, 120 Stat. 1730, amending the Trademark Act of 1946.

33  Dilution by blurring is "association arising from the similarity between a mark or trade name and a famous mark that impairs the distinctiveness of the famous mark."

34  Dilution by tarnishment is "association arising from the similarity between a mark or trade name and a famous mark that harms the reputation of the famous mark."

35  15 U.S.C. §1129.

36  *Internet Corporation for Assigned Names & Numbers*, ICANN Referrals Page, http://www.ICANN.com (last visited Dec. 10, 2009).

## 9  Other Ways to Protect "Ideas"

1  *Int'l. News Service v. Associated Press*, 248 U.S. 215, 250 (1919).

2  765 ILCS 065/2 (2005).

3  Unif. Trade Secrets Act §1 (1985).

4  *See* 764 ILCS 1065/3 (a).

5  *See* N.C. Gen. Stat. §66–152 (1) (2005).

6  Pepsico, Inc. v. Redmond and the Quaker Oats Co., 54 F.3d 1262, 35 U.S.P.Q.2d (BNA) 1010 (7th Cir. 1995).

7  E.I. du Pont de Nemours & Co., Inc. v. Rolfe Christopher, 431 F.2d 1012 (5th Cir. 1970).

8  Kewanee Oil Co. v. Bicron Corp., 416 U.S. 470 (1974).

9  Dow Chemical v. United States, 476 U.S. 227 (1986).

10  Ruckelshaus v. Monsanto Co., 467 U.S. 986 (1984).

11  Id. at 1005.

12  See International News Serv. v. The Associated Press, 248 U.S. 315, 39 S. Ct. 68, 63 L. Ed. 211 (1918).

13  Columbia Broadcasting System, Inc. v. Melody Recordings, Inc., 341 A.2d 348 (N.J. Super. 1985).

14  Id. at 353–354.

15  Id. at 354.

16  See, e.g., Cheney Bros. v. Doris Silk Corp., 35 F.2d 279 (1929), cert. denied 281 U.S. 728 (1930).

17  Nadel v. Play-By-Play Toys & Novelties, Inc., 208 F.3d 368 (2d Cir. 2000).

18  Id. at 371.

19  Id. at 372.

20  Id.

21  Id. at 373.

22  Id.

23  Id.

24  Id. at 380.

25  Donahue v. Ziv Television Programs, Inc., 245 Cal. App. 2d 593, 54 Cal. Rptr. 130 (Ct. App. 1966).

26  Id. at 597.

27  Id.

28  Id. at 600.

29  Id.

30  Id. at 601.

31  The concept of consideration evolved significantly in the early twentieth century, embracing the concept that past acts could not serve as consideration for a future contractual arrangement. Justice Benjamin Cardozo addressed this rule in the oft-cited contract case of Dougherty v. Salt, 227 N.Y. 200, 125 N.E. 94 (1919). In the case, a woman issued a promissory note due upon her death to her nephew for several thousand dollars (an exceptional sum during the time period) because the boy had always treated her well. When the nephew sought to enforce the promissory note upon her death as a valid enforceable contract, Justice Cardozo wrote that the note was little more than an executory (to be performed in the future) gift and not an enforceable contract, because the boy's past acts had no present value as consideration.

32  Phillips v. Avis, Inc., No. 95 C 1566, 1996 U.S. Dist. LEXIS 7342 (N.D. Ill. May 29, 1996).

33  Id. at 13–14.

34  Id. at 14.

35  Id. at 15.

36  Id. at 15, citing Apfel v. Prudential-Bache Securities, Inc., 81 N.Y. 470, 477–478, 600 N.Y.S.2d 433, 436, 616 N.E.2d 1095 (1993).

37  See, e.g., Webb v. McGowin, 27 Ala. App. 82, 168 So. 196 (Ct. App. 1935).

## 10  The Federal Trade Commission, the Food and Drug
## Administration and the Securities and Exchange Commission

1  Sherman Anti-Trust Act, 15 U.S.C. §§1–7 (1890).
2  15 U.S.C. §45 (a). (See for current version.)
3  *Id.*
4  15 U.S.C. §53. (See for current version.)
5  *Valentine v. Chrestensen*, 316 U.S. 52 (1942).
6  *Pittsburgh Press Co. v. Human Rel. Comm'n*, 413 U.S. 376 (1973).
7  *Va. State Bd. of Pharmacy v. Va. Citizens Consumer Council*, 425 U.S. 748 (1976).
8  *Id.* at 770.
9  *Id.* at 771.
10  *Id.*
11  *Young v. American Mini Theatres, Inc.*, 427 U.S. 50 (1976).
12  *Id.* at 69 n. 31.
13  15 U.S.C. §45 (a)(6).
14  *Id.* at §52 (b).
15  *Id.* at §55 (a)(1).
16  *Levitt Corp. v. Levitt*, 201 U.S.P.Q. (BNA) 164 (E.D.N.Y. 1978), *aff'd* 593 F.2d 463 (2d Cir. 1979).
17  *Levitt Corp. v. Levitt*, 593 F.2d 463 (2d Cir. 1979).
18  *Smith-Victor Corp. v. Sylvania Electric Products, Inc.*, 242 F. Supp. 302 (N.D. Ill. 1965).
19  *Id.*
20  *Chrysler Corp. v. Federal Trade Com.*, 182 U.S. App. D.C. 359 (D.C. Cir. 1977).
21  45 Antitrust and Trade Reg. Rep. (BNA) no. 1137, at 684 (Oct. 14, 1983).
22  *In re Cliffdale Assoc.*, 103 F.T.C. 110 (1984).
23  K.A. PLEVAN and M. L. SIROKY, ADVERTISING COMPLIANCE HANDBOOK 109 (2d ed. 1991), citing *In re International Harvester Co.*, 104 F.T.C. 949, 1056 (1984).
24  *In re Southwest Sunsites, Inc.*, 105 F.T.C. 7, 149 (1985); *aff'd* 785 F.2d 1431 (9th Cir. 1986); *cert. denied*, 479 U.S. 828 (1986).
25  *Id.*
26  2–18 George E. Rosden & Peter E. Rosden, *Part V: Basic Principles of Federal Trade Commission Control of Advertising*, in THE LAW OF ADVERTISING §18.03 (Matthew Bender & Co., Inc. 2004).
27  Federal Trade Commission File No. 912 3336 (11/7/96). See Federal Trade Commission Press Advisory No. C-3582 (6/7/95).
28  *See Get the Scoop: Haagen-Dazs Not Low Fat*, Lexington (Ky.) HERALD-LEADER (The Washington Post), Nov. 22, 1994, at A-5, col. 3.
29  *Id.*
30  *See Followup: Bogus Health Drink, Latecomer Air-conditioner*, 60 CONSUMER REP. 447 (1995).
31  *In re Third Option Laboratories*, 120 F.T.C. 973 (1995).
32  15 U.S.C. §1501.
33  *In re International Harvester Co.*, 104 F.T.C. 949 (1984).
34  *Id.* at 1059.
35  *Id.*
36  *Id.*
37  *F.T.C. v. Colgate-Palmolive Co.*, 380 U.S. 374 (1965).
38  *Id.*

39 *Id.*
40 *In re Campbell Soup*, 1970 F.T.C. LEXIS 116 (May 25, 1970).
41 *Id.* at 4.
42 H.R. 2243.
43 *See Hooked on Tobacco: The Teen Epidemic*, 60 CONSUMER REP. 142 (1995).
44 *Cigarette Ads Found to Affect Teen-agers Most*, Lexington (Ky.) HERALD-LEADER (Associated Press) Aug. 18, 1994, at A3, col. 4.
45 *See Hooked on Tobacco, supra* n. 43.
46 *Can First Amendment Save Camel's 'Old Joe'?*, Lexington (Ky.) HERALD-LEADER
47 *See Hooked on Tobacco, supra* n. 43. at 144.
48 2–18 Rosden, *Unfair Methods of Competition*, in *The Law of Advertising* §18.06 (Matthew Bender & Co., Inc. 2004) (citations omitted).
49 *Id.*
50 *In re Pfizer, Inc.*, 81 F.T.C. 23 (1972).
51 *Id.* at 24.
52 *Id.* at 24–25.
53 *Id.* at 62.
54 *Id.*
55 *In re Natl. Comm'n on Egg Nutrition*, 88 F.T.C. 84 (1976); *modified, Nat'l. Comm'n on Egg Nutrition v. F.T.C.*, 570 F.2d 157 (7th Cir. 1977); *cert. denied*, 439 U.S. 821 (1978).
56 *Id.* at 191 (citations omitted).
57 *Id.* n. 14.
58 47 Antitrust and Trade Reg. Rep. (BNA), n. 1176 at 234 (Aug. 2, 1984).
59 PLEVAN at 114. *See*, e.g., *Firestone Tire and Rubber Co. v. F.T.C.*, 481 F.2d 246 (6th Cir. 1973).
60 *See*, e.g., *Leon A. Tashof v. F.T.C.*, 14 F.2d 707 (D.C. Cir. 1970).
61 *Pfizer*, 81 F.T.C. at 66.
62 *Id.*
63 *Firestone Tire & Rubber Co. v. F.T.C.*, 481 F.2d 246 (6th Cir. 1973).
64 *U-Haul International, Inc. v. Jartran, Inc.*, 522 F. Supp. 1238, 1245 (D. Ariz. 1981); *aff'd* p. 127.
65 *In re Dannon Milk Products*, 61 F.T.C. 840 (1962).
66 *In re Better Living, Inc.*, 54 F.T.C. 648 (1957); *aff'd* 259 F.2d 271 (1958).
67 *Id.* at 653.
68 *Gillette Co. v. Wilkinson Sword, Inc.*, 1991 U.S. Dist. LEXIS 21006 (S.D.N.Y. 1991).
69 *Id.* at 54.
70 *In re Thompson Medical Co., Inc.*, 104 F.T.C. 648 (1984).
71 *Id.* at 844.
72 *Id.* at 723.
73 16 C.F.R. §419 (1989).
74 16 C.F.R. §225 (a) (1987).
75 *Id.* at §255 (b).
76 *In re Cliffdale Assoc.*, 1984 FTC LEXIS 71, 103 F.T.C. 110 (1984).
77 *Id.* at 36.
78 *Id.* at 169.
79 *Id.* at 171–172.
80 *In re Cooga Mooga*, 92 F.T.C. 310 (1978).
81 16 C.F.R. §255.3 (b) (1987).
82 *In re Leroy Gordon Cooper*, 94 F.T.C. 674 (1979).

83 *Id.* at 680.
84 *Niresk Industries, Inc. v. Federal Trade Com.*, 278 F.2d 337 (7th Cir. 1960).
85 16 C.F.R. §233.1–5 (1990).
86 *Id.* at §238.
87 15 U.S.C. §§160–1614 and 1661–1665 (a) (1990).
88 15 U.S.C. §7701 et seq.
89 15 U.S.C. §7701 et seq.
90 *The CAN-SPAM Act: A Compliance Guide for Business.* Available at http://www.ftc.gov/bcp/edu/pubs/business/ecommerce/bus61.shtm. Last accessed May 4, 2010.
91 MCL §752.1061 et seq. and UTAH ANN. CODE §13–39–101 et seq.
92 MCL §752.1061 et seq. and UTAH ANN. CODE §13–39–101 et seq.
93 15 U.S.C. §45 (b) (1973).
94 *Sears, Roebuck & Co. v. F.T.C.*, 676 F.2d 385, 391 (9th Cir. 1982).
95 Codified in the Federal Cigarette Labeling and Advertising Act, 1965.
96 *Warner-Lambert Co. v. F.T.C.*, 562 F.2d 749 (D.C. Cir. 1977); *cert. denied*, 435 U.S. 950 (1988).
97 *Id.* at 762.
98 *F.T.C. v. Pharmtech Research, Inc.*, 576 F. Supp. 294 (D.D.C. 1983).
99 15 U.S.C. §45 (m).
100 *United States v. Reader's Digest Assoc.*, 464 F. Supp. 1037 (D. Del. 1978); *aff'd*, 662 F.2d 955 (3d Cir. 1981).
101 *Chrysler Corp. v. F.T.C.*, 561 F.2d 357 (D.C. Cir. 1977).
102 *Id.*
103 *Id.* at 364.
104 *Id.*
105 *ITT Continental Baking Co. v. F.T.C.*, 532 F.2d 207 (2d Cir. 1976).
106 *American Medical Association v. F.T.C.*, 638 F.2d 443 (2d Cir. 1980).
107 *Id.* at 452.
108 *Standard Oil Co. v. F.T.C.*, 577 F.2d 653 (9th Cir. 1978)
109 *Id.* at 659.
110 F.T.C. Guidelines §b—ACH, 1993 Cumulative Supplement, at 96.
111 *Id.*
112 *Id.* at 22.
113 BRUCE E. H. JOHNSON & KAUSTUV M. DAS, *Recent Developments in Commercial Speech and Consumer Privacy Interests* (Communications Law 2006, Vol. 2, Practising Law Institute).
114 http://www.epic.org/privacy/consumer/states.html
115 15 U.S.C. §45(a)(1).
116 *In Re Matter of BJ's Wholesale Club*, F.T.C. Case No. 042 3160 (2005).
117 *Id.*
118 http://www.ftc.gov/bcp/edu/pubs/business/alerts/alt050.shtm
119 *Id.*
120 21 U.S.C. §352.
121 *Id.* at §353 (b)(1)(g).
122 *Id.* at §353 (b)(1)(c).
123 *Id.* at §321 (m).
124 *Nature Food Centres, Inc. v. United States*, 310 F.2d 67 (1st Cir. 1962).
125 *United States v. Articles of Drug, etc.*, 263 F. Supp. 212 (D. Neb. 1967).
126 *United States v. Guardian Chemical Corp.*, 410 F.2d 157 (2d Cir. 1969).
127 *United States v. Diapulse Mfg. Corp.*, 269 F. Supp. 162 (D. Conn. 1967).
128 *Va. St. Bd. of Pharmacy v. Va. Citizens Consumer Council*, 425 U.S. 748 (1976).

129 *Abbott Laboratories v. Celebrezze*, 352 F.2d 286 (3d Cir. 1965)
130 21 C.F.R. §202.1 (e).
131 *Id.* at §202.1 (e)(3)(iii).
132 *Id.* at §202.1 (3)(i).
133 *Id.*
134 *Id.* at §202.1 (3)(iii)(a).
135 *Id.* at §201.6 (i).
136 21 C.F.R. §202.1 (6)(xiv).
137 *Id.* at Ch. 1 (4–1–94 Edition) §202.1 (6)(xv).
138 *Id.* at (7)(v).
139 *Id.* at (6)(xiii).
140 *Id.* at (6)(xvii).
141 *Id.* at (6)(xix).
142 21 U.S.C. §352 (n).
143 *Id.* at (7)(viii).
144 21 U.S.C. §352 (n).
145 *Id.*
146 15 U.S.C. §77z.
147 *Id.* at §78gg.
148 *Id.* at §78c (a)(18).
149 Sarbanes-Oxley Act of 2002, Pub. L. No. 107–204, 116 Stat. 745, 758 (2002).
150 SECURITIES AND EXCHANGE COMMISSION, THE WORK OF THE SECURITIES AND EXCHANGE COMMISSION (1974) at 1.
151 *Ernst and Ernst v. Hochfelder*, 425 U.S. 185 (1976).
152 *Id.*
153 15 U.S.C. §77 (a)(8), at §78 (c).
154 17 C.F.R. §230.134.
155 *S.E.C. v. Arvida Corporation*, 169 F. Supp. 211 (S.D.N.Y. 1958).
156 *In re Carl M. Loeb, Rhoades & Co.*, 38 S.E.C. 843 (1959).
157 *Id.* at 851.
158 *Id.* at 853.
159 *Arvida*, 169 F. Supp. at 215.
160 17 C.F.R. Ch. 11 (4–1–94 Edition) §240.10b-1.
161 15 U.S.C. §§78 (m), 78 (n).
162 *Gillette Co. v. RB Partners*, 693 F. Supp. 1266 (D. Mass. 1988).
163 *Long Island Lighting Co. v. Barbash*, 779 F.2d 793 (2d Cir. 1985).
164 *Id.* at 794.
165 *Id.* at 797.
166 *Long Island Lighting Co. v. Barbash*, 625 F. Supp. 221 (E.D.N.Y. 1985).
167 *Id.* at 226.
168 *Barbash*, 779 F.2d 793.
169 *Id.* at 796.
170 *Id.*
171 *Id.*, citing Rule 14a–6 (g), 17 C.F.R. §240.14a-6 (g).
172 *Id.*, citing *Medical Comm. for Human Rights v. S.E.C.*, 432 F.2d 659 (D.C. Cir. 1970).
173 *S.E.C v. Texas Gulf Sulphur Co.*, 401 F.2d 833 (2d Cir. 1968).
174 *Id.* at 845.
175 17 C.F.R. Ch. 11 (4–1–94 Edition) §240.10b-5.
176 *Texas Gulf Sulphur*, 401 F.2d at 856.
177 *Id.* at 852.

178  *Id.* at 848.
179  *Id.* Citing 17 C.F.R. Ch. 11 (4–1–94 Edition) §240.10b-5.
180  *Carpenter v. United States*, 484 U.S. 19 (1987).
181  For further discussion, *see* I. B. Bromberg, *Disclosure Programs for Publicly Held Companies—A Practical Guide*, Duke L.J. (1970), 1139.

## 11  Other Federal and State Regulation of Commercial Speech

1   15 U.S.C. §1125 (1946) (also referred to as Lanham Act §43(a)).
2   *Id.*
3   *Id.*
4   15 U.S.C. §1125(1)(b) (1992).
5   *Id.* §1125(1).
6   *Id.* §1125(2).
7   *Serbin v. Ziebart Int'l Corp.*, 11 F.3d 1163 (3d Cir. 1993).
8   *Balance Dynamics Corp. v. Schmitt Indus.*, 204 F.3d 683 (6th Cir. 2000).
9   *Balance Dynamics Corp. v. Schmitt Indus.*, 1997 U.S. Dist. LEXIS 17253 (E.D. Mich. 1997).
10  *Pizza Hut v. Papa John's Int'l*, 227 F.3d 489 (5th Cir. 2000).
11  *Pizza Hut, Inc. v. Papa John's Int'l, Inc.*, 80 F. Supp. 2d 600 (N.D. Tex. 2000).
12  *Kasky v. Nike, Inc.*, 119 Cal. Rptr. 2d 296 (Cal. 2002).
13  42 U.S.C. 3603(b).
14  *Id.*
15  *Ragin v. New York Times* Co., 923 F.2d 995 (2d Cir. 1991); *cert. denied*, 112 S. Ct. 81 (1991).
16  Pub. L. No. 88–352, §70 et seq., 78 Stat. 241, Title 42 U.S.C. §2000e et seq.
17  *Hailes v. United Air Lines*, 464 F. 2d 1006 (5th Cir. 1972).
18  *Pittsburgh Press Co. v. Pittsburgh Comm'n. on Human Relations*, 413 U.S. 376 (1973).
19  Pub. L. 90–202, 80 Stat. 602 (29 U.S.C. §621), as amended in Pub. L. 95–256 (A.D. in Employment Amendments of 1978), 92 Stat. 189.
20  42 U.S.C. §12101 et seq.
21  *Housing Opportunities Made Equal v. Cincinnati Enquirer*, 943 F.2d 644 (6th Cir. 1991).
22  *Id.* at 646.
23  Pub. L. 96–240, 90 Stat. 257 (1976); codified at Table 15 U.S.C. §§1667–1667e (1982).
24  Id.
25  Id.
26  Pub. L. 93–495, Title V, 88 Stat. 1521 (1974); codified at 15 U.S.C. §§1691–1691f (1982).
27  15 U.S.C. §1811 (1982).
28  *See Housing Opportunities Made Equal v. Cincinnati Enquirer*, 943 F.2d 644 (6th Cir. 1991).
29  49 U.S.C. §303 (1956).
30  23 U.S.C. §131 (1965).
31  *Metromedia, Inc. v. City of San Diego*, 453 U.S. 490 (1981).
32  15 U.S.C. §§1601–1614 and 1661–1665a (April 1990).
33  U.S. Const. amend. XXI.
34  *Central Hudson Gas & Elec. Corp. v. Public Serv. Comm'n*, 447 U.S. 557 (1980).

35  *Rubin v. Coors Brewing Co.*, 514 U.S. 476 (1995).
36  *44 Liquormart v. Rhode Island*, 517 U.S. 484 (1996).
37  *See* G. E. ROSDEN & P. E. ROSDEN, THE LAW OF ADVERTISING (Matthew Bender & Co. Inc., New York, 1991).
38  *See* CAL. BUS. & PROF. CODE §17200 et seq.; CAL. BUS. & PROF. CODE §17500 et seq.
39  ROSDEN at vol. 2, §13–14.
40  *F.T.C. v. Sperry & Hutchinson Co.*, 405 U.S. 233 (1972).
41  ROSDEN at vol. 2, §13–29.
42  *Id.* at vol. 3, §26–47.
43  *Id.*
44  *Id.* at vol. 4, §57–29.
45  Unif. Sec. Act §§101–102 (1956) (amended 2003).
46  ROSDEN at vol. 4, §57–30.
47  *Code of Responsible Practices*, The Distilled Spirits Council of the United States, *at* http://www.discus.org/industry/code/ (visited Nov. 7, 2004).

## 12  Access to Information, Free Press/Fair Trial, Journalist Privilege and Other Issues Related to News Gathering/Dissemination

1  *Pell v. Procunier*, 417 U.S. 817 (1974).
2  *Saxbe v. Wash. Post Co.*, 417 U.S. 843 (1974).
3  5 U.S.C. §552, as amended by Pub. L. No. 99–570, 1801–1804 (1986).
4  5 U.S.C. §552a, as amended by Pub. L. No. 97–365, 96 Stat. 1749 (1982).
5  5 U.S.C. §552a (1974).
6  5 U.S.C. §552 as amended by Pub. L. No. 104–231, 110 Stat. 3048 (1996).
7  *Chrysler Corp. v. Brown*, 441 U.S. 281 (1979).
8  *See United States Dep't of State v. Wash. Post Co.*, 456 U.S. 595 (1982); *New York Times Co. v. National Aeronautics & Space Admin.*, 287 U.S. App. D.C. 208 (D.C. Cir. 1990).
9  5 U.S.C. §552b.
10  Generally attributed to Col. Edward C. Raleigh according to Army Public Affairs, http://www4.army.mil/ocpa/resources/HOF/2002/index.html.
11  *Miranda v. Arizona*, 384 U.S. 436 (1966).
12  *Sheppard v. Maxwell*, 384 U.S. 333 (1966).
13  *Id.*
14  *Nebraska Press Assn. v. Stuart*, 427 U.S. 539, 553 (1976); quoting *Sheppard v. Maxwell*, 384 U.S. 333, 363 (1966).
15  *Id.* at 542.
16  *Id.*
17  *Id.* at 543.
18  *Id.* at 547.
19  *Id.* at 548.
20  *Id.* at 555.
21  *Id.* at 561.
22  *Id.*
23  *Id.* at 565.
24  *Id.* at 568.
25  *Gannett Co. v. DePasquale*, 443 U.S. 368 (1979).
26  *Id.* at 375.
27  *Id.* at 376.

28  *Id.* at 393.
29  *Richmond Newspapers v. Va.*, 448 U.S. 555 (1980).
30  *Id.* at 560.
31  *Id.* at 564.
32  *Id.* at 573.
33  *Id.* at 576; quoting *First Nat'l Bank of Boston v. Bellotti*, 435 U.S. 765, 783 (1978).
34  *Id.* at 577.
35  *Id.* at 580; quoting *Branzburg v. Hayes*, 408 U.S. 664, 681 (1972).
36  *Globe Newspaper Co. v. Superior Court*, 457 U.S. 596 (1982).
37  *Press-Enterprise Co. v. Superior Court of California*, 464 U.S. 501 (1984).
38  *Press-Enterprise Co. v. Superior Court*, 478 U.S. 1 (1986).
39  *Id.* at 4.
40  *Id.* at 7.
41  *Id.* at 8.
42  *Id.*
43  *Id.* at 10.
44  *Id.*
45  *Id.* at 11.
46  *Id.* at 12.
47  *Id.*
48  *Chandler v. Fla.*, 449 U.S. 560 (1981).
49  Quoted in COMMUNICATIONS LAW (Vol. 3 1994) at 432.
50  COMMUNICATIONS LAW (Vol. 3 1994) at 429.
51  *Branzburg v. Hayes*, 408 U.S. 664, 690 n. 29 (1972); quoting B. J. WIGMORE, *EVIDENCE* (McNaughton rev. cd.), 1961, §2192, at 73.
52  *Id.* at 692.
53  The case consolidated *Branzburg* with *In re Pappas* and *U.S. v. Caldwell*.
54  *Id.* at 669; quoting *Branzburg v. Pound*, 461 S.W.2d 345 (1970).
55  *Id.*
56  *Id.* at 672.
57  *Id.* at 674; quoting *In re Pappas*, 266 N.D.2d 297, 299, 358 Mass. 604, 607 (1971).
58  *Id.* at 675.
59  *Id.* at 681.
60  *Id.*
61  *Id.* at 682.
62  *Id.* at 685.
63  *Id.* at 685.
64  *Id.* at 690.
65  *Id.* at 704.
66  *Id.* at 709.
66  *Cohen v. Cowles Media Co.*, 501 U.S. 663 (1991).
67  S.C. CODE ANN. §19–11–100.
68  *State v. Smith (In re Decker)*, 322 S.C. 215 (1995).
69  *Alton Telegraph v. People*, No. 09-MR548 (Ill. Cir. May 15, 2009).
70  *Mortgage Specialists, Inc. v. Implode-Explode Heavy Indus. Inc.*, No. 08–E0572 (N.H. Super. Ct., March 11, 2009).
71  *Doe v. T.S. et al.*, No. CV08030693 (Or. 5th Jud. Cir. Sept. 30, 2008).
72  *Doty v. Molnar*, No. DV07–022 (Mont. 13th Jud. Cir. Sept. 3, 2008).

# Table of Cases

# Index